BIG JIM EASTLAND

Big Jim Eastland

THE GODFATHER OF MISSISSIPPI

By J. Lee Annis Jr.

UNIVERSITY PRESS OF MISSISSIPPI / JACKSON

www.upress.state.ms.us

Designed by Peter D. Halverson

The University Press of Mississippi is a member of the Association of American University Presses.

First printing 2016

∞

Library of Congress Cataloging-in-Publication Data

Names: Annis, J. Lee (James Lee), 1957– author.
Title: Big Jim Eastland : the godfather of Mississippi / by J. Lee Annis Jr.
Description: Jackson : University Press of Mississippi, 2016. | Includes
  bibliographical references and index.
Identifiers: LCCN 2015049967 (print) | LCCN 2015050103 (ebook) | ISBN
  9781496806147 (cloth : alk. paper) | ISBN 9781496806154 (epub single) |
  ISBN 9781496806161 (epub institutional) | ISBN 9781496806178 (pdf single)
  | ISBN 9781496806185 (pdf institutional)
Subjects: LCSH: Eastland, James O. (James Oliver), 1904–1986. |
  Legislators—United States—Biography. | United States. Congress.
  Senate—Biography. | United States—Politics and government—1945–1989. |
  Mississippi—Biography.
Classification: LCC E748.E135 A85 2016 (print) | LCC E748.E135 (ebook) | DDC
  328.73/092--dc23
LC record available at http://lccn.loc.gov/2015049967

British Library Cataloging-in-Publication Data available

Contents

Key to Abbreviations

AFL-CIO	American Federation of Labor and Congress of Industrial Organizations
CDGM	Child Development Group of Mississippi
CIO	Congress of Industrial Organizations
DPOWA	Distributive, Processing, and Office Workers of America
FCG	Federation for Constitutional Government
FDR	Franklin Delano Roosevelt
FEPC	Fair Employment Practices Commission
GOP	Grand Old Party (Republican)
ITT	International Telegraph and Telephone Company
LBJ	Lyndon Baines Johnson
MFDP	Mississippi Freedom Democratic Party
MSSC	Mississippi State Sovereignty Commission
NAACP	National Association for the Advancement of Colored People
OPA	Office of Price Administration
PBC	Peoples Bicentennial Commission
SCEF	Southern Conference Educational Fund
SCHW	Southern Conference for Human Welfare
SISS	Senate Internal Security Subcommittee
SNCC	Student Nonviolent Coordinating Committee
TVA	Tennessee Valley Authority
UN	United Nations

Acknowledgments

ANY MANUSCRIPT OF BOOK LENGTH IS A COLLABORATIVE ONE, AND THIS one is no different. More than anything, I need to thank the Eastland family, particularly the senator's son, Woods, and his cousin, Hiram, for their help with this project. At the outset of this project, none of the Eastlands knew me. All are aware that not everything in James Eastland's background or career will appear noble or edifying in the more socially egalitarian climate of the twenty-first century. Even so, Woods and Hiram Eastland patiently and charitably made time often in the midst of busy schedules to answer any questions I had or cajole reluctant friends of theirs to talk with me. They perused drafts but did not so much as even suggest a change unless they spotted a clear error of fact. I also benefitted from a discussion with James and Libby Eastland's daughters, Nell Eastland Amos, Anne Eastland Howdeshell, and Sue Eastland McRoberts. I am grateful especially to Mrs. McRoberts, for she heard that I had accepted as fact what appears to have been some artful embellishment by a ghostwriter for a non-Mississippian involved in one of the seminal events of Mississippi history of which she had some direct knowledge, and she called to save me from a particularly egregious mistake.

I am nearly as obliged to the thoroughly outstanding staff of the Special Collections Department at the John D. Williams Library of the University of Mississippi, where the Eastland papers are stored. Especially helpful was Leigh McWhite, the very able head of the political portion of that shop who processed the Eastland collection and did her best to guide me to what would be most helpful within its 1040 boxes. But I also need to thank Jennifer Ford, the department's able director, and assistants Chatham Ewing, Greg Johnson, Jason Kovari, Stephanie McKnight,

Lauren Rogers, John Wall, Pamela Williamson, and others for gracious assistance that extended even to lining up hair appointments in Oxford. Over the course of five years, my research took me all over Mississippi and to libraries from Boston, Massachusetts, to Yorba Linda, California. I thank the always helpful staffs at the Library of Congress; the Mississippi Department of Archives and History; the National Archives; the Roosevelt, Truman, Eisenhower, Kennedy, Johnson, Nixon, Ford, and Carter Presidential Libraries; the special collections departments of the libraries at Clemson University, Delta State University, Hanover College, Mississippi College, Mississippi State University, the University of Memphis, the University of North Carolina, the University of Southern Mississippi, and Vanderbilt University; and the public libraries of New Orleans and of Belzoni, Clarksdale, Cleveland, Forest, Greenville, Greenwood, Indianola, and Jackson, Mississippi. And, I am grateful that Fred Smith, the semi-retired proprietor of Choctaw Books, was always willing to spend a few minutes sharing his broad array of knowledge and stories.

I would also like to thank all those who interacted with Senator Eastland who were kind enough to take the time to sit for interviews. I was fortunate to speak with most of the living people who knew James Eastland best. The only two I truly missed speaking with who were alive at the outset of this project were Senator Ted Kennedy and Larry Speakes, who were beginning to suffer from the afflictions that took their lives. Even so, I'm grateful that many of their associates recalled well so many of the stories they had passed down. Many who knew James Eastland were eager to share reminiscences of him. Discussions with presidential counselors of both parties, Judiciary Committee and Justice Department staff, and his Senate colleagues and staff were particularly fruitful. For this project, David Bowen, Clarence Pierce, and Herb Montgomery were especially generous with their time and valuable counsel. Gil Carmichael and Wally Johnson graciously read chapters on matters of which they possess a bit of expertise. Some, like Senators Jim Abourezk, Fred Harris, and John Tunney, who did not sit for interviews, were still kind enough to pass along helpful information. Others I profited from speaking with include Joe Allen, Cub Amos, Bobby Baker, Howard Baker, Frank Barber Jr., Haley Barbour, Birch Bayh, James Biglane, G. Robert Blakey, Leon Bramlett, Howard Brent, Bill Brock, Owen Brooks, Rex Buffington, Hank

Burdine, Harry Byrd Jr., Robert G. Clark, Thad Cochran, Marlow Cook, Eph Cresswell, John C. Culver, Danny Cupit, Maurice Dantin, John Davis, Kenneth Dean, Ben Dixon, David Dixon, Winfield Dunn, Brad Dye, Rufus Edmisten, Macon Edwards, Charles Evers, Kenneth Feinberg, Jim Flug, Webb Franklin, Jim Free, Al From, David Gambrell, Steve Guyton, Orrin Hatch, Mark Hazard, Jim Herring, Ernest Hollings, Frank Hunger, Pete Johnson, Seymour Johnson, Bennett Johnston, Nicholas Katzenbach, Robert Khayat, Edwin King, Tom Korologos, David Lambert, Thurston Little, Robert Livingston, Trent Lott, James Meredith, Frank Mitchener, Walter Mondale, Frank Moore, Chip Morgan, Johnny Morgan, Robert Morgan, Walter Nixon, Walker Nolan, Maybeth Ormond, Casey Pace, Liz Johnston Patterson, Robert "Tut" Patterson, Steve Patterson, Eddie Payton, Billy Percy, Charles Pickering, Clarke Reed, John Rouse, Katherine Ruth, Ira Shapiro, Craig Shirley, John Siegenthaler, Bill Simpson III, Britt Singletary, John Sobotka, Dan Tate, William Threadgill, Kathleen Kennedy Townsend, Joseph Tydings, William Waller, Taylor Webb, William Winter, Wirt Yerger, and Jim Ziglar.

In addition, I have benefitted from discussions and communications with some of America's most distinguished historians and journalists. Always of great value are the recollections of Dick Baker and Don Ritchie, the two prodigious scholars who headed the Senate Historical Office over its first four decades of existence under Democratic and Republican majorities alike. For a thoughtful first reading, I was incredibly fortunate to have a seventeen-page analysis from Jere Nash, the coauthor of the most thorough history of recent Mississippi politics. I also benefitted from the truly incisive thoughts of my colleague John Riedl, who made a habit of posing thoughtful questions that always deserved contemplation, and Christi Holliday and Layla Hashemi, for raising some issues that need to be addressed. And, I had the pleasure of engaging in discourse with some of the best scholars in the American historical profession. The U.S. Senate, the modern South, and the state of Mississippi have had their share of able chroniclers. I'm grateful that Chris Myers Asch, Jack Bass, Hodding Carter III, Charles E. Cobb Jr., Joe Crespino, Reid Derr, Kari Frederickson, Beverly Gage, John Herbers, Phil Jones, Bill Minor, Jerry Mitchell, Bo Morgan, K. C. Morison, Todd Moye, Roger Mudd, Sid Salter, Greg Taylor, Jason Ward, Curtis Wilkie, and Maarten Zwiers have made time to handle any and all inquiries. At Montgomery College, I benefitted from conversations with Connie and Tony Morella, Rodney Redmond, and Alonzo Smith. I also need to thank friends like Brian Annis, Jack Gelin, John Godwin, Richard Houston, Lorraine Kuchmy, Fred Marcum, Rusty Morgan, Martha Scott Poindexter, and David Stewart for helping me secure access to some wonderful sources. And, I am also truly grateful for the thoughtful counsel of editor Craig Gill, his assistant Katie Keene, managing editor Anne Stascavage, manuscript editor Lisa DiDonato Brousseau, and a scholar who remains anonymous to me.

More than anyone else, I thank Tony Edmonds. In regaling thousands of students over a remarkable academic career of two generations with a tale of how he, as an eighteen-year-old Yale freshman, was "set up," perhaps in more ways than one, he inspired this book, which is dedicated to him.

BIG JIM EASTLAND

Introduction

"PUT HIM UP," THE CIGAR-CHOMPING, ROUND-FACED SOLON THIRD (AND for six months, second) in line to the presidency would command a top aide one or two late afternoons each week from August 1972 to December 1978. That assistant would proceed to call those legislators their boss wanted to cajole, inviting them to either share a bottle of Chivas Regal (often supplied by the Cotton Council) or, for the handful of teetotalers among them, merely listen to other colleagues talk about what concerned them, be it the state of the world, the fate of a legislative program or a particular bill, or musings about who might win an upcoming football game. On occasion, members might ask for advice about problems with their wives or rebellious kids. But few would drink too much, for they knew they would have to drive home. And they knew as well that Libby Eastland, the wife of the host, would call at about 7:00 P.M. if she knew the Senate had adjourned for the day. "Come on home, Jim," she would say with more than a hint of authority.[1]

Other afternoons, James O. Eastland would spot his closest friend within his own caucus, John O. Pastore, the moderately liberal Rhode Islander, on the Senate floor. Uncommonly eloquent, unlike Eastland, and a foot shorter, Pastore seemed to have little in common other than a shared middle initial and party identification with his onetime segregationist colleague. Yet their eyes would meet and they would leave the Senate chambers through different doors, as being seen with the other might hurt one or both in their home states. When they met up in Eastland's hideaway office or, just as often, that of Senate Secretary J. Stanley Kimmitt, there might be senators ranging in philosophy from high-minded liberals like Walter Mondale, the future vice president, and Gaylord Nelson, the father of Earth Day, to staunch conservative Republicans like Roman Hruska. Others might make their way in for a few minutes of conviviality or negotiation. But Tom Korologos, a top lobbyist in the Nixon and Ford administrations, would report that this group "got to where we got more legislating done than we ever did on the floor."[2]

Well before ascending to a perch on the ladder of presidential succession, Eastland was known as one of the Capitol's preeminent movers and shakers. To the nation as a whole, he was best known as one of the most durable and, at times, one of the more intransigent leaders of the southern resistance to what he branded as the "Second Reconstruction." Here was an image Eastland wore proudly for the first quarter century of his service in the Senate, and one that properly characterizes much of the academic treatment of his career. One purpose of this work is to illuminate the parts of Mississippi's past that spawned his ideology, as well as to explore how Eastland reacted for the third of a century after World War II to changes in the American consciousness, which, particularly in the area of race relations, he saw as revolutionary. But James Eastland was a blunt man of many dimensions and more than a few contradictions who dealt with many issues.

As important as it is to chronicle his lingering attachment to the values of the white-dominant rural Mississippi of his youth and examine his accommodation to the presence of African Americans in his state's electorate in the last decade of his Senate tenure, one must note, thankfully, that Eastland was on the losing side of those questions. Any comprehensive biography should be a warts-and-all portrait, rather than one merely of warts. And, in the case of James O. Eastland, there were some very real achievements. Most notably, for two of the most pivotal decades in the history of our country and his Southland, no one played a larger role in the confirmation of federal judges at all levels than Eastland. Well before, it was a rare degree of success protecting some key local economic interests during an initial eighty-eight-day stint in the Senate that won Eastland sufficient support statewide to propel him to a career spanning nearly four decades and friendly estimates of his abilities in Washington. Never a great orator, Eastland relished the opportunity to work, particularly behind the scenes, with colleagues, who he said, "with very few exceptions . . . have been good and great men[3] of high character and ideals, loyal to their states, and dedicated to the public good."[4] But what he valued most about the Senate was the chance he got to act as a quiet patron for the common white men and women of the Magnolia State, be they ginners or farmers, peckerwood sawmill operators or poultry producers, or even those African Americans who respected his authority as a white man.

Without question, anyone who would have been elected to statewide office from Mississippi during the heyday of the civil rights revolution would have borne the reputation of a racist or a white supremacist. A Harris Poll taken in April 1964 indicated that while 54 percent of southern whites opposed that year's civil rights bill, that last stand was the desire of fully 96.4 percent of the whites in Mississippi. Differences in image in the Magnolia State could only be measured in gradations. Even William Winter, often very appropriately described as the *beau ideal* of Dixie liberals, found himself ranked as the most progressive statewide Mississippi pol in the 1950s and 1960s more because he preferred to change the subject to the economic issues he deemed more integral to the state's future than from any aversion he took publicly against segregation. What Mississippians needed more than anything, Winter would say, was "peace and quiet."[5] Yet, when asked about Eastland's attitudes on race, Winter agreed that the outlook of the man he drove all over Mississippi in 1942 was one that most accurately could be termed a kind of paternalism that mellowed considerably over his six terms in the Senate. Whereas any number of sources who worked with Eastland told this writer that they did hear Eastland refer to African Americans in politically incorrect terms, their collective sense (with a few exceptions) was that his choice of words reflected thoroughly ingrained habits rather than any sense of hatred.

Although few of those interested in stronger guarantees of civil rights for African Americans in the heyday of the civil rights movement could be convinced that Eastland bore them or their cause any benevolent attitudes, there were nuances that distinguished one degree of elected segregationist from another. For example, almost as soon as he learned of the assassination of the state leader of the National Association for the Advancement of Colored People (NAACP) leader, Medgar Evers, Eastland told reporters that he hoped that justice would be "meted out to the guilty party." Here was a reaction sharply at odds with that of Governor Ross Barnett, who entered the courtroom in front of the jury during the first trial of Byron De La Beckwith, the man later convicted of murdering Evers, and shook his hand. Some point out that Eastland occasionally privately derided some colleagues who overstated their case on race-related measures that came before the Senate. "Listen to Ole Strom," he once told future State Auditor Steve Patterson. "He really believes all that ole shit."[6]

Better than any other categorization academics insist on using, Eastland fits the profile of a unique brand of political animal known as the Bourbon Democrat who permeated the electoral landscape of the Black Belts of the Deep South for much of the century following the Civil War. Often, pols of the Bourbon stripe were wealthy and devoted to the interests of the planters within their midst as well as to those of the merchants and professionals who provided the economic infrastructure that supported them. Generally courtly and refined, Bourbons more often than not shared the white supremacist values of their neighbors. Still, for much of the first two-thirds of the twentieth century, they took what historian James C. Cobb termed "a more businesslike approach to the race issue."[7] One can readily differentiate them from some of the populist demagogues who claimed to better represent the hopes and aspirations of lower-class whites by a readily apparent paternalistic streak and an abhorrence of violence. In the early twentieth century, the exemplary Mississippi Bourbon was Senator LeRoy Percy, who, while excusing the initial Ku Klux Klan of the Reconstruction era as a "a desperate remedy for a helpless, scourged and torn people," found much to condemn in the more powerful manifestation that grew after World War I. In 1922, he learned that four hooded Klansmen had entered a black church in nearby Helena, Arkansas, headed for the courthouse in his native Greenville, and then lambasted a spokesman for the hooded order there. "When you are going to do a lawful thing, a righteous thing, a brave thing," he lectured, "you . . . do it in broad daylight, and you don't have to cover your face to do it."[8] Just six years later, a young Jim Eastland, who lacked Percy's aristocratic refinement, joined a contingent of Mississippi Democrats at their party's national convention who formed the majority over the objections of the Klan and their allies to signify their approval of nominee Al Smith, the first Catholic either major party had nominated for president. Within a generation, Eastland, who resided in a modest six-bedroom home built in the 1920s on a 5800-acre plantation, became the most visible Bourbon leader in Mississippi, perhaps even the South.

The "Duke of Doddsville," as Ernest "Fritz" Hollings of South Carolina liked to call Eastland, was the man leaders of the Delta Council, a virtual chamber of commerce for Mississippi's northwestern quadrant, called their "go-to guy" for virtually all legislation involving their crops, roads, and markets. Eastland invariably took a lead in pushing to extend highway systems, particularly those linking rural areas to nearby towns. And, for two generations, he was largely responsible for the building of every means of flood control in a region where fortunes were governed more than any other in America by the whims of Mother Nature and the rhythms of nearby waterways. While David L. Cohn, a writer nurtured in Greenville, defined the parameters of the Yazoo-Mississippi Delta as extending from the lobby of Memphis' Peabody Hotel to Catfish Row in Vicksburg, Eastland took an interest as well in areas bordering Mississippi that provided markets for his state's produce. Tennesseans often called him their third senator. For forty years, he had his suits made by Joe Aquino, the house tailor at the Peabody Hotel, then at One Commerce Square in Memphis. He bought other clothes at Oak Hall and even sent his Panama hats to be cleaned in the largest port between New Orleans and St. Louis.[9]

Yet Eastland retained close ties to the plebeian white majority in Mississippi as well. He liked to tell tillers of the soil that he was a John Deere farmer and boast that he had gone to but one embassy party during his six terms in the Senate. He kept his home phone numbers in both the Washington, D.C., and Sunflower County phone books. Some constituents knew that they could get him to attend to their problems even if they called after midnight or drove to his plantation. Often he got his best political intelligence at home, one governor noted, from farmers, ginners, and sawmill operators without a day of secondary education who had amassed considerable fortunes through diligence and knowhow. When he spoke in Mississippi during his first four terms, he often would arrive with prepared remarks, work the crowd from back to front, then dispense with the speech he had prepared and talk about those concerns that seemed to mean most to those constituents he had just encountered.[10]

Central to the imagery Eastland created for himself was an ever-present cigar, a prop with both Freudian and Machiavellian dimensions. For a man who ordinarily was shy almost to the point of timidity in private, a stogie added a trace of masculine authority. Some colleagues were aware he had a soft touch, but this was a trait he did not advertise. Those he did not know who were called before panels he chaired were often bewildered by the image of an aging, round-cheeked, bespectacled authority figure puffing away on a long Cuban cigar while shooting intimidating queries their way. Jean Allen, his longtime personal secretary, told friends that Eastland heightened the menacing nature of this image by inserting a wire through his stogies to keep the ashes from dropping. This was a tack he learned from his father, a prominent Delta attorney who customarily lit up cigars upon concluding his closing statement to distract the attention of juries away from the arguments of opposing counsel.[11]

To many colleagues, particularly younger ones like longtime Senate GOP leader Howard Baker, Eastland appeared as a "giant, quiet Buddha." He was the kind of legislator who said little but read voraciously, observed carefully, and missed little that proceeded before him. "Nobody knows what Jim's thinking," a friend told Willard Edwards of the *Chicago Tribune*. "His secretary doesn't know. His own wife doesn't know." While usually economical with his words, Eastland was invariably direct with whomever he dealt. But, as Calvin Coolidge had long before advised, he was just as careful with what he did not say as with what he did. "What you don't say," he often told people, "couldn't come back to haunt you." And, saying as little as possible publicly gave him plenty of room to maneuver behind the scenes, "the best way," he found either to shape policy or to help constituents. "Never do directly," he liked to tell Nixon aide Wally Johnson, "what you can do indirectly." According to Macon Edwards, the longtime lobbyist for the U.S. Cotton Council, Eastland "could walk through wet concrete and not leave a mark."[12]

Senators of opposite ideological stripes often found Eastland an invaluable ally. A master of the legislative process, he knew he had to deal with colleagues from both parties to get what he needed for Mississippi. Like his friend Lyndon Johnson, he was also quick to make younger colleagues aware that he knew their interests better than they did. Eastland relished the give-and-take of congressional horse trading and had a keen sense of when senators would compromise. As early as 1944, his second full year, Scott Lucas, the Illinoisan who later became Senate Democratic leader, noted admiringly that Eastland had swayed two votes from him on a measure facilitating the right of soldiers to vote. "You are the damnedest conniver," he told Eastland, he had ever seen, especially for someone who had been a member for such a short time. Eastland respected differences of opinion, and he expected colleagues with whom he dissented to fight as ardently for their constituents as he did for his. "You don't fall out with a person" he liked to say, "because you disagree with them." "More often than not," he told Ted Kennedy and others of all partisan stripes early in their careers, "you can work something out." When Birch Bayh, then Indiana's junior senator, got a request from the Pipefitters Union that the home of Eugene V. Debs, the socialist railroad union leader, be made a national monument, he asked Eastland for his assistance. "Don't worry about it," the chairman assured him. "I'll take care of it." At the next opportunity, Bayh moved to authorize the monument. William Scott of Virginia, a Republican known for holding a press conference to deny a report that he was "the dumbest member of Congress," objected. It fell naturally upon Eastland to try and reason with Scott that Debs and Bayh both hailed from Terre Haute, Indiana. "He's from his home town, boy," Eastland said before pounding the gavel and ordering Scott to cease and desist. Once Scott restated his dissent, Eastland commanded, "Sit yo' ass down," and then gaveled him down twice more. And, Eastland was a shrewd judge of character. This two of his "boys," as he designated the bright young men on his staff, learned that a bill increasing the number of judgeships in 1961 did not contain an agreed upon additional judge for Minnesota. Once his ideological opposite Hubert Humphrey called the inadvertent omission to his attention, Eastland confronted his staff. "Hubuht don't lie!" he told them.[13]

Brad Dye, a former three-term lieutenant governor and Eastland's driver during his 1954 campaign for reelection, found him more astute in knowing which government button to push to get what he wanted done than anyone else with whom he ever dealt. He would tell constituents, Cabinet members, or even presidents what exactly he could and would do, and what he could and would not. If someone brought to his attention something he found unethical, he would cut in and say, "They've got a word for it. It's called frawwwd: F-R-A-U-D. If I'd do that, they'd put both of us in jail." Eastland proved equally astute in telling the powerful what might pass and what would not. He could expound if need be why those measures would not pass, but seldom did anyone see a need to ask. Were a bill viable, he would let advocates of a bill know whose approval they needed to secure passage.

As he aged, Eastland came to enjoy mentoring junior members. For some he was a valued guide to the practical intricacies of the legislative process. "You understand," he once told a liberal colleague, "I don't approve of what you're doing, but if you insist on trying it, this is the way to do it." And, when a young Joe Biden wanted to rise to the chairmanship of the Criminal Laws and Procedures Subcommittee, he came to Eastland. "Did you count, boy?" Eastland asked. Biden responded that he had, and that he sensed a tie. Quickly, Eastland asked, "You want to be chairman." "Yes sir, Mr. Chairman," "OK," Eastland declared twice before Biden realized that he would see that the future vice president chaired that panel. Bill Simpson, Eastland's highly regarded legislative aide over the last decade of his Senate tenure, added that Eastland "understood power and its proper application better" than anyone he had ever seen. Eastland "understood what it was and how to use it properly and in the right degree," Simpson added. "He never pounded on a table, never screamed or hollered. He just got the job done."[14]

Indeed, Eastland relished nothing more than exerting his influence behind the scenes in usually subtle but still intimidating calls to appropriate officials of government or industry on behalf of constituents, regardless of how rich or poor.[15] Typical is the tale of Lamar Hooker, a young cotton farmer from Kosciusko, who, like Eastland and many other Mississippi farmers, was having trouble selling his crop in 1968. Several mill owners told him no one was buying. In the course of one conversation, Hooker mentioned to a merchant in Greenville, South Carolina, that he knew Eastland. "How well?" came the reply. "He'll call back," said Hooker.

Quickly, Hooker phoned Eastland's office at 10:30 P.M. and reached Courtney Pace, Eastland's chief aide. The senator was in a meeting, Pace said, and would return the call. A half hour later, Hooker answered the phone and heard a familiar voice. "Wha' chu wan," Eastland opened. Hooker told Eastland he needed to sell 4500 bales of cotton. "I haven't sold mine yet," said Eastland, but he would get back to Hooker as soon as he could.

Just prior to 8:00 A.M. the next morning, Hooker picked up the phone again. "You have an appointment with a mill broker at 10:30 today," Eastland told him. "Dammit, don't be late." Hooker arrived on schedule and found that not only had Eastland called the broker, but so had his junior colleague John Stennis and G. V. "Sonny" Montgomery, the congressman from Meridian, Mississippi. "I'll be expecting a call from LBJ any moment," the broker continued, before giving Hooker a favorable price, then declaring incredulously, "I've heard of deals like this, but I've never been in one."[16]

Eastland was equally quick to go to bat for friends of greater consequence, even infamy. Most instructive was his handling of the last wishes of Leander Perez, the boss of Plaquemines Parish, Louisiana, and his associate in several ventures involving Charolais cattle. Perez, long known as one of America's most vocal segregationists, had been excommunicated several years earlier by the Louisiana Catholic hierarchy after he had loudly pressed local white Catholics not to attend the newly integrated parochial schools near New Orleans. While those who followed the leading potentate of Plaquemines into rogue houses of worship came to be known as "Perezbyterians," Perez' foremost desire was to be buried next to his wife in the consecrated ground of a Catholic cemetery. Eastland was a Methodist, but had known for years of his friend's wishes for his remains. Shortly after Perez' passing, he had aides find all they could about the staff of the papal legation in America. Upon learning that the legation had several priests who had overstayed the length of time specified in their visas, Eastland got Edward Foley, a former aide to Harry Truman, to send for the Vatican's highest representative in Washington and tell him that he would see that those of his subordinates who had stayed beyond the schedules on their visas were deported. The papal ambassador asked how he could avert that. Lift the excommunication, Eastland replied, and let his bones rest in peace where he wanted. Only after Perez' remains were set six feet under a huge monument in St. Joseph's could the pope's legates rest assured that they could stay in the states as long as they were needed.[17]

Eastland could be far more generous than much of the general public might expect. Some around him noticed a soft spot in his heart for the multitude of street vendors who sold their wares around the Capitol to solons and tourists alike. If Eastland learned that any of them, many of whom were foreign nationals, were having trouble with the Immigration and Naturalization Service or another federal agency, he would intercede quietly on their behalf.[18] Even more telling was his reaction when an associate of relatively modest means informed him that he was afraid that his young son might be suffering from a rare blood disorder. "Look," Eastland responded quickly, "don't worry about anything, hospitals—NIH, Bethesda Naval—or anything else. You take him and I'll pay for it."[19] At least one civil rights leader has credited him with finding the attorney who got him acquitted after a charge of income tax evasion. Here was the kind of not infrequent gesture that engendered an extreme degree of loyalty, and not just from colleagues and staff in Washington. To Eastland, this was key. "In politics," he often told his "boys," "loyalty is everything."[20]

Eastland also endeared himself to colleagues by sharing credit with colleagues of any partisan or ideological stripe. At one point, he told junior members of the Judiciary Committee that he saw it as his duty, regardless of party, to help them get reelected. Once, he invited a freshman Democrat to sit beside him at a televised hearing. "Sit down here beside me, boy," he suggested, "I'm gonna get you some publicity." When a young Eastern senator told him of his interest in a bill that would allow many more Italian immigrants to be admitted, Eastland informed him that the leadership of the Judiciary Committee had already agreed upon a compromise almost identical to the solution his colleague sought. Even so, he encouraged his colleague to get some favorable publicity by introducing the bill committee elders had agreed upon. "I'll do what you want," Eastland assured him. "But you make me do it."[21]

By virtually all accounts, Eastland had the best political organization in Mississippi over the middle half of the twentieth century. He staffed his state and Washington offices with astute men and women, many of whom had served or were serving concurrently in the Mississippi General Assembly. While Eastland liked to say that bootleggers were his most loyal supporters, because they always needed him to get them out of trouble, Trent Lott found Eastland's political operation much simpler. In each county, Eastland, whom he termed the "Godfather" of Mississippi, relied upon but three key people. One was his local finance chairman, who often was the wealthiest person in that jurisdiction and could, if needed, raise the money for an effective campaign. Just as important was the local official who he deemed best placed and most effective in helping him serve the people of the Magnolia State as well as providing him sound political information. That official was a county supervisor more often than not, for Eastland knew that they were the politicos who came into contact with more people on a daily basis than any others. But Eastland's chief political operative in any county was not always the most prominent citizen in any town, but a loyalist, often a soul of blue collar background who was dedicated to serving him. In Lott's Jackson County, that operative made his living as a barber; in other counties that leader might be a pharmacist, a gas station owner, or a rural mail carrier, the kind of person who would come into contact with hundreds of voters a day. Some might own fairly seedy small-town hotels, where Eastland would stay during statewide tours out of loyalty. Eastland "knew the man at the crossroads," declared Larry Speakes, Ronald Reagan's chief spokesman between 1981 and 1987, who started his Washington career in the same role with Eastland. The secret of his success was simple, said Robert Everett, who shared a law office with Eastland in Ruleville. "He just delivers the goods."[22]

And, Eastland's distinct accent was enough of a subject of amusement that wags of the mid twentieth century loved to joke that the most southern points on the map of the United States were Eastland and Key West, Florida. That sense is borne out by a tale a young Joe Biden told Eastland's daughter Sue. Needing to get some work done, Eastland asked an aide, "Feel hot in heah?"

"The thermostat's at 72, Senator," came the reply.

"Feel hot in heah?" Eastland reiterated.

"Not to me, Senator, but I'll lower the thermostat," the seemingly helpful young man replied.

"Damn it, son! Is Sen-a-tah Feel, P-H-I-L, Hot, H-A-R-T, in heah?"[23]

Still, there was no part of the legislative work of the Senate that Eastland so relished than his role as a defender of the legitimate economic interests of his home state. Members from states bordering Mississippi fondly recall his and John Stennis' initial approaches to them for funding for the Tennessee-Tombigbee Waterway, a project that it took many a while to discover did not enter their states for even an inch. But it was the interests of the Magnolia State's cotton planters, large and small, that aroused his particular attention. "That's the reason I came up here," he would tell anyone who cared to listen. What first made his reputation in the Senate was his advocacy for them during his initial eighty-eight-day stint in the Senate in 1941. In part, his concern reflected self-interest. Phil Hart, the Michigan liberal whose integrity led Eastland to respect him as much as anyone with whom he had ever served, once said that the only thing that he ever saw Eastland worry about was his cotton crop. But Eastland was just as interested because cotton, the "white gold" of the Yazoo-Mississippi Delta, had provided the underpinnings of his state's socioeconomic system and the foundation of its agrarian heritage. "They make a lot of money off them sy'beans," he told Larry Gibson, one of the first African-American professors at the University of Maryland of Law, "but I don't care how much money it makes. I got to have some cotton around for sentimental purposes."[24]

CHAPTER 1

The Beginnings of a Southern Solon

IN HIS CLASSIC 1949 BOOK *SOUTHERN POLITICS*, THE YALE POLITICAL
scientist V. O. Key Jr. described struggles for statewide office in Mississippi as a seemingly biennial struggle of candidates from the Hills of the
Magnolia State against those from the Delta, with the victor almost always
determined in the Democratic primary. Aspiring politicos from the Hills
commonly crafted their appeals to their "redneck" base of small farmers
and working-class white voters with the socially conservative but populistic anticorporate rhetoric associated with James G. "The White Chief"
Vardaman and Theodore G. "The Man" Bilbo. Those from the Delta, often
termed "Bourbons," generally shunned the virulently racist appeals of
Vardaman and Bilbo, but adopted policies designed to further business
interests and maintain the rigid social and racial hierarchy so ingrained
in the Deep South. In James O. Eastland, who did not rate a mention in
Key's *Southern Politics* even though he was entering his second term in
the Senate at the time of its publication, Key would have found a paradox.
Here was a pol born in the plantation-based Delta hamlet of Doddsville,
who lived the brunt of his adult life there and ably advocated that area's
agribusiness interests, but was raised and buried in the Hill town of Forest,
and as former Governor William Winter noted, always identified in his
own mind with the "hill yeoman folks of Scott County."[1]

The first Eastland in America was Thomas Eastland, a Quaker migrant
who arrived in Pennsylvania in the early nineteenth century. Over time,
his descendants drifted down the Great Wagon Road south through the
valley of Virginia and the Cumberland Gap into MacMendel, Tennessee.
The first of Jim Eastland's ancestors to distinguish himself in Mississippi
was his great-grandfather Hiram Eastland, who settled in Scott County,

a locale in the heart of the piney woods 40 miles east of Jackson, and became its first sheriff. Hiram Eastland first settled his family in Ludlow, Mississippi, then moved them to Hillsboro prior to the Civil War. There, the Eastlands stayed until the devastation brought to his home and farm by the army of William Tecumseh Sherman forced them to move 8 miles south to the larger town of Forest. Hiram Eastland's son Oliver had even more success in the pharmaceutical world. He not only established a small chain of drugstores in Scott County, but concocted the antibiotic known throughout central Mississippi as "Eastland's Antiseptic." In years to come, the Eastlands sold their creation to the Tischner family of New Orleans, who marketed it as their own product throughout the South for much of the first half of the twentieth century. Still, Jim Eastland, an authentic Civil War buff, was always proudest to tout his lineage from Captain Richmond Austin, his maternal grandfather, who was wounded while serving under Robert E. Lee at Gettysburg, then transferred to the command of Nathan Bedford Forrest, where he rode in the cavalry.[2]

The idealization of the "Lost Cause" as a noble, chivalrous defense of the southern way of life was inculcated into Jim Eastland from his earliest days. His mother, Alma Austin Eastland, was weaned on firsthand reports of Yankee brutality and bitter and one-sided, often misguided, even hysterical accounts of "Negro rule" during Reconstruction. A kindly if shy daughter of a physician, she was never known to pass anyone while in her carriage without offering them a ride. Still, her passion was her work as president of the Scott County chapter of the United Daughters of the Confederacy, whose members, the group's historian Karen Cox wrote, "aspired to transform military defeat into a political and cultural victory where states' rights and white supremacy remained intact." Not only did she raise large sums of money for a monument to the women of the South on the grounds of the Capitol of Mississippi, but she impressed upon her son and anyone else who cared to listen the importance of distrusting federal authority and most if not all "Yankees."

It would have been hard for anyone to have been a more attentive listener than Jim Eastland, and he absorbed unquestioningly virtually every crumpet of the historical doctrine known to academics as the Dunning school of history, which most white Southerners and all too many Northerners swore to in the first half of the twentieth century. Although

William A. Dunning himself was New Jersey born and an Ivy League–trained scholar, he and his doctoral students at Columbia crafted the first historical treatments of the Reconstruction era. Each narrative followed the image depicted by Dunning himself in which newly freed slaves were placed "on the necks of their former masters." Acolytes of Dunning repainted a set of images they derived by unquestioningly accepting the attacks rendered by embittered white politicos in the decade after the Civil War and ignoring any evidence from blacks or others without ties to the antebellum southern establishment that might discredit fallacious and bizarre claims of "Negro rule." Those Southerners who imbibed these portraits almost always used them to buttress their own prejudices and fight any change in the racial order of the Deep South. Few were as socialized as Eastland to echo such claims. Before a Mississippi Democratic convention in June 1948, for example, he proudly exalted the examples of the Democratic leaders of 1875 like James Z. George, Lucius Q. C. Lamar, and Edward C. Walthall, whom many saluted as "Redeemers." It was they, he said, who "redeemed our institutions, reclaimed the good name of our state" and drove "from control of public affairs the grafters, thieves, carpetbaggers and social equality demagogues, who had fastened themselves upon a prostate and bleeding South." What he had not told fellow Democrats was these onetime Confederates had retaken their state from the Reconstruction Republican coalition through a campaign of terror, fraud, and chicanery rarely matched in the annals of America. Even more telling was his statement at an informal gathering of leaders of the Democratic establishment on August 8, 1974, just hours before Richard Nixon announced his resignation. Eastland asked everyone present who they would name as the greatest in American history in any number of categories. He would not allow Edward Foley, a former aide to Harry Truman who was his best friend in Washington, to voice his opinion on whom he deemed our best general ever, for Foley had been personal attaché to General George C. Marshall during World War II. But when those present got to Eastland, he ended discussion by slowly chirping, "No, suh. You are wrong. The greatest general in American history was a man . . . by the name of R. E. Lee."[3]

Virtually all in the Eastland orbit agreed, however, that the single dominant shaping influence upon young Jim Eastland was Woods Caperton

Eastland, his father. The second of Oliver Eastland's six children, Woods Eastland was a blunt, gregarious, stocky man who made friends easily. In his days at nearby Harperville College, Eastland roomed with Paul B. Johnson, a future governor of Mississippi. Around the same time, he came into contact with Bob and Tom Hederman, who came to manage the *Jackson Clarion-Ledger*, Mississippi's largest newspaper, and members of the McMullan family, who ran Deposit Guaranty, one of the state's largest banks. Unlike his father, Woods Eastland chose the law for a career. He specialized in personal injury suits, an apt decision in Scott County, an area laden with sawmills. But he also made enough suing railroads on questions like those involving rights-of-way that one of them placed him on retainer so he could not sue them again. Like many lawyers, he got involved in politics, first as an operator behind the scenes, then as district attorney of Scott County between 1912 and 1920.[4]

If Woods Eastland had a dream, it was to acquire more prime cotton land in the Delta. A generation earlier, his father had begun speculating in land in the hamlet of Doddsville near the Sunflower River, which in 1882 went for merely $1 an acre. Oliver Eastland and his sons snapped up hundreds of acres at slightly inflated prices over the next three decades. When there, the Eastlands loved to ride their horses to and from nearby towns like Ruleville and Shaw. By the time of his death in 1899, Oliver Eastland had accumulated some 2400 acres. It fell upon Woods Eastland to supervise the clearing of the family land of woodland and cane. This was no small task. In the late nineteenth century, the Delta remained a swampy depository well known for regular floods and high rates of malaria, yellow fever, and violence, not to mention wild hogs, wolves, panthers, bears, and snakes.[5]

Early in February 1904, one of those instances of violence took the life of an Eastland and several others. Albert Carr and Luther Holbert, black laborers who had worked for years for the Eastlands in Forest, had followed Woods' younger brother James to Doddsville, where he, soon after graduating from Mississippi College, took up managing the plantation. Carr and Holbert took to quarreling, almost certainly over a woman. The disturbances grew louder until the twenty-one-year-old Eastland found it necessary to investigate. His probe led him to side with Carr and to order Holbert to leave the plantation. Holbert's delay in departing prompted

Carr and Eastland to ride their horses to Holbert's cabin to enforce their decision on Wednesday, February 3. Who shot first and why cannot be ascertained with certainty, but Eastland and Carr were found dead and Luther and Mary Holbert, perhaps the woman whom he and Carr had fought over, had fled the scene.[6]

Within hours, Woods Eastland offered a $1200 reward for the capture of Luther Holbert and recruited a fifty-man posse to avenge the murder of his brother. That night, he killed a man he suspected of abetting Holbert's escape. Another Doddsville woman died from the accidental discharge of a gun from a member of the mob. Within three days, three other African Americans totally unconnected with the incident had been killed at points as far away as Itta Bena and Belzoni. In a Delta that was still largely wilderness, the Holberts eluded capture through that Thursday and Friday. But, while Luther had shaved his distinctive mustache and Mary had cut her hair and dressed as a man, the well-armed Holberts were spied asleep a few miles west of Greenwood that Saturday. When they arose, they were wounded and subdued by two men who were aware of the reward. Quickly, the two turned over the Holberts to the deputy sheriff of Sunflower County. But once the three returned to Doddsville, the mob overpowered the deputy and took the Holberts to a site in the yard of a black church directly adjacent to the Holbert's cabin. "Burn them! Burn them!" the thousand-man mob shouted. But before the flames could be lit, the mob proceeded to dismember the fingers and ears of both Holberts, then inserted and bored a corkscrew in several portions of the torsos and limbs of both.[7]

The gruesome lynching of the Holberts spawned outrage. Booker T. Washington, the one African-American leader known throughout the United States at the time, even while an accommodationist, lamented that the killings might have a deleterious effect "on the friendly relations which should exist between the races." Sunflower County prosecutors brought charges against Woods Eastland in September 1904 and convinced an all-white grand jury to indict him for murder. But while Eastland so obviously had taken the law into his own hands, the chances of an all-white jury convicting a white man "for lynching a Negro" in the Delta of 1904, as the *Greenwood Commonwealth* editorialized, were virtually nonexistent. Just as the editors prognosticated, a judge bought the arguments of

Eastland counsel Anselm McLaurin, a former U.S. senator, that there was no evidence that Woods Eastland had personally set the Holberts on fire and that the lynching of the Holberts was justified given the nature of their crimes. Before the case got to an all-white jury, the judge threw it out of court.[8]

Woods and Alma Eastland immortalized his deceased brother by giving their first and only child his name. James Oliver Eastland first saw the light of a Delta morning on November 28, 1904, little more than two months after his father won his freedom. Less than a year later, the Eastlands left Doddsville to return to Forest, which, unlike Sunflower County, had plenty of schools, doctors, electricity, and businesses. It was in Forest where young Jim Eastland was reared among the considerably less well-off hill farmers of central Mississippi. Even so, he spent most summers at what he called the family "plan'ation." It was on these day-long jaunts along the railroad, first from Forest west to Vicksburg, then along the Illinois Central to Doddsville, where Eastland first came to see large parts of Mississippi. Yet it was in Sunflower County where he acquired the paternalistic streak he shared with his father and all too many planters toward most African Americans. In 1942, for example, Woods Eastland recommended one Walter Flowers as a teacher by writing Governor Paul Johnson that he was the kind of trustworthy black man who would "teach the young negroes to be truthful, honest, and industrious and to know their place in life." For much of his life, Jim Eastland, too, as his daughter Anne Eastland Howdeshell told historian Christopher Asch, was convinced that blacks "would always need strict control."[9]

It was Woods Eastland who was the dominant figure in young Jim's life. Jim Eastland at some point became aware of his father's involvement in the lynching of the Holberts. He was embarrassed enough by the story to shield his own children from knowledge of it until well into their adulthoods. Only when his son Woods learned of the incident from some college friends in the 1970s did Jim Eastland acknowledge to any of them that his father indeed had been responsible, and then only with the bare facts. Being an only child, young Jim was showered with attention from his parents, and grew accustomed to lengthy man hugs from his father whenever he was away for more than a couple of days. In his early school years, one grocer found him "uppity," perhaps because the

Eastlands formed part of the upper crust of the society of Forest, a town then holding some 1500 people. As he grew older, the envy of Eastland turned to respect, as he, being the one kid in school with a car, could drive his classmates through town to anywhere they might want to go. Yet those who observed Jim Eastland almost to a soul recalled the family dynamics almost exactly as he explained a half century later. "My father," he said, "controlled me."[10]

In the all-white public schools of Forest, Mississippi, Eastland fared well in the subjects he enjoyed, particularly history. One teacher, Knowles Archer, called him an "outstanding" student, but others found that he did not apply himself in the subjects that bored him. While he was not much of an athlete, he was tall for the time, and his gawky 5 foot 11 inch frame helped land him a slot on the basketball team. His aloofness some likened to timidity, but he liked people, and was known to help fellow students whose families were struggling to make ends meet. He had a habit, childhood friend Oliver B. Triplet said, of appearing where there was a discussion going on and assuming a leading, even dominant role. "Whatever he said," Kenneth Archer, another of his teachers, declared years later, "went," even if he did like "to see a little scrap as much as anyone." And even at an early age, Eastland exhibited a real interest in politics. "He liked to pull strings," said W. E. Anderson, another high school friend, "but he didn't seek anything himself."[11]

Eastland got his first taste of state politics at the tender age of eighteen. Then, he took on the duty of sporting Democratic gubernatorial candidate Henry L. Whitfield around Mississippi in his Model T during his runoff primary against former Governor Theodore G. Bilbo, the longtime champion of Mississippi's poor whites. Not only did young Eastland gain a horde of new contacts in the campaign of Whitfield, an education-oriented business progressive, but he gained a keen insight into the friends-and-neighbors approach so pivotal in the politics of the rural South. Whitfield's election, he learned, came because he "knew how to get to the people" and "knew how to get close to the people." Never an overpowering orator, Eastland recognized he would have to do the same were he ever to seek office.[12]

In college, Jim Eastland relished campus politics far more than any of his studies. Although Woods Eastland initially thought the Virginia

Military Institute might be the best place for his son to matriculate, he changed his mind and started Jim at the University of Mississippi in Oxford. Then Woods Eastland convinced his son that the case study method of studying law being used at Vanderbilt University in Nashville, Tennessee, would provide him a more practical legal education than the textbook method being used at Ole Miss. Young Jim then transferred to Vanderbilt and finished a course of law that normally took a year to complete in a semester, right before finishing his schooling with a year in Tuscaloosa at the University of Alabama. "I just studied what I wanted to study," he later told reporters, rather than following any prescribed curriculum. Each time, his own children noted, Eastland transferred before he would have to fulfill the mathematics requirement. A member of Alpha Tau Omega fraternity, the Greek Club, the Phi Sigma Literary Society, and the Hermaean Society, a debating club, young Jim Eastland engaged in more than his share of on and off campus hijinks. He and a friend from Forest, Pat McMullan, later one of Mississippi's most influential bankers, ventured down to Cuba, a rite of passage for well-to-do southern youth in the half-century prior to the rise of Fidel Castro. They spent so much money that they had to wire home for additional funds only their mothers would provide. It was said that he broke open a ballot box to fix the election for a friend of his as the "prettiest girl" in the class as well as to steal the votes of those declaring him to be the "biggest liar." He managed the campaign of a friend, Raymond Zeller, for student body president, and another for the entire editorial board of *The Mississippian*, so they might hire him as their business manager. "We ran everything," he later boasted. Even so, he never graduated from any college. After reading the law in his father's office, he took the Mississippi bar exam in the spring of 1927 and scored the highest grade of anyone who took it that year, then dropped out.[13]

Jim Eastland was ready to run for public office. He was not yet twenty-three.

CHAPTER 2

Bilbo's Lieutenant

AS WITH SO MUCH ELSE IN JIM EASTLAND'S EARLY LIFE, RUNNING FOR THE
Mississippi House of Representatives seemed to be more of his father's
idea than his own. The attraction was hardly the pay. State legislators have
never made much money, and that was particularly true during the late
1920s in Mississippi. Members received $750 for each biennial session,
plus another $10 per day if they returned for a special session. In the view
of Woods Eastland, legislative service would give a newly minted attorney
like his son invaluable practical experience in dealing with some of the
leading figures in Mississippi as well as additional standing in his own
home town of Forest.[1]

Ironically, Jim Eastland had a reputation as a liberal during his first
venture into elective politics. Then a resident of the hill country of Mississippi and thus running for office in a district where Forest, with 1500
people, was easily the largest community, one could hardly expect anyone
to win who did not champion farm and public power legislation. Even for
a bottom-rung position like a state representative, it is rare for someone
just twenty-two years of age to emerge victorious. Yet so it was with Eastland in 1927, when he shocked his closest opponent, Forest banker W. D.
Cook, a man closely tied to the farming and commercial communities of
Scott County.[2]

In years to come, Eastland routinely described the Mississippi legislature as a "fast" track that more than amply prepared him for the U.S.
Senate. At the time, he aligned himself with the "books and bricks" agenda
of incoming Governor Theodore G. "The Man" Bilbo. Chester M. Morgan,
Bilbo's biographer, described his subject as a "redneck liberal" who voters
had brought back for a second term after an eight-year hiatus. In the years

between 1928 and 1931, Eastland embraced much of Bilbo's populistic approach that was reflected in programs to provide additional funding for schools, lengthen the school year to eight months, pave state highways with vitrified brick, reform the state's prisons, reforest Mississippi lands, and add $1 a day to pension programs for each of the state's surviving Confederate veterans. It was Eastland who floor-managed the legislation to provide free textbooks to the state's African-American students for the first time. Almost always, he was one of the more vocal spokesmen for the Bilbo program, and he did what he could to move it from his perches on the important Agriculture, Judiciary, Registration and Elections and Ways and Means Committees as well as the Board of Trustees of the State Insane Hospital. By the end of Bilbo's term, Fred Sullens, the editor of the *Jackson Daily News*, was deriding Eastland and legislative contemporaries Courtney Pace, who later would serve as Eastland's administrative assistant for all six of his terms in the Senate, and Kelly J. Hammond, a fellow freshman from Marion County, as Bilbo's "Little Three."[3]

At age twenty-three, Eastland proved an eager young legislator, determined to make his mark quickly. In later years, he often marveled at his own greenness as a lawmaker. "There never was a more ignorant man elected than I was," he told a group of legislators a half century later, adding that he was not even aware that he could go to the attorney general's office for help drafting bills. Bilbo's critics noted that the "Little Three" were often outmaneuvered by the more established, fiscally conservative powers who dominated the lower House: Speaker Thomas L. Bailey, Ways and Means Committee Chairman Joseph W. George, Appropriations Committee Chairman Laurens Kennedy, and Judiciary Committee Chairman Walter L. "Red" Sillers. In his first years, Eastland attached his name to a bevy of bills. Some, even if responsible fiscally, were ill advised politically. Bilbo even warned his "Little Three" that they should let senior members with specific jurisdiction thereof propose unpopular measures like sales taxes, rather than lead such efforts themselves. And, some colleagues were quick to judge those with whom they disagreed. "That was the impeachingest legislature in history," Eastland said later. A few of his colleagues even tried to impeach a dead man, he told reporters, before pointing out that they were unsuccessful. Still, Eastland determined from watching Bilbo handle the governorship that any further political career he might have would be in the legislative rather than in the executive branch. "For every one you make happy," he observed, "you make a whole lot unhappy."[4]

Eastland got his first taste of national politics as a delegate to the 1928 Democratic National Convention. While the Mississippi delegation was considerably tamer than the one the Ku Klux Klan controlled in 1924, the contingent Eastland served with at the Democratic gathering in Houston was sufficiently rowdy that humorist Will Rogers flatly refused to attend one of their meetings. They liked to fight so much, Rogers quipped, that they had run out of opponents. Tellingly, Delegation Chairman Homer Casteel rued that the drys were going to "drink up all of our whiskey" if the voting on the nomination lasted longer than one ballot. Prior to the convention, delegates fended off a challenge by the forces of drydom led by the Women's Christian Temperance Union and the Klan to instruct them to vote against Governor Al Smith, the "Happy Warrior" from New York whose intent of ending Prohibition was anathema to many. Once Franklin D. Roosevelt, then best known as the losing Democratic nominee for vice president in 1920, placed Smith's name in nomination, a fistfight erupted when Eastland and a few other Mississippians attempted to join the demonstration for Smith. When Mike Morrissey, a Vicksburg Democrat, grabbed the Mississippi banner, he was caned by Hubert Stephens, the state's junior senator. In the melee, a woman who was not part of the delegation picked up the Magnolia State banner. Eastland took it from her, then led the small Mississippi contingent for Smith in a few laps around the convention floor.[5]

As it was a Mississippi tradition to invoke the unit rule binding all delegates to the choice of the majority at either party's national convention, Eastland, like all delegates, answered the first call of the roll of the states by voting for Senator Byron P. "Pat" Harrison, who ran as their "favorite son." Once the votes were tabulated, frontrunner Smith had garnered the requisite two-thirds to become the nominee. While Harrison and Eastland followed tradition by moving to make the nomination unanimous for Smith, the first Catholic ever nominated for president by a major party, only seven and a half of Mississippi's other eighteen votes followed them to Smith's camp. Theodore Bilbo, who had given his proxy to a Baptist minister who served as secretary of the state's Anti-Saloon League, and

Speaker Thomas L. Bailey, a future governor, would not budge from their stands for Harrison, even in the wake of rumors that Harrison would get a Cabinet post if Smith were elected. Another delegate did switch his vote to Bilbo, of all people, a self-described "dry, . . . Baptist, . . . Klansman." Bilbo resolved his own doubts about who should be elected by declaring the Democratic nominee preferable to Mississippi GOP leaders Perry Howard, Mary Booze, and Courtney Redmond, all African Americans.

As for the general election, Bilbo was the chief Democratic spokesman in Mississippi, and he assuaged fears about Smith's Catholic faith by claiming the New Yorker lacked "enough religion to hurt anyone or anything." What he did for the first time was to accentuate the white supremacist strand of his philosophy. When speaking, Bilbo reveled in highlighting the fallacious line that GOP nominee Herbert Hoover had once danced with Booze, Mississippi's Republican National Committeewoman, and had courted other black women while overseeing relief after the devastating Mississippi River flood of 1927. He was hardly the only Mississippi Democrat to play the race card. "A vote for the Democratic ticket," Fred Sullens editorialized, "will be a vote for the preservation of white supremacy." His counterparts at the *Jackson Clarion-Ledger* hailed the Democratic ticket as the "White Man's Ticket." Pat Harrison, in contrast, refrained from going any farther than to reassure whites that "Governor Smith does not believe in the marriage of whites and blacks." From a twenty-first century standpoint, it is easy to applaud the ecumenical approach of Pat Harrison and Jim Eastland, two relatively conservative Mississippians, in declining to disparage Al Smith's religion. Sadly, the chief lesson virtually all Magnolia State Democrats, and in no small way Eastland, took away from the 1928 election was one Bilbo taught them. While Al Smith prevailed in Mississippi by a six-to-one margin over Herbert Hoover, he and his fellow Democrats had carried neighboring Alabama by only 7000 votes. Indeed, the Mississippi of the 1920s was a state with a sizable Ku Klux Klan population where Bilbo campaigned extensively, and one where pundits attributed Smith's win to the undisguised appeals of Bilbo and other surrogates to the basest of racial fears.[6]

At some point during his single stint in the state legislature, Eastland developed reservations about Bilbo. What offended Woods Eastland was Bilbo's vitriolic, crass, even coarse, style of demonizing his opponents, be they individuals or powerful special interests. "I trust to God," he later wrote his son, that "you will lay off of demagoguery," as it would "drive all of the intelligent people of the state away." Yet neither Eastland could mistake Bilbo's pattern of grasping for additional power, and some would say full control for the office of the governor that took hold well before Bilbo left office and continued long afterward. Perhaps the first Bilbo measure to arouse extensive opposition was his unsuccessful attempt in 1928 to spend $500,000 to build a state textbook printing plant, a project loudly condemned by commercial publishers and printers alike. Even more controversial were Bilbo's bids to bring all parts of Mississippi's system of higher education under his control. Bilbo critics led by Chancellor Alfred Hume of the University of Mississippi opened fire on his plan to move Ole Miss from Oxford to Jackson. With Hume rallying legislators, many of them Ole Miss graduates, to keep the state's flagship university in Oxford, Bilbo opted to try another tack. In May 1930, he used his power of appointment to name three undistinguished sycophants to the state board governing higher education. His appointees gave him a majority on the panel, which quickly acted to remove Hume; counterparts at the Mississippi Agricultural and Mechanical College (now Mississippi State University), the Mississippi State College for Women, and the Mississippi State Teachers' College; and many key administrators and faculty members. Once replacements were installed, the Southern Association of Colleges and Secondary Schools promptly disaccredited each of the Magnolia State's largest colleges. While Bilbo's successor, Governor Martin S. "Mike" Conner, ended the controversy by depoliticizing higher education, the incident and similar ones led the often colorful, even more often venomous editor Fred Sullens of the *Jackson Daily News* to chide the governor as "Theodough Graftmore Bilbo." Eastland was rarely so judgmental, especially not in public. Still, the controversy gave him some insight into the human condition, and perhaps even more into a man who later would become his most vitriolic critic on a strictly personal level. Power itself was not evil, he later told a key aide, "only its misuse is evil."[7]

To an even greater degree than the nation as a whole, Mississippi was in dire straits at the end of Bilbo's second term, and any incumbent would have had a tough road to reelection. The Great Depression hit the Magnolia State hard indeed. Farmers, who still formed the bulk of the state's population, averaged but $71 per capita in 1930, with cotton farmers faring even worse than those who grew food. Factional bickering had left the state's schools tattered from the university level down through the first grade, and the state was nearly bankrupt. Mississippi had a $13 million debt, and at one point, a mere $1376.27 in the treasury. In the eyes of fellow "Little Three" member Courtney Pace, who represented Delta areas due west of Cleveland like his own hometown of Pace, Eastland likely would have been reelected, whereas he would have been defeated had either sought reelection. In later years, Eastland told John Holloman, his Senate counsel, that he suspected he would have been defeated as well had he sought a second term.[8] But the idea of a career in the Mississippi legislature did not appeal to Eastland. Long before, Woods Eastland had implanted within him the notion that the purpose of an early stint in the state House of Representatives was to give him experience, a degree of name recognition, and an acquaintance with the movers and shakers in the state. That accomplished, he did not want Jim forever "scratching a poor man's hip pocket." Instead, it was Woods Eastland's idea that it was time for him "to get married and learn something about business and the law profession."[9]

Eastland hardly abandoned his interest in politics. By 1932, the year of the most precipitous economic decline in American history, he was embracing a plan of Senator Huey P. Long, the earthy, flamboyant "King-fish" of Louisiana, to ban cotton farming for a year so as to raise prices for farmers by reducing surpluses and allow time to eradicate the boll weevil. Long even brought Eastland to Baton Rouge to appear on his radio program to explain farming conditions in his Scott County district and report on how the cotton holiday movement was progressing in Mississippi. In later years, he recognized what was known as the "No Cotton" or the "Louisiana" Plan would have proved to be folly. "It was not practical and would not have worked," he acknowledged. "The prohibition of cotton would not have freed the price of cotton up because there was no money available to buy cotton." It was a different presidential contender to whom Eastland pledged his allegiance in 1932, when Magnolia State Democrats again elected him to represent them at the Democratic National Convention. In Chicago, Eastland heeded the state convention's instructions to vote for the ultimate victor, New York Governor Franklin D. Roosevelt.

But with instructions or without them, Eastland still would have voted for Roosevelt, a man he admired profoundly and later saluted as "the greatest domestic president in the history of this country."[10]

It was Sunflower County where Eastland spent much of the rest of his life. In 1930, Woods Eastland had moved his family to the plantation in Doddsville, a town that year's census recorded as having 317 people. On one visit, Jim Eastland got better acquainted with Elizabeth "Libby" Coleman, a strong-minded, 5 foot 6 inch, brown-haired doctor's daughter with a degree from Sophie Newcomb College in New Orleans and impeccable southern values. The attraction is not completely clear, for Libby made her living teaching mathematics, unquestionably his least favorite academic discipline, at nearby Ruleville High School. Still, the young legislator was impressed and began courting Libby, even if communicating wasn't always easy. With all Doddsville residents linked by one party telephone line, Eastland took to having a field hand ride his horse from his home half a mile west of town to hers a half mile east to carry messages to her. Were she spotted at the local drug store, Jim would race his horse there so he would run into her. His first proposal came while he still represented Scott County in the legislature. Not ruling anything out, she suggested that he "would have to get a job first." Once he began practicing law full time, he proposed to Libby in true Victorian fashion, while sitting next to her on the swing on her front porch. He used what he had saved from his earnings as a legislator to buy her engagement ring. The two married in the Coleman home, with Eastland's lifelong friend, colleague, and assistant Courtney Pace as his best man. They honeymooned on the Gulf Coast, with Depression conditions dictating that just one other couple could afford to share the hotel where they were staying.[11]

With cotton ranging in price from 4½ to barely 6 cents a pound in 1932, the Eastlands could hardly afford to start their wedded life in Sunflower County. Instead, they made their home in Forest, where Jim opened a law practice with his cousin Seaborn Ormond. With the piney woods area so full of sawmills, not to mention a few cotton gins, it was natural for him to specialize in personal injury cases. A man of few words, save with those to whom he felt close, Eastland was hardly a natural litigator. Even so, he developed a talent for trying cases, in part because of some rather rigid coaching from his father. Once, after thinking he had finished a solid argument to a jury, he returned to his chair. Before he could sit down, the ever-blunt Woods Eastland grabbed his son and practically commanded him to "get back over" to the jury and "look 'em in the eye." While not the master of courtroom psychology his father was, Jim Eastland was a superior legal researcher who came to sense that his clients appreciated him at least as much if not more than his father. Times were tough enough in the early 1930s that Eastland would seldom charge merely to give legal advice and would even draft *pro bono* simple contracts for the indigent. Like many professional people in the rural South in the early 1930s, he would often take food from clients who could not afford to pay him in cash. He and Libby would shop for fruits and vegetables on Saturdays so they might receive good deals on produce that grocers would otherwise let go to waste. It was in these years that Eastland's appreciation for home-cooked southern meals grew. Grits were his favorite food, he told one correspondent, and one colleague told his kids that they should dress their grits with soy sauce just like Senator Eastland. A chef who cooked for him noted that Eastland particularly enjoyed the pot likker from the greens he prepared. To be sure, Jim and Libby Eastland found some diversions in Forest. Eastland read voraciously, sometimes studying maps or atlases, but usually opting for history, particularly that of the Civil War, or detective novels or magazines. Each Saturday night, he and Libby would go to the movies. And, it was in Forest that the Eastlands started their family. There, daughter Alma Eleanor, who answered to Nell, was born in 1933.[12]

The next year, the Eastlands returned to the Delta for good. While the rise in cotton prices to 10 cents a pound had made the move feasible, even desirable economically, what dictated Jim Eastland's change of plans was that he was needed to help manage the family plantation, which had grown substantially with the purchase of an adjoining farm. His father's blood pressure had risen to a dangerous level, and Jim would have to take control of the financial side of the operation. There was no doubt as to who really ran things. "My father is the boss," he wrote in 1940, "and I am subject to his orders." While he seemed to spend more time at the law practice he opened in Ruleville with Robert Everett, Jim Eastland came to love his life as a planter. He especially enjoyed advising local farmers like close friend Otha Shurden of nearby Drew, Mississippi, as to what techniques had worked for him and how he could cut costs on his farm. In their first days in Doddsville, the Eastlands moved in with Libby's mother, known to all as "Eddie," in the house where Eastland was born. After a year, the four moved to a large if not ornate three-bedroom house Woods Eastland had built for them using yellow pine lumber from Scott County. In time, the house, located due west of the Sunflower River bridge just off State Highway 442, would expand to six bedrooms and the Eastlands would have three additional children: Anne, who was born in 1938, Sue, who followed in 1943, and little Woods, who today is happy to note that he was an "unplanned surprise" of 1945.[13]

Eastland's progeny remember something of an idyllic early childhood in Doddsville. Three grandparents and several aunts and uncles lived nearby, and Nell and Anne fondly remember eating breakfast and sometimes even dinner with the elder Eastlands with some degree of regularity. Immediately thereafter, Woods Eastland often treated them to a ride on his horse. Jim and Libby Eastland occasionally partook of casual games of bridge, he hunted, and the kids engaged in scavenger hunts and dances throughout the Delta. Sundays were a time for church socials, where Libby Eastland's oyster soup, devil's food cake, and cheese straws were in high demand. "It was a fun place to be white and . . . of a certain social class," Anne told historian Chris Myers Asch, the author of *The Senator and the Sharecropper*, where he thoughtfully juxtaposes analyses of the lives of Jim Eastland and civil rights leader Fannie Lou Hamer, a Ruleville native, in a work just as devoted to treating Sunflower County society as it was to considering either protagonist.[14]

Yet there were sharp schisms in Sunflower County society separating the white minority from the overwhelming black majority. In rural communities like Doddsville, whites and blacks lived near each other, but African Americans were expected to know that they were inferior and to show deference to all whites. Such a consciousness took hold in the minds of young Delta residents, the younger Woods Eastland said later, "from the time you decipher your first sounds." While the young Eastlands grew up learning from and even admiring the African-American women who cooked many of their meals, cleaned their laundry and scrubbed their floors, and the men who tended their yard, those African Americans who worked the Eastland homestead and others nearby always carefully observed the informal boundaries that permeated the Jim Crow society of rural Mississippi. Well understood, for example, was that black men who were close to the Eastlands were never to touch their daughters when they took them for horseback rides.[15]

It was hardly those in the immediate surroundings who concerned the Eastlands, however. Sunflower County, like much of the Delta, retained a frontier character replete with frequent outbreaks of violence for much of the first half of the twentieth century. On the Eastland plantation, the most obvious manifestation was the murder of one of their plantation managers by another white man not long after they returned to Dodds-ville. But the adult Eastlands, like many aristocratic Delta whites, always were quick to note the more frequent instances of black-on-black violence in their vicinity. Plantation bookkeeper Robert Ormond, a cousin, once wrote Eastland in Washington that he was happy that there were "no fights or killings" in his absence. More commonly, Eastland field hands got into trouble for cases of theft or unlawful visits to Delta stills. Aware of the need of all planters for field labor, local judges often suspended sentences or kept them light. The young Eastlands witnessed some fist-fights among the workers, but were far more likely to hear their parents and adult neighbors relating the proclivity of their field staff to get into trouble. Having sensed that their elders saw blacks "as children or as if they were not civilized," Anne Eastland Howdeshell told Asch that it "was understood that they didn't have the visceral values we had" and that it was necessary "to cut them some slack."[16]

Among his own almost entirely African-American work force, Eastland was known for a relatively rare paternalistic benevolence. With mechani-zation like that in the form of John Rust's cotton picker rendering large numbers of field hands, who almost always were African Americans, increasingly unnecessary, dozens on the Eastland plantation, like many thousands of others in the Delta, left the farm for more fruitful opportuni-ties. They often made their way to more densely populated areas of the Magnolia State, like Jackson or the Gulf Coast, but some found their way north. By the mid-1960s, sixty families remained on the plantation with little if any work to do. Still, Eastland continued to pay for the rent, the water, and part of the electricity for those who remained in the homes, a pattern continued by his offspring after his death. "He never told anyone to move off his place," said one of them, Wiley Caples, "no matter how old." Eastland, to be sure, was particularly generous to Caples, to whom he gave land to use on which to build a Missionary Baptist church where local blacks could worship, $1500 to buy a used Thunderbird, and spare change fairly regularly to buy cigars. He went even further in his later years, replacing the tar-paper shacks many of his aging workers lived in with small but sturdy brick homes. "Nobody," Woodrow Wilson, an elderly worker, told a twenty-first century scholar, "suffered on this place for nothing."[17]

It was this paternalistic outlook Eastland developed in the Delta that he would take to Washington when a call came in 1941. And it was this static racial order that Jim Eastland sought to preserve for the better part of his long political career.

CHAPTER 3

Cottonseed Jim

SCHOLARS OF HISTORY, LAY OR ACADEMIC, RELISH FEW DEBATES MORE than those portending to establish one date rather than another in a given period of time as the one around which all others revolved. Americans who chronicle the year 1941 with an eye toward events emanating from war almost always cite the primacy of December 7, the infamous date on which the Empire of Japan launched not just its foolhardy attack on Pearl Harbor that precipitated America's entry into the bloodiest war in history, but others on more populated sites throughout the South Pacific. Students of race relations would agree. Still, they would also award a strong honorable mention to June 25, the date President Roosevelt revolutionized race relations in the United States by using his power as commander-in-chief to issue Executive Order 8802. This order not only barred racial discrimination by any firm holding a contract with the federal government to produce war materials, but effectively ended his party's tradition of ignoring and even fighting the "equal protection" clause of the Fourteenth Amendment. Others, particularly European scholars, would make a claim for June 22, the date Adolf Hitler began his ill-advised bid to stretch the boundaries of the Axis empire with his invasion of the Soviet Union, the Communist power he had linked with less than two years earlier to divide and conquer Poland. Many Mississippians, however, especially at the time, found the same day equally momentous in that it was the day they lost their senior senator, Byron Patton "Pat" Harrison, to "exhaustion" brought on by a bout with colon cancer just a few months before he reached the age of sixty.[1]

Replacing Harrison, a man Washington correspondents had named just two years earlier as the "most influential" of all ninety-six senators, would be no small task. While he had lost a bid in 1937 to become Senate majority leader by a mere one vote, Harrison was at the time of his death chairman of the Senate Finance Committee and president pro tempore of the Senate, a largely honorific post that placed him third in line to the presidency. In the early years of the New Deal, Harrison had steered to passage such vital legislation as the Federal Emergency Relief Act, the National Industrial Recovery Act, the 1933 bill to relegalize beer, the Reciprocal Trade Act, and the Social Security Act. His backing for the New Deal had waned a bit by the onset of Franklin D. Roosevelt's second term. Harrison, his biographer Martha H. Swain explained, "viewed the New Deal as an approach to the exigencies of extreme depression" and was "not interested in adding provisions for social control."[2] In 1937, his lack of ardor for further New Deal programs prompted Roosevelt to lend his support to the candidacy of Alben Barkley, the future vice president from Kentucky, for the leadership. While some credited last-minute administration help for Barkley's win, Harrison intimates attributed the one vote verdict to the absence of home-state loyalty exhibited by Theodore Bilbo, by then Mississippi's junior senator, a Barkley backer. Still, by 1941, it was a dying Harrison who Roosevelt called upon to secure passage of his then-controversial Lend-Lease Program, which in time provided enough military and economic aid to allow millions of those who survived fierce Nazi and Japanese attacks to withstand those offensives.[3]

It is hardly surprising that Eastland would hail him upon his passing as a "great man, a big man, and a good man," a sentiment widely shared in Washington, D.C., and in the Magnolia State. On the day Harrison was laid to rest, 10,000 people flocked to his home church in Gulfport, one of the more impressive demonstrations of respect for a fallen legislator in all of American history. Vice President Henry Wallace and thirty of Harrison's Senate colleagues had taken a special train to the Gulf Coast to be present. Dozens of state legislators had arranged for their own train to bring them in from Jackson. Dignitaries and family members sat inside the church, and all others heard the services beamed outside over a loudspeaker placed in the parking lot. Jim Eastland made the six-hour drive from Doddsville to Gulfport to pay his respects. But it was telling that even with the offer of free train fare, Theodore Bilbo, who had become Mississippi's senior senator upon Harrison's passing, could not be found.[4]

It fell upon Governor Paul Johnson to name the person who would serve for the eighty-eight days it would take before an election could be held to fill the remaining sixteen months of Harrison's term. Johnson did not intend to pick from among the state's congressmen, as choosing any would likely alienate the others. He had made it known previously that it would be his policy in the event of vacancies to appoint loyalists who would serve Mississippi quietly and without controversy. Honoring a promise not to make an appointment until after an official period of mourning had passed, Johnson waited until June 28, six days after Harrison's passing, to phone Woods Eastland, his old Scott County associate, and offer him the seat. But the elder Eastland was in his sixties and ailing, and he told Johnson that he preferred to remain in the Delta. "Paul," he replied, "I don't want to go up to Washington, but I'd like for you to appoint my boy, Jim." Johnson responded that he next felt bound to offer what he thought would be a largely honorary position to *Jackson Clarion-Ledger* publishers Robert and Thomas Hederman, who also grew up in rural Scott County. Upon hanging up, Eastland phoned one of the Hedermans and got both to agree to decline the seat and to recommend Jim, which they were happy to do, for they had just begun to thrive in the newspaper business. That left Jim Eastland. Johnson found him at his law office in Ruleville at noon, and got Eastland's promise that he would not run to fill the remainder of Harrison's term and that he would do nothing to embarrass either him or the state of Mississippi. It was no surprise that Johnson would be appointing a loyalist, but it surprised many when he gave the interim seat to Jim Eastland, who at thirty-six would become the body's youngest member. Johnson introduced him as a "man of great ability, culture and refinement," who was "splendidly educated, . . . ideally suited for the job," and "very aggressive."[5]

Eastland accepted the appointment humbly, saying he wished he "were qualified" to fill the seat so recently held by a senatorial giant like Pat Harrison. He was quick to note that his trip to Washington with Libby and his daughters marked both his first visit to the nation's capital and his first ride on an airplane. His flight was sufficiently rough to force him to lay over for a day in Atlanta. When he arrived, he took the oath from Vice President Henry A. Wallace on July 3, clad in a gray three-piece suit with a blue striped tie and brown and white two-toned shoes. At that time, he became not just the youngest Mississippian ever to hold a seat in the upper chamber, but the youngest member of anyone serving in the Senate. It was hardly lost upon him that the *Jackson Daily News*, the organ of the anti-Bilbo, neo-Bourbon faction of Mississippi Democrats, had editorialized that he was not of "senatorial caliber."

As the winds of war blew stronger in Europe as well as in Asia, Eastland pledged little more than to follow Franklin D. Roosevelt's lead, especially on questions of foreign relations. Acting on Governor Johnson's advice, he would devote his time to making contacts that might help him in the future rather than running in the special election to fill the remainder of Harrison's term. To anyone who would listen, Eastland declared that he would be in Washington to do his "best for Mississippi." Over the next eighty-eight days, he patterned a work day whereby he would arrive in the office by 7:30 A.M. and keep at his duties until 9:00 or 10:00 P.M., a regimen that allowed him to lose ten pounds. Upon arriving in Washington, he rented a room in the Raleigh Hotel. A few weeks later, he moved over to the Wardman Park Hotel, and Libby took their daughters back to Doddsville. At the time, she expected that Eastland would join them permanently in the Delta once a successor was elected. It was her hope that her husband would always be the country lawyer she had married.[6] Unbeknownst to either, Eastland was not destined to be a temporary caretaker. Matters arose that not only affected thousands of Mississippians directly, but, if left unaddressed, would have hurt quite a few. On these issues, particularly those relating to his fellow cotton farmers, Jim Eastland would never remain passive.

To be sure, Eastland's presence at first was a bit inauspicious. Being the newest senator, he got only those offices that all other senators had passed over. That left him and his small staff, as always headed by former Mississippi House colleague Courtney Pace, with a small office in the basement of the only Senate Office Building at the time, which held but two desks, a leather couch, and a few chairs. Early on, he wrote his father to tell him that he was in bed early, at work by 7:30 each morning to answer his mail, cordial to visitors, and present at each session of the full Senate. Woods Eastland, in turn, used his letters to urge his son to stay away from hard liquor, to implore him to spurn any form of demagoguery, and to keep him posted of developments on the family plantation. The hundred drums of poison the elder Eastland paid for in July 1941 indicate that the boll weevil was still a substantial problem for the Eastlands and other Delta planters. But more than anything, Woods Eastland pumped his son for inside information about cotton and cottonseed oil, matters of prime import to any Delta farmer of any size.[7]

Enemies of Johnson and his friend Woods Eastland expected that Jim Eastland would be just a typical caretaker senator who would fade into oblivion after his brief stint. *Jackson Daily News* editor Fred Sullens, a man who had once knocked Johnson over a chair after Johnson pummeled him with a cane in the back of his head, printed a poem by reporter Kathleen Sexton, which assumed just that.[8]

> Just ninety days, not long enough
> For one to get acquainted
> And find Washington's half bluff
> And life not what it's painted.
>
> Where puppets prance to party strings
> And dance to lobby lyres
> And politics is God of things,
> And privilege works the wires.
>
> He'll cast a futile vote or two
> But ere he can grow dippy
> He'll have to pack his duds and blow
> Back to Mississippi.
>
> Then time will tell if one brief term
> Has spread its sly infection
> And stung him with that fatal germ
> The urge for re-election.

Indeed, where Jim Eastland intended to have a role during his brief stay was on legislation affecting cotton, a crop he maintained had "long been treated as a stepchild." Speaking from notes on a yellow legal pad, he first targeted a decision made in June 1941 by Leon Henderson, the head of the Office of Price Administration (OPA), to cap cottonseed prices at $25 per ton. For Eastland and others all over Mississippi, the losses would be enormous, as many planters made as much selling cottonseed, which was used to make oil, as they did from selling the fiber. In preceding months, Eastland had become intimately familiar with the degree to which many of his neighbors would be hurt. He and fellow planters had been planning on getting $60 a ton for their crop, and their losses would be substantial. But he was just as moved by the plight of small farmers who could produce but a few bales a year. Eastland took the occasion of his maiden speech to blast the decision as a "contemptible, malicious stab at the South," and carefully targeted OPA Chief Henderson, rather than the Roosevelt administration he served, for the directive he found so ill-advised. In truth, what Henderson aimed to do was limit the price-gouging he believed had proved so detrimental to the Allied cause during World War I. Still, Henderson seemed oblivious to the suffering many Delta residents had experienced over the previous decade. Eastland readily painted Henderson as part of "a crowd of bureaucrats . . . who fight the cotton South every chance they get." Indeed, Henderson's New Jersey origin made an apt political foil, as Eastland could thus concentrate his rhetorical fire upon him, a heretofore unknown Yankee, as opposed to the president he served. Roosevelt could thus quietly prompt Henderson to rescind the offending limit, with no appreciable political effect on him or his party. Within a few days, cottonseed prices reverted to nearly $60 a ton, and Jim Eastland had captured the allegiances of cotton farmers of all sizes throughout the Delta, a group that would form his most loyal bloc of supporters for the remainder of his career.[9]

Eastland proved equally quick to advocate for others in his home state if he thought any of Roosevelt's appointees had forgotten their interests. In mid-August, he learned that Henderson had set the price of Mississippi pine lumber at $27 per 100 feet, or $3 below the common going rate in recent weeks. With Theodore Bilbo, who hailed from Poplarville in the heart of southern Mississippi's lumber country, Eastland called upon Franklin D. Roosevelt at the White House and told him that lumbermen could not operate their businesses at a profit if they could earn no more than $27 for their pinewood. Roosevelt listened with a degree of apparent sympathy that few others could muster, then had Henderson arrange to meet a delegation of lumbermen at the Roosevelt Hotel in New Orleans. Here was an overture that became necessary once farm-bloc and southern senators let it be known that they were considering legislation to strip Henderson or any successor at OPA of authority to fix the prices of any agricultural commodity.[10]

At the same time, Eastland allied himself with the Senate's premier experts on cotton questions, John H. Bankhead II of Alabama and Ellison D. "Cotton Ed" Smith of South Carolina. It was these two he joined in pushing to ban the Commodity Trade Corporation from disposing of surplus cotton until prices reached 30 cents per pound on ten leading exchanges. In Eastland's view, the measure had become necessary once he learned that Agriculture Department officials were passing over American cotton when they received orders from Canadian mills and letting them buy cotton from Brazil to make uniforms for American troops. Initially, he suggested that the government place a floor for cotton at 20 cents per pound, an idea that led to an immediate upward spike of nearly 40 percent in cotton futures. But while farm-bloc senators led Congress to approve such a bottom line, Franklin D. Roosevelt vetoed a bill containing such a program at the end of August. In doing so, the president followed the advice of Treasury Secretary Henry Morgenthau, who maintained that a failure to control prices on cotton, wheat, and other crops would spur inflation that might harm any future war effort. Eastland found Roosevelt's position not just absurd, but discriminatory, but was careful to blame Morgenthau rather than his patron in the White House. Morgenthau, he said, had "always been prejudiced against the South, opposed to any cotton program, and totally ignorant of all problems relating to cotton and the South."[11]

If there was any issue traditionally identified with both the Democratic Party and the South where Eastland was quick to add his voice, it was that of free trade. Like so many predecessors, he felt certain that subsidies given to northern manufacturers in the form of protective tariffs effectively made it more difficult for southern farmers to sell their crops abroad and thereby limited their profits. Once that summer, he spied a Cadillac on Capitol Hill bearing Massachusetts plates and told Courtney Pace that Southerners were "paying for that car with this damn tariff." Early in August, he joined John Bankhead in introducing a bill that would allow duty-free imports of foreign goods to any country that used the money they would be saving to buy American cotton and other products. Within a month, he was meeting Secretary of State Cordell Hull, a fellow free trader, to secure passage of his measure.[12]

The Bankhead-Eastland bill, as it came to be known, embodied a theme that Eastland would proclaim for the rest of his term and indeed the rest of his political career. "These Yankees," he would tell one correspondent, "have been imposing on the South since the Civil War, and I will fight them as long as I hold public office." He would resist "any mistreatment," he told another, "whether it comes from Democrats, Republicans, Socialists, or Communists." His near dogmatic belief that the South had been abused worse during Reconstruction than any occupied people since the beginning of the American republic intensified after a visit to Gettysburg, his first, in early September. To be sure, he would never be shy about pushing programs like parity and the Rankin-Russell Rural Electrification bill, which inordinately benefitted the still-agrarian South. Yet he adamantly and persistently pushed the doctrine that the South remained poor largely because of Interstate Commerce Commission policies that gave preferential rates to northern producers and protective tariffs that had much the same effect. Prior to the Civil War, he was quick to note, the system of free trade in place had made Charleston and Natchez two of the busiest and wealthiest ports east of the Mississippi. By 1941, those towns flourished more from tourism than from trade, and their surrounding areas languished from inactivity.[13]

By the end of his eighty-eight days in the upper chamber, Eastland had made quite a reputation as a defender of Mississippi's peculiar interests. He had ignored those who had tried to tell him that interim senators could not accomplish much, believing instead that it would hardly hurt his constituents if he adopted a more active role than was the norm. He had made many friends around the chambers of the Senate, among members, their staffs, and even some pages. He had made even more in Mississippi. Fully 3500 constituents wired him to applaud his work to remove the cap on cottonseed prices. Eastland did suffer a bit of a setback in the special election to fill the remainder of Pat Harrison's term. He had backed Ross Collins, the congressman from Lauderdale County who had arranged for Ida Eastland Ormond, his aunt, to be named the postmistress for Scott County. But Collins had lost by a narrow 569-vote margin to Wall Doxey, the Holly Springs resident who represented northern Mississippi. Still, Eastland's appetite had been whetted for further service in Washington. Less than three weeks after his return home, he began to traverse Mississippi to "get the lay of the land" for a future bid. He discounted what seemed to be the conventional wisdom in Mississippi that voters in the rest of the state were determined to block the election of any denizen of the Delta. In one letter, he made it clear that he agreed with a correspondent who wrote that a Delta resident could be elected to the Senate who could "shed the Pharisee attitude of the average Deltaite and see eye to eye with the little man from the hills."[14]

Eastland even seemed to reestablish a relationship with Mississippi's senior senator. Bilbo invited Eastland to his apartment for a gumbo supper. Eastland got his father to lend Edward P. Terry, Bilbo's press secretary, the use of his family's vacation home at Lake Hamilton, near Hot Springs, Arkansas, for a weekend.

"He is all wool," declared Theodore Bilbo, "and a yard wide. God never made a true and better friend than Jim Eastland."[15]

The two would not speak again for another five years.

CHAPTER 4

Bilbo's Nemesis

EASTLAND'S INITIAL EIGHTY-EIGHT-DAY STINT LEFT HIM WITH A PASSION for the life of the Senate that would linger for nearly four decades. Within days after Representative Wall Doxey had been elected to fill the remainder of Pat Harrison's term, senators he had befriended let him know that they hoped he would seek a full term in 1942. While his wife and mother would have preferred that he resume a career in the Delta, Woods told his son that this might be his one chance to move up and that he hoped he would seriously contemplate running for a full term. By mid-October, Eastland had notified a select few friends that he had begun to take the pulse of fellow Democrats throughout Mississippi. He was hardly a novice. He could call upon contacts he had made across the state as far back as the 1923 Whitfield campaign and hundreds more from Paul B. Johnson's 1935 and 1939 campaigns for governor, in which he had been quite active, and even some from both of Theodore Bilbo's bids for the Senate, where he had been on the periphery. Eastland had made many powerful and wealthy friends in the Delta, and he still could rely upon the many less-well-off denizens he had grown up among and represented in Scott County. And he was hardly averse to scanning Ole Miss yearbooks to find classmates he had forgotten to ask for help. One friend even submitted a list of names for him to contact that he had acquired from an inmate at Parchman State Penitentiary.[1]

It was the outbreak of World War II that would provide the backdrop for Eastland's initial race for the Senate. Unquestionably, the most prophetic words Jim Eastland ever spoke came at a Chamber of Commerce banquet in Indianola on November 3, 1941. One of these mornings, he warned in the largest town in his home county, "we are going to wake up to find that the United States is at war with Japan." More than a month before the Japanese attack on Pearl Harbor, he predicted "one of the most startling naval battles in history" would be fought near the Hawaiian Islands.[2]

Eastland hardly had a clear field. It had gnawed at Theodore Bilbo since he entered the Senate in 1935 that Pat Harrison had enjoyed considerably more influence in Washington than he did. It irked Bilbo even more that the Roosevelt administration had granted Harrison a near monopoly of patronage in Mississippi. With Harrison's passing, Bilbo was determined to gain unquestioned control of all federal hiring in the Magnolia State. Right after Harrison's death, he prompted the Roosevelt administration to oust state Works Progress Administration director Roland Wall, a Harrison loyalist and four-term mayor of Brookhaven, so he might determine who the organization hired and who it did not. But Wall confounded Bilbo by entering the Senate race against Bilbo's ideal colleague, Wall Doxey, who had served northern Mississippi in the House of Representatives since 1928. Still, the limited scope of Doxey's victory for the last fifteen months of Harrison's term convinced Ross Collins, the man he had just narrowly defeated, that he might be more successful in a second bid for the seat than he had been during his first.[3]

Bilbo recognized that Eastland would be a formidable challenger to Doxey. As early as October 24, 1941, he contacted Governor Johnson, whom he had backed in his 1939 campaign, to urge him to push both Woods and Jim Eastland to join him in anointing Doxey as the new senator for life. Johnson was noncommittal, but Bilbo should have known that he would hardly oppose a friend from Scott County for any office, much less one he had initially appointed. By early 1942, Bilbo was antsy. His man Doxey was an amiable sort who had entered the upper chamber with the commonly found mindset among new senators that he was to be seen and not heard, even if he had chaired the House Agriculture Committee. Whereas Doxey patterned his course to reap legislative successes in years to come, Eastland entered his three-month stint in the Senate with the psychology that he would try and solve the few problems he could in his short stay, fully aware that he might not ever have another opportunity. His unusual productivity won him a following that Bilbo came to envy. Indeed, Bilbo wrote Johnson in January of 1942 and told him to tell the

Eastlands that he would support Jim for governor in 1943 if he would only sit out the 1942 Senate race. One thing that Bilbo could not know was that Eastland's experiences during Bilbo's governorship had convinced him that he would never seek any executive position. Another matter that Bilbo would not learn until the end of January was that Governor Johnson not only had not tried to talk Eastland out of the Senate race, but had promised him that he would call all of his county chairmen and put them to work on his behalf.[4]

Six months prior to the election, Bilbo sensed that a Doxey victory was far from certain. One way to ease Doxey's path was to reduce the field, and in a letter of February 18 Bilbo called upon Eastland to undertake a more patriotic course than merely seeking a Senate seat. After opening with a seemingly friendly "Dear Jim," Bilbo proceeded to urge his onetime legislative leader to "lose no time in rendering your all to your country and put on its uniform and help defeat . . . Hitler, Tojo . . . , and Mussolini," as Eastland fell between the prescribed military ages of twenty and forty-four. Libby, Nell, and Anne, Bilbo added, could be "abundantly provided for by your own means and that [sic] of your family." If Eastland acted as Bilbo suggested, he could avert being censured for "being a slacker when your Country was calling and needing your services to save our all" and eventually, if he survived the war, rise to be "the great leader . . . that you are destined to be." Bilbo closed in a page and a half long postscript by saying that he did not believe the reports he was hearing that Eastland was being "misled" into jumping into a fight that might precipitate a rupture between him and Governor Johnson.[5]

Eastland found Bilbo's letter an incredibly petty bid to intimidate him into leaving the race. Woods Eastland had never much appreciated Bilbo's long record of demagoguery. He had done his duty as a Democrat to make a perfunctory donation to Bilbo in 1940, but was so unenthusiastic that he would not make the trip from Doddsville, where he then resided, to Forest, which was still his legal address, to cast his ballot. In this missive, he found "manna from heaven."[6] Both he and his son sensed that if Bilbo's initial salvo became public and Jim added just a bit of his own political one-upmanship, he would gain considerable traction among the anti-Bilbo bloc of Mississippi voters that seemed to be growing daily. Unlike Bilbo, Eastland did not begin by feigning friendship. "Dear Senator," he began before he proceeded to lambaste his former colleague for his presumptuousness in telling him what his patriotic duty was. Bilbo was twenty-one when America went to war with Spain, he wrote, but he did not enlist in the fight against that decadent empire. Even though he would not be born for another six years, Eastland added, "I killed just as many Spaniards as you" and "freed just as many Cubans as you." Moreover, both Bilbo and Doxey were of military age in 1917, and neither had families, yet neither saw fit to take up the fight against the dreaded Kaiser of Germany.

In continuing, Eastland laid the foundation of the themes of his Democratic primary campaign, which still was tantamount to victory three generations after the end of Reconstruction in a state where Republicans were seen as the party of both the Union and the Depression. His fundamental target would be Bilbo, not Doxey, who he painted as an ineffectual Bilbo acolyte. Eastland charged that Bilbo had sent his original missive solely because of his desire to have as his colleague a Senator he could "dominate and control." The year before, he added, both Bilbo and Doxey had voted to add to their own pensions rather than use those funds for legitimate purposes that would benefit all. He refuted as sheer mythology Bilbo's point that it was customary to return senators to office for a full term who had first been elected in a special election. Not altogether truthfully, as he had accepted Paul Johnson's appointment as an interim one only, Eastland declared that he would have liked to have run for a full term in 1941. Had he done so, "there would have been no one to represent Mississippi," he said, as Bilbo spent the summer of 1941 campaigning for Doxey. In taking this tack, Eastland highlighted his own record while blasting Bilbo for what he described as a habit of inattention to legitimate duties. For most of that time, Bilbo had not been in Washington to help fight the dumping of federally owned cotton on the market or cut the price of cottonseed below that of the market value or even allow Brazilian producers to ship their cotton into the United States via Canada and thus cut the prices paid to Mississippi planters. Nor had Bilbo seen fit to return to the Capitol from his "Pearl River country estate" to vote to declare war on Japan after Pearl Harbor. Perhaps, Eastland added, Bilbo did not want constituents to know why he had allied with the Senate's leading isolationists in not just voting against, but filibustering, the bill repealing the Neutrality Act. But his principal aim was to cast himself as a worthy successor to the vaunted

Pat Harrison, and he was quick to recall both Bilbo's lack of loyalty to this accomplished Mississippian and his inability to match his legislative productivity.[7]

Eastland continued by telling Bilbo that his letter came as no surprise. "Regardless of how one might have befriended you in the past," Eastland wrote, "when you could no longer use that friend, you would turn against him with Japanese treachery as you did against the late beloved Senator Pat Harrison, who not only had a fat job created for you when you were down and out, but when you were elected to the Senate made it possible for you to get the little temporary standing that you once had in Washington."[8] Eastland would not be deterred by any thinly veiled threat, he promised. "If Wall Doxey can endure your praise, I can stand your censure." And though Eastland's postscript was but two sentences long, its sarcasm carried considerably more bite than Bilbo's. "In your letter," Eastland concluded, "you tell me that I must 'help defeat the Dictators Adolf Hitler of Germany, Tojo of Japan, and Benito Mussolini of Italy.' Why did you fail to mention the fourth—Theodore Bilbo of Mississippi?"[9]

Eastland's four-page retort infuriated Bilbo, who long had been known for his vindictiveness. Eight days after Eastland released his letter, Bilbo wrote a friend asking for dirt on Eastland and declared that he "made a flop in the Senate" and "wrecked himself with the Roosevelt Administration." Soon thereafter, Bilbo asked a friend in Drew, Mississippi, to comb public records to see who served on the Sunflower County draft board. To his chagrin, Bilbo found that those on that body were Eastland's friends and allies, so any attempt to get them to draft Eastland would not be successful. This should hardly have been surprising to Bilbo, for Eastland himself had served as an appeal agent on that panel until July 1941, the month he began his initial eighty-eight-day stint in the Senate. The dwarfish "Man" of Mississippi recognized that Eastland, and Ross Collins and Roland Wall as well, would try and make him an issue, perhaps even *the* issue in the election. But he reserved a special spite for Eastland, whose mention of his questionable financing of the materials and labor for his "dream house" had greatly perturbed him. In public, Bilbo would declare that Eastland's campaign was little more than a bid for a "permanent draft exemption." What Bilbo could not fathom was that his popularity in Mississippi was not transferable and was never as devoted as he imagined. Some of those whom he assumed would back any candidate he recommended were solid for Eastland from the beginning, even if Bilbo delivered sixty-four speeches over the course of the campaign deriding his onetime floor leader as a "little upstart."[10]

From today's perspective, the degree to which race was not an issue is remarkable. While the Old South ethos of patriarchal white supremacy may not have been, as Charles W. Collins argued, "rooted in the very fibre of the Southern soul," it was ingrained enough in Mississippi that all those who stood for statewide office until the 1970s were careful to honor its precepts. In 1942, Eastland was careful to hail his fellow Southerners as "the purest strain of Anglo-Saxon blood" in several widely circulated pamphlets. "It was Southern brains which formed this government," he added, "and which gave to the world democracy." On matters of racially directed policy, he was content merely to state his support for a poll tax. This to him was the "great bulwark of white supremacy" in that it discriminated against black would-be voters, who less likely could afford the nominal fee for the franchise. In that all of his opponents heartily concurred, there would be no political benefit if he opted to stress the issue.[11]

Where Eastland would wage battle was on issues relating to World War II. He pronounced himself thoroughly in accord with the programs of President Roosevelt and General Douglas MacArthur, the commander in the Pacific theater where more Americans were then engaged in battle. Indeed, he cast the war against the Axis powers as a war for "civilization and Christianity," and he said that his only immediate concern would be to "win the war." It was his strategy to knock out Ross Collins in the primary so he might engage Bilbo's ally Wall Doxey in the runoff, and Collins's record as chairman of a military construction subcommittee of the House Appropriations Committee gave him plenty of ammunition. On the stump, Eastland painted Collins as MacArthur's chief heckler "in and out of Congress." He had Courtney Pace supply surrogates with research indicating that Collins had opposed several defense measures beginning with MacArthur's request for a preparedness plan. "Tonight," he told an audience in early July 1942, "thousands of men sleep beneath the sands because they had too little and that arrived too late." For that, he blamed Collins and other members of Congress who had voted against funding defense measures like the fortification of Guam and Alaska, the naval construction bill of 1938, and expanding the Army Air Corps.

Eastland was especially harsh on Collins for backing the Ludlow Act in 1938, a proposed constitutional amendment he termed "Pacifist" and "Communist," which, had it passed, would have forbidden any troops to be sent abroad even after a congressional declaration of war until voters ratified that decision in a national plebiscite. He was nearly as critical of Collins' opposition to the Selective Service Act, and called attention to a *Readers' Digest* article Collins had written in June 1941 entitled "Do We Need a Mass Army?" From time to time, he got in shots at Wall Doxey for never having spoken for an important defense bill on the floor of either house of Congress. Still, he particularly relished contrasting his ideas with Collins', knowing that many Mississippians could be persuaded, if they were not already convinced, that Collins had voted in a way antithetical to the national interest. Restating their differences would give Eastland a chance to reiterate ideas he knew meshed with those of the majority of Mississippians. To avoid future wars, he declared often, the United States would have to be "fortified, equipped, and ready."[12]

Eastland was equally quick to blast those he deemed insufficiently vigilant in their commitment to the war effort. Throughout the campaign, in both public appearances and campaign literature, he spoke for the right of working men and women to protect themselves "from unscrupulous employers and from the greed of labor racketeers." His primary target was United Mine Workers chief John L. Lewis, a man who several times had breached a good-faith "no-strike" pledge most union leaders had forged with the Roosevelt administration for the duration of the war. Work stoppages that limited the availability of products as necessary as coal effectively harmed the war effort, Eastland believed, and he frequently painted those who perpetrated them as "traitors" who were "knifing the country." Not only did he slam Congressmen Collins and Doxey and Senator Bilbo for not lifting a finger against Lewis, but he also blasted Doxey for joining Lewis in pushing price control measures and in effectively smothering legislation banning wartime strikes. On occasion, he jabbed at Collins for not moving to deport the Australian-born west coast longshoremen's chief, Harry Bridges, who long had been alleged to be tied to the Communist Party. And Eastland relished any chance he got to snipe at Bilbo, whose sole contribution to the war effort, he said, was drafting a bill "to teach soldiers how to swim so they could swim across the Pacific."[13]

Still, Eastland, in planning his first statewide campaign, was just as careful plotting how he would frame his message as he was in determining what that message would be. That meant that he would traverse the state and appear in virtually all eighty-two of Mississippi's counties, often delivering four or sometimes even six speeches a day. He repeated his standard appeal often enough that William F. "Billy" Winter, his nineteen-year-old driver, rehearsed for his own future political career by reciting Eastland's speeches to his family's herd of cattle. Eastland shunted aside his essentially shy demeanor and developed what the future governor described as a "very intense, hard-driving" persona as a candidate. As much as one might like to idealize the political arena as a battleground of ideas, the politics of Mississippi, one of the more rural states, epitomized the notion expressed by Thomas P. "Tip" O'Neill that "all politics are local." Particularly in the pre-television age, retail politics at the "friends and neighbors" level were crucial to any candidate's success. Eastland in years to come often told volunteers that it was important to meet with Rotary Clubs and country club members for their help in fundraising. Ever more important to political success in Mississippi, he added, was gaining the support of county supervisors, as their closeness to the people better situated them to get people to the polls, and the Farm Bureau, the best organized group representing the largest profession in the state.

Eastland had a gift for quickly sensing whom he could trust enough to delegate authority and get a positive result. Many in at the outset were old friends like campaign manager Joseph E. Brown, a Natchez attorney he had given the nickname of "Varmint" at Ole Miss, or Oxford businessman John Lee Gainey, who specialized in figuring ways to get Eastland on radio to discuss each day's headline. His finance chairman was E. O. Spencer, the owner of the Walthall Hotel in Jackson, where most campaign meetings were held and that also had the largest safe in the state to keep donations. His most active fundraiser was Woods Eastland, who knew enough Delta planters and small-city businessmen he could hit up for hefty sums that would be used to air his son's speeches on the radio. The Eastlands also charged their hand-picked county organizations with raising $5 and $10 donations from less-well-off Mississippians. From the coffers of these entities, funds would be taken to pay for slick multipage ads that would be placed in the multitudes of daily and weekly newspapers operating in the state at the time.[14]

Eastland signaled the image he intended to project in his choice of Forest, where he was raised, as the site where he would open his campaign. In doing so, he reminded voters that this hill town was the one constituency he had ever been elected to represent, even if he had moved to the Delta. For the announcement held on June 20, 1942, he brought the high school band of Ruleville to play alongside that of Forest, and had the two towns bet a cotton bale as to which would produce a higher percentage for him in the initial primary. Also present were Governor Johnson, Lieutenant Governor Dennis Murphree, Congressman W. Arthur Winstead, and several state legislators. The agenda he announced hardly surprised anyone who had followed the campaign. His every act in the Senate would be to help small farmers and small businessmen, he said. He would fight to maintain the poll tax. He would be his own man rather than the rubber stamp of any politico, an obvious jibe at Wall Doxey. On military matters, he would back Franklin D. Roosevelt, his commander-in-chief, against anyone who would put their own special interests ahead of the war effort. In virtually every speech, Eastland spoke of his aim to prepare returning veterans to reenter civilian life by paying them six months of their regular salary so they might reestablish themselves at home. He would do his part to remove all federal discriminations against Southerners, particularly those replete within preferential freight rates and protective tariffs. He would try to end nonessential federal spending, including from New Deal programs like the Works Progress Administration, which he thought had outlived their usefulness. The one politician he took care to salute was the late Pat Harrison, whose work to raise teachers' salaries he pledged to continue. But Eastland also took care to reserve his clearest swipe not for any opponent, but for "the Man" who once seemed to be his patron. Were he elected, Eastland promised there would not be time for any attempt to "create a dictatorship in Mississippi."[15]

Ironically enough, the most influential Mississippian other than Bilbo who was quick to blast Eastland after his opening was *Jackson Daily News* editor Frederick Sullens, Harrison's chief ally in the press who long had been known as the most important Bourbon Democrat in the state. "His

few weeks of sitting around in Pat Harrison's seat," Sullens wrote of Eastland, "no more fits him for the Senate than one trip in an airplane would
qualify him to sit at the controls of a bombing plane." The wrath of Sullens,
who was also known for his fiery barbs at Bilbo, was hardly unexpected,
for he had never forgiven Woods Eastland for representing Paul Johnson a
decade earlier in a slander suit he brought against the *Daily News* wherein
a jury awarded the future governor $15,000 in damages. So whereas the
often-punchy Sullens could deride Eastland as a "playboy" and a "stooge"
and declare that his election would give the Magnolia State "the first and
second most useless" members of the Senate, his editorials were "cotton
spitballs," as the Eastlands termed them, which had a decidedly different
impact than he, a supporter of Ross Collins, intended. Those Bourbons
who were already in the Eastland camp, particularly those in the Delta,
could not be broken from their allegiance by a missive from a big-city editor. If anything, the Sullens pieces may have reinforced the image Eastland
aimed to convey: while he had come to manage the family plantation, his
heart remained with the interests and sentiments of the white hill farmers
among whom he was reared.[16]

From the beginning, Eastland predicated his campaign on the notion
that neither he nor Ross Collins nor Wall Doxey nor Roland Wall would
garner the 50 percent of the vote necessary to avert a runoff. With Collins
and Doxey both in Congress, it came easy for him to paint them as professional politicians who had cast several ill-advised votes against defense
measures prior to Pearl Harbor. Doxey was particularly vulnerable to such
a charge, for he had voted for a pension for members of Congress, never
a popular stance but a particularly controversial one during wartime.
Eastland avoided personal attacks on either opponent, but particularly
Collins, for he assumed that he would need the votes of Collins' backers
in the runoff. His opponents reciprocated for the most part. Roland Wall
did little more than to suggest that Eastland's moves of 1941 to raise ceilings on cotton and cottonseed prices helped but a few Delta farmers, an
easily refutable point. Doxey tried ridiculing Eastland as the "chief brag-
gart" with the "loudest clamor" and the "most promises." Perhaps Doxey
could have fared better when it was found that Texas Democrat W. Lee
"Pappy" O'Daniel had used his senatorial frank to send 140,000 envelopes
stuffed with copies of Eastland's Senate speeches to Eastland's Jackson

headquarters. While he and Bilbo cried foul, Eastland pointed out that he as a former senator could not use the frank. Once Eastland assured voters and the press that the assuredly tacky practice had been done without his sanction, the issue lost all salience.[17]

Regardless of the relatively small differences on the issues of the day and the give and take between the campaigns, the fact was that Eastland was the only candidate with an effective organization statewide. Wall enjoyed far less prestige from his Works Progress Administration experience than he expected. Collins had a base in his east-central Mississippi district, but only there. According to Orbrey Street, a Ripley attorney, Doxey had considerable support in northern Mississippi, but he had to carry all of it or he would not be able to pull it off. That proved to be the case, for in the initial primary, Eastland ran nearly 12,000 votes ahead of Doxey, who narrowly edged out Collins for second place and a position in the runoff.[18]

With quite a cushion, Eastland approached the main contest with confidence. He had created very little anti-Eastland sentiment in the initial race, and knew he stood to pick up the votes of many Collins backers statewide. Accordingly, he could have his father decline the traditional Mississippi way of winning the support of primary opponents by paying off their campaign debts. So while Doxey won the official backing of Collins and Wall in that time-honored manner, Eastland won the active assistance of their campaign managers and much of their organizations.[19]

What Eastland, with his keen political antennae, had discerned was that Doxey's particular vulnerability lay in the fact that Bilbo was backing him. While Doxey had benefitted from Bilbo's support in the initial race to a degree, his backing was a two-edged sword. Too many onetime Bilbo friends had come to see him as an ingrate and found themselves, as one wrote Eastland, "tired, sick, sore and disgusted" that Bilbo was "coming back to Mississippi and trying to tell intelligent people who to vote for and telling falsehoods on every street corner." Many outside the Doxey camp had come to share such sentiments, and Eastland was hardly shy about exploiting it by campaigning more against Bilbo than Doxey, his actual opponent. "This is our chance to get rid of Bilbo," Eastland started telling crowds. Bilbo's constant presence in the vicinity of Doxey made it easy for him to paint Doxey as Bilbo's "hen-pecked" puppet. His barbs grew more pointed as the election drew near. "In the gravest hour of our history," Eastland told one audience, "Bilbo has deserted his post of duty and is meddling in a political campaign. A matter like a world war and the confusion imposed by drafting the biggest tax bill in all history doesn't interest him. He isn't interested in anything except the election of his little Charlie McCarthy."[20]

Bilbo indeed was obsessed with beating Eastland, and he went about it in ways that harmed rather than helped Doxey. He recruited sixteen colleagues, most of them Southerners, to sign a letter countering Eastland's claim that he alone had prompted the OPA to lift cotton and cottonseed price ceilings in his initial eighty-eight days. Here was no endorsement of Doxey, even if some signers privately hoped for a Doxey victory. But any astute senator recognized that not adding their name to the letter would possibly lose them favor with two senators, particularly Bilbo, and perhaps votes for future projects in their states. But in challenging Eastland, Bilbo made himself rather than either Eastland or Doxey the issue. Here was a particularly counterproductive move, as it allowed Eastland to turn the tables on Bilbo in ways that reminded voters that he had been away from Washington in the summer of 1941. "My friends," he said in mock agreement with his former colleagues, "no one man can accomplish anything—God almighty is the only one that I know—singlehanded and without any help—God almighty created the world in six days, and on the seventh day he rested, but Bilbo wasn't there."[21]

Only Fred Sullens rivaled Bilbo in consequence among Eastland's critics. After Ross Collins, his favorite, had been eliminated in the initial primary, Sullens shifted his backing to Doxey. Eastland, he wrote, was an "emotionally immature, intellectually undeveloped, spiritually short-changed" soul with the "character of a buffoon and a bombastic playboy." But readers or followers of Sullens' who might have been motivated to switch had to be aware of Bilbo's support for Doxey and equally assuredly had to have imbibed some of Sullens' long-stated mistrust for Bilbo. Switches like Sullens' accordingly were few. With the firm support of the *Jackson Clarion-Ledger*, a daily with a much larger circulation, Eastland could relax and put out small fires. He could visit the Gulf Coast and reassure members of railroad brotherhoods that he would vote their interests and aspirations in Washington as he had in the legislature. He could refute the claim of an African-American newspaper that aides to "The Man" Bilbo were circulating that he only used African-American labor on his plantation. Eastland closed by pledging an investigation of the way Bilbo had funded the construction of an island "dream house" on a manmade lake on his Poplarville property. His election, he promised, would spell an end to "Bilboism."[22]

Eastland prevailed in the runoff with an impressive 56 percent of the vote. He carried sixty of Mississippi's eighty-two counties, running second only in Doxey's northern Mississippi congressional district, the areas surrounding Bilbo's Pearl River County stronghold and Hinds County, with Jackson, the state's largest. Doxey wired his congratulations as soon as his fate was certain, a characteristic act of gentility that Eastland appreciated. In return, he phoned Doxey, thanked him, then hailed him as a "gentleman" and a "worthy opponent," and avowed that he carried "no brief" against those who supported Doxey.[23] Here was a pledge he kept even for Bilbo, for he never pushed the investigation he had promised into the highly questionable financing he had used to finance his dream house and its surroundings. And he respected Doxey enough to join his new Senate Democratic colleagues in each of the next two Congresses in voting to make him their sergeant of arms.

Bilbo, unlike Doxey, would not bury the hatchet. He saw Eastland's caustic public reply to his suggestion that he enlist in the armed services as the "most dirty, insulting, . . . and insinuating, contemptible" response he had ever received. When Eastland approached him in Washington on his first visit to the Capitol, Bilbo turned his back. He told friends that he would "let this little playboy weed his own row, and with his own damn hoe." If nothing else, the election had made it clear that Bilbo's grip on Mississippi voters had loosened. In some eyes, Bilbo had lost much more in search of his holy grail of political omnipotence in Mississippi, even any sense of a moral compass.[24] Now he and Eastland were effectively equals, even if Bilbo was the more visible and senior of the two. Neither question of status concerned Eastland. His immediate priority lay in helping his fellow farmers, whether their holdings were small or large.

Still, the march of history dictated that he, in the not too distant future, would have to address more volatile questions that had plagued the Magnolia State visibly ever since the days of Reconstruction, but in actuality, even since the first Americans with English backgrounds be-gan to encroach upon the lands first occupied by the Chickasaw and the Choctaw. Eastland at his best would not try and replicate the Bilbo model of addressing such problems. Then again, those representing constituen-cies under attack often cannot hide a defensive tone in ways that scholars of the future will not find attractive, much less applaud. What seemed to supplant resolving the problems of rural America in Eastland's mind as the foremost challenge for the next generation was preserving the lost cause of retaining a paternalistic Delta society from any semblance of change. In the public eye, this dictated that he would be treated by virtu-ally all pundits outside the Deep South as Bilbo's heir. But unlike Bilbo, Eastland's general *modus operandi* with just a few noteworthy exceptions until the advent of the civil rights era was to work quietly on most issues and pay as much attention to the needs of his colleagues and those they represented as he did to the sound of his rather distinctive voice. That choice let Eastland focus his attention upon the needs of his home state. It also determined that he would have far more impact upon the workings of the Senate than Bilbo ever dreamed of having.

CHAPTER 5

The First Full Term of a Deep South Solon

EASTLAND ENTERED HIS FIRST FULL TERM DETERMINED TO ADOPT THE role of a tribune for the white South. Necessities imposed by World War II relegated civil rights issues to the background for the time being. Eastland would add his voice to those who had long condemned policies they believed hurt their native Southland, chief among them the high tariffs and discriminatory freight rates they saw as favoring northern industry at the expense of agriculture in the South and the Great Plains. Eastland could pursue his case for more equitable regional freight rates from his perch on the Interstate Commerce Committee. But like most freshman senators, his influence would be limited, for he had no special expertise on issues before the other panels to which he had been assigned: Territories and Insular Affairs, Education and Labor, Claims and Post Office and Post Roads.[1]

Like many younger senators, Eastland got some of his most valuable lessons in entirely different venues. One came late in 1942, when Majority Leader Alben Barkley invited him to the White House. Upon making his way to Roosevelt, the president greeted the young planter with a grin and a chuckle, then telling him to "sit down there in the corner." Once he greeted the rest of his guests, the president steered his wheelchair next to Eastland. In his previous eighty-eight-day stint, FDR noted, Eastland "jumped on" his "price man and raised the price of cotton." The tenor of his primary campaign, he added, made it abundantly clear that Eastland would not be a down-the-line New Dealer. But how Eastland got to the Senate did not concern FDR, who knew both men were "good Democrats" who had to get along. "You can come see me whenever you want to," Roosevelt added. "If you want something for your state, come on in that door over there, and I'll give you two minutes to tell me what you want, and I'll see to it that you get what you want. Then I'm going to spend fifteen minutes telling you what I want from you and you are going to do it. Understood?" "Yes, sir," Eastland replied. In truth, Roosevelt rarely if ever asked Eastland for anything.[2] But his message never left Eastland, who quickly learned how important it was to the people of Mississippi and his own standing in the Senate that he maintain a cordial relationship with the occupant of the Oval Office, be they a Democrat or a Republican.

What was most obvious about the new senator was the contentious-ness of his relationship with his senior senator. After Eastland won the primary, he approached Bilbo, who completely turned his back upon him. "I just won't pay any mind to him," he added. Eastland backers showed equal disdain for Bilbo. Swep J. Taylor wrote that Bilbo was incredibly un-scrupulous and that a common "cur" dog would make a better legislative partner. Bilbo seemed to prove this in an unheard of breach of tradition when he, as Mississippi's senior senator, refused to escort Eastland to the well of the Senate floor to be sworn in by Vice President Henry Wallace. Instead, Kenneth "K. D." McKellar, the aging curmudgeon from Tennessee, stood with Eastland. Bilbo's sniping never relented. As early as February 1943, he was lambasting Eastland for being "absent from his post of duty" for ten days, not mentioning that Eastland was home comforting Libby as she was giving birth to their daughter Sue. Privately, Eastland did feel the slight. In several handwritten memos to Courtney Pace, he confided a desire to steal the thunder of the man he referred to as "a certain party" by getting in front of movements to fight legislation he deemed anti-South.[3]

If there was any realm of public policy that truly interested Eastland, it was that involving agriculture. That was his "passion," agree those aides who survive.[4] While he did not sit on the Agriculture Committee at the outset of his service, he forged alliances with neighbors like John Bank-head of Alabama, then the leader of the cotton bloc, and fellow freshman John McClellan of Arkansas on most issues affecting the rural South. Over the next few years, they introduced legislation to raise the loan rate on cotton to near parity and limit the ability of the OPA to establish ceilings on cotton and cottonseed prices. They had some success when they lobbied officials in the Food Administration and the OPA to raise caps for cotton and dairy products. But Eastland was concerned that those responsible for cotton prices at OPA, while Harvard graduates, were too removed from farmers to be able to understand their plight. Too few, he thought, had ever been near a plantation or had any practical business experience to set policy as sensibly as they might. He recoiled at insinuations that cotton growers were making windfall profits, and rued that many southern textile mills were operating at a loss. His concerns were sufficiently strong that he called upon his colleagues in the winter of 1944 to create a special committee to study the efficiency of postwar agriculture, and often admonished state commissioners of agriculture in years to come to organize so they might better serve their farmers.[5]

More than anyone else, United Mine Workers chief John L. Lewis drew the wrath of Eastland in his first full term. His disdain reflected the exigencies of the war, for Lewis had threatened to have his workers lay down their tools to get higher wages. Eastland truly found "no right to strike in time of war," and he was quick to sign on to proposals that would let the government draft strikers. As time went on, he came to fear that the labor movement was moving rapidly to the left. He suggested on occasion that Lewis' aim was to have the government nationalize the coal industry. But Eastland was growing ever more annoyed with the growing involvement of union leaders in movements for racial equality. Even during the war, he was quick to chastise those linked to left-wing organizations, especially those with any perceived Communist ties. Remembering lessons he had absorbed as a child, he saw the Congress of Industrial Organizations (CIO), the leading federation of left-wing unions, through the prism of Reconstruction. In his view, carpetbaggers were using scalawags to control his home state.[6]

The first question on which Eastland crossed swords with the Roosevelt administration was that of ensuring that the men and women in uniform could vote in the presidential election of 1944. FDR and the national committees of both parties preferred a bill of Democrats Theodore Green of Rhode Island and Scott Lucas of Illinois to create a federal program to conduct voting by American troops. To Eastland, the Green-Lucas bill was dangerous, as it allowed federal authorities to usurp the constitutional authority of the states and even overturn the practice of many southern states of requiring all voters to pay poll taxes. Moreover, Eastland told the Senate in November 1943, the Green-Lucas proposal would "send carpetbaggers into the South to control elections" and allow men to vote, who, not withstanding the Fifteenth Amendment, "have never had the right to vote before." He, John McClellan, and K. D. McKellar crafted a substitute that they deemed more constitutional that called upon states to enact laws guaranteeing that soldiers be allowed to vote. While Roosevelt called the proposal of the three Southerners a "fraud" and Paul Prattis of the *Pittsburgh Courier*, one of the more widely read African-American newspapers, maintained it was motivated by Eastland's "fear of the Negro" being "stronger than his love of America," conservative coalitions in both houses of Congress opted for variations of Eastland's bill. In the end, the measure that passed without Franklin Roosevelt's signature prompted states to expand absentee ballot programs for soldiers but left intact the discriminations of the South, the course Jim Eastland preferred.[7]

Eastland, too, adopted a vocal role in denouncing any move to alter any practice that helped preserve white dominance over southern society. He was outraged by the Supreme Court's 1944 ruling in the case of *Smith v. Allwright*, which declared unconstitutional the practice in Texas and other southern states of allowing only whites to vote in Democratic primaries. With other discriminations that rendered statewide Republican victories impossible in most parts of the South, denying the right to vote in the primary that effectively determined the outcome of elections left African Americans without a voice in how they would be governed. Eastland was even more active in southern efforts to quash legislation that would ban states from requiring payment of a poll tax, which almost always served to keep poor blacks and whites from voting. As a junior member, Eastland followed the lead of senior Southerners led by Tom Connally of Texas, who their informal caucus had charged with formulating strategy. His initial contribution lay in drafting dozens of amendments to attack inequitable election laws he had found north of the Mason-Dixon line. "You'd be surprised," he told reporters. "Some of these Northern states' qualifications are pretty strict. They ought to be in a bill." Yet as the debate proceeded, Eastland introduced tactics he would use over the next quarter of a century to try and defeat any and all civil rights legislation. Inevitably, he argued that the Constitution vested all authority for setting qualifications for voting to the states. He attacked any and all legislation of the sort by alluding to support for such bills by various elements of the furthest left elements of the American body politic. He was quick to try and discredit the anti-poll-tax bill by noting that some of the bill's backers favored intermarriage and by describing the CIO, the largest federation of left-wing dominated unions, as both the "driving force" behind the bill and a body controlled by "alien Communists." Senators in 1944 were scarcely ready to break down barriers to suffrage. When they cast ballots in mid-May, thirty-six backed the invocation of cloture on the bill to ban the poll tax, while forty-four voted against cutting off a filibuster. For a time, the South had prevailed. But Eastland was too shrewd to think that the South's victory would be permanent. "We were able to defeat the anti poll tax bill this time," he wrote a constituent. "However, it is only a question of time . . . until this measure will pass."[8]

Still, Eastland remained a loyal Democrat, and he played a key role in determining who would be the next president. He recognized that the precarious state of Franklin D. Roosevelt's health meant that the man delegates chose for vice president was likely to accede to the helm before the end of FDR's fourth term. Like many Southerners, he deemed incumbent Henry Wallace far too strong of a supporter of civil rights and too unpredictable to trust as president. Unlike the past half-century, when conventions have served as coronations for each party's nominee and who he desires as his running mate, delegates prior to 1960 often had a real voice on the floor as to who would get the second slot on their ticket. Eastland came to the convention intent upon voting for James Byrnes, the South Carolinian then known as the "domestic czar" who had served his party in both houses of Congress, on the Supreme Court, and as head of the Office of War Mobilization. Once Byrnes withdrew from consideration after garment union leader Sidney Hillman, FDR's closest labor ally, promised to veto any Southerner, Eastland got Mississippi's delegation to cast their lot on the first ballot to Alabama Senator John Bankhead, his partner in drafting most cotton legislation. Bankhead realized as well as anyone that he was merely "a hitching post" for southern delegates. The real contest was between Wallace and Harry S. Truman, then best known as a onetime haberdasher from Missouri who chaired the Senate committee overseeing America's war effort. On the first ballot, Wallace led Truman 429–319, far short of a majority. Before the roll was called again, Robert Hannegan, the chairman of the Democratic National Committee told Eastland and Mississippi Democratic chief Herbert Holmes that the time had come to get behind Truman. It was Eastland who told his state's delegates that they needed to switch to Truman if they aimed to block a Wallace nomination—and perhaps even a Wallace presidency. Quickly, he grabbed the mic, demanded recognition, and announced Mississippi's intention to switch to Truman. While party officials ruled him out of order, other Bankhead followers joined Mississippi on the second ballot. Once other delegates sensed or in some cases learned that a Truman nod had the explicit approval of the commander-in-chief, an avalanche of delegates shifted their support to Truman, giving him an overwhelming victory on the second ballot.[9]

For Eastland, the Truman nomination seemed a godsend. Truman, he told correspondents, was a "warm personal friend" who sat directly in front of him in the Senate and was "level headed and utterly fearless." While the two occasionally disagreed, Eastland felt confident that Truman better than anyone else could bring the several Democratic factions together. And, were Truman to become president, Eastland told Mississippians that he felt certain that the Missourian would lead a fundamentally conservative administration.[10]

Family business effectively kept Eastland from much of a role in the fall Democratic campaign of 1944. In late summer, Woods Eastland, the father he idolized, traveled to the Mayo Clinic to have some gallstones removed. For the elder Eastland, any surgery was risky, for he had long suffered from high blood pressure. While he seemed to be in good spirits when he emerged from sedation that afternoon, the strain of the operation was just too much for the elder Eastland, and his heart gave out the next day. With the Senate out of session, Jim Eastland would remain in Mississippi for much of the fall to manage a big crop at the plantation that he and his father had expanded.[11]

Whether Jim Eastland ever knew it or not, at the time of his death Woods Eastland was quite proud of him. In Mississippi, Jim Eastland had supplanted state House Speaker Walter Sillers as Mississippi's dominant Bourbon. He had brought to an end his family's feud with *Jackson Daily News* editor Fred Sullens, who was lauding him by 1945 as one who held a "place that usually takes two terms for a member to gain."[12] And, Mississippians who needed help from their government knew to go to

Eastland, for his office was well known for the quality of its constituent service. Within the Senate itself, Eastland's favored role was as a tribune for the interests of his rural white constituents. This was true be they cottonseed oil mill producers, who feared that refiners of their products were manipulating prices through near monopolies on their market; oilmen, who wanted states rather than the federal government to own the mineral rights in coastal waters; postal carriers, for whom he advocated pay raises; or Gulfport-based fishermen, for whom he convinced the Army to move a bombing range away from one of their prime fishing sites.[13]

More visibly, Eastland joined John Bankhead in pushing to restore subsidies to planters not to grow certain crops, a practice that he believed had guaranteed surpluses that limited profits for hardworking Southerners. He was just as intent upon removing regulative clamps he thought had limited the earnings of long-suffering farmers and producers. Most culpable in his view was the OPA, which had capped textile prices at artificially low rates and effectively left some less-fortunate cotton growers struggling to make ends meet. By early 1946, he was demanding that the OPA be terminated and that its duties be transferred to other agencies. As a Mississippian, he quite naturally focused on the mistakes of those he called "the OPA boys" with northeastern backgrounds and no experience with or expertise in the practices of the textile industry, and he made a point to back all those with an axe to grind with the OPA. He was anxious to see sugar rationing end, Eastland wrote, and he joined other Democrats in pushing a measure to end the OPA's power to control oil prices. And, he said shortages had prompted his own family to change their household practices. Shortages, he said, had prompted Libby to make butter out of cream, for butter was hard to come by in Washington, D.C., and next to impossible to find in the Delta.[14]

Once Truman acceded to the presidency on April 12, 1945, the bills that most aroused Eastland's consternation were those funding and making permanent the Fair Employment Practices Commission (FEPC), the agency Roosevelt had created to enforce his ban on discrimination in war-based agencies. Like many Southerners, Eastland had become increasingly defensive on questions of race. With the *Pittsburgh Courier* encouraging African Americans to wage a "Double V" campaign for victory against fascism abroad and Jim Crow at home, Eastland had begun voting against appropriations bills in 1944 that included funding for the FEPC. Albeit in more restrained tones than those of Theodore Bilbo, Eastland ventured into anti-FEPC filibusters in the next two years with gusto, occasionally shouting that the FEPC "exemplifies the ideology . . . of Harlem and the Bronx." It was backed, he added, by the CIO, a "carpetbag organization," coupled with Communists and fellow travelers. Allowing the FEPC to continue, he added, might let federal authorities force quotas on manufacturers and might force white girls to "take dictation from a group of burr-headed Negroes in the departments." As less than 10 percent of the complaints were initiated against employers in Dixie, Eastland termed a permanent FEPC an attempt to "destroy Southern institutions." While challenged by New Mexico liberal Dennis Chavez, Eastland and fellow Southerners managed to end funding for the FEPC, a far less powerful body than they claimed, in February 1946. Even so, he feared that liberals would have enough votes to reconstitute the body under a different name within a few years.

Even more ominous to him was the notion that a vote to recreate the FEPC might embolden northern senators to pursue further civil rights legislation. In 1947, he found himself the lone Democrat on a three-member panel formed to study antilynching legislation. Any of these proposals Eastland would have fought with mettle, for he deemed them anti-South in motivation as well as "not the way to stop lynchings."[15] But the fact that none of these measures passed prior to 1964, when that year's monumental Civil Rights Act authorized the creation of the Equal Employment Opportunity Commission, is a testament to the effectiveness of the obstructionism of Eastland and other southern Democrats.

Even in the 1940s, Eastland believed that the Supreme Court was the body of government that had most usurped its power. In 1946, he joined Styles Bridges, the very conservative New Hampshire Republican, in introducing a constitutional amendment limiting any president to selecting no more than three Supreme Court justices. The proposal would be retroactive in character, and thus allow Congress to "unpack" the high court by removing its four most recent appointees, Justices William O. Douglas, Robert Jackson, Frank Murphy, and Wiley Rutledge. Here was a measure designed to call attention to the fact that Franklin D. Roosevelt had placed seven of the sitting justices on the Supreme Court. With them being the ones who had united behind some of the court's more controversial rulings, Eastland declared that he was merely trying to address the public's lack of confidence in the Supreme Court. While the Eastland-Bridges proposal did attract some attention, not all of it was positive. Some ventured that the idea conflicted with the spirit of the constitutional ban on *ex post facto* laws. More appropriately, wags quipped that the chances of the amendment being approved were about as good as Mae West's of being named president of the Women's Christian Temperance Union.[16]

In the public eye, the most notorious of the southern members remained Bilbo, whose words in print and in public grew steadily more vituperative as he aged. His was bombast with few parallels in the annals of the Senate. It had not been lost upon anyone that Bilbo in 1945 had addressed a letter to the sister of three Italian-American soldiers, one of whom had been killed in battle, as "Dear Dago." Not long thereafter, he had tried to dispel reports that he was anti-Semitic by declaring that he was "for every good Jew from Christ on down." Still, he targeted African Americans with the bulk of his more vitriolic rhetoric. Modern Bilbo scholars note a steady upswing in the intemperance of his anti-black harangues beginning in 1938, the year he began to forward his infamous "back to Africa" proposal, which, had it passed, would have empowered Franklin D. Roosevelt or any other president to divert funds from Works Progress Administration projects to finance the return of any African American who desired to return to the continent of his or her ancestors. Near the end of his life, he published a polemic entitled *Take Your Choice: Separation or Mongrelization* that provided more than ample evidence for those who deemed him the "archangel of white supremacy." Not long before, he had been heard decrying Congresswoman Claire Booth Luce as the "greatest niggerlover in the North except Old Lady Eleanor Roosevelt," and that what set the former First Lady below Luce was that she in Washington "forced our Southern girls to use the stools and the toilets of syphilitic nigger women."[17]

The events that precipitated Bilbo's downfall occurred during his successful fight for renomination in the 1946 Democratic primary. In that race, Bilbo called "on every red-blooded white man to use any means to keep niggers away from the polls" and told audiences they were "just plain dumb" if they did not understand. Clearly, he intended such rhetoric to incite violations of the Fifteenth Amendment at a time, wrote historian Robert L. Fleegler, of a "growing intolerance among many whites toward public racism and anti-Semitism." Senate Republicans aimed to expose patterns of intimidation, and they forced the majority to create a committee to investigate whether Bilbo had violated Senate rules. Members held hearings in Jackson in December and heard testimony from several African Americans that Bilbo partisans had forcibly prevented them from voting. Witnesses provided testimony at the same hearings that Bilbo had shaken down war contractors to donate to Wall Doxey, Eastland's chief opponent in 1942, and also failed to pay others who helped build his "dream house" in Poplarville and planned to seek future federal contracts. Onetime staffers let it be known that Bilbo had threatened their lives if they blew the whistle on their former boss. It was fortuitous for Bilbo that the senator who chaired the panel was Allen Ellender of Louisiana, his best friend in Washington, and that three of the five members were fellow Democrats. But while Democrats could block any findings against Bilbo as long as they controlled the Senate, they got a sense of what might come when they lost control of the upper chamber in the minority views of Republicans Styles Bridges of New Hampshire and Bourke Hickenlooper of Iowa. Never, the two wrote, had a senator employed such "vile, contemptible, inflammatory and dangerous language" as Bilbo had in a bid for reelection. While their claim could be disputed on historical grounds, the Senate was about to change hands. Be it because northern Republicans were interested in regaining some of the black vote, as Ellender charged, or merely attempting to preserve the dignity of the Senate, most in the new majority and even a few Democrats had become less than forgiving toward the foibles of one of their least popular colleagues.[18]

Eastland's relationship with Bilbo had not improved. When Bilbo was to be escorted to take his oath, he insisted that John Overton of Louisiana walk with him rather than Eastland. While Bilbo assumed that Republicans would try to block him from being seated, it surprised him when folksinging Idaho Democrat Glenn Taylor objected to his being sworn in. Taylor agreed that states had a right to choose their own representatives, but was determined to see that the Senate did not honor the election of anyone who had been elected in part because voters had been intimidated. Thus proceeded a two-day flurry of parliamentary activity where only eighteen senators joined Eastland in favor of Overton's motion to seat Bilbo. For Eastland, the question had no personal dimensions. While he was silent during the caucus meeting Democrats convened to consider the matter, he told the full Senate that what was involved was simply Mississippi being granted equal standing. There had been "no fraud and no coercion" in the 1946 election, he added, as literacy tests were equally administered to all. If senators suspected that Bilbo had profited unethically from defense contractors, he should still occupy his seat until the Senate conducted a trial. The speech was one Eastland gave perfunctorily only because Bilbo was a fellow Mississippian. Still, it was a cue for Bilbo to end a feud that once had him tagging Eastland with what Fred Sullens termed "the vilest epithet in the English language." He approached his onetime friend and extended his hand. "Thank you, Jim," he said in what may have been their last words.[19]

Debate over Bilbo's fate continued but a few hours longer. Right after the vote, Louisiana Democrat Allen Ellender, at 5 foot 3 inches one of the few members who could look "The Man" in the eye, took the floor to decry the "Gestapo tactics" he said the new GOP majority was employing to oust Bilbo. He was interrupted soon after by Minority Leader Barkley, who announced that Bilbo would be flying to New Orleans for surgery on a growth inside his mouth. Barkley was frank for the time, providing a note from the Senate physician saying that Bilbo was being treated for the cancer that would take his life. Robert Taft agreed for the GOP majority to delay further action upon Bilbo through the parliamentary device of tabling his credentials, but to continue to allow Bilbo and his staff to draw pay until the matter was resolved. When Bilbo did pass away on August 21, 1947, more than 5000 mourners joined Eastland, five southern colleagues, and the Mississippi House delegation at the services in Poplarville.[20]

Five Democrats vied to succeed Bilbo. The first to enter the race was Judge John C. Stennis of DeKalb, who had a solid base of support among fellow alumni of Mississippi State as well in his native east-central part of the state and the Delta. Not far behind were two House members: William Colmer, the low-key seven-term conservative from the Gulf Coast, and John Rankin, the fourteen-term economic populist from Tupelo who many joked was trying to "out-Bilbo Bilbo." The man most renowned in legal circles was Jackson attorney Forrest Jackson, who had argued some cases for the state NAACP but was best known for handling Bilbo's legal work. The man many assumed Eastland would support was Paul B. Johnson Jr., the thirty-one-year-old son of the governor who had appointed him to his first stint in the Senate. In the end, Eastland hailed all five as "fine gentlemen" and kept his preference to himself. While many tried to depict the contest as one pitting two remnants of the Bilbo tradition—Jackson and Rankin—against two calm and collected politicos in Colmer and Stennis, what in fact was at work was a classic case of "friends and neighbors" politics. While each of the five carried their home parts of the state, Stennis picked up enough ballots in other areas to prevail in the winner-take-all contest with 26.9 percent of the vote, less than 7000 votes ahead of Colmer, who came in second. That the race had been free of the rancor that had governed Mississippi senatorial politics over the past dozen years was best demonstrated when Colmer walked to Stennis' hotel room on election night to concede defeat and emerged arm-in-arm moments later with the senator-elect.[21]

Regardless of whether Stennis or any of the others had been elected, Eastland was determined to ensure a smooth working relationship with the new senator. The noncooperation that had characterized his relationship with Bilbo, and for that matter, Pat Harrison's relationship with Bilbo, had not helped the people of Mississippi. Once the people made their choice, John Stennis used his victory speech to reciprocate the sentiment by "extending the hand of friendship and cooperation." Eastland had Courtney Pace contact Stennis and instruct him on the logistics of the work life of a senator. This was important for Eastland, for he did not intend to spend any further time working at cross purposes with a home-state colleague of his own party. His delegation of authority to Pace hardly reflected any enmity toward Stennis, for the two—and Pace, for that matter—had served together well in the Mississippi House. But Pace's ties to Stennis were even stronger than Eastland's, for the two had been friends since their undergraduate days at Mississippi State. Pace extended to Stennis the use of Eastland's office, made reservations for him for his first days in Washington at the Raleigh Hotel, and advised him on how to hire a staff. Here indeed was the beginning of one of the longest and more successful partnerships in the history of the Senate.[22]

Eastland and Stennis served Mississippi longer than any previous pair of senators ever served their states, and longer than any until their record was surpassed by Strom Thurmond and Ernest F. "Fritz" Hollings in the 1990s. They conferred frequently, not just as to how they would vote but as to how each would explain his vote. When possible, they worked in tandem, knowing a united front gave Mississippi a stronger voice on Capitol Hill. They were dissimilar in interests, in political style, and in temperament. Eastland, unlike his wife Libby, was not all that religious; Stennis helped start the Congressional Prayer Breakfast. "I take care of John Stennis' politics," Eastland quipped, "and he takes care of my conscience." Stennis revered the orderly processes of the legislative branch, spent time in the Library of Congress, and took the time to master the rules of the Senate. Eastland was far more oriented toward winning results for whomever he saw as his clients at any given time. Stennis told one friend that he liked to go "straight at things . . . but when Jim could do something easily and with entire propriety, he seems to love to make it look like he did it by some shady backroom process." While the two seldom socialized, they were inseparable allies who colleagues saw almost as a single entity representing the Magnolia State. At one point in 1953, Stennis let Eastland's daughter Anne board with he and wife, Coy, in Washington while the Eastlands remained in Doddsville. Counter to what might be expected when one senator put up the teenaged child of another, the Stennises came to see Anne as a "practical, down to earth" young lady who was becoming a part of their family. Of her father, Stennis declared much later that "we got to the point that we didn't have to tell each other what we were thinking—we just knew." But Mississippians who wanted to hear a thoughtful discussion of public policy knew they should visit Stennis; those who needed help invariably called Eastland.[23]

Washington insiders often relate a tale about a Mississippi group who came to the Capitol to meet their congressional delegation. When they reached the Senate side, they called upon Stennis first, who, as always, was courtly and considerate. He spoke with the group about the importance of the Constitution, then took them to lunch, then up to the gallery to watch a session, then finally over to Eastland's office. There, they met Eastland, who was sitting in the dark smoking a cigar with his heels on his desk. Over the next few minutes, puffs of smoke arose with Eastland mumbling scarcely more than a word or two. After the group excused themselves, one of its leaders was heard to say, "That Senator Stennis was awfully nice to us, but Mr. Jim, he's our kind of guy."[24]

CHAPTER 6

Reconstructing Europe

LIKE SO MANY SOUTHERN DEMOCRATS INTERESTED IN EXPANDING markets for their produce abroad, Jim Eastland firmly maintained that the internationalist approach of Woodrow Wilson was the ideal way to create prosperity in the postwar world, thereby molding a lasting peace. In the election year of 1944, he regularly blasted Republicans for sabotaging the League of Nations and made it clear that he hoped that, after World War II, the United States would join an organization like the one Wilson promoted so boldly in 1919. Eastland served on a bipartisan delegation in early 1945 to conferences in San Francisco charged with creating the United Nations (UN). He told the Senate a year later that the UN would be a "powerful weapon in the preservation of peace," even while he feared that the veto given each of the five permanent members would render the UN Security Council less effective. He was quick to laud those in the State Department who promoted reciprocal trade agreements among member nations and thereby resisted temptations to wage "economic warfare."[1] Still, paramount in Eastland's so deeply held *weltanschuung* was his determination not to allow postwar Germany to experience the same cruel occupation he believed his native South had undergone after the Civil War.

Eastland's grounding in the South's mythology of Reconstruction was thorough. Southerners, wrote historian David Sansing, "don't learn about their past; they absorb it." Eastland was weaned in the doctrine of the "Lost Cause" by his mother, a county president of the United Daughters of the Confederacy. He read the history of the Civil War voraciously and devoured long-since-discredited works on the subsequent Reconstruction period. His favorite of these tomes, he assured correspondents, was *The Tragic Era* by Claude G. Bowers, a journalist turned popular historian who one of the South's leading liberal scholars of recent years called "an unapologetic racist." In *The Tragic Era*, Bowers, who never attended college but did keynote the 1928 Democratic National Convention, depicted Reconstruction in not just partisan but melodramatic, nearly Manichean, terms as a struggle between benighted white Southerners and ravaging Yankee invaders assisted by inferior, insolent one-time slaves solely motivated by ignoble desires for revenge and profit. This image Jim Eastland never lost. Nor did he ever lose his reverence for the bravery of the Confederate soldier. The South, he told the Senate in February 1946, had been defeated solely because of starvation, not by any force of arms.[2]

It was Eastland's dogmatic acceptance of these myopic stereotypes that led him in 1945 to air the most outrageous charge of his career. Like many from the Deep South, Eastland seemed eager to credit scattered reports by unnamed generals (albeit not Dwight Eisenhower, Douglas MacArthur, George Patton, or Mark Clark, all of whom praised their African-American troops) that black soldiers from any country were an "utter and abysmal failure" in combat. But Eastland went further, first airing his charges on the Senate floor in the latter part of June after touring Europe for three weeks with eight colleagues from the Naval Affairs Committee. He declared that black troops had performed a majority of the sexual assaults on French women in the 1944 Normandy campaign. Even more inflammatory were charges that black Africans serving in Stuttgart in the French occupation army had gang-raped nearly 300 women in a nearby tunnel. In truth, while several women were raped in Stuttgart in 1945, the rapes had come by individuals in private homes rather than in a tunnel. Whereas the troops were Africans, they were either Algerians or Goums from northern Morocco, who were of Arab extraction. It could hardly have been otherwise, for there were but four French troops with black African ancestry anywhere near Stuttgart at the time.[3]

Still, while blundering so egregiously in his identification of the perpetrators, Eastland gained knowledge from the same tour of Europe that would lead to public policy that he always considered one of his central accomplishments. With eight colleagues, five of whom (Harry F. Byrd of Virginia, Burnet Maybank of South Carolina, John McClellan of Arkansas, Richard B. Russell of Georgia, and A. Thomas Stewart of Tennessee) were southern Democrats, he met with generals and soldiers, and received a first-hand view of a Germany in shambles. Tens of thousands of buildings, factories, and homes had been reduced to rubble. Railroads had been destroyed, and refugees were roaming city streets in search of food and shelter. Some women were prostituting themselves for cigarettes or nylons. Hundreds of German males were being sent to Soviet work camps arbitrarily. This was no time for the United States to withdraw from Germany, each concluded, as the Soviet Union had started "to communize everything" they had liberated from the Nazis.[4]

What Eastland observed equated almost exactly with the images he had grown up imbibing of Mississippi during Reconstruction. Yet as Timothy Snyder noted in his recent and magisterial *Bloodlands: Europe between Hitler and Stalin*, the barbaric behavior of Soviet troops toward fellow Slavs, particularly women, in the lands between their homeland and Germany in the latter stages of the war was far more brutal than anything ever imagined by General William Tecumseh Sherman, the South's *bête noire*. Widely accepted reports estimated that vengeful soldiers raped 130,000 Berlin *fraus* and *frauleins* over the last ten days of the war, many of them repeatedly. Theft was just as common among the army from the east, with bicycles and wristwatches favorite targets. "Not since the days of Nero," Eastland declared after leaving Germany, "have Christians been treated so cruelly."[5]

If there was any postwar idea that drew Eastland's enmity, it was that of Treasury Secretary Henry Morgenthau to reduce Germany from an industrial giant to a pastoral nation too weak to threaten its neighbors. Indeed, he boasted often that he was the first member of Congress to oppose the Morgenthau Plan, which he deemed a "cold, calculated, selfish policy to destroy the German people," rather than one that would effectively serve the West by establishing a new Germany that might serve as a bulwark against any further Soviet expansion. Not only would it would wind up starving millions of German women and children, but it would also injure the American economy as well as have the more parochial effect of depriving southern producers of much needed markets for their food and cotton.[6]

Like Supreme Allied Commander Eisenhower, Eastland feared that American occupation policies would add to starvation in Germany. As might be expected from a legislator from a predominantly agricultural state, he was quick to advance measures to expand the UN Relief and Re-habilitation Administration so as to expedite food shipments to Europe. By late 1945, Eastland and thirty-three other senators of both parties, in a measure applauded by the American Civil Liberties Union, appealed to President Truman to intercede with Soviet strongman Joseph Stalin to expedite the resumption of mail services so westerners might send needed food. Soon, he joined Democrat Dennis Chavez of New Mexico and Nebraska Republican Kenneth Wherry in calling for a probe of American food policies toward Germany.[7]

Eastland aired his misgivings on the Senate floor. Sparing no hyperbole in a lengthy address, he blasted the "sadistic" approach toward the German people embodied in the Morgenthau Plan, which he charged the Treasury Department had developed without the slightest consultation with the far more knowledgeable staff of the State Department's Central European Division. Having just a few months earlier been denied entry into the Soviet zone of Germany where reports of rape, looting, pestilence and even mass murder ran rampant, he made his case in stark terms. Aside from the aberration of the Hitler years, he declared, Germany had served historically as a "neutralizing agent" and as a "barrier between the Orien-tal hordes and a western civilization two thousand years old." Germany would have to be quickly rehabilitated to assume that geopolitical role, for the "predatory aggressor" Soviet state that occupied the lands called Russia had begun to follow "the same fateful road of conquest . . . with which Adolf Hitler set the world on fire." And, people would have to be fed. Infant mortality rates in Austria and Berlin had skyrocketed. East-land feared the same would ensue in Poland, Czechoslovakia, Greece, and elsewhere in Europe without rapid attention from the United States. The only beneficiary of such "vast human suffering" would be Communism, and the final result would be "the cremation of Christianity" throughout the continent. "We should not make the children pay for the sins of their elders," he said.[8]

Once the Truman administration introduced its program of containing Communism, Eastland became one of its staunchest senatorial advocates. "Stalin is on the march," he warned, and containment was thus a "program of peace and not of war." "By stopping Russia now," he wrote one corre-spondent, "we will prevent another terrible war." The United States needed to begin to prepare immediately for war, he told another, for the Soviets would for the next ten years be trying to add enough industrial capacity to reach a semblance of parity.[9]

Well before Truman appeared before Congress in March 1947 to ask for money to help the governments of Greece and Turkey defeat challenges from Communist insurgents, Eastland was urging a program of massive aid. He steadfastly supported Truman when he requested $400 million for the Greeks and the Turks, as well as the Truman Doctrine, which committed America to defending any government resisting subjugation by Communists of any stripe, be it the relatively small band of Titoite partisans from Yugoslavia or the massive Soviet army. Seeing aggressive Communist behavior everywhere from the Baltic to the Balkans to Korea to Finland, Eastland echoed Truman in calling for resistance on every front. He was quick to take on anyone critical of Truman's containment strategy. Loudest in 1947 was former Vice President Henry A. Wallace, who blasted what he saw as an excessive reliance on military aid in London, and called instead for the United States to join in a ten-year UN program to extend $50 billion in aid to all countries in Europe including the Soviet Union. Less than three days later, Eastland took to the Senate floor to lambaste Wallace, whose approach he found similar to that of French Communist party chief Jacques Duclos, one of his hosts in London. "No American citizen," Eastland said, "has the moral right to conspire with foreign peoples in order to undermine and to weaken the hand of his country." While Wallace tried to dismiss Eastland as a mere "representative of a backward state," it was Eastland's words that found favor. Arkansas Democrat J. William Fulbright, hardly a Redbaiter, speculated that someone in the Kremlin might have written Wallace's speech. Arthur Vandenberg, the chairman of the Senate Foreign Relations Committee who many consider the father of the bipartisan foreign policy, went even further, describing Wallace's words as "treasonous."[10]

To be sure, Eastland had some qualms with the Truman approach to the Soviet Union. He called upon fellow senators to reject the Allied peace treaty with Italy, saying that it would give Yugoslavia's Communist dictator Josip Broz Tito control of 80–90 percent of what had been Italy's supply of hard coal. With Communist control of Hungary tightening in the wake of a coup, Eastland declared that the United States needed to take "decisive action against Russian aggression" even if it meant expelling the Soviets from the UN. Eastland's concerns were geopolitical and parochial. He could not understand why the U.S. Army was blowing up nitrogen fertilizer plants in Germany when a fertilizer shortage in the United States seemed to be limiting production of more than a few crops.[11]

As always, paramount to Eastland were concerns about cotton. He and other legislators from the Deep South made their case to anyone who would listen, even going so far as to lobby Harry Truman at the White House in June 1947 that German and Japanese textile mills should be barred from using any cotton other than that grown in the United States. Being a planter himself, he knew instinctively what the Delta Council, the principal organization promoting economic growth in the Mississippi-Yazoo Delta, had been reporting that competition from rayon and other synthetics had rendered the future of cotton "precarious." As early as May 1945, he had begun pushing with fellow Wilsonians Kenneth D. McKellar of Tennessee and Ernest McFarland of Arizona not just for lower tariffs but for a surplus export subsidy program that would use federal money as well to buy cotton and other crops and then give them to the war-torn countries of Europe to help rehabilitate their economies. While none of the standard histories of the era credit any of the three for influencing anyone in the hierarchy of the Truman White House, it is very clear that their ideas quite neatly parallel those developed within that administration between 1945 and 1947 for the recovery of Europe.[12]

In the early spring of 1947, most within the State Department concurred with Eastland that a peace could not be won without allowing Germany and Japan "prosperity, high living standards, if they can earn them, and freedom to work and prosper." This would be done by inviting all European nations to apply for credit to buy needed goods from American producers. Such a program would both benefit American manufacturers and farmers and hasten the revival of Europe. The true architect of the program embodying their ideas was Undersecretary of State for Economic Affairs Will L. Clayton, a 6 foot 6 inch native of Tupelo, Mississippi, who had risen from an eighth-grade education to run the world's most lucrative cotton brokerage firm. President Truman was set to unveil his administration's program in a May speech at the annual meeting of the Delta Council in Cleveland, Mississippi, but fears that his appearance

might be seen as favorable to one of the prospective aspirants to the Senate seat of the dying and as-yet-unseated Theodore Bilbo led him to send
Undersecretary of State Dean Acheson instead. Acheson's call to provide
"further emergency funding" to Europe to end further dislocation, wrote
cotton chronicler D. Clayton Brown, "resonated throughout the Cotton
Belt," but it took a more formal, better advanced and publicized appeal by
Secretary of State George C. Marshall during his June 1947 commencement address to give the plan a more national and bipartisan appeal, not
to mention its name.[13]

For the duration of 1947 and 1948, Eastland proudly lauded the Marshall Plan as "the one hope for permanent peace" in the face of the ex-
pansionism of the Stalinist Soviet Union. Seemingly forgetting the Nazi
Germany of the recent past, he described the Soviet Union as the "most
cruel dictatorship the world has ever known." Any attempt to limit the
extension of Marshall Plan aid, he told Rotary Clubs and correspondents
across Mississippi, would leave an open door for Communism throughout
Western Europe. He had reluctantly concluded that he would have to
support universal military training, as the United States was engaged in
a vital conflict of propaganda and ideology with the Soviet Union. The
only way to avert a deadly shooting war, he said, was to rehabilitate the
European economy.[14]

While Eastland steadfastly backed the Truman containment policies
at the outset of the Cold War, he occasionally advised the administration
to be even firmer. The Soviet blockade of Berlin instituted in June 1948
struck him as little more than a bluff. While ardently backing the airlift
of food and supplies to the once and future German capital, Eastland
believed that a credible threat to the Soviets, even an extreme one like
the dropping of nuclear weapons on several Soviet cities, would have
compelled the Soviets to withdraw their blockade much earlier. "We've
got to call a halt to Communist expansion," he said.[15]

In light of what has been known about the cruelty of the Stalinist regime and its successors at least since 1956, the year Soviet strongman
Nikita Khrushchev both detailed the crimes of his predecessor in his
secret speech to the Soviet Politburo and brutally quashed a Hungarian
revolution, Eastland's general support for the containment policies of the
Truman administration seems wise. But one has to wonder if he came

to equate what was so evil about the sins of the Communists with what he had been socialized since birth to regard as the sins of the Radical Republican regimes that had governed each of the southern states in the 1860s and 1870s. Often in the next few years, Eastland found the seeming Soviet heirs of the carpetbaggers he so despised lurking within any move to reshape the traditional southern society he venerated. On its way was what many scholars have termed the South's Second Reconstruction, and Jim Eastland was determined to resist its intrusion as ardently as any Georgian fought General Sherman.

CHAPTER 7

Dixiecrat

AS HISTORIAN KARI FREDERICKSON DEMONSTRATED IN HER SEMINAL discussion, the appearance of the States' Rights Democratic "Dixiecrat" Party in 1948 merely served as the culmination of discontent among the ruling classes of the Deep South with Democrats in other parts of the country who aimed to pursue policies consistent with the Fourteenth Amendment guarantee of "equal protection."[1] Permeating the consciousness of white Southerners after World War II was a fear that the dynamics of relations between the races were about to undergo profound, even revolutionary, changes. The valor of African-American soldiers like the famed Red Ball Express and Tuskegee Airmen truly buttressed the case of Swedish scholar Gunnar Myrdal in *An American Dilemma: The Negro Problem and Modern Democracy* that America's failure to live up to its ideal of civil equality portended a period of racial strife ahead. Especially illuminating was an encounter soon after the war ended between the Magnolia State congressional delegation and Lieutenant Van Barfoot of Carthage, the most decorated of all Mississippi soldiers. When asked by Theodore Bilbo, the most notorious of those present, if he had "much trouble with the nigras over there," Barfoot's reply caused the diminutive Bilbo to turn red. "I found out after I did some fighting . . . that the colored boys fight just as good as the white boys," he retorted. "I've changed my ideas a lot about colored people since I got into this war and so have a lot of other boys from the South."[2]

Few denizens of the Deep South who remained at home developed any similar degree of enlightenment. Walter Sillers, the Rosedale planter who served for a generation as Speaker of the Mississippi House, wrote Eastland just three months after his first election to the Senate and urged him to organize a southern bloc. "Let them betray us no longer," he wrote, "but stand firm for white supremacy and Southern Democracy." The paternalistic outlook Eastland took on racial questions resembled Sillers', but he resisted all appeals to split his state's Democrats from those elsewhere in America for the duration of the war. Roosevelt was as "strong as horse radish," in Mississippi, he wrote in 1943, and he knew such efforts would be futile, if not counterproductive. When a few delegates to the 1944 Democratic National Convention, with the blessing of former Governor Martin S. "Mike" Conner, suggested withholding three of the state's electoral votes from Franklin D. Roosevelt, Eastland joined Governor Thomas L. Bailey in resisting stoutly. "A vote for Byrd," Bailey declared, "is a vote for Dewey." In Eastland's mind, such a move was almost as certain to alienate other Democrats as accomplish anything he found desirable. While he had concluded that most New Deal agencies had completed the jobs they were created to do and were prime for termination, he remained strongly for Roosevelt in the face of all suggestions that he not seek a fourth term. Eastland never elaborated on his reasoning, but it is hard not to surmise that he saw no wisdom in changing presidents in the midst of the deadliest war in history.[3]

Even during the war, other Democratic leaders of the Deep South had begun to consider breaking with their national party. As early as March 1943, Governor Sam H. Jones of Louisiana wrote in the *Saturday Evening Post* that many were "rumbling" that both parties treated the South like "an orphan stepchild." That sense was illuminated in 1936, when the South effectively lost a veto on the Democratic nomination when their national party ceased requiring their nominee to secure two-thirds of the votes of convention delegates rather than a mere majority. "Our elected officials," wrote New Orleans rope manufacturer John U. Barr, "still had the power and prestige to hold in check the *revolutionary radicals*, the long-haired *New York communists* who were attempting to force an *unnatural* solution of the race problem in the South" (emphasis his). While critical of northern Democrats for channeling the majority of war industry to the North and maintaining freight rate structures that discriminated against the South, Jones was quick to assert that too many in the North had forgotten why the South had remained solidly Democratic for the past three generations. He praised Franklin D. Roosevelt for keeping tariffs relatively low, but bemoaned his sense that his party was condoning the "mongrelization" of the races and abandoning its commitment to the principle of states' rights. What Jones demanded that Democrats do to remain competitive nationally was a "complete reversal of attitude toward the South." Without the 115 votes the states of the Confederacy customarily provided his party, Democrats would be hard-pressed to capture a majority of the 531 electors.[4]

Four years later, the Alabama-born lawyer, banker, and librarian Charles W. Collins published a tome called *Whither Solid South*, which became the roadmap for those citizens of the Deep South intent upon fighting what they liked to call the "Second Reconstruction." Collins premised his argument on the notion that "no person could be elected to any sort of public office in the South who failed to subscribe" to the doctrine of white supremacy. With segregation "rooted in the very fibre of the Southern soul," Collins called upon the South to organize to resist the "misguided humanitarianism" and "religious fanaticism" of those who would disrupt the social system predominant in Dixie. There could be no compromise this time, he argued. Collins, for starters, revived a generally discredited idea of Theodore Bilbo and Marcus Garvey that all African Americans be moved to a forty-ninth state to be created in either Baja California or Africa. More popular was a suggestion that southern Democrats hold a regional convention to unite upon a candidate who could capture the votes of the states that had once formed the Confederacy as well as a few in the border South. They could not hope to win outright, but they could win enough votes to give the South the balance of power in the electoral college.[5]

At the time *Whither Solid South* appeared, an infrastructure was in place to set Collins' ideas into motion from among a group of Southerners who had tried to draft conservative Senator Harry F. Byrd of Virginia for president at the 1944 Democratic convention. While Byrd himself knew that their aim had no chance of fruition, their leaders, especially John U. Barr, held onto their lists, first in the hope of using them as a foundation to prompt Byrd to run against a successor to Roosevelt, then as a means to rally the South if they came to fear that northern Democrats were excluding them from their deliberations. An activist within the Southern States Industrial Council, Barr expanded the list of regional leaders he consulted. He drove to Ruleville to meet with Eastland in the summer of 1947, but did not find a groundswell of concern until word came that former Vice President Henry Wallace might challenge President Truman, a man they deemed far less likely to accelerate the pace of racial integration, in the Democratic primaries of 1948. While Wallace implicitly acknowledged that he had no chance to win the nomination when he took his followers to the fledgling Progressive Party, Barr and several around him developed an overriding fear that he might prevail or prompt President Truman to move sharply to the left. It thus became his mission to rally the leadership of the South to fight any change to its way of life. "The Democratic Party Should Be the Servant of the South," he wrote in a missive sent to thousands of small-town editors throughout the region, "Not Its Master."[6]

In the winter of 1948, Barr came to suspect that Truman aimed to move in the same direction as Wallace. He and other leaders of the Deep South were shocked by the publication of *To Secure These Rights*, a report of December 1947 that recommended strengthening the guarantees of civil rights seemingly granted to all Americans in the Fourteenth and Fifteenth Amendments. Little found in *To Secure These Rights* stood any chance of passage, for southern strength in both chambers of Congress was sufficiently strong to block any civil rights proposal. But what it meant, historian Harvard Sitkoff noted, was that Truman aimed to compete for black votes with likely Republican nominee Thomas E. Dewey, the governor of New York who had guided the creation of the first state fair employment practices commission, and Henry Wallace. To Eastland, this was a call to arms. Almost immediately, he bought a copy of *Whither Solid South* and passed it on to Governor Fielding L. Wright. Over the next few weeks, the two purchased 300 more copies and distributed them throughout the region.[7]

Like Walter Sillers, Eastland wanted Wright to be the public face of the southern revolt in Mississippi. A governor in his view had far more opportunities to organize and direct public sentiment than did a senator based in Washington. There were more personal elements to Eastland's sentiment. Not only had Libby Eastland suffered a heart attack in 1947, but he had long before ruled out ever seeking an elective executive position. More importantly, he would hardly abandon a safe Senate seat to take a position on the national ticket of a fourth party. Unlike Eastland, Wright, a onetime semipro baseball player from the Delta town of Rolling Fork, had no reelection concerns, having been elected to a full term in November 1947 after having taken over a year earlier upon the death of Governor Bailey. An attorney known for a stern personality, Wright had served with Eastland in the legislature. There, he had focused on transportation issues, but had taken issue with Theodore Bilbo and other populist-tinged politicos often enough to be labeled a Bourbon. But on January 20, 1948, he laid down the gauntlet for white Mississippians in what was his inaugural address as governor.[8]

Wright opened his full term with a plea to the legislature to preserve "vital principles and eternal truths." Truman's inclusion of a civil rights program in his State of the Union Address was merely part of a "campaign of abuse and misrepresentation . . . by those who wanted to tear down and disrupt our institutions and our way of life." "The time had come," he added, for the "militant people of the South and the Nation . . . to band together" to preserve "true Americanism." Eastland endorsed his appeal in a brief address to the Senate, and repeated his opposition to the Truman proposals. John U. Barr echoed them in an address to the venetian blind industry and warned that the South would no longer condone "class and racial boondoggling."[9]

On January 29, 1948, Eastland hailed Wright in an address to the Mississippi General Assembly for standing "against sinister encroachments in states' rights and our way of living." Southern society, he said in opening an hour-long address, was "built on segregation" and, like any other "country with a color problem," was "being swept to its destruction." "Every decent Southerner wants the Negro to have a square deal and enjoy the fruits of his labors," he added. "The only rule we have is that he stay out of politics, because he will use the power of the ballot to destroy our laws." To his chagrin, blacks were becoming more aggressive in demanding that federal government protect their rights. Even worse than NAACP leader Walter White having more influence than "all the Southern states," he said, was that Republicans and "mongrel Democrats" were trying to "punish" Southerners for adhering to the "time honored principles" of their party. He was even harsher on those around the president, who he feared would barter southern institutions for the votes of the "red mongrel minority groups" of the North. Their insistence on pushing for measures he felt certain they knew to be unconstitutional had resulted in the South having "their backs to the wall." There could be no delay, he wrote one correspondent. The South would "be destroyed, unless her people act."[10]

Here was Eastland's first salvo in a multifaceted year-long campaign to compel national Democrats to pay more attention to white Southerners. Charleston congressman L. Mendel Rivers termed Truman's program a "premeditated and inexcusable" attack on the South. John McMillan, a more volatile South Carolina congressman, charged that Presidents Roosevelt and Truman were "always ready to sacrifice any and all the Southern sacred rights for a few colored and Jew votes in New York and Chicago." John Rankin of Tupelo pronounced that Truman was trying to shove the Communist Party platform down the throat of the American people. But neither they nor anyone else could forge a united front. Fielding Wright attended a conference of southern governors at Wakulla Springs, Florida, over the first weekend in February and tried to swing his cohorts behind a proposition to make it clear that they would condone no further attempts to push civil rights legislation. Wright found colleagues as opposed to Truman's program as he, but unwilling to contemplate seceding from the national party. All they would agree to was to create a panel recommended by Strom Thurmond of South Carolina that would seek a compromise during a forty-day "cooling off" period.[11]

Eastland echoed Wright's position on the Senate floor two days later. As always, he berated the North for policies he thought effectively relegated the South to colonial status, like existing discriminations on freight and tariff rates. But the focal point of Eastland's address remained his disdain for the measures pushed in *To Secure These Rights*. Here to Eastland was a program almost identical to the Reconstruction era policies that the Republican Party had pushed in the post–Civil War era to "destroy the white race in the South." But the South had options. It could refuse to vote for the national ticket. Playing "hard to get" might allow the South to elect one of their own, or, at the very least let Dixie residents "dictate" their party's policies. Southerners in other offices met in other venues over the next month, but few were anxious to operate outside of their ancestral party. "Where does he think we would go?" asked Congressman Robert L. F. Sikes of the Florida Panhandle. Paul Brown of Georgia wrote Strom

Thurmond and asserted that history showed that South Carolina's best previous defender of the southern way of life was Pitchfork Ben Tillman, whose policies had gone into effect because he waged his fight within the Democratic Party. Senators Harry Byrd and Burnet Maybank agreed that no good could come out of a third party race. For Eastland, the notion that Southerners should accept the outcome of any internecine struggle within their own party had become anathema. "This is what the northern bosses of the Democratic Party want us to say," he wrote a friend. "We are a hopeless minority, and they will pay no attention to us as soon as they are sure that they will receive our electoral votes."[12]

In Washington, Eastland spent considerable time fighting a law that would have made it a federal crime for any individual to participate in a lynching or for a law enforcement official not to do all possible to block one in progress. Here in his view was pernicious legislation that would not limit actual lynchings but merely escalate regional tensions. Not mentioning the historic disinclination of southern juries to convict white defendants, he said that prosecuting lynchers was a state issue and noted that there had been but six lynchings in all forty-eight states in 1946. With the number receding, antilynching bills seemed to Eastland to be rooted in what Robert Penn Warren termed a "treasury of virtue" among Northerners who bashed the South for problems they had not solved in their own communities. When he found that a sizable number of those advocating such a measure came from New York City, he drafted amendments to address the faults of the "Big Apple," a center not just of commerce but also crime, where 325 people had been murdered in 1947. The addenda included measures to make gangsters and union figures who engaged in mob violence as culpable as lynchers in Dixie, render law enforcement figures liable for any property damage suffered during northern race riots, and subject those in positions of power who did not chase down the perpetrators of nonracial political violence to the same fines equally negligent southern racists would have to pay. None of his addenda were approved, and Eastland alone of the three-man subcommittee voted against the Truman antilynching measure. While he could claim that he had raised doubts about the constitutionality of the measure with some conservatives and that the full Judiciary Committee had gutted the bill that reached it, Eastland was just as quick to warn friends that he was afraid that a similar bill might be approved in the very near future.[13]

Outside of the Senate, southern leaders had not agreed upon the form their movement should take. Eastland was certain that he and his allies should stress what they saw as the constitutional roots of their movement. Strom Thurmond wrote Arkansas Governor Ben Laney that Southerners should wage their fight on "state sovereignty" rather than "on the theory of white supremacy." Other issues like tariff and freight rates always formed part of their agenda. Many backing them, especially those from Louisiana and Texas, had oil and gas interests and wanted to ensure that states continued to own the petrol in the tidelands 3 miles off their shores rather than the federal government. Since 1939, producers had drilled 12,000 oil wells in Mississippi as well, and many of their owners had assets in the two states due west. So while the Dixiecrat movement commenced around the issue of the pace of racial change, it quickly attracted others, particularly in the Deep South, discontented with the national Democratic Party.[14]

Those southern senators disenchanted with Truman had not agreed upon an alternative to him, much less recruited one. John McClellan of Arkansas recommended Harry Byrd of Virginia. Olin Johnston of South Carolina suggested trying to attract the thoroughly apolitical George C. Marshall, the former chairman of the Joint Chiefs of Staff, who was serving Truman as secretary of state. Once the apolitical Marshall declined, Eastland made it clear like Johnston, Senators John Stennis, Richard Russell of Georgia and John Sparkman of Alabama, and Governors Ben Laney of Arkansas and Strom Thurmond of South Carolina that he found the notion of Eisenhower as a prospective candidate intriguing. In time, Eastland tempered his enthusiasm for Eisenhower, when he came to suspect that Eisenhower might be acting as a stalking horse for Truman.[15] Yet neither he nor anyone else suspected that Eisenhower not only had not yet acquired the fire in the belly for political life just yet, but was born and raised a Kansas Republican.

Eastland never entertained the option of becoming a Republican. Memories ingrained in him of the alleged horrors of Reconstruction and the realities he had experienced during the Depression and blamed on the exorbitant Smoot-Hawley tariffs still rang strong. He made it clear to one correspondent that he appreciated the international approach of Republicans who backed the Truman containment policy more than the isolationist outlook of Senator Robert Taft and others who wanted America to limit its commitments abroad. But preeminent in his mind was his devotion to his state's farmers. Like every other Mississippian who had ever served in the Senate, Eastland adhered to the principles of free trade, and he was proud to extol the virtues of policies like Franklin D. Roosevelt's Reciprocal Trade Act that embodied those principles. He, too, had a ready network of southern Democrats who would vote with him on any measure to benefit the regional economy. One such bill emerged on the floor in the early summer of 1948, when Eastland moved to create a $150 million revolving fund for the Army to use to buy cotton, wool, mohair, and flax that would be sold primarily to Japan and Germany, but also to South Korea and Austria. Once textile industries were rehabilitated in those countries, the initial loan could be repaid. Here was an amendment to the Marshall Plan that Harry Truman happily embraced and signed into law less than two weeks prior to the opening of that year's Democratic National Convention.[16]

Eastland's primary aim in the spring of 1948 remained the creation of an organization that would forward what he saw as states' rights principles. In the long range, he wanted to form a Washington, D.C.–based lobby that would present the case for preserving what he saw as the southern way of life. Without one, he wrote a friend, his homeland would "be crushed." His immediate task was to build a core group that would aim to manifest itself into a viable political force by November. The first Southwide meeting of states' rights Democrats opened at the Heidelberg Hotel in Jackson on Saturday, May 10. The principal speaker that day was host Governor Wright, who Eastland counseled in a lengthy memo to formulate a program that would unite Southerners and what he hoped were "millions of allies" in the North in a "fight to preserve for our children's children the Caucasian blood stream which is responsible for all civilization and culture." The past few years had been harmful to his party and to the United States, he advised. "We now have a government dominated by organized minorities, racial demagogues, refugees, cranks and crackpots." "The fight is to depose them and return this government to the millions of Americans of all creeds who built America and made it good." Wright took Eastland's ideas and went him one better, telling African Americans in no uncertain terms that they should leave the South if they did not subscribe to the Jim Crow laws of their region. Following Wright was Strom Thurmond, the forty-five-year-old governor of South Carolina many Mississippians were pushing to seek the presidency, who even then was known for his legendary vigor and virility. Whereas Wright had been stern, even somber, Thurmond challenged those present to launch an unending fight for the southern way of life. "We will not lay our armor down," he promised, "until the present leadership of the Democratic Party is repudiated and the South is again recognized as a political entity of these United States."[17]

Just six weeks later, Eastland keynoted the state Democratic convention. He would not discount the possibility of a walkout from the Democratic National Convention, for he deemed such a move the "only weapon" the South had against "those who would destroy us." He again painted attempts by those from outside the region to pass an antilynching bill, create a "so-called Fair Employment Practices Commission," and end dual school systems as attacks upon his homeland. If anyone were not clear, he then laid down the gauntlet. "We must make it plain," he told delegates, "that we will not be kicked around, embarrassed, humiliated or imposed upon by any group of politicians."[18]

National Democratic leaders were fully aware that Mississippians and some other southern delegates would consider a new form of secession if some of their demands were not met. To try and stave off a rebellion, they named Eastland and John Stennis to the committee to notify the nominee of his selection. Democratic National Committee Chairman Howard McGrath agreed to meet with Governors Fielding Wright and Ben Laney. But McGrath could not control all delegates. George Vaughan, an African-American delegate from Missouri, moved to unseat all delegates from the Magnolia State and won the votes of more than a quarter of the delegations. Then, the full convention voted down a plea of Walter Sillers and other southern leaders calling upon Democrats to revert to what they called their party's traditional states' rights principles. His motion united the South, but won just eleven votes outside the Confederacy. For those in the Deep South, the denouement came when Mayor Hubert Humphrey of Minneapolis challenged Democrats "to get out of the shadow of states' rights and walk forthrightly into the bright sunshine of human rights" by endorsing the Truman civil rights program. Once the national party went on record for the first time in history for a measure calling for the enforcement of the Fourteenth and Fifteenth Amendments, Alabamans started shouting at convention chairman Sam Rayburn. When Rayburn would not recognize them until after a recess, Alabama delegate Handy Ellis and twelve cohorts bid their colleagues from the forty-seven other states farewell, all the while promising that they would never vote for a Republican or Truman or back a civil rights program. Eastland and every other Mississippian followed them even before they got a chance to cast a futile ballot for Georgia Senator Richard Russell in his last-minute challenge to Truman. When Dorothy Vredenburgh, the secretary of the national party, got to her native state as she called the roll of the states, someone shouted "Mississippi is gone home."[19]

Actually, Eastland stopped in Birmingham, Alabama, before he made it back to Doddsville. That was the site Fielding Wright chose for States' Rights Democrats to convene to nominate two of their own to challenge the Truman-Barkley ticket. Once he learned of Wright's machinations, Eastland booked two Pullman cars to carry him and the other Mississippi delegates to Washington. There, they picked up their automobiles, then drove 800 miles largely over two-lane highways from the nation's capital to the "Pittsburgh of the South." Dixiecrats met there in the largest available venue, the 6000-seat City Auditorium, the décor of which reflected the professional wrestling exhibition staged there a few days before. States' righters opened their deliberations just three days after regular Democrats adjourned. Organizers needed to fill the arena, and they admitted anyone, not just to the galleries but even onto the floor. Bands were primed to play "Dixie," "Suwanee River" and "Carry Me Back to Old Virginny" while dozens of newly appointed delegates snuck in Confederate flags and portraits of Confederate legends that conveners had tried to discourage. For Wallace W. Wright, a Jackson attorney and the owner of the largest grocery firm in Mississippi, the meeting was merely "the beginning of our electoral fight to save the South." While Eastland agreed that there were means by which Southerners could "win this fight yet," he and others knew that the only viable strategy would be one designed to throw the election into the House of Representatives. For while the meeting was billed as a gathering of a cross section of southern Democrats, those present hailed largely from the three states of the Black Belt with the largest African-American proportions of the population: Alabama, Mississippi and South Carolina.[20]

As one might expect, the leadership at the Birmingham convention fit the Bourbon profile. Planters and those entrepreneurs and lawyers who serviced their interests proliferated and dominated each of the sessions. The only two southern senators present were Eastland and Stennis, whose junior status left them freer than they would ever be to publicly back a presidential candidate of another party, as stripping them of their seniority would have little consequence. While permanent chairman Walter Sillers epitomized the term Bourbon, and John Rankin, a man of populist temperament without shame in resorting to virulent racist and anti-Semitic appeals, was the only member of the Mississippi congressional delegation absent, some who fit any definition of the word crackpot were present. Former Oklahoma Governor "Alfalfa Bill" Murray declared America great because of "Christian principles and white men's brains" and boasted that it was he who had "introduced Jim Crow in Oklahoma." Texas state legislator Lloyd Price blamed New England merchants for all of America's racial problems, for they had taken "howling, screaming savages" from Africa by the thousands. J. E. Perkins, the author of a tract called *The Jews Have Got the Atom Bomb*, got in, but Reverend Gerald L. K. Smith was notorious enough in his anti-Semitism that he felt compelled to use the pseudonym S. Goodyear. Far more dangerous in years to come was Jesse B. Stoner, an anti-Semite and Klansman later known for his conviction for bombing a Birmingham church, his description of Hitler as "too moderate," and his legal representation of James Earl Ray after his conviction for assassinating Martin Luther King Jr. Here were men whose company Eastland shunned and whose sanity Ben Laney questioned, but they would get nowhere near any lever of power at any point during the convention or any time during the rest of the campaign.[21]

It was the Bourbon elite of the Dixiecrat movement who picked the national ticket. By most accounts, the favorite of many delegates was Laney, the outgoing business-oriented two-term governor of Arkansas. Alas, he hid out in his hotel room when leaders explored the availability of potential standard-bearers. When Eastland and former Governor Frank

Dixon of Alabama let it be known that they were not interested in running, only Governors Thurmond and Wright were left. Wright had been in office less than two years and said that he did not feel ready to head the ticket. Thurmond was just as inexperienced, but made it clear that he was only comfortable as the Dixiecrat standard-bearer. Thus by accident was formed one of the more impactful third party tickets in American history.[22]

Eastland seconded the nomination of the tandem of Thurmond and Wright. He was not as colorful as convention keynoter Frank Dixon, who lambasted his national party as an "unholy alliance of left-wingers, pseudoliberals and radicals of as many hues as Joseph's coat," nor Beulah Waller, the seventy-nine-year-old "wool hat" delegate from Georgia who got up on the stage and danced a jig. It was his job to echo clarion calls that had already been trumpeted for candidates who pledged to fight for resolutions heralding the Constitution. The choice the South had, Eastland told delegates, was either to "stand together and fight" or "surrender our culture and civilization." At this time, he expected the South to unite as it had four generations earlier and deny Truman every "single electoral vote." From there, Thurmond and Wright could "invade Missouri and Kentucky" and perhaps even Maryland and Delaware in the aim of garnering enough electoral votes to throw the election into the House of Representatives. Electing a president would then be possible, he said. "Northern Democrats would still prefer a Southern Democrat to a Republican," he assured his southern brethren, "and Republicans would prefer a Southern Democrat to a Democrat."[23]

Eastland's words seem like pipedreams today, but at the time he appeared just mildly optimistic. Reputable polls taken at the end of September showed that GOP nominee Thomas E. Dewey would defeat Truman in a landslide. Two months earlier, Dixiecrats posited that if that pattern held up until the time of the election, southern Democrats who feared a GOP victory would move their support to the Dixiecrats. At the convention, Eastland expressed doubt that Truman and Barkley would win any electoral votes, guessing Dewey would sweep the lands north and west of the Mason-Dixon line and that Thurmond would emerge equally strong in Dixie. He miscalculated in two major ways. First, he assumed that Dixiecrats would acquire the Democratic label on each state ballot, an advantage he thought would give States' Rights Democrats an insurmountable edge in the eleven states of the Old Confederacy. But Dixiecrat leaders could not acquire that badge of legitimacy save in four states, effectively limiting their electorate to true believers or those casting protest votes. More importantly, Eastland badly underestimated the appeal of Truman's "Turnip Day" challenge to Republicans in his acceptance speech. "More bark than bite," he declared. The failure of the GOP congressional leadership to act upon the promises in their platform served to legitimize Truman's derision of them as a "do nothing Congress." While Truman would never be mistaken for a Missouri model of a Cicero, his newfound assertiveness catalyzed the transformation of his image from that of an unsatisfactory successor to Franklin D. Roosevelt to that of a gutsy fighter for the causes and interests of their party. "Give 'em Hell, Harry," became a popular shout even in many parts of the South, for Democratic spokesmen took care to stress the value of New Deal and Fair Deal programs to the southern economy.[24]

Dewey, in contrast, suffered from the outset from his identification as the nominee of the party identified with both Reconstruction and the Great Depression. The unpleasant memories of those eras coupled with Dewey's support for a civil rights program at least as expansive as Truman's guaranteed that he would remain anathema to Southerners outside of the traditionally Republican Appalachians and Ozarks. To a far greater degree than Eastland or any of his fellow Dixiecrats imagined, partisan loyalties still trumped regional or even racial ones in many parts of the South, and the appeal of the Dixiecrats would be confined to the Cotton Belt.

Eastland for his part waged the good fight for the states' rights cause. With reelection assured by his victory in the Democratic primary, he could venture all across the South to speak for Thurmond and Wright, starting with the acceptance speeches the two delivered in Houston on August 11. He hailed Thurmond in early September as the "best qualified man" for the presidency and taunted Dewey by declaring that Thurmond did not "have to wear a little moustache to look important." The month before the election, he barnstormed Texas with a bevy of Cotton Belt congressmen and former governors, speaking everywhere from Houston to Wichita Falls for their national ticket. For races lower on the ticket,

Thurmond-Wright surrogates invariably sided with Democrats. Eastland was no different. In Tennessee, for example, he made clear that he backed his fairly conservative friend Tom Stewart in the Democratic primary. But once Stewart was toppled by the fairly liberal Estes Kefauver, who later became a bit of a *bête noire*, Eastland wired his campaign manager and endorsed Kefauver as an "able and sincere" aspirant for the open seat. "Democratic control of the Senate," he added, "would be for the best interests of the country and the South." Over the course of the late summer and early fall, Eastland worked arduously. He lost 10 pounds before being told by his doctor that he should limit his traveling as he was suffering from nervous exhaustion.[25]

In the end, the Dixiecrats won but 2.4 percent of the vote nationwide and carried only Alabama, Louisiana, Mississippi, and South Carolina, the four states with the largest proportions of their populations. The fact that few blacks in those states could vote led many black leaders at the national level to demand that Congress not seat those elected in those four states. Their ire extended not just toward Eastland, the one Dixiecrat who stood for election to the Senate that year, but also to John Sparkman of Alabama, Russell Long of Louisiana, and Burnet Maybank of South Carolina, all of whom had stuck with Truman and Barkley. Edgar Brown of the National Negro Council charged that the four had been elected only through the use of "Hitler white supremacy tactics." Brown was correct in saying that the number of African Americans in the electorate was limited because the Jim Crow laws passed near the turn of the last century effectively denied them suffrage. But, with Southerners still a sizable minority within the Democratic caucuses of both houses of Congress, no such move would be considered. Even the most liberal Truman partisans recognized that they from time to time would need southern votes for their Fair Deal measures, a reality that dictated that they not introduce their own new brand of disenfranchisement.[26]

Had Truman completely denied patronage to those who had backed the Dixiecrats, he would have had to do the same to Senator Glen Taylor, the folksinger from Idaho who had been Henry Wallace's running mate. Still, he gave preference to regular Democrats where the two sides preferred different people. J. Howard McGrath, the Rhode Island senator who chaired the Democratic National Committee, worked to see that

Mississippians in Congress received no patronage without prior clearance from the state's Truman organization. In time, he modified his directive to give John Stennis' choices priority, as his role was far smaller than Eastland's in the Dixiecrat campaign. The enforcer of Truman's wishes was Majority Leader Alben Barkley, who prior to being sworn in as vice president saw to it that Truman loyalists Olin Johnston of South Carolina, Guy Gillette of Iowa, and Clinton Anderson of New Mexico got preference over Eastland for vacant seats on the Agriculture Committee. Eastland in turn was relegated to bodies with jurisdiction over matters less related to Mississippi. While Eastland had worked closely with Tom Stewart, the panel's leading authority on cotton questions, and developed relationships with members like Oklahoma Democrat Elmer Thomas and Vermont Republican George Aiken that proved indispensable to those who tilled the soil in Mississippi, his being denied the vacancy left by Stewart's defeat left him without a vote on the panel integral to the interests of his state's farmers. But when Thomas and Majority Leader Lucas lost their reelection bids in 1950, Eastland finally got his seat on the Agriculture Committee. By March 1951, Truman and Barkley recognized that they could not keep Eastland in their doghouse forever. When national Democratic leaders felt compelled to remove Mississippi's committeeman on a charge of selling administration patronage, the only plausible solution was to restore Eastland's perks, as he was in a position to help them on many other matters.[27]

While the States' Rights Democratic Party lasted but one election cycle, its impact was enormous. Civil rights issues, Eastland and other leaders knew, were growing in intensity. Strom Thurmond wrote Eastland that the prime significance of the first and last stand of the States' Rights Democratic Party had demonstrated that the South would no longer be a "political doormat of any party." In many ways, Kari Frederickson noted, "the Dixiecrats weakened the Democratic Party's grip on presidential elections in the Deep South."[28] This in time meant that Democratic strength would weaken at the state and local level as well. That decline moved fastest in burgeoning small urban and suburban areas replete with substantial and growing middle classes. Some circumstances were truer of South Carolina than Mississippi, facilitating Thurmond's switch from the Democrats to the GOP in 1964. Ever loyal to the party of his forbearers and the Confederacy, Eastland would never make such a move. Yet it was always within him to ally with others of any party who shared interests or ideology.

To a far greater degree than ever before, the Dixiecrat campaign forged and even tightened bonds among conservative Southerners that lingered even on issues with no racial connotations. Some would argue that the conservative movement that gelled in the nomination of Barry Goldwater by Republicans in 1964 with near unanimous support in the Deep South sprung largely from roots planted in 1948. By 1956, Dixiecrat financier John U. Barr was predicting that states' righters would try to take control of one of the two major parties.[29] This breed of conservatism hardly restricted itself to a myopic opposition to racial equality. Most who adhered to it paradoxically and some might say hypocritically were just as committed to what they saw as the cause of freedom for those subjugated in other parts of the world by those they feared were shoveling the seeds of social upheaval in their back yards. Jim Eastland found the Communists of his time as diabolical as he had been taught the Radical Republicans of the Reconstruction Era were. He had seen some of the horrors perpetrated by Joseph Stalin during and after World War II, and it was easy for him to transfix in his own mind the image of every Marxist-Leninist, however harmless, trying to impose similar abuses upon Americans, particularly Southerners. Eastland did all in his power to expose and condemn the very real abuses of Communists abroad. And he did all he could to try and discredit those at home intent upon transforming his way of life, particularly those with any association, however inconsequential or inadvertent, with groups or individuals who had ever espoused or even entertained any connection with a doctrine like that of Marx.

CHAPTER 8

Great Southern Commie Hunter

JIM EASTLAND WAS EMPHATIC IN HIS OPPOSITION TO ANYTHING THAT could even remotely be described as Communism. Replete within his mindset was a near congenital resistance to the oft-violent nature and accelerating pace of change demanded by the most doctrinaire followers of Marx and Lenin. To be sure, Eastland had experienced very real chaos in Germany during the immediate aftermath of World War II, and he fully suspected that Joseph Stalin might try and exploit such disarray to expand his empire. But any coalescence of political forces backing that most violent of Soviet dictators rested solely on the European side of the Atlantic. It long concerned anti-Communists that Stalin and his hench-men might create Fifth Columns in every conceivable group, who would seek to undermine the foundations of their world. With the sturdiest pillar of Jim Eastland's worldview—the need to fortify the hierarchical segregated society from which he sprang— under challenge, he spent hundreds of hours probing whether some critics of his semifeudal Delta homeland were acting on behalf of Stalin or his agents, with no concern for the general welfare of its people, white or black. Still, on a day-to-day basis, Eastland stood with those most fiercely determined to resist Com-munist expansion, rarely questioning if those opposed to the forces of Marx and Lenin might constitute even less humane alternatives.

As one might expect, Eastland took a stiffer anti-Communist line than Truman. Like many Bourbons, he approached foreign policy with a "belligerently isolationist sense" of nationalism. Eastland regularly cosponsored a proposed constitutional amendment by Ohio Republi-can John Bricker to deny any president the power to negotiate treaties that contradicted part of the Constitution. He regularly backed aid to non-Communists, be they those who protected the human rights of their citizens or those who did not. He proposed making West Germany an "equal partner" in the global fight against Communism and rearming Japan. More conspicuously, he urged Truman to extend Marshall Plan aid to Spain, the one country whose leader, Generalissimo Francisco Franco, had ever collaborated with Hitler and Mussolini. Doing otherwise, he said, less than prophetically, might avail the Soviets of a vacuum they might exploit.[1]

One issue on which Eastland took on a more contentious role was on the number of displaced refugees the United States should admit. Eastland had a personal stake on this issue. He and Libby took in a Latvian couple as domestic servants in 1949, and seven years later adopted a German family endorsed by the National Catholic Welfare Conference as well as a Russian couple recommended by the Romanian-Lutheran Refugee Review. His approach differed from Truman's. The refugees Eastland knew best were ethnic Germans who had been driven from their homes in places like the Sudetenland by decisions made at Yalta and Potsdam. "No branch of the white race," he told the Senate, "has suffered as these people have suffered." In contrast, the Truman administration, while firmly committed to containing Communism, was just as sensitive to pleas to admit European Jews still suffering after the liberation of the Nazi death camps. In 1949, they drafted a bill to expand the number of refugees who could enter the United States and got veteran New York City legislator Emmanuel Celler to introduce it in the House of Representatives. Wary of Pat McCarran, a short, fiery Nevadan with an anti-Semitic streak who chaired the Senate Judiciary Committee, Truman's team prompted J. Howard McGrath to introduce their bill. McCarran replied by stacking a subcommittee with those like Eastland, who had seen FBI and CIA evidence that Communists were infiltrating America through the displaced persons program. Eastland often echoed McCarran's charge over the next year that the well-funded Citizens Committee on Displaced Persons was driving the push for a bill. But unlike McCarran, Eastland framed his arguments around the notion that an expanded program might let some Communists filter into the country. He and McCarran drafted 130 amendments, most of which were defeated, but his most conspicuous role was to denounce European officials of the UN's

International Refugee Organization, who he feared might have more of a say over who entered the United States than officials of our own government and declared "guilty of moral treason" for letting Communists enter. Newly elected liberal Democrat Herbert Lehman from New York derided what he saw as "misstatements" and "inaccuracies." This to Eastland was a breach of decorum, less because of the charges themselves than because Lehman had made them while he was not on the floor. But while questions of honor and etiquette may have favored Eastland, the view favored by Lehman and Truman carried the day when a vote finally came.[2]

Later that year, Eastland took a harder line than Truman when North Korean Communist forces invaded South Korea. He eschewed the Truman description of a proper U.S. response as a "police action" to halt the aggression of the forces of Kim Il-Sung and called instead for the "all out or get out" approach of the China lobby. Just as he had urged Truman earlier in 1950 not to recognize Mao Zedong's new Chinese Communist government, Eastland joined Pat McCarran in demanding that defense appropriations be doubled and that diplomatic relations be broken with the Soviet Union and its East European satellites. Over the Korean War's first nine months, his positions resembled those privately pushed by General Douglas MacArthur. That pattern continued even after the Chinese, angered by a counteroffensive exceeding a UN mandate and pushed at some points even to their border, entered the war and quickly drove MacArthur's troops south of the thirty-eighth parallel, which had previously separated the two Korean states.

Soon thereafter, Eastland called upon Truman to destroy transportation and industrial networks on China's mainland, blockade its ports, and unleash the Nationalist Chinese army of Jiang Jieshi, now restricted to Taiwan, upon the country he once ruled. Eastland predicated this notion on his assumption that Jiang's government had fallen in China because American policymakers had followed the "Lattimore line." It was true that the maneuverings of Asian scholar Owen Lattimore, who had worked during World War II in the Office of War Information, were a bit curious and that his proximity to many Communist leaders should have raised eyebrows. But Eastland's suggestion that the armies of Jiang, who had proven impotent in the Asian theater of World War II and even more so while defending their control of Chinese territory between 1945 and

1949, could even inconvenience Mao's forces relied upon an extremely optimistic notion of Jiang's power. Just as faulty was his sense that a large number of Chinese might rally behind Jiang if he were to invade his homeland. While those who calculated the strength of the two armies always estimated the number backing Jiang as at least three times those of Mao, the shallowness of the commitment of Jiang's supporters had been evident since the end of World War II. Eastland's position reflected a commonly felt frustration with the course of a war where he found no "real effort" to win, and he often told friends as the war lingered that America should either go all out for victory in Korea or withdraw.[3]

For much of Truman's second term, Eastland believed that Secretary of State Dean Acheson deserved much of the blame for what he deemed a weak U.S. posture toward East Asia. Although Eastland appreciated the fact that Acheson had previewed the Marshall Plan at a meeting of the Delta Council, he noted that it was on Acheson's watch in 1949 that America had withdrawn troops from South Korea. A year later, Eastland concluded that America had reentered the Korean peninsula without sufficient troops or arms to complete its mission, and he called for Acheson and others he deemed negligent to resign. And, as early as the winter of 1946, he and others turned over FBI files to Secretary of State James F. Byrnes indicating that onetime State Department lawyer Alger Hiss had doubled as a Soviet spy in the 1930s. Such warnings came nearly three years before Richard Nixon rose to fame when he looked into similar allegations repentant ex-Communist Whittaker Chambers made before the House Un-American Activities Committee late in the summer of 1948. Those findings came fully nine years after Chambers alerted Adolph A. Berle, Franklin D. Roosevelt's assistant secretary of state, that Hiss had, at best, conflicting loyalties. But Acheson's refusal in January 1950 to distance himself from Hiss even after Hiss was indicted for perjury served to buttress Eastland's call for Acheson's resignation at the end of that year.[4]

By this time, Eastland was enmeshed with those demanding probes of alleged Communists within the United States. The first vehicle he backed was one introduced by Republican Congressmen Karl Mundt and Richard Nixon in 1948, which did not outlaw the Communist Party as Eastland would have preferred, but denied Communists passports and required them to register with the government. Mundt- Nixon also created a Subversive Activities Control Board to determine which groups were Communist fronts and dictated that any group so labeled disclose the source of any information they aired or published. Here was a bill that aroused the enmity of Communists and many civil libertarians, who thought it smacked of a denial of any freedom to associate. Several witnesses took the stand to state their opposition. One witness with whom Eastland engaged in a civil exchange in May 1949 was Arnold Johnson, executive secretary of the Communist Party of the United States. Not so disposed was C. B. "Beanie" Baldwin, a longtime aide to Henry Wallace, who intended from the witness chair to denounce the Mundt-Nixon bill as a prime example of the anti-Communist hysteria he said had "been whipped up since the end of the war." Baldwin, who secretly was a Communist, met with committee attorneys privately, then asked the panel to resume its proceedings in public. After Baldwin refused to answer if he was or had ever belonged to the Communist Party, Eastland inquired if Baldwin would swear to uphold the Constitution. Baldwin flipped the question, declaring he would take an oath of allegiance to the United States, particularly if it enforced the Fourteenth and Fifteenth Amendments. After adding that he doubted that Eastland could take the same oath "with a clear conscience," Baldwin called him a "narrow-minded bigot" who represented only the Cotton Council and "fought every measure that would have helped the Negro people." It was less Baldwin's attack than its context that offended Eastland. Even if he was questioning Baldwin's patriotism, Eastland had accommodated his requests to conduct some of their business behind closed doors. What he got in return was an *ad hominem* assault unrelated to the hearings. Just a few moments later, Eastland rose and unloaded angrily, replying "You're a goddamned son of a bitch and a goddamned liar," before he had Capitol police remove a shouting Baldwin from the room. Later, Baldwin inflamed matters even more by declaring that Eastland's methods had been "borrowed lock, stock and barrel from . . . Hitler and Mussolini." Almost immediately, the National Committee to Defeat the Mundt-Nixon Bill demanded that Eastland be ousted from his subcommittee chairmanship for his "foul and abusive language."[5]

This sort of theatrical excess commonly highlighted the carnival atmosphere pervading many of the anti-Communist probes of the postwar era.

Both Eastland and Baldwin played to narrow constituencies, and neither swung many converts. Eastland remained a loyal follower of Pat McCarran, and both worked closely with FBI Director J. Edgar Hoover. By the end of 1950, they had resurrected the Mundt-Nixon bill and recrafted it into a passable form, even if a unanimous Supreme Court later declared unconstitutional its portions requiring Communists to register and denying them passports. Three months after Congress passed the bill that had become known as the McCarran Act, Eastland drafted and introduced a measure creating what would become the Senate's version of the House Un-American Activities Committee. The resolution, one pushed ardently by McCarran and other Judiciary Committee anti-Communists, created a subpanel charged with investigating the "extent, nature, and effects" of Communist and subversive activities in the United States. Known to the public as the Senate Internal Security Subcommittee (SISS), this group became the repository of several of Hoover's most sensitive leaks after he came to realize that Joseph McCarthy's alcoholism was too advanced and his personality too reckless for him to be trusted. Much earlier, Hoover had concluded that many other members of McCarthy's committee were more interested in headlines than national security. In contrast, he knew that he could trust McCarran and Eastland and GOP colleagues William Jenner and Homer Ferguson not to reveal that their information came from FBI files. Hundreds of times, Hoover favored SISS with blind memos replete with leads and clues as to how to pursue them, and he charged ten senior aides with meeting their requests. Moreover, top Hoover aides not only recommended candidates for jobs on SISS, but vetted anyone members thought of hiring. And, while the panel did air considerable amounts of material about Communist activities over the next quarter century, often using witnesses suggested by Hoover, the occasional missteps and oversteps of members—and Eastland made his share—provided considerable embarrassment to those who aimed to limit Communist influence in America.[6]

Only with the creation of SISS did Eastland's role become important. SISS was a congenial group, both personally and ideologically. Eastland ranked second in seniority behind McCarran and before fellow China lobby backers Herbert O'Conor of Maryland, a former governor, and Willis Smith of North Carolina, a conservative best remembered for bringing a campaign aide named Jesse Helms to Washington as his administrative assistant. Committee Republicans Homer Ferguson of Michigan, William Jenner of Indiana, and Arthur Watkins of Utah were just as reflexively anti-Communist. Eastland, to be sure, would participate in most investigations SISS conducted over its first four years of existence. But his special focus was never too far removed from the question of if and how Communists might be trying to uproot the traditional racial order of the South.[7]

By the early 1950s, Eastland had come to fear that Communists aimed to organize blacks into unions they controlled. Ex-Communists who the FBI found and sent the way of SISS buttressed this conclusion. Manning Johnson, an African American who once had worked as a porter, told the panel during a probe of the Dining Car and Railroad Food Workers Union that the party to which he once belonged aimed to foment "armed rebellions of blacks, after which they would create an independent and autonomous Negro republic in the black belt." The one ex-Communist Eastland placed an inordinate amount of faith in was Paul Crouch, who he, like the FBI, deemed an expert on the party's activities in the South. The son of a North Carolina preacher, Crouch joined the party in 1925 while a serviceman in Hawaii. Soon after, he tried to start a Communist League and was quickly caught and court-martialed. Though sentenced to forty years, he served less than three. Upon his release, Crouch served his party in a variety of ways, from interviewing Lenin's widow to consulting with Marshal Mikhail Tukhachevsky, the Soviet commander-in-chief later purged by Stalin, to organizing Communist-led unions and editing Communist publications. Crouch had gained a wealth of information about America's archenemy. Some of it was quite valuable to lawmakers and law enforcement officials, but, as Eastland and others would learn to their dismay, not all of it was accurate. The one academic to treat Crouch's experiences in total, Gregory S. Taylor, titled his work, *The Life and Lies of Paul Crouch: Communist, Opportunist, Cold War Snitch*.[8]

Crouch seemed credible to Eastland the first time he employed him as his star witness in an October 1951 probe of the Distributive, Processing, and Office Workers of America (DPOWA). The DPOWA was a 65,000-member union formed in 1950 by the merger of the United Office and Professional Workers of America with the Food, Tobacco and

Agricultural Workers of America after both were expelled by the CIO. For Eastland, there was no better venue for such a probe than Memphis. Not only was the river city a most familiar haunt, it also was home to many members of Local 19 of the DPOWA and hordes of businessmen who were uncomfortable with black-majority unions of any sort, much less one dominated by Communists. It was Crouch's position, as he stated at the hearing, that DPOWA took "its orders from the Communist higher-ups in this country, who in turn take their orders from their bosses in Moscow."[9]

Eastland found it clear that DPOWA was a "Communist organization" and that "the Negroes who belong to it are dupes." Even if there was no legitimate legislative purpose to his probe, he intended to expose the ties of several DPOWA leaders to groups dedicated to revolutionary change in his southern homeland. He buttressed Crouch's claims by calling on Reverend James McDaniel, the executive secretary of the Memphis Urban League, to testify that he had warned fellow African Americans against Local 19. But those from DPOWA subpoenaed to tell their stories found Eastland intimidating. Some he hectored relentlessly; others he sought to draw information from. "We on the committee are your true friends," he told Local 19 president Lee Lashley, an African American. But the record of the hearings reveals that Eastland often addressed him simply as "Lashley" without the title of Mr. and called him "boy" at least once. *Memphis Press-Scimitar* correspondents reported that he used "boy" more often than the record indicates. Eastland and other Southerners, to be sure, did use "boy" as a racial slur, but Eastland, it must be said, also used it as a term of endearment while addressing younger aides and even a colleague or two. After two days of intensive questioning, two panel investigators testified that Lashley admitted that he was a Communist. Lashley thereupon assented to Eastland's suggestion that they meet behind closed doors. There, Lashley told Eastland that he had belonged to the Communist Party but was less than familiar with its doctrine or practices. Edwin McCrea, the business agent for Local 19, had persuaded him to join, Lashley said. Once the two returned to the hearing room, Eastland hailed Lashley for being forthright, even if he was much more impressed with Lashley's integrity than his sagacity. At the end of the second day of hearings, he described the African-American witnesses as "dumb" souls who were being used by nefarious "designing people," all of whom were white.[10]

Eastland showered these "designing people" with the most contempt. When he called upon Paul Crouch to point out DPOWA's business agent, that onetime Communist bigwig identified McCrea as his successor as the organizer of the Tennessee Communist Party. Crouch went on to charge that McCrea answered directly to Soviet spy boss J. Peters. Their fundamental aim, he added, was to spur southern blacks to secede and start their own republic, a goal that had been unsuccessful because few blacks had swallowed their bait. At one point, Crouch told Lee Lashley that he was being used by Victor Rabinowitz, the union-provided lawyer, and "some people in New York." "Mr. Rabinowitz," he said later, was a "very able lawyer who always shows up representing big-time Communists." When Rabinowitz tried to block documents from being made public that SISS staffers had acquired following the enforcement of a subpoena, Eastland got testy. "Throw that damn scum out of here," Eastland ordered two guards. "Get rid of him."[11]

Later, Eastland admitted that he had been occasionally "discourteous" to some witnesses. Rabinowitz and some of his allies reciprocated this understatement with comparable hyperbole. Eastland had browbeaten witnesses, they said, and engaged in "outrageous interference" to secure Local 19's records. Predictably, Pat McCarran and Homer Ferguson endorsed Eastland's findings. DPOWA, a union with a $3 million annual income, had prospered "by preying on the gullibility of Negro workers and the fear and helpfulness of small businesses," McCarran wrote. SISS did ask the Justice Department to consider perjury charges against a few witnesses and called upon Congress to pass laws allowing employers to fire workers with subversive affiliations and barring Communists from holding offices or jobs with any union. But while critics alleged that the purpose of the hearings was to keep African Americans in a rather docile place, the one practical result of the probe in any part of the South was to prompt Local 19 to leave DPOWA and affiliate instead with the more conservative Retail, Wholesale, and Department Store Union.[12]

Of far greater notoriety were hearings Eastland conducted into the activities of the Southern Conference for Human Welfare (SCHW) and its offshoot, the Southern Conference Educational Fund (SCEF). He described SCEF as a "very vicious organization" that was "attempting to penetrate the schools of the South" by supporting a class-action suit before the Supreme Court against five school districts accused of racial discrimination. In the winter of 1953–1954, he convinced SISS chairman Jenner that they target SCEF, and Jenner was soon telling reporters that SISS would be probing supposed "Communist activities" within that group. SCEF Chairman Aubrey Williams feared little, for he knew his group held few Communists. If any were tolerated, the African-American historian Linda Reed wrote years later, "it was because they, too, were considered outsiders to most white Southerners." As such, Williams wired Jenner to condemn a "dishonest, . . . contemptible" charge of "subversion and disloyalty." If Jenner had evidence that someone within the SCEF had engaged in disloyal activity, he should provide it to prosecutors. That way, those charged could confront their accusers, and the patriotic majority of SCEF's predominantly liberal body of donors would not be tarnished "by inference and innuendo."[13]

It was Eastland who presided over the hearings. As late as March 8, 1954, the night he was feted in Memphis by a bipartisan group giving him four awards for his anti-Communism work, he expected to be joined in New Orleans by Democrats Pat McCarran and John McClellan. Alarmed, Virginia Durr, a founder of SCHW who was a sister-in-law of Justice Hugo Black, called her senator, Lister Hill, and tried to get him to intercede to temper the probe. When Hill proved unsuccessful, Durr phoned her friends Lyndon and Lady Bird Johnson to see if they could get him to stop the hearings. It was too late, said Johnson, who did not know what Eastland had in mind. She wondered if he might get McCarran and McClellan to skip the hearing. That he could do, knowing McCarran was not up for reelection and that McClellan had no serious challenger. No Republicans planned to participate, but Mrs. Durr called Ohio Republican George Bender to make sure. Presiding without colleagues, particularly from a site near Mississippi, afforded Eastland no trepidation. SISS members often heard witnesses alone. A year and a half later, he wrote that his central aim was to air enough material to prompt the Justice Department to label SCEF as "subversive."[14] Even if those on the stand were not Communists, he could return home at the outset of an election year with a stroke added to his image as one who was fighting for the heavy white majority of the electorate against those who would alter their segregated way of life.

As early as a year before the hearings, Crouch wrote Eastland to suggest witnesses for a probe of SCEF and urged that James Dombrowski and Aubrey Williams be named as Communists. Eastland had sufficient confidence in Crouch at this point that his two prehearing executive sessions with his primary witness were devoted solely to matters related to potential Communist influence in Hawaii. Crouch's information on DPOWA was valid, but staff director Ben Mandel, who had written the House Un-American Activities report on SCHW, told Eastland that this strategy for probing SCEF carried risks. A "small hard core of Communists and a very wide circle of fuzzy-minded liberals," Mandel believed, constituted the membership of both SCHW and SCEF. While deeming it desirable to expose the few Communists, Mandel warned that Communists would exploit any misfiring of the committee by rushing to any reporter within earshot to denounce any abuse they found in the probers' tactics.[15]

Eastland gaveled the hearings to order at 10:00 A.M. on March 18 in a courtroom inside the Post Office Building in New Orleans. On his right was investigator Richard Arens, who moonlighted as a consultant to New England textile manufacturer Wickliffe Draper on a project aimed at proving that blacks were genetically inferior to whites. Also in tow was the ubiquitous Paul Crouch. There were many procedural questions from counsel for the accused, as neither Eastland nor Arens had apprised any witnesses but their own as to the rules. And while Eastland pledged to run the hearing "in a fair manner," he announced at the outset that lawyers for those subpoenaed would not automatically be allowed to cross-examine other witnesses. The proceeding was not a criminal trial, he said, so there was no inherent right for any witness to have his or her own advocate examine the claims of any other witness. "I will announce them (the rules) as I desire," he declared when asked about the rules under which the hearings would take place.[16]

Two leaders of the New Orleans Young Men's Business Club, a body that had declared SCHW a "Communist front" group as early as 1946, were the first witnesses called. They maintained that SCEF was simply the same body as SCHW under a different name. As was perfunctory for the age, Eastland then called two witnesses, Miami lawyer Leo Scheiner and Miami contractor Max Schlafrock, who asserted their rights, which Scheiner said meant not just the Fifth Amendment protection against self-incrimination but also the rights covered in the First, Fourth, Sixth, Eighth, Ninth, and Tenth Amendments. Next up was SCEF Director James Dombrowski, a Methodist minister who had helped found the Highlander Folk School in Monteagle, Tennessee. Dombrowski gave the panel the names of SCEF's officers as well as its financial statement, but refused to turn over a list of its contributors. Here was a request, he said, that violated the Fifth Amendment's protection against being deprived of property without due process of law. Matter-of-factly, Eastland replied that Dombrowski's refusal to surrender a list of SCEF's donors rendered him vulnerable to a contempt of Congress charge.[17]

Next to be sworn in were Paul Crouch and fellow ex-Communist John Butler, who, like Crouch, was a paid informant. His motives were sketchy. Not only had he been convicted for bootlegging several times, but he had left the party about the time he had been expelled from the Mine, Mill and Smelter Workers Union for embezzling funds from its treasury. Still, he said under questioning from Arens that he had met Dombrowski in 1942 at a Birmingham hotel in the room of Alton Lawrence, a Communist union leader, "to discuss the party line." Then, he testified that he had met Dombrowski at Highlander in 1938, where he said Dombrowski told him that he preferred to be called a "left Socialist" as opposed to a Communist and that he could serve the left better if tagged as such. Dombrowski replied that he could not recall meeting Butler and stated flatly that he had never been introduced by anyone as a Communist. Had he been, he said, he would have corrected the record on the spot. He vaguely remembered meeting Crouch when both protested a move to restrict Florida's Democratic primary to whites. On this trip, however, Crouch said the two had ridden together from "Miami to Winter Haven," even though the protest was in Winter Park. And, while Crouch supposedly had left the Communist discipline in 1942, five years before the fateful ride, he said the two had sung the "Internationale" en route to Winter Park. Here, Dombrowski acknowledged amusement, for while he had managed the glee club in college, "they wouldn't let me sing." But when Crouch went on to declare that the two had discussed the hideouts of various Communists at Highlander, Dombrowski blurted, "That is a lie, sir." After nearly five hours, Eastland went through a list of groups to which Dombrowski had attached his name, either as a member or a donor. Dombrowski averred that he remembered joining some and did not recall others. Right before the panel adjourned for the day, he did acknowledge that he was the kind of soul who would give to any group with a program he found admirable, without investigating if those groups might be Communist fronts.[18]

High drama ensued the next morning. First up was Virginia Durr, who would testify only that she was married to attorney Clifford Durr and that she was not then nor had she ever been a Communist. Mrs. Durr hoped that she could open by reading an inflammatory statement, but Eastland told her she could only do that if she answered questions he and Richard Arens put to her. She answered all other queries by saying that she stood mute or doing so while powdering her nose. Once Eastland and Arens raised all of their questions, they called in Paul Crouch and John Butler. Crouch testified that Mrs. Durr had subscribed to *New South*, a publication he had edited for the Communist Party in the late 1930s. Here was a curious charge, for the fact that *New South* was a Communist organ could be found on the mastheads of the first two issues only. He also alleged that the Durr home in Washington had been a Communist hangout in the late 1930s, and that Virginia Durr had arranged for Joseph Gelders, a left-wing physics professor from Alabama, to meet with both Eleanor Roosevelt and Justice Hugo Black, her brother-in-law. Butler could add little more save that Mrs. Durr had not been identified to him as a Communist, but had joined him and Alton Lawrence, his Communist former union head, for dinner. Faced with such a paltry amount of circumstantial evidence, Mrs. Durr waited nonchalantly until the hearing recessed to approach reporters and hand them copies of a statement that professed her "total and utter contempt of this committee."[19]

Next up was SCEF Chairman Aubrey Williams, who, while far too liberal for Eastland to back when Franklin D. Roosevelt nominated him to head the Rural Electrification Administration in 1945, Eastland still respected, as he had organized a federal relief program in Mississippi in the 1930s. Still, this proved a contentious afternoon. Clifford Durr, Williams' attorney and Virginia's husband, entered the proceedings almost immediately after Williams was sworn in to proclaim the hearing a "trial" and a "bill of attainder." In the first hour, Williams corrected the record by saying that Virginia Durr was not a director of SCEF and declared that his organization's primary purpose was to fight discrimination against the black population of their homeland. As far as Williams knew, there were no Communists in SCEF. He could not recall ever having met Paul Crouch. He had met union leader Alton Lawrence, but had never been in his home and did not know he was a Communist. He was also acquainted with Joseph Gelders and Robert F. Hall, who gave to SCEF, but was not aware that either man had ever been a Communist.[20]

Fireworks were in the air when Butler and Crouch returned to the stand to charge that Williams had been in the Marxist-Leninist camp. Butler alleged that he had been introduced to Williams in 1942 as a secret party member and met him at a closed party meeting in Nashville. The charge stunned Williams, who called upon Butler to repeat it in a venue where he might be sued.[21] Crouch also declared that he had met Williams at several party functions, had been reliably informed by party member Rob Hall that Williams was a Communist, and that his activities always coincided with the "interests of the Communist Party." Once Crouch concluded, Eastland yielded to Clifford Durr's motion that he be allowed to cross-examine Butler and Crouch. Eastland assented, noting that Williams, unlike previous witnesses, answered every question he and Arens posed except those related to the names of those who gave to SCEF. What Eastland could not have predicted was how deeply Durr's queries would penetrate the charges of the two ex-Communists.

Durr pored into Crouch's life as a Communist, and repeatedly hinted that Communist practice required its agents to be "trained in deception." He demonstrated that Crouch's memory was faulty, particularly about his supposedly frequent meetings with Williams. Then Arens, sensing that Crouch was losing credibility, asked Crouch if he thought Durr was a Communist. Crouch was not sure that Durr remained with the party, but knew he had belonged once. This remark brought raucous laughter to the room, even, Williams later wrote, from Eastland, if not from Durr. Still chuckling, Eastland thought of striking the reply, but Durr convinced him that the remark should remain in the record, as it was made under oath. Eastland then let Durr ask Crouch about his claim that Durr was a Communist. Crouch replied that he had met Durr at several party events between 1938 and 1941. While he could not pinpoint the number or any particular time, Crouch did say that Communists had used Durr to transmit several messages to Justice Black over the years. Stunned, Durr asked Eastland to swear him in as a witness so he might respond. This Eastland did, and Durr pronounced that any notion that he had ever been a Communist was a "complete and absolute falsehood." "One of . . . us should be indicted for perjury," he added before explaining to Arens that he was not aware that Gelders was a Communist nor had he ever subscribed to the *Daily Worker*.[22]

When the panel adjourned, Eastland sensed that the public session scheduled to open the next morning at 9:30 might bring even more drama. At lunch, Eastland and Arens arranged for Myles Horton, the executive director of the Highlander School in Monteagle, Tennessee, to testify in executive session so they might discern whether Horton might provide enough useful information to justify calling him to answer questions in public. After denying that he was a Communist and declaring that he did not recall meeting Crouch, Horton said that he had been wrong to discuss Crouch, as doing so ran counter to his intention to answer questions about his activities alone. The next morning, Horton arrived for the public hearing he had requested with Clifford Durr acting as his attorney. Eastland opened by asking if Horton knew Mildred White, who he said was a Communist who had attended Highlander. This charge came from Paul Crouch who had told him that Horton and James Dombrowski had allowed White to enter so she might spread propaganda there. Horton replied that he did not recall her and that Highlander did not admit Communists, so she must have been admitted as a union member. For Eastland, this did not suffice. Raising his voice, he asked Horton how he could explain her presence if he did not recall her. Arens then queried Horton if Dombrowski worked for the school. Durr responded that Dombrowski had already answered that question. Eastland then asked if there was a reason Horton could not reply. Horton tried to justify his refusal, but this Eastland would not countenance, just an answer. After further jockeying, Horton started to lecture Eastland. "You listened to an ex-Communist who is a paid informer. Why don't you listen to the testimony of an ordinary American?" When Horton prolonged his sidestepping and began reading a statement from Dwight D. Eisenhower on civil rights, Eastland ordered two federal marshals to take Horton from the room. Neither were gentle. "They're treating me like a criminal," Horton shouted, while the marshals grabbed Horton by his arms, took him outside and dropped him on the floor. As they did so, Eastland declared that he would not allow any "self-serving declarations." Here indeed was what Horton had planned. In a statement he later released to reporters, he was prepared to tell Eastland that "the hysteria spread by your committee and others like it has substantially contributed to the fiction that the only dynamic force in the world is Communism" and that he had "never been tempted by Communism" because he believed in democracy.[23]

One last display of theatrics ensued after Eastland recalled Paul Crouch for a final bombshell. This time, Crouch alleged that five southern Communists had fed him information in 1938 that they had received indirectly from First Lady Eleanor Roosevelt through Virginia Durr, who had "full knowledge" of their intentions. Clifford Durr was irate, even though he was nursing a heart condition serious enough to prompt a doctor to advise him to skip the hearing. Minutes after the hearing adjourned, he darted around a railing in front of a witness bench toward Crouch. "You dirty dog," he blared firmly while lunging at Crouch and grabbing his arm. "I'll kill you for lying about my wife." Attorneys and U.S. marshals in the vicinity had to move quickly to separate the two.[24]

Few papers sent reporters to cover the hearing, but those that did pummeled Eastland. One of the first to write a letter to any editor was *New York Post* reporter Joseph Lash, one of five suspected Communists Crouch had named, who wrote the *New York Times* to deny the charge almost as soon as Crouch made it. Only after he soured on the Soviet Union once it entered into an alliance with Nazi Germany in August 1939 had Lash ever had much contact with the Roosevelt administration, and he had never been a member of any Communist group. Predictably, the most negative was the *Daily Worker*, which blasted Eastland for a "Ku Klux mentality" and opined that his true aim was to get Crouch to spread "tall tales" about the Durrs and thus neutralize Justice Hugo Black, right before the *Brown v. Board of Education of Topeka, Kansas* ruling. More reflective of the body politic was a telegram signed by Eleanor Roosevelt and 200 prominent liberals protesting what they deemed "an attack upon the Negro community of this nation." Eastland fared little better with moderate Southerners. "Eastland Follows McCarthy," the *St. Petersburg Times* titled its editorial. More temperate was the conservative *Montgomery Advertiser*, which printed Eastland's statement to a reporter that he did not think either Williams or the Durrs were Communists, but also ran a piece by columnist Allen Rankin chiding him for putting the Durrs and Williams on trial for alleged heresies. And, when the *Advertiser* polled nine reporters covering the hearing as to who posed "the greatest threat to American ideals," four chose Eastland, two Crouch, and one each took Arens, Dombrowski, and Max Schlaforth.[25]

Virginia Durr never forgave Eastland. While her depiction of him as "as common as pig tracks" can be found in her account of the hearings in *Outside the Magic Circle*, her autobiography, the impassioned nature of her animus toward Eastland included gossipy, even offensive tales of him by unnamed women who she said had explained to her that the Eastlands were Southerners of the Snopesian variety who had recently migrated to the Delta from "northern Mississippi." But this account, uncorroborated in other literature, is suspect as no one directly related to Eastland ever resided in northern Mississippi other than while many attended Ole Miss. Eastland, to be sure, did deride her as "that woman" in a chance encounter with Benjamin Smith, Dombrowski's lawyer, on a flight from Houston to New Orleans. But, a generation later, Hiram Eastland Jr. recalled his cousin cutting short a conversation when Mrs. Durr's name arose by saying that he understood her disdain, then signaling that he would not elaborate further.[26]

In contrast, the discrepancies in Crouch's testimony as well as his friendship with McCarthy counsel Roy Cohn raised the eyebrows of many on and off the committee. Attorneys fighting the deportation of Pulitzer Prize–winning cartoonist Jacob Bourck, who Crouch alleged had been a Communist in the 1930s, submitted nineteen affidavits contradicting portions of Crouch's testimony before various tribunals. While key Justice Department officials had called on him sixty times as an expert witness, they now questioned his veracity. Only once more would he be called upon to testify. This to Crouch was a breach of a pact that usually paid $25, and occasionally $100 per testimony, not a bad gig for the early 1950s. He, in turn, demanded that Attorney General Herbert Brownell and William P. Rogers, his deputy, be probed for giving "aid and comfort to the enemy." Even SISS Chairman Jenner, a conservative often at odds with the Eisenhower administration, derided this notion as "absurd." Lyndon Johnson and Lister Hill eventually convinced Eastland that any further hearings would be counterproductive. Pat McCarran, after consulting Eastland and other Democrats, urged Jenner to create a task force to investigate Crouch's multitude of allegations and "let the chips fall where they may." In effect, Crouch had become *persona non grata* to virtually everyone in Washington. Even his death less than two years later went little noticed.[27]

It ironically was another Crouch lead that provoked an even more fateful probe. Roy Cohn cited a seven-page document Crouch drafted on the "Communist infiltration of the American Armed Forces" as the inspiration for a probe of alleged subversion by a cell at Fort Monmouth, New Jersey, launched by Joseph McCarthy. Here was the genesis of the televised spectacle that paralyzed the body politic for much of 1954. From this arose McCarthy's badgering of Brigadier General Ralph Zwicker, an authentic hero of the D-Day invasion and the Battle of the Bulge, as a man who was "not fit to wear that uniform," his insinuations that there were hundreds of Communists in the military, and the denouement of his abrogation of a gentleman's agreement not to mention that Fred Fisher, a law partner of Army counsel Joseph N. Welch, had once belonged to the National Lawyers Guild, a group often listed as a Communist front. A spontaneous overwhelmingly favorable public response to Welch's quaint but penetrating retort to McCarthy's bullying, "Have you at long last, sir, no sense of decency?" rendered McCarthy, however bombastic, relatively harmless by the middle of June 1954.[28]

It was not certain how Eastland would vote when the elderly Vermont Republican Ralph Flanders, McCarthy's most outspoken Senate critic, introduced his resolution to censure the Wisconsinian. McCarthy had less of a following in the South than in any other region. His most fateful blunder was in targeting the U.S. Army, the most revered institution in an area populated by tens of thousands employed by what Dwight D. Eisenhower later called the "military industrial complex," not to mention veterans and their families. While some Bourbons, like Fred Sullens, detested McCarthy, others such as State House Speaker Walter Sillers urged Eastland to stand by him. By mid-September 1954, only one Democrat was openly opposed to censuring McCarthy, Pat McCarran. While McCarran might have influenced Eastland's vote, his sudden death on September 28, a day after a special panel voted unanimously to censure McCarthy, removed any pressure within his caucus that might have led him to contemplate a break with his party.[29]

Well before, Lyndon Johnson ensured that McCarran would have little help from Democrats by stacking his forces with men on the right of his caucus who had not taken a public position for or against McCarthy. His ranking member was Edwin Johnson of Colorado, who was close to southern senators like the two junior to him on the panel, John Stennis and Sam Ervin of North Carolina. The Minority Leader also finagled GOP counterpart William Knowland to designate three respected senators of judicious but solidly conservative temperament led by Arthur Watkins, a quiet but tough Mormon. When they completed their work, they voted not to chastise McCarthy for any specific abuse, which all knew would lose them perhaps ten votes, but rather for behavior that "tended to bring the Senate into disrepute." Such was the tack members took when they arose on the floor to make their case. Most compelling was Ervin, a gifted raconteur who sprinkled his oration with stories from North Carolina. Ervin ended with the tale of Ephraim Swink, an octogenarian afflicted with a crippling brand of arthritis who a revivalist asked to testify as to what the Lord had done for him. "Uncle Ephraim arose," said Ervin, "with his bent and distorted body, and said, 'He has mighty nigh ruint me.'" And that, said Ervin, "was about what McCarthy has done to the Senate."[30]

Eastland rarely spoke many words when few would suffice. He kept his own counsel and was far more loyal to his party and Lyndon Johnson than most knew. Like Johnson, Eastland could not have condoned McCarthy's description of fellow conservative Watkins as "stupid" and "cowardly." Even less appropriate to him was McCarthy's suggestion that a committee where fellow southern conservatives Ervin and Stennis sat had "done the work of the Communist Party." With no one able to see an end to the verbal bullying of McCarthy, especially when his bombast was fueled by an ever more crippling bout with alcohol, powerful Republicans like General Jerry Persons, who headed Eisenhower's congressional liaison office, and Chief Justice Earl Warren provided counsel to McCarthy's critics of both parties. Even some eminent military men were helping those who thought it necessary to rein in the Wisconsin Republican. One aide to SISS Chairman Jenner, a close McCarthy ally, noted that General George C. Marshall was working behind the scenes with the Eisenhower administration to sway southern senators like Harry Byrd and Richard Russell against McCarthy. Drew Pearson reported that Lyndon Johnson had promised Eastland that, if he voted for censure, he would become chairman of SISS in the event Democrats retook the Senate. While Pearson's reports were inaccurate often enough that one should be skeptical, it is probable that Johnson reassured Eastland that he would get the gavel of SISS. Here was hardly something Eastland sweated, for Johnson was not one to deny senators chairmanships accorded by seniority, especially Southerners at a time when Dixie denizens held nearly half of the seats in his caucus. Perhaps more than anything, Eastland had seen FBI evidence indicating that some of what McCarthy was saying was, at best, exaggerated. Ever the institutionalist, Eastland on the whole had concluded in the way of the immortal Ephraim Swink that McCarthy had damn near ruined the Senate.[31]

Like most of his colleagues, Eastland got along well with McCarthy away from the cameras or the floor. The two bonded during the last year of McCarthy's life, after Eastland called on the Wisconsin Republican to testify for a bill to nullify a 6–3 decision in the case of *Kendrick M. Cole v. Philip Young et al.*, which declared the federal government could only dismiss a federal worker with ties to Communists or other subversive groups if they held jobs with clear responsibility for national security. There, McCarthy made clear that he agreed with Eastland that the Warren court was rendering one pro-Communist decision after another, even if he stopped short of accusing Warren, the GOP's 1948 nominee for vice president, of being a Communist. To be sure, giving McCarthy an official forum afforded Eastland credibility among McCarthy's diminishing group of friends and even more ignominy among his growing number of enemies. It helped little when Eastland tried to clarify that he was not charging Warren "with being a party member" but found it curious when he took "the same position they do when he says the Communist Party is just another political party."[32]

A half century later, Arthur Herman, one of McCarthy's few apologists in the historical profession, described Eastland as the only influential friend McCarthy made in Washington after his censure. Eastland indeed came to regret his vote to condemn the senator. Like much of official Washington, Eastland recognized that the excesses in McCarthy's drinking were increasingly self-destructive. The day he read McCarthy's obituary in the *Washington Evening Star*, May 2, 1957, Eastland lamented to his son Woods that the "press had hounded him to death." When it came time for senators to eulogize McCarthy three months later, Eastland saluted him not just for "great courage and deep and abiding convictions," but a "pure" heart. In his view, McCarthy had a "noble" purpose that had been aroused by his recognition that the "Trojan Horse" replete within Communist tactics lay in the "infiltration within the free state, espionage and subversion of the minds of men." To Eastland, the righteousness of McCarthy's aims was best demonstrated by the fact that most of McCarthy's critics had launched broadsides against his methods rather than his broader objectives.[33]

For Eastland, the fall of McCarthy had other implications. Barely a month after the Senate censured the man some called "Tail-Gunner Joe," Eastland, with his Democratic Party having retaken control of the Senate, assumed the helm of the panel empowered with the broadest authority to probe anyone accused of subverting the government. But for Eastland, a far more pressing matter was the preservation of a way of life. Such held true both for agrarian denizens less economically secure than ever as a result of mechanization and for his white neighbors against Yankee-led demands that the post–Civil War additions to the Constitution be enforced.

CHAPTER 9

Mississippi Bourbon Politics in the Age of Eisenhower

ON JANUARY 29, 1949, JIM EASTLAND BECAME THE SENATE'S PRIMARY arbiter of civil rights legislation. That day, Pat McCarran named him chairman of the Civil Rights Subcommittee of the full Judiciary Committee, a perch from which he could kill all civil rights legislation. McCarran's move reflected the awareness of Democratic leaders that their caucus was split sufficiently on questions of race that having Eastland at the helm of that panel to squirrel away civil rights bills and take the blame would shield all Democrats from any political fallout. Black leaders widely criticized his ascension. Executive Secretary William Patterson of the Civil Rights Congress called his choice a "calculated insult and affront to the Negro people and all progressives."[1]

There had been no crack in Eastland's segregationism. In the late spring of 1949, he tried to get the Senate to ban the District of Columbia from changing any law mandating a segregated capital city without the approval of both Congress and a plebiscite of District voters. The 49–27 vote against his amendment was hardly the first signal that the forces of Jim Crow were declining in all parts of the country.[2] And, as with Bourbon Democrats before him, Eastland's tone and ardor in defense of the society from whence he sprung varied from situation to situation, depending upon the nuances of socioeconomic circumstances and the intricacies of interpersonal relationships at any given moment.

Still, Eastland realized that maintaining any clout depended upon the good will of Democratic colleagues. On a personal level, he got along well with all members of both caucuses save newcomer Herbert Lehman, but he knew that he needed to support the national ticket to keep his chairmanship.[3] Equally instinctively, he recognized that the position of Mississippi was enhanced in Congress by the presence of a seasoned group of legislators with seniority on several committees, and he aggressively discouraged primary challenges to any of the state's incumbents. The member most susceptible to such a contest in the 1950s was Frank E. Smith of Greenwood, the congressman deemed Mississippi's most liberal. But, at least twice that decade, Eastland helped scotch the notion of a challenge to Smith. Most serious was one contemplated in 1958 by Charles Sullivan, a dynamic young conservative lawyer from Clarksdale whose father had managed Eastland's 1954 campaign. But while Sullivan's ideology may have been more akin to Eastland's own, the losses that might befall Mississippi from the loss of Smith's seniority and the strains Eastland feared might accrue upon Democrats from a divisive contest led him to quietly discourage a challenge. Where Eastland would almost always take overt roles were the gubernatorial campaigns of Paul B. Johnson Jr., the son of the man who had initially appointed him to the Senate.[4] Johnson's first of three bids for the state's highest office came in 1951, when he was a young assistant U.S. attorney. Johnson vied against the rest of an eight-member field, the best known of whom was Hugh White, the former governor, who at seventy was more than twice his age. To some, Eastland's backing seemed implausible, as Johnson, unlike White and others in the race, had been one of the few prominent Mississippi Democrats to back Truman in 1948. Eastland found such matters immaterial. "A political debt is never paid," he would tell anyone who cared to listen. And while White eventually prevailed, the size of his victory was the smallest of any in the Magnolia State since 1907.[5]

Eastland kept his own counsel as to national politics. At the outset of the 1952 presidential primary season, Eastland remained friendly with the president on a personal level. Still, the fact that Truman had once pushed a civil rights program rendered it unlikely that Eastland would embrace any ticket with him at its head. He was even less enthusiastic about Estes Kefauver, the fairly liberal senator from Tennessee who upset Truman in the New Hampshire primary, whose backing for measures he deemed anti-southern, such as anti-lynching and anti–poll tax bills, rendered him "too far to the left" for Eastland. As a man of the old South, Eastland, like the rest of the Mississippi delegation, found a natural home in the camp of Richard Russell of Georgia, even if he knew that Russell's chances of getting the nod were nonexistent. C. B. Curlee, who served as his political eyes and ears in northern Mississippi, told him in early April that Russell could expect to prevail in a general election against any prospective GOP candidate only in Dixie. Senator Robert A. Taft, the leader of GOP conservatives, might run ahead of Truman in Mississippi if the two faced off in November, Curlee continued, but would fall to any other Democrat. The wild card Curlee and other Eastland hands feared most was that Republicans would nominate General Dwight D. Eisenhower, as the presence of a national hero like Eisenhower might hasten splits among southern Democratic parties. With several factions and a nascent Republican Party all looking for new voters, such a development might prod one or more to appeal to African Americans. That would require them to contemplate registering black voters, a change that not only would limit the Democrats' dominance of the state's politics, but accelerate the end of the traditional southern way of life.[6]

While some opined that he was not as enthusiastic in support of the national party as Governor Hugh White and Lieutenant Governor Carroll Gartin, Eastland volunteered right after the convention to speak any time, anywhere during the fall for the Stevenson-Sparkman ticket. He was comfortable with the tacit Democratic agreement that their strategy on civil rights issues would be drafting a bill strong enough to excite Northerners, but guaranteeing that it did not pass so as to placate the South. Still, he noticed early on that several prominent Democrats, including many Dixiecrats, had aligned behind Eisenhower, the most prominent being Speaker Walter Sillers and former Lieutenant Governor Sam Lumpkin. In early fall 1952, Eastland wrote Sillers that both Eisenhower and Stevenson were "good men" but he was certain that the general would prevail by a substantial margin. He resisted several overtures to back Eisenhower, telling friends that he would have to become a Republican were he to do so, as his own party would certainly ostracize him if he stood against their national nominees in two successive elections. But if the general's coattails extended to other Republicans, Democratic hegemony in the Magnolia State might end. There was no reason for such fears in 1952, for most Mississippi Democrats clung tightly to their political heritage. While

Eisenhower ran well ahead of the performance of any Republican since Reconstruction in the Magnolia State, he still could not garner even 40 percent of the vote statewide, even as he carried Florida, Tennessee, Texas, and Virginia. He did raise some eyebrows in Sunflower County, where he ran just eighty-two votes behind Stevenson. Still, only one of those votes came from nearby Ruleville, where the railroad supervisor who cast it was thereafter known to all as Eisenhower.[7]

With Eisenhower's accession, Eastland moved to highlight those parts of the Democratic brand that would resonate in Mississippi. Once he learned Majority Leader Ernest McFarland had been defeated for reelection by Barry Goldwater, then known as the scion of a Phoenix department store chain, he set himself firmly behind the ascension of Democratic Whip Lyndon Johnson to the leadership. Six months later, he brought Johnson to Jackson to address the state party's Jefferson-Jackson Day dinner. Ever shrewd, Johnson declined to blast the popular new president, but called attention to the "rude awakening" that Eisenhower received when the Republican "Old Guard" fought his attempt to extend the Reciprocal Trade Act. Johnson's excoriating of the new GOP congressional majorities reminded those present that their party was not just the party of the Confederacy, but the one that had pursued low tariff policies that had greased the paths for the past century for their food, forest, and fiber products to foreign markets. But there were also more recent New Deal programs for which nearly all Magnolia State Democrats would fight. Chief among them was the Tennessee Valley Authority (TVA), which had brought cheap energy to northern Mississippi since the 1930s. While not convinced that public power was wise everywhere, Eastland thought that the TVA had served his people well. Just as aware that most Republicans opposed its creation, he feared that some might try and let it fall into private hands and joined Estes Kefauver and Lister Hill in bashing Republicans for putting TVA on a "starvation diet." While GOP leaders tried to reassure the public that neither Eisenhower nor they intended to sell TVA, Eastland retorted that Eisenhower had appointed Dean Clarence Manion of the Notre Dame Law School, who had long advocated the sale of TVA, to chair his Commission on Intergovernmental Relations. On questioning from moderate Republican John Sherman Cooper, who, like Hill and Kefauver, hailed from a TVA state, Eastland had to admit that Manion merely served on a temporary panel. Even if the charge was flimsy, more credibility accrued upon the overall notion that Eisenhower was anti-TVA when the Atomic Energy Commission bought power from two private power companies rather than TVA to fuel its plants near Memphis. Eastland was quick to join fellow Democrats in a filibuster that blocked what came to be known as the Dixon-Yates affair until their party retook control of both Houses of Congress after the 1954 election.[8]

Still, the one issue that Bourbons had prioritized for the three generations since Reconstruction was farm policy. After Eastland moved onto the Agriculture Committee, he quickly earned a reputation for expertise on these questions. Aides to Allen Ellender, who outranked him in seniority, often sent Louisiana farmers to Eastland to untangle their problems within the bureaucracy. Eastland's principal concern was cotton, and he was quick to speak up when administration programs seemed less farmer friendly than those espoused by candidate Eisenhower during the 1952 campaign. As soon as Agriculture Secretary Ezra Taft Benson, a free-market purist, likened parity programs to "disaster insurance" less than a month after his confirmation, Eastland joined several Democrats in taking the floor to expound upon the need for such a program at a time of falling farm income. Farmers who voted Republican, Eastland said, "had the rug pulled out from under them." He would not prolong a dispute with Benson or any officer of the new administration for he knew that Mississippi farmers would only benefit if the two worked in tandem. In weeks to come, he not only backed Eisenhower on a plan to reorganize the Agriculture Department, but secured for Benson the coveted spot of keynoting the annual meeting of the Delta Council. There, Benson pledged to join Eastland temporarily in calling for 90 percent parity for most food and fiber products. Yet, the secretary added, it was even more necessary for American farmers to expand their markets, and he warned them not to stick with programs that priced their commodities so high that they could not sell abroad. Eastland agreed, but remained intent upon buying time for farmers to accept the flexible price supports Benson preferred. With Republicans Edward Thye of Minnesota and Milton Young of North Dakota, the Senate tribunes for wheat farmers, he began pushing to let America dispense with its farm surpluses by trading them for military supplies from countries too poor to pay for goods the United States could not sell elsewhere. While a committed free trader, Eastland would not call for resuming trade with Communist China, as he feared they might enter and complicate the ongoing conflict in Indochina. Still, he firmly favored expanding exports of Mississippi farm products, even to the Soviet bloc.[9]

While southern members of Congress prior to 1954 had blocked every piece of legislation with a civil rights designation, many white Southerners feared that the Supreme Court might radically alter their way of life. By mid 1953, Mississippi politicos sensed that a class-action suit brought by five groups of plaintiffs could be the one to permanently transform all social relationships in their part of Dixie. Eastland was as apprehensive as anyone. He "was a product of a world that did not change," his son Woods said more than half a century later, "and segregation was one of the pillars of that world." He and top aides including Courtney Pace told political associates in Mississippi that it was next to impossible to discern any exact reading on what the justices were thinking. Their pragmatism could not hide their trepidations, which were readily visible when the Judiciary Committee met to consider the nomination of California Governor Earl Warren to the chief justiceship. After Chairman William Langer, a maverick from North Dakota, convened closed-door meetings to hear flimsy charges against Warren from witnesses who were a bit eccentric, and, in one case, a fugitive from justice, Eastland voted to report Warren's nomination to the full committee. He then joined only Olin Johnston of South Carolina in voting against reporting Warren's name to the full Senate, and defended his viewpoint by saying that the Californian lacked judicial experience.[10]

When a united Supreme Court ruled on May 17, 1954, in *Brown v. Board of Education of Topeka, Kansas* that in the field of education "separate but equal was inherently unequal," Eastland stood defiantly. He remained firmly committed to the mindset of relatively humane Delta planters that both races were content with the *status quo* and warned that any attempt to enforce the *Brown* ruling would "cause great . . . turmoil." While Governor Hugh White vowed not to "pay any attention to the . . . decision" and Congressman John Bell Williams from Hinds County tagged the date as "Black Monday," their reactions and Eastland's were hardly universal, even in the South. Russell Long of Louisiana urged the South to accept the decision. Far more emphatic were the ordinarily conservative editors of the *Knoxville Journal*, who opined that "no one fitted by character and intelligence to sit as a Justice of the Supreme Court, and sworn to uphold the Constitution . . . could have decided it other than the way it was decided." Richard Russell, who would become the effective leader of southern senators for the duration of the civil rights era, contrastingly urged his colleagues and other Dixie officeholders to study the legal authority of states to disregard a Supreme Court decision. Eastland demanded an even bolder stand for a cause he feared might soon be lost. "The South," he told reporters, "will not abide nor obey this legislative decision by a political court."[11]

Eastland elaborated at length ten days later. His audience was less the near-empty Senate he spoke to than the nearly all-white Democratic primary electorate in Mississippi that he reached by having more than 100,000 copies of his speech made. One home state potentate he took care to quote was Fred Sullens, a onetime critic, who termed the decision a "prize piece of poppycock and piffle." But, Eastland added, the court had not created new "civil rights." Rather, it had created "social rights" by putting the races together, physically, upon a plane of social equality. Eastland hailed blacks for their "great contribution" to the South, but insisted segregation was the one system that promoted "racial harmony." America's greatness, he declared, "depended upon racial purity and the maintenance of Anglo-Saxon institutions." He targeted both the Supreme Court as a whole and members as individuals, saying no jurist ought to accept any award other than an honorary doctorate. While he was harshest on Hugo Black, the Alabaman who had accepted an award from the SCHW, a group he termed a Communist front, he also blasted Justices Felix Frankfurter and Stanley Reed for acting as character witnesses for Alger Hiss, whose denial that he had been a Communist got him convicted for perjury; William O. Douglas for contributing to the NAACP and advocating that the United States recognize the Communist government of China; and Sherman Minton for speaking at an interracial banquet of the SCHW. The South was making progress on civil rights, he continued, without "Northern meddlers" and was graciously adding funding for black schools. If anyone missed his intent, he asserted that the North was in for a long struggle. "One is naïve, indeed, to think that Southern people will permit all of their social institutions to be swept away on the distorted and, in my judgment, politically inspired decision of the Court."[12]

To a far greater degree than reported at the time, Eastland's intransigence on issues of race was exacerbated by the presence of a viable challenger in the Democratic primary. It was a longstanding Dixie tradition, his revered predecessor Pat Harrison once told a reporter, for senators to don a statesmanlike posture for the first five years of their terms, then return home the sixth year to "sling the shit." But the challenge itself came primarily because of Eastland's indecision as to whether to seek a third term. In early 1953, he told State Senator Brinkley Morton that he was unlikely to seek reelection. His reticence sprang from Libby's discomfort with continuing to school Anne, Sue, and Woods for the first semester of each school year in Ruleville, then bringing them to Washington for the winter and spring, a practice they feared was leaving their kids behind those their age in Washington. In the meantime, Pat McCarran, at the time the ranking Democrat on the Judiciary Committee, pointed out to Eastland that the two Democrats senior to him—he and Harley Kilgore—were much older than him and not in good health. That effectively meant that it would not be long before he might become chairman and thus truly well placed to serve his home state. Eastland resolved this dilemma by promising Libby that he would buy a house in the District of Columbia, where his children could complete their secondary education. Then and only then could he announce that his desire to help alleviate continuing problems on America's farms had prompted him to seek a third term.[13]

Eastland's opponent was Lieutenant Governor Carroll Gartin, an able forty-year-old veteran and two-term mayor of Laurel. Yet many believed that it was less Gartin pushing a challenge than Hugh White. Little separated White and Eastland on matters of policy. Eastland got behind the governor's proposed constitutional amendment later in the year to allow the state legislature, by a two-thirds vote of both houses, to close all public schools and dispose of their property if integration seemed inevitable.[14] But White had nursed a grudge against Eastland since the summer of 1951, when Eastland had backed Paul B. Johnson Jr. rather than him in the Democratic runoff. For Eastland, supporting thirty-three-year-old Johnson was merely an opportunity to repay the Johnson family. White was hardly placated. In prevailing upon Gartin, White found an able man young and energetic enough to wage a credible challenge and one who had been a loyal second-in-command. Gartin's base was strong in southern Mississippi and among fellow veterans, and he was amply financed by the CIO, the further left of the two major industrial federations. He also was backed by many mayors across the state who thought he might more aggressively press for gas tax revenue for their towns and cities. Still, the unlikelihood that his challenge might find success should have been apparent early in the race, when more members of the state Senate, the body he served as president, sided with Eastland than with him.[15]

Publicly and privately, Eastland never sweated any suggestion that he might lose. His network of supporters throughout the state remained uncommonly loyal, particularly among those for whom he had done favors. Eastland had always fared well with the Mississippi business community, and the railroad brotherhoods and the Farm Bureau Federation were just as solidly behind him. While he feared that northeastern Mississippi, always the battleground statewide, needed some work, he deemed southern Mississippi in "better than excellent shape." He had the backing of the state's two largest newspapers. Fred Sullens opined that Eastland had "grown" since he first sought a full six-year term, and he put the weight of the *Jackson Daily News* behind him. Support from the *Jackson Clarion-Ledger* was never in doubt, considering the long relationship of the Eastland family with its publishers. Still, even Carroll Gartin might have been surprised had he known that the Hederman brothers had sent their draft endorsement to Eastland so he might clarify and improve the message he was trying to sell to voters on their editorial page.[16]

It was hardly lost upon the Eastland team that Gartin could spend more time campaigning. His campaign manager C. Arthur Sullivan told reporters later that Gartin shook more hands most days than Eastland would all summer. Still, Eastland realized that he needed to get out and traverse the state. Knowing he tired easier than he had during his last strenuous campaign, his staff braced themselves for a tumultuous two months. Twenty-year-old Brad Dye, the 6 foot 6 inch son of a state legislator, served as Eastland's driver and found the job "a pretty good grind." Eastland would venture from town to town, often giving half a dozen speeches a day. A sound truck would go ahead to the next town and a barker would announce that their senior senator would soon arrive. Upon finishing, Eastland would plunge into the crowd and pump the flesh until Dye butted in to tell him that it was time to go. The senator would chew Dye out in public, then follow him to the campaign car and commend the future lieutenant governor once inside for breaking in at just the right time. Dye would not turn on the car's air conditioning, not even when it reached 108 degrees in McComb, because Eastland feared that he might lose his voice. And Dye was prepared for other idiosyncrasies. Eastland wanted the radio to be tuned to a news station rather than one that played music or a ballgame. He insisted on fresh Triangle cigars, which one could get in Mississippi only in the Heidelberg Hotel in Jackson, or cigarettes on the rare occasions he might prefer them. He wanted club soda, which was only sold at the time on the Gulf Coast, to dilute the Ballantine scotch that he favored for his two nightly drinks. And, Eastland's senior aides made clear one last request. "If he wants to pee," they told Dye, "he wants to pee right now. You don't have to wait to get to the next service station. Just pull off to the side of the road."[17]

It had been Eastland's intention to focus his campaign on the needs of small farmers in Mississippi, but the Supreme Court's ruling in *Brown v. Board of Education* changed that. Race became the pervasive issue almost to the omission of all others. "Not since the post-bellum period," wrote historian Neil R. McMillen, "was it so consuming an issue as in the years after the Second World War." On a trip to Pearl River County, Erle Johnston, Eastland's publicist whose copy often appeared as news stories in dailies and weeklies, large and small, throughout the state, asked if Eastland would like him to insert a line or two about tung oil, an important product of southern Mississippi, in his standard speech. "The hell with tung oil," Eastland replied. The primary, indeed overriding, issue in this race was "segregation, segregation, segregation."[18]

Eastland formally opened his campaign in Forest, the larger of the two towns he could call home, on June 26, 1954. Aides served 5000 barbecued chicken lunches to the largely white audience, and animated the festivities by revving up jukeboxes to blare "Roll On, Mississippi." After Judge Percy Lee introduced him and his family, Eastland took the stage to describe the fight he would wage to preserve the southern way of life. Using a phrase popularized a few years earlier by President Eisenhower, he pledged that he was "about to embark upon a great crusade to restore Americanism," which in his view entailed the "untainted racial heritage, their culture, and the institutions of the Anglo-Saxon race." To be sure, with but thirteen senators having served longer than he, Eastland took care to trumpet the benefits his seniority could bring. He promised to fight for programs like TVA and the Rural Electrification Administration that had created so many opportunities for rural Mississippi. He pledged a "square deal" for labor and management, but hinted which side he would take in the event of conflict when he told the crowd that the CIO was doing all it could to defeat him. But his focus remained the fight he pledged to wage for a segregated society. Jabbing his fist, then one arm, then the other, Eastland called for a national movement to "combat the biased and incompetent . . . decisions of the United States Supreme Court." "Tell him about it, Jim," yelled many, before he assured the crowd that he did not intend to create another third party like the Dixiecrats. And he could hardly fail to mention his clout in Washington simply by his standing as chairman of the Subcommittee on Civil Rights. "I had special pockets put in my pants," he declared with just a bit of hyperbole, "and for three years I carried those bills around in my pockets everywhere I went and every one of them was defeated."[19]

Gartin had opened his campaign two weeks earlier. While his endorsement by the CIO signified that he was the champion of more liberal Democrats, Gartin opted to challenge Eastland on virtually every front from every side. He hoped to sway some hill county farmers by attacking Eastland for allowing western farmers more acreage for their crops. In truth, few votes from tillers of the soil were ever available to anyone but Eastland, as Eastland and his team could reply that bills he supported and helped write had actually given southern farmers additional acreage. More often, Gartin reminded voters of his status as a veteran and castigated Eastland as "the man who's seldom there." He pointed to an attendance record that indicated that Eastland had been present much less often than the congressional norm, a point some found unfair as Eastland had been legitimately bedridden during some of the absences. But, most curiously, Gartin, in a bid to sway some of the redneck vote, took to castigating Eastland as less than a "real Southerner" for "failing to stand by" Theodore Bilbo, when senators would not seat him after his reelection in 1946. But while fans of "The Man" had to agree that the dwarflike senator with the big voice had been "the greatest voice of white supremacy" of their generation, they could hardly have found Eastland soft on segregation. Those fond of neither Eastland nor Bilbo were put off, even horrified, by Gartin's amplification and sharpening of his critique. Especially shocked was Ira Harkey, the publisher of the influential and moderate *Pascagoula Chronicle*, who withdrew his paper's endorsement from the lieutenant governor for that reason alone.[20]

With Gartin blasting away at Eastland's alleged absenteeism, Eastland aides crafted a rebuttal. C. B. Curlee wrote Eastland that the jibes of the man they liked to deride as "Little Carroll" would not be accepted because Mississippians, particularly farmers, were fully aware of his work on their behalf. Courtney Pace had a knack for devising stratagems that would sell in Mississippi, and he came up with the slogan that Eastland used for the rest of the campaign. "Just name the fight when Jim wasn't there," Eastland backers began to chant, until the constant repetition of the phrase allowed them to shorten their mantra to the first four words. Every bit as important were circulars Pace and Erle Johnston put together to insert in the state's newspapers just prior to the election. In these, the two trumpeted Eastland's fights and votes for any number of popular measures, from the GI bill to the Hill-Burton hospital construction bill to battles to keep parity rates high, and placed the dates of each battle alongside. And Eastland was not above using the perks of incumbency. While he hated to fly, he flew often to Washington during the summer of 1954 to cast key votes or deliver well-covered addresses on matters of importance to white Mississippi. He and John Stennis cast the deciding votes to continue Rural Electrification Administration appropriations and important ones to raise price supports. On another trip, he gave a long speech where he called for lower tariffs to expand the access of farm products to foreign markets and bashed the justices of the Supreme Court as a group of "parasitic politicians" who he charged in *Brown v. Board of Education* had begun to strip power from the states in an unprecedented way.[21]

Eastland also benefitted considerably from timely help from his Republican Senate colleagues. When Gartin derided the value of Eastland's time in office, Karl Mundt of South Dakota, who had chaired the hearings probing Joseph McCarthy's charges that Communists had infiltrated the

Army, wrote Mississippians that seniority was the foundation of Senate power. Vermont moderate George D. Aiken, Eastland's frequent partner on farm bills, met a Gartin charge that western farmers were getting higher acreage for their cotton allotments than Southerners by writing a farmer to say Mississippi had been allotted 320,000 additional acres in a recent cotton bill.[22] Aiken also answered a Gartin attack on Eastland's absence from the floor on a vote for final passage of a farm bill by noting Eastland's presence for all controversial parts of the measure, including a vote against Eisenhower's program for flexible supports for many commodities that Aiken backed.[23] And when Gartin questioned Eastland's commitment to segregation, Courtney Pace carried out one of the greatest counterintuitive tricks ever. He went to Everett Dirksen, who prided himself on having represented the area Abraham Lincoln had served in Congress. Might Dirksen, who knew Mississippi would not elect a Republican in 1954, condemn Eastland's intransigence, Pace asked. Indeed he would, Dirksen replied. Within minutes, the organ-toned Illinoisan signed a letter Pace drafted deriding Eastland as the man who did more to obstruct civil rights than any other senator.[24]

By the end of the campaign, Eastland was declaring the main issue as being "whether the national CIO, the Americans for Democratic Action, and the NAACP can elect a senator in Mississippi." Gartin tried to answer by painting Eastland as a "part-time senator who votes Republican as much as he does Democratic," denying that he was controlled by "pressure groups" and condemning Eastland's "flimsy campaign tactics." Still, Eastland won easily, carrying seventy of the state's eighty-two counties. While Gartin ran fairly well in the cities, Eastland amassed a huge majority among rural whites. He carried 93 percent of the vote in his native Sunflower County, although not one of the registered black voters there cast a vote for either he or Gartin. He indicated a particular joy in winning a solid bloc of the Chinese minority in the Delta.

Gartin, in turn, heard often from voters all over the state that they knew and liked him, and while they did not know Eastland, they still felt obliged to vote for him.[25] However close their ties with Gartin, the bonds they felt as the clientele of Eastland registered stronger at the time it came down to casting their vote. Here were patronage relationships like those forged by leaders of big city machines with those in their communities. And, while the distance separating him from his constituents was considerably larger than that dividing mayors from their people, the key to the perseverance of any southern Bourbon like Eastland had as much to do with the quality of the services he provided as his ideology.

Organizing against integration was virtually nonexistent in the Delta prior to *Brown v. Board of Education*. Robert "Tut" Patterson, a onetime Mississippi State football star from Itta Bena, wrote Eastland before the decision to ask about a Washington-based group called the National Association for the Advancement of White People. Eastland knew nothing of this group, but he read literature Patterson forwarded with headlines like "Racial Separation Is No Sin—Hatred Is" and hoped it might "serve as a propaganda medium."[26] To their dismay, the association, led by New Jersey native John Kasper, was one that asked followers to break up any gathering of integrationists, "physically, by whatever means necessary." The National Association for the Advancement of White People soon wreaked havoc from Milford, Delaware, to Poolesville, Maryland, to Clinton and Nashville, Tennessee. Once the violent tactics Kasper excused became public, Mississippi segregationists let him and others they deemed extreme know that they could handle their own affairs without the help of "outside agitators." "There is no place in Mississippi," declared Attorney General Joe T. Patterson in 1956, "for a revival of the Ku Klux Klan, John Kasper or Asa Carter." New Governor James P. Coleman echoed Patterson's message the same year when he invoked a law barring "fomenting and agitating of litigation" to keep Kasper from airing his appeals to hate and violence in the Magnolia State.[27]

The kind of group most Delta segregationists pined for was one dedicated to preserving their world that would give them an air of respectability. It had begun to irritate a few in Indianola even before *Brown v. Board of Education* that the Supreme Court was contemplating mandating the integration of schools. Just two years earlier, they had heeded Hugh White's requests to build a new high school for the three quarters of Sunflower County kids who were black and move to equalize funding for facilities and salaries for those who taught in black schools. It mattered to few that William Faulkner, the state's best known literary figure, had written the editor of the *Memphis Commercial Appeal* to note that existing schools were "not even good enough for white folks." Some, like Patterson, were truly concerned about what they saw as the "mongrelization" of their society and the "federalizing of our public schools." In July 1954, a dozen of them met at the home of cotton compress manager Dave Hawkins to form such a body. A week later, a hundred Deltans met at Indianola's city hall to charter the first Citizens' Council and elected banker Herman Moore as their president. Hawkins and Patterson joined Moore on a board of professionals chosen to evoke an image of respectability for a group designed to be, as their first pamphlet proclaimed, "the South's answer to the mongrelizers." Well aware of the ignoble heritage of the Ku Klux Klan, they renounced violence. One Eastland aide who watched the growth of the Citizens Councils with interest was Brad Dye, whose father, a state legislator, enlisted in his local chapter near Grenada. The Magnolia State bourgeoisie took care to organize their movement, Dye believed, to keep the "damn riffraff" from controlling it. Campaign publicist Erle Johnston was the only Eastland aide to join, and he stayed for just a few weeks. To him, council meetings were "an emotional purgative" where members gathered at courthouses and heard pleas for money. Some gave, but rarely solved any problems, let alone agreed on a course of action, but always seemed to leave meetings feeling better. James P. Coleman much later declared that the Citizens Councils, however inadvertently, served to limit violence by giving members an outlet to vent their outrage verbally and disavow any malicious intent.[28]

Citizens Councils sprouted throughout Mississippi, then across the South. By January 1955, 110 chapters had formed in Mississippi; a year later, a full 250,000 people belonged, with 80,000 of them in the Magnolia State. Members hailed largely from the middle class and especially from small towns in areas where blacks outnumbered whites by more than two to one. They placed applications in banks, service clubs, and restaurants throughout the region. Eastland never joined and discouraged those close to him from doing so, sensing membership might become a political liability. Rather quickly, *Delta Democrat Times* publisher W. Hodding Carter Jr., a liberal by southern standards, took to labeling the Councils "uptown Ku Klux Klans." Others chimed in "hoodless Klan," "country club Klan," and a "Ku Klux Klan with deodorant." Still, Eastland found the Citizens Councils were important allies in the short run, and he had aides correspond with their leaders. He and John Bell Williams interceded to let the councils film their weekly fifteen-minute *Citizens Council Forum* at the official Capitol studios, thus facilitating access to guests and saving them money. Aide L. P. Lipscomb wrote "Tut" Patterson to suggest that he highlight pro-segregation statements from noted blacks like novelist Zora Neale Hurston or editorials that appeared in conservative black organs. But while Eastland and others endorsed the mission of the Citizens Councils, they carefully absented themselves from their inner workings.

Indeed, some less savory Delta chapters engaged in some truly sordid misdeeds. The town most tarred for its Citizens Council's violence was Belzoni, known as the "catfish capital of the world," where Reverend George Lee, the vice president of the Regional Council of Negro Leadership, was killed gangland style in May 1955 after he refused to remove his name from the voter registration rolls. Six months later, Gus Courts, the president of the Humphreys County NAACP, was hit by three bullets while making change at the grocery store he managed. More commonly, councils conducted what the *Montgomery (AL) Advertiser* called "economic thuggery." E. J. Stringer, the state NAACP chairman in 1954, saw black patrons of his Columbus practice pressed to find other sources of dental care. Black farmers who tried to register to vote or join the NAACP found it next to impossible to secure credit and sometimes found loans called in well before they were due. Fifty-three Yazoo City blacks who signed a petition calling for the integration of local schools saw their names in Citizens Council ads and found themselves without jobs or boycotted by whites who once were their customers. While "Tut" Patterson denied that Mississippi councils ever intended to exert economic pressure so brazenly, he declared it "their business" if employers chose to fire their help.[29]

Almost always in the post–*Brown v. Board of Education* decade, Eastland echoed the Citizens Councils. They reprinted at least one of his speeches, so few found it unfair when NAACP leader Roy Wilkens derided him at the end of 1955 as their "chief spokesman." While many in the South breathed a sigh of relief when the Supreme Court in a decision often called *Brown II* essentially placed the pace of integration in the hands of district court judges and thus afforded many school districts a bit of a delay, Eastland was not placated when the court inserted the ambivalent phrase "with all deliberate speed." Soon after, he took the Senate floor to pledge that the South would defy "those who would destroy our system of government" in courts, in legislatures, and by their ballots. His reaction was intuitive rather than calculated. He was quick to bash social scientists the Supreme Court had cited for "false and insidious propaganda." Some once belonged to Communist front groups, he said, while others had been saluted in the *Daily Worker*. The court, he argued, had ignored the Constitution and substituted "psychological, sociological, and anthropological" considerations. Still, not every Washington hand saw Eastland as the most intransigent opponent of integration. Veteran *New York Times* columnist William S. White assigned that distinction to Strom Thurmond, who had been elected to the Senate in 1954. Any perception of the public behavior of the two rests upon minor nuances, but a private communication affirms White's impression. Thurmond learned in February 1956 that Sidwell Friends School, the Washington, D.C., school Eastland's three younger children attended, had decided to desegregate. Almost immediately, he wrote Eastland indignantly and attached the *New York Times* article reporting the change. "I thought *you* were *opposed* to integration," he proclaimed.[30]

In truth, there was no change in Eastland's outlook. He often saw seemingly unrelated questions through the prism of their effect upon the preservation of the southern way of life. He gave Supreme Court nominees tighter scrutiny than ever before, particularly Republicans from states that once had been abolitionist havens. The first to experience a thorough examination on ideological matters rather than those of capability or integrity was John M. Harlan II, Eisenhower's choice to replace Robert Jackson. At first, Eastland told Attorney General Herbert Brownell that he feared Harlan had "Communist sympathies," but recanted when he learned that a staffer had provided him data on another John Harlan. He then confided to Justice Department lawyers that he considered Harlan an "improvement" over Jackson and a "high class fellow." Still, he feared that Harlan, the grandson of the justice who had cast the one dissenting vote in *Plessy v. Ferguson*, the 1896 case that established the doctrine of "separate but equal," might emerge as another regular vote for the bloc led by Earl Warren. Harlan in the end turned out to be a rather cautious and conservative jurist, even if he had been the choice of moderate New York Governor Thomas E. Dewey. It would be Harlan's ties to Dewey around which Eastland focused his public opposition. Harlan's inexperience as a judge reminded him of Warren's, and his connections fortified Eastland's belief that the Supreme Court was too susceptible to the political winds of the day. Eastland used his time to pursue two lines of inquiry. Did Harlan believe that a treaty could supersede any authority granted by the Constitution? Like many facing similar inquiries in the future, Harlan declined to answer, saying he would not comment upon matters that might come before the court. And, when asked if he should decide cases on the basis of the authority of the Constitution or in accordance with his own views on political, sociological, or economic questions, Harlan declared that the Constitution, the law, and the facts would be his guides. His declining to go further and suggest that he might tinker with Supreme Court rulings in cases like *Brown v. the Board of Education* that had annoyed the South meant that Harlan would not get Eastland's vote. But Eastland was in a very decided minority, as the Senate voted 71–11 to install Harlan on the Supreme Court.[31]

As much as other Southerners made of what they deemed the abuses of the Supreme Court, it was a gruesome murder 22 miles due east of Doddsville in an even smaller hamlet of Money, Mississippi, that multiplied demands for racial progress. In late August 1955, a fourteen-year-old African-American visitor from Chicago, Emmett Till, was lynched by storeowner Roy Bryant and half-brother J. W. Milam after he allegedly came on to his wife and left her with a wolf whistle. It was days before the two set out to avenge Carolyn Bryant's honor, but they found Till, pistol whipped him, ordered him to carry a cotton gin fan to the bank of the Tallahatchie River, and then demanded that he strip. Once Till was naked, they killed him with a single bullet, then tied the fan to Till's head so the body would sink to the bottom when they threw it in the river. Till's mutilated corpse was recovered, then shipped in a coffin to Chicago. Once the casket was opened for Till's mother to identify her son, Mamie Bradley insisted that it remain open throughout the funeral so all could see the attack's sheer brutality. Oblivious to the perpetrators was the reality that it was not just Emmett Till's friends and relatives who would witness the outcome of their terror, but all of America, for *Jet* magazine, the best-selling African-American weekly, ran images of Till's corpse in their September 15 issue.[32]

Editorially, Fred Sullens, the colorful and occasionally volatile publisher of the *Jackson Daily News*, spoke for much of Bourbon Mississippi when he decried the lynching as a "brutal senseless crime." Governor White promised a "vigorous prosecution." Even "Tut" Patterson termed the murder "very regrettable." Still, the unapologetic acquittals of Bryant and Milam made it seem that white Mississippians and indeed Southerners were more incensed by suggestions that reaction to it reflected legitimate criticisms of the society that spawned his killers. Sullens wrote that he sensed that the NAACP was trying to use the lynching to "arouse hatred and fear," and he got Eastland and John Stennis to look into the war record of Private Louis Till, the victim's father. What they found was that the elder Till had been hanged after being court-martialed and convicted of the murder of one Italian woman and the rape of two others ten years earlier. But the millions who saw *Jet*'s photograph of Till's mutilated corpse had to wonder why such an irrelevant detail about a man who had been punished when the victim was but four years old was raised or even probed.[33] Indeed, that picture evoked better than any other the reality that African Americans had long suffered not just from inequities or indignities but barbarities from many segments of southern society. Just three months later, a bus boycott organized in Montgomery, Alabama, after seamstress and church secretary Rosa Parks refused to give up her seat to a white patron indicated that many would no longer accept further injustices of any sort. Many took to using their First Amendment rights to petition for a redress of grievances and assemble peaceably to insist that their Fourteenth Amendment right of "equal protection" be honored.

In turn, Eastland alluded to memories of the southern past to suggest his next course. "You'll remember the Confederate Army made a token capture at Gettysburg," he told one audience in a somewhat biased version of the seminal battle of what he called the War Between the States. "Some of Pickett's men reached the top of the ridge. But who won the battle? Since the decision in 1954, we've had token integration in some places, but the South has not been breached." A few years later, he promised that the fight would go on with an allusion to the end of the first Reconstruction. "How long did it take the South to win the war?" he asked. "Eleven years, wasn't it?"[34]

CHAPTER 10

Chairman of the Senate Internal Security Subcommittee

IT HAS OFTEN BEEN TRUE IN THE STORIED HISTORY OF THE U.S. SENATE that seemingly innocuous moves of personnel have had great impacts. So it was in 1955, when Majority Leader Lyndon Johnson got Eastland to leave the helm of the Civil Rights Subcommittee and take charge of the SISS. The switch from Eastland to Thomas Hennings of Missouri on the civil rights panel symbolized that Senate Democratic leaders were moving away from their previous practice of skirting divisive debates over matters of race relations that might impair their party's unity on economic issues. But the presence of a McCarran loyalist like Eastland at the chair of SISS also served to dispel GOP suggestions that Democrats might be "soft on Communism."[1]

Within the committee itself, Eastland opted to keep the staff he had inherited from McCarran and William "Wild Bill" Jenner, his two predecessors. As Democrats again held the majority, the lead counsel again would be Julien "Jay" Sourwine, an intimidating, husky interrogator who had made scores of enemies while working for McCarran. At his side was minority counsel Robert Morris, an even more conservative aide to ranking Republican Jenner. Neither was close to Eastland, who even offered to fire Sourwine, if that were the preferred course of Alan Bible, McCarran's popular, moderately conservative successor from Nevada. That was not necessary, Bible told Eastland, even as Sourwine challenged him for renomination in 1956. When Sourwine left SISS to wage an extraordinarily unsuccessful campaign, Eastland brought back Morris, who served until leaving in 1958 to wage an equally futile bid for a GOP Senate nod in New Jersey. Eastland then rehired Sourwine for the duration of the panel's existence, even if Sourwine's abrasiveness was pronounced enough at one after-work session that Eastland told his staff never again to invite him for a drink. Still, Eastland delegated upon him an inordinate degree of influence over the panel's work. Far more than before he took the helm of the full Judiciary Committee, Eastland was focusing upon judgeships, civil rights, and the unique problems of Mississippi farms.[2]

There was no dearth of potential probes for SISS in the hypercharged Cold War atmosphere of the mid-1950s. Well before Eastland became chairman, Sourwine scoured the political landscape for groups that might have experienced some Communist penetration. His and Eastland's ideas were hardly pipedreams. J. Edgar Hoover had long favored them with choice leads, knowing that they would not let information leak that might compromise ongoing investigations. But while the *Daily Worker*, the Communist house organ, liked to opine that Senator Joseph "McCarthy has changed his name to Eastland," some scholars of the McCarthy era note that the names of many probed by SISS and the House Un-American Activities Committee appeared in both the Venona project and Soviet archives that were revealed two generations later. This does not render SISS blameless. Some ex-Communist witnesses like Paul Crouch and the even shadier Harvey Matusow[3] often were reckless with the facts of their pasts. Eastland, in turn, was always quick to air allegations that Communists were influential in the civil rights movement. For his part, Sourwine not only could be more partisan than judicious if the man probed was a Republican, but also had a strange penchant for trying to tag pacifistic groups of long vintage as pawns of the Kremlin. At one point, Thomas J. Dodd, the Connecticut Democrat, not only lambasted him publicly for labeling the Quaker-run American Friends Service Committee as a "well-known transmission belt for the Communist apparatus" in a SISS published pamphlet, but also ordered that all uncirculated copies be destroyed. What SISS did was air material well known to the intelligence and defense communities, recognizing full well that they would not get instant gratification. An assistant once told Sourwine that the aims of any SISS hearing were to provide the next day's news story and to give allies a record that would fortify their own anti-Communist positions. "We lose more than we win in tomorrow's papers," he argued. Victory would come when the public concluded from the evidence they gathered and published that Communism was as dangerous inside the United States as they deemed it to be.[4]

It was always Eastland's and Sourwine's fear that Communists would try to infiltrate any American institution they deemed vulnerable. In Eastland's view, one of the most susceptible groups was the press, and they came to suspect that Communists had found their way onto the staffs of several major newspapers. But not all Democrats thought it wise to hunt for Communists in the press. Price Daniel and Olin Johnston, Eastland's fellow Southerners on SISS, rendered their opposition quietly, but onetime reporter Richard Neuberger of Oregon argued that such an investigation would open a Pandora's box of threats to the freedom of the press. While Neuberger's position was the dominant one within the Democratic caucus, they were outvoted by Eastland and the panel's three Republicans on SISS.[5]

Eastland's star witness when hearings opened in June 1955 was Winston Burdett, a CBS correspondent who as a young reporter had belonged to the Communist Party while working for the *Brooklyn Eagle*. An erudite journalist hired by Edward R. Murrow during World War II, Burdett broke completely with the Communists in 1942 and let his superiors know of his odyssey away from the party as early as 1951, the year many news executives began requiring employees to sign anti-Communist affidavits. Soon after becoming chairman, Eastland moved to shield Burdett from the "mud guns of vilification" of those who felt betrayed, especially the twelve he implicated as having been part of his cell at the *Eagle*. He saluted Burdett in letters to CBS news executives, thus buttressing their intent to protect him. Twelve witnesses followed Burdett to the stand over the next two days. Ten asserted their rights against self-incrimination. One of the two who testified at length was Charles Grutzner, a reporter for the *New York Times* who had been part of Burdett's cell. The principal reason for calling Grutzner rested on an Air Force general's claim that Grutzner had reported classified information while covering the Korean War and thereby aided and abetted the enemy. But what Eastland did not know was that Grutzner had cleared each of his stories with the Pentagon before sending them to the *Times*. When spokesmen for the Defense Department corroborated Grutzner's account, Eastland was forced to concede that Grutzner had not harmed the security of American troops.[6]

Two weeks later, SISS heard from onetime *Eagle* reporters who had moved on to bigger New York papers. Two who belonged to the Communist Party when they worked for the *Eagle*, then left in 1942, invoked their Fifth Amendment protections rather than answer Jay Sourwine's queries about their associations. Both found themselves immediately dismissed by the *New York Daily News* and the *New York Times*. In contrast, Ira Freeman, a *Times* reporter who rehashed his experience as one who joined the party through a union it dominated, then left that union when he found them inept as a bargaining agent, kept his job after coming clean to the panel. Over the next few months, Sourwine got more dossiers on journalists somehow connected with left-wing groups from FBI Assistant Director Louis Nichols. Eventually, SISS subpoenaed thirty-eight whom they deemed overly close to some on the left. The fact that twenty-five of those called worked for the *New York Times* led many to suspect Eastland of pursuing a vendetta against that paper, as it often took stands on racial questions at odds with his. But Sourwine was the driving force for the probe of the New York press, and he was often cued by J. Edgar Hoover, who feared Communists had become "more brazen" by 1955, the year Nikita Khrushchev completed his rise to the top slot in the Soviet hierarchy. *Times* executives took the probe seriously and encouraged all employees to come clean about any association they had with the Communist Party or any front. When SISS reconvened on January 4, 1956, witnesses used a variety of tactics in response to committee inquiries. Some asserted their Fifth Amendment rights. Others, like *Times* reporter Clayton Knowles and editor Benjamin Fine, chronicled their own involvements in the party and reluctantly gave SISS the names of a few cohorts. These witnesses Eastland saluted. Knowles, for example, regretted having to tell SISS in public what he had told staff privately, that he had joined the party in the midst of a long strike at the *Long Island Press*, where he worked nearly a generation earlier. "I made a bad mistake and rectified it as soon as I could," he said. It thus came easy for Eastland to echo liberal Thomas Hennings, who called Knowles "an exceedingly accurate, factual, able reporter." But Knowles, in his testimony, explained that in the 1930s he found the appeal of the Communist Party to young journalists like himself more rooted in the dynamics of struggles within his union than any external events, for he had seen no evidence of sabotage or intrigue by any left-wing group within the New York newspaper world.[7]

Witnesses called on the third day of hearings adopted different tacks. Three asserted their Fifth Amendment right against self-incrimination. Three more said that the free speech protections implicit in the First Amendment spared them from having to name others, a ploy that had not kept the Hollywood Ten out of jail in the late 1940s. Three other *Times* employees—music critic Robert Shelton and copy editors Alden Whitman and Seymour Peck—each acknowledged that he had been Communists for a time but all declined to answer further questions, invoking what they called their right of press protection not to have to answer any questions regarding their associations or their methods. While a poll by the then-liberal *New York Post* indicated editors and publishers nationwide split evenly on whether the probe threatened any liberties, the panel pushed to charge Shelton, Whitman, and Peck and three others who scoffed at the notion that SISS or any congressional panel could ask any journalist about their affiliations or opinions, past or present, with contempt of Congress. The full Senate approved the citations unanimously, and a grand jury returned indictments late in 1956. When Peck called for a jury trial, Eastland asked the Senate to allow him to testify. While Dennis Chavez of New Mexico objected, Peck's lawyers opted to bring Eastland to the stand. It was Eastland's position that SISS would never consider legislation that would infringe upon the freedom of the press. He and the staff initiated the probe after they were told that the Soviet Union might be trying to recruit reporters. No one in the employ of SISS, he added, had examined the content of any newspaper that members believed the Communists had infiltrated. Federal District Judge Luther Youngdahl wrestled with the question of whether the Constitution permitted any such inquiry into the practices of the press before ruling that there was ample precedent to rule for SISS. The jury, in contrast, deliberated for but half an hour before convicting Peck on five counts of contempt of Congress.[8]

To be sure, nothing could prompt Eastland into moving SISS into probing left-wing activity quicker than suggestions that Communists were trying, however ineptly, to establish beachheads in the Deep South. Over the winter of 1955–1956, SISS staffers unearthed information linking a number of New Orleans professionals to the Communist Party. Although most had left the party, few would testify about any past activities. Neither Eastland nor anyone connected with SISS disputed that anyone they called could invoke their Fifth Amendment rights. Yet many asserted that Eastland's query invaded their right to keep their associations and beliefs private. As with many hearings in the infancy of television, SISS sessions were marked by frequent outbursts by witnesses and counsel for both the panel and its witnesses. Eastland was content to direct witnesses to answer questions, allowing them to decline only if they asserted their right against self-incrimination. Most prominent was Herman Liveright, the program director of a New Orleans television station, who would not answer questions from the committee's staff, claiming that the inquiries improperly intruded into his personal beliefs. As no federal court had accepted that argument without a prior assertion of the right against self-incrimination, the committee readily pursued a contempt of Congress charge. Liveright, who once had worked for publishing firms and a New York television station, found himself without a job less than a day after he appeared before SISS.[9]

The real drama that punctuated this session came near the end. It had come to Eastland's attention that some of the attorneys for witnesses suspected of ties to the Communists had experienced discourtesies and even threats of violence, and he accorded the three lawyers present a chance to proclaim that they were loyal to America and merely representing clients. Liberal attorneys Ben Smith and Abraham Kleinfeldt took this opportunity. In contrast, Philip Wittenberg, Liveright's counsel, snapped that he did not have to make a statement because he was "not ashamed of anything" he had done. "You misunderstand," Eastland shot back. "I did not ask you to make a statement. I am merely granting you the opportunity, just to be fair." Here, Wittenberg lit into Eastland. "I don't have to make a statement . . . I am not a Communist and have never been and I have respect for the United States Supreme Court. You are the only one who preaches sedition," he added, shaking his fist. Whatever offense Wittenberg took to Eastland's segregationism, his reply bore no resemblance to any matter under discussion. "Put him out," Eastland ordered three deputy marshals, who then surpassed Wittenberg's excesses by grabbing

him and pushing him out of the hearing room. Wittenberg's friends took
to deriding the police as "hoodlums" and demanded that they "turn him
loose." In turn, Liveright saw his counsel being manhandled and ran to
pull the lawmen off his lawyer, but not before they inflicted a mild sprain
on Wittenberg's wrist and aggravated a previous shoulder injury. Seconds
after he untangled Wittenberg from the paws of the police, six deputies
grabbed Liveright and guided him into a nearby elevator to shield him
from a crowd urging that he be thrown down the shaft. The scene may
not have been the near "riot" the *Washington Post* described, but it deci-
mated the decorous image usually prescribed for congressional hearings.
A month later, the left-wing National Lawyers Guild urged the Senate to
discipline Eastland for ejecting Wittenberg from the hearing.[10]

Even more histrionics followed when Eastland resumed hearings on
April 12. The witness around whom the greatest controversy developed
was Hunter Pitts "Jack" O'Dell, an African-American veteran who, being
employed as a bus boy, hardly seemed a major source of information.
But when SISS process servers ventured to the cafeteria where O'Dell
worked, he fled out the back door. Police drove to his apartment, thinking
he might be there. When no one answered the door, investigators entered
his room and found a voluminous private library of the literature of Communists and their fronts. Also present were two Social Security cards
not in O'Dell's name and instructions to Communist organizers to join
groups where they might come into contact with workers, like churches,
the NAACP, PTAs, unions, and the Democratic Party. It begs credulity
from the standpoint of the twenty-first century to imagine that anyone
in the confines of New Orleans circa 1956 aligned with any party with
a revolutionary ideology might have made more than a little headway
outside the dockworkers' unions. But there was a very real fear among
Eastland and the considerably more ideological staff of SISS that a small
cell in the Big Easy might mushroom.[11]

Although Eastland and his counsels demonstrated that onetime Communists had worked their way onto the staffs of several papers and even
onto the staffs of some television stations, they had not proved that any
had managed to move the editorial stance of their papers in any direction, much less that of the heirs of Lenin. Many outside of SISS took to
questioning if congressional panels should be empowered to probe any

outside groups, especially the press. Some liberal journalists like *Arkansas Gazette* publisher Harry Ashmore went even further, declaring that the press had a duty to fight such investigations through its "pulpit."[12]

It was staff who embroiled the subcommittee in some truly embarrassing peccadillos. While running for the Senate in 1956, Jay Sourwine charged that Justice Department officials had evidence that New York Attorney General Jacob Javits was the "protégé" of some important Communists. His claim rested upon charges ex-Communist Bella V. Dodd gave to several groups suggesting that Javits in 1945 and 1946 had met with several Communists during his initial campaign for the House. The fact that Dodd told at least one rabbi that lifelong New Yorker Javits was a Communist she had brought from San Francisco to "bore from within" led Attorney General Herbert Brownell to denounce Sourwine's resuscitation of her charges as a "straight smear job." But Sourwine could not be deterred in his bid to sway some more conservative "yellow dog" Democrats in Nevada. After chiding Javits as an "anti-anti-Communist" candidate, he went on to declare that "the Republican Party under President Eisenhower had done more for the advancement of Communism than any other administration."[13]

Nearly a month before Sourwine aired Dodd's charges, Javits phoned Robert Morris to clear his name. Eastland at the time was on a fishing vacation that kept him engaged until Democrats convened in Chicago to renominate Adlai Stevenson to challenge Eisenhower. Only on September 5 could Javits answer the Dodd-Sourwine charges, first at an executive session at Eastland's home, then in a public hearing in the Senate caucus room. It was hardly Eastland's aim to alienate a man who soon might join him in the Senate, and he kept his own counsel in assessing if Dodd's claims had merit. He received wires from staunch anti-Communists who had served with Javits, including Walter Judd of Minnesota and James Richards of South Carolina, attesting to Javits' patriotism. The brunt of the questioning thus fell upon Morris, who had bought into each of Dodd's claims. To Morris' suggestion that he associated with Communist journalist Frederick Vanderbilt Field, Javits replied that he merely spoke with him on a San Francisco ferry and did not consider him a "traveling companion." Then, when Morris had Benjamin Mandel, himself an ex-Communist, mention Javits' connection with wealthy San Francisco

Communist Louise Bransten, Javits replied that he had been set up for an eminently forgettable date with Miss Bransten and met her years later by accident at a New York grocery. The friend who mismatched him with Bransten told Javits he thought he might have gone to a party at Bransten's home, but that was not Javits' memory. Morris then turned to Javits' acquaintance with Bella Dodd, whom he had met with in 1946, thinking he could learn from her experience with the New York Teachers' Union. Javits replied that he did not know that Dodd was a Communist. He added that he had not seen some newspaper clippings from 1945 labeling Dodd as a Communist, and that a *Life* magazine photograph Morris held up was published after he met Dodd. And when Morris declared that it had been testified that Javits had said that he could get the support of the left-wing American Labor Party if he desired, Javits said that that the party had backed a candidate in both 1946 and 1948 who had nearly defeated him. Eastland saw that some of the charges against Javits were overblown, and agreed to Javits' request that the panel publish some anti-Communist letters he had written in the record of the hearings. But while Morris' allies on the staff and William Jenner, his chief patron, spoke of "inconsistencies" in his testimony, the degree to which he was exculpated can be seen in his nomination by a 17–8 vote of the New York GOP State Executive Committee five days later.[14] This proved a lesson for SISS. They would investigate matters with ideological implications in the future, but would shun those like the Javits matter with partisan or intrapartisan implications.

One other incident initiated during a Morris instigated probe caused SISS considerable embarrassment. It occurred in the course of inquiries in March 1957 into why American diplomat John K. Emmerson, a onetime civilian advisor to General Douglas MacArthur, had recommended in the fall of 1944 that Japanese Communists be used to help restore order in Japan after the war. Robert Morris, who never got over blaming people other than the government of Jiang Jieshi for the fall of China, knew from past interviews that one foreign service officer had testified that Emmerson and Canadian diplomat E. Herbert Norman had been not only anxious to release two high-ranking Japanese Communists from jail but had chauffeured them around Tokyo. Emmerson replied that MacArthur had ordered the two discharged, and he denied that either had been accorded any special treatment. But, in a 1951 probe, SISS heard that Norman had belonged to a Communist study group at Columbia University, then joined the Canadian Communist Party, and lied to the FBI in 1942 when he said he was working for the Canadian government while trying to secure the possessions of one of the Communists. One finds instructive an account by SISS special counsel William Rusher, who with some cohorts saw some foreign service officers who had ties they did not approve in the Far East in the 1940s now stationed in the embassies of the Middle East. To them, it was more than coincidental when Canada sent Norman to Egypt as its ambassador and the United States named Emmerson deputy chief at its embassy in Beirut.[15] But such a circumstance reflects the hysteria of the age as well as anything in the inordinate concern about Emmerson's associations, forged in the matrix of World War II, or unproven suspicions of that time, a rekindling of which would be possible only through infrequent 350-mile trips or secure telephone calls.

What ended in tragedy started innocently on March 12, when Emmerson testified behind closed doors about his ties to Norman. Neither the questions nor the replies gave SISS any new evidence, albeit what members and staff knew about Norman had never been aired publicly. Two days later, SISS voted to release the transcript once it was cleared by the State Department. Officials at Foggy Bottom were amenable until Emmerson informed SISS that he would like to "amplify" on some testimony at a hearing on March 21. Before the panel could accommodate him, a copy of his first round of testimony reached the Associated Press. Members scrambled to prod the wire service to withdraw their account after the story had been out for twenty minutes, but to no avail. Even so, coverage was limited until Lester Pearson, Canada's foreign secretary and the Liberal Party's standard-bearer for prime minister, declared that the testimony about his friend Norman repeated slanders that his government had previously discounted, even if much of SISS' evidence had come from the Royal Canadian Mounted Police. Still, Emmerson appeared for a second executive session on March 21 and painted a more favorable picture of his and Norman's activities. Acting Secretary of State Christian Herter asked SISS to suppress the record to placate Canada. This, members said, would not be fair to Emmerson or Norman, and they voted to publish the complete record. Here spelled trouble for Norman, a man under considerable stress. Fearing that he would have to testify in both America and Canada about matters that he had expounded upon lengthily in private, Norman suspected that he might be forced to expose questionable deeds by dozens of officials in both countries. By April 4, the one way he saw to avoid what he saw in his exhausted state as an act of dishonor was to leap from the roof of a nine-story building in Cairo.[16]

Initial sorrow quickly transformed into widespread anger at SISS, both in Canada and in the United States. After the *Toronto Globe and Mail* attributed Norman's death to the persistence of "liars and calumniators," University of Toronto students burned Eastland, Morris, and Joseph McCarthy in effigy. In a sermon at New York's Episcopal Cathedral, James Pike blamed Norman's passing on "assassination by insinuation." A few Senate liberals were nearly as fearful that the tragedy might imperil U.S.-Canadian relations, and they prevailed upon Majority Leader Lyndon Johnson to rein in Eastland and SISS. Johnson called Eastland into his office and demanded to know what had prompted the release of the report. While he had suspended the probe, Eastland assured his leader that he would investigate. He went to Frank Barber, a young clerk from Mississippi, and asked him what he knew. Barber replied that Morris had told him to hand-deliver the report to the Associated Press. When Morris denied giving the order, Barber told Eastland that Morris had told a "goddamn lie," but offered to resign. That would not be necessary, Eastland replied. He believed Barber and learned that he could rely upon him for sound judgment. In contrast, he retained Morris to placate William Jenner, but his faith in him dissipated. When Richard Neuberger posed the question a week later in a colloquy, Eastland gave a long dispassionate account of his panel's proceedings where he blamed neither Morris nor Barber. When one cuts through the pompous moralism so prevalent throughout the 1950s, it can be seen that little that unraveled about Ambassador Norman proved untrue.[17] But it is every bit as legitimate to ask why SISS or any other panel devoted so much time to probing what foreign nationals were doing fifteen years before.

Like many anti-Communists, Eastland discounted any suggestion that the Communist threat was any less menacing after Stalin's death. He felt certain that Nikita Khrushchev, the new roly-poly Soviet strongman, would be as repressive and expansionistic as Stalin had been. Particularly after the Soviets brutally quashed a rebellion in Hungary in the fall of 1956, he eagerly aired testimony from defectors from their Eastern Europe satellites. Not placated by the thousands of departures from the Communist camp by European leftists who were horrified by the violent Soviet crackdown, Eastland saw a "vicious revolutionary core" east of the Elbe. He was even less ready to embrace detente with the Peoples' Republic of China, whose Communist leaders, a SISS report charged, had executed 15 million people since taking over and placed millions more in slave labor camps.[18] For these reasons, he slammed as "astonishing" and "ominous" Vice President Richard Nixon's proposal to repeal the Connally Amendment, which limited the World Court's jurisdiction within the United States to matters not covered by the Constitution. Surrendering sovereignty to the World Court, he said, might empower judges from the Communist world to use that tribunal as "forums for Communist propaganda."[19]

In truth, there was no maneuver that Eastland believed that the Soviets would not employ. His position rested upon his digesting of hundreds of FBI and staff reports as well as his memories of Soviet postwar maneuvers. It also reflected a bit of a fear that the American people might be susceptible to a doctrine that preached, while hardly practicing, universal equality. SISS reports warned that the Russian majority had used "genocide, massive discrimination, and abuse of power" against other nationalities. They indicated that many Orthodox churchmen doubled as spies for the KGB, and that Soviet government employees often accompanied cultural and athletic delegations on trips abroad. Other SISS reports noted that Soviet Communists had made the Communist Party of the United States a virtual subsidiary. Eastland feared that U.S. audiences might be unable to dispel subliminal messages Soviets and their satellite states might insert into propaganda they snuck into films they exported. He thus called for "more effective safeguards" upon which films were shown in the United States. But what truly annoyed him were any suggestions that Communists might be behind a move to push blacks to demand the integration of their homeland. Staff like Ben Mandel played upon this fear by letting him know the *Daily Worker* and other Communist organs were prescribing stronger enforcement of existing laws. Eastland, in turn, took to warning opponents of civil rights that the Soviet Union was against them, too. "Moscow," he told the States' Rights Council of Georgia in 1961, "presses a button and sets race against race and the working man against his employer."[20]

By 1956, Eastland was also exploring if SISS should probe where else the Soviets were trying to extend their tentacles. His first concerns about the Middle East, ironically, were more parochial than geopolitical. Like most Southerners, he opposed the Eisenhower plan to build a dam on the Nile at Aswan, as the improved irrigation would allow Egypt to increase by 100,000 acres the land it could use to produce the thicker variety of cotton grown there. He asked if one colleague knew that the Egyptians subsidized their cotton exports. To constituents, he asked why America developed waterways like the Nile, but not those at home like the Tombigbee. One saw no remorse from him when an effective cotton state veto led Egyptian President Gamel Abdel Nasser to nationalize the Suez Canal. The United States, he declared in May 1957, would have no problems in the Middle East had President Eisenhower let France, Britain, and Israel retake the canal in October 1956. From the prism of the bilateral view common during the Cold War, Eastland's view that Nasser was a "stooge of the Kremlin" appealed to many. But it is now clear that Nasser was a nationalist with aspirations to grandeur who would have given preferential treatment to whatever nation paid for the dam, the prime symbol of his dreams. That power was the Soviet Union, the source of much mischief Eastland observed and some he imagined. It thus is hardly surprising that Eastland backed Eisenhower's July 1958 landing of troops on Lebanese beaches, a move he believed bolstered that government in the wake of the assassination of the king of Iraq, an American ally, at a time when some Muslims were attempting to guide it into the United Arab Republic, the recent and temporary union of Egypt and Syria. Just as important to him was that Eisenhower's move blocked the Soviets from trying to cut off the supply of oil to Western Europe.[21]

Perhaps because of Latin America's proximity to Mississippi's Gulf Coast, Eastland and SISS were far more attuned to the chicanery of Communists in the southern hemisphere. Even before SISS was created, Pat McCarran and he warned that Cuba was a focal point for Communist operations in the west. Neither they nor any other member of Congress devoted much time to examining the systemic weaknesses of the corrupt, repressive Batista regime that rendered that island susceptible to a revolution by insurgents. When a left-wing oligarchy headed by Fidel Castro deposed Batista, Eastland and Thomas Dodd, to whom he had delegated much of his authority, began inquiring as to how a group replete with a number of open Communists could come to power. While it was not clear in early 1959 that Castro followed Marx, onetime ambassador to Cuba Spruille Braden, had told SISS that two of his top lieutenants, brother Raul Castro and Ernesto "Che" Guevara, indisputably were under Communist discipline. Richard Nixon, the highest-ranking American to meet with Castro in 1959, also concluded after spending two hours with the new Cuban *jefe* that he was either "naive" or taking his lead from Khrushchev. Clarence Pierce, an Eastland aide on the payroll of SISS, notes that members and staff can be credited for being among the first to recognize that Castro and his associates were hardly Cuban Robin Hoods. Only later that year was it clear that Castro was indeed a Communist and that Cuba had become, as Eastland put it, "Khrushchev's leading outpost in the western hemisphere." In July 1959, SISS heard from Major Pedro Luis Diaz Lanz, Castro's initial head of the Cuban Air Force, that Communists had infiltrated the Cuban armed services and that he felt certain that Castro was determined to impose Communist rule upon Cuba. Even before, U.S. officials had noticed that Raul Castro had rejected demands that citizens be compensated for the hundreds of millions of dollars of property his brother's regime had expropriated.[22]

It would be another year before Eastland and Dodd held hearings aimed at assessing which Americans were responsible for the fall of Cuba. The method they employed was similar to that the China lobby used a few years earlier, assuming that only U.S. complicity could explain the demise of a corrupt and repressive pro-American government. Their two star witnesses were the two U.S. ambassadors to Cuba who had served over the six years prior to Batista's demise. On August 27, 1960, Dodd and the staff of SISS took testimony at the home of the ailing Arthur Gardner, the principal U.S. emissary between 1953 and 1957 who had been close to Batista. Gardner deemed those to blame as a few of his superiors at the State Department and Herbert Matthews of the *New York Times*, who had romanticized Castro's plight in a memorable piece of 1957 and minimized the role of the Communists. Three days later, they returned to Washington to join Eastland in hearing Earl T. Smith, Gardner's successor, add to the picture of Castro's duplicity and even more on how Matthews influenced the American public to prefer any alternative to Batista. It mattered little to Eastland and Dodd that William Wieland, the lead officer at the State Department's Caribbean desk, told SISS that he and his colleagues often disagreed with Matthews the few times they met. Their final report lambasted low-level officials at the State Department for a fall of Castro they likened to the surrender of China. They were not unanimous. Kenneth Keating, a New York Republican often allied with them on ways of confronting Communism, denounced the report as injurious to the cause of peace in the region. Secretary of State Christian Herter went even further in terming the charges "shocking and unfounded." While a Latin American diplomat who would not identify himself termed the report an example of "McCarthyism," SISS's report is better understood as one more partisan than ideological. Indeed, Jim Eastland was using its findings less than a month before that year's hotly contested presidential election to disparage Richard Nixon's conservative bona fides.[23]

SISS continued to monitor several left-wing groups with an interest in the Caribbean. Eastland knew enough about a pro-Castro group called Fair Play for Cuba to characterize it as "substantially Communist-financed and . . . dominated." Were it up to him, he would embargo trade with Cuba, with, not coincidentally, the one exception being on tobacco, as he thought that such sanctions would endanger the jobs of 600 cigar workers in Tampa.[24] But what once was known as the Pearl of the Antilles would be the site of the most obvious setback of the next president of Eastland's party at its Bay of Pigs, as well as that of his greatest triumph.

CHAPTER 11

Massive Resistance, Bourbon Style

MERELY A WEEK AFTER THE DEATH OF SENATOR HARLEY KILGORE OF West Virginia, who had been chairman of the Senate Judiciary Committee, second in line Jim Eastland met with an all black delegation from Mississippi at a National Assembly on Civil Rights. Among those present at this gathering of March 6, 1956, was C. R. Darden of Meridian, who told Eastland that he believed both parties should stop "kicking civil rights around" and take positive action to improve the lot of the African-American minority. Much more conspicuous was Gus Courts, who five months before had been shot after refusing to remove his name from the voter registration rolls and provide a list of local NAACP members to the local Citizens Council. Courts found Eastland more sympathetic than most southern members of Congress his group had tried to visit. Right after the visit, he told reporters that Eastland "seemed very interested in me" and "very sorry that what happened did happen in Belzoni." Curiously enough, perhaps with partisan considerations of 1956 in mind, Eastland advised the group that the president was the one official with the authority to act on such matters. "What you should do in the future," he continued, "is elect a President who will act."[1]

What transpired illustrates Eastland's paternalistic view of black Americans. Outside of the public view, Eastland extended many private kindnesses to blacks who respected his authority as a senator and a white man, whether in Washington or on his plantation. He would never acknowledge those gestures publicly. Like most in Congress, he saw his first responsibility as representing the wishes of those who put him in office, and in the 1950s that electorate was nearly all white. Eastland realized that change was in the works, but deemed it his duty to do all he could to prevent any excesses of the Second Reconstruction from being as destructive as he imagined those of the first had been. His comments to Courts reflected the completeness of his commitment to his party. When but eighteen months later, a Republican used the power Eastland told Courts only the president could exert, Eastland excoriated that chief executive for what he termed an abuse of power. In time, when presidents of his party faced similar challenges, Eastland publicly was as critical as he was of Eisenhower, but he worked with officials of those administrations privately to ensure that whatever change came was peaceful. And, to a larger degree than most recognized, Eastland understood that southern society was in a state of transition. "You know good and well I got to get and win the votes of these rednecks," he told Percy Greene, the relatively conservative black editor of the *Jackson Advocate* who had been his friend since the two had taken the bar exam in the same room. "Y'all ain't got no money and you ain't got no votes, but there ain't no way for me to help you, no kind of damn way if I don't get elected."[2]

In the fall of 1955, however, Eastland and others among the nonviolent foes of integration fumbled for a strategy to fight integration until he and Harry F. Byrd opted to revive the time-worn doctrine of interposition. Here was a ploy that some allies like former Georgia Governor Herman Talmadge thought the Civil War had resolved. But interposition found considerable support. In the first days of 1956, Virginians approved a referendum creating a constitutional convention to consider allowing their counties and cities to fund segregated private schools within their boundaries. Later that year, their legislature voted to cut off support to any public school system that moved to integrate. Even if Justice Department lawyers had not begun to target Mississippi schools, interposition found enough support in Mississippi for Courtney Pace to tell a reporter a generation later that it served primarily to buy time for the South to accept the changes their leaders knew would ensue. But Virginians would take the lead, for they, unlike those from the Deep South, had never borne the stigma of being the extremists who had cast the first votes to secede. The man who initiated the juxtaposition of this doctrine from its eighteenth-century origins to the politics of the 1950s was James J. Kilpatrick, the editor of the *Richmond News Leader*. Not only did he commence peppering his readers in December 1955 with editorials reminding them of that long moribund practice, but he also sent reading lists to Eastland and others so they might sharpen their own arguments. There was one reaction Eastland would not follow. "We have to be practical," State Senator W. B. Alexander wrote Eastland, "and know that Mississippi cannot secede from the union of the states."[3]

Inside the Senate, the initial vehicle Southerners used to promote their new dogma was an infamous document they called their "Statement of Constitutional Principles." This missive, known as the "Southern Manifesto," pledged signers to "use all lawful means" to overturn the *Brown v. Board of Education* decision and preserve the traditional rights of states to run their own affairs. While the document was the brainchild of Strom Thurmond, it was drafted by Sam Ervin, Richard Russell, and John Stennis, and introduced by Walter George, the dean of southern senators. Eastland proudly affixed his name, as did all members from the states that once constituted the Confederacy other than Majority Leader Lyndon Johnson and moderate-to-liberal Tennesseans Albert Gore and Estes Kefauver. Outside the upper chamber, Eastland, more than any other southern senator, spent time rallying the forces who aimed to preserve their segregated society.[4]

It was Eastland's belief that white Southerners who wanted to preserve their way of life needed to "move from a defensive position to one of offense." He and other onetime Dixiecrats began exploring the feasibility of creating an organization to coordinate the efforts of states' rights groups as early as January 1955, when a group met that came to be known as the Federation for Constitutional Government (FCG). While organizers aimed to win some backing nationally, their choice of John U. Barr, who had laid much of the groundwork for both the draft-Byrd campaign of 1944 and the 1948 Dixiecrat effort, effectively limited its appeal to the regional level. The first formal FCG gathering came late in December 1955, when thirty-five prominent segregationists, most from Alabama or Mississippi, met at Memphis' renowned Peabody Hotel. Strom Thurmond was the only senator other than Eastland present, but Governor Marvin Griffin of Georgia attended, as did four former governors and six members of the House of Representatives. Eastland told attendees that they were about to "embark upon a great crusade to restore Americanism and return the control of our government to our people." He added that the FCG would serve as a "peoples' organization to fight the Supreme Court, ... the NAACP, and . . . all conscienceless pressure groups who are attempting our destruction."[5] It, too, would take on those who might try to socialize industry or medicine and do all it could to preserve the "untainted racial heritage, . . . culture, and . . . institutions of the Anglo-Saxon race." While such language was strident enough to prompt the New York NAACP to demand that Attorney General Brownell put the FCG on his list of "subversive" organizations, the limited funding it received guaranteed that it would never much affect policy. Headquartered in New Orleans and identified as an organization of elites, the FCG had little appeal to common people of the towns and hamlets of the Deep South and even less to those in the border South.[6]

Eastland, for his part, found himself traversing the South far more than he had expected to wage his campaign to allow the states to nullify unpopular federal statutes and court rulings within their boundaries. His first stop was in Jackson on December 1, 1955. Outgoing Governor Hugh White and Governor-elect James P. Coleman also appeared, but it was Eastland who keynoted this gathering of their state's Citizens Councils. In a speech entitled "We've Reached the Age of Judicial Tyranny," he pronounced that there was nothing in the Constitution allowing the Congress, the president, or the Supreme Court the "right or power to declare that white and colored children must attend the same school." He went on to warn an audience of several thousand of a campaign in which children were indoctrinated and college students "brainwashed" by liberal pressure groups, foundations, and churches. There could be no compromise. Those present needed to fight "not only to maintain and perpetuate the law, customs, tradition and the culture of our way of life, but to restore and revitalize the republic." But, as he would in every address he gave counseling interposition over the next two years, Eastland warned against "violence and lawlessness," as any instances of either would harm "the cause of the South."[7]

Eastland followed his home state debut by touring the "Jim Crow circuit." He ventured into the Carolinas two months later and found his most ardent supporters at a Citizens Council rally in Columbia, the capital of the first state to secede in 1861. Flanked by Olin Johnston and Strom Thurmond, he was interrupted by applause some twenty-nine times. As always, he berated the influence of those he called "pressure groups." He was hardest on the NAACP, which he said was backed by "organizations of all shades of red, . . . from the blood red of the Communist Party to the almost equal red of the National Council of Churches." It was imperative, he told those present, for the South to counter the images those groups were painting by creating a more positive portrait of Dixie.[8]

An even larger crowd appeared at the State Coliseum in Montgomery, Alabama, in early February. There, 10,000 to 15,000 people flocked to hear him rail against integration. Eastland arrived in a police cruiser. In comparison with local police commissioner Clyde Sellers, who declared that their battle cry should be "states' rights and white supremacy," and Georgia Attorney General Eugene Cook, who termed the *Brown v. Board of Education* ruling a "mulatto decision," Eastland was fairly restrained in his appeal for a "united Southern front." The group Eastland demonized most was the NAACP, who he asserted was trying to "take over your schools." But as always, Eastland reiterated his exhortations to attendees to shun physical force, an admonition some listeners did not heed. Later in the year, State Senator Sam Engelhardt, the Alabama executive secretary of the councils, wrote Eastland that members of a rogue faction in his state were using vulgar anti-Semitic rhetoric and recruiting like-minded souls from the Ku Klux Klan and other groups with a penchant for violence. At the event itself, some of their followers, almost certainly without the knowledge of its organizers, were handing out uncommonly inflammatory pamphlets that explicitly condoned racial violence.[9]

Two months later, Eastland declared in Forest, the town where he grew to manhood, that the South could not hold against the onslaught of the forces of integration if states were "picked off one by one under the deplorable doctrine of gradualism." He counseled those from the American Legion and the Citizens Councils that there was no imminent danger that any state among the Dixiecrat bloc would yield. Even so, he expressed regret that President Eisenhower had used his power to desegregate the schools of the District of Columbia, where he said the educational standards of the public schools "had to be lowered to meet the average intelligence of the Negro school children." He rued the fact that black and white kids had begun to attend the same schools in sixty communities in Texas, and lamented it just as loudly that there were some dents in the armor of Arkansas and Tennessee. The South needed a commission, he said, to defend itself from a "rising crescendo of vicious propaganda inspired and financed by Communist front and race-minded groups." He particularly wanted that body to have a speakers' bureau that could send representatives all over the nation to explain the southern way of life to those in other regions or, at least, to "get off Mississippi's back."[10]

In May 1956, Mississippi acted on Eastland's suggestion and created a Mississippi State Sovereignty Commission (MSSC) charged with protecting the Magnolia State and its agencies from federal encroachment. In the administration of J. P. Coleman (1956–1960), who thought interposition "legal poppycock" and signed the bill creating it reluctantly, the MSSC was funded scantily and caused few problems. Coleman even vetoed a bill granting MSSC funds to the Citizens Councils. But his successor, bitter-end segregationist Ross Barnett (1960–1964), expanded the power and the resources of the MSSC in such a way that reminded some of the 1956 warning of State Representative Philip Bryant of Oxford that the body had the potential to become a "private Gestapo" to conduct "character assassinations." During those years, the MSSC funneled $200,000 to the Citizens Councils. That money it used to send speakers north to trumpet the virtues they saw in segregation or produce and air the Citizens Council Forum, a regularly scheduled fifteen-minute television show distributed to stations across Dixie. They also gave tens of thousands of dollars to a group created to oppose civil rights legislation. MSSC agents combed the parking lots of NAACP meeting sites so they might record the license tag numbers of those present, then forwarded the names of some to Eastland and other Mississippi legislators. They planted stories and killed others in both Jackson dailies and the *Jackson Advocate*, the largest black owned and operated paper in Mississippi. They created a Mississippi Negro Citizenship Association where more conservative blacks could congregate. MSSC agents also helped defense lawyers scrutinize prospective jurors prior to the second trial of Byron De La Beckwith, the man convicted nearly three decades later of the murder of Medgar Evers. Altogether, the MSSC kept files on some 250 groups and 87,000 people. But not all of the work was of high quality. In 1962, the MSSC paid for more than a million postcards it gave to friends to send to President Kennedy to protest James Meredith's admission to Ole Miss. Journalist Curtis Wilkie, a native

Mississippian, later opined that some of the Sovereignty Commission agents "were about as useful to the forces of segregation as the German guards on *Hogan's Heroes* would have been to the Third Reich."[11]

By late winter of 1956, Eastland had the perch that served as his foundation of authority for the rest of his career. His elevation to the chairmanship of the Senate Judiciary Committee was to most Democrats a formality. Dennis Chavez, the first Hispanic ever to serve in the upper chamber, happily placed his name in nomination. But Eastland's rise scared many in left-of-center groups like the New York Liberal Party, the Americans for Democratic Action, and the NAACP, which called him "an accessory to murder and treason." Still, only Paul Douglas, Herbert Lehman, and Wayne Morse, three very liberal Democrats, dissented when the matter came to a vote. America would not survive, said Morse, if the Senate beat a "retreat to the doctrine of nullification." Lehman declared that Eastland had acted in ways that were "un-American and dangerous to American democracy." While John Stennis lambasted him and other critics for ignoring Eastland's qualifications, far more in sync with the caucus was former Vice President Alben Barkley, who had been elected to a final stint in the Senate less than two years earlier. The ever-eloquent Kentuckian found fault with Eastland's suggestion that the South ignore the *Brown v. Board of Education* decision, but told colleagues that tinkering with the system in place would do even more harm. The electioneering that would result from choosing chairs by means other than seniority would bring even more "jealousies, ambitions" and other "frailties of human nature" into the legislative process. Republicans reveled in the Democratic split. California moderate Thomas Kuchel blasted Morse for his party switch of 1953, which gave Democrats the one-vote majority that allowed them to elect Eastland and all Democrats as chairmen. A few days later, GOP National Chairman Hugh D. Scott Jr. chided counterpart Paul D. Butler as to what Democrats planned to do about Eastland. Eastland took the debate in somewhat amusedly. Once the voice vote was cast in his favor, he walked over to Paul Douglas and thanked him for the "no" vote he mouthed, as an objection from a principled liberal such as him might add to Eastland's clout with the still virtually all-white Mississippi electorate.[12]

Rather quickly, Eastland became a target for both liberal Democrats and northern Republicans. Clarence Mitchell, the chief lobbyist for the

NAACP, described him as a "stinking albatross around the neck of the Democratic Party." Adam Clayton Powell, Harlem's flamboyant congressman, called upon blacks to repudiate "Eastlandism" and cast their ballots for Eisenhower. Labor leaders like United Auto Workers head Walter Reuther declared the issue of raising Eastland to the helm of the Judiciary Committee a "basic moral question" and declared that his party could not "have Mr. Eastland and us at the same time." GOP leaders, in turn, advised Eisenhower surrogates and their Senate candidates to woo African-American and liberal voters by arguing that a vote for any Democrat was a vote to keep Eastland at the helm of the Judiciary Committee. Liberal Republican Jacob Javits was as quick to blast opponent Robert Wagner, the mayor of New York City, for his ties to Eastland as he was to hail Eisenhower, his ticket's standard-bearer, for ending segregation in the nation's capital. Just as adamant was Connecticut Republican Prescott Bush. "Adlai and the Democrats in the North," he declared, "know . . . that their promises are hollow and deceptive so long as the senior senator from Mississippi must be their party's choice as chairman."[13]

The most controversial and pressing bit of committee business at the time of Eastland's ascension lay in acting upon Eisenhower's nomination of Solicitor General Simon Sobeloff to be chief judge of the Fourth Circuit Court of Appeals. Southerners for months had blocked a hearing upon Sobeloff, a moderate-to-liberal Marylander who had prepared the administration's briefs in *Brown II*. Eastland publicly characterized Sobeloff as "frank" and "open," but said that he feared that he might "carry on the erosion of our Constitution," rhetoric designed for consumption in Mississippi. The real source of the holdup was Olin Johnston, who had wanted the post to go to a fellow South Carolinian and feared a challenge in the Democratic primary if he appeared mild in opposing a Baltimorean. The identity of the culprit mattered little to Lyndon Johnson, who, fearing that rejecting an able attorney like Sobeloff would expose all Democrats, implored Eastland to press Johnston to allow a vote. Such a task proved easy once Johnston's one primary challenger withdrew from the race. In the end, Eastland and Johnston cast their ballots against Sobeloff in committee and on the floor and preserved their credibility with the segregationist majorities of their party in their home states. But just seventeen senators joined them, all but four of them southern Democrats.[14]

In truth, it was Johnson's aim as majority leader to foster unity within his caucus, particularly in an election year, an image that would not be served if he allowed bills to be considered just so "Jim Eastland and Herbert Lehman can insult each other, or . . . Paul Douglas and Albert Gore can exercise their lungs." An internecine congressional bloodbath, he sensed, was just a GOP strategist's dream. While contemplating the idea of Spessard Holland of Florida to have the majority of his party forward a constitutional amendment banning a poll tax, Johnson feared that even this tack might hamper his party's cohesion. He, too, maneuvered to keep a House-passed civil rights bill off the floor prior to the election, telling Senate GOP Leader William Knowland that he would allow debate on that measure only if he put off action on Eisenhower's foreign aid package and a bill granting executive department officials a pay raise. While Johnson calculated that Knowland might deem it necessary to delay action for a year, he aimed to send the bill to the Judiciary Committee for Eastland to bury. Douglas sensed that their leader might take this course and walked to the House of Representatives to meet the messenger carrying the bill. But Johnson sabotaged this ploy by having allies sneak the bill in through a side door of the House. When the bill did reach the floor ahead of schedule—and without Douglas—Johnson was waiting. With a few more sleights of Johnson's legislative hand, the bill was sent to Eastland to keep it dormant for the rest of the year.[15]

Eastland was much more loyal to his party then most believed. While he could not support the bid for president of New York Governor Averill Harriman, whom he found too liberal, he, like John Stennis and Governor Coleman, let it be known that he could accept likely nominee Adlai Stevenson, whom he deemed a "man of moderation." With Mississippi Democratic leaders making it clear that they would be loyal, national party leaders saw fit to roundly defeat moves at the convention to require their delegates and South Carolina's to pledge their loyalty. When he cast his ballot, Eastland opted for Lyndon Johnson, whom he hailed as the best Senate majority leader ever. When Stevenson opened the choice of his running mate to the convention, Mississippi delegates aligned behind Albert Gore, whom they deemed closer to their outlooks than fellow Tennessean Estes Kefauver. With Gore's support restricted to Tennessee and the Deep South, however, they joined a switch to John F. Kennedy, the thirty-nine-year-old senator from Massachusetts. But Kennedy's initial bid for national office fell just short, and Eastland joined John Stennis and Governor J. P. Coleman in promising to do everything in their power to help their ticket win once the convention settled upon Stevenson and Kefauver.[16]

Eastland knew by 1957 that he could no longer block civil rights legislation. He could count on but four of fifteen votes from the Judiciary Committee. It was not lost on Democrats, particularly those eying the 1960 presidential nomination, that Eisenhower had increased his share of the black vote in 1956 to 39 percent and performed even better in the South. He had won clear majorities among blacks in Jackson and Memphis. He carried the all-black Delta town of Mound Bayou by a margin of 118 to 38. Here was a factor Lieutenant George W. Lee, the very eloquent black GOP leader of Memphis, credited to concerns that "Eastland, [Georgia Governor Herman] Talmadge, and the White Citizens Council" dominated southern Democratic parties. Majority Leader Johnson was particularly emphatic that the state of affairs would have to change if Democrats were to succeed nationally in future elections. "Listen," he told Eastland, "we might as well face it. We're not gonna be able to get out of here until we've got some kind of nigger bill."[17]

Eastland hardly acquiesced. "Let me be frank," he told Paul Douglas, who backed the strong bill the Eisenhower administration was pushing. "I am opposed to the bill." "I gathered as much," Douglas replied with a grin. Early in the new Congress, Eastland used his power to expand the Civil Rights Subcommittee he had once chaired from three members to seven. He gave the newly created seats to Southerners Olin Johnston and Sam Ervin and GOP conservatives Arthur Watkins of Utah and Roman Hruska of Nebraska. When the administration's bill arrived, Subcommittee Chairman Thomas Hennings tried to expedite consideration, but could not get a majority to vote a report to the full panel for two months. Once Hruska and Watkins budged, Eastland took control of the measure and began a unique brand of obstruction. Each Monday morning at 10:30, he would open the scheduled meeting by calling on a fellow Southerner, usually Sam Ervin. Just as regularly, he ignored Hennings' pleas to open discussion on Eisenhower's bill his body had approved. Eastland ran the meetings until noon, when Senate rules required all committee business to cease. He allowed a vote on Ervin's proposal to dilute the bill by eliminating the provisions creating a Civil Rights Division of the Justice Department and a Civil Rights Commission. And, he and others from Dixie tried to amend the bill with sections guaranteeing jury trials to those charged with denying the right to vote. As expected, the only senators to back either amendment were the four from the Deep South. So while the addenda were defeated, there was no committee action on the subcommittee bill, and a civil rights measure could not be placed on the calendar until the House passed its version on June 18, 1957. A united southern front and a few Republicans aligned behind a move of Richard Russell to assign the bill to the Judiciary Committee, where Eastland could bury it just as he had all others. But their votes were not enough, as the full Senate voted down Russell's maneuver by a vote of 45–39.[18]

Eastland's course thereafter rested as much upon partisan considerations as it did racial ones. While State House Speaker Sillers pressed him to filibuster the "outrageous Communist inspired" measure, Eastland joined Richard Russell and other Southerners in impressing upon Johnson that they would not filibuster a bill to protect the right to vote if it allowed a trial by jury to those charged of denying the franchise. Johnson soon pressed Democrats to show good will toward colleagues from other parts of America. After Robert G. "Bobby" Baker, the powerful secretary of the Senate, convinced Speaker Sam Rayburn that a southern filibuster would kill any civil rights bill if it did not include a jury trial provision, Adam Clayton Powell, the chairman of the House Education and Labor Committee, used a sermon in his Harlem Abyssinian Baptist Church to signal John F. Kennedy and other Northerners that the inclusion of any amendment was less important than passing the first civil rights bill since 1875.

Johnson knew that several western Democrats aimed to build a dam in Idaho's Hells Canyon. He had elderly Montanan James Murray approach Eastland, who in 1956 had opposed authorizing construction. "I need help on civil rights," Eastland replied, before telling Murray to see Richard Russell. When he met Russell and Johnson, Murray learned that he might get some southern votes if westerners used restraint debating civil rights. Even as five westerners voted not to place the House measure on the calendar, recruiting Southerners was difficult, as many did not relish using tax revenues for a public power system. Surprising many, Eastland listened in part because of the benefits the TVA had conferred upon northern Mississippi. But his pragmatic streak let him understand implicitly that voting for the dam did not mean that it would pass, for both President Eisenhower and the House of Representatives could still kill the project. Still, if switching course to cast his lot with such a bill would heighten the probability that a civil rights measure might be watered down or even defeated, he would do so. In the end, the Senate approved the dam, with the votes of Southerners Eastland, Russell, Sam Ervin, Russell Long, and George Smathers, all of whom had opposed the measure in 1956, being determinative.[19]

As Senate debate opened on the House-passed civil rights bill, Eastland took the floor to attack the measure in a fifty-page speech as a "sly, scheming attempt to circumvent our Constitution." He told colleagues that he remained convinced that only a small portion of the black community wanted such legislation, which he said violated the Tenth Amendment by letting the attorney general nullify state laws. Privately, he was considerably less fearful that the bill might alter the social structure of the South than he let on in public, even if he knew that the Senate would take the rare step of voting to bypass his Judiciary Committee. He wrote Walter Sillers, an even firmer states righter than Eastland, that he knew that those who backed civil rights would "whip us," even while the Senate was likely to soften the portions of the House-passed bill that threatened to accelerate the transformation of the southern way of life most completely.[20]

The issue on which Eastland and Richard Russell chose to wage their fight was the question of letting Southerners accused of violating the voting rights of blacks have a jury trial. Northerners in both parties insisted that the bill keep this portion, for they knew that all-white southern juries were unlikely to convict those who discriminated. To Eastland and Russell, the right of jury trial was paramount. In a speech of thirty typed pages, Eastland argued that the privilege of a trial by one's peers had been central to all constitutional systems for two centuries. But it was not a Southerner whose name was attached to the amendment preserving that "right." Lyndon Johnson recruited Clinton Anderson of New Mexico to introduce that addendum and GOP moderate George Aiken of Vermont to be his cosponsor. Thus presented, preserving a jury trial attracted all but thirteen Democratic liberals and split the Republicans, with eighteen backing the measure and twenty-five joining the administration against it. To Paul Douglas, the victory was a personal one for Eastland and Russell. Eastland was less certain. The bill had been improved more than he had hoped, he wrote, but still was "stronger than is being indicated in the press." Still, he did not join Strom Thurmond's day-long filibuster. Even if many constituents echoed a writer who declared Thurmond "ten miles tall" while "all others ought to be in hell," Eastland and others knew that they could get no more than eighteen of the thirty-two votes needed to keep debate going and that any ill-timed move might prompt northern solons to apply stronger remedies. He could paint the measure as a GOP bill and, even as amended, as "part of an attack . . . against the people of the South." Still, he was one of but fifteen senators, all Southerners, to vote no, and he knew all too well that this was only the beginning. In a metaphor that many copied, civil rights lawyer Joseph L. Rauh likened what had happened to the Senate "losing its virginity" on civil rights issues. As any Southerner recognized, further temptations would be even harder to resist.[21]

Even in these years, Eastland seldom spent much time cultivating any media outside of Mississippi, Memphis, or New Orleans. Rare exceptions came in the summer of 1957, when he submitted to the interrogatories of Dave Garroway of NBC and Mike Wallace, then of ABC. The Wallace interview almost did not occur, as Eastland, after he agreed to do the show, took issue with a teaser a week before the program saying that Wallace would try to find out from him if "the Negro is an inferior race." This line Eastland had ceased using, and he called Wallace to object.[22] But on July 28, Eastland went on as scheduled after Wallace introduced him as the "voice of the white South." This was a misnomer. Eastland was hardly the voice of liberal whites; he was often their target. He was also not the voice of the small but growing southern white GOP population centered in the region's cities and suburbs; he thought they threatened the region's political and racial harmony. Nor did he speak for John Kasper's Seaboard Citizens Council or the Ku Klux Klan, which he said promoted "racial and religious prejudice, hatred and bigotry." He was the most visible voice of the Bourbon South, a sizable part of Dixie's body politic as resistant to change in the way the races related as any other. As usual, he took the occasion to blast Northerners for their hypocrisy in not ending de facto segregation in reputedly liberal areas like New York City. He noted that his state's black middle class had grown a bit and added, accurately, that racial strife plagued Communist countries. He was on less solid ground in blaming Radical Republicans, whose regime he said, inaccurately, had been controlled by "members of the Nigra race," for the laws establishing segregation. But he was truly mistaken when he denied that voting discrimination existed in the Magnolia State. While insisting that "everyone who is qualified to vote should vote," he declared that a tale that a registrar had asked a black voter how many bubbles were in a bar of soap was a fable concocted by *Nation* magazine in the 1920s. What he may not have known was that some blacks had sent affidavits to Attorney General Brownell charging Forrest County registrar Luther Cox with pelting aspiring black registrants with that query for nearly a generation. When Wallace pointed out that only 4 percent of the adult black population had voted in the latest Democratic primary, Eastland attributed that to most Mississippi blacks being Republicans and thus unable to vote in the races that effectively determined elections. Eastland did not sugarcoat his positions, Wallace pointed out, a tack he followed to the end. Would there be an integrated South in his lifetime? "No," Eastland said emphatically. Two months later, he told Garroway that segregation was the product of "three hundred years of history" and conceded that the major objection of most white Southerners was the prospect of interracial marriage.[23]

School desegregation began in a major city in a state bordering Mississippi soon thereafter. In the summer of 1957, Eastland began to chide Governor Orval Faubus of Arkansas, then known as a moderate-to-liberal governor, for being slow to resist a federal court order to desegregate schools in Little Rock. "If . . . Southern states are picked off one by one under the damnable doctrine of gradualism," he said, "I don't know if we can hold or not." As the school year began, local officials admitted nine students to Central High School. When mobs formed to block their entrance, Faubus activated his state's national guard to defend the protestors, a move he had led the president to believe he would not take. For Eisenhower, the crisis had international implications. How might the governments of newly independent nations in Africa and Asia side with America under any circumstance, he asked, if he did not enforce a court order because of pressure from the governor of a small state? His concern led him to activate the 101st Airborne Division and federalize the Arkansas National Guard. Eastland joined many southern leaders in expressing outrage. The president's decision made "Reconstruction II official," he said. A few months later, he likened Eisenhower's use of troops to the Soviet invasion of Budapest in the fall of 1956 and declared it an unprecedented "attempt to destroy the social order of the South" that he hoped would "boomerang" to where it might prompt a future Supreme Court to nullify the *Brown v. Board of Education* decision. His words reflected the mindsets of most Mississippi whites. Editor Jack Tannehill of the *Neshoba County Democrat* called Eisenhower's move "the boner of the century." Clifton Langford of the *Bolivar County Commercial* went him one better by declaring that "the Supreme Court has assumed dictatorial powers . . . and the President is carrying out their orders." In the short run, Eastland was certain that Eisenhower's order would solidify the South and did what he could to let that impression linger. After W. Wilson White, Eisenhower's choice to be assistant attorney general, refused to deny that a president could use troops to "uphold the integrity of the judicial process," Eastland delayed consideration of his nomination by six months. But, just as importantly to someone who always identified as a Democrat, Eastland knew that the posture Eisenhower had taken as a bit of an invader would resound locally to the benefit of his party, even while the policies of his national party were moving farther from his own preferences.[24]

More commonly, Eastland attacked the Supreme Court. Late in the 1950s, he drafted a constitutional amendment requiring the Senate to reconfirm each sitting justice every four years. From time to time, he put up measures stripping the court of jurisdiction to hear certain cases, measures he knew would not be approved. He wrote friends that he would like to see Chief Justice Warren impeached, a step he knew was implausible. But the ploy that truly irked colleagues was his compiling a rating index on the basis of the number of times members of the Supreme Court ruled the same way the Communist Party recommended. This tack was taken as early as 1953 by Eugene C. Gearhart, a former editor of the *American Bar Association Journal*, in the *New York University Law Review*. Eastland updated Gearhart's contentions on the floor of the Senate first in 1958 and then in 1962, and he rather cagily declared that he did not mean to suggest that the justices had been wrong, merely that they had voted as the Communists had wished. In that these "Pro-Red Batting Averages" were forwarded with little discussion of the merits of each case and served to buttress occasionally wild claims by extreme groups like the John Birch Society, these assertions were roundly condemned by moderates and liberals of both parties. Hubert Humphrey, while frequently allied with Eastland on agricultural issues, nevertheless spoke for many when he declared this line of attack one that was "grossly wrong" and could "not be justified."[25]

Like many white Southerners, Eastland used the prism of the segregation issue to guide his thinking on many seemingly unrelated matters. To him, adding either Alaska or Hawaii to the union was an attack on the South, for those members either state elected to Congress were certain to support any civil rights bill proposed. Eastland had argued this point since 1949, when he vowed to try to substitute the Mundt-Ferguson bill—which would have banned Communists from holding public office and required all Communists to register—for any that would bring either territory into the union. While Majority Leader Scott Lucas concluded then that discussion of the measure might divide Democrats and kept Alaska statehood off the calendar, Lyndon Johnson decided in 1959 that Alaska should be granted statehood, even if many Texans resented it that the new state would surpass them in size. Accordingly, Johnson retreated to his ranch to avoid the debate and charged Majority Whip Mike Mansfield and Bobby Baker with breaking the filibuster.[26]

When Mansfield and Baker began running the Senate all night, Eastland called their course a disgrace. "You're likely to kill a bunch of old men here," he declared. "You ought to be ashamed of yourself. . . . If a senator's heart fails him because he's fatigued, you'll be marked for life." "Well, senator, I can't stop the filibuster," Baker replied. "But there are those who can. It seems to me . . . if a senator died and I . . . had the power to stop the filibuster, but . . . refused to use it, maybe then I'd have blood on my hands." "Alright I hear you," Eastland conceded. "But we've got to make a substantial record for our home folks, so I can't call it off immediately. But . . . if you'll see to it that the Senate adjourns early tomorrow morning until 10 A.M. on Monday, I'll give you my word that the unlimited debate won't run past Tuesday." He and Baker shook hands. As Eastland promised, no filibuster materialized, and only Strom Thurmond took any time to protest.[27]

Eastland fought considerably harder to keep Hawaii out of the union. He told friends as early as 1950 that the senators elected from Hawaii would cast two votes for "socialized medicine, . . . two votes for government ownership of industry, two votes against all racial segregation, and two votes against the South on all social matters." Less clairvoyantly, he predicted those two senators would be Republicans. Eastland also feared that admitting Hawaii would be a precedent that would allow the entry in future years of territories like Puerto Rico and the Virgin Islands, which also held ethnic mixes not reflective of the U.S. population, and might lead America into an unwise and unprecedented imperial direction. More commonly, he aired a fear stoked by the right-wing Hawaii Residents Association that anyone elected from Hawaii would come under Communist influence. He posited his case on the heavy role exerted over the Hawaiian economy by the International Longshoremen's and Warehousemen's Union, whose head, Harry Bridges, had been convicted of perjury for denying that he was a Communist. Here was a popular line of attack in the 1950s that Eastland pursued when he conducted hearings in Honolulu in December 1956. Yet as early as 1953, the *Honolulu Star-Bulletin* pointed out that more than a thousand Hawaiians had been killed or wounded fighting Communism in Korea, and others recognized that few of Bridges' charges shared his party affiliation. By the time of the vote in 1959, Eastland was privately conceding that "we lost this fight when we lost the fight on Alaska."[28]

Eastland did use his power as chairman of the Judiciary Committee to more thoroughly scrutinize Eisenhower nominees to the Supreme Court. In part, he aimed to remind southern Democratic voters that it was this GOP president who had put Chief Justice Earl Warren on the bench. Yet he was equally determined, over the advice of Attorney General William Rogers, to put judicial nominees on record to uphold each part of the Constitution. He was tougher on Republican than Democratic nominees and hardest upon moderate-to-liberal Republicans. Early in March 1957, he expedited the consideration of William Brennan, a Democratic jurist from New Jersey whom Eisenhower picked to replace Robert H. Jackson. He did the same for Kansas conservative Charles H. Whittaker, whom

Eisenhower chose to succeed Stanley Reed. But in 1959, Eastland length-ened the consideration of Justice Potter Stewart, who had been seated via a recess appointment until hearings could be held on his confirmation. Enough questions were put to Stewart about his view of the *Brown v. Board of Education* decision to make Stewart feel compelled to tell John McClellan that he would not like him to "vote for me on the assump-tion or the proposition that I am dedicated to overturning that decision, because I am not." In casting his own vote, Eastland told Stewart that he was an "able lawyer and a man of integrity." Yet he would cast his ballot no, citing a need to take a stand against recess appointments and a sense that Stewart believed that the Supreme Court could "amend the Constitution and the statutes of the United States in order to meet modern conditions." On the floor, only sixteen southern senators joined him in voting no.[29]

At the beginning of 1960, Southerners expected Eisenhower and his allies to push another civil rights bill, but did not know what one might contain. A few feared proponents of a new bill might try to fully eradicate segregation, but those from the Deep South opened their defenses by blasting plans they feared would eliminate the poll tax, which lingered only in five states. Eastland led with a three-hour speech on this question and was seconded by Strom Thurmond, Lister Hill, and John Sparkman. This was a matter for the states, he said, and he would not chide those in that huge majority of states who had eliminated their charges. But in the Magnolia State, he said, the revenues derived from poll taxes went to financing public schools, and he denied that any tax upon the franchise was discriminatory. "A person who does not care enough to pay a poll tax as a qualification should not be permitted to vote," he told the Senate, "because I do not believe he cares about his citizenship."[30] He crafted his arguments toward fellow Bourbons for they historically could always spare enough cash six months prior to an election to pay their taxes. Poor whites and blacks were rarely so secure, and as all knew, for this reason and others their numbers were likely to be fewer at the polls in proportion to their numbers in the population than any other groups.

Only on February 15, 1960, did Lyndon Johnson make his first move, when he opened a Senate resolution covering the leasing of an army base to a school district in Stella, Missouri, to nongermane civil rights amend-ments. Two weeks later, he and Everett Dirksen initiated round-the-clock sessions to break the filibuster they knew would ensue. Richard Russell countered by organizing Southerners into six-member teams he charged with being on or near the floor at all times throughout a 125-hour debate. Eastland, in his initial ninety-two-page speech, described the "so-called civil rights bill" as the "most vicious, iniquitous, revolutionary and un-constitutional series of measures . . . ever . . . proposed in the Congress of the United States, except for that period of time when the Southern states were divided into military districts, . . . operated by the military governors in a status which equaled . . . sheer tyranny." Here was hyper-bole long used by Deep South solons to lambaste anyone connected with Washington. Eastland, as always, chided the Supreme Court for the *Brown v. Board of Education* decision and scored the Civil Rights Commission for "highhanded and sanctimonious tactics" that required Louisiana to produce election results before charging anyone with any wrongdoing. But what had to surprise many of the senators on the floor were his cita-tions of Radical Republicans, who Eastland said were not as harsh on the southern states as his own colleagues. The Missouri Radical Carl Schurz, he said, had written about the problems integrated schools had in the troubled 1860s. Eastland was proud to report that even onetime abolition-ist Charles Sumner, the Massachusetts Radical who a southern extremist had caned in 1856 and other Dixie denizens had just as thoroughly vilified for the next century, had not seen fit to require that schools be mixed at the time of his death in 1874.[31]

When Everett Dirksen tried to publish a Supreme Court ruling af-firming the constitutionality of the 1957 act in the *Congressional Record*, Eastland objected, saying that he did not want the record "cluttered up with that crap." Paul Douglas cut in to point out that the court acted unanimously. "That doesn't mean anything," Eastland replied, as the deci-sion reflected an ignorance of the Constitution. Like many with argu-ments that had begun to lose favor, Eastland tried to change the subject. Colleagues would better serve the public, he said, if they switched their focus to a growth in "rape, muggings, murder, and crime" in the District of Columbia and other cities. But, hours after giving his speech and engag-ing in many colloquies, Eastland resorted to a then common practice of seeing that the Senate clerks replaced the words "crap" and "tripe" that he had used to describe recent Supreme Court rulings with the more socially acceptable term of "claptrap."[32]

Only at this time did Majority Leader Johnson and Dirksen opt to restrict their bill to one providing further protections to the right to vote. Just what they intended to include they kept to themselves. Eastland was uncertain as to what ideas he should attack and which southern practices he needed to defend. Sometimes, he quoted black-run papers that lauded expanded funding to build new gymnasiums, classrooms, and cafeterias in black Mississippi schools. On other occasions, he debated the intent of the Radical Republicans. His reading of the Fifteenth Amendment, he said, convinced him that the authors did not intend to establish a general right of suffrage, but merely deny states the right to accord preference to one citizen over another on the basis of race. He was especially harsh on expected moves to let those designated as federal referees register voters. And, as always, Eastland did not hesitate to argue the relative treatments of African Americans in North and South. Almost as soon as Douglas brought to the Senate's attention records from South Carolina indicating that not a single nonwhite citizen was included on one county's roll of voters and a recent boast of Mississippi's new Governor Ross Barnett that only 4 percent of black adults in Mississippi were registered, Eastland shot back that a minority of blacks voted in Illinois. He denied that Eisenhower was delinquent in filing suits in Mississippi by saying that there were no grounds for such litigation. He and other Southerners took heart in a preliminary cloture vote of March 8 in which those who wanted to close debate could muster but fifty-three votes for cloture, nowhere near the two-thirds needed. But what neither he nor Douglas knew was that Johnson and Dirksen had decided not to open debate on what they intended to be the main vehicle to protect civil rights until the House of Representatives had approved its version.[33]

Once the House bill passed, Johnson moved to send the bill to the Judiciary Committee with instructions to report a measure back after five days. Jacob Javits suspected that Eastland might try and obstruct the bill. Suppose Eastland did just that, he asked the majority leader. Johnson trusted Eastland's commitment to the rules of the Senate and assured Javits that there was no precedent. Eastland then sought to get the bill assigned to his committee without instructions. His maneuver won the votes of eighteen Southerners, including Johnson, and Milton Young, a North Dakota Republican who favored the bill but had never before voted to limit debate. With this move derailed, just four bitter-enders from the Deep South joined Eastland in voting against limiting the bill's stay in the Judiciary Committee.[34]

Once the Eisenhower bill reemerged on the floor, senators from outside the South moved to render the bill more palatable to moderates and conservatives from outside the South. They approved Everett Dirksen's measure to make violations of court orders federal crimes, not just those involving school desegregation. They modified an amendment by Estes Kefauver so that it would require any hearings on who would vote to be held in public, a practice many feared would result in the harassment of black applicants for the franchise. More traditional Southerners continued to pick at the bill, but they did not filibuster. Not infrequently, they joined more cautious members of the upper chamber in voting down amendments by more liberal senators to accelerate change in the South. Just ten days after the measure left Eastland's panel, the Senate gave its approval by a margin of 74–18.[35]

Many liberal Northerners found the watered down bill a mere pittance of what might have been passed. Jacob Javits swore it was a "victory for the Old South." Democrat Joseph Clark found the outcome suggesting that the roles of Ulysses S. Grant and Robert E. Lee had been reversed. Conservative champion Harry Byrd of Virginia echoed them, declaring that the limited bill passed "demonstrated the effectiveness of courageous massive resistance." Eastland was less certain. While he would never concede as much publicly, he suspected that that the days of Jim Crow were soon to pass. On the day of the vote, he wrote Elmore D. Greaves, one of the more extreme segregationists in Mississippi, that the forces of the South had succeeded in keeping all matters relating to school desegregation out of the bill, but still had been defeated by a better than four to one margin.[36]

Not long after Eisenhower left office, Herbert Brownell appeared before the Judiciary Committee to endorse a Kennedy nominee to a lower court. When he finished his testimony, Eastland invited Brownell to his office for a drink. After taking a seat, Brownell asked Eastland how he was "getting along in the appointment of federal judges." "It's much better than when you were here," Eastland replied. He and other Southerners had far better luck in getting judges with segregationist backgrounds approved than they had over the previous eight years. To the chagrin of Eastland, Eisenhower appointees to lower courts including John Brown of Texas, Frank Johnson of Alabama, Elbert Tuttle of Georgia, and John Minor Wisdom of Louisiana were the "unlikely heroes," as journalist Jack Bass described them, who rendered decisions that jumpstarted the civil rights revolution. But while Eisenhower had created the Civil Rights Commission, a body Eastland detested, the prosecutors in his administration were quite passive in using the authority granted them by the Civil Rights Act of 1957. Some hesitated to take on Eastland in Mississippi, fearing he might take out his wrath on other parts of their program. Alluding to Brownell's successor, Eastland later asked Robert Kennedy if he knew "that he [William Rogers] never brought a case in Mississippi?"[37] Whether Eastland sought to suggest that the new attorney general limit his attention to civil rights or was boasting that he had intimidated Rogers into submission is far from certain. What is clear is that the heightened expectations of those interested in racial progress was prompting many to accelerate the timetable by which they wanted to see their demands—which had been part of the Constitution since Reconstruction—carried out by all legal authorities anywhere in the United States.

CHAPTER 12

Big Jim and the Kennedys

AT NO TIME IN HIS POLITICAL CAREER DID JIM EASTLAND EVER CONTEM-
plate leaving the Democratic Party, though the principles of its national
leaders departed increasingly from his. He was acutely aware that the
partisan realignment shepherded by Franklin D. Roosevelt in the 1930s
had, as historian Dewey W. Grantham wrote, transformed Southerners
from "a majority faction in a minority party to a minority faction in a
majority party." By 1960, an older and shrewder Eastland recognized that
he could no longer engage in a quixotic stand as he had with the Dixiecrats. Keeping his chairmanship dictated that he would have to stay
loyal to his party publicly. Indeed, the South's position within the national
Democratic Party, not to mention the nation, rested upon him and several
senior colleagues remaining in charge of the committees they chaired.
Were too many seats to change hands, he told friends, "the total defenses
of the South would collapse like a house of cards."[1]

While Eastland, like John Stennis and most southern Democratic senators, strongly and proudly supported Johnson's presidential candidacy at
the outset of the 1960 campaign, theirs was not the dominant position
within the Mississippi delegation.[2] Walter Sillers and others thought it
was time for Mississippi to run another slate of independent electors,
hoping that such a course, if matched by likeminded southern electors,
might throw the election into the House of Representatives and force
both parties to make concessions to positions more commonly held in the
Deep South. Eastland thought such a course futile, for he knew that only
Alabama might follow. While Congressmen William Colmer and John
Bell Williams announced that they could not support the national ticket
because of its plank on civil rights, Stanley Posposil, the chairman of the

States' Rights Party of Florida, went even further and encouraged Eastland to run as his party's candidate for president. This was not an option for Eastland, who not only was resolute for Johnson but had proclaimed his confidence as early as June 1957 in Kennedy's ability to serve as president.[3]

Eastland and Stennis erred in trusting that Governor Ross Barnett would follow their lead. On the opening day of the Democratic National Convention in Los Angeles, they took Barnett to meet Johnson in his hotel room. There, the governor startled them by telling Johnson that he could not back a "liberal." With Barnett having virtually handpicked the delegation prior to the convention, it went without saying that his view, not Eastland's and Stennis', would prevail among Mississippians when the roll was called. Yet, Barnett may have inadvertently done the Democratic ticket a favor. By taking what seemed like such an extreme position, he demonstrated that whoever won the nod had not yet sewn up the South's electoral votes, a consideration not lost upon eventual nominee John F. Kennedy. One virtue Kennedy found in choosing Johnson as his running mate was that his selection would bind Southerners like Eastland, Stennis, and colleagues including Richard Russell and Herman Talmadge of Georgia—not to mention their loyalists—behind his candidacy. And without a scion of Dixie balancing the ticket headed by a son of Massachusetts, Eastland calculated, every southern state might vote Republican.[4]

During the 1960 campaign, Jim Eastland's pragmatic partisan considerations and Ross Barnett's absolute commitment to segregation were not reconciled. In Barnett's view, a vote for either Kennedy or Vice President Richard Nixon, the GOP nominee, would result in the integration of all schools by 1963 and allow African Americans "to mingle socially with our white sons and daughters." Almost immediately after the Democratic National Convention, the governor pushed state Democrats to put his unpledged elector slate on the ballot under the Democratic label. Mississippi Democrats met him partway, by placing both his slate and that designated by the Kennedy-Johnson campaign under the Democratic line.[5]

Eastland and Stennis pledged to support the Kennedy-Johnson ticket the day of Mississippi's Democratic convention. In a statement where they acknowledged that they found the civil rights and several other planks in the Democratic platform at best unseemly, they urged Mississippians to ignore a slate of unpledged electors Ross Barnett put together. As they remembered from their days as Dixiecrats, the "independent elector" plan did not have "sufficient strength in the South to be effective." In early fall, Eastland, secure in his own reelection, took to Magnolia State airwaves to tell voters that Johnson had taken "everything relating to integration out of those civil rights bills." In appearances from Jackson to New Orleans on the "Cornpone Special," Johnson's campaign train, and others around the state, Eastland would introduce the Texan and salute him as one of the Senate's "most effective leaders." He then hailed Kennedy for having a "keener mind" than Richard Nixon, declared that the vice president was not a conservative, and blasted him for backing an amendment to deny a trial by jury to those accused of civil rights violations. Kennedy's religion would not be an issue, he assured voters. And, noting that Cuba had fallen to Communist Fidel Castro under the Republican Eisenhower administration, he was quick to salute the anticommunism he found implicit within Kennedy and, indeed, most Catholics.[6]

Despite the best efforts of Eastland, Stennis, and the state's relatively weak American Federation of Labor and Congress of Industrial Organizations (AFL-CIO) contingent, the slate of unpledged electors ran ahead of the Kennedy-Johnson ticket by nearly 8000 votes and cast their ballots for Senator Harry F. Byrd of Virginia. In Eastland's mind, the victory margin resulted from a shift of votes that many white conservatives had planned to cast for Richard Nixon to the unpledged slate after GOP vice presidential nominee Henry Cabot Lodge pledged that Nixon would place an African American in his Cabinet were he elected president. The weakness of the Mississippi Republican Party at that time was reflected as much in Eastland's victory for a fourth term, with more than 90 percent of the vote, as it was in the state GOP's failure to garner even one-quarter of the vote for their nominee for president. But while Eastland could not bring the Magnolia State into the Democratic column, his support for the national ticket meant that a move being planned by some liberals in and outside of his caucus to strip him of his chairmanship would fail.[7] Not only would Eastland remain at the helm of the Judiciary Committee but his advice and help would be solicited often by those at the highest levels of the new administration.

Although Eastland would never admit it at home, he was as devoted to the institution of the Senate and its traditions as to his native South. As with any committee chairman of an incoming president's party, Eastland saw his first duty as steering Kennedy's nominees through the confirmation process. First on his committee's docket was action upon the selection of Robert F. Kennedy, the president-elect's brother and campaign manager, to be attorney general. Eastland had frequently encountered the younger Kennedy in the preceding decade and quickly cited his quite visible public profile as counsel to Democratic senators during the Army-McCarthy hearings and to John McClellan during his probes of the abuses of the Teamsters' Union. It thus was easy for him to declare that the Kennedy often described as ruthless had performed each job he had taken "with credit above and beyond the call of duty." And he was quick to reply when Colorado conservative Gordon Allott, a relatively junior GOP senator, tried to embarrass Kennedy with selective excerpts from his testimony. Everett Dirksen and Roman Hruska, the two committee Republicans charged with examining the nominee, Eastland boasted, were both merely honoring Senate custom and giving a new president his choice of people to staff his administration.[8]

Kennedy hands were quick to express their gratitude during the inaugural week festivities, with no one more demonstrative than family patriarch, Joseph P. Kennedy, the onetime ambassador to the Court of St. James. Still more instructive of the kind of quietly constructive collaboration Eastland would exhibit toward the new president's family for the duration of his career was an incident during Kennedy's inaugural parade. Those Democrats who had opted the previous year to back a slate of independent electors arranged for the official Mississippi car in the parade to be covered with stickers for Governor Ross Barnett, the highest ranking of the renegades. Like John Stennis, Eastland flatly refused to ride in the car or even be seen in its vicinity. That dubious honor went to a group led by Biloxi lawyer Walter L. Nixon Jr., ordinarily an Eastland loyalist, but one bold enough to josh him, if in a courtly manner. "You could have ridden with us," the future federal judge ribbed Eastland. "Go to hell," Eastland replied immediately.[9]

To be sure, many northern liberals led by economist John Kenneth Galbraith and historian Arthur M. Schlesinger Jr. tried to push the Senate Democratic caucus to strip Eastland of his chairmanship. Civil rights lobbyist Clarence Mitchell was heard bemoaning that Kennedy's New

Frontier looked "suspiciously like a dude ranch with . . . Eastland as the general manager." Their point man inside the caucus was Joseph Clark of Pennsylvania, who found next to no support when he moved to oust Eastland. The maneuver found no favor with the new president, who appreciated Eastland's support against the "unpledged electors" slate and realized that comity was imperative, even tantamount within the Senate. On a personal level, Eastland was quick to assure friends that Kennedy would not be as "liberal as many expected." And, on many occasions, Eastland proved quite helpful to Kennedy, particularly among southern Democrats. In the first few months of the New Frontier, he guided to passage Robert Kennedy's anticrime package, which made it illegal to cross state lines to assist gamblers, racketeers, or those involved in other illicit businesses. In 1962, he introduced the Kennedy bill to make it easier for the attorney general to authorize wiretapping of those suspected of espionage, murder, kidnapping, extortion, drug offenses, or bribery. The same year, he steered Supreme Court nominees Byron R. White, who replaced Eisenhower appointee Charles Whittaker, and Arthur J. Goldberg, who succeeded Roosevelt pick Felix Frankfurter, to confirmation almost effortlessly. And Eastland wasted no time in doing all he could to expedite the passage of programs both Kennedys championed. Foremost was Kennedy's Food for Peace initiative, which Eastland knew would stimulate employment and economic stability and develop renewable resources in rural America while making food available to some of the poorest areas of the world.[10]

On occasions when Kennedy feared that hastily considered calls for action might lead to bad public policy, Eastland could prove an invaluable ally. A case in point was a bill reforming the pharmaceutical industry offered by Estes Kefauver, which many feared was overly punitive toward the industry in ways that might harm the consumer via higher costs. Had it passed, the Kefauver measure would have limited patents for new drugs to three years and required that drug producers be licensed, display generic names for their products, and demonstrate the safety of their products before putting them on the market. While one might observe that Eastland had once called Kefauver a "renegade Southerner," it is more appropriate to note that Eastland was close to several pharmaceutical industry lobbyists. Onetime Truman aide Edward Foley was his closest friend in Washington, and he, like frequent allies Everett Dirksen and Roman Hruska, had strong working relationships with New Deal veteran Tommy "the Cork" Corcoran and Lloyd Cutler, who later served at the highest levels of the Carter and Clinton administrations. Aware that Kefauver wanted Kennedy to highlight his bill in his State of the Union message of 1962, Eastland phoned White House head of congressional liaison Larry O'Brien and asked to meet with the president. Fifteen minutes later, O'Brien returned the call and suggested that Eastland meet Kennedy early the next morning. "Goddamn, Larry," Eastland shot back, "I wouldn't fight this Washington traffic to meet Jesus Christ at 7:30." From another line, he heard a familiar laugh with a Boston aristocratic tinge roaring. "Jim," Kennedy cut in, "I'll see you at 11:30."[11]

What became the administration's bill did not emerge until the spring, and it diluted the safety portions of the Kefauver bill and maintained the existing length of drug patents at seventeen years. During a June meeting, Eastland, Dirksen, and representatives of the Department of Health, Education, and Welfare and the pharmaceutical industry met and mapped out strategy for the bill's final passage. As they expected, Kefauver resented being excluded. Eastland was hardly apologetic, saying that he doubted that Kefauver would agree to any proposal but his own and that several of his amendments had previously been rejected in committee by 12–3 votes. For Kefauver, this was an excuse to have his staff leak evidence that German mothers who had used the insufficiently tested drug thalidomide had babies born without arms or legs. What the media-savvy Kefauver accomplished was to raise a public outcry that pressed the Senate to reinstate his original safety provisions. But he could only sway twenty-seven colleagues to join him behind provisions limiting the time patents for new drugs applied to three years. So, while the Kefauver-Harris drug reform bill, as it came to be known, passed unanimously in the Senate, the proposed features most offensive to the pharmaceutical industry, not to mention Eastland and Kennedy, were not approved.[12]

When the interests of the Kennedys and Eastland converged, positive action usually came quickly. Especially revealing was action on a bill the Judicial Conference proposed in March 1960 to create dozens of new district and appellate judgeships to meet growing caseloads. Eastland had been convinced of the need for the bill in the latter days of the Eisenhower administration by his friend Lawrence E. Walsh, the assistant attorney general. Walsh and other Justice Department officials agreed to consult with Democratic senators just as they would with Republicans as to who would be appointed. But the deal unraveled when William P. Rogers, Walsh's boss, wrote Eastland in a somewhat harsh tone that there was no agreement on the nature of the consultation. Political considerations alone dictated Rogers' letter. Not only did the attorney general not want anyone in the Eisenhower administration seen as caving to a man perceived as the Senate's leading segregationist, he was just as cynical of circumstances that might arise just before an election from one or both nominees. The release of the letter prompted Eastland and Majority Leader Lyndon Johnson to withdraw the measure from the Senate calendar. This maneuver squared with a previous request from dozens of House Democrats who wanted to allow a new Democratic administration to make the nominations. Obstruction on either side ended the day Kennedy entered the White House. Within a month and a half, Eastland steered to passage a bill creating sixty-nine new judgeships in all parts of America.[13]

What the bill meant for Mississippi was that it would get another federal district court judge. Kennedy had Deputy Attorney General Byron White and aide Joe Dolan go to Eastland's office to ask who he wanted to see nominated. Eastland gave Kennedy's men the same name he had given Eisenhower's lawyers in 1955, that of corporation lawyer W. Harold Cox, a former chairman of the Hinds County (Jackson) Democratic Executive Committee who had been his friend since college.[14] But while his ardor for Cox gave pause to Eisenhower's civil rights team, led by Deputy Attorney General William P. Rogers, Kennedy felt obligated, even after Eastland fended off queries about Cox. "I ain't gonna tell you a thing, boys," he said. "You find out for yourselves." Inquiries for the Justice Department, like one conducted by Leon Jaworski of the American Bar Association, inspired so little confidence that Robert Kennedy took it upon himself to interview Cox. He, too, felt a bit uneasy, and directed Byron White to ask Eastland if Cox might prefer an appointment to the Fifth Circuit Court of Appeals, where they knew he would be outvoted on a regular basis. Cox, it turned out, aspired only to the position of a trial judge. Kennedy made Cox's the first nomination he sent up to the Senate in early June, and Eastland saw to his confirmation by the end of the month. By the end of

Cox's tenure, even Eastland concluded that the Kennedys' apprehensions had been justified. In a voting rights case of 1964, for example, Cox called several African-American plaintiffs "niggers" and told them that they were acting "like a bunch of chimpanzees." Public comments of that sort proved embarrassing and frequent enough that Eastland near the end of his own career felt compelled to plead with Cox, without success, to enter into senior status on the court.[15]

Even so, if there is one purported Eastland statement chroniclers on the left more commonly declare factual than any other, it is that of Eastland's alleged offer to Robert Kennedy in this instance. "Tell your brother," Eastland supposedly told the attorney general, "that if you give me Harold Cox, I will give him the nigger," in reference to Thurgood Marshall. Here is a statement liberal journalists like Juan Williams and Curtis Wilkie, with no disposition to herald Eastland for anything, are quick to cite as apocryphal. For while the language reflected that Eastland used for much of his life, the deal so reported could not have happened because Marshall was not nominated for a perch on the Second Circuit Court of Appeals until September 23, 1961, three months after the Senate confirmed Cox.[16] Eastland privately assured Kennedy that he would allow Marshall and other black nominees to be voted out of his committee and then be confirmed. But that would only occur after Southerners used an initial delay to oppose the nominations loudly enough to derive some political benefit from their seeming intraparty dissent.[17]

It surprised no one that Eastland's initial inattention lasted long enough to prompt the Kennedys to grant Marshall a recess appointment. To hear testimony on Marshall, Eastland named southern Democrats Olin Johnston and John McClellan and his close friend Roman Hruska, who, like many midwestern Republicans of the time, maintained that the party of Lincoln should remain one devoted to equal rights for all. Only Hruska appeared for the first day of hearings. Just as Eastland anticipated, a southern Democratic colleague was immersed in a hotly contested primary. Johnston was facing a stiff challenge from then Governor Ernest F. "Fritz" Hollings, and in the political climate of the time did not want to appear soft on integration. Having Eastland's word, the Kennedy brothers tried to assure Marshall that confirmations "take time." But Marshall, having been the NAACP's top lawyer for more than a decade, knew of Eastland's record intimately and would not be placated. When Robert Kennedy urged him to make a courtesy call upon Eastland, Marshall refused to "genuflect to that man." While liberal Republicans Jacob Javits and Kenneth Keating praised Marshall at the initial hearing in April, there was no hint of pressure from Democrats until August, when four liberals—John Carroll, Thomas Dodd, Philip Hart, and Edward V. Long—wrote Eastland to criticize the length of the hearings and vow that they would move to spring Marshall's nomination. Under normal circumstances, such overt pressure would increase Eastland's determination not to bend. But once Johnston was renominated, Eastland could keep his word, a move expedited by a visit from Marshall's friend Henry Luce, the founder of the *Time-Life* empire, who knew that Marshall was developing anxieties that he would soon no longer be receiving biweekly paychecks because his recess appointment was about to expire. Thinking such a process demeaning to any nominee, Luce encouraged Eastland to expose any negative material he had found right away. He also pledged to run pro-Marshall stories in each of his publications, then deemed fairly conservative ones, until the Senate acted. With off-year elections but two months away, Eastland knew it was time to honor his promise to the Kennedys. There would be no negative ramifications from voters in his home state, virtually all of whom were white. He could tell them he had called attention to Marshall's onetime memberships in left-wing organizations like the National Lawyers Guild and the International Juridical Association and put each senator on record for or against Marshall, even if only fifteen fellow southern Democrats would join him in voting nay.[18]

Privately, Eastland made it clear to the Kennedy Justice Department and congressional liaison staff that he would continue to oppose all efforts to expand rights for African Americans. He counseled White House lobbyists in the spring of 1961 that he believed that extending the life of the Civil Rights Commission for two years was a mistake. Still, he assured the Kennedy staff that he would not hold up any nominations to the panel. He joined other Southerners in lengthy proceedings against submitting a proposed constitutional amendment to bar states from requiring the payment of a poll tax as a prerequisite for voting. To be sure, Eastland was always candid with the Kennedy team as to how he would deal with civil rights matters. When Robert Kennedy brought by Burke Marshall, his brother's nominee to head the Civil Rights Division of the Justice Department, for a courtesy call, he jibed Eastland that Marshall would be the man who would "put the Negroes in your white schools in Mississippi." Eastland chuckled and vowed not to stand in the way of Marshall's confirmation, while assuring him that he would "vote against Jesus Christ if he was nominated for that position."[19]

The Freedom Riders was the first civil rights group to prod the new administration to accelerate the pace they intended to use to spur compliance with the Fourteenth Amendment. These predominantly youthful idealists boarded buses in Washington in early May 1961 and aimed to integrate the lunch counters and waiting rooms at southern bus stations and the seating patterns on the buses themselves. Eastland quickly disparaged them to one correspondent as "Friction Riders." While fellow Democrats distanced themselves from such brash rhetoric, surprisingly few—certainly none in the Kennedy administration—were much more eager to embrace the Freedom Riders. That changed in mid-May when the Ku Klux Klan and their allies unleashed a rash of violence in Alabama. In Anniston, Klansmen dented the frame, slashed the tires, and broke the windows of a bus carrying the Freedom Riders, then threw flaming rags through the windows, all the while shouting "Burn them" and a host of vulgar racist slogans. When another bus of Freedom Riders reached Birmingham, Commissioner of Public Safety Eugene "Bull" Connor let Klansmen and their allies have fifteen minutes to assault anyone who got near the lunch counter or the white waiting room. Only then did Robert Kennedy dispatch Special Assistant John Seigenthaler, a Nashvillian with a soft southern accent, to Alabama to confer with Governor John Patterson and his top law enforcement officials. At Seigenthaler's request, Patterson agreed to protect those Freedom Riders who were ready to head toward Mississippi. Seigenthaler then drove to the Montgomery Greyhound terminal, where he saw a teenaged kid punching a young white Freedom Rider. He got out of his car and identified himself. Within seconds, a man hit him in the back of his head with a lead pipe. A few others kicked him in the midsection, leaving him unconscious with a fractured skull and several broken ribs.[20]

While Eastland predictably was quick to lash out at the Freedom Riders on the Senate floor, he was determined to guarantee that his state would not be the site of mob or police violence like that which had occurred in Alabama. To be sure, he did use intemperate language to oppose a measure forwarded by Jacob Javits that saluted the administration's relatively limited interventions. The Freedom Riders, he said, were "Communist inspired," and the Congress of Racial Equality, the primary group funding and organizing the generally youthful riders, should be considered "the war department of the integration movement." His particular target was James Peck, who had been bloodied in Birmingham and, at forty-six, was one of the older Freedom Riders. Eastland noted that Peck in the past had worked alongside Communists and associated with some from front groups, then called him "disloyal" and a "Communist agitator and organizer of the worst kind." Peck, who had been jailed in Danbury federal prison for three years during World War II for refusing to register for the draft, found the charges laughable, for he had never backed any sort of dictatorship. Harsher were the editors of the *New York Post*, then a liberal organ, who said that Eastland "should have learned the distinction between a pacifist and a Communist."

But unknown to them, Eastland was in regular contact with Robert F. Kennedy and his chief deputies, Byron White and Nicholas Katzenbach, sometimes even using the back elevator in the Justice Department. While the Freedom Riders boarded buses, other Mississippians close to the Kennedys, like Jackson Mayor Allen Thompson and former Governor James P. Coleman, warned Kennedy aides that Governor Barnett was too much of a loose cannon to be trusted. Consequently, Robert Kennedy called Eastland several dozen times over the next three days to tell him that his "primary interest was to see that they weren't beaten up." Eastland told Kennedy what he could and could not do, then pledged to do all he could to see that Mississippi did not embarrass the United States in the court of world opinion. Eastland notified Kennedy, who thought him easier to deal with than some closer to his own brand of thinking, that, once he leaned on Barnett, he could guarantee the physical safety of the Freedom Riders. Even so, he told the attorney general that he would not be able to stop them from being arrested in Jackson or sentenced to Parchman State Penitentiary for sixty days. Here was a godsend for the Kennedys, as it limited strife among Democrats, a party still loaded with white Southerners, even if civil rights leaders sensed that it was merely another side deal that postponed the appearance of racial justice. It is interesting to note that the National Guard lieutenant colonel who commanded the bus from the Alabama line to Jackson was G. V. "Sonny" Montgomery, who later came to represent the state in the House of Representatives for three decades. And, once the Freedom Riders were convicted and sent to Parchman, Eastland saw to it that the hierarchy at Parchman kept them isolated from other prisoners. While this meant that some felt dehumanized by their lack of exercise and contact with others, it also meant that there were few cases of guards harassing or beating these impassioned idealists and none of them being put to hard labor breaking rocks.[21]

The Kennedys were less fortunate when they had to enforce a court order to desegregate the University of Mississippi in September 1962. Rumors were rampant that Robert Kennedy, hardly a popular man in the Magnolia State at that time, would go to Ole Miss to personally oversee the admission of James Meredith, the thirty-year-old African-American veteran who had brought the suit. Once Bill Minor, the nearly authoritative head of the Mississippi bureau of the *New Orleans Times-Picayune*, apprised Eastland of such reports, Eastland called the attorney general to inquire. "I'll go down there, Jim," Kennedy said laughing, "if you'll go with me." Eastland retorted that he would go only "as far as Memphis."[22]

Publicly, Eastland sided with the leaders of his state, even while sensing that Ole Miss would erupt in violence as soon as the Justice Department tried to enforce the order to admit Meredith. Privately, he was in close contact with Robert Kennedy as well as many on the scene, especially his youngest daughter Sue, then a sophomore at Ole Miss. To Sue, like the bulk of the student body, the events were a curiosity, indeed almost a sport, and she joined her classmates at the Grove each day to observe the ongoing theater. Eastland called her from Washington nightly to get her reports. His calls were as much those of a father as those of a senator. He feared for her safety enough by Friday September 28, 1962, to tell her that she needed to leave campus. By that time, he had lost confidence in Ross Barnett, an open Citizens Council member who had no plan to block the court's dictate other than to try and bluff the Kennedys into letting the matter die. While Eastland had taken the Senate floor two days earlier to laud Barnett for his "deep courage" in opposing a dictum of a federal court of appeals that he said had arrogated unto itself the powers of a district court, another senator told the *Washington Post* that Eastland had crafted his speech solely for home consumption. Two days later, Eastland joined all but one colleague in his state's congressional delegation in signing a letter to President Kennedy urging that he remove the federal troops he had sent to Oxford. One "successful registration," they asserted in a plea to the chief executive, was not worth the cost of the "holocaust" they saw in the making.[23]

At no point in the crisis was Barnett's approach less than bombastic, a tack urged on him by Citizens Council leaders William Simmons and M. Ney Williams, two of his closest advisers. Hours after the Fifth Circuit Court of Appeals ordered Ole Miss to admit Meredith, Barnett took to the airwaves to promise that no school would be integrated while he was governor and called upon citizens "to stand up like men and tell them NEVER!" A week later, he named himself acting registrar at Ole Miss and personally denied Meredith admission. He directed the MSSC to print more than a million postcards letting John F. Kennedy know senders "resent[ed] the unnatural warfare" being waged against Mississippi and distributed them that weekend at college football games in states throughout the South. Barnett's defiance emboldened the extreme right. An especially inflammatory radio broadcast by General Edwin Walker, who even Citizens' Council leaders found extreme, condemning the "anti-Christ Supreme Court," prompted many to drive hundreds of miles to Oxford. The first few dozen arrived on Saturday September 29, the night the Ole Miss football team took on the Kentucky Wildcats at Veterans Memorial Stadium in Jackson. More important—and exhilarating—to thousands of those present than the Southeastern Conference showdown was Barnett's dramatic appearance at halftime. "I love Mississippi," the governor told the crowd. "I love her people, our customs. I love and honor our heritage." His words aroused much of the all-white crowd to lustily hoist Confederate flags and more than a few to prepare to head to Oxford to join General Walker.[24]

Eastland convened a meeting of the Mississippi congressional delegation in his Washington office at 2:00 P.M. on Sunday the 30th. All were present for most of the afternoon, except Frank Smith, the moderate six-term veteran from Greenwood who had been defeated in a primary.

Those gathered knew that Barnett had proposed scenarios involving many federal marshals pointing pistols at Barnett to secure Meredith's admittance, a scheme the delegation found foolish. Some suggested that Eastland or John Stennis assume the role of a mediator, as Congressman L. Brooks Hays had during the Little Rock crisis. Neither man was interested. Eastland was especially dismissive, remembering that Hays could not move his governor to do the right thing, nor was his credibility as an honest broker enhanced, nor did he survive the next primary against a committed segregationist. Having been in touch with Robert Kennedy, Eastland remained hopeful that bloodshed could be averted. But his confidence receded once he started trying to reach Barnett in Jackson. He received busy signals for three hours, then asked several operators to cut into Barnett's line and tell him that his state's congressional delegation needed to reach him. Disturbed, Eastland called attorney John C. Satterfield, a longtime ally, in Yazoo City, and asked him to intercede with the governor. Within twenty minutes, Barnett did call Eastland, but his words were scarcely reassuring.[25]

Barnett's incendiary words the previous night had prompted thousands of the South's most intransigent racists to head for Oxford. Accounts from the next day indicate that hundreds of cars with out-of-state license plates had reached Ole Miss by noon. Matters were volatile enough by 4:00 P.M. that football coach Johnny Vaught felt compelled to tell his players to stay away from the Lyceum, where Meredith or any other student would register. By nightfall, federal authorities had federalized the Mississippi National Guard to try and calm the vigilant. While President Kennedy had hoped that anger would subside and trusted, mistakenly, at several points that he had agreements with Ross Barnett to register Meredith in a roundabout way, he was sufficiently concerned to go on television at 8:00 P.M. and call upon Mississippians to uphold their traditions of honor and courage by "preserv[ing] both the law and the peace." All but 300 of the student body of 4800 complied. Some who did not began to taunt the troops. A few others hurled lead pipes and bricks, leading some guardsmen to fire canisters of tear gas into the crowd. A few of the most zealous in the mob fired back. Even before learning that two spectators—a French journalist and another innocent bystander—lay dead, Deputy Attorney

General Nicholas Katzenbach phoned the president and convinced him to send in federal troops.[26]

Employing federal troops to quell the demonstrations was a course Kennedy had sought to avoid. Indeed, when Dwight D. Eisenhower had sent the 82nd Airborne Division into Little Rock to desegregate Central High School, Kennedy had thought the display of force excessive. Now events prompted him to employ a tactic he had previously condemned. While only two Mississippi House members, Karl Wiesenburg of Pascagoula and Joseph Wroten of Greeneville, voted against a resolution of late September hailing the Barnett approach—and paid for it by being branded as "traitors" by the *Jackson Daily News*—quite a few Mississippi officials privately concluded that their governor had overreacted. The matter had been "poorly handled," State Representative Brad Dye declared much later. Even more emphatically State House Ways and Means Committee Chairman John Holloman, while watching Barnett's halftime speech, looked at his son, a future counsel to Eastland, and rued in a somber tone that, "We've gone too far."[27]

Eastland, for his part, continued to monitor events at Oxford. University officials blamed the marshals for the trouble on their campus and prompted him to ask his colleague Sam Ervin to launch an investigation of the riot. Ervin was willing, but Eastland soon deferred to Ross Barnett's request to intercede and halt that probe. Even Barnett had recognized that the only kind of inquiry that would accept his version of the events that week was one he could control, and that result did ensue when the Mississippi legislature the following winter blamed the Kennedys and "trigger happy marshalls."[28] By this time, Eastland knew that his best source of information was not Barnett but Nicholas Katzenbach, the assistant attorney general who had overseen federal operations at Ole Miss. There could be no safer place anywhere, Katzenbach replied, unless someone feared that 22,000 soldiers, many of them African American, were now stationed on campus. Eastland chuckled, but would not allow daughter Sue to return to school until the Thursday after what came to be known as "the Battle of Oxford." Even then, guards searched her car, as they did any other, for guns or other contraband. In time, Eastland invited Katzenbach to visit him in Doddsville. To Eastland's great surprise, the balding Rhodes Scholar and World War II prisoner of war ventured the two-hour drive from Oxford to his plantation. Eastland asked the soft-spoken Katzenbach a few questions, grunted a bit, then let it be known that he thought Robert Kennedy erred seriously when he thought he could negotiate in good faith with Ross Barnett.[29]

In retrospect, Kennedy hands quickly concede that Eastland, unlike many of the more flamboyant segregationist governors of the time— Barnett and John Patterson and George Wallace of Alabama—kept his rhetoric to a temperate level during the early 1960s, rarely going farther than making a single speech on any issue other than on the Senate floor to placate his state's segregationist bloc. Even this was too much for some of Kennedy's critics in the Magnolia State. One was Charles Sullivan, an eloquent and dynamic young attorney from Clarksdale whose father had managed Eastland's 1954 campaign. In 1960, Sullivan backed Ross Barnett's slate of independent electors; thereafter, he made it clear he believed that Eastland was too close to the Kennedys. Once, after having too much to drink at a fish fry, he sought out Eastland and blasted him loudly in full view of dozens of Delta Democrats with repeated taunts of "no guts, no courage, no convictions." More than a bit perturbed, Eastland puffed his cigar, then walked away, and quietly concluded that Sullivan was too intemperate to occupy higher office.[30] Even while Sullivan would be elected lieutenant governor in 1967, he would never again run with Eastland's blessing, even if observers noted that the two seemed philosophically and geographically akin.

Alabamans further right also made it known that they had bones to pick with Eastland. His sin in their eyes was joining John Stennis and the Georgians Richard Russell and Herman Talmadge in signing a letter urging the reelection of Lister Hill, who voted a rather populistic line on economic issues but always sided with them on racial ones. Many of those most committed to segregation in Alabama signed on with Republican James W. Martin, who was using the notion that Hill was "soft on integration" and too close to the Kennedys. Several among them wired or wrote Eastland (or, in some cases, "Easterling") and demanded to know why he was backing an alleged liberal like Hill. "Why, Senator," wrote Robert M. Shelton, the Imperial Wizard of the United Klans of America, "do you support Lister Hill? His record is greater than Javits.'" For Eastland, the answer was simple. Hill was a regular ally on agricultural issues, the ones that meant the most to him, and racial ones, the most salient of the time, not to mention a Democrat and a friend. As important to Eastland as any other quality was loyalty, and he practiced it even more than he preached it. For Hill, the letter from his senatorial neighbors in Georgia and Mississippi was a godsend, for he prevailed in the only spirited campaign of the seven he waged by less than 2 percent of the vote.[31]

As Lister Hill's critics recognized, Eastland maintained a close professional relationship with John and Robert Kennedy for the rest of their lives. He was closest personally to the attorney general, but once led a visitor to his office to the door the moment that man described the president as a "pinko Commie liberal." Still, the Kennedy whose career Eastland impacted most profoundly was the youngest, Edward M. Kennedy, better known as Ted, who became the most accomplished legislator of the three. Eastland "nearly adopted Ted," remembered Hodding Carter III, the publisher of the Greenville-based *Delta Democrat-Times*. In years to come, if Eastland saw Kennedy at a committee meeting smoking one of the short thin cigars he preferred, he would look over to an aide, catch his attention, then hand him one of his vintage Havana cigars a friend sent him from Europe and tell him to give it to Kennedy and chide him to "to smoke a man's cigar." A meeting that Kennedy loved to recount in a drawl miming Eastland's was one where Eastland called Kennedy in to give him his subcommittee assignments. In an initial meeting, Kennedy walked to Eastland's office, found Eastland greeting him warmly, then suggesting that the thirty-year-old freshman use the weekend to decide which panels he preferred. Kennedy called those he respected most, including his brother Jack, and determined that he would like to work on issues like civil and constitutional rights. Still, he suspected that his chances of landing on any of his desired committees were limited, both because of his inexperience and his status as the president's brother.[32]

The very next Tuesday, Eastland called Kennedy in to see him just before 10:00 A.M. Upon entering his chairman's office, the newest and youngest senator heard a query well known to older colleagues, but one usually delayed until after 5:00 P.M. "Bourbon or scotch?" Eastland asked. "Scotch," Kennedy replied sheepishly, upon which an Eastland aide pulled out a bottle of Chivas Regal and poured him a scotch on the rocks, which Kennedy quickly realized was considerably stronger than the drinks he poured himself. "I think I know wha chu wan," Eastland led. "You've got a lot of I-talians up there in Boston, don't you? . . . Drink that drink," he commanded, "and you're on the immigration subcommittee." Kennedy raised his glass to Eastland, then waited for his chairman to walk around his office and turn his back, so he might find a moment to surreptitiously dump what was left of his fiery cocktail into a nearby plant.[33]

Eastland poured Kennedy another semilethal Chivas Regal and water, and continued. "You Kennedys always care about the Nigras," he said. "Finish that off, and you're on the civil rights subcommittee." This was not a problem for him, Eastland knew. "We don't kill the bills in subcommittee," he told Kennedy. "We kill them in full committee." Kennedy nodded, then searched for another chance to dump part of this potent potable into another potted plant. If he desired, Kennedy could be a member of a third subcommittee, even if few senators generally opted for that many. "You're always caring about the, you know, Cons'tution," Eastland said. "Kennedys always talk about the Cons'tution. . . . Finish that and I'll put you on the Cons'tution subcommittee." Kennedy was elated, and more than a bit high on life. He had said next to nothing and wound up with seats on the panels where he could best serve Massachusetts and trumpet the causes dearest to him.[34]

Then, Eastland proceeded to lecture the youngest member of the Senate on how best to get along in the upper chamber. "You want something," he told Kennedy, "you come on over to me. I don't ever want to get a letter from you." Eastland paused before adding that Kennedy's brother Jack was never as effective as he might have been in the upper chamber because too many colleagues believed that he was using "the Senate to run for President." "You may want to run for President someday yourself, but you'll be happier here and make more friends if you'll do your homework. Don't try to avoid the ditch-digging. It's part of the job." In time, the youngest Kennedy came to recognize that he rarely got better advice from anyone. That day, he left Eastland's office after two hours and weaved a path back to his own office after his first nips of the senatorial scotch, just hoping that reporters would accept his assurance that he had been getting his subcommittee assignments rather than broadcast the story that he had zig-zagged with more than a mild buzz.[35]

For the duration of his career, Eastland maintained a close relationship with the family nearest to royalty among Democrats. When Robert Kennedy won a Senate seat from New York in 1964, Eastland insisted that he follow the time-honored traditions of the upper chamber for his first few months on his new job. "Young man," he once said, "be quiet and listen to the committee." But Eastland soon found that Kennedy's experience at the Justice Department was an invaluable resource, and he tapped it freely. Often he was heard saying "Bobby suggests this" or "Bobby thinks that" to buttress his side of a discussion or merely provide a point of information. And, it was clear that the third Kennedy brother appreciated his tutelage, for he gave a copy of *To Seek a Newer World*, a book that he had written, to Eastland and inscribed it, "Jim, it's not too late" just above the title. Eastland found work for the youngest Kennedy as well. It had been his intention to resist mightily a bill to transform immigration law by allowing the admittance of many more newcomers from many other parts of the world than Europe. But once he determined that there was no way he could block it, he ceased all such efforts and allowed a young Ted Kennedy to steer it—and take credit for steering it—to its approval.[36]

It was Eastland's practice for much of his career to drive the thousand miles home from Washington once a year, primarily to take his car back so he might use it over the Christmas holidays. Friday, November 22, 1963, was the day he embarked on his traditional Thanksgiving journey. He reached U.S. Route 11 in the Shenandoah Valley of Virginia by mid-afternoon, then peered out windows on either side of his car and noticed one and then several flags at half staff. Quickly, he turned on his radio. The man being honored was not a fallen local soldier or policeman, he learned, but the leader of the free world, John F. Kennedy, whose all-too-short life had been taken in a "senseless and dastardly" assassination. Like the rest of America that dark day, Eastland was stunned by the loss of a man he found a "rare combination" of a "scholar and . . . man of action," endowed with unmistakable "intelligence, courage, energy, compassion, determination, and dedication." Yet Eastland was enough of a Washington insider to recognize that passing legislation had never been John F. Kennedy's strong suit, either as a senator or as president. For Eastland, the change was ominous, for he and Southerners felt certain they had civil rights legislation "blocked" for at least as long as Kennedy was president. But that would soon change. Lyndon Johnson, in contrast, the man who would take Kennedy's place, was the most formidable manipulator of Congress since the days of Franklin D. Roosevelt, if not the most formidable ever. "Good God," Eastland was heard to exclaim, "Lyndon's president. He's gonna pass a lot of this damn fool stuff."[37]

CHAPTER 13

Big Jim and a Larger-Than-Life Texan

ON A PERSONAL LEVEL, NO PRESIDENT WAS CLOSER TO EASTLAND THAN Lyndon Baines Johnson. Even more than Eastland, LBJ relished the behind-the-scenes approach to lawmaking. "Lyndon wouldn't ask you to do something," Eastland would say, "he'd tell you." Over the dozen years the two served jointly as senators, Johnson tended to defer to Eastland on questions relating to the interests of the cotton farmers who formed such a large portion of their constituencies. Until 1956, both fought all efforts to guarantee the protections in the Fourteenth and Fifteenth Amendments. But that year, Johnson determined that their party's interests and his national ambitions rested on his ability to pass laws strengthening mechanisms that protect those rights. Once the egalitarian strains of the Johnson persona took hold, the "Sage of the Pedernales" was often heard while strategizing to pass those bills deriding Eastland's single-minded opposition. "Jim Eastland could be standing here in the middle of the worst Mississippi flood ever," he would declare, "and he'd say the niggers caused it, helped out some by the Communists." Still, Eastland believed Johnson was the shrewdest politico he ever encountered, and the two remained friendly. One of the few invitations the thirty-sixth president extended in the last two months of his life was to Eastland and oilmen D. A. Biglane and H. L. Hunt to visit his ranch for a weekend of hunting.[1]

In the immediate aftermath of the Kennedy assassination, Eastland and Johnson were in close contact. The Judiciary Committee was one of several panels one would assume might hold hearings on the killings of the late president and his likely assassin, Lee Harvey Oswald. Several senators had gone to Eastland and encouraged just that course. For his part,

Eastland used the occasion to introduce legislation making the assassination of a president a federal crime. Johnson feared the bill might call up a significant states' rights issue, but he told Eastland six days after assuming office that he was even more certain that too many investigations would open up a Pandora's box replete with "very explosive" leaks that might harm America's national security. Eastland concurred and agreed to defer action until Johnson got back to him about the superpanel he would create to probe the matter. The next evening, the new president phoned Eastland, read him the text of his announcement that he would be forming a commission chaired by Chief Justice Warren, and explained why he chose each member. Eastland listened intently until Johnson announced who would be in charge, then interjected that he would have preferred the selection of Associate Justice John Harlan to Warren. There, Johnson butted in to say he had to give the panel credibility by putting the chief justice in charge rather than a mere associate justice. Eastland understood and acquiesced without complaint to the new president's near command that he protect his "flank over there in the Senate."[2]

Blind opposition to any president was never Eastland's *modus operandi*, and this was especially true in these tragic circumstances. He had supported a Kennedy-Johnson bill to cut taxes 30 percent across the board, telling a friend that he had "found that the best way ... to curtail spending is to curtail revenues." He managed the cotton section of Johnson's 1964 farm bill, saying that the new proposal would cost the taxpayer $118 million less and subsidize textile mills in a way that would make cotton competitive with artificial fibers like rayon so that cotton farmers could "compete with the DuPonts." And when Johnson used his vacancy on the Supreme Court to nominate longtime Democratic consigliere Abe Fortas, it was Eastland who effectively burst the balloon of one hapless critic. Having known Fortas, a politically astute liberal from Memphis, for a while, he retained hope that Fortas might develop into a judicial conservative, much as Felix Frankfurter had. So, when Marjorie Shearon, the publisher of an obscure right-wing tome known as the *Challenge to Socialism*, tried to lambaste Fortas because some who served alongside him in the Agricultural Adjustment Administration of the 1930s were Communists, Eastland effectively quieted all dissent by demanding to know what that had to do with the nominee.[3]

Yet there were many pieces of legislation during the early 1960s that Eastland could not support. While he often voted with Kennedy and Johnson's moves to expand trade, he remained unalterably opposed to any new agreements with the Soviet Union like the Nuclear Test-Ban Treaty of 1963. While he objected to the Appalachian Regional Development Act because it eliminated language that had funded projects in Mississippi, he strongly opposed Medicare and Medicaid and repealing Section 14B of the Taft-Hartley Act, which allowed states to enact right-to-work laws. Eastland was especially opposed to any federal aid to education. Here was a program he found "parasitic," as the national government through an "erosive usurpation of power" might eventually take children from their families and make them "ward[s] of the state." Any time between 1961 and 1969 when it appeared that the Office of Education might acquire more in the way of authority or funding, Eastland resisted. "I wouldn't vote a red turd to Doc Howe," he said in 1966 of Harold Howe II, Johnson's commissioner of education who ended funding for federal programs in some Mississippi counties that continued to delay compliance with desegregation orders. Still, Eastland took care as to how he worded his critiques. "Lyndon reads the *Congressional Record*," he told aides. Clearly, however, his was one of the more conservative voting records in Congress, one he trumpeted for home consumption as that of just "another Southern reactionary."[4]

On no issue was Eastland's posture more obvious than on civil rights. In his first address to Congress as president, Lyndon Johnson made it clear that he would force the issue, appealing powerfully to members that they could give their "fallen leader" no greater tribute than to enact his legislative program, especially his civil rights bill. All along, Eastland warned that the South was "in for a fight." He called one bill drafted in the Justice Department the "greatest single executive grasp for power" in history. There would be all-night sessions, he knew, and he reveled in pointing out that it was northern senators who cried "calf rope" the last time that this tactic was employed. Thinking that it would take "time for the implications of this program to sink in," he opened hearings and recruited some of America's more respectable segregationists to make their case. When Robert Kennedy took the stand to testify for the measure, Sam Ervin engaged the attorney general in a lengthy question-and-answer session that ended only when Eastland resorted to using an archaic Senate rule that required him to adjourn the hearing while the full Senate was in session. Kenneth Keating, a liberal Republican from New York with an eye for publicity, suggested that committee sessions be held at night, after floor business had concluded. When Eastland denied this request, Keating suggested that the panel hear witnesses in Birmingham, Alabama, where Eugene "Bull" Connor, that city's outgoing sheriff, just three months earlier had subjected demonstrators, many of them mere teenagers, to attacks by police dogs and sprayings from quite powerful fire hoses. Just as Eastland intended, action on the bill reflected Keating's view that the hearings were "rapidly approaching the appearance of a committee filibuster."[5]

Majority Leader Mike Mansfield knew Eastland far too well to suspect that he would do anything other than try and bottle up the House-passed measure in his Judiciary Committee. He thus awaited the messenger from the junior chamber carrying the bill at the door of the Senate so he could physically intercept it before Eastland could move that it be referred to his panel. Once Mansfield took control of the measure, he took it to the well of the Senate and asked the body to put the bill on the calendar immediately. "The reasons for unusual procedures," he said, "are too well known to require elaboration."[6]

Here was the fight of fights that segregationists would wage to preserve their way of life. All knew the stakes. "When they get the vote," Eastland told Washington lawyer Lloyd Cutler one afternoon, "I won't be talking this way any more." In contrast, Hubert Humphrey, the bill's manager, had worked closely with Eastland on many farm bills over several years and realized that he would have to use every resource at his disposal. "They have to die in the trenches," Humphrey told a reporter. Obstruction was "what they were sent here for. They're old and they haven't any recruits. They know it—one of them said to me you simply have to overwhelm us, and so we have to beat them to a pulp." Just as determined was Lyndon Johnson, who knew his onetime colleagues represented electorates with white majorities far greater than their white proportions of their states' populations and depended on their votes. The president saw part of his job as determining when the solons of segregation had earned their salaries and then ending debate at just that point. He told Richard Russell early in 1964 that he knew he owed Russell for facilitating his rise, but there would be no compromise or "falling back" on this measure. He would see that it would pass.[7]

Eastland was well aware that his side would lose. When he first came to the Senate in 1941, he wrote a friend, the South could count not just on the votes of senators from the eleven states that comprised the Confederacy but also those of Kentucky, Maryland, and Oklahoma. That had long since ceased to be true. Neither he nor any of his cohorts expected to bring around anyone from outside the South, nor would they exert pressure behind the scenes. "You never ask a politician to do something he cannot do," he often admonished younger associates. The quiet bravery of civil rights demonstrators, some old and some in their early teens, the previous year in Birmingham had swung national opinion away from any further sympathy with the defenders of the old order. What Southerners could do would be to try and delay the inevitable as long as possible and create a legislative record that would serve them well with their constituents or possibly point out the errors of those pushing for a more integrated society. The only other way the South might "ride the storm," he wrote friends, would be if his colleagues from other parts of the country inserted provisions that would scare away moderate-to-conservative swing votes. That he knew would not happen, for Senate leaders were as determined as Johnson to secure passage of a bill that would not just win popular approval but bring America closer to its promise of equal opportunity for all.[8]

Eastland enjoyed nothing more during the course of a civil rights debate than pointing out northern hypocrisies. As far back as 1946, he had phoned *Delta Democrat Times* publisher Hodding Carter Jr. to inquire about a reference Carter had made in a *Saturday Evening Post* piece to de facto segregation in Ohio. This debate was no different. Once speeches began, Eastland employed this tack often. In an early colloquy, he told Jacob Javits that "If we are to have integration, it must apply in New York and in other states as it would in Mississippi." A month later, he bemoaned the lack of coverage reporters devoted to beatings of civil rights demonstrators in New York City. Had they happened in Mississippi, he said, there would be a plethora of charges of "police brutality." And, he took the time to air a conversation with Allen Ellender, perhaps the single fiercest Senate opponent of civil rights, about their sense that many southern blacks who had moved north from their states to cities like Chicago were returning home as they could not abide the horrid "slum conditions" they found. But unlike previous debates, proponents of civil rights had senators on the floor at all times to counter the claims of their opponents, and they conducted themselves with a gentility often associated with the South. The member present while Eastland and Ellender were airing their opposition was Paul Douglas, the aging Keynesian economist from Illinois, who pointed out graciously that thousands of the migrants were staying in the north both because of better opportunities and that conditions in even the worst neighborhoods offered more hope than those they had left.[9]

There would be no facet of the bill that Southerners would not challenge. From years of practice, all knew their roles. Their leader was Richard Russell, a Georgian with an aura of authority and an unmatched knowledge of the body's rules. A Senate stalwart for more than three decades who acknowledged that he did not feel comfortable living in the twentieth century, Russell shepherded his flock into platoons. Younger men from states from the Upper South were expected to be a bit more restrained. Sam Ervin would emphasize the Constitution. Members like Eastland from the Deep South might employ a bit more bombast. They would resist everything, beginning on February 26, 1964, the day Russell objected to Mike Mansfield's motion to place the House-passed bill directly on the Senate calendar. Once the upper chamber voted 54–37 to overrule Russell, Southerners talked for sixteen days on whether to move to consider the bill. Eastland participated early and often. In one memorable early exchange, he argued that the absence in the bill of a definition of the word discrimination rendered possible the notion that some bureaucrat could gain the power of a "Khrushchev, Nasser, or Hitler" and assume a blank check no member of Congress had ever contemplated. Such authority, he said, enhanced the chances that the American government might become one of men rather than laws.[10]

Over the next dozen weeks, Eastland interjected himself frequently into the longest debate in the history of the Senate. While he conceded that few blacks were registered to vote in Mississippi, he denied there was any discrimination. Such a statistic could not be measured because the Magnolia State did not keep voting records by race. He described the

House-passed bill as the most "monstrous and heinous piece of legislation that has ever been produced." It was unconstitutional in that its limiting the literacy test denied the rights of states to determine the qualifications of their electorate, and because its provisions allowing certain cases to be moved from state to federal courts constituted a "star chamber" and violated rights guaranteed by the Seventh Amendment. Moreover, Eastland declared that the bill was equally dangerous in that it conferred unprecedented authority upon the Justice Department and an Equal Employment Opportunity Commission.[11]

As Eastland knew, the bill's fate rested upon Johnson's ability to bring aboard GOP Leader Everett Dirksen, the one man who could sway enough senators to carry a vote to cut off debate. Eastland and Dirksen were not just friends but allies in an ongoing fight to delay compliance with Supreme Court orders requiring states to move toward a "one man, one vote" standard of legislative apportionment. But neither Eastland nor any other Southerner could mistake Dirksen's intent when he told reporters of Victor Hugo's admonition that "Stronger than any army is an idea whose time has come." The substitute Dirksen introduced with Mike Mansfield was no compromise, Eastland told colleagues. It was crafted to address the doubts of waverers from the Midwest and West, among them some who had never before cast their ballots to close debate. While Eastland continued his arguments, there would be a 76–18 vote to substitute the Mansfield-Dirksen measure for the House-passed bill and a 71–29 vote to cut off debate. Once cloture was voted, each member could speak but one hour more under the rules. Seventy-three senators cast their lot with Johnson and the Senate leadership. The result was a bitter pill for many Southerners, but one they accepted, as they not only had ample time to make their case, but each proponent had made it a point to treat them kindly. In Eastland's case, both Humphrey and John Sherman Cooper, the moderate Republican from Kentucky, saluted his talents as an attorney. He and other southern solons could go home with their heads held high, knowing that they had given as much for a legislative lost cause as their forbearers had for a military one. They, in turn, would be gracious in defeat, with most rushing to shake the hand of Hubert Humphrey, the happy legislative warrior with a masters' degree from Louisiana State University who had captained the fight against them.[12]

Just two days later, reports appeared that three civil rights workers, James Chaney, a black plasterer from Meridian, Mississippi, Michael Schwerner, a Brooklynite who headed the Meridian office of the Mississippi Summer Project, and Andrew Goodman, a Queens College student, were missing. The three had been arrested by a Neshoba County deputy on the afternoon of June 21, and they were released at 10:00 P.M. that night. The next day, civil rights workers contacted the office of the Congress of Racial Equality in Jackson and told them they had heard nothing more. Concern mounted as friends and family of the three men began calling for help. Eastland phoned Johnson at 3:59 P.M. on June 23 and told the president that he presumed that the disappearance of the three was a "hoax." His sense that the incident might be a "publicity stunt" arose both from his distrust of the civil rights community and initial reports he attributed to the Congress of Racial Equality that the men were missing. The part of east-central Mississippi where the three were heading had not been as much the focal point of racial violence as some parts of southwestern Mississippi had been in the immediately preceding years. Over the past six months, five blacks had been murdered in Amite County, without a single indictment being presented. The unsolved case that attracted more attention from law enforcement officials than any other was the disappearance of two nineteen-year-old black males unconnected with the civil rights movement last seen hitchhiking near Meadville fifty days before. Still, Klan membership and activity had skyrocketed statewide over the first half of 1964. The White Knights of the Ku Klux Klan had infiltrated the state highway patrol and many county police forces. One was Neshoba, where Klansmen had initiated a new round of cross burnings.[13]

Minutes after Eastland got off the phone with Johnson, the president learned from FBI Director J. Edgar Hoover that a Choctaw Indian had found Schwerner's car smoldering a full eighty feet off the highway. When LBJ called at 4:25 to relay the news, Eastland told him that Governor Paul B. Johnson Jr. suggested that he send "some impartial guy" with an air of *gravitas* to look into the disappearances. Eastland and the governor felt sure that the president and whoever he sent would get the surprise of their lives that there was "nothing, no violence" whatsoever. Whenever asked publicly over the next few weeks, Eastland and Governor Johnson kept their disbelief that anything of the sort could occur in their state. Only in early August when the bodies of Schwerner, Goodman, and Chaney were unearthed would Eastland and Governor Johnson find out just how wrong they had been.[14]

Former CIA Director Allen Dulles, the man LBJ chose to lead the probe, discerned almost immediately upon his arrival a considerably greater spike in Klan activity than anyone in Washington was aware. Contrary to images evoked in the film *Mississippi Burning*, there was virtually no FBI presence in the state prior to the two disappearances. Dulles returned after two days, urging, among other things, immediate action to "control and prosecute terroristic activity" by the Ku Klux Klan and the Americans for the Preservation of the White Race and greater collaboration between state and federal law enforcement authorities. Within two weeks, J. Edgar Hoover gave Paul Johnson ninety names of Magnolia State Klansmen and opened an office in Jackson. The governor reciprocated by handing Hoover a list of 1100 members of the hooded order and urging Hoover to have the Justice Department prosecute those responsible for the disappearance, knowing a state jury was unlikely to convict the culprits. Soon, he commenced proceedings to fire the two Klansmen on the state highway patrol and sent some high-ranking officers on the force to the FBI National Academy for thorough training.

As several black churches were bombed in Mississippi the same summer, the point had been reached where neither Johnson, who had been elected in 1963 on a segregationist platform, nor allies like Eastland or John Stennis would excuse further violence. "There will be no hate or prejudice during my administration," he had proclaimed in his inaugural address. He would fight not "for a rearguard action of yesterday, but for our share of tomorrow." Governor Johnson, the one with enforcement authority, made known his intent to maintain "law and order" and traveled to areas where violence seemed eminent and leveled with their leaders about how counterproductive this would be. Allies like Bolivar County Sheriff Charlie Capps got friendly editors not to publish stories about out-of-state demonstrators that might escalate aggravations segregationists might feel, then went to Klansmen and threatened to jail any who burned a cross or circulated even a single leaflet. He reined in the MSSC by cutting funding for the *Citizens Council Forum* and seeing to it that the MSSC withdrew from circulation *Oxford USA*, a documentary that blamed federal marshals for the rioting at Ole Miss in 1962. Eastland, for his part, took to seeing that prominent civil rights workers like a grandson of onetime Connecticut Republican Senator Hiram Bingham were protected so conspicuously by state highway patrolmen that it made organizing black neighborhoods like those in Sunflower County next to impossible. And, he advised mayors like Charles Dorrough of Ruleville to ensure that young black women were taught to work in local factories so as to placate federal investigators and because they soon might need black votes. When Dorrough complied and found a cross burning on his lawn, Eastland drove to Ruleville and lauded Dorrough at that town's white school. And while the MSSC collected information on the Council of Federated Organizations, a student-based coalition of civil rights groups dedicated to serving the interest of poor blacks in the Delta, it devoted just as much time to keeping tabs on the Ku Klux Klan and Americans for the Preservation of the White Race by the end of 1964. In prior years, it would behoove any civil rights leader to contemplate such actions, but Elmore D. Greaves, the publisher of the Jackson-based *Southern Review*, a neo-Confederate biweekly, was chastising both Johnsons and Eastland as scheming "leftists."[15]

Yet while Eastland, Johnson, and the rest of the state's elected leadership had repudiated violence, they had not embraced a biracial society. They reflected the large majority of their white constituents in their continuing critiques of any move toward "racial balance." While violence subsided somewhat over the next year, freedom schools were burned to the ground in Laurel and Indianola and several cars carrying Freedom Summer volunteers were run off the road. The degree to which things had not changed was reflected in the Indianola incident, where police not only arrested the arsonist in early 1965 but eight civil rights workers who they said had obstructed their investigation. Many who complied with the Civil Rights Act did so reluctantly. The Mississippi Economic Council delayed urging compliance with the new law for nearly a year. Greenwood drained both its white and black public pools rather than allow whites and blacks to swim together. Jackson's Robert E. Lee Hotel closed its doors rather than house a single African American. But like a key part of the business community that appeared during the Ole Miss crisis and reemerged in the shame of the Neshoba County killings, Eastland had to face the reality that national firms would not relocate to Mississippi until it fully renounced violence. Just as importantly, he and other leaders of white Mississippi recognized that they faced an emboldened black community. By midsummer, Aaron "Doc" Henry, the Clarksdale pharmacist who had replaced the slain Medgar Evers at the helm of the state NAACP, vowed to boycott any business that did not treat African Americans as equals. And within the year, Governor Johnson was conceding that some who had fought integration were "not only the architects, but we helped build the doghouse we now find ourselves in."[16]

Though it all, Eastland and SISS continued to monitor civil rights groups. He was particularly anxious to hear about Communists who might have joined the movement, be they men or women, with or without consequence. Mississippi state officials regularly sent him information that they found damning. In June 1961, M. B. Pierce, the top detective in the Jackson Police Department, provided him with a list of those involved in that year's freedom rides. Later that year, Courtney Pace had SISS look into a request from a McComb resident as to the affiliations of freedom riders Tom Hayden and Paul Potter, but had to advise him that it was unlikely that Hayden at twenty-one or Potter at twenty-two belonged to any Communist groups or fronts. Later in the decade, it was almost an annual rite for Eastland to lament that men and women of the left were "invading" the South and detail each pernicious affiliation he found. Communists were pressing for a "Negro revolution," he would say. One SISS report chided Fidel Castro for trying to "subvert the American Negro against his own government," for example, without adding that they had little success. But most of those he named with information provided to him in some cases from the MSSC were either unknown to the public or well-known to political insiders as attorneys who made their livings defending those on the left.

It was hardly true that SISS did not probe the activities of the more prominent civil rights leaders. J. Edgar Hoover's hatred for Dr. Martin Luther King Jr. guaranteed that SISS would closely scrutinize King's movements and associates. SISS files at the National Archives are full of publications by those who aimed to preserve a segregated society. On Hoover's recommendation, SISS subpoenaed Stanley Levison, a top

King aide whose ties to the left aroused some suspicion. But like many previous witnesses, Levison denied being a Communist, then asserted his Fifth Amendment rights to decline to answer further questions. For his part, Eastland in late 1964 asked Francis McNamara, who managed the House Un-American Activities Committee staff, if King were tied to any Communists. Although there was no evidence that King ever belonged to any Communist group, McNamara replied, he had met with several Communist fronts and sent messages to others allied with his movement. Eastland answered similar inquiries with a summary of articles hailing King from the *Daily Worker* and the *Southern Patriot*, the journal of the SCHW. In some ways, what they did not find flustered Eastland and his staff. Courtney Pace conceded in 1965 that King had been "comparatively careful about keeping any guilty connections with the Communist conspiracy," and that Eastland would not air any material suggesting as much that was not impeccably documented.[17]

Lyndon Johnson had even more trouble with Mississippians in the summer of 1964 as he sought the presidency in his own right. More than 2500 Democrats traveled to Jackson's Masonic temple to elect an alternate delegation to their national convention. To Eastland, the prospect of a challenge under the auspices of the Mississippi Freedom Democratic Party (MFDP) was frightening. Still, his immediate concern was that delegates to his party's national convention might unseat the contingent elected at the virtually all-white state convention, most of whom were considering a vote for GOP nominee Barry Goldwater. Eastland would not attend the convention in Atlantic City, but was determined to keep any political residue from falling upon John Stennis' campaign for reelection or his own bid in 1966. A week prior to the convention, he phoned Johnson to inquire if his state's delegation would be seated. LBJ hemmed and hawed, then said he could not be certain, adding that some radicals remained upset about the murders of Schwerner, Chaney, and Goodman, and their allies on the Credentials Committee were looking favorably upon those aiming to seat MFDP members. The president conceded that Paul Johnson had been "judicious and cooperative" in moving to rid the state of those perpetuating racial violence and prosecuting those who engaged in it. He credited Eastland for intervening with his governor to insure that any further terror would be curtailed. But he expressed chagrin that so few white Southerners backed him, one of their own. East-land assured the president that he had the "red hot" support of Greenville attorney Douglas Wynne, the son-in-law of his ambassador to Australia, and some backing from railway brotherhoods and other unions. While Johnson appreciated his assistance and knew Eastland was doing all he could behind the scenes, he remained fearful that any misstep in the Mississippi controversy might spoil the week he hoped would end with a kind of coronation.[18]

Eastland and Johnson spoke nine times over the next week. At one point, Eastland told LBJ that either Hubert Humphrey or Mike Mansfield would be a good vice president, but advised the president that Mansfield might be a better fit, as his Catholic faith would be an asset in the wake of the Kennedy assassination. Johnson told Eastland that he hoped Mississippi delegates would pledge their loyalty to the nominees, as it might facilitate the acceptance of their credentials. Eastland relayed his message to Paul Johnson, who told him to let the president know that the two of them and John Stennis had exerted every sort of muscle they could to stop their state party from backing Goldwater. When Eastland got back to LBJ, he learned that delegates Douglas Wynne and E. K. Collins had impressed the Credentials Committee, and that that panel would probably seat the official delegation if members signed a loyalty oath. An apprehensive Johnson feared that a potential southern walkout would dampen enthusiasm and thus threaten his chance to earn legitimacy with a huge win of his own. He knew Eastland well enough to know that he could vent. "I'm going to let Goldwater cut out all your subsidies," LBJ blurted, half in jest, "and stop your six billion dollar cotton program." Eastland again phoned Paul Johnson and found that he would go no further than to tell the official delegation to use their own judgment. Upon reporting back, he found LBJ prepared to seat Mississippi close to the door so reporters would find it difficult to cover any departures. In the end, all but three Johnson backers walked out of the convention hall, and even they, feeling uncomfortable, left early. After an impassioned appeal by Fannie Lou Hamer, the MFDP spokeswoman, delegates awarded two seats to MFDP delegates Aaron Henry and Rev. Ed King, a compromise that MFDP leaders rejected. National Democrats assured the MFDP that they would never again condone a segregated delegation from Mississippi or any other state.[19]

Eastland kept a low profile in the fall of 1964. Earlier that year, he was among the many who prompted Ross Barnett not to challenge John Stennis in the Democratic primary. He was surely aware of the appeal of GOP nominee Barry Goldwater, who like him had voted against the Civil Rights Act. In a state where less than 7 percent of the blacks cast ballots, Goldwater carried every county and more than 87 percent of the vote. While Eastland admired Goldwater, whom he knew to be a conservative of principle and candor, he remained loyal to his Democratic roots. Staffers at the Democratic National Committee not only got Eastland to join John Stennis and Governor Johnson, a Goldwater supporter, in meeting the "Lady Bird Special," the name they gave the first lady's four-day whistlestop tour of the South, in Biloxi, but privately saluted him for helping to organize it.[20]

Late in the year, Johnson made known his intention to raise Nicholas Katzenbach to permanent status as Robert Kennedy's replacement as attorney general. Eastland had no objection, even if Katzenbach's positions were almost always well to the left of his own. Still, when Republican Jacob Javits, the liberal from New York, moved for a roll call vote, Eastland felt duty-bound to vote no. Once Katzenbach returned to his office, Eastland gave him a shout. "That goddamned Javits, asking for a roll call," he opened the conversation, "Nick, you know I wanted you to be Attorney General." "That's all right, Senator," the shrewd but intensely diplomatic Katzenbach shot back. "It's [Eastland's no vote] probably good for both of us."[21]

What emerged as a primary order of business of the new Congress resulted to a large degree from the fact that only 6.6 percent of black Mississippians had voted in 1964. Noting similar results in other Deep South states, civil rights leaders highlighted their concerns in a campaign to end discriminatory practices in Selma, Alabama, a black-majority city where ten times as many whites cast their ballots as blacks in 1964. Early in 1965, Justice Department lawyers began working with Mike Mansfield and Everett Dirksen on a measure to expand federal authority to protect the rights of blacks aspiring to register to vote. While they aimed to move quickly, public revulsion to the murders of three civil rights workers and a brutal Sunday afternoon attack by the Alabama State Police on many more who crossed the Edmund Pettus Bridge en route to Montgomery spurred them to hasten efforts to send a consensus bill to Congress. In a speech the Friday after the Selma police riot, Lyndon Johnson presented the package to a joint session of Congress. What made the speech so memorable was the president using the occasion to chant his Texas-trilled vow that "We shall overcome" the horrors even many northern conservatives decried. But Johnson was uniquely astute tactically. While Dirksen had wanted the president's voting rights bill to be referred to the Judiciary Committee, he made his wishes public before Eastland made it known that he was "opposed to every word and line" and would do all he could to block it. Dirksen abruptly changed his mind and joined Mansfield in adding language requiring the panel to report a voting rights bill within three weeks.[22]

From the outset, many Southerners conceded that they could not win. "I'll have to do my part," Harry Byrd, the elderly Finance Committee chairman told a reporter, "but . . . you can't stop this" and keep denying blacks a "basic constitutional right." Publicly, Eastland declared the three-week limit "wholly inadequate" and promised to fight what he considered "unheard of . . . regional legislation" that mandated action against violators in but six Deep South states, thirty-four North Carolina counties, and parts of Alaska and Arizona where Native Americans formed a large part of the population. As in the past, Eastland sought to rekindle memories of the harsh occupation he believed his homeland had suffered. Not since the time of the "Force Acts of the Reconstruction era," he declared, had any bloc in Congress forwarded such a "heinous and oppressive measure." But while his rhetoric was as strident as ever, the *Washington Post* reported that only Allen Ellender among the southern Democrats was inclined toward a filibuster.[23]

Eastland did go through the motions of fighting the bill. When Nicholas Katzenbach testified before the committee, Eastland tried to deny that some counties still discriminated against black would-be voters. To his chagrin, the attorney general came armed with figures disputing his contention. In Hinds County in 1964, for example, Katzenbach asserted that 92 percent of eligible whites were registered to vote, but only 15 percent of the blacks. Eastland continued and found that Katzenbach had statistics for even his state's smallest counties indicating similar incriminating patterns. The attorney general left the committee room fearing that he had effectively ruined a relationship with a chairman he could not afford to alienate. Not five minutes after he got back to his office, he heard the phone ringing. It was Eastland. "Nick," he said chuckling, "you know too goddamned much about Mississippi," and then hung up.[24]

At various points during the debate, Eastland recycled previous discussions of case law surrounding voting rights, noted the presence of a handful of Communists among those marching for civil rights, declared that the measure deprived affected states of their rights to establish qualifications for their voters, and denied that those who initially imposed poll taxes and literacy tests in the southern states had done so to discriminate. But he had long since abandoned hope that Southerners might block a measure aimed at ending abuses like those Sheriff Clark and others engaged in at Selma. By 1965, Eastland was less apt to try defending segregationists if their rhetoric surpassed any realm of reason. Thus, he murmured not even a grunt when Everett Dirksen lambasted Leander Perez, the longtime boss of Plaquemines Parish, Louisiana, for telling the Judiciary Committee that the Voting Rights Act was part of a "Communist plan." "Now, Mr. Perez," Dirksen exclaimed in his unmistakable baritone, "that is about as stupid a statement as has ever been uttered in this hearing, and it is a reflection on members of the Senate."[25]

Contrary to any prior experience with a civil rights bill, the Senate passed the Voting Rights Act little more than two months after it was introduced. Ever the pragmatist, Eastland was far more engaged by the end of this debate in steering to confirmation James P. Coleman, who Johnson had nominated for a vacant seat on the Federal Court of Appeals. Some billed Coleman's choice as a sop to Eastland, as Coleman had backed him in 1942, but Coleman always described himself as more a part of John Stennis' political family than Eastland's. And, even before 1942, Coleman had befriended Lyndon Johnson. So while Johnson may have wanted to placate Eastland and Stennis, he knew that Coleman was perceived at home as a relatively moderate white Mississippian. His record bore out LBJ's conclusion. Like anyone Mississippi would have elected statewide, Coleman advocated segregation throughout the 1950s. In his

1955 gubernatorial campaign, he promised never to close a public school or allow one to be integrated. Once in office, he signed a law affirming the doctrine of interposition and declared that blacks were "unprepared" to assume the duty of voting. Yet there was another side to Coleman. In 1958, he traveled to Arkansas to campaign for moderate Brooks Hays in his unsuccessful bid for renomination against a segregationist challenger. A year later, he got the FBI's help in finding the lynchers of Mack Charles Parker. When he sought election to a second term after a state mandated four-year hiatus, he was heard declaring that the state's hard line on desegregation had hurt its ability to recruit industry. Indeed, some attributed his narrow loss to Paul Johnson Jr. in 1963 to his calls for an end to "hatred, distrust, rancor, and spite."[26]

Eastland surmised that some civil rights groups would try to paint Coleman as a racist. He quickly took control of the process. He said little in public other than to describe Coleman's talents as those of a "very fine judge" and got conservatives Sam Ervin and Roman Hruska to join him on a subcommittee to consider the choice. While many from the Congress of Racial Equality and the Student Nonviolent Coordinating Committee (SNCC) testified against Coleman, his staunchest critic was Detroit Congressman John Conyers, who described him as a "dedicated and effective segregationist." Eastland opened by calling upon Nicholas Katzenbach to salute Coleman as a man of "genuine political courage." The attorney general added that ten federal judges had certified Coleman's fitness for the bench, and liberal historian James W. Silver, the author of *Mississippi: The Closed Society*, had praised Coleman for keeping extremists "at arm's length." Eastland let Coleman's opponents testify and found time for his liberal colleagues to question him and his critics. The nominee they saw was hardly the caricature some painted. Indeed, Coleman's declarations that segregation was "dead in this country, finished and over as a legal proposition" and that the Civil Rights Act had done "more good toward working our problems out than anything in the past ten years" reassured most. Only liberals Phil Hart and Jacob Javits cast their lot against Coleman in committee. Once the nomination reached the floor, Eastland let the young senator who knew him best manage his confirmation. That member was Robert F. Kennedy, who had dealt with Coleman on matters affecting both the Freedom Riders and the showdown at Ole Miss and sensed that Coleman was not just wise in advising him not to trust Governor Ross Barnett but also a "man of his word." More than anyone alive, Robert Kennedy could reassure skeptics that Coleman would be guided by the law rather than any lingering attachment to the remnants of the *weltanschuung* of the antebellum South. His words assured that only eight liberal idealists would oppose Coleman.[27]

As always, Eastland remained focused on conditions at home. While longtime ally Paul Johnson used his power to urge compliance with the Voting Rights Act to such a degree that segregationists were deriding him as "Crawling Paul," it came to Eastland's attention in the spring of 1966 that those he called "civil rights agitators" aimed to register the black workers on his plantation to vote. He would not stand for such a provocation, and he phoned the attorney general to tell them he would have them arrested for trespassing if they carried out their threat. The way to avert that, Katzenbach replied calmly, was to let local authorities register his work force and those in all other counties. Those on his plantation, he told Eastland, were certain to back him. "I'll do it," Eastland replied. Katzenbach, seeking comity and trusting Eastland, kept federal registrars out of Sunflower County as long as the local registrar followed the guidelines set forth in the Voting Rights Act. Eastland let Katzenbach know he intended to spare himself, his county, and his state any embarrassment. "If she doesn't," he told the attorney general, "you let me know before you send anyone into Sunflower." So while by the spring of 1966 thirteen Democratic congressmen were urging the Justice Department to beef up its crew of registrars, Katzenbach had not received even one complaint from the African-American majority in Sunflower County. Those pressures to enforce the law would come from local blacks affiliated with the MFDP, who took county officials to federal court for continuing to collect poll taxes and not letting black residents know when municipal elections would be held. And although Judge Claude F. Clayton, a jurist originally recommended by Eastland, denied petitions against officials in Doddsville and Ruleville, he did find that authorities in nearby Moorhead and Sunflower had violated the Voting Rights Act and ordered new elections to be held in May of 1967.[28]

Eastland remained a defender of traditional Mississippi practices whenever they came under challenge. Especially conspicuous in 1966 was his opposition to continued funding for the state's Head Start program, which provided food, health care, and preschool education to poor children through the Child Development Group of Mississippi (CDGM). Here, Eastland resorted to his time-tested tack of trying to discredit those groups by using documents provided him by the MSSC to name the radicals among them. While most he named were little known and had even less standing in Moscow, they did fall into his categories of "subversives," "radicals," and "outside agitators." The number of those far to the left of most Americans was sufficient that NAACP Executive Secretary Roy Wilkins, no friend of his, lamented that "Chinese communist elements" were having some effect upon SNCC, Council of Federated Organizations, and other groups. Eastland thus had cover to back John Stennis' effort to deny money to the CDGM, arguing that those funds were sustaining some CDGM workers who were participating in demonstrations. Appropriating money for CDGM, he argued, could "funnel funds into the extreme leftist ... beatnik groups." The proximity of both the CDGM and the MFDP headquarters in Mount Beulah and other towns near the capital and the Delta lent credence to this view. In time, Peace Corps Director R. Sargent Shriver and others opted to steer Head Start funding to a biracial group known as Mississippi Action for Progress that included nationally known local moderates like Hodding Carter III and Aaron Henry. This proved a much safer course politically for Johnson and his men, as some blacks had grown frustrated by the slow pace of change after the hopes raised by the enactments of the Civil Rights and Voting Rights Acts. Never was this more evident than after a racist assailant shot James Meredith on June 6, 1966, in the midst of what began as a solitary "March against Fear." In the wake of the wounding of such a civil rights icon, aggressive young leaders adopted extreme tactics. SNCC, once the most visible of the biracial groups employing nonviolent means to secure rights guaranteed all, began replacing their founders with more radical voices and found money harder to raise. Stokely Carmichael, SNCC's new chairman, proceeded to bar whites from SNCC, renounce his group's nonviolent coda, and employ chants of "black power." His switch led Martin Luther King Jr. to fear that it would blunt the effectiveness of a once nonviolent movement. But, for Eastland, the influx of those from the farther shores of the left was a godsend, as it rendered it more likely that others in all parts of America might find credible his suggestion that some espousing "black power" might be plotting an eventual "Communist invasion" of America.[29]

In 1966, Eastland faced a challenge from an entirely different source. The performance of GOP presidential standard-bearer Barry Goldwater in 1964 led Mississippi Republicans to think they could defeat Eastland. Many in the GOP hoped that chairman Wirt Yerger Jr., one of the few Republicans with contacts in all parts of the state, would make the race. But Yerger opted not to run once Congressman Prentiss Walker, a gregarious forty-five-year-old grocer and poultry farmer from Mize, announced that he would run. While Walker had gained some visibility in Washington when he rode Goldwater's coattails in 1964 to narrowly unseat eleven-term incumbent W. Arthur Winstead, he foolishly assumed that Mississippians had been convinced of his merits as a candidate as much as Goldwater's. Although he had once served on the executive committee of the state Game and Fish Commission and thought that his base in eastern Mississippi and his ties in the poultry community and among fellow fox hunters would make him a viable challenger to Eastland statewide, a more realistic assessment came from conservative columnist Holmes Alexander. To stand a chance of winning, he wrote, Walker needed to fuse all unenthusiastic about Eastland, including not just Republicans, but the NAACP, the Ku Klux Klan, and the AFL-CIO.[30]

Walker never understood the enormity of his task. He described the choice voters would face as one pitting "a conservative Republican" against "a double-standard Democrat." In aiming to convince voters that he stood well to Eastland's right, he made a curious choice, as Eastland had a 93 percent lifetime rating from the American Conservative Union. He blasted Eastland for "hobnobbing and prancing with the Kennedys" in Washington and voting to confirm Justice Abe Fortas; Housing and Urban Development Secretary Robert Weaver, the first African-American Cabinet member; and Francis Morrisey, a Kennedy associate whose nomination for a judgeship Lyndon Johnson had needed to withdraw. But Walker was on truly dubious ground when he tried to get to Eastland's right on racial grounds. Some blacks like Charles Evers, the brother of the slain state NAACP head Medgar Evers, let it be known that they would back a Republican rather than an African American if he stood the best chance of defeating Eastland. "You just don't outsegregate Jim Eastland," declared state AFL-CIO chief Claude Ramsey. Still, Walker, a man with an inflated sense of the numerical strength of the Ku Klux Klan, tried to do just that, making it known that he had attended a meeting of the Americans for the Preservation of the White Race, which many saw as a Klan front.[31] Eastland declined a similar invitation and was proud to boast that both the AFL-CIO and the Klan opposed him. Walker had no more interest in union backing than Eastland, but knew that others ideologically akin to the Ku Klux Klan were upset with Eastland. *Southern Review* publisher Elmore D. Greaves lambasted Eastland for plotting with President Johnson to have a panel looking into the workings of the Klan subpoena him. "The President is trying to wipe out the Ku Klux Klan," he said. "Next will be the John Birch Society." Thinking many in the Magnolia State were just as strident, Walker took to bashing Eastland for not being able to stop any of the four civil rights acts of the previous decade and for voting to confirm seven of the nine judges who sat on a Supreme Court that had outlawed prayer and Bible reading in the schools.[32]

As it turned out, Eastland had ineffectual opposition in his own primary. Some MFDP activists recruited Reverend Clifton Whitley Jr. to challenge him. Their effort received some national attention, as black registration had jumped statewide in less than a year from 30,000 to 130,000. But this was far from enough blacks for Whitley or anyone else the MFDP might have recruited to have stood a chance. Although Whitley surprised many by carrying Claiborne and Jefferson Counties southwest of the Delta, Eastland prevailed in the primary by a better than six-to-one margin, winning, as one wag put it, more votes in both Sunflower County and in the Delta than legal liquor.[33]

At one point in 1966, Eastland got his liberal friend Phil Hart to condemn him in the midst of a Judiciary Committee meeting as an obstructionist. Sam Ervin of North Carolina broke in to interject that Hart was breaching Senate decorum with a personal attack. "For God's sakes, Sam," Eastland commanded, while arching his head to look directly at his committee's next most senior member. "Shut up and sit down. You're ruining the whole thing."[34]

It would have been out of character for any Mississippi Bourbon to refrain from GOP bashing. Eastland feared that a two-party system would harm his state by rendering congressional veterans more susceptible to challenges and forcing both parties to compete for the votes of African Americans, a possibility he found daunting. There remained enough of the post–Civil War world view in Eastland for him to bash the party whose presidential nominee had carried nearly seven-eighths of the state's vote two years earlier as the party of "black Reconstruction, . . . the Hoover rabbit days, school integration, and Earl Warren." Were anyone to miss his intent to cling to his image as the primary Senate voice of die-hard Deep South conservatives, Eastland promised in a newspaper ad run statewide that he had opposed every step of the "Great Society" and would continue to do so. Eastland blasted Walker for not repudiating the support of the "national Republican Party" because it favored integrating hospitals and public schools. He furthered that image by bringing in several well-known critics of all civil rights legislation. Alabama Governor George Wallace campaigned for him in Meridian. Judge Tom Brady hailed him as the man "hated by more minority groups and subversive groups than any other" and one whose loss would cause celebration in the Kremlin. Even more emphatic was Judge Leander Perez, who Eastland brought in to speak in southwestern Mississippi, the area of the state with the largest Ku Klux Klan membership. In one speech, Perez declared that LBJ was still a conservative when both he and Eastland were senators. In an address punctuated by a mere three uses of the word "nigger," a new low for Perez, the longtime boss of that part of Louisiana southeast of New Orleans, bemoaned what a "double-crosser" the president had become.[35]

Eastland opened his formal campaign in Forest on September 29, 1966, with virtually all of the state's Democratic hierarchy present. While Paul Johnson and John Stennis were present, the man Eastland tapped to introduce him was Carroll Gartin, his rival from 1954. As he had before, Eastland defined himself as a "Mississippi Democrat" and pledged never to become a "political prostitute for any national political party." He called for funding to modernize the interstate highway system, particularly those roads that ran through Mississippi, and recalled the work he and other southern Democrats had done since the days of Franklin D. Roosevelt to provide electricity to rural America. As in other parts of the state, he argued for a pet bill to require television networks to institute a blackout of any NFL or AFL football game at times that conflicted with the Friday nights customarily reserved for high school or junior college games. But more than anything, Eastland sought to identify himself as a traditional Mississippi Democrat. Key in conveying this image was Leander Perez, whom Eastland had pooh-pooh the fact that Barry Goldwater would be flying in to speak for Prentiss Walker. Perez also heralded Alabama Governor George Wallace rather than Goldwater (the "Mr. Conservative" of 1964) as the "greatest living conservative."[36]

It thus became imperative for Walker to prove that Eastland was tainted with Great Society liberalism, and he brought Goldwater to Jackson to show gratitude before a crowd of 3500. "I can't remember my friend Jim supporting Goldwater," he said, recalling Eastland's pledge two years earlier to go down the line for the Democratic ticket, before wondering aloud how long Eastland could hold on to his base of power, even if Democrats retained control of the Senate. "Seniority doesn't mean anything," he went on. "It depends on whether his party still wants him." Without Goldwater around, Walker bashed Eastland often for employing the wife of Bobby Baker, the controversial former secretary of the Senate, to manage the records of SISS and for misleading the Citizens Council by telling them that they need not worry about civil rights legislation being passed. Other Republicans reinforced that idea by circulating pictures of Eastland shaking hands with Robert Kennedy. State GOP Chairman Clarke Reed offered a $1000 reward to any voter who could get Eastland or any other local Democrat to sign a pledge not to back any leader of their national party. But many national Republicans grew uneasy with some facets of Walker's approach, particularly his claim that Eastland had been unresponsive to a group like the Citizens Council. GOP Senate Campaign Committee Chairman Thruston Morton denied Walker all but the bare minimum his group could grant. That Walker had failed to impress even many moderate souls who had long been critical of Eastland can be seen in the decision of Greenville's *Delta Democrat Times*, long the state's largest voice for moderate Mississippians, not to endorse either candidate.[37]

The one concern some close to Eastland had was that African Americans might unite behind an opponent. Some black leaders made it clear that they would back anyone but him. But Walker would not even defend himself when Eastland allies pointed out that he, if inadvertently, had awarded Marvell Lang, an African-American constituent, a seat in the Air Force Academy. Even so, some feared that a divided white vote might allow a strong third party candidate to win by a plurality. Most thought that the matter was decided when Eastland trounced Clifton Whitley in the primary. While state law barred unsuccessful primary candidates from appearing on the ballot as independent candidates in the general election, civil rights groups sued to win him a slot. Although they prevailed in court, the verdict came little more than a week prior to the election, hardly time to raise money or mount a campaign, thus ending any chance that Eastland might be defeated.[38]

There was but one downside to Eastland's bid for reelection. Just prior to the election, his campaign manager, Jimmy Walker, was killed after his car slid down an embankment on the Natchez Trace Parkway and hit a tree. At the time of his death at but thirty-one, Walker had accumulated enough respect over his seven years in the State House to chair the Joint Legislative Investigating Committee. Eastland was quick to tell whoever cared to listen of the stage presence and political acumen that he thought would make Walker an ideal candidate for statewide office in this television age. "He has it all," Eastland often told associates and his family, and Walker's tragic death was the only stain that besmirched his campaign.[39]

Eastland worried so little about the election's outcome that he opted to spend election afternoon dining and sipping scotch in downtown Jackson with Bob Hearin, the president of the First National Bank of Mississippi. He could discern how the election would turn by asking one question, "How we doing in the counties?" Whoever answered would give the results of Adams (Natchez) and Alcorn (Corinth) Counties, which were both the first two alphabetically and bellwether domains. If results were as expected, Eastland would know "we're gonna be fine." As anticipated, Magnolia State voters returned him for a fifth term with 65.6 percent of the vote. The 91,175 votes won by Prentiss Walker amounted to but 26.7 percent of the total cast. Clifton Whitley rounded out the field with but 7.7 percent. Although Walker fared best in rural areas, he mustered as much as 31.5 percent only in the Fourth District he had represented. Few eyes were raised when results showed Eastland capturing nearly two-thirds of the white vote, but even he had to be startled when he won a full 47 percent from African Americans.[40]

The Senate Eastland returned to had five fewer Democrats, even if his party retained sixty-two seats. Still, A. Willis Robertson's narrow loss

in Virginia's Democratic primary led many southern Democrats to recognize that they could not remain dominant for much longer. Eastland
wrote a former colleague that the forty-nine seat GOP gain in the House
and concurrent five-seat Senate pickup reflected a "backlash" against the
Great Society and the growing militancy of some protest leaders. The
smaller number of Democrats, he knew, dictated that the pace of the
reforms of the Great Society would decelerate. While he welcomed this,
he insisted that his state get its share of any funds of any federal program,
most notably while working to insure that eighteen northeastern Mississippi counties got funding from programs to aid Appalachia. And, he
recognized that the relative moderation of most elected in 1966 indicated
a public acceptance of those reformers who used traditional channels of
power. No better example could be found than when LBJ chose Thurgood
Marshall, the longtime counsel for the NAACP, to fill a vacancy on the Supreme Court. That Eastland would vote against Marshall, the first African
American ever chosen for the high court, was never in doubt, as Marshall
was too liberal for his tastes. But it was his duty to preside over Marshall's
confirmation hearings. He saw to it that Sam Ervin and John McClellan
got three days to ask Marshall about the rights of defendants and Strom
Thurmond an hour to query him about the history of the Thirteenth
and Fourteenth Amendments. For his part, Eastland asked Marshall no
question more difficult than if he had known when he cited the work of
Herbert Aptheker in an opinion that Aptheker had clear ties to the Communist Party. Once Marshall replied in the negative and that he would not
knowingly reference a Communist in any future ruling, Eastland ceased
his questioning. The vote on Marshall was virtually identical to that taken
on his 1962 nomination for a seat on a federal appeals court. Only ten colleagues joined Eastland in voting against him, all southern Democrats.[41]

At much the same time, Eastland managed the administration's farm
bill, one that contained the provisions extending payments to farmers
who cut their acreage for cotton by roughly one-third and subsidizing the
same farmers a dime a pound on the "white gold" they did sell. In many
ways, this represented a continuation of New Deal programs in which the
government paid farmers not to grow cotton and thereby limited supply, thus raising prices for that prime Mississippi commodity. What this
meant for Eastland and many fellow Delta planters were hefty payments

from Washington. While his father's will stipulated that his grandchildren would inherit the land when the youngest reached twenty-one, Eastland waited until 1971 before he formally gave his children their land. Here was a convenient interval, for many in both parties were pushing to cap such payments at $20,000. In the 1960s, critics often chided Eastland for taking more than $13,000 a month not to grow cotton at a time impoverished residents were getting a welfare allotment of no more than $9.50 a child. Eastland, to be sure, was hardly the only Delta planter pocketing significant amounts. Seventy-seven collected more than $25,000 in 1967 to limit their cotton plots. Eastland spokesmen defended such practices by noting that some funds trickled down to their work forces. But the adoption of mechanical cotton pickers had diminished the number of hands needed to work a plantation. Fewer than half the 400 who worked the Eastland homestead in the 1940s still resided there by the 1960s. Such circumstances were common throughout Mississippi, where half a million fewer African Americans lived in 1950 than had fifty years earlier. Like their white neighbors, young blacks had begun to leave for sites where they could speak and vote their mind and follow their dreams, closer to cities and further to the north.[42]

Eastland's outlook began to budge when he was confronted with dire poverty less than 15 miles from his home. It took Robert Kennedy's visit to the Delta town of Cleveland in the summer of 1967 to showcase widespread hunger that until then had escaped national attention. What aroused Kennedy's interest was a visit by staffer Peter Edelman designed to build support for Head Start programs for poor communities. Edelman learned from Marian Wright, the NAACP Legal Defense Fund attorney he married the next year, that hunger was far more pervasive than he knew. When Kennedy arrived in Cleveland, he visited homes with empty refrigerators and met children with swollen bellies who ate but one meal a day and suffered from rickets, anemia, and malaria. Upon returning to Washington, Kennedy saw to it that the Subcommittee on Employment, Manpower, and Poverty expanded its scope to hear evidence of what they saw, primarily from doctors who treated some of the starving. Eastland and Stennis sat quietly for much of the six-hour session. They took on a defensive air when Dr. A. L. Gray, the head of the state board of health, told Kennedy that any medical volunteers who came to Mississippi would need in-state licenses before they could treat patients in the Delta. Neither Eastland nor Stennis reacted until they thought the doctors had over-stated their case. What spawned their outrage was a claim by Charlotte-based physician Ray Wheeler that some in the state's power structure were trying to drive blacks out of the Delta. While Stennis termed the charge a "gross libel and slander" upon Mississippi, Eastland, more accustomed to living near blacks, however paternalistically, displayed incredulity. Were there a mass outmigration of blacks from the Delta, he said, "I would move out." In time, he signed on as a cosponsor of Stennis' bill to pro-vide $10 million to treat malnutrition where it was proven to exist. This was hardly the sum Kennedy desired, but he deemed it a start—and a change—for both Eastland and Stennis. "We'll take that," he told aides. But while the two could get the bill through the Senate, they could not compel action by the House.[43]

Within his own family, Eastland saw other signs of change. Hiram Eastland Jr., his seventeen-year-old cousin, had been sponsored by the Mississippi American Legion as their representative to the Boys Nation convention and was considering a race for the presidency of that group. There, Hiram encountered an African-American youth from Texas with rare eloquence, Alan Keyes, who later achieved ambassadorial status and ran several times for the Senate and the presidency. A realist, Hiram rec-ognized Keyes' forensic skills and threw his support to Keyes' presidential candidacy at a crucial time. The first Eastland aide to hear what he had done was Clarence Pierce, who happened to be near the convention. He would have to tell his boss, Pierce said. Not sure what to expect, Hiram perspired a bit the next time he visited the chairman of the Judiciary Committee. "They tell me you supported a nigra for president of Boys Nation," Eastland declared. "Why'd you do that?" Keyes, Hiram replied, was the most articulate and most qualified of any of the youths being considered. Jim Eastland thought for a moment, then pulled his cigar from his mouth. "Well, I just want to tell you, you did the right thing."

The very next day, young Hiram got a similar message at the White House. "Young man," said Lyndon Johnson, "that was the right thing you did for the great state of Texas." The president then leaned down and in-quired if Hiram could "get Jim to help me out on civil rights." Two genera-tions younger than his cousin and considerably more enlightened, Hiram

Eastland had no problem telling Johnson that he would try, however futile such efforts would be. He told the senator of his inquiry and got him to chuckle. "That's just like Lyndon," Jim Eastland said to his young cousin. "He never misses a political opportunity."[44]

To Eastland's chagrin, Johnson had another civil rights bill in mind. Unlike previous bills, the fair housing provisions of this one affected northern as well as southern domains and the votes of their solons were not certain. Everett Dirksen was one Eastland knew to believe that the new measure had to be tweaked, and Dirksen's support for the two prior bills had been determinative. "Big Dirk," Eastland asked one day, "how about those real estate provisions?" On those, Dirksen admitted "grave doubts." His concerns reflected those of the real estate lobby, as the sections denying discrimination in the sale of a house violated the private property rights of individuals. Eastland sympathized on legal grounds, but he was far more happy to stoke anxiety about the increasing visibility of those like Stokely Carmichael. At first, he forwarded amendments to bar anyone from boycotting firms they believed were discriminatory or blocking entrances to public offices. Here were measures designed to direct public ire at those in dissent, rather than win support. In a few weeks, he adopted a path of obstruction, crafting four dozen amendments. But the inability of members to reconcile principles of open housing and private property meant that Republicans and southern Democrats had blocked an end to debate for a while. But such a coalition was short-lived, for younger GOP senators concluded that another bill was needed to calm tensions like those so evident in the deadly riots in Detroit and other cities in 1967 to dispel the idea that they were not just an obstacle to racial progress, but the principal one. Chief among them was Howard Baker, then best known as Dirksen's son-in-law, who began putting their ideas on paper. After contemplating all options, Dirksen realized that he could push a measure that preserved the right of individuals to sell their homes to anyone they desired, but made part of any realtors license provisions that they not discriminate against any potential buyer on the basis of race. As he had on past civil rights bills, Johnson yielded to Dirksen's judgment, even on which further appendages had to be added to secure the votes of enough members to invoke cloture. Here Eastland could forward legislation forcing the North to live under the same rules he thought that its members had forced upon the South. But even he had to relent once he realized that Johnson's acceptance of Dirksen's compromise meant that the last of the monumental civil rights legislation of the 1960s would become law.[45]

While Johnson remained resourceful, his appeal among Democrats had declined because of public discontent with America's continuing involvement in what seemed to be a no-win war in Vietnam. Uncertain he could be nominated again, he phoned Eastland the last day of March 1968 to tell him he would announce that he would not seek another term. Only weeks before that year's Democratic convention did Johnson and Eastland have a chance to meet at length. With many Democrats distancing themselves from Johnson, the president tracked down Eastland in Mexico, where he was scouting stud Charolais bulls for the cattle ranch he operated in Warren County with D. A. Biglane, the largest oil producer in Mississippi, and Otha Shurden, his closest friend in Sunflower County. On their way home, Eastland heard Johnson insisting that they visit him at his ranch, and they agreed reluctantly to call on their increasingly isolated president. It was Lady Bird Johnson who was waiting when they landed. When she gave them a tour of the ranch, the first lady was surprised to hear Eastland suggest that her husband accept a draft if one emerged and she firmly dispelled Eastland of any notion that LBJ might accept the nomination even it were offered. The president was more interested in hearing the thoughts of Shurden, a scarcely educated farmer, than either Biglane or Eastland, as Shurden had a rare capacity for sizing up the value of a piece of land. But he was also interested in the perceptions of each as to how southern whites were handling civil rights laws, as he had become frustrated with the militancy of the black community. In Johnson's view, the civil rights revolution "simply got out of hand." Few understood Johnson's anxieties better than denizens of the Deep South, and they took care to be gentle in explaining the costs local communities had to bear to comply with federal guidelines. This merely added to Johnson's concerns, for he could not be certain in these troubled days if he could maintain the egalitarian "Great Society" as a civil society as well.[46]

Without question, the Johnson decision of 1968 that most perturbed Eastland was that to elevate Associate Justice Abe Fortas to succeed retiring Chief Justice Earl Warren, then to nominate federal Court of Appeals

Judge Homer Thornberry, a former Texas congressman, to fill the seat Fortas would be leaving. On June 15, the day before LBJ announced that he would nominate the two, Eastland told White House congressional liaison Mike Manatos that Fortas could not be confirmed. Eighteen Republican senators had already announced that they believed that the next person selected for the Supreme Court should be chosen by the president elected the following November and hence would oppose any Johnson nominee. Even more intended to follow the same course. Not at all happy, Johnson tracked down Eastland en route to a wedding in Hattiesburg and laid upon him a fifty-minute dose of the "Johnson treatment," long enough to get the chairman to fear that he might miss the wedding, albeit not to change his mind. "Jim," Johnson said, "I've done you a lot of favors and I want you to have Abe Fortas confirmed." Nothing doing, Eastland responded. It would be "political suicide" for him or any Mississippian to vote to elevate any regular ally of Earl Warren. Not only was there no chance that the Senate would confirm Fortas, he told Johnson, the nomination would "tear this country up." Under normal circumstances, Johnson would have taken Eastland's advice to heart, for he knew him as one of his best sources on what Republicans might do. But this time, Johnson's loyalty to Fortas rendered him unable to fathom what Eastland meant. The president pondered Eastland's reply, then opted to assess the degree of Eastland's opposition. "Will you let him out of the Judiciary Committee?" "Yes," Eastland responded, "at my own time."[47]

In the midst of the hearings, Eastland found himself an unwitting participant in one of the more peculiar instances among the bevy of airplane hijackings that plagued American travelers that summer. Eastland as always worked until midafternoon, then had an aide drive him to the Baltimore airport. His trip of July 12 seemed routine, until he ran into a traffic jam. Get on the shoulder of the road, he told James W. Ziglar, then just twenty-two but a future Supreme Court clerk and Senate sergeant of arms. That's against the law, Ziglar replied. Step on it, Eastland ordered, and Ziglar got Eastland to Baltimore in plenty of time to catch his flight to Houston, the first stop on a trip to Mexico.[48]

Once the plane took off, Eastland ordered a drink. After about an hour, as the plane was flying over Nashville, he got up to answer the call of nature. But before he reached the restroom, he felt a silver-plated .45

automatic in his back and heard an unfamiliar voice saying, "I'm going to kill you." Unlike many other hijackers of 1968, the perpetrator was not a left-wing dissident who wanted asylum in Cuba, but a former mental patient. Eastland determined quickly that the man, Oran Daniel Richards, had not pointed his gun at him because of his position, but because Eastland stood between the cockpit and him, and so he returned to his seat. Other passengers stayed calm even while they were certain from the way the plane was turning and the position of the sun that they were en route to Havana. Once a flight engineer persuaded Richards to hand over his gun, the pilot could bring the plane down in Miami. While not the destination most had in mind, the passengers were relieved. Eastland opted to return to Washington, knowing he, the most prominent American to experience the hijacking other than television host Allen Funt, would have to meet reporters as soon as the plane landed. He approached the microphones upon arriving in the terminal and tried to describe what happened quickly. He resisted attempts to call for sweeping new legislation and rehashed a standard theme that lenient Supreme Court rulings had made it possible for "criminals to run wild." Here was a point where Eastland thought voters would understand if he were as blunt on camera as he was in meetings with colleagues. Still, staff and friends recoiled when he said not once, but twice, what was foremost on his mind. "I gotta pee," he blurted.[49]

A day or two later, Ziglar cringed a bit. He told his wife what he knew Eastland would say his first day back at the office and could only smile internally when Eastland did just that. "God damn it, Jimmy," Ziglar knew he would hear from his boss, "if you hadn't broken the law, none of this would have happened to me."[50]

In fighting Fortas, Eastland and other conservatives opted to stress a number of the Warren court's decisions on obscenity cases they found permissive. Eastland dispatched new press secretary Larry Speakes to a photography shop on Capitol Hill to make some 8 × 10 prints of the more graphic scenes from some of the more explicit films. Day after day, they found senators stopping by the Judiciary Committee's offices for thorough and intensive reviews of the evidence that Speakes had developed. One senator was heard saying that one of the films was "so sick" that he "couldn't even get aroused." Senate Democratic Whip Russell Long sympathized for a different reason, finding "one Fortas film ... enough."[51]

As Eastland promised, he delayed hearings until after both parties held their conventions. His tack gave critics time to develop their cases, privately and in the court of public opinion, and Fortas had given them plenty to work with. Eastland opened by asking Fortas if he while a justice had recommended several Johnson aides for higher executive branch posts. Fortas denied the suggestion, an assertion many senators suspected was less than candid. As it turned out, Fortas not only had suggested that several aides be promoted, but had also advised Johnson on political questions as sensitive as the steel strike and Detroit riots of 1967 and even Vietnam policy. But many to the right of center were even more concerned about the general drift of the Warren court. For them, Eastland wrote that the court had "swept aside principles and shattered precedents" that had "formed the foundation of our system for almost two centuries." Strom Thurmond spoke for that bloc at the hearings when he tried to pound into Fortas the notion that the court's decisions in cases like *Mallory v. United States* where convicted criminals, even some who had confessed to what they had been accused of, were set free on technicalities. Eastland also picked up the mantle of groups like the Citizens for Decent Literature who declared that Fortas had cast the decisive vote in forty-nine cases where the court would not sanction films deemed obscene or their makers. "The upsurge in smut literature," Eastland said, was "poisoning our society." But what hammered the last nail in the coffin of Fortas' nomination was the finding that the $30,000 he had taken to teach a course at American University had been put up not by the law school, but rather by five businessmen who might some day have business before the Supreme Court. The committee sent Fortas' name to the full Senate by a mere 11–6 vote, hardly a ringing endorsement. Indeed, the only shaky votes on the panel were from some who had voted for Fortas, like Everett Dirksen and Roman Hruska. When Democratic leader Mike Mansfield tried to get the full Senate to shut off debate in early October, he could muster but a 45–43 margin, far short of the two-thirds majority needed to invoke cloture and compelling enough to prompt Fortas to ask Johnson to withdraw his nomination.[52]

The choice of a new chief justice would thus fall upon the next president. On the question of who that president should be, Eastland was quiet. The safe position at home was to back former Alabama governor George Wallace, the nominee of the American Independent Party who carried more than 67 percent in Mississippi. But backing Wallace would have subjected Eastland to charges of party disloyalty and rendered him vulnerable to a challenge to his chairmanship. The same would be true if he backed GOP nominee Richard Nixon. Publicly, Eastland still held that the development of a viable second party might result in the splitting of the white vote in Mississippi. Outside of the South, he had often quietly assisted the campaigns of friendly GOP colleagues, especially those on the Agriculture and Judiciary Committees. As early as 1947, he saluted Herbert Hoover, long the principal target of Democratic rhetoric, for providing relief to those affected by the Mississippi River flood of 1927 and those rendered homeless and near starvation by World War I. But Eastland also recalled that the GOP was not just the party of those responsible for Reconstruction but also that of those who enacted the first civil rights bills. His place was still the Democratic Party. During the Johnson presidency, Eastland always supported his foreign policies, especially those towards Southeast Asia. However much Eastland admired Robert F. Kennedy until the day of his assassination, he would not align with Kennedy's steadily sharpening critique of America's involvement in Vietnam. Thus, once Johnson withdrew from the race, Eastland and John Stennis privately promoted the candidacy of Vice President Hubert Humphrey, however liberal he remained on domestic issues. By late July, Eastland was heard ruing that Humphrey's candidacy had not caught fire and guessed that only LBJ among potential Democratic nominees could carry more than one or two southern states. Still, Eastland remained loyal to his party. One can never discern exactly how another might act in the privacy of the voting booth, especially if that soul never so much as suggests publicly how he or she may have marked their ballot. While twenty-three-year-old son Woods Eastland used his first vote to join just 13 percent of Mississippians in casting their ballots for Richard Nixon, there is not a scintilla of evidence to suggest that Eastland in 1968 did anything but hold true to his Democratic heritage and cast his vote for Humphrey.[53]

Eastland remained loyal to fellow southern Democrats. One faced with an interparty challenge in 1969 was Majority Whip Russell Long, his neighbor from Louisiana whose alcoholism had become increasingly visible. The man liberals pegged to contest Long in late 1968 was Edward M. Kennedy, whose stature had grown with the assassination of a second of his older brothers. When Kennedy tracked Eastland down at his cattle ranch near Vicksburg, he heard a familiar, "Wha' chu wan', Kenn-dy." Kennedy was running to be Whip. "That job ain't vacant," Eastland replied before inquiring about why. "I think I should," Kennedy replied. "Shee-it," Eastland retorted, not expecting that the thirty-six-year-old would dislodge a respected Senate veteran like Long by a vote of 31–26.[54]

Neither Kennedy's victory nor Richard Nixon's disheartened Eastland. The "Southern Strategy" Nixon employed to win the Republican nomination in 1968 gave him hope that the Deep South might stave off desegregation for another few years. But those observing Jim Eastland from strictly the prism of civil rights generally missed another key truth. Whereas the notoriety of Jim Eastland sprung from his commitment to fighting what he described as the Second Reconstruction, he was every bit as determined to install in high offices in both the executive and judicial branches of government men and women committed to his law-and-order philosophy. On these issues, Richard Nixon would prove a staunch ally.

CHAPTER 14

The Best Chairman

THE ONE AREA WHERE JIM EASTLAND TRULY DISTINGUISHED HIMSELF IN the eyes of his peers was at the helm of the Judiciary Committee. "You will have the best chairman in the Senate," Nicholas Katzenbach told liberal Maryland Republican Charles McCurdy "Mac" Mathias, after Mathias learned he would get a seat on that panel in 1969. In any given year, the Judiciary Committee conducted between 45 and 60 percent of all Senate committee business, handling everything from antitrust matters to the confirmation of every nominee to a federal prosecutorial office or judgeship in every state and territory. Civil rights issues were most often the salient ones during the first decade of Eastland's chairmanship. While the *Washington Post* opined when he retired that he did all he could to "block or retard the ... liberation of his region and then of the country as a whole from the shackles of government-sanctioned, culturally blessed institutional racism," their frequently liberal editorial board also saluted him for a standard of fairness that successors like Edward Kennedy would be "hard-pressed" to uphold. Playing it "fair down the line" was as much a strategy as a practice for Eastland. "Because he is so zealous in interpreting the rules fairly," Courtney Pace wrote, "they cannot become irked when he uses those same rules themselves." Eastland, one liberal declared thankfully, was "not like some of those high-minded ones who beat you by calling a vote when you are in the men's room."[1]

Still, in the eyes of some like Ernest F. "Fritz" Hollings of South Carolina, Eastland "controlled that committee," in part by crafting a gruff public image. His chief prop was a cigar, and he was quite generous in sharing his Havana treats with favored colleagues like Robert and Edward Kennedy and committee staffers like Rufus Edmisten, Sam Ervin's eyes and ears. At executive sessions, some lit up less expensive stogies that would fill the room in a manner that brought to mind the oft-derided smoke-filled rooms of a previous century. The air was thick enough one day that Howard Metzenbaum, the fairly junior Ohio liberal, looked at Joseph Biden, the first member he spotted, and asked him to put "that out." Yet while the air remained thick and musty, the only one puffing when Metzenbaum made his request was Eastland. Metzenbaum backed off when he recognized this was the case. "Oh, not you, Mr. Chairman," he backslid sheepishly.[2]

The prime executive branch nominee who came under the purview of his committee was the attorney general. Eastland, from the moment each nominee was chosen, took care to create a collegial relationship with all who would serve as the chief law enforcement officer of the American government. In his initial meeting with each, he made it clear that he needed two promises. He urged them to keep his friend John Duffner high on their staff, for Duffner had long been his top source of information on who was being considered for judgeships. And, he insisted that they return his phone calls. "I'll be calling you from time to time on something I want done," he told Elliott Richardson, the third man to serve Richard Nixon in that post, for example. That could mean he might be carrying a request from a friend or a constituent. Even so, he asked them merely to hear him out and do what they thought what was right. In his memoir, Richard Kleindienst, Nixon's second attorney general, reported that Eastland made but one such request. And Richardson, whose tenure in the Justice Department was cut short after but five months when he resigned rather than break a promise not to fire Watergate Special Prosecutor Archibald Cox, made it clear in his autobiography that Duffner was just as helpful to him as he was to Eastland.[3]

The one nominee who Eastland did not warm to immediately was Edward H. Levi, the president of the University of Chicago whom Gerald Ford nominated in early 1975. It was Ford's idea that times demanded a Justice Department divorced from political considerations and that circumstances called for choosing someone without partisan credentials. Levi was suspect to some conservatives because in the 1940s he had belonged to the National Lawyers Guild, a group later determined to be a Communist front. For Eastland, this mattered little. The two had met but once, back in 1955, when Eastland subpoenaed Levi to testify before SISS. The issue then was why Levi had as dean of the Law School allowed his faculty members to participate in a study of a Wichita jury whose proceedings were taped by a hidden microphone. An academic at heart, Levi replied that he had let the proceedings be recorded as part of a project he hoped might "strengthen the jury system." His response did not satisfy either Eastland, who believed that the study "violated the very reason that we have juries," or Attorney General Herbert Brownell, who verbally reprimanded him for the study. A generation later, Eastland remained skeptical. Still, Levi made a point to lunch with him and provide both him and Gerald Ford all records from the project that he had come to regret.

Neither Eastland nor Roman Hruska was placated until Ford brought them to the White House and told them how Levi had handled a fifteen-day sit-in at the University of Chicago in 1968. Levi did not initiate a confrontation or call for outside help, Ford told them, but met with students to discuss how to address their grievances. Levi did not promise amnesty to those who broke the law, and he even expelled forty of the leading provocateurs as soon as they left his office. Eastland and Hruska were thus assured that Levi was "not a bushy-haired liberal" like Johnson's Attorney General Ramsey Clark. American Bar Association President Lawrence E. Walsh testified that Levi would exert a high degree of independence, prompting them to fall in line, even if they had preferred a more conservative nominee. As it turned out, the only two witnesses to testify against Levi were lobbyists for the Liberty Lobby and U.S. Labor Party, who forwarded bizarre conspiratorial notions from the far right and left, respectively, that Levi, having rather distant tertiary ties to the Rockefeller family, would be disinclined to pursue charges against the family of the vice president. As such, Levi went through by voice vote.[4]

Those senators who wound up on the Judiciary Committee while Eastland was chairman quickly found that he would look out for their interests. One of the first to learn this was New Hampshire Republican Norris Cotton, who Eastland urged to seek a seat while the two were riding the underground train between the Senate office building and the Capitol in late 1958. Happy with the seats he held at the time, Cotton was reluctant. "Oh, you come on the committee," Eastland pled. "I'll give you some patronage." Such a procedure Eastland found only right. "If I've got a man on that committee who needs to place a fellow to help him with his committee work," he continued, "why he gets it." That was obvious from the numbers of staff who worked directly or indirectly under him. While the average Senate committee employed twenty-eight people in the late 1960s, fully 137 men and women worked for the Judiciary Committee, all but fourteen on the payrolls of its twelve subcommittees. A champion of the legislative branch at every level, Eastland declared that this was quite fair as the executive branch was superior in its ability to develop policy with its advantages in staff. "My conscience doesn't bother me," he would tell fellow conservatives who cited the costs. But he would not be so generous if liberal members ventured into areas he found truly inadvisable. "Don't y'all need some more staff on that committee?" he would suggest. "Staff? That's money," would be a likely reply. "Yeah, hell, sure. I'll be a good boy."[5]

Eastland also made it a policy to find subcommittee chairmanships for each Democrat on the committee. With Estes Kefauver's death in August 1963, for example, many senators wanted to eliminate the Subcommittee on Constitutional Amendments that the Tennessean had chaired. The one Judiciary Committee Democrat who did not chair a subcommittee at that time was Birch Bayh, the newest member of the panel aside from Ted Kennedy. Even at thirty-five, Bayh was quite savvy, and he arranged to meet with Eastland to make his case for securing control of the Subcommittee on Constitutional Amendments. Not yet aware of the panel's protocols, he, a teetotaler at the time, declined the glass of scotch Eastland offered him. But he soon learned that his chairman was inclined to assent to the wishes of Allen Ellender, who chaired the Subcommittee on Legislative Appropriations and wanted to shut down the panel. Money was not a problem, Bayh assured Eastland, for he would use his own staff to conduct the panel's business. Discouraged when he left Eastland's office, Bayh picked up the phone the next morning to hear Eastland tell him that he had changed his mind and knew that Bayh would "make a good one."

For Bayh, the new post conveyed prestige, but it took on a whole new context after the assassination of President Kennedy. Previous hearings conducted as to how a vice presidential vacancy should be filled had almost always produced high-minded discussions of the ideal means of acting much more than any concrete proposal to address the concerns of enough legislators at both the federal and state levels so it could become part of the Constitution. Kennedy's death brought urgency to the matter. Next in line to the presidency were seventy-two-year-old Speaker John McCormack and eighty-six-year-old Senate president pro tempore Carl Hayden, both of whom looked older than their years. It was Bayh who would conduct the hearings on questions that had become integral to the workings of American democracy. In tandem with cagy veterans like Everett Dirksen and Sam Ervin, Bayh crafted the Twenty-Fifth Amendment, which created processes to fill vacancies in the vice presidency and handle any potential cases of presidential disability. All the while, Bayh acted not just with Eastland's consent, but with his proxy, both within the full Senate and the conference committee.[6]

A few years later, John Tunney, a law school classmate of Edward Kennedy from California, won a seat on the committee and found himself the one member without a subcommittee chairmanship. He called upon Eastland in his office and asked if he might find him one. Eastland found his close assistant Bill Simpson and told him to bring in John Holloman, the committee's chief counsel. "Make Tunney a subcommittee," he commanded. "What would it be called?" someone asked. "How about John's subcommittee," Eastland replied. In time, Eastland let Holloman strip a small amount of jurisdiction from other panels and gave it to Tunney under the moniker of the Representation of Citizens Interest Subcommittee. On occasion, he could be just as generous with one or two favored Republicans. He granted ranking member Roman Hruska a subcommittee on Federal Charters, Holidays, and Celebrations as a means to see that Hruska got additional staff.[7]

Just as importantly to colleagues, Eastland, on matters other than civil rights, did not make a practice of blocking votes on bills that had gone through the ordinary legislative process, even on matters where he disagreed strongly. In 1959, he was the only member of the Subcommittee on Constitutional Amendments to vote against allowing residents of the District of Columbia to vote for president, but it soon became the Twenty-Second Amendment. Eleven years later, he, in both the committee and on the floor, opposed a proposed constitutional amendment eliminating the electoral college and thereby allowing for the direct election of the president. Still, counter to the practice of some chairpeople since, he allowed a vote, perhaps realizing that a majority of his colleagues might back the measure but enough legislators from small states would oppose it at some level to keep it from becoming the law of the land.[8]

Informally, Eastland made it a practice to notify all senators that if they objected to any presidential nominee to the federal bench from their home state, they should merely hang on to the piece of paper known as the blue slip that indicated that they approved of a prospective judge. Unless he received blue slips from both senators from any state, he refused to hold hearings on that nominee. Senators would not even have to state their reasons, a departure from previous practice. If a senator put a hold on a nomination, Eastland would notify those in the Justice Department who that senator was, so they might try and convince that senator to change his or her mind. He clung to these practices for all senators. When William Scott of Virginia opposed a respected judge Gerald Ford nominated and Independent conservative Harry F. Byrd Jr. backed, Eastland moved to table the nomination. He did the same for senators who were his ideological opposites. When Wisconsin liberal Gaylord Nelson heard that Congressman Glenn Davis was being considered for a vacancy on the federal bench, he went to Eastland and asked him to discourage those in the Nixon White House who urged his selection. Labor, African-American, and Jewish groups all opposed Davis, he said, as did the Wisconsin Bar Association. "Gaylord, you're telling me all the reasons I ought to be *for* him. What do you want?" Nelson said that best for all, even Davis, was for Nixon to choose someone else. "Awright," shot back Eastland, as he stuck his cigar back in his mouth and proceeded to let Justice Department officials know that he would honor his policy, even for someone as different from him as Nelson. On the other hand, he would back a nominee backed by any state's two senators even if a majority of the panel's Democrats opposed him or her. In the early days of the Ford presidency, he backed Connecticut Governor Thomas Meskill, a Nixon nominee for the U.S. Court of Appeals, who six committee Democrats joined the American Bar Association and the New York City bar in deriding for insufficient judicial experience. If a member found that a judicial candidate recommended by a senator ran into opposition from other politicos, Eastland might intercede with the attorney general. In the early days of the Kennedy administration, his message to Robert Kennedy about the rationale for some opposition to a potential jurist backed by Oklahoma Democrat Robert Kerr prompted Kennedy to dispatch two aides to Oklahoma to determine the rationale for their dissent. Their finding that the jurist's critics were moved by political considerations alone led Kennedy to side with Kerr and see that his brother opted for his choice. And, if a president and a state's senators approved of a nominee he aimed to oppose, Eastland still would expedite a vote. Once, Phil Hart approached Eastland to query how he might consider an African-American nominee from Michigan. "Don't worry about your boy," he told Hart, a veteran of D-Day whose courage and integrity he admired. "He'll go through all right, but you understand we [southern senators] got to put on a little show."[9]

If responsible parties in an administration felt strongly enough about one of their nominees, Eastland might even work with their agents to help them overcome objections a few senators may have developed. One early aim of the Nixon Justice Department, for example, was to find qualified black attorneys to install on the bench. A name that came to the fore was that of Barrington Parker, an attorney from the District of Columbia with advocates across the political spectrum. While Deputy Attorney General Richard Kleindienst expected rapid confirmation, he found that a well-placed Republican had raised doubts in Strom Thurmond's mind about Parker's fitness for the bench. Surprised, Eastland called Kleindienst and Thurmond into his office and prompted Kleindienst to tell Thurmond about Parker. After he made his case, Eastland peered at Thurmond just as the assistant attorney general concluded. "Does that satisfy you, Strom?" he asked. It did, and the nomination of Parker, who presided with quiet dignity over the trial of John Hinckley, the man who shot Ronald Reagan, went through with little discussion and without dissent.[10] That outcome served both Eastland and Thurmond well, too, for the white majorities that had elected these two onetime segregationists got little sense that the two had not only not objected to but had facilitated the elevation of an African American to the federal bench.

In the early days of the Carter administration, Congressman Thomas Foley, a future Speaker of the House, sought out Eastland and told him he had an outstanding attorney from his district near Spokane, Washington, who he would like to see on the federal bench. "All right," Eastland replied.

Who should he see to assure his friend was nominated and confirmed, Foley inquired earnestly. "I told you all right, didn't I?" Eastland grunted before he returned to the other regulars in Senate Secretary Stanley Kimmitt's hideaway office off the floor. Both Gaylord Nelson and John Culver had similar experiences with Eastland when they wanted Carter to select a highly respected liberal attorney from their states. At separate times, over drinks in Eastland's office, they started detailing their friends' best qualities and the high points of their resume. In both cases, Eastland butted in after about a minute and a half. "Does your boy do what you tell him to do?" he asked. The response of Nelson belied a bit of incredulity. "We're not talking about justices of the peace," he replied. "Mine do," Eastland shot back with a smile.[11]

Eastland's liberal colleagues respected him enough to reciprocate on occasion. In the fall of 1969, he prompted President Nixon to nominate Charles Clark to a seat on the Court of Appeals for the Fifth District. Over the previous decade, Clark had served as assistant to the attorney general of Mississippi and thus wound up representing Governor Ross Barnett during the Ole Miss crisis of 1962 and several school districts seeking to delay desegregation thereafter. To some, Clark's position as counsel for those on the wrong side of history should have disqualified him from the federal bench. Eastland and others countered that Clark was merely the lawyer for those who intended to slow the inevitable. Senate liberals may have disagreed, but few were inclined to pick a fight with Eastland and many owed him a favor. Those on his Judiciary Committee agreed to allow Clark to be confirmed, but asked Eastland to find a way to consider his nomination so that they would not be seen on record as having backed one of his recommended judges. Eastland chose Saturday, October 15, 1969, the day of one of the largest moratoriums held by opponents of the Vietnam War. With many liberal senators away and having given him their quiet approval, Eastland could ask for a voice vote, one where no member could be recorded for or against, or even present or absent. With Quentin Burdick of North Dakota presiding, Eastland asked for and got a voice vote to confirm Clark, just eight days after he was nominated.[12]

As Eastland got older, he particularly relished counseling younger members as to the ways of the Senate. At times, he would invite favored junior senators to join him for a drink, sometimes in his office and sometimes in the hideaway of Senate Secretary Stan Kimmitt. In his last few years in the upper chamber, he found himself serving alongside more teetotalers than before, particularly among fellow conservatives. Orrin Hatch, for one, was quick to tell Eastland that his Mormon faith dictated that he "abstain from alcohol products" and heard Eastland querying of him, "What the hell kind of church is that?" Just a few months later, Hatch felt honored when his chairman invited him to join him for dinner after a particularly contentious conference committee meeting. The two men ordered, then ate slowly, with neither man saying much for half an hour. Then Eastland, after slurping a mouthful of soup, inquired of Hatch what he thought of the day's events and related developments. Just having turned forty and uncommonly earnest, Hatch answered with a paragraph long reply that he was hopeful that things would improve within the Senate for those who shared their conservative philosophy. "Hatch," Eastland interrupted in an inimitable frank rejoinder, "*bullshit.*"[13]

On other occasions, although not one to look back, he would answer the questions of colleagues considerably younger than him about the history and traditions of the institution he revered. One who sought him out frequently after committee meetings was Joe Biden, then that body's youngest member. What was the biggest change he had seen over his tenure in the Senate, Biden once asked. "Ay-uh conditionin'" he replied, explaining that the sun would hit the glass on the Capitol dome so sharply in late May that it would heat the Senate chambers to such unbearable levels that members would agree to return home for the rest of the year. Then, Biden recounted to biographer Jules Witcover, Eastland lamented that "we put in ay-uh conditionin', stayed year round, and ruined America."[14]

The portion of his responsibilities as chairman of the Judiciary Committee that he deemed most important, however, was his duty to hold hearings on anyone a president might choose to fill a seat on America's highest court. The president whose nominees Eastland did more to help than any other was that of a former Senate colleague from the party of Abraham Lincoln, Richard M. Nixon.

Eastland (right) next to his father, Woods Caperton Eastland. Courtesy Woods E. Eastland.

Libby Coleman Eastland was known for her impeccable southern values and for delectable cheese straws and devil's food cakes. Courtesy Archives and Special Collections, University of Mississippi Libraries.

Governor Paul B. Johnson (here) appointed Eastland to the seat left vacant by the death of Senator Byron "Pat" Harrison in 1941. Thereafter, Eastland made a point to support Johnson's son, Paul B. Johnson Jr., for any office he sought. "A political debt is never repaid," he would say. Courtesy Archives and Special Collections, University of Mississippi Libraries.

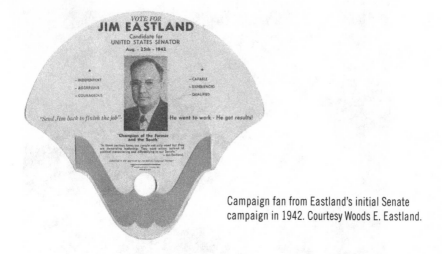

Campaign fan from Eastland's initial Senate campaign in 1942. Courtesy Woods E. Eastland.

Early in Eastland's career, two of the most formidable southern power brokers in Congress were Senators Kenneth "K. D." McKellar (D-TN) (center), who in 1943 escorted Eastland to be sworn in when Theodore Bilbo refused, and Walter F. George (D-GA) (far right). Courtesy Archives and Special Collections, University of Mississippi Libraries.

Eastland (left) and Jackson hotel magnate E. O. Spencer flank a field hand carrying their haul after a hunt in the late 1940s. Courtesy Archives and Special Collections, University of Mississippi Libraries.

Eastland traveled to Germany in 1945 as part of a Senate delegation. From this trip, Eastland's suspicions of Communism were exacerbated and his sense grew that war-torn Europe needed vast infusions of goods and cash like those that came through the Marshall Plan. In the back row (left to right) are Eastland, John McClellan (D-AK), Chapman Revercomb (R-WV), A. T. "Tom" Stewart (D-TN), Richard B. Russell (D-GA), and Burnet Maybank (D-SC). In front (left to right) are Chan Gurney (R-SD), Lieutenant General Jacob Devers, CG, 6th Army, General Omar N. Bradley, 12th Army Group, Harry F. Byrd (D-VA), and Clyde Reed (R-KS). Courtesy Dwight D. Eisenhower Presidential Library.

Eastland spent much of his time throughout his career working on agricultural legislation. Eastland joins other key congressional advocates of cotton in observing as Dwight D. Eisenhower signs into law a bill fixing the national cotton acreage allotment. Salt Lake City Tribune file (AP photo) 73-862, courtesy Dwight D. Eisenhower Presidential Library.

Pat McCarran (D-NV) was the first chairman of the Senate Internal Security Subcommittee and an important mentor to Eastland as both chairman of SISS and the full Judiciary Committee. A man with a fiery temper, McCarran was as zealous as Eastland in his search for Communists and, like Eastland, got many leaks from FBI Director J. Edgar Hoover and other FBI personnel. Courtesy Archives and Special Collections, University of Mississippi Libraries.

Eastland stands with Richard Russell (D-GA), the acknowledged leader of southern senators during the 1950s and 1960s, in front of the statue of Confederate President Jefferson Davis in the Capitol's Statuary Hall. Courtesy Archives and Special Collections, University of Mississippi Libraries.

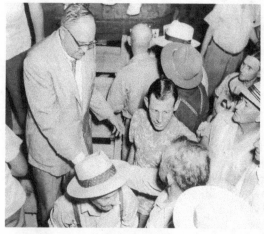

Eastland presses the flesh with voters during his hard-fought but successful bid in 1954 to be nominated by Mississippi Democrats for a third term. Courtesy Archives and Special Collections, University of Mississippi Libraries.

(left to right) Eastland, Judge Thomas Brady, Robert "Tut" Patterson of Indianola, and Governor Ross Barnett were some of Mississippi's most visible segregationists in the 1950s and 1960s. Courtesy Archives and Special Collections, University of Mississippi Libraries.

Eastland and other Judiciary Committee members join Senate Majority Leader Mike Mansfield, Attorney General Robert F. Kennedy, and Vice President Lyndon B. Johnson in observing President John F. Kennedy signing the Interstate Anti-Crime Act of 1961. Courtesy Woods E. Eastland.

Longtime state NAACP leader Aaron "Doc" Henry joins supporters in singing freedom songs at an October 29, 1964, rally in Hattiesburg. Henry, a Clarksdale pharmacist, was the gubernatorial candidate of the Mississippi Freedom Democratic Party that year and eventually was elected to the Mississippi State Senate. In the last decade of his life, Eastland forged a close political relationship and strong personal friendship with Henry. Courtesy of the Archives and Records Services Division, Mississippi Department of Archives and History.

On a personal level, the president with whom Eastland enjoyed the closest relationship was Lyndon Johnson. Here Eastland meets with Johnson, whom he believed to be the sharpest politico he ever dealt with, in the Oval Office in November 1967. Courtesy Lyndon Baines Johnson Presidential Library, photo by Yoichi Okamoto.

Longtime colleague John C. Stennis and Eastland join the rest of the Mississippi congressional delegation to meet with President Richard Nixon (bottom left) and Attorney General John Mitchell (upper right) on Air Force One prior to inspecting the Gulf Coast in September 1969 after Hurricane Camille. The visit spawned a close political alliance thereafter between Nixon and Eastland on most issues other than civil rights. Courtesy Archives and Special Collections, University of Mississippi Libraries.

As president pro tem of the Senate, Eastland assumed the seat of the vice president on occasions when that office was vacant. Here, he and House Speaker Carl Albert (D-OK) oversaw the swearing in of Gerald R. Ford as vice president in December 1973. Courtesy Archives and Special Collections, University of Mississippi Libraries.

As president pro tem, Eastland was part of the joint congressional leadership. To his left are House Minority Leader John J. Rhodes Jr. (R-AZ), House Majority Leader Thomas P. "Tip" O'Neill (D-MA), and President Gerald Ford. To his right are Senate Minority Leader Hugh D. Scott Jr. (R-PA) and Senate Minority Whip Robert P. Griffin (R-MI). Courtesy Archives and Special Collections, University of Mississippi Libraries.

Eastland using the ceremonial office of the vice president during one of the two periods when he was second in line to the presidency behind House Speaker Carl Albert. Courtesy of Woods E. Eastland.

CHAPTER 15

Big Jim and the Nixon-Ford Supreme Court

THE PRIMARY CONSTITUTIONAL TASK THAT FALLS UNDER THE PURVIEW of the chair of the Senate Judiciary Committee lies in devising the process by which the upper chamber will give its advice and consent to presidential nominees for vacancies on the Supreme Court. This duty Jim Eastland relished, as he had long been convinced that the Supreme Court of Earl Warren had been too generous in accepting the claims of those aggrieved at injustices they saw, not to mention too willing to make law rather than merely interpret existing statutes. It was hardly lost upon Eastland that Richard Nixon did not share his opposition to any further grants of civil rights to African Americans. As Kevin J. McMahon demonstrated in a thoughtful recent analysis, it was not Nixon's aim to build a right-wing court, but merely to temper the liberalism he saw in the Warren court. Still, Eastland took comfort in Nixon's view that the Warren court had been too generous in granting rights to criminals as well as in his commitment to a strict constructionist philosophy of constitutional interpretation. It thus became easy for Eastland to agree to do all he could to secure the confirmation of any Nixon nominee who he thought more conservative than the justice he would be replacing.

The Senate's failure to elevate Abe Fortas to the Chief Justiceship dictated that the first seat Nixon would fill would be that of Warren. Noting that short lists of potential replacements included northern Republicans with moderate-to-liberal civil rights records like Thomas E. Dewey and Herbert Brownell, Eastland was grateful when Nixon chose Warren Burger, the chief judge of the federal Court of Appeals for the District of Columbia, to head the high court. Burger would not decide every case as he would, Eastland told reporters and colleagues, yet was an "outstanding" lawyer and judge and much more conservative than his predecessor or others whose names were suggested. Still, Eastland used Burger's confirmation hearing to prompt the Minnesota-reared jurist to affirm his respect for the Tenth Amendment, which gives states an important role in the American system. While Nixon was still enjoying the honeymoon that Congress generally grants new presidents, all but three of Eastland's colleagues joined him in voting for Burger.[1]

Senators would not be so charitable in considering nominees for the next opening. That vacancy emerged after Abe Fortas left in disgrace once it was learned that he, while on the Supreme Court, had taken $20,000 (which he later returned) from convicted financier Louis Wolfson to advise his family's foundation on how to use its money. While Eastland urged a "thorough investigation," he did not go as far as other senators, even some liberal Democrats like Walter F. "Fritz" Mondale of Minnesota, who called upon Fortas to resign as soon as they learned of the ill-advised payment. Yet while Fortas' ethical lapses attracted a bipartisan bevy of critics, it was not lost upon more progressive Democrats and their supporting interests that the justice who had had to leave was a regular ally of Chief Justice Earl Warren.[2] Already having lost two members of their majority in the first six months of the Nixon administration, they exhibited considerable anxiety that the Burger court might overturn many of the verdicts that endeared them to the Warren court.[3] In the immediate wake of the Fortas debacle, they would do their best to mandate that anyone selected to fill the next vacancy would not only have to pass the normal tests of qualifications and philosophy, but also be free of even the slightest scintilla of any ethical transgression.

Nixon's choice to replace Fortas was Clement Haynsworth, a fifty-six-year-old jurist from Greenville, South Carolina, who had served since the Eisenhower administration on the Fourth Circuit Court of Appeals and earned the respect of fellow judges, the American Bar Association, and law professors. Contrary to popular belief, Haynsworth was less the choice of Strom Thurmond, then seen as the most conservative Republican in the Senate, than of moderate South Carolina Democrat Ernest F. "Fritz" Hollings. What convinced Eastland at the outset that Haynsworth could be confirmed without much rancor was that Everett Dirksen had lined up behind Haynsworth. To be sure, some civil rights and labor leaders had stated their opposition. The day the choice was announced, Washington attorney Joseph Rauh, who had close ties to both groups, denounced Haynsworth with far more than a usual degree of ideological hyperbole as a "hard core segregationist." Still, Dirksen's civil rights credentials in Eastland's view were sufficiently strong to give the moderate and liberal Republicans who still formed a sizable chunk of the GOP caucus a reason to lend Haynsworth a vote if they found their decisions a close call. If Republicans held firm, Eastland felt certain that he could bring not just his fellow Southerners, but a few moderate Democrats as well.[4]

Dirksen's sudden death on September 7, 1969, portended trouble for the Haynsworth nomination. While much of official Washington mourned the passing of Dirksen, a man of gravitas and humor revered across party lines, leaders of organized labor spent the hours following his death hiring forty fulltime lobbyists to mount a full-scale campaign against Haynsworth. Less than a week after the choice of Haynsworth was announced, AFL-CIO chief George Meany wrote Eastland that the nominee was "not fit to be an Associate Justice." Meany's case rested on a 1963 charge by a Textile Workers Union lawyer that he received an anonymous phone call after an antiunion ruling by Haynsworth alleging that Haynsworth had been bribed. Less than two months after the charge was made, that attorney recanted it in a letter to Simon E. Sobeloff, the presiding judge of the Fourth Circuit Court of Appeals, who forwarded the finding to Robert F. Kennedy. It came easy for Kennedy to then declare his "complete confidence" in Haynsworth, thus eliminating these objections. With that avenue of attack gone, some Democrats requested Haynsworth's financial records. Eastland had a Justice Department team headed by William H. Rehnquist, then a assistant attorney general in the Office of Legal Counsel, prepare a twelve-page report detailing those matters. This was a document Rehnquist compiled hurriedly, for he at the time was "terrified" of Eastland, a man who often displayed a gruff demeanor to those he barely knew. But Rehnquist's arguments impressed Eastland, who gained confidence in his judgment and proudly released his statement to the full Senate.[5]

To be sure, Haynsworth's performance as a witness was less impressive than many expected. The South Carolina jurist had a bit of a speech impediment that led senators who did not know him to suspect that he was less than candid with them before the committee. This impression took hold slowly among those in the middle. It was Eastland's standard practice to call for a count as soon as he thought that he had enough ayes to carry a vote. Thus, thinking he could win, he ended testimony from pro-Haynsworth witnesses before all of the jurists and law professors who had signed up to speak on his behalf testified.[6]

Haynsworth's opponents, in contrast, did not relent. Eight black House Democrats led by John Conyers of Michigan told the Judiciary Committee broadly that confirming Haynsworth would embolden those who wanted to reverse advances in civil rights. Perhaps their claims furthered fears about Haynsworth's southern origins, but the sparseness of rulings from Haynsworth that could be considered antagonistic to civil rights limited their impact.[7] Conversely, union leaders found several Haynsworth rulings they opposed, but opted not to wage their campaign against the merits of those decisions, for they knew the general public did not always side with them. Nor could they attack the character or qualifications of Haynsworth, who even today opponents call a "fine man" and eminent legal scholar.[8] But they could credibly wage a campaign against Haynsworth on the basis that he was insufficiently attentive to questions of conflict of interest, for this was the very issue that prompted Abe Fortas to resign.

It was Birch Bayh who most pointedly took up the union mantle when Haynsworth appeared before the Judiciary Committee. Bayh first elicited a promise from the nominee that he would recuse himself from any cases involving J. P. Stevens, the large textile firm long known for antiunion practices. Not only did Haynsworth hold $24,000 worth of stock in J. P. Stevens, but the textile giant had long retained Haynsworth's onetime law firm as its counsel. Bayh appreciated Haynsworth's guarantee, even if he thought Haynsworth was "asking for trouble" by holding onto his stock. But Bayh and Edward Kennedy were not completely mollified by Haynsworth's assurances that he would avoid conflicts of interest. Indeed, they suspected that the late Robert Kennedy's previous profession that he had confidence in Haynsworth extended only to charges of bribery and not to less serious allegations of conflicts of interest. Bayh, in his questioning of Haynsworth, refocused his inquiries on the 1963 case, where, in a decision that was eventually overturned, he ruled with a 3–2 court majority that the Darlington, South Carolina, plant of the Deering-Milliken textile firm could close for antiunion purposes. What unions claimed improper was that Haynsworth, before becoming a judge, had helped organize Vend-a-Matic that operated vending machines in three Deering-Milliken plants and remained a director of that firm until the federal Judicial Conference suggested in 1963 that all jurists leave corporate boards on which they served. Haynsworth resigned as asked, but Vend-a-Matic soon was bought out by a national firm, and Haynsworth emerged $450,000 wealthier.[9]

Under normal circumstances, those charging a conflict of interest based upon an association with a party doing business with a firm involved in a lawsuit would receive little credibility. But this was the first fight of the post-Fortas era, and those who had found Fortas a regular ally were determined to see that anyone who would replace their friend, especially someone of a different philosophy, would be subject to the same standards. At the time, Bayh was convinced that Haynsworth would be confirmed, and he gave him a chance to say that he would adhere to post-Fortas era standards and recuse himself if ever again faced with an identical case. The query by this point had become more political than ethical. Still, Haynsworth, in replying that he would still "feel compelled to sit," conveyed a sense that he appreciated the letter of existing doctrines covering judicial ethics more than he valued the new sensibilities. Furthering the same impression was a revelation that Haynsworth had purchased $16,000 in stock in the Brunswick Corporation in 1967 six weeks after joining in a unanimous ruling for the bowling alley manufacturer, but well before the verdict was announced. This was hardly a major ethical transgression, save to those who demand that all jurists remain purer than Caesar's wife. But Bayh was right on the mark when he told reporters that the purchase "sure looks bad to the general public."[10]

It was never Haynsworth's merits or perceived shortcomings that concerned Eastland; it was the appearances permeating the politics of the nomination. He told one GOP senator that enough Democrats were still sufficiently annoyed at the early and ardent opposition of rising stars Howard Baker of Tennessee, Everett Dirksen's son-in-law, and newly elected GOP Whip Robert Griffin of Michigan to the Fortas nomination that it was unlikely that either at that time could get Jesus Christ confirmed. He tapped instead newly elected moderate conservative Marlow Cook to manage the fight for confirmation. Cook and ranking Republican Roman Hruska put together a twenty-eight-page booklet defending Haynsworth's record against charges from civil rights lawyer Joseph Rauh that he was a "laundered segregationist." The thrust of the anti-Haynsworth lobby had become that he had ruled upon cases where he had a conflict of interest, charges similar to those which had forced Abe Fortas' resignation. To Eastland. Haynsworth's conflict of interest was far less serious than Fortas'. Still, he sensed by September 19 that the nomination was in "deep trouble." He invited deputy White House counsel Clark Mollenhoff into his office and told him that he could not understand why a few top officials—namely Attorney General John Mitchell and White House Counsel John Ehrlichman—had effectively muzzled Haynsworth. Their policy of barring the judge from answering written inquiries from any senator other than Eastland or Hruska, both of whom were firmly committed to the nominee, needlessly antagonized any number of senators. Many of those critical were Republicans as stalwart as first year Senator Bob Dole of Kansas, who were looking for reasons to justify a vote for Haynsworth. "The folks they have working at the Justice Department don't know what they are doing," Eastland counseled Mollenhoff, and Haynsworth would be defeated unless the administration changed its practices.[11]

Publicly, Eastland pronounced that Haynsworth's judicial and financial records had been examined like no other nominee's. It was his policy as chairman to try and report judicial nominees to the full Senate if they had the support of both members from their home state. On October 6, the Judiciary Committee reported Haynsworth's nomination by a 10–7 margin, but the vote was deceiving, as two of the ayes—GOP Leader Hugh Scott and Democrat Thomas Dodd—were shaky. With two noes coming from Republicans—GOP Whip Robert Griffin of Michigan and Charles McCurdy "Mac" Mathias of Maryland—astute politicos began to predict that the nomination might be defeated. Eastland privately began contacting civic leaders from the home states of undecided senators whose support might influence them to vote for Haynsworth, a time-honored technique of coalition building that might have paid dividends had the White House employed it from the start. But some administration hands had taken responsibility for getting Haynsworth confirmed from their seasoned chief of congressional liaison Bryce Harlow, and given it to many new to the Capitol who were seen as heavy-handed and occasionally clumsy. GOP maverick John Williams of Delaware took the White House to task for not stressing Haynsworth's general pattern of integrity. The single most ill-advised move from the White House came from deputy White House counsel Clark Mollenhoff, who asked a GOP state chairmen's advisory panel to endorse Haynsworth. Many state chairmen would have advised against had they been asked, as such resolutions historically had been confined to matters of public policy. But, when the request was ruled out of order, the press portrayed his decision as an affront by GOP loyalists to their nominee. Less devastating than what became known as the "Mollenhoff cocktail" but equally demonstrative of the ineptitude of the White House lobbying campaign were post-midnight calls from Martha Mitchell, the outspoken alcoholic wife of Attorney General John Mitchell, to at least two senators deemed likely to approve a nonextreme southern nominee.[12]

Eastland tried to project a positive impression about the likelihood of Haynsworth being confirmed. Privately, he knew labor groups had chiseled away what he had expected to be a huge majority for the South Carolinian. Most susceptible was the seventeen-member bloc of moderate Republicans from the Northeast and Midwest, of whom fourteen opposed Haynsworth. According to Ralph Smith, the Illinois Republican filling the vacancy left by Everett Dirksen's death who wound up backing Haynsworth (and losing his bid to fill the remainder of Dirksen's term), "Anyone who is up for election next year" felt compelled for political reasons to oppose Haynsworth. Fully aware of the politics of the moment and the desire of many Fortas allies to avenge his fall, Eastland recoiled at a speech by Ernest Hollings that he feared portended a negative outcome. Eastland declared that Hollings, the young South Carolinian with a foghorn-like voice, had "loused up" in that his depressing outlook was like "peeing in the milk bucket." In two addresses to the Senate, he heralded Haynsworth as a man of stoic-like "dignity, restraint and courage" who had withstood a "trial by ordeal" within his committee and a "trial by rumor" from outside. Eastland hailed the support given Haynsworth not only from his own judicial colleagues, but also that of multitudes of eminent law professors and bar association leaders that former American Bar Association President Lewis Powell lined up for him. He depicted Haynsworth as a man of moderate philosophy and lambasted some who had painted him out of the mainstream. Rather, he argued, it was the "liberal establishment" that was out of touch with the rest of America, for it had "always painted everyone with a dissenting view as a racist, a bigot, or a fascist."[13]

Eastland's speech changed no votes. While liberal journalist Tom Wicker later wrote that Haynsworth "went on to long and reputable service on the Fourth Circuit and is widely regarded today as having been worthy of confirmation," he went down to a 55–45 defeat in November 1969. What Eastland had done was to trumpet themes that would be repeated each time a fairly conservative nominee, be they, like Haynsworth, qualified for the job they were chosen to fill or less than desirable for any public office, came under fire for any reason from critics to their left. One who echoed them often in years to come was the far less conservative Richard Nixon, who reveled in reminding southern audiences that the Senate had defeated his nominee. In the immediate aftermath of the Haynsworth debacle, a somewhat obsessive Nixon aimed to reinforce the message in a manner that ultimately had a political upside, but just as surely called into question public respect for many of his judicial nominees. "Go out," he ordered some of his closest associates, and "find a good federal judge further south and further to the right."[14]

There was, to be sure, no shortage of qualified, even talented, southern GOP jurists from whom Nixon could choose. Most were Eisenhower appointees who had been quiet on civil rights questions prior to being put on the bench, but followed the precedents implicit in *Brown v. Board of Education* once they took their seats. These were Jack Bass' "unlikely heroes," men like John Brown of Texas, Frank Johnson of Alabama, Elbert Tuttle of Georgia, and John Minor Wisdom of Louisiana, who effectively accelerated the pace of desegregation.[15] They hardly fit Eastland's ideal of what a judge should be, which much resembled the description replete within Nixon's directive to look deeper in the South and farther to the right. Eastland accordingly was encouraged when Nixon chose G. Harrold Carswell, a Florida judge strongly backed by respected Southerners Richard Russell, a Democrat, and Edward Gurney, a Republican. Eastland quickly predicted that Carswell would be confirmed and got him to vow privately to carry out his oath to uphold the Constitution. What Eastland did not know was that what seemed to have sealed the choice of Carswell was less his merits as a federal judge, but, what in the post-Fortas aftermath seemed even more important, the fact that he owned no stocks or bonds.[16]

While few members relished another fight in the immediate aftermath of the Haynsworth debacle, many soon developed doubts about Carswell's fitness for the high court. Lawmakers noted that higher tribunals had reversed several Carswell rulings. Others found it curious that seven of Carswell's colleagues on the Fifth Circuit Court of Appeals refused to sign a telegram recommending that he be confirmed. What especially troubled senators was that Carswell's attitudes had not seemed to change over his eleven years on the bench. It wasn't just that Carswell belonged to an all-white country club; many senators did as well. Nor was it that Carswell as a candidate for the Georgia legislature in 1948 had avowed a perpetual belief in white supremacy; many from the Deep South at that time had done likewise. Eastland could rebut some testimony before the Judiciary Committee as secondhand. But much harder to discount were accounts from those like civil rights attorney LeRoy D. Clark, who told senators that Carswell had been "insulting and hostile" to black Americans who appeared in his court. Maryland Democrat Joseph Tydings, a junior senator, heard privately from a Justice Department lawyer that Carswell was considerably less than civil to lawyers for those trying to register black voters. Struck by the absence of judicial temperament displayed by a nominee for the nation's highest court, Tydings went to Eastland and informed him that he had some information that needed to be considered. Eastland understood and agreed not to resist Tydings' call for a right of holdover, a device allowing any senator a one-week delay on any vote. That intermission gave the civil rights community time to build a case against Carswell. While the committee voted 13–4 to report the nomination, several members made it clear that they had not committed to voting for Carswell. One, Marlow Cook, came to question whether Carswell was even qualified to be a lawyer, much less a justice, after hearing his inept description of the judicial doctrine of *stare decisis*. Another, Hiram L. Fong of Hawaii, usually a stalwart Republican, even approached one of Carswell's most ardent supporters and told him that he considered the judge a "jackass."[17]

"That fellow Carswell," Eastland declared, "is his own worst enemy," a sentiment many key Nixon staffers came to share. Other southern senators who wound up voting for Carswell privately concurred. Staunch conservative John McClellan of Arkansas was heard declaring "that man is not qualified." Ernest Hollings rued that Carswell was "not qualified to carry Judge Haynsworth's law books." And, Nixon chief of congressional liaison Bryce Harlow told White House associates that senators of all stripes thought Carswell was "a boob, a dummy. And what counter is there to that? He is." But what sealed Carswell's fate was an inadvertent aside Roman Hruska made to a radio reporter that summed up what many on both sides were thinking. "Even if he were mediocre," Hruska asserted, "there are a lot of mediocre judges and people and lawyers. They are entitled to a little representation, aren't they?"[18]

Once it became clear that Carswell would be rejected, Nixon and his allies moved to paint the vote as the result of anti-southern bigotry. Eastland professed himself "keenly disappointed" that a Southerner could not be confirmed by the full Senate and guessed that a Northerner even with the same limitations as Carswell would have been approved "without a whimper." They scrambled to find someone who could win confirmation quickly and accepted the suggestion of Chief Justice Burger that they forward the name of his lifelong friend Harry Blackmun, who at the time was serving on the Eighth Circuit Court of Appeals. Unlike the two previous nominees, Blackmun, who many called the second "Minnesota twin," enjoyed the enthusiastic backing of a liberal Democrat from his home state, Walter Mondale, and another from the Judiciary Committee, Quentin Burdick of North Dakota, and confirmation would be unanimous. Still, the opening of the hearings always gave Eastland a chance to ask nominees what they thought was the proper function of the Supreme Court. This single day of hearings proved no different. Once Blackmun placated him by replying that the duty of a justice was to "interpret" the law rather than make it, Eastland told anyone who cared to listen that he would be voting in the affirmative. To be sure, the hearings did go a bit longer than expected, and Blackmun feared for a time that they might go on for another day. What should he do? "If I were you," a supremely confident Eastland told Blackmun, "I'd eat a good supper, take a slug of whiskey, and go to bed."[19]

Just sixteen months later, Nixon got a chance to add two more justices. On the same day in mid-September 1971, two ailing Supreme Court mainstays, Hugo Black and John M. Harlan, announced their retirements. Their departures left the administration unprepared, even if Nixon was determined to fill both seats with "strict constructionists." After a panel convened by the American Bar Association found the first two names Nixon submitted less than ideal, Nixon asked allies to suggest candidates with considerably more gravitas. Chief Justice Burger knew of no more qualified legal scholar than Lewis F. Powell Jr., a fairly conservative Richmond attorney who had been president of the American Bar Association and the American College of Trial Lawyers and had also chaired the local school board and served on Lyndon Johnson's Crime Commission. After an American Bar Association panel found him "one of the best qualified lawyers available," Nixon settled upon him once his men broke down Powell's reluctance to leave his law practice.[20] An offer for the other seat was extended to Howard Baker, a man whose lack of enthusiasm for judicial work was best demonstrated in oft-repeated comments that he found mausoleums livelier than the Supreme Court. Baker found after a hasty visit with Justice Potter Stewart that he would feel obligated to Nixon to accept the nod if he so desired, but would prefer that Nixon honor someone else. As Baker took his time considering what some might have found the opportunity of a lifetime, many close to the administration privately began to inquire who else was being considered.[21]

Eastland could not understand why Nixon would risk losing an able loyalist like Baker, and he recommended that Nixon opt for a lesser-known potential justice on the list. "The man for the job," he told Attorney General John Mitchell, was William H. Rehnquist, a assistant attorney general he had found "smart as a whip" in the three most recent confirmation struggles. Eastland's thinking was shared by many in the White House. Who, they thought, could oppose someone of Rehnquist's background as both a clerk to Justice Robert Jackson, an appointee of liberal icon Franklin D. Roosevelt, and a high official in the presidential campaign of his fellow Arizona conservative Barry Goldwater?[22]

Although he had not met Powell prior to his selection, Eastland's sense of the Senate quickly told him that he was the more respected and popular of the two among his colleagues. Powell himself was not even sure that he would be approved until Eastland assured him his confirmation was certain as they dined together over his frequent lunch of a bacon, lettuce, and tomato sandwich with buttermilk. "Do you know why the liberals will take you and they won't take Rehnquist?" Eastland asked

the sixty-four-year-old Powell. "No," said the bespectacled Richmond attorney. Eastland paused for a good half-minute, then shot back, "Cause
they think you're gonna die." According to Larry Speakes, then Eastland's
press secretary, Powell gulped and nearly choked on his sandwich.[23]

Eastland was not the only one who discerned quickly that Rehnquist
was the more controversial of the nominees. He sensed a haughtiness
among the retinue around Powell who wanted him and Rehnquist be
considered separately. One ally was overheard saying that Powell was not
seeking confirmation, but canonization. Eastland's antennae convinced
him that public opinion in America preferred that the high court recon-
vene as soon as feasible with a full nine-member contingent. Accordingly, he crafted a strategy with the Nixon Justice Department, in which
the Judiciary Committee would consider the two nominees virtually in
tandem, with hearings on Rehnquist to be held first. His decision to make
Powell's nomination being considered contingent upon an assurance of
Rehnquist's being acted upon rendered it next to impossible to deny
Rehnquist confirmation. When Birch Bayh assured Eastland that he and
other liberals would readily vote for Powell, Eastland played his trump.
"You will not get Powell," he told Bayh, "without Rehnquist." "Oh," sighed
Bayh, recognizing that Rehnquist would be confirmed unless he and his
allies uncovered an incredibly damning skeleton in his closet.[24]

When hearings opened, Powell emerged unscathed. Eastland said later
that he had never known anyone with as much "enthusiastic support"
from the legal profession as Powell. Rehnquist fared nearly as well, with
Birch Bayh, a leader of the opposition, conceding that he was a "man of
integrity." The closest Bayh came to placing a chink in Rehnquist's armor
was his lament that Attorney General Mitchell would not waive Rehnquist
from the attorney-client privilege as a Justice Department official. Still,
Rehnquist had some ardent critics. AFL-CIO lobbyist Andrew Biemiller
termed him a "right-wing zealot" who favored "executive supremacy" and
limits on personal freedom. More strident were civil rights advocates
Clarence Mitchell and Joseph Rauh, who cited reports uncorroborated
by any witness who appeared before the committee that Rehnquist had
participated in "ballot security" programs in Arizona. When Mitchell cited
rumors that Rehnquist belonged to the extreme right-wing John Birch
Society, Eastland produced an affidavit signed by Rehnquist affirming he

was "not now and never has been a member of the John Birch Society." Rauh followed by interjecting that that disclaimer did not refute a suggestion that Rehnquist might be linked to the Birchers. Surprisingly, it was Edward Kennedy who decried this "completely unwarranted and . . . uncalled for" guilt-by-association tactic. It fell upon Eastland and Roman Hruska to refute charges that Rehnquist belonged to right-wing groups like the John Birch Society and Arizonans for Arizona (a small group of elderly xenophobes). In a twenty-page argument, they castigated Rauh and Mitchell for "highly misleading and exaggerated statements" they found a "malicious and deliberate attempt to distort a good faith statement." Eastland and Hruska depicted memos Rehnquist wrote Justice Jackson a generation earlier opposing Linda Brown and others who sought the integration of public schools as the work of a clerk providing a bevy of arguments to the jurist he served. But when Rehnquist's opponents proved persistent, Eastland agreed to let the FBI investigate further. As he had a substantial majority and doubted there was more incriminating evidence, Eastland would not reopen hearings. While California liberal John Tunney used his right to delay a vote for a week, only twenty-two senators backed a bid to hold off a vote on Rehnquist until the new year. Confirmation was as certain for the Stanford-trained assistant attorney general as it was for the Virginian, even if twenty-six dissenters cast their lot against Rehnquist while but one lone Oklahoman voted against Powell.[25]

This outcome serves as a testament to the shrewdness of Jim Eastland. Perhaps more than any other piece of legislative business outside the agricultural realm in his nearly four decades in Washington, the confirmation of William Rehnquist owed itself primarily to his skill and ingenuity. For his part, Rehnquist remained grateful, even on days when Eastland would use his lunch hour to walk the quarter of a mile between his Senate office and the Supreme Court, climb the steps to Rehnquist's chambers, tell him to "get a haircut," then retrace his path back to his office immediately.[26]

There would not be another vacancy on the high court until 1975, when the aging New Deal liberal William O. Douglas announced his retirement. Hardly surprisingly, Eastland let it be known that he would prefer that President Ford fill that vacancy with an able Mississippi jurist like federal Judges Charles Clark or James P. Coleman. But Ford would only get the Senate consensus he sought with the choice of a centrist, and the one he chose was highly regarded jurist John Paul Stevens of Chicago, who served on the Seventh Circuit Court of Appeals. When asked about Stevens' chances of confirmation, Eastland told reporters that the Illinoisan should be approved both easily and quickly. He was familiar with Stevens' FBI reports, having seen them once before, and hailed him as an "able lawyer . . . who did not blindly follow socialistic theories." As became the norm after the Haynsworth nomination went down, Stevens initiated a set of meetings to get acquainted with senators, beginning with Eastland and ranking Republican Roman Hruska. Eastland seemed to Stevens to be cordial if noncommittal, and he got no hint of which way the chairman was leaning until the third day of hearings. Then, a critic of Stevens took the stand and proceeded to read a lengthy prepared statement condemning his service in 1967 as counsel to a commission probing the ethics of two members of the Illinois Supreme Court. Eastland walked over to Stevens and asked if he cared to respond or even listen. Not really, Stevens replied. Thereupon, Eastland looked to the committee reporter, asked him to make a thorough record, and then invited Stevens to his office for a drink. What else transpired Stevens declined to relate in his recent memoir, but he was confirmed without dissent within a month of his nomination, a near record for any nominee to the high court.[27]

Ironically, when Stevens retired in 2009, he was considered one of the more liberal members, if not the most liberal member of the Supreme Court. Yet in 1975, virtually all observers deemed him well to the right of outgoing Justice Douglas. Thus, Gerald Ford's one nominee fit the pattern of all four Nixon appointees as well as the two the Senate denied confirmation for being well to the right of the Warren court jurist they replaced. For Eastland, his work to secure approval of each, other than Carswell, was a source of some of his greatest pride of his work in the Senate. While none of the five who went on the Supreme Court save Rehnquist was in any way as conservative as Eastland would have liked, all were less likely to expand interpretations of constitutional rights in ways majorities on the Warren court did regularly between 1954 and 1969. To Eastland, this was a mark of honor, one he could trumpet in both Mississippi and outside the South, where many had begun to resent and resist additional grants of rights imposed by the one branch of government not elected by the people.

CHAPTER 16

Of Camille and Richard Nixon

OF THE THREE REPUBLICAN PRESIDENTS ON WHOSE WATCH HE SERVED, Jim Eastland developed the closest working relationship with Richard Nixon. Even though the two had been colleagues between 1951 and 1953 and Nixon had presided over the upper chamber for the rest of the decade, the two men were never personally close. Both were renowned for shunning the Georgetown party circuit. They kept their own counsel and shared a suspicion of left-wing foes, imagined and real, even if Eastland was far more secure within his own skin and more in control of his envies and anxieties than Nixon. Still, Eastland realized that Nixon's record on civil rights issues was considerably more progressive than his own, even while hoping that his administration decelerated the pace of integration from that of the heyday of the "Great Society." It was hardly lost upon Nixon that he had to cultivate Eastland on patronage. Eastland indeed made it clear to Nixon aides in the early months of his administration that there would be no new U.S. attorneys or any other personnel connected with law enforcement or the federal judiciary for Mississippi whom he did not select.[1] Yet by the middle of August 1969, the fates of the two became intertwined, not as some might have suspected by pressure from Yankee liberals, but rather by devastation from an uninvited Category 5 hurricane from the Caribbean.[2]

Few storms ever assaulted the Gulf Coast with the ferocity of Camille. "The most intensive hurricane on record" in the eyes of the U.S. Geological Survey, Camille packed winds that blew more than 200 miles per hour at their apex and lifted tides more than 33 feet above most sea walls. While Camille spared New Orleans, the hub of the coast, the storm killed more than 400 people in Mississippi alone and destroyed 19,000 homes over a span 60 miles wide by 60 miles long. Fully 211,900 acres in the Magnolia State were flooded, and 6000 Mississippians alone lost their jobs. Especially hard hit were Bay St. Louis and the port of Gulfport, from which pleasure and commercial boats were swept inland to points as far away as Pass Christian and Long Beach, towns Governor John Bell Williams felt compelled to evacuate. Large piles of debris in Pass Christian were common as far away as four blocks from what had been the coast. U.S. 90, the largest coastal artery, was either blocked or underwater in many places, making the transport of medical supplies or food virtually impossible.[3]

Hours before Camille struck the mainland, Vice President Spiro Agnew contacted Williams to let him know that the administration would help as much as possible. The next day, President Nixon declared twenty-six counties as major disaster areas and designated former GOP National Committeeman Fred LaRue, an unpaid White House aide from Mississippi, as his liaison to officials in the affected areas. Eastland arrived the same day, driving part of the way then riding in a helicopter, to oversee a scene Governor Williams likened to that in Hiroshima the day after the first atomic bomb was dropped. Almost immediately, he and John Stennis began drafting legislation to provide relief to those harmed by Camille, as did colleagues from the other affected states of Alabama, Louisiana, Virginia, and West Virginia, and the chairmen of several key committees.[4]

Birch Bayh, who chaired a subcommittee on disaster relief, had pushed for a comprehensive bill since a tornado killed 135 people in northern Indiana on Palm Sunday of 1965. At that time, he got Congress and President Johnson to approve a measure that provided relief to those left homeless during that tragedy. Even so, Bayh tenaciously warned that the federal government needed to prepare to deal with the consequences of all strikes of Mother Nature before the next "big blow" left tens of thousands more virtually helpless. When Congress returned from its summer recess, Bayh found a House-passed bill granting relief to those affected by a relatively small storm in California and adopted it as the vehicle to establish a relief program for victims of Camille and future storms of similar magnitude. Quickly, he incorporated most of the provisions included in the Eastland-Stennis bill that veteran Democrat William Colmer was introducing in the House and expedited its consideration by the full Senate. The bill, which Eastland liked to compare to a "miniature Marshall Plan," provided funds to, among other things, permanently repair state highways, give food and housing assistance to those affected, ease the processes by which Farmers Home Administration and Small Business Administration loans were awarded and remove debris from private land.[5]

Mississippi soon received more attention at the federal level than it had in generations. Spiro Agnew, Secretary of Housing and Urban Development George Romney, and seven members of the House Public Works Committee all visited the state within the next two weeks to inspect the devastation. Bill Simpson, a brilliant Eastland aide from Pass Christian, one of the most affected communities, had gone to the White House on September 7 to work out a thorough measure. The next day, Richard Nixon flew to Gulfport with Eastland, John Stennis, Attorney General Mitchell, and much of the state's congressional delegation in tow. Nixon had agreed to the proposal Simpson had hashed out, but had not told everyone. So when Stennis started to describe the bill he had in mind, he spoke long enough that Nixon found it nearly impossible to get in a word. Aware that Nixon would tell both that more than half a billion dollars in relief would be coming soon to Mississippi, Eastland looked at Stennis and asked him to "just hush and let the boy talk." The event itself was momentous. As the first stop by a sitting president in Mississippi since Franklin D. Roosevelt visited Tupelo in 1936, the visit signified to many that the national government had removed their state from pariah status. Trent Lott, William Colmer's young chief of staff, described the sight of Air Force One landing in Gulfport as "the prettiest sight" he had ever seen. Nixon was just as grateful and he told Eastland that he had never been so warmly received nor had he seen such devastation since he toured Essen, Germany, as a first-term congressman on a trip that had convinced him to support the Marshall Plan. Eastland was appreciative, even if one correspondent lambasted him for standing behind Nixon with his arms crossed when he wasn't puffing away at his cigar.[6]

Almost as soon as Eastland and the others got back to Washington, both houses of Congress approved the bill. "People needed help," Birch Bayh said later, and he and others charged with passing the measure pressed those who wanted to use the bill to push their own agenda to find another vehicle. Eastland, for his part, was quick to denounce officials in the Department of Health, Education, and Welfare who aimed to deny all funds to schools hit by Camille for what he called their "heartless and vindictive" aim to use the schools "as an experimental laboratory for their theories of forced integration." More quietly, he did all he could within legislative and administrative channels to guarantee that Mississippi firms would perform the cleanup. Once others cleared up a few more technical glitches, the Senate approved what became the most comprehensive disaster relief bill ever by voice vote.[7] Thus, Eastland forged a relationship across party lines that would not just last but strengthen for the duration of the Nixon presidency.

On foreign policy issues, Eastland attached himself firmly to the goals of Richard Nixon. Always a proponent of the adage that politics stopped at the water line, Eastland trusted Nixon's instinctive anti-Communism, and he was as supportive of Nixon's handling of the U.S. war effort in Vietnam as he had been of Lyndon Johnson's. He had had some initial misgivings about deploying American troops in Indochina, saying in 1954 that "American boys cannot be the policemen of the world" and that he did not want America involved in "another hopeless war like Korea." As France prepared to leave her colony of Indochina, comprised of Vietnam, Cambodia, and Laos, Eastland told Mississippians that Southeast Asia was too far outside our natural defense perimeters to justify sending troops. Once American troops were committed, he, like many on the right, was convinced that first Johnson and then Nixon "should turn our Air Force loose, destroy North Vietnam, and bring the boys home." Unconcerned with the practices of America's allies in South Vietnam, he clung to his conception of the fundamentally diabolical nature of the Communists to their north. In defending the intrusion into Cambodia in April 1970, for example, Eastland said that Nixon had been confronted with "cold, calculated, callous aggression and endless maneuvering of the latter day oriental khan." As the war wound down, he stuck with Nixon through every nuance of his ever-evolving strategy to bring the war to a halt. He defended each expansion of the bombing of North Vietnam and insisted that America should not withdraw from Southeast Asia until all prisoners of war had been returned. He supported Nixon's move to build an anti-ballistic missile system and thought his initial moves toward détente with the Soviet Union were a "sincere effort" toward world peace. Yet he had grave doubts about Nixon's reopening of relations with China.

Aware that millions of people had died needlessly since the Communists took power, Eastland hoped that Nixon was exploiting a weakness in the Sino-Soviet relationship and demanded that geopolitical policy in the region be conducted with "our eyes open." He was equally quick to mention that he backed the regime of Jiang Jieshi, the anti-Communist but hardly democratic leader of the Republic of China, which had had to take refuge on the island of Taiwan. If Nationalist China was to be ousted from the UN, Eastland urged that the United States immediately suspend all financial aid to that group.[8]

The countries outside of Nixon's focus where Eastland took a particular interest were the apartheid regimes of South Africa and what then was known as Rhodesia. Like many members of Congress from the Deep South, he toured those troubled lands at his own expense. He was hardly interested in the sites. Upon arriving at Victoria Falls, he observed that wonder of the world for about fifteen seconds and then declared, "OK, I've seen it."[9] Eastland met with Prime Ministers Ian Smith of Rhodesia and John Vorster of South Africa and made it clear that he admired their systems. "I believe in segregation," he declared in Johannesburg. He found the low veldt land as fertile as that of the Mississippi Delta and was even more impressed by the prosperity, stability, and racial harmony he saw, even in the midst of guerilla attacks. He bristled at America's refusal to recognize the Smith regime and repeatedly blasted American administrations for what he called "inhumane, illegal, arbitrary, unfair, harmful and costly" policies. The sanctions applied against Rhodesia, he said, were not only stiffer than those against China, but geopolitically and economically foolish as well as they denied America its best potential source of chrome. In consequence, the United States had to get its higher-priced store of chrome from the Soviet Union, and the Soviets profited even more on that portion of the chrome they bought from Rhodesia.[10]

Eastland's reflexive anti-Communism on questions involving southern Africa had always been part of his outlook. It mattered little if countries who shunned the rhetoric of Marx and Lenin protected basic human rights within their borders. He would be with them. In 1960, he hailed Dominican dictator Rafael Trujillo as a "true friend" of the United States and argued that abandoning him might create a vacuum Communist Cuba could fill. A year later, he joined conservatives William F. Buckley and Barry Goldwater in raising money for the American Committee for Aid to Katanga Freedom Fighters, a group trying to prevent the Congo from falling to the Communist-supplied forces of Patrice Lumumba. And, more than a decade later, he, unlike most in his caucus, proudly told colleagues that he had utterly no regrets with the Nixon administration's use of the CIA to depose the democratically elected Marxist government of Salvador Allende in Chile.[11]

On matters of civil rights policy, the matters long deemed to be central in the eyes of most Mississippians, Nixon was much less of an ally. Eastland was initially distressed by the appointments of James Farmer, the onetime head of the Congress of Racial Equality, as assistant secretary of the Department of Health, Education, and Welfare, and New York Commissioner of Education James E. Allen Jr. to a similar position within the department. He called Farmer a "militant civil rights worker" and blasted Allen for backing affirmative action and busing. Fifty-seven percent of the American people, he told the Senate, had voted for candidates (Nixon and George Wallace) who advocated a slower pace of desegregation than pursued during the Johnson years. Eastland, like other Southerners pushing "freedom of choice" as an alternative to full desegregation, expressed alarm at the statement of Health, Education, and Welfare Secretary Robert Finch that he would reject any plan that did "not secure full integration." He told a correspondent that delegations from Dixie would step up pressure on Nixon to slow integration. In Eastland's view, Nixon had abandoned a pledge to institute the kind of "freedom of choice" plans that many liberals feared allowed white parents to choose the schools their children would attend, then denied black parents the same opportunity. Nor was he pleased that Nixon would not find time for months to meet with him and the rest of the Mississippi delegation on racial questions. While he believed that the heart of new Attorney General John Mitchell was "in the right place," Eastland found the early days of the Nixon administration "very, very disappointing."[12]

Even at this late date, Eastland told Leon Panetta, the young head of the civil rights office in the Department of Health, Education, and Welfare, "You are never going to integrate schools in the South." He felt certain desegregation could be delayed indefinitely, and he was grateful that Secretary Robert Finch sided with Mississippi lawyers who called upon the Fifth Circuit Court of Appeals to let them delay submitting plans for schools until December 1, 1969. But while that motion carried, a Supreme Court ruling of October 29, 1969, in *Alexander v. Holmes County* (Mississippi) effectively ended the Deep South's stall by ordering all southern states to desegregate their public schools by the beginning of the 1970–71 school year. For Eastland, the ruling was an unmitigated disaster. Still, he and all other Mississippi politicos realized that the decision barred the state from preventing black students from attending previously all-white schools. White parents in Mississippi could enroll their children in what quickly became known as "segregation academies" and began building them across the state. By fall 1970, enough parents withdrew their children from public schools in Sunflower County to leave them but 15 percent white. While Eastland had not been a favorite of the Citizens Council since he boarded the Lady Bird Special, he continued to argue that racially mixed schools had never worked "at any place, at any time," and gave hefty sums to the Indianola and North Sunflower Academies in his home county. He and State Supreme Court Justice Tom Brady were named honorary cochairmen of a Citizens Council–sponsored foundation in the summer of 1970 that built private schools around the state that would be open to any white child. The same year, Eastland also launched plans to convince Congress to nullify an order by a lower federal court to deny tax-exempt status to any of these new "segregation academies."[13]

For the duration of his fifth term, Eastland engaged in what historian Joseph Crespino called a "strategic accommodation" with those accelerating the pace of desegregation. He would not assist the work of the committees the administration had created in many counties to guide the desegregation of the schools, but he would not obstruct their work either. He did back a bid by John Stennis to equalize practices for school desegregation in all parts of the country and thus end a system that permitted de facto segregation in the North while condemning the de jure variety prevalent in Dixie. To the surprise of many, the Senate passed this measure. While some northern and midwestern liberals conceded that their own states had not adequately integrated their schools, they opposed the Stennis addendum, arguing that it would take funds away from larger problems of longer vintage in the South. But their arguments did not prevail this time, for Abraham Ribicoff of Connecticut, once John

F. Kennedy's secretary of the Department of Health, Education, and Welfare, broke with his progressive brethren to condemn the "monumental hypocrisy" of those who opposed uniform enforcement procedures in all parts of America. What resulted were not further delays in enforcement in the South, as Eastland had hoped, for Richard Nixon was determined to carry out the letter of *Alexander v. Holmes County*, if as quietly as possible. Nixon, as noted by Dean J. Kotlowski, the most thorough academic student of his civil rights record, "gave the South the opportunity to comply with the Court's mandate peacefully." In doing so, he allowed them to "retreat with dignity rather than continue fighting." Nixon's major objective in traveling south in 1970 was to meet with media representatives to urge them to desensationalize their coverage of integration and to nudge a panel his administration formed in Louisiana to hasten its negotiations, so schools might open on time without incident. Southern leaders like Eastland would not be helpful, but the lack of overt moralizing left them feeling less compelled to lead another charge against any modicum of change.[14]

Busing was one issue with racial connotations that Eastland raised for the rest of his tenure in the Senate. In truth, the amount of busing had changed little from the heyday of the Jim Crow South, when black children were often bused from one end of a county to another to get to an all-black school serving their grade. But, like those of other segregationists, Eastland's attitudes changed when the students being bused were white. In 1970 and 1971, he came out for measures barring busing and stripping from federal courts jurisdiction over any question involving education. Only mischief could ensue when "bureaucrats assumed the function of parents" and "suicidal social theories were substituted for the sound principles that undergird the educational process," he said. Once the Supreme Court in April of 1971 ruled in *Swann v. Charlotte-Mecklenberg County* that school boards could employ busing as its principal means of achieving racial balance in its schools, Eastland gained latitude. He rued that the court put the impetus only on a southern school system to gain proportional equity and not all those throughout the land. With more than a few crocodile tears, he got in a bit of Yankee bashing when he declared that he could not understand how a "ten year old colored" student in Harlem, South Chicago, or Watts was not protesting the lack of similar measures to impose integration upon other parts of the country. Later in the decade, courts ordered schools in northern cities, among them Boston, Detroit, and Louisville, to use busing to bring balance. Such rulings aroused controversy outside of the Deep South among those who still resisted any integration and others who resented the less than rational means by which some busing plans were being set into motion. In Nashville, for example, school officials adopted a system whereby some schools created a two-shift schedule and some students were bused past several schools serving their grade. For the rest of his tenure, Eastland found opportunities to hold hearings on antibusing measures, knowing none of the constitutional amendments being floated would be ratified. In this way, he put northern legislators on notice that their hypocrisies were being observed. Yet he also came to recognize that whereas some he called social engineers believed that their egalitarian aims justified busing, many parents of all partisan, ideological, and religious stripes, some who had backed all previous means of integration, had concluded that busing had detrimental effects upon the education of their children. On this issue with racial connotations, if this one alone, time was on his side.[15]

At home, Eastland remained a force, even if he was never the omnipotent "Godfather of Mississippi" many projected him to be. It was rare that he involved himself prior to a runoff in any gubernatorial primary campaign other than those of Paul Johnson Jr., whose father had appointed him to his Senate seat. Even these Libby tried to dissuade him from, saying that his debt had been met many times. Eastland would have none of it. "A political obligation is never repaid," he always replied.[16] Consistent with his practice, Eastland took no public position in the initial gubernatorial primary of 1971. His supporters divided among several candidates, and the leader after the first plebiscite was Lieutenant Governor Charles Sullivan, a Clarksdale attorney, who ran more than 60,000 votes ahead of William Waller, the district attorney best known for having unsuccessfully prosecuted Byron De La Beckwith. But while Champ Terney, Eastland's son-in-law, backed the lieutenant governor, Sullivan near the end of the first primary began painting Waller as a tool of the old order, primarily because many of Eastland's principal money men and supporters backed him. "If you vote for that candidate," he said, "you'll get a change all right, . . . you'll get a change right back to the way things were ten years ago." His words clearly were aimed at Eastland and former Governor Paul Johnson Jr. and reopened wounds first inflicted a decade before. Astutely, Waller began driving to Doddsville often to seek Eastland's advice. Eastland listened more than he spoke, but he ended most visits by cataloguing a list of influential people in virtually every county for Waller to contact. And, he made a few phone calls on his own. One was to Frank Barber, who had worked for Governor Johnson before he signed on with Eastland. "Frank," he commanded, "go tell Paul that I know what he wants and he knows what I want." He also dispatched longtime associate Martin Fraley to travel the state and give the backhanded assurance that Sullivan's "drinking problem is not as bad as it was." Waller prevailed in the end by virtually the same margin as he ran behind Sullivan in the initial primary. Not long before his death in 2011, Waller made it clear to at least one writer that he could not have been elected governor "without his [Eastland's] help."[17]

Waller had opposition in the general election, but not from a Republican. The challenge came from Charles Evers, who when elected mayor of Fayette in 1969 became the first African-American mayor of a biracial town in the South. Evers had intended to run as the nominee of the Loyalist Democratic Party, the body recognized by the national Democratic Party, but Secretary of State Heber Ladner ruled that only the Regular Democratic Party had legal standing in the state. He would have to run as an Independent. Eastland discounted his chances as much as anyone. "A two year old," he told a Tupelo dinner gathering, had "a better chance to dig the Tennessee-Tombigbee Waterway with a teaspoon than our opponent has to defeat Bill Waller." The point where Eastland chose to attack Evers lay in his sources of funding, as too much of it had been raised in the District of Columbia and New York City "on the fancy cocktail party circuit" from "curious, smelly long-haired people." These were mild barbs in what for the Magnolia State was a unique and pioneering race almost entirely devoid of racial content. "It's a good time to be a Mississippian," Hodding Carter III, the moderately liberal editor of the *Delta Democrat Times* pronounced, right before Waller trounced Evers by a better than three-to-one margin.[18]

As always, Eastland took time to counsel aspiring young politicos who had been friendly in the past. He offered his support in a contested

Democratic primary to David R. Bowen, a bright young political scientist who had run the state's federal liaison program for Governor John Bell Williams, with the only caveat that Bowen had to seek a seat on the House Agriculture Committee. And, he made time for Trent Lott, who unlike William Colmer, his boss, was running as a Republican, a seeming demerit in a district where only 8 percent of the voters identified with the party of Lincoln. Lott walked to Eastland's office and waited for what seemed an eternity. Once invited in, he declined a Chivas Regal and then, realizing that a Democrat could not actively support him, asked Eastland with a considerable stammer not to work actively against him. "Oh hell, boy," Eastland said, emerging from his gruff demeanor, "I ain't gonna oppose you."

Even so, Eastland had begun to contemplate how long he wanted to continue his political career, and he needed a push to seek a sixth term. Libby, never relishing political life, would have been content to return to Doddsville. Were he to retire, Eastland still believed he had a duty to recruit an electable successor of some gravitas. The only one he believed fit that bill in 1972 was James P. Coleman, and he sent an aide to notify Coleman that he would defer to him if he wanted to make the bid. Coleman, who had lost his last statewide election in 1963, considered the offer briefly, then declined, knowing that he would have to abandon a rewarding federal judgeship for a race where he would have to wage a spirited effort even to secure the Democratic nomination.[19]

Eastland did draw token opposition in the primary from two little-known challengers: Louis Fondren, a state representative from Moss Point, and Taylor Webb, a Leland businessman who had once headed the state Economic Council. Webb, the more serious of the two, believed that no one should go unchallenged and maintained that the state's black minority deserved a more sympathetic ear. He berated Eastland for missing votes to hike Social Security benefits and increase funding for higher education or crime control and for failing to compel Birch Bayh to hold hearings that might lead to legislation to curb what both he and Eastland called "forced busing." But more commonly, he rued Eastland's dominance of the state. "If you're going to get rid of boss politics," he would say, "you've got to get rid of the boss." Webb won the support of the *Leland Progress* and the *Winona Times*, but could not compete with Eastland, who long before had captured the loyalties of most Mississippi whites, as much from his work to meet the human needs of ordinary constituents as from his commitment to any issue. Still, Eastland took no chances. He hired a campaign consultant for the first time, Deloss Walker, a Memphis-based strategist who had designed the successful gubernatorial bids of Democrat Dale Bumpers of Arkansas and Republican Winfield Dunn of Tennessee in 1970 and Democrat William Waller of Mississippi in 1971. In contrast, a Houston-based agency Webb hired dropped him as a client at the behest of Texas Republican Senator John Tower, who almost certainly acted on behalf of the Nixon White House. Although Webb thought he was making progress, Eastland won 70 percent of the vote. Once the campaign ended, Webb spotted Eastland at Lillo's restaurant in Leland and walked over to extend his congratulations. Eastland was magnanimous, a trait Webb respected, but he let his vanquished opponent in on a secret. "You never knew it," he told Webb, "but I had a man sitting up in your campaign telling you what to do."[20]

Eastland had been led by White House hands to expect that he would have no GOP opposition in 1972. Thinking Eastland unbeatable, many agreed that the best course was to leave their Senate slot blank and concentrate upon electing their candidates to seats being vacated by three retiring House members. That was what many state GOP leaders intended, but that changed when James Meredith let it be known that he would file to run against Eastland. To America as a whole, Meredith was the hero of the battle of Oxford. But he had no standing among Mississippi Republicans and, having lived in New York for the past three years, little among Mississippi blacks. Because Meredith had not confided in them, state GOP leaders could not predict the course he might take. Some suspected he was using the race to establish himself as a rival among the state's blacks to Mayor Charles Evers. More common was a fear that Meredith, if nominated, would spend the fall trashing Richard Nixon and thus harm not just Nixon, but all party-building efforts, and they began searching for an alternative.[21]

The man state chairman Clarke Reed recruited was Gil Carmichael, a forty-five-year-old Volkswagen dealer and community activist from Meridian with ties to all parts of the state. Over the previous five years, the articulate entrepreneur had been named Mississippian of the Year by the state Broadcasters Association, served as president of the East Mississippi Council, cofounded Highways: Our Pressing Emergency, chaired the Meridian Industrial Foundation, served on the Emergency Council Governor John Bell Williams had formed to direct aid after Hurricane Camille, and taught a Sunday school class for adults. A sixth-generation Mississippian, Carmichael had an appeal to youth that was reflected later in the year in victories in straw polls at colleges and universities across the state. He also had some credibility with black voters, for he had served on Nixon's state advisory Committee on Education and in 1964 had financed the replacement of the shattered windshield of civil rights worker Michael Schwerner. In what was the first statewide Republican primary ever in Mississippi, Carmichael outpolled Meredith by a nearly four-to-one margin. But those analyzing the results were quick to note that GOP turnout was but one-tenth of that for Democrats.[22]

At sixty-seven, Eastland was entering the new media-driven age of politics. He had lost some of his vigor, and regretted that he could not wear the two-button charcoal gray suits that were the staple of his wardrobe. His handler Deloss Walker forced him to wear tighter three-button brown and blue suits that he came to call his "uniforms" for the duration of the campaign and dispensed with immediately thereafter. He hardly looked forward to an endless schedule of speeches. In lieu of those, friends organized a series of Eastland Appreciation Dinners around the state to allow him to conserve his energy. From time to time, he planned to plunge into crowds for short intervals to press the flesh. But one hour-long stint in the sun outside of a new banana terminal in Gulfport was exhausting enough that he ordered press secretary Larry Speakes not to let that happen again. And, when asked who he backed in the Democratic primary for president, Eastland replied that he would cast his ballot for George Wallace, who stood no chance of winning. Whenever asked if he would support the eventual nominee, he ducked the issue by saying he would wait to "discuss that when we know who it is."[23]

Carmichael, for his part, made a strong impression in what would be a good Republican year. Some outside of the formal leadership of the GOP guessed that any money that went to a challenger to Eastland would be money that would not go to three blue chip candidates—Carl Butler of Columbus, Thad Cochran of Jackson, and Trent Lott of Pascagoula—who were vying to fill vacancies created by the retirements of congressional veterans Thomas Abernethy, Charles Griffin, and William Colmer, respectively. Mississippi River tugboat magnate Jesse Brent, a close friend of Eastland albeit a Republican, even sought out Carmichael and offered to help him pay any debts incurred up until that point and guarantee him some future support from the Eastland organization if he withdrew. Less subtle was Fred LaRue, who warned Carmichael quite bluntly that he would have trouble raising money for any future campaign unless he left the race. Taken aback at first by LaRue's heavy-handedness and then emboldened, Carmichael smiled and said he was in the campaign to stay.[24]

Still, Carmichael did not have a united Republican Party. Prentiss Walker, the ultraconservative former congressman Eastland had trounced in 1966, was running as an Independent, thinking Carmichael the "most liberal" Republican of any stature in the state party. Jackson businessman Jack Breed, the recently ousted chairman of the Hinds County GOP Executive Committee, and Columbus attorney Hunter Gholson both signed on with Eastland with no rancor toward Carmichael, thinking he as chairman could do more to advance the conservative causes that mattered to them. A far more prominent recruit for Eastland was Rubel Phillips, who had run credible races as the GOP nominee for governor in 1963 and 1967. For Phillips, who had worked on Eastland's 1954 campaign, the choice was clear. Richard Nixon seemed satisfied with Eastland being in the Senate and his position was "more valuable to the state now than ever."[25]

Eastland's principal selling point was his clout. "When Jim Eastland speaks," one newspaper ad led, taking off on a then popular television spot for the E. F. Hutton brokerage firm, "Presidents listen." Another met a contention of the Carmichael campaign head on by pointing to the billions of dollars Eastland and John Stennis had brought into the state. "Jim Eastland has been working: just look around and see." The one issue he highlighted was his work to expedite aid after Hurricane Camille. "The Morning after the Storm," bold print in another statewide ad read, "Eastland was there." Counter to his past, he centered his appeals to conservatives by heralding his credentials as an anti-Communist and trumpeted the declaration of the *Red Star* that he was the chief opponent of Communism in America. He sought to counter Carmichael's appeal to youth by reminding those of college age that he had backed the Twenty-Sixth Amendment, which had lowered the voting age to eighteen. And, faced with more blacks in the electorate, he stressed his work as a national leader rather then one determined to wage war for any further lost regional causes. Those on the dais at one dinner saluted more than a dozen prominent black leaders in attendance. No longer would "Dixie" be played at each event. At an appreciation dinner in Hattiesburg, an integrated Baptist choir sang "The Battle Hymn of the Republic," the last tune anyone connected with the Confederacy would have wanted to hear in any year of the previous century.[26]

While Eastland had long maintained that a two-party system would harm the South as it would dilute the black vote, he adopted a stance as a voice of bipartisan harmony in 1972. That option came to him from Richard Nixon, who found his help on the Judiciary Committee invaluable. When Nixon asked if Eastland might help him in his reelection bid, the choice came easily for Eastland, who was just as appreciative of Nixon's rapid response to the needs of his state after Hurricane Camille. "All right, Mr. President," Eastland told Nixon. "You don't need any help in the state, but you can get it." In the unspoken language of politics, the obvious quid pro quo was that Nixon would do nothing to help Carmichael. Nixon installed Eastland intimate Jesse Brent as chairman of the state branch of the Committee to Re-elect the President. Three months before the election, Eastland told friends that Carmichael was getting no money from national GOP sources, and that Brent would spend considerable time having Democrats for Nixon instruct voters how to split their ticket. "Vote for the man, not for the party," Eastland workers would say, and he made sure to cast himself as a "Mississippi Democrat." Were he to lose and the GOP to control the Senate, power would move to members from just south of the Canadian border, as Margaret Chase Smith of Maine would get the chiefdom at the Armed Services Committee, Roman Hruska would chair the Judiciary Committee, and Milton Young would assume the helm of the Agriculture Committee. Whenever asked if he was supporting George McGovern, the Democratic nominee, he deflected the question by saying that he was "running for the Senate just as hard" as he could. Privately, he conceded that McGovern was a drag on the ticket in the South and that his ticket mates would have to work harder because of his presence. "I'm not a party hack," he would say, sensing that most realized that he was leaning toward Nixon. Aware that most knew that polls showed Nixon well ahead, he used his ads to stress his clout as well as the limited impact Carmichael would almost certainly have if he were elected. Sending a freshman to represent Mississippi, he said, would be like "adding another Chinaman to the population of China."[27]

Eastland shadowboxed with Carmichael for much of the campaign. When he first met Carmichael, he feigned uncertainty. "Are you that fellow who's running against me?" Eastland asked. "Since I'm running against you," Carmichael retorted, "I just wanted you to lay eyes on me." Eastland continued to stand as a Bourbon. By 1972, that meant that he would deemphasize issues with racial connotations other than busing and that he would advertise in black newspapers. He backed revenue sharing programs that would allow state and local officials even in the smallest of communities much more control over how federal money would be spent where they lived. He called upon the federal government to add funding for interstate highways and a system of four-lane highways in Mississippi. And, just as importantly to the predominantly rural denizens of the Magnolia State, he vowed to fight any effort to use federal funds previously set aside for the federal highway system to build mass transit systems in America's urban centers.[28]

Carmichael, for his part, trekked 40,000 miles by car and logged 400 hours in the air, just by mid-September. Like New South pols of a century earlier, he heralded a vision of a more prosperous Dixie centered around vibrant commercial centers fueled by clean industries staffed by the ablest native young people who no longer would leave the state for higher-paying jobs elsewhere. He painted himself and his party as champions of the working men and women of Mississippi, even blasting Eastland for voting against raising the minimum wage. Other times, he cited a report published in *Field and Stream* magazine, hardly a haven for radicals, that condemned Eastland's record on environmental issues as the worst of any senator. Here was a message tailor-made for a border-state Whig of the 1840s or Republican of the 1970s. But, sadly for Carmichael, his state remained a land of small cities and large plantations, whose prosperity depended on the whims of the weather and whose outlooks remained akin to those of their rustic forbearers. He hoped that he might appeal to the populistic strains embedded in some of those of middle to lower incomes by lamenting that Eastland had made more in subsidies some years than they had made their entire lives. "He's supposed to be better-ing the people," Carmichael would say, "and not his own cotton-picking wealth." His polls showed that a majority of Mississippians wanted both the choices afforded by a two-party system and a change. One Democrat told Carmichael that he was ahead at the beginning of October, but that mattered little in 1972. By all measurements, the clearest choice on the ballot that year was between Richard Nixon and George McGovern. Car-michael had the easy choice of backing a popular incumbent of his own party. Eastland privately backed Nixon, but knew that overtly supporting him would place his chairmanship and thus the major source of his power in jeopardy. Carmichael noticed Eastland's discomfort and admired the shrewdness of his straddle. "That old booger is a better politician that he was six months ago," he marveled. Still, he continued to taunt Eastland as to who his choice for president was, assuming that a single misstep might turn the election in his favor.[29]

Astute politicos had no trouble discerning who Nixon preferred. When Vice President Agnew came to Jackson to speak on September 29, seated behind him were the three Republican congressional candidates who he praised effusively, many of Mississippi's best-known Democrats, a group of Nixonettes, and several bands. Carmichael was kept away from the podium in front of the old State House, even if he was in the eyes of many GOP leaders one of the ablest newcomers anywhere. While dozens of Republicans waved Carmichael signs anyway, their candidate was left to watch the proceedings across the street from the fifth floor offices of the state Republican Party. State GOP Chairman Clarke Reed had to explain to reporters that Nixon and Agnew could not afford to alienate someone like Eastland who had been helpful in the past. Carmichael in return took the occasion to lambaste the Committee to Re-elect the President and White House aide Fred LaRue, often Nixon's liaison to Eastland, for back-ing a "bogus Republican candidate" who had once described Republicans as "rattlesnakes."[30]

Many state Republicans remained demoralized by Nixon's tacit sup-port for Eastland, even if it gave Carmichael the image of a David taking on an aging Goliath. That state of affairs lingered, particularly after John

Mitchell and Richard Kleindienst, the two men who had served Nixon as attorney general, and Clifford Hardin and Earl Butz, their counter-parts at the Agriculture Department, traveled to Mississippi in October to make it clear that they were for Eastland. A few national Republicans lent their support to Carmichael. Tennessee Governor Winfield Dunn and fourteen GOP senators endorsed him, as did some with enduring resentments of Eastland like Charles Sullivan and a niece of Wall Doxey. But the ambivalence projected by the White House continued to resonate. While Nixon had daughter Tricia Nixon Cox endorse Eastland on a trip to Mississippi, Harry Dent, the architect of Nixon's "Southern Strategy," told reporters before a Committee to Re-elect the President event in Jackson that he backed Carmichael but would not knock Eastland. In a letter to Julie Nixon Eisenhower, who would appear on the Gulf Coast two days later, Dent acknowledged that Eastland had backed Nixon "on some very critical issues," he wrote. But while Carmichael had no chance of winning, she might, even should, endorse him to restore some morale to the state GOP who still were figured to have good shots at picking up a seat or two in the state's House delegation, so long as she did not utter a word implying a criticism of the chairman.[31]

Eastland closed his campaign trumpeting a solid Bourbon tune. "We've destroyed the Warren Court and . . . I helped do it," he boasted at a rally right before the election. "Do you think some Republican got 'em through?" In truth, he had much GOP help securing the confirmations of Nixon's nominees. It was as well the national Republican Party who cut off the money spigot to Carmichael, leaving him but $155,000, barely one-fifth of what Eastland had raised. While Carmichael could run ads in smaller markets, he could not afford an ad on even one television station in the Baton Rouge, Memphis, Mobile, and New Orleans media markets. His brief late summer rise in the polls did perturb Eastland enough for him to lament that "that son of a bitch cost my friends a half million dollars." Still, Carmichael carried but eleven counties near his Lauderdale County home. He fared better than most Republicans among African Americans, but still won but 47 percent, a showing that demonstrated how thoroughly the GOP had slipped among them over the last decade. Among all other voters in this still agriculture-dominated haven, Eastland prevailed handily. The 375,102 votes he garnered, 57.8 percent of the total, nearly tripled the number of votes received by George McGovern, a performance demonstrating that white Mississippi voters strongly approved of him and Richard Nixon and wanted to keep them working together for another four years.[32] Yet the victories of young attorneys Thad Cochran and Trent Lott in congressional districts centered in Jackson and along the Gulf Coast demonstrated a growing appeal of the brand of Republicanism in the commercial hubs of Mississippi. Some even surmised that Carmichael might have given Eastland quite a challenge had his own party's hierarchy been as loyal to him as they had been to less viable nominees in other states. Were such demographic trends to accelerate, the southern political species of the Bourbon Democrat would become extinct.

To Eastland's way of thinking, what had happened was a reconstitution of the conservative coalition of Republicans and southern Democrats that had first appeared in Franklin Roosevelt's second term. With Nixon having won 61 percent nationwide and carried 49 states, conditions appeared ripe for the generation of peace Nixon had promised and a decentralization of federal power. What neither man counted on was that a foiled burglary the White House had originally termed a "third rate break-in" would by the middle of 1973 manifest into a presidential scandal without precedent.

Eastland's first involvement with what his friend John Mitchell described as the "White House horrors" came months before five burglars were arrested in the Watergate headquarters of the Democratic National Committee. A task he assumed would be perfunctory lay in confirming Richard Kleindienst to succeed Mitchell as attorney general. While some liberals hurled sharp queries at Kleindienst in the initial round of hearings, they uncovered nothing terribly embarrassing. It was Eastland's practice to hold a vote whenever he knew he had the votes to win, and a united committee approved Kleindienst in the latter part of February 1972. At this point, there were but two opponents in the Senate, Fred Harris and George McGovern, both of whom in running for president were tailoring their appeals to the most liberal elements of the Democratic Party. But, as confirmation seemed assured, muckraker Jack Anderson published stories charging Kleindienst with lying that he had not been involved in an antitrust settlement where the International Telegraph and Telephone Company (ITT) would acquire the Hartford Fire Insurance Company if it made significant contributions to GOP causes. As Anderson was hardly the most respected journalist in the capital and the statement in question was not made under oath, the story as it stood had little chance of impacting anything. Still, Kleindienst took it as an attack upon his honor and asked Eastland to reopen the hearings so he might defend himself. "Are you out of yo' mind?" Eastland asked Kleindienst. No, Kleindienst replied, I just want to clear my good name. In doing so, he made certain that much more information would come out that would embarrass the administration and eventually get him convicted of perjury for testifying that he had received no pressure from within the government to drop antitrust litigation against ITT. This statement would be proven patently false when a White House tape of April 19, 1971, made clear that Nixon himself had phoned Kleindienst to order that he cease scrutiny of ITT.[33]

The hearings Eastland conducted lasted twenty-four days, one of the longest confirmation probes in history. The procedures employed were bizarre. The key piece of evidence Jack Anderson turned up was a memo written by ITT lobbyist Dita Beard informing ITT president Harold Geneen that a large contribution to the GOP had rendered it likely that the Justice Department would not challenge their firm's acquisition of Hartford Insurance. If the panel's probe is remembered for anything, it was its pursuit of Beard, a colorful woman with a reputation for hard drinking, all the way to a Denver hospital where second-tier Nixon aides tried to hide her beneath a mass of makeup and a reddish wig. Upon finding her, senators and staff questioned her in her bed, where she answered questions in a hospital gown while smoking cigarettes, then sucked in air through an oxygen mask. Eastland did not make that trip, but did all he could to see not only that Kleindienst got a chance to make his case, but that his critics had ample time to make theirs. At the time, the reopening of the Kleindienst hearings gave Judiciary Committee liberals an opportunity to probe at great length for the first time allegations of sordid behavior within the Nixon administration.[34]

Only after Nixon's reelection would senators begin to contemplate a probe of all matters categorized under the heading of Watergate. As chairman of the Senate Judiciary Committee, Eastland held a perch that seemed to make him a natural choice to chair an investigation of Watergate. Majority Leader Mike Mansfield was not so sure. He wrote

Eastland and Sam Ervin and told them that one of the two, rather than a younger member with presidential ambitions, would have to chair a select committee that would study what went wrong and take legislative steps to see such events did not recur. Recognizing that Ervin's aptitudes as a raconteur as well as his constitutional acumen made him a natural for a job demanding a bit of a media presence, Eastland deferred gladly to Ervin, knowing many in his party thought him too close to Nixon. But he would not be able to avoid Watergate as it unfurled. On his docket in early March 1973 was the nomination of acting director L. Patrick Gray to replace J. Edgar Hoover. Eastland at first thought Gray a cinch for confirmation, but many longtime Hoover hands, some hoping one of them would replace Hoover, began leaking reports of what they saw as Gray's mistakes to friends in the press and in Congress. Senators began to explore how the FBI would make available their files on the Watergate break-in to them. Upon being queried by Eastland, Gray agreed to let every senator inspect the documents. This offer was open for but a few days, as Nixon, annoyed with Gray's habit of answering all queries, forced his nominee to rescind his proffer. By mid March, committee Democrats found that Gray had burned documents from Watergate figure E. Howard Hunt at the behest of White House counsel John Dean. Eastland opined that the panel could not subpoena Dean, but that he could and should appear voluntarily. Nothing doing, said Dean, who unknown to Eastland or Gray, but with Nixon's acquiescence, had decided it best that Gray not be confirmed. Eastland then passed along an offer from Dean to answer written interrogatories, but Sam Ervin and liberal Republican Charles Mathias scotched this by saying that Dean would have to appear if Gray were to be confirmed. Eastland recessed the hearings for two weeks in the hope of calming tensions. But there was no chance Dean would testify, which guaranteed that the best Gray could expect was a tie vote in committee, a reality that prompted him to ask Nixon to withdraw his nomination.[35]

Eastland recognized that interest in Watergate had heightened when he noticed that he would have to find a bigger room to conduct the Gray hearings. It was then that Dean's participation in the Watergate cover-up became public, after which Dean hired lawyers to protect his own interests. For Eastland at the outset of the investigation, the Watergate affair did not prompt a "need for national self-immolation," as it was simply an "incredibly stupid act by a few men" that Nixon's critics had "blown out of proportion." At the dedication of the Everett McKinley Dirksen Library in June 1973, Eastland assured Nixon that he would support him in the event of an impeachment regardless of if he were innocent or not. Once it became known that Nixon had taped many presidential conversations in the White House and elsewhere, Eastland suggested that he go before the Ervin committee and announce that he had destroyed the tapes in keeping with what he saw as the principle of executive privilege. By the end of August 1973, Eastland was telling correspondents that he would like to see the Senate Watergate Committee end its hearings and publish its final report as quickly as possible.[36]

Eastland's support for Nixon remained constant throughout the Watergate ordeal. He was one of the few members of Congress Nixon would phone during the middle of the night to seek counsel. Those who talked with Eastland about Nixon's approaches then or thereafter got no sense that he believed Nixon was drinking more than he could handle, as Bob Woodward and Carl Bernstein reported in *The Final Days*. Rather, they suspected Eastland found a bit of paranoia in Nixon when he phoned him in Doddsville to ask how he might avert impeachment. "You gotta help me," Nixon would practically beg him. "You gotta save me." Eastland then put the phone down, went to fix himself a drink. "Dick," he would say as he would to any other former colleague, "now, you've gotta get ahold of yourself. I'm not going to abandon you under any circumstances."[37]

Even as others began lamenting Nixon's delays in complying with requests from the Ervin committee or the Watergate special prosecutor or the language he was caught using when some of the transcripts of tapes were released, Eastland held just as strongly for the president as he did privately. In late April 1974, he, John Stennis, Governor William Waller, three of the state's congressmen, and Ole Miss football icon Archie Manning, then quarterback of the New Orleans Saints, hosted Nixon and his wife Pat in Jackson for one of his few public appearances that year. Here, Nixon could speak among friends about everything but Watergate. Mississippians appreciated that he had expedited his approval of disaster relief after an array of tornadoes had devastated parts of their state. But Nixon was just as quick to reward Eastland by promising to approve a bill many congressional fiscal watchdogs termed as useless pork. The bill in question indemnified the state's poultry and egg producers, who had to remove nearly 22 million of their birds from the market and slaughter them because they contained residue from dieldrin, a pesticide suspected of being a carcinogen. Eastland told colleagues the plight of the producers "was not of their own making." What many wondered was if such a special measure would have a chance with a conservative president if he were not facing impeachment.[38]

Nixon's legal position fell irreparably after the Supreme Court's 8–0 decision in *United States v. Nixon* ordered the president to surrender tapes sought by Special Prosecutor Leon Jaworski. "It's all over," White House lobbyist Tom Korologos was heard saying in the Senate Judiciary Committee office. Not long thereafter, Alexander Haig, Nixon's chief of staff, determined that he would have to examine the tapes. He listened to one of June 23, in which Nixon acceded to a suggestion that he order the CIA to block the FBI investigation of the Watergate break-in and sensed that Nixon's days in the White House were numbered. Thus forewarned, Haig headed to the Capitol to approach Eastland and other loyalists and show them the incriminating transcripts. Before Haig left, Larry Speakes, by then an assistant in the White House press office, gave him one piece of advice he reserved for only conversations of the highest sensitivity. Eastland's practice was to offer any guest a drink, almost always of his favorite Chivas Regal. Eastland would pour himself a drink in a small glass and dilute it with club soda to half of its potency. Drinks he or Courtney Pace served in much larger iced tea glasses almost always had a considerably higher percentage of alcohol than his own. To guarantee that Haig maintained his command of the discussion, Speakes warned Haig to make sure that his Chivas was as weak as Eastland's. Haig took Speakes' message to heart and insisted that his drink be watered down when he entered Eastland's office. Eastland had never been one for small talk, and this was no time for him to change. Once he saw the transcript, Eastland told Haig that Nixon would be removed from office if he did not resign, even if he himself would be with Nixon to the end.[39]

There were few qualities Eastland appreciated as much as loyalty, and he customarily reciprocated. Not even a set of scandals as tawdry as those connected with Watergate could prompt him to break his allegiance to Nixon, a man who had been his colleague and friend as well as one he credited for expediting hundreds of millions of dollars to alleviate the suffering of thousands of Mississippians after one of the worst hurricanes in history. To him, Nixon's only sin was "to try to cover up." Late in the afternoon of August 8, 1974, he hosted a meeting with a number of longtime Washington hands, mostly Democrats like Johnson Defense Secretary Clark Clifford, Tommy "the Cork" Corcoran, and Ed Foley, that some likened to a "wake" for our government. As president pro tem, Eastland was invited to Nixon's meeting with the joint congressional leadership an hour and a half before he took the air that night to announce that he would resign the presidency at noon the next day. Of those present—Eastland, Senate Majority and Minority Leaders Mike Mansfield and Hugh Scott, House Speaker Carl Albert, and Minority Leader John Rhodes—Eastland was the only one the president any longer found a kindred spirit. He alone would join four dozen other Nixon loyalists at a second meeting a half hour later. Eastland listened intently as Nixon said farewell. "You've been a damned good president," he assured the disgraced commander-in-chief.[40]

That Nixon appreciated Eastland's loyalty is indisputable. One of his first stops anywhere in America when he emerged from his self-imposed exile in 1978 was at a Veterans Day celebration in Gulfport that Eastland and Trent Lott were hosting. Even a few years after Eastland's death, onetime press secretary David Lambert attended a talk by the former president and stood in line to shake hands with Nixon, the only president he had not met since coming to Washington a generation earlier. Lambert found Nixon unimpressed that he had worked for Ron Ziegler, his own spokesman, but ready to chat at length when he mentioned that he had flacked for Eastland. Indeed, the week after he resigned, a despondent Nixon phoned Eastland, one of the few men in Washington in whom he still believed he could confide. "Don't let [Special Prosecutor Leon] Jaworski put me on trial with Haldeman and Ehrlichman," the former president begged the man who once again was second in line to the presidency. "I can't take any more." Eastland immediately phoned Jaworski, whom he knew well from the special prosecutor's stints on American Bar Association panels assessing the merits of nominees to federal courts, and told him Nixon was "in bad shape." Jaworski listened empathetically but noncommittally, not relishing the prospect of bringing a former president to court. Would Congress pass a resolution like one being advanced by

Massachusetts Republican Edward W. Brooke opposing the prosecution of Nixon, he asked, that might provide him a bit of political cover. "We'll think on it," Eastland replied, sensing that members of Congress, particularly his fellow Democrats, were torn on the question.[41]

While Eastland never got back to Jaworski, the question for both became moot when new President Gerald Ford issued Nixon a full and complete pardon on September 8. Still proud to claim Nixon as a "personal friend," Eastland told correspondents that he thought Nixon had "been punished enough" and that a trial demanded by some of Nixon's most vehement critics would be "detrimental to the best interests of our nation" in that it would limit attention from the "many other problems that require our attention." It was his hope that Watergate might have the benefit of stripping some of the power that had devolved upon the executive branch over the past two generations and thus restore the "legislative branch to its rightful place in our constitutional system."[42] Here, Eastland could have a major role, for no longer was he merely chairman of the Senate Judiciary Committee. The departure of Richard Nixon had for the second time in less than a year made him as president pro tempore of the Senate second in line to the presidency behind only Speaker of the House Carl Albert.

CHAPTER 17

President Pro Tem

WHILE JIM EASTLAND'S POWER STEMMED LARGELY FROM THE AUTHORITY
he embodied as chairman of the Judiciary Committee, the most impressive title he ever bore was that of president pro tempore of the Senate.
This was a post Pat Harrison, his revered predecessor, had once held and
one customarily awarded to the senior member of the majority party.
As almost always happens, Eastland fell into this particular job with the
death of the previous occupant, Allen Ellender, on July 27, 1972. For his
part, Eastland was quick to note the criteria as to how one ascends to that
post, pronounced himself "humble and proud," and called it recognition
"of a state and a people." Governor William Waller called his pending
elevation a "bright day for Mississippi." Hardly as happy was Mississippi
NAACP head Aaron Henry, who lambasted Eastland at this time as a
"racist" and promised to monitor Eastland's commitment to his party in
the years to come.[1]

Preparations for what seemed a perfunctory ascension began once
senators returned from Ellender's funeral on Air Force One, where Eastland swapped war stories with President Nixon and a few colleagues.
On his return to the Capitol, he was met by Phil Hart, a man known as
the liberal conscience of the Senate and one who placed but one picture
on his own office wall, Eastland's. Hart startled him by telling him that
he could not support him. When the caucus convened, Hart took issue
with his opposition to civil rights. "Jim Eastland would make an excellent
president pro tem," Hart said, but an "outrageous president. I do not believe Jim Eastland is qualified to govern our country." Several Democrats
commended Hart for his conscientiousness, but none joined him. When
the question went to the Senate, Majority Leader Mike Mansfield placed

Eastland's name in nomination. By custom, Minority Leader Hugh Scott immediately moved to substitute the name of George Aiken of Vermont, the senior Republican. Minutes after the Senate perfunctorily nixed that motion, Jim Eastland stood third in line to the presidency behind only Vice President Spiro Agnew and Speaker of the House Carl Albert.[2]

While Eastland continued to vote a fiscally conservative line not terribly dissimilar to that pushed by the Nixon administration, he did in 1973 side with Senate Democrats on several questions reining in what Arthur M. Schlesinger Jr. called that year "the imperial Presidency." He joined fellow committee chairmen in suing to block Nixon from impounding previously appropriated funds, saying Mississippi was in dire need of money for the Farmers Home Administration and roads. Eastland had always had qualms about sending American boys to Vietnam, even if he had dutifully backed the Johnson and Nixon policies to prosecute the war there. As such, he voted to override Nixon's veto of the War Powers Act, which limited any president's ability to take America to war without congressional approval. When Nixon at around the same time ordered a 4.77 percent salary increase for high-ranking officials in the executive branch, Eastland decreed the same for officers and employees of the Senate. And, although a Nixon loyalist throughout the Watergate debacle, Eastland took care to insist that the orderly processes of government continue. After the infamous Saturday Night Massacre of October 1973, in which Attorney General Elliott Richardson resigned and Deputy Attorney General William Ruckelshaus was fired when they would not dismiss Special Prosecutor Archibald Cox, Eastland joined the rest of the Judiciary Committee in recommending that a new special prosecutor be named to replace Cox and demanding that access to all evidence collected by Cox be limited to just a few authorized people.[3]

A sad occasion occurred for Eastland early in his tenure. In late January 1973, two young hoodlums accosted John Stennis, then robbed him and pumped bullets into his leg and chest. Stennis crawled up the sidewalk and steps of his Washington home and then walked for the door; his wife Coy soon hailed an ambulance to take him to Walter Reed Hospital. Eastland rushed to be with his colleague, and he made it to the hospital as Stennis was wheeled into the operating room. Dozens of senators and the state's House delegation were not far behind. Oregon Republican Mark

Hatfield, Stennis' closest Senate friend, even stayed overnight several times to answer press queries about the prognosis for Stennis. Eastland and Bob Dole established a fund to provide money to anyone who gave information leading to the arrest of the shooters. And it was Eastland alone who represented Mississippi's interests for the next three months. Although it was never his way to milk such a tragedy for personal publicity, there was one point on which Eastland assured instate correspondents who shared his rural values and feared that such an incident might spur any change in policy they abhorred. He would fight each and every bid "to take our guns away from us."[4]

The duties and potential duties that Eastland's new position entailed first became real to him on October 10, 1973, the day Spiro Agnew resigned the vice presidency after pleading *nolo contendre* to a charge of income tax evasion. Like most in Washington, Eastland discounted any notion that the allegations against Agnew might be founded in fact, and thus was surprised when he learned of his departure. But now only Speaker Albert stood between him and the presidency. In immediate terms, his salary rose from $47,500 to $62,500 while the vice presidency remained vacant. The thirty-five member staff of the office of the vice president came under his control. He decided which committees to refer each piece of legislation, signed all bills passed by the Senate, assented to the membership of all delegations representing the Senate on missions abroad, and approved just who could use the Capitol. While he was afforded the use of the vice president's jet, he opted to fly commercially because of the energy crunch that developed after the Yom Kippur War. And, he was granted the use of a second limousine, but ordered it parked.[5] Here were duties—and perks—he had never sought. "There's plenty to keep me busy," he told reporters. "It's another full time job," he added that he would not miss once Congress confirmed a successor to Agnew.[6]

As president pro tem, Eastland was in the room with others in the bipartisan leadership of Congress when Richard Nixon asked for advice as to who the next vice president should be. After Nixon opted for one of their own, House Minority Leader Gerald Ford, Eastland was one of several Democrats the FBI interviewed when they looked into Ford's fitness for the nation's second highest office. Ford's innately open demeanor registered strongly with Eastland, as did his fiscal conservatism and his orientation toward a muscular defense. Even if they had not, it is hardly likely that Eastland would have opposed anyone Nixon or any other president would have nominated except under extreme circumstances, especially with Nixon so enmeshed in trying to untangle the ongoing conflict in the Middle East. The fact that Ford's nomination was the first to be considered under the Twenty-Fifth Amendment made it doubly important to Eastland that he expedite the process. Eastland joined Senate Democratic Leaders Mike Mansfield and Robert Byrd in pushing for the Senate Rules Committee, a panel with little business under normal circumstances, to conduct the hearings. Eastland wrote a friend that he was happy that Ford had made a "great impression" upon that body and the House Judiciary Committee, which conducted its own hearings. He had no problem with Speaker Albert remaining second in line to the presidency, he said, but that was not what the drafters of the Twenty-Fifth Amendment had intended, nor was it good for American democracy. In the radioactive atmosphere of the time, particularly in the House, Eastland recognized that some younger firebrands might try to prolong the hearings so they might score some partisan points. Yet he appreciated that senior House Democrats, recognizing that the ardor of their more determined liberal members might antagonize the center of the electorate, were moving to focus what already was as thorough of an investigation as any American leader had ever received. In the end, majorities of better than 90 percent formed for Ford in both the House and the Senate, and Eastland could return for a while to being a mere third in line to succeed to the presidency.[7]

Eastland's relationship with President Ford was perpetually cordial, even if it lacked the links provided by Mother Nature that bound him so tightly to Richard Nixon. Such could be seen as early as the week after Ford's swearing-in when the new president called Eastland to ask his advice on who should succeed him as vice president. Eastland thought for a moment, then suggested a man whom he and many senators in both parties deemed one of their ablest colleagues. "Lloyd Bentsen," said Eastland, naming a fifty-four-year-old Texan of moderate outlook who had been close to Lyndon Johnson. At the time, Cotton Council lobbyist Macon Edwards was visiting Eastland and noticed from Eastland's end of the conversation that Ford had reservations about naming Bentsen or any other Democrat. Neither he nor Eastland was aware that House Democratic Leader Thomas P. "Tip" O'Neill had counseled Ford against such a course well before. But there were some obvious potential benefits to Eastland's suggestion, for a Bentsen choice might resurrect the coalition for Ford that had appeared in what Nixon described in 1972 as his "New Majority" and been crippled in the aftermath of Watergate. Forever tight with his words, Eastland added only that choosing Bentsen might guarantee Ford a win in Texas in 1976 were he to stand for election in his own right.[8]

When Ford chose Nelson Rockefeller to fill the vacancy, Eastland went along reluctantly and voted to confirm him, even if Rockefeller's unwavering support for civil rights did not endear him to many white Mississippians. Even so, it was always Eastland's belief that any president should enjoy considerable latitude in selecting those who would become his working partners. Once Rockefeller was confirmed, the two came to work in tandem as president of the Senate and president pro tem to make the upper chamber work, and Eastland came to respect Rockefeller's "tremendous experience and unusual talent." The two forged a friendship, and Eastland was quick to salute Rockefeller upon his departure from Washington for his years as vice president, which he said were marked by an "unusual spirit of harmony and accomplishment."[9]

Just as he had with Nixon, Eastland proved a regular ally for Ford. On the Judiciary Committee, he joined a conservative coalition in trying to bottle up a bill sponsored by Phil Hart to give the Antitrust Division of the Justice Department new authority to institute new suits against oil and natural gas companies. Unlike most Democrats, Eastland was inclined to sustain Ford's vetoes of bills he deemed excessive in spending, particularly those with no funds for Mississippi. He had no interest in any plan to risk any more American lives or treasure in Vietnam. Still, as one who had always had what an aide called a "soft spot" for the Chinese minority in his native Delta, he, like Ford, took an interest in the plight of South Vietnamese children, who he feared might be abandoned to the vengeance of the Communists were they not admitted into the United States, and he moved to expedite visas for those kids. But he would not stand for Communist attacks on any Americans. When a group of the Khmer Rouge seized the American merchant ship *Mayaguez* in international waters less than three weeks after they took over Cambodia, Eastland had but one piece of advice when the president called him to the White House. "I'd bomb 'em," he told Ford and forty other members of Congress.[10]

Much more often than before, Eastland could be found swapping yarns in public with colleagues with whom he often disagreed. One day in the mid 1970s, he spotted George McGovern, who he almost certainly voted against for president, in clear view across the Senate floor, then shouted the one question he most wanted him to answer about a heckler he had encountered. "Jawge," he asked, "did you really tell that guy . . . to kiss your ass?" When McGovern grinned and nodded, Eastland smiled and then complimented him for the "best line in the campaign." And Eastland was quicker to taunt some of his more liberal friends like Birch Bayh. "'Bo'tion, prayer, the women's thing, the black and white thing," he would kid Bayh. "How in the hell do you do it, boy?"[11]

Eastland was particularly anxious to mentor young members. One favorite over his last term was Joseph Biden, who then was best known for having lost his wife and young daughter in a tragic automobile accident. Aware that Biden shared his opposition to busing and admiring that he had contemplated resigning his seat to take care of his two surviving sons, Eastland took an interest in him. He saw to it that Biden got seats during his first year in the Senate on panels that could help his state of Delaware as well as one on the powerful Democratic Steering Committee. Two years later, Eastland guided Biden to a seat on the prestigious Foreign Relations Committee. Yet he could be as frank with Biden, who showed him considerable deference, as he was with anyone else. Like most Democrats, Eastland was a bit disconcerted when Biden took the floor at a caucus meeting to argue at length for the full public financing of congressional campaigns. The speech drew enough silence to stun Biden. Then, Eastland looked at Biden, still with a cigar in his mouth. "They tell me you're the youngest man in the history of America ever elected to the U.S. Senate," misstating the fact that Biden was merely the second youngest. "You keep making speeches like you made today and you gonna be the youngest one-term senator in the history of America."[12]

Still Eastland recognized that his world was changing, in Washington and in Mississippi. Nothing better symbolized the receding power held by southern senators than a 1975 change in the rules from a requirement that two-thirds of the members present be needed to invoke cloture to a mere sixty senators. Reports surfaced with Sam Ervin's retirement that Eastland was beginning to lose control of the Judiciary Committee. But even while a very liberal freshman like James Abourezk took Ervin's seat, Eastland retained a bevy of legislative tools and a mastery of procedure that he could use to rein in Senate liberals who threatened his turf. He, unlike much of his caucus, took an interest in the plight of fellow conservatives, even some Republicans, who felt threatened by challenges from Democrats. After charges of influence peddling led Florida Republican Edward Gurney to retire from the Senate, Eastland contributed to his defense fund and apprised Gurney as to who to call for legal help. When Democrats tried to delay the seating of Henry Bellmon, an Oklahoma Republican who prevailed in his bid for reelection in the decidedly Democratic year of 1974 by less than 3000 votes, Eastland stood with him and advised him privately as to how to resist their challenge. In the even closer race for an open New Hampshire seat, Eastland was one of but five Democrats to vote for a new election after post-election recounts first showed Democrat John Durkin winning by ten votes, then Republican Louis Wyman prevailing by an even narrower two-vote plurality.[13]

Eastland got a sign of his own mortality later that year when he fell at his Doddsville home and broke or cracked six ribs. He lay immobile in the nearby Cleveland, Mississippi, hospital for two weeks before he returned to his plantation to recuperate further. This determined that he could not be present when the Senate took up his pet bill to restore the citizenship of Robert E. Lee. More importantly, he was bedridden at a time when the Judiciary Committee moved to take up the bill to extend the life of the Voting Rights Act for another seven years. For the first time in the twentieth century, it was a liberal Democrat in Phil Hart rather than a Southerner who presided over the consideration of a major civil rights bill, and the extension of the Voting Rights Act would be passed and on the way to Gerald Ford's desk for his signature in record time.[14]

Eastland's recovery was sufficient enough by fall 1975 that he could appear at Democratic unity rallies. As usual in a gubernatorial primary where no Johnson was on the ballot, he told friends that he was letting them make up their own minds. Some intimates like Jesse Brent backed Lieutenant Governor William Winter, a relative liberal on racial questions.

While Winter ran first in the initial primary, he fell far short of the majority needed to avert a runoff. Holding office himself, he was susceptible in tough economic times to a campaign waged by an outsider perceived as a populist, a tack taken that year by second place finisher Cliff Finch, a former state legislator who made his living as a personal injury lawyer. A onetime segregationist, Finch augmented his campaign by working a blue collar job a day a week to demonstrate an empathy with small farmers and laborers. Winter avoided what wags called a blackneck-redneck race, declaring that he was "convinced that the people do not want a clown or stuntman leading them for the next four years." But this remark gave Finch the opening around which he tailored the rest of a campaign, which found support from both Charles Evers and the founder of the Americans for the Preservation of the White Race. "If they call them rednecks, clowns or whatever, I'm proud to be one of them," Finch replied, on his way to a better than 100,000 vote victory in the runoff.[15]

For Eastland, Finch was hardly an ideal candidate. Yet he barely wavered when called to speak at Democratic functions in the Delta. His attachment to his party had strengthened. Not only had more liberal colleagues and interest groups impressed upon him the need to remain loyal, but it was hardly lost upon him that fellow Democrats in Congress had voted more in what he deemed the interests of Mississippi farmers than had Republicans. Earlier that year, House Democrats had provided a majority for cotton price supports, while GOP votes were scarce. Grain and soybean farmers were even more irked by a Ford embargo of September 1975 upon sales of their produce to the Soviets, a move prompted by the refusal of Gulf Coast longshoremen to load their goods until the Soviets used more American ships to haul it. Eastland placed the blame upon the union leaders who prodded them to walk off the job. Still, he wrote one correspondent that it was a sad state of affairs when AFL-CIO George Meany determined "U.S. foreign and agricultural policy." By the end of September, he was expressing gratitude that Ford had lifted the embargo. But once he hit the campaign trail, Eastland, true to his Democratic heritage, lambasted the GOP as the "party of high price goods and cheap fiber," and exhorted farmers to take out their anger on "every Republican in sight."[16]

In truth, the general election was the first Mississippi gubernatorial contest since 1871 in which the GOP candidate was taken seriously.

Republicans nominated Gil Carmichael, who made a good impression on many in his challenge to Eastland. Carmichael ran an issue-oriented campaign, pledging, among other things, a new state constitution, reform of Mississippi's mental health and prison systems, and added aid to education at all levels. His approach contrasted sharply with that of Finch, which the *Delta-Democrat Times* editorialized had "no more substance than meringue." Still, the business-oriented ideology of Carmichael, which included calls for gun control and ratifying the Equal Rights Amendment, was better-suited for a more urban state. In many ways, Eastland vivified Carmichael's tack by playfully mocking him. Finch had "some little Republican opposition," he would say. "How swell it is." Some expected Eastland to demonstrate rancor toward Carmichael, but he did little more than stand with his state party's nominees. The fairly conservative rural denizens and county level officeholders he brought with him were imperative for a Finch win. While Jackson-based civil rights activist Henry Kirksey ran as an Independent, Carmichael got far more African-American votes than most Republicans, a factor best symbolized by the endorsement given him by State Representative Robert Clark of Holmes County, the state's sole black legislator. His inroads would not be enough, for Finch's margins in the blue collar and rural areas of Mississippi carried him to an unusually narrow 52 to 45 percent victory. Gil Carmichael was not the only Mississippian to credit Eastland as much for the Democratic win as Finch, but he was the most colorful in crediting the work of an "old guard political machine." "Eastland represents the old political system and I ... the new," he declared. "We naturally tend to fight each other. I sort of enjoy it, and I hope he does, too."[17]

Another symbol that Eastland's power had declined somewhat was the diminishing role of SISS. Two Supreme Court decisions of 1967 had restricted the powers SISS could exert by barring probes not approved by the full subcommittee and allowed staff, if not senators, to be sued for abuses committed in the course of any investigation. Fewer members aspired to serve on SISS. Kentucky Republican Marlow Cook was heard saying that the half million dollars the panel spent each year was "just too damn large," and a staffer declared that the group's continuance was just a way to "employ ... ex-McCarthyites who sit around thinking evil thoughts ... about the Communist conspiracy." While William F. Buckley Jr. noted that SISS had compiled thoughtful reports on the Weather Underground, the international drug trade, terrorism, the human costs of Communism, and the misdeeds of Fidel Castro between 1970 and 1975, other congressional panels and several outside groups were conducting similar studies. Critics like Mark Hatfield replied pointedly that SISS in the same time period held just eight days of hearings on pieces of legislation, the very foundation of what should be the work of any congressional committee.

What especially illuminated the obsolescence of SISS was a probe of the Peoples Bicentennial Commission (PBC), a well-funded group who aimed to employ the symbols of the American Revolution to promote the idea of economic democracy. The PBC did employ a number of those prominently involved in protests against the Vietnam War. They heckled President Ford at a bicentennial-related appearance in New Hampshire in 1975, and burned him in effigy in a nearby courtyard at another stop. To Eastland, the PBC was a "propaganda and organizing tool" for those affiliated with the New Left whose views were "far closer to those of Castro and Mao than . . . to those of our Founding Fathers." The PBC offered rewards of $25,000 to secretaries at Fortune 500 companies who gave them information about any criminal practices indulged in by their bosses. They hedged their bets more than a bit when they made clear that they would pay up if and only if that data provided "concrete evidence" that resulted in the conviction and incarceration of those chief executive officers. Here was a stunt reminiscent of some conducted in the late 1960s by Abbie Hoffman and other antiwar leaders better known for their audacity than any results. Then again, Eastland's statement reflected an exaggerated evaluation of the potential impact of the PBC that mirrored some of the paranoia replete within all too many of the anti-Communist probes of the 1950s. It hardly added to the probe's credibility when SISS heard from but two obscure monitors of radical groups and no one connected with the PBC. Still, the statement of PBC spokesman Jeremy Rifkin painting Eastland's statement as "McCarthyism" was just as reflective of many samples of the rhetorical overkill of some on the left during the same period.[18] By the second generation of the television age, potshots of this sort no longer provided much even in the way of theatrics. SISS never had produced much in the way of actual legislation. With its oversight functions having been assumed by other bodies, SISS had become a relic of the 1950s overseeing less than impactful relics of the 1960s, and most of its legitimate functions were being duplicated by the Senate Intelligence Committee.

It was during these years that Eastland began to develop relationships, and in the case of Aaron Henry, a very real friendship, with some of the more prominent leaders of his state's African-American community. To be sure, there were many who would never forgive Eastland for any of the sins they ascribed to him. Yet the Voting Rights Act had made possible the franchise to thousands of African Americans who had heretofore been denied the rights granted them under the Fifteenth Amendment. It was not long before they commenced using their votes to elect scores of their own to offices in all parts of the state. By 1975, even Pace, the Bolivar County hamlet from whence Courtney Pace sprang, had not just a black mayor but an all-black town council and a black town marshal.[19]

A year earlier, Kenneth L. Dean, a white Baptist minister and veteran of the MFDP, was among the many who let it be known that he had noticed a change in the way Eastland dealt with those like him who had been active in the civil rights movement. While contemplating a race for Thad Cochran's House seat, Dean was advised by state Democratic chairman Thomas Riddell to go to Washington to see "the Man" and ask for help. When he arrived at Eastland's office, he watched the chairman spend the first half of his three-hour visit taking constituent calls relating to the proper location of the frost line vis-à-vis the soybean crop. Then, Eastland assured Dean of his commitment to the Mississippi Democratic Party and advised him which of his friends he could call for contributions.[20]

Eastland was also far more accessible to leaders of Mississippi's African-American community. If firsts are landmarks, one important distinction belongs to Robert Clark, who when elected to the state House of Representatives in 1967 became the first African American to win a seat in the Mississippi legislature since 1890. More visible to the nation at large was Fayette mayor Charles Evers, the brother of slain NAACP leader Medgar Evers. In both cases, Eastland recognized that there would be a cultural bridge that he would have to cross. Upon meeting Evers, he asked if he was the one "raising all that hell." Evers smiled, then Eastland continued, "Let me tell you something, man. We don't hate nigras. We've just been taught different. We try to do what's right." In a follow-up, Eastland showed Evers around his plantation, then boasted that blacks "run all that stuff." Evers took in what he heard from Eastland, whom he would need on occasion to do his bidding in Washington. By 1976, on the day Evers, comedian Dick Gregory, and Aaron Henry were named honorary Mississippi colonels, he noted some positive change in Eastland, even if he still described him as "the same racist bigot" he always had been when it served his interests. Such a tack he knew would help him with the liberal black voters who would form his base in any statewide race as much as it helped Eastland with whites who had not abandoned their prejudices. But privately, he found Eastland a "politician" who had to cater to his electorate, taking to heart an admonition of his father. "If your word ain't no good," James Evers had told him, "you ain't no good." As mayor, he needed help from the Nixon administration, particularly for a health clinic that would serve all of Jefferson County. To get it, he went through Natchez oilman D. A. Biglane, one of Eastland's closest friends who touted him as his "black son." A trust developed, particularly after Nixon signed a bill that funded the facility that Evers had sought, money he knew would not have come without Eastland's intervention. In time, the two would meet more often without a shred of an adversarial demeanor, and Eastland would counsel Evers as to how blacks could advance. "You all just keep getting educated," he would say. "You gotta vote."[21]

Eastland's first encounter with Robert Clark came out of necessity. Not long after Clark entered the House, he found that a summer youth program funded by the Small Business Administration was being transferred out of Holmes County. He tried phoning the official responsible for the decision in Atlanta and heard nothing but doubletalk. Confounded, Clark called Eastland, who had long been known as a seldom surpassed legislative fixer. Clark gave Eastland his side of the story, or the requisite "facts" Eastland always asked for, then heard one question. "Whea are you, Mr. Clark?" In the lobby of the downtown Jackson Holiday Inn, Clark replied. Eastland, as spare with words as ever, told Clark to stay where he was for fifteen minutes. It wasn't Eastland he heard from a quarter of an hour later, but a voice on a loudspeaker paging him. When he picked up the phone, the voice he heard was that of the young bureaucrat who had been obstructive. "Your program will remain in Lexington," he said. It was hardly true that Clark and Eastland would become close allies; neither supported the other in any future electoral venture. But fate had thrown them together to serve the same constituents. Both were determined to get as much as possible for their people, and both usually succeeded. One surprise for Clark was that Eastland, whom he found something of a treacherous character for much of his life, made a valuable working partner and always treated him "with dignity and respect." Even today, Clark relishes one left-handed compliment from Eastland. "Clark," Eastland said, grinning, "you're awright, but you ain't no Aa-ron Henry," a remark he appreciated for he knew Eastland held Henry in as high esteem as he did himself.[22]

Eastland's dealings with Aaron Henry commenced inauspiciously. He knew well that the Clarksdale pharmacist had often derided him from his perch as head of the Mississippi NAACP as a racist. It took a while for Eastland to see Henry as a pragmatist dedicated to the economic uplift of his people. The delay sprung in part from the underpinnings of Eastland's Victorian upbringing. He was a man's man who could not have been comfortable with the greetings of Henry, who often greeted male acquaintances not just with a bear hug but also by rubbing his head against theirs and occasionally giving them pecks on the cheek. Such habits raised suspicions that Henry was bisexual.[23] Henry's hellos were disturbing enough that Eastland had Larry Speakes assemble two to three dozen chairs around his desk whenever he heard Henry might be visiting so he could get no closer than to shake his hand. Even so, the bond between Eastland and Henry grew, particularly as Henry became a cochair of the state Democratic Party.[24]

In years to come, Henry liked to say that it was "just as hard for Senator Eastland to be around some of us as it is for some of us to be around him." Only in March 1976 would Henry hint publicly that they were friends at a dinner honoring Eastland in Jackson, where the University of Mississippi Law School unveiled a scholarship program in his name. On the dais that night were Chief Justice Warren Burger, the featured speaker, and Attorney General Edward Levi. John Stennis was there, as were thirty-three other Senate colleagues ranging in ideology from Jesse Helms on the right to Hubert Humphrey on the left and in geography from Ted Stevens of Anchorage, Alaska, to Lawton Chiles of Lakeland, Florida. Senators present saw the occasion as a chance to honor a senior colleague who had done them a favor. In some ways, the event provided a forum to demonstrate a sense of reconciliation. Humphrey, who in a matter of weeks was diagnosed with terminal bladder cancer, saluted Eastland as a "great" Mississippian. Eastland reciprocated by expressing the possibility that a divided Democratic convention might turn to the happy warrior from Minnesota as a consensus nominee that summer. That notion had to elate Henry, who as the state's Democratic National Committeeman realized that his party would need all the strength it could muster. But Henry had paid to attend. While he defended himself by saying that Eastland had backed more legislation of interest to blacks than at any time in the past, in part because he and some others had explained their positions to him, some civil rights leaders thought his presence a sin bordering on treason. Particularly upset were leaders of the Delta Ministry, a group established by the National Council of Churches to work with lower-class blacks. Executive Director Owen Brooks wrote Henry and charged that he had "sacrificed the integrity" of the NAACP and "done irreparable harm to the cause." Russ Barber, his associate, derided any discussion of a "unity" that he believed meant merely that "Big Jim gets patted on the back by some prominent blacks." Prior to his death, Brooks saluted Henry for a Christian demeanor and sincere desire for racial reconciliation that allowed him to forgive Eastland for his decades as a segregationist, a posture that he could not bring himself to grant. Tensions were sufficiently charged at the time that Henry felt compelled to explain that Eastland was merely using his name to promote contributions to scholarships that would go to deserving young lawyers-to-be of both races.[25]

Still, what the developing Eastland-Henry relationship signified was that a truly biracial state Democratic Party was emerging in Mississippi, something few people could have imagined even a decade earlier. The fracture separating Regular Democrats and those loyal to the national Democratic Party, known as Loyalists, had been sufficiently broad that both Eastland and John Stennis avoided going to national conventions so as not to be seen as taking sides. While Democrats seated all but two of the all-white Regulars at their national convention in 1964, a compromise reached there dictated that no contingent other than a biracial one loyal to the national ticket would ever again be seated by the national party. Some Regulars would never be comfortable with most of the Loyalists, either for racial reasons or those of a more economic nature. Moreover, Loyalists had their own splits, with a predominantly black group of those who had been among the firebrands of the MFDP often at odds with a more pragmatic and moderate biracial band, among whom the best-known members were Charles Evers, Aaron Henry, and Hodding Carter III. Over the course of the previous decade, such spats were often debilitating and always exhausting. And, with the obvious growth of a state Republican Party seen in and around the cities of the Magnolia State in both Carmichael campaigns and all presidential races since the 1950s, any failure to limit such internecine disputes would hasten the fall of Jefferson Davis' party as Mississippi's majority party.[26]

With John Stennis characteristically avoiding state politics, it effectively fell upon Eastland to prod conservatives who intended to stay Democrats to devise structures that would facilitate participation by all wings of the Democratic Party. His allies, led by State Chairman Tom Riddell, began meeting with Aaron Henry and other Loyalist leaders who were tired of having some influence at the national level but none whatsoever at home. As Patricia M. "Patt" Derian, the state's Democratic National Committeewoman, explained, it was in the interest of all Democrats to work together, be they her Loyalists or Jim Eastland's Bourbons. By 1975, the two sides agreed both to double the size of the state Democratic executive committee to include both factions and to initiate a delegate selection process in which every Democrat could participate at the precinct level.[27] To be sure, GOP growth was steady enough that future Democratic wins in Mississippi would depend on their finding candidates at home and nationally who could bridge the many long-standing divides. Yet, fortuitously for Eastland and even more so for Derian and future husband Hodding Carter III, there was such a candidate in the race in 1976, a peanut farmer from Georgia with a deep-seeded interest in human rights that any Loyalist could admire.

CHAPTER 18

Eastland Prepares to Go Home

IT WAS ALWAYS EASTLAND'S HOPE THAT IN 1976 HIS PARTY WOULD TURN to someone friendlier to the South and more defense-oriented than 1972 nominee George McGovern. One might have expected him to join former Governors Barnett, Johnson, and Williams in backing fellow onetime segregationist George Wallace, who again announced for the presidency. But, while he expected Wallace to make a "strong race," Eastland realized that his paralysis from a would-be assassin's bullet in 1972 rendered his chances of being nominated next to nil. He considered backing Henry "Scoop" Jackson, the Washington senator known for his strident critiques of the Soviet Union, and secured for him a coveted slot keynoting the annual meeting of the Delta Council. But he also placed allies in early 1976 on the statewide staffs of Lloyd Bentsen and Robert Byrd, colleagues who were waging halfhearted bids for the nation's highest office, and that of Jimmy Carter, the fairly obscure former Georgia governor who was waging a full-fledged battle. While Wallace won the state's precinct caucuses handily, the moderate candidate who emerged was not Bentsen, Eastland's initial first choice, but Carter. Eastland wrote a friend at the outset of the race that he found Carter a "fine man" even if he had left his home state "nearly bankrupt." But when the primaries concluded and it was clear that Carter had secured a majority of the delegates, Eastland joined John Stennis in saluting Carter for "one of the best planned and executed national campaigns in history," and in heartily endorsing him.[1]

Contrary to what many assumed, Eastland eagerly embraced what Aaron Henry called the "Peaches and Cream" ticket of Carter and Walter Mondale, his liberal colleague from Minnesota. But he was as quick as ever to declare that neither the fairly liberal Democratic platform of 1976 nor any other was "binding on anyone." What truly mattered to Eastland was that Carter was campaigning in Mississippi. Never prior to Carter's mid-September visit to the Gulf Coast had Eastland ever campaigned in his home state with his party's nominee for president. Past standard-bearers had avoided Mississippi, certain that the Magnolia State was either in the bag or a lost cause. What had changed was that black votes made possible by the Voting Rights Act had put Mississippi in play for both parties for the first time since Reconstruction. While Carter kidded that East-land and he had bonded because both were "small farmers," he was ever sensitive to the fact that he, who painted himself as a champion of a South free of discrimination, was campaigning alongside Eastland, Stennis, and Aaron Henry. The South, Carter said, was desegregating peacefully faster than the North, and the Civil Rights Act of 1964 was the "best thing that ever happened to the South." Eastland and Stennis, he continued, were to be commended for adapting to the changes it brought with "success and with courage." Typically, reporters got no comment from Eastland after Carter's speech, but noted that he puffed on his cigar on the dais.[2]

Where Eastland truly proved helpful was in putting together Carter's field organization. Jim Free, the young operative who managed Carter's campaigns in Mississippi, Alabama, and Tennessee, quickly discerned that Eastland was still the man who could pull the strings that would make a difference in the Magnolia State. Three times a month that fall, he visited Eastland at his home in Doddsville and found Eastland going through a list of major activists in each of his state's eighty-two counties. If Free had yet to call anyone Eastland deemed important, he would find a distant glare implying significant disappointment as well as a rising mist of cigar smoke, neither of which he ever aimed to see again. Within the state, Jackson attorney Danny E. Cupit called Eastland every morning to get six or eight names of people to contact with instructions to call back with the response. Those not firm for Carter soon would get calls from Eastland himself. The race was far closer in Mississippi than anyone suspected. Steady GOP development among professionals in the state's small cities was supplemented by the endorsements of Gerald Ford by four Mississippi Democrats who had served with him in the House of Representatives. The Ford forces sent in Strom Thurmond, the face of the original Dixiecrats, to Laurel and Hattiesburg to suggest that Eastland

and Stennis backed Carter only because they feared that they might be stripped of their chairmanships if they did otherwise. But far too many of the rural denizens of Mississippi who such appeals might have swayed were more directly connected with Eastland and Stennis than Thurmond. Over the campaign's last week, Eastland and Stennis effectively refuted such contentions by stumping in Mississippi not just with Carter's wife, Rosalyn, but also with "Miz Lillian," his mother, and Jack, his son. The outcome on election night was not clear until past 3:00 A.M., when all three networks declared that Carter would narrowly carry the state. The seven electoral votes Carter garnered in the Magnolia State were the seven that gave him more than the 270 needed to prevail in the Electoral College. Even though Carter fared more poorly in Mississippi than any southern state other than Virginia, he never forgot how much he owed their people. "Just so nobody has doubts," he told a gathering in Yazoo City in mid-July of 1977, "Mississippi put me over the top."[3]

While skeptical of too much change, Eastland did intend to see that Carter had a chance to institute some of the reforms he had promised for selecting federal judges or prosecutors. In mid-December 1976, he met with Attorney General-designate Griffin Bell at the Georgia governor's mansion and let him know that he was skeptical of the merit commissions Carter aimed to create to give him larger pools of potential nominees. Even so, Eastland assured Bell that he would not obstruct the new president's initiative for federal courts of appeals. His opposition to stripping U.S. attorney nominations from the patronage pot was strong enough to prompt Carter to shelve this part of his promise. While Eastland and Bell reached no agreement on how the new administration would handle nominations for vacancies on federal district courts in general, Eastland did make it clear that he would insist on traditional patronage procedures for any opening on a lower court in Mississippi. "I'll hand you a slip of paper with one name on it," he told Bell, "and that'll be the judge."[4]

As was usual with a president of his party, Eastland was also determined to see that Carter got a chance to staff his administration with his own people. For this reason, he voted for Paul Warnke, Carter's controversial choice to be his chief arms control negotiator, after Carter assured him and others with doubts about Warnke that he would be in charge of U.S. foreign policy and not Warnke. It was Eastland's particular duty to steer the nomination of Griffin Bell to approval. While Bell had compiled a moderate record on the Fifth Circuit Court of Appeals over fourteen years, some civil rights leaders expressed concern because Bell had campaigned for segregationist Ernest Vandiver in his successful 1958 bid for the governorship, signed petitions recommending that the Senate confirm G. Harrold Carswell for the Supreme Court, and still belonged to private clubs that had not yet opened their doors to blacks. Some moderate-to-liberal Republicans who hoped that they might recapture some of the black vote took up their cause. Charles Mathias of Maryland compared the vote on Bell to the votes he had cast against Carswell and Clement Haynsworth and challenged Democrats to uphold the principles they had espoused in their campaigns against those two Nixon nominees. But while Eastland saluted Bell as an able and honorable jurist, he let Birch Bayh, a man civil rights leaders trusted, manage the floor fight for Bell. Once Bell promised to leave the clubs and Bayh vowed to "sensitize" Bell to the mindsets of African Americans, all but five of the sixty-two Democratic senators were sufficiently placated to side with Bell.[5]

More than most senators, Eastland was determined to place key associates in plum federal patronage positions in Mississippi. Soon after the inauguration, he learned that there had been no action on his suggestion to make Mark Hazard head of the state Farmers Home Administration, in part because John Stennis had his own candidate for the job. But it was Eastland, with a seat on the Agriculture Committee, who had much more clout on those issues. Eastland called Boswell Stevens, Hazard's grandfather and the longtime head of the state Farm Bureau Federation, and Stevens called Stennis to inquire as to why he favored another candidate. Stennis heard Stevens out, then told Stevens that he feared that Hazard at twenty-six was too young. "Hell, John," Stevens replied, "you were mighty young" in 1947, when the Farm Bureau put all of its resources behind his candidacy. With Stennis thus resigned to Hazard getting the post, Eastland began calling those he discerned most influential on farm questions in Carter's White House and asked if they were "gonna make me waste the president's time to come all the way down there to get this boy appointed to this position or can you take care of it yourself?" In less than an hour, he picked up the phone to hear the voice of Secretary of Agriculture Bob Bergland reading the press release he had drafted announcing Hazard's appointment. Within minutes, Eastland phoned Hamilton Jordan, Carter's top political aide, to let him know that he would not need to speak with the president.[6]

One Carter nominee who found a hold on his nomination was W. Hodding Carter III, who had been designated as the new president's spokesman at the State Department. Congressional liaison Frank Moore told Carter he would have to talk to Eastland if he aimed to win confirmation. Apprehensively, Carter trekked to Eastland's office and found him sitting behind his desk. "Boy," Eastland said, "they tell me you think that I'm keeping you from being confirmed. I don't give a good goddamn about you, son. But you see that guy right there?" Eastland said, pointing to a portrait of Leander Perez, his deceased friend. "Now Leander hates your daddy and he hates you," Eastland added. "Is that so," Carter shot back, all the while remembering Perez's unbridled segregationism and the fact that he had backed Huey Long, who Hodding Carter Jr. had often depicted as corrupt. Carter listened to Eastland for a few more minutes and then left warily. The next day, Carter was stunned. Eastland had dropped his hold.[7] What Eastland had done was impress upon Carter the notion that he needed to respect all senators, regardless of any previous disagreements, especially the two from his home state.

Eastland's access to Carter expanded after his inauguration. He remained part of the Democratic leadership team that met with Carter each week and had an assistant with him as well. To honor the terminally ill Hubert Humphrey for the final year of his life, Democrats made him Eastland's deputy and gave him a $100,000 budget to staff his portion of his office. Curiously enough, the two men who were seemingly ideologically incompatible combatants on civil rights, the greatest moral issue of the day, strengthened a longstanding friendship forged around their need to work together on questions governing the lives of Minnesota and Mississippi farmers. It was Eastland who best described the kind of bond that could link him in what author Ira Shapiro termed "the last great Senate" with the irrepressibly gregarious "Happy Warrior" in a fairly benign atmosphere. Saluting Humphrey's legislative skills and his rare capacity for reaching voters in open air venues, Eastland rued that "he should have been President." But then again, Eastland had memories of which he could now kid. "The first time I saw him," Eastland waxed nostalgically about their confrontation in Philadelphia in 1948, "he made a speech to kick me out of the Democratic National Convention."[8]

Eastland's and Stennis' most expensive project was a waterway linking the Tennessee and Tombigbee Rivers that would allow more traffic to reach the Gulf Coast from the Ohio Valley. Eastland had joined John Bankhead of Alabama as early as 1944 in arguing that Tenn-Tom, as it became known, would serve as a vital commercial artery for producers throughout the American heartland. From the beginning, sponsors, chiefly Gulf state lawmakers, recognized that the project would be as expensive as any the Army Corps of Engineers had ever built. For that reason, Congress in 1951 effectively blocked further work on Tenn-Tom for a generation. But under the radar, residents of Alabama and Mississippi and tribunes like Eastland in and out of Congress continued to press for the waterway. They found an ally in Richard Nixon, who almost certainly opted to revive Tenn-Tom as part of his Southern Strategy to bring more denizens of Dixie behind his bid for reelection. Even so, environmental and budget concerns, not to mention those raised by attorneys for railroads that would lose business if Tenn-Tom were built, slowed construction. Many who backed Carter in 1976 saw the key point in the race for Mississippi as when Gerald Ford alienated many in east-central Mississippi by rescinding replacement funds for highway bridges over the project. Ford sensed that he had made a major faux pas and restored money for the bridges just days before the election, too late to save him. Eastland and Stennis perceived that they had to move quickly, in light of Carter's desire to curb exorbitant water projects, to let him know that they saw the waterway's completion as a proper payback for Mississippi's role in his victory. By early 1977, key Tenn-Tom backers had ascended to important positions in the House. Jamie Whitten of Mississippi now chaired the full Appropriations Committee, and Tom Bevill of northwest Alabama held the helm of its subcommittee on water resources. Stennis shrewdly chose Columbus, Mississippi, a town convenient to interested parties in both states, to hold a daylong hearing on Tenn-Tom where supporters comprised the majority of the crowd of 5000, in prompting Carter to purge the largest project from his hit list.[9]

While Eastland relished his work on projects he believed would ease the lives of his fellow farmers, large or small, he remained a defender of

Victorian values on many of the more volatile issues of the day. Those most salient in the late 1970s involved questions of gender. On these, too, Eastland almost always sided with the forces of tradition. From early 1973, he put himself on the side of those who faulted the Supreme Court for its decision in *Roe v. Wade* giving women more of a choice in whether to carry their pregnancies to term. And, while he had written friends previously that "discrimination because of sex is equally or more obnoxious than discrimination because of race" and had at one time cosponsored the Equal Rights Amendment, he was one of but eight senators to cast his ballot against that proposed addition to the Constitution in 1972. Some called his attitude paternalistic, while others used the term sexist. His attitudes resembled the more traditional view taken a generation earlier by liberal women like Eleanor Roosevelt and Frances Perkins. "I have a wife, three daughters, and a little granddaughter," he wrote Liz Carpenter, Lyndon Johnson's secretary, near the time of that vote. "I would gladly give my life for either of them, but I cannot vote to repeal the statutes of my state under which women have more rights than men." His protective streak toward the fairer sex had other facets, too. Then, as in previous years, he heralded his support for measures to punish those who engaged in child pornography and to let states define what constituted pornography within their borders.[10]

As always, Eastland also heralded the common ground he found with his state's more conservative voters on issues some identified as those of patriotism. Almost immediately, he let it be known that he strongly opposed Carter's blanket pardon of Vietnam-era draft evaders. He trumpeted calls for a more assertive foreign policy and clung to his support for the governments of Rhodesia and Taiwan, thus reminding voters of his longstanding anti-Communism. In other venues, contrary to the position of the Carter administration, he told listeners that America needed the B1 bomber, as its fleet of B52s was increasingly obsolete. But no issue occupied more of Eastland's fervor than those involving negotiations Carter conducted with the government of the Central American nation he called "Panny-maw." Even before Carter signed pacts restoring control over a 10-mile stretch of land through the heart of Panama to that nation, Eastland professed his undying opposition to any change in the U.S.-Panamanian relationship. "In the words of that Japanese senator from California, Sam

Hayakawa," he said, "we stole it fair and square." Before Mississippi business and veterans groups, Eastland reiterated his position often, budging
only to say that America should voluntarily increase the amount of rent it
paid to Panama to operate the canal and inhabit the Canal Zone. On occasion, he plied his appeals with warnings that Panamanian leader Omar
Torrijos, who he derided as a "tinhorn dictator," was too close to Cuba's
Communist government. While he excited fears with that unfounded
claim, Eastland's position was at one with Mississippi. Not only did the
state's entire congressional delegation quickly announce their opposition to the pacts once Carter signed them, all but twenty members of
both houses of the state legislature joined them. In Eastland's eyes, it was
imperative for America to project a sense of strength. "I don't think a great
nation should surrender anything," he said.[11]

Eastland also saw an opportune time with a Georgia Democrat in the
White House to push a pet matter that appealed to his southernmost
instincts. He always rued the fact that Radical Republicans had used their
supermajority status to strip Confederate President Jefferson Davis, a
fellow Mississippian, of his citizenship during Reconstruction. Aware that
his name as lead sponsor of a measure restoring Davis' citizenship would
render it dead on arrival, he searched for a northern sponsor to forward
the bill. In early 1977, he learned that Mark Hatfield would soon be hos-
pitalized. Eastland approached Hatfield and gave him a copy of Hudson
Strode's *Jefferson Davis: Confederate President*, one of the friendliest analyses of Abraham Lincoln's southern counterpart. The Oregon Republican
read Strode's account as he recuperated, learned that Davis had served
America capably in many positions, concluded that no useful purpose
justified Davis' continued absence from the rolls of the citizenry, and
agreed to let Eastland use his name. Eastland synchronized the scheduling
of the measure's placement on the calendar of the Judiciary Committee
so that passage would come at a time when Jimmy Carter was out of the
country, and the president's signature would be less likely to antagonize
some of his more liberal supporters. He put the question first on the
committee agenda one April day and heard Edward Kennedy asking if
the panel could "talk about this." "We not gonna talk about this," Eastland
replied, knowing Kennedy understood most elements of his constituency,
"we gonna do it."[12]

Less certain at the time was Eastland's view of his own political future, for he had sent conflicting signals. He confided to GOP Congressman Thad Cochran early in 1977 that he felt "too old" to seek and serve another term. Half a year later, he said he had reconsidered and began to attend the county and state Jefferson-Jackson Dinners he had forsaken over the previous fifteen years. Still, at seventy-three, Eastland did not relish the prospect of a race against a viable challenger, especially within his own party, and was uncertain if he would carry through with those plans if he were faced with a serious challenge. His base remained strong among the Mississippi Association of Supervisors, the Farm Bureau, the Cotton and Delta Councils, and much of the state's business establishment. Not so happily for him, younger entrepreneurs had been trending Republican in the state's small but growing towns over the previous decade. Seeing slow but certain growth, Republican National Committee Chairman Bill Brock traveled to Mississippi in early November 1977 to promise that the GOP would present Eastland with a strong challenge the next year. While Thad Cochran was making appearances around the state, always keeping secret what Eastland had shared, he made sure Eastland knew that he would not try to move up to the upper chamber until he or John Stennis publicly announced his retirement. Trent Lott, the state's other GOP congressman, likewise was thought to have his ambitions under control, but State Senator Charles Pickering, the state Republican chairman, was planning a race whether or not Eastland sought a seventh full term.[13]

The growth of the southern Republican Party dictated that Eastland was more in need of a united Democratic Party than ever. For that to come, he needed to accentuate his ties with national Democrats, an easier task than before because of the presence of a southern fiscal conservative in the White House. Like Carter, Eastland was what longtime counsel John Holloman called an "REA [Rural Electrification Administration], TVA kind of guy" who had cosponsored bills like the Hill-Burton Hospital Construction Act and the GI Bill. But the foundation of his base had always been his success in getting those in federal agencies to help his constituents, primarily those in rural Mississippi. Surrogates could trumpet the fact that Mississippi got 99 percent as much funding from the Farmers Home Administration as the entire state of Texas even though it had but a quarter of its population. Even so, Eastland recognized that the subsidies his family had received for not growing cotton allowed potential challengers to claim that he sympathized with the dreams and aspirations of fellow planters alone. To rectify his image among small growers, he let it be known that he sympathized with the aims of a somewhat radical new organization called the American Agriculture Movement, whose leaders were forwarding the ideas of a nationwide farm strike and payments of 100 percent parity if the somewhat dismal plight of the small farmer did not improve. Eastland would not commit himself to a timetable for such actions, preferring instead to urge farmers experiencing problems with Farmers Home Administration to contact him and his staff.[14]

Where Eastland needed to improve his standing was among blacks. Here was a task state NAACP Executive Secretary Aaron Henry told two chroniclers in 1974 would be impossible, for he was convinced that Eastland had built his political empire on racial discord. It was not lost upon Henry that Eastland had not broken a habit of using racially offensive language. When Eastland met Egyptian President Anwar Sadat, a man he admired, and noted his dark complexion for a man from North Africa, he was heard saying he was not aware that Sadat "was a nigger." Yet Henry had built his own relationship with Eastland and concluded that he was in a far better position to help his people than anyone who might replace him. As he and Tom Riddell had started working with Eastland to revive the state Democratic Party, Henry detected a bit of a switch from Eastland on issues like funding for Head Start, food stamps, Medicare, and Medicaid. To be sure, African Americans in Mississippi were not the only ones pushing such a change; Morris Lewis, the head of the Indianola-based Sunflower Grocery chain, told Eastland that the food stamp program was largely responsible for his profit margin. Henry also found Eastland willing to help him and entrepreneur Charles Young acquire a license from the Federal Communications Commission for a television station. This would not be all Henry demanded. Peace was "not necessarily the absence of turmoil," he told reporters. "It is the presence of love and justice, and we ain't got it yet." Henry and Young then suggested that Eastland hire a black staff member. None had ever applied, Eastland responded. But by early February, Edward Cole, a veteran experienced in economic development programs who had managed Charles Evers' gubernatorial campaign of 1971, had joined Eastland's staff. At this point, Henry told reporters, he could publicly begin to help Eastland "rehabilitate himself" with the African-American community of Mississippi.[15]

Publicly thereafter, Henry called upon predominantly black groups like the Greenwood Voters League to put Eastland "to the test" without letting him get off easy. Privately, he counseled Eastland that his chances of getting much of the black vote were "poor at best" because of the "master-servant philosophy" with which they believed he had looked upon their aspirations. Eastland understood, but knew that he would have to try and court all Democratic constituent groups were he to discourage challengers. His debut as a would-be champion of the dreams of African Americans came when he keynoted a dinner to raise funds for the Mississippi Industrial College (now known as Rust College) just prior to Christmas of 1977. Here was an apt choice for an initial appearance, he said, for a study made by the United Negro College Fund indicated that 75 percent of black professionals with degrees had graduated from historically black colleges. But in this venue, where he could show a preference for Booker T. Washington's self-help doctrines over those of more militant black leaders, he took care to quote a friend who the civil rights community saw as an ally. "Many things go into education," he quoted Vice President Walter Mondale as telling the editors of *Jet*, "but the one you can't do without is money." Here were words that accentuated his success in bringing home federal pork for Mississippi, and those Henry reiterated in a letter to the state's civil rights community to suggest that they should give Eastland a chance. After all, he would say in other venues, Eastland might not have felt comfortable with them. "Son," Eastland said to Henry, half in jest in the early stages of a friendship that would strengthen until the end of his life, "do you realize you never did invite me?" Henry would get chuckles when he reiterated the conversation, but he received a rash of criticism from African-American leaders who saw Eastland's apparent change of heart as less than sincere. "In the long list of betrayals of Black people by Black leaders," wrote Owen H. Brooks, the leader of the Delta Ministry, "this has to be foremost." J. H. Hill, the chairman of the Alcorn County NAACP, called upon Henry to resign as state chairman of the NAACP, saying he was "too tied up politically" with the Democrats to lead his people effectively.[16]

Eastland had no problem finding room for additional politicos who sought a place on his campaign. But many who had long been part of his organization were not comfortable with newcomers, and they took pains to show off their superior value to Eastland to anyone who might be interested. Disagreements about the form the campaign would take intensified, less for ideological reasons than among those who preferred a traditional organizationally based race and those who wanted a more up-to-date media strategy. Eastland made it clear that he sided with those urging more inclusiveness. "You never kick anyone off the wagon," he would say. "You just wait for more to get on." While Tom Riddell and Aaron Henry had done a herculean job of reuniting Mississippi Democrats in both Cliff Finch's race for governor and the Carter campaign, Eastland was spending more time trying to manage the infighting. Both Jimmy Carter and Walter Mondale urged him to make the race, and not just because they preferred him to Carter's archrival Ted Kennedy at the helm of the Judiciary Committee.

More influential was Libby Eastland, who had never enjoyed life in Washington and knew that his blood pressure had risen to 220 over 110. For her, 1978 was an apt time to return to the Delta. He did not flinch when little-known aspirants, like Henry J. Kirksey, an African-American cartographer, and Robert Robinson, a former state chairman of Public Welfare, made it known they were contemplating challenges. Were any viable challenger to appear, however, Eastland would be content to retire to the Delta. Two rivals were preparing challenges, Eastland learned in mid-March. The one who jumped the gun was former Governor Bill Waller, who had sensed after visiting Eastland that he would only run without serious opposition. Waller got wind that his successor, Cliff Finch, would challenge Eastland if the state legislature did not approve his bill to allow governors to succeed themselves. While Waller may have announced to get an edge on Finch, the wording of his declaration contained a clear shot at Eastland that few Eastland supporters would forgive, then or ever. "We need a sixty hour a week man in Washington," he said, referring to Eastland's age and his frequent trips home, "not a six hour a week man." While backers took note, Eastland did not finalize his decision until he peered at a lengthy schedule of events his campaign staff had set up. "I am just not up to it," he told Jesse Brent. He was resolute once he made up his mind. One of the few phone calls his staff allowed to reach him came from Chicago Bear running back Walter Payton, a native of Columbia, Mississippi, who had just been named NFL Player of the Year. But Payton had no more luck in swaying Eastland than anyone else. Few were surprised when Clarence Pierce, the head of Eastland's state office in Jackson, confirmed reports that he would not be seeking reelection.[17]

Reaction was quickest from among those officeholders who depended upon Eastland to help them secure federal help for their projects. State Senator Robert Crook of Ruleville declared that Waller would never be elected to statewide office again. Bill Burgin of Columbus derided Waller as a "tadpole." State House Speaker Buddie Newman got one hundred legislators to sign a petition urging Eastland to reconsider, which Crook hand-delivered to Eastland. But many outside of the regular Democratic hierarchy were not so complementary. The Greenville-based *Delta-Democratic Times* berated him as a "crotchety old man" who had "served . . . too long" and "threw up roadblocks when he could have built a highway." And Ralph David Abernathy, the successor of Martin Luther King Jr. as chairman of the Southern Christian Leadership Conference, applauded Eastland's departure, saying he hoped the Magnolia State would elect someone inclined to distribute wealth "more evenly."[18]

Some always deemed thirty-three-year-old Woods Eastland the logical heir to the seat. In the few previous years, the younger Eastland, an amiable and erudite graduate of Vanderbilt University and the University of Mississippi Law School who managed the family plantation and later served as president of Staplcotn, the world's largest cotton-producing cooperative, had spoken in his father's stead in venues across the state. His easygoing nature and talents were impressive enough for officials of both parties to try and recruit him at various times over the next three decades to seek statewide office on their ticket. In 1978, Jim Eastland's first instinct was to try and keep peace within his family. "Ask your mother," he told his son. Libby Eastland had experienced the ups and downs that afflict many political wives and wanted no part of it for her son, at least for the moment. "Wait 'til your kids are grown," she told her son, "then you can think about it." Woods Eastland pondered a race for a few hours more, then came to believe that he did not have the subtlety his father possessed in droves. Contemplating such a race at such an early age, he now says overly humbly, had been a matter of ego and perhaps his mother's advice had been in his and his young family's best interest all along.[19]

Those around Eastland quickly learned that there were three experienced officeholders who he considered appropriate successors. One was William Winter, the moderate former lieutenant governor who had chauffeured him around the state in his initial campaign of 1942 but was committed to running for governor in 1979. Brad Dye also heard Eastland out, but told him that family considerations dictated that he would seek only offices in state government. There remained Maurice Dantin, a former mayor of Columbia and district attorney who had gained some recognition statewide during an unsuccessful bid for the governorship in 1975. An accomplished chef and the youngest mayor in the state when first elected in 1957, the forty-eight-year-old Dantin traveled to Doddsville to pay homage to Eastland. He prepared an exquisite meal for the senator, who, as usual, listened more than he spoke. Dantin left Doddsville knowing he had the tacit support of state Democratic chairman Tom Riddell, as well as that of Wayne Edwards, who would have run Eastland's campaign had he stayed in the race. "No one poured oil over my head," Dantin told reporters later, even if he did know that he was the only major contender who had not at one time or another alienated Eastland in no small way.[20]

Subsequent developments in the spring of 1978 dispelled common claims of Eastland's omnipotence within his home state. Mississippi politics, William Winter told one budding scholar, was a "politics of . . . personality and emotion." Alliances were cast with individual politicos solely and often did not transfer to the friends, even the protégés, of those individuals. Friends of Eastland swung to the camps of several potential successors. Farmers aligned quickly behind Cliff Finch, who did not make his intentions known until Eastland withdrew. Former Lieutenant Governor Charles Sullivan was championed by a conservative bloc based in Coahoma County that included both former Governor John Bell Williams and Eastland's son-in-law Champ Terney. Dantin, a substantive man with a moderate posture, had ties with the state's unions and also funding from Eastland backers like banker Paul McMullan and, more conspicuously, Walter Payton. But to a far greater extent than many had expected, the political and demographic profile of the Magnolia State had changed since 1972. Republicans were considerably greater in number than before.

While some Eastland backers and intimates like Jesse Brent got behind Republican Congressman Thad Cochran, others rallied to the standard of GOP State Chairman Charles Pickering. Those left on the farms and the communities that served them were fewer. While Finch deemed his standing among them to be sufficient to afford him a victory in the initial primary, changing demographics meant that he had to find other supporters were he to win outright. Unlike Dantin, who benefited from being the one denizen of southern Mississippi to run, Finch had to vie with Sullivan for votes north of Jackson. And while Finch's demeanor appealed to a biracial coalition, others, like Waller, the first governor to name blacks to key positions in state government, had ties in the black community that readily transferred to votes. So while Finch's visibility as governor was an advantage, the presence of scandal within his administration—and there were several small scandals—would limit his appeal however he used the perks of his office. As expected, he ran better than 20,000 votes ahead of Sullivan and Waller, who finished third and fourth, but still 4000 votes behind the lesser-known Dantin, who seemed to emerge from nowhere to run ahead of the field.[21]

Dantin's surprise win prompted Finch to highlight the populistic strains of his rhetoric so as to win the votes of those who had backed Waller. In doing so, Finch effectively conceded Charles Sullivan's conservative backers to Dantin. But the way he made his pitch demonstrated that he did not understand why Waller had fared so poorly. Finch eschewed a programmatic approach to the better natures of the working class and declared that Waller would have been his opponent had it not been for the last-minute tactics of "the machine." In doing so, Finch seemed to forget that Eastland had been instrumental in Waller's initial election and his own, and many who backed both of them for governor still held Eastland in considerable esteem. Finch added fuel to the fire not just by saying that Dantin represented the "country club set" and the oil companies, but by having an actor ask in one of his television ads where he could find some Chivas Regal and cigars. Finch's heavy-handedness energized Eastland's allies much more than Finch's own. It had not been Eastland's intention to make any calls for Dantin, he said later, but he changed his mind when he "was made an issue of." Within half an hour of the polls closing, Dantin led by a two-to-one margin, enough for Wayne Edwards to begin handing out Chivas Regal and cigars at Dantin's victory party. In the end, Dantin carried seventy-three of the state's eighty-two counties and prevailed by nearly 110,000 votes.[22]

Here was the last hurrah of Jim Eastland and his order. He would appear at public gatherings and make calls for favored Democrats, if health permitted, but he had made his peace with the notion that others would lead the fights for Mississippi aspirants to appointive office, projects, and other interests. Perhaps Bill Waller was the first to learn this. Purely by chance, Waller showed up at an event where Eastland was present a few weeks after his withdrawal. Waller walked over, put his hand out, then tried to engage Eastland in small talk. Eastland thought for a moment, then grasped Waller's hand awkwardly. "What are we going to do about cotton prices?" Waller asked, almost out of habit. "I don't know what you're going to do about it," Eastland replied, "but I'm not gonna do a damn thing about it because you drove me out of the race."[23]

On the other hand, Eastland was eager to appear at ceremonial events, if they involved friends and were held in Mississippi. Still, the nature of those rites had changed. In late summer of 1977, he took a call from Edward Kennedy and heard a request to get him invited to speak at Ole Miss. Once he hung up, Eastland told associates that Kennedy would challenge Jimmy Carter for their party's nomination in 1980, as there could be no other reason for such a request. The ideologies of the two were far too disparate for Kennedy to expect Eastland to endorse him. On more than one occasion, Kennedy had told Eastland that he could be for him or against him, whichever would help him more. "You know I want you to be against me," Eastland always retorted. But in May 1978, the speech Eastland got Kennedy to give was the commencement address on the site of the campus where his brother had to federalize the state national guard to maintain order sixteen years earlier. It was Eastland who met him at the airport, introduced him, and joined him at a country club reception thereafter. But there was one event that never could have happened even a decade earlier. As soon as Aaron Henry saw Eastland, he marched over to plant a peck on his cheek. More startled than Eastland was Kennedy, who told reporter Curtis Wilkie that he pined for a picture of Henry kissing Eastland and another "of Jim Eastland when he realized someone had a picture of Aaron Henry kissing him."[24]

Equally momentous changes could be found in the race to succeed Eastland. While the national Democratic Party quickly rallied behind Maurice Dantin, some wounds opened in the primary were slow to heal. At a time when the number of Mississippians who would flock behind the standards of Eastland or others was declining, here was an ominous portent. Even if a putative Democratic newcomer like Dantin could assert the value of belonging to the majority party, this packed less of an electoral punch than the argument a chairman could make that his position offered even more benefits. But farmers who were the core of Eastland's constituency were fewer in number and those closer to the cities and towns had begun to swing toward a party more akin to their bourgeois values. Moderate-to-conservative Mississippians found much to admire in the positive campaigns Thad Cochran and Charles Pickering waged for their party's nod in 1978. Once the primary votes were counted, Pickering and his more conservative supporters rapidly switched to Cochran. In contrast, Democrats were slow to unite behind Dantin. While Eastland acknowledged his work behind the scenes for Dantin in the runoff and heralded him "a very worthy successor," his own camp divided as soon as he announced his retirement. While most stayed true to their Democratic heritage, some moved to Cochran. Easily the biggest surprise was the decision of D. A. Biglane, the self-made oil millionaire from Natchez who was one of Eastland's closest friends, to become the treasurer for the Independent candidacy of Charles Evers.[25]

It had been Jim Eastland's position for his first four terms in the Senate that the rise of the Republican Party would not be good for Mississippi, as it might hasten the fall of a society built on a foundation of white supremacy. By 1978, that political order was in tatters. Not only did Thad Cochran court the white elements of the state's body politic, but he mixed easily with blacks and took a moderate posture on issues with racial implications. Charles Evers' entrance into the race brought additional volatility to a changing political climate, for the mayor of Fayette combined a powerful bearing as the brother of a civil rights martyr with a social and cultural conservatism that appealed to many whites. In truth, the real reason Evers entered the race, he later said, was to deny the black vote to Dantin, whom he despised, and thus guarantee that either he or Cochran would be elected. He did go through the motions of berating

Eastland, whom he saw privately as a friend, for "keeping us down for all those years." But even more compelling was his personal story. "I know what it's like to drive a mule all day and not have anything to show for it," he would say to some audiences. "You need somebody who looks like you and talks like you and has suffered like you," he told others. Alone among the aspiring black politicos in Mississippi, most of whom were more liberal than him, Evers was endowed with the kind of charisma that could inspire blacks in the Delta and other parts of Mississippi. He drew naturally from blacks who might otherwise have been drawn to the Democratic nominee or stayed at home. And he was astute enough to employ celebrities to campaign alongside him. One was boxer Muhammad Ali, who was in Natchez shooting a film based loosely upon the life of Reconstruction-era Senator Hiram Revels, the first African American ever seated in the upper chamber. The champ who liked to call himself "The Greatest" not only led a parade of 40,000 supporters for Evers through Jackson, but cut a commercial for him. "If you don't vote for Charles Evers," Ali declared, half-smiling, "I'm going to bop you."[26]

With votes leaving Dantin from both left and right, Eastland stepped up his activity for his party's nominee in the last month of the campaign. He made calls for Dantin and recruited twenty-one Democratic colleagues to appear at a Capitol Hill fundraiser for Dantin. He conceded that Cochran was ahead, but tried to rally his longtime backers by forecasting that Dantin would ultimately prevail. He was not a prophet, he said, so he would not make any predictions. Such was a wise course, for a poll published in mid-September had Cochran ahead of Dantin by 23 points and Evers not far behind. On occasion, he and Dantin revived rhetoric of the New Deal era blaming Republicans for most farm foreclosures over the past half-century and reminded voters that Democrats had created the Farmers Home Administration. While he liked and respected Cochran and did not chide him by name, Eastland used his appearances in the Delta to pledge, as most Democrats did by the 1970s, that Dantin, unlike Cochran, would never vote against raising the minimum wage or for hiking interest rates on disaster loans. Still, his best argument remained that voters would be getting a "zero" if they defeated either Dantin or David Bowen, the congressman who represented the Delta. Eastland reasoned that a new member of the minority party could not enjoy the clout carried by a senator in the majority, who would hold at least a subcommittee chairmanship from the outset. But voters who had been accustomed to the power Eastland exercised for a generation knew that it would take time for Dantin to garner a similar degree of authority. Cochran, for his part, focused his barbs more on the troubles facing the Carter administration than the divisions separating his opponents.

With Evers' appeal strong enough for him to carry ten African-American-majority counties and a full 23 percent of the vote, the ballots Dantin could muster were not enough to win. Cochran prevailed with 45 percent of the vote, carrying the state by 80,000 votes over Dantin. Ever astute, Eastland knew the result arose in part from migrants to the towns of the Magnolia State who would be naturally receptive to the appeals of a neo-Whig like Cochran, who had carefully courted all classes. But he also had worked with Cochran and appreciated not just his positive campaign to win "fair and square," but also the characteristic diligence of his legislative work and constituent service. It thus came very easy for Eastland to wire Cochran before midnight on election night and congratulate him for a "wonderful victory."[27]

Before leaving the Senate, Eastland aimed to complete one bit of unfinished business. Since 1962, he had been trying to change the composition of the federal courts in the Fifth Judicial District that served Mississippi. At first, his objection was that judges in that locale tended to rule for those suing states and localities for civil rights violations. He was never louder than after a three-judge panel levied $10,000 fines per day against Ross Barnett and Paul Johnson for every day they blocked James Meredith's admission to Ole Miss. Some liberals suspected for the next decade and a half that Eastland aimed to split the Fifth Circuit Court of Appeals. Were that to happen, John R. Brown and John Minor Wisdom, two jurists known for affirming complaints by those charging civil rights violations, might not again be assigned a Mississippi case. In these troubled times, their contentions had merit. Yet this was not the sole reason for Eastland's position, as questions of size had a role as well. "It's not a court," he once declared. "It's a convention." Three years later, Brown, by then the circuit's senior jurist, endorsed Eastland's and Chief Justice Warren Burger's pleas for additional judgeships. Even more tellingly, he did not oppose Eastland's plan to split the circuit in two and place Mississippi with Florida,

Alabama, and Georgia in the Fifth and allow judges from Louisiana and Texas to form a new circuit. Civil rights groups, however, still feared that his offer might allow allies like J. P. Coleman to control the work of the court and obstruct progress on issues of concern to them. They in turn leaned on House liberals like Judiciary Committee Chairman Peter Rodino and Barbara Jordan to block such a move in a conference committee. It fell upon Attorney General Griffin Bell, a former judge trusted by both sides, to devise a compromise that could be presented as an appropriate measure to honor Eastland's service. As Eastland desired, thirty-five new judgeships would be created, eleven of them in the Deep South. Moreover, any circuit with more than fifteen members could assemble *en banc* panels as the chief judge wished to hear cases under their jurisdiction.[28]

It was always Eastland's aim to serve out the entirety of his term. But the election of a number of midwestern Republicans caused agricultural bigwigs in the Deep South to fear that one of those new GOP senators might not only get a seat on the Agriculture Committee but also be seated before Cochran and thus gain seniority over him to the detriment of Mississippi. Delta Council leaders Seymour Johnson and Frank Mitchener realized Cochran was hardly presumptuous enough to go to the third man in line to the presidency and ask him to leave. That being the case, they prevailed upon Eastland to depart so as to benefit not just Cochran, but their state. Eastland agreed readily, and the two then convinced Governor Finch to name Cochran to fill the last week of Eastland's term. Once that was accomplished, Cochran had no qualms in accepting the appointment for the last uneventful week of Eastland's term.[29]

What Eastland had done, in effect, was facilitate the process by which a successor of the other party could accumulate seniority and thus derive benefits for Mississippi in droves, much as he had. This decision came easily for Eastland. Late in the afternoon in his last day on the job, he shared a drink and a cigar with only Hiram Eastland Jr., a cousin who worked in the Justice Department. The two talked about family and their Christmas plans, before the chairman began to rib Hiram for opting not to fly home to the Delta but rather to drive home so he could get his sheepdog back. They chatted a bit longer before Eastland slapped his chair. "Well, son," he said, "I've been here thirty-six years. It's time to go home." They walked to Hiram's car, and his cousin drove him to what was then known as Washington National Airport, from which Eastland would fly to Memphis, then return to his home. At that point, Eastland got his initial firsthand lesson about the fleeting nature of power. As he walked toward the waiting area, he heard a man shout out to any who cared to listen, "There he goes. That's the great senator from the great state of Mississippi, John C. Stennis."[30]

CHAPTER 19

Home to the Plantation

EASTLAND ADJUSTED EASILY TO LIFE AFTER THE SENATE. HE WAS ALWAYS more at home in the Delta than in the District of Columbia, and he identified more as a farmer than a legislator even when he was third in line to the presidency. Eastland was no more given to small talk than when he was in office. He was a bit more open with close friends, always asking Libby to fix his guests a "real drink" as opposed to a watered down one. "Hiram wants another drink," he would tell his wife. "Aw, Jim," she would reply, "you're not fooling me." Like his friend Lyndon Johnson, he preferred excreting outdoors well into his seventies. Former State Auditor Steve Patterson was hardly the only associate who heard him bemoan the fact that he could no longer "piss all the way across this truck." Guests he knew just slightly who visited his home would always find Libby ready to engage in conversation, but rarely Eastland, who did not miss having to glad-hand relative strangers. Just prior to returning to Washington for one final night of whiskey with his colleagues, he drove to a Sunflower County barber shop. Upon entering, he was greeted by another patron. "You don't remember me," said the man. "You're damn right," Eastland retorted, "I don't."[1]

Eastland was content to settle down to a life of farm and family. He hiked across his plantation daily, always racking up at least three miles. He found time to spend with male friends at haunts like Lusco's Restaurant in Greenwood, where Booth #2 was known as his second Delta office, Lillo's restaurant in Leland, where he found the best salads in the Delta, Doe's Eat Place in Greenville, or the Merigold Hunting Club. Twice a week, he drove from Doddsville to Cleveland for lunch and drinks at the country club. He enjoyed watching friends play poker, but never partook himself, being content to watch while puffing on the Cuban cigars a friend still sent him regularly from Geneva. Chip Morgan, the executive vice president of the Delta Council who sometimes acted as the designated driver for Eastland and Jesse Brent, termed him a "man's man" who would say less than anyone present but enjoy himself more. Eastland would drop by cattle sales on occasion or hunt and fish. He told reporters who tracked him down in the Delta that what he missed most about Washington was "mah friends," but he seldom sought out onetime colleagues. A few of his closest associates like Roman Hruska and John Pastore would call often, or in Hruska's case, join him for a fishing trip at his favorite site, the mouth of the Mississippi. More often, he preferred the company of fellow Delta planters and a group of not terribly well educated but unusually intelligent entrepreneurial Mississippians who had risen from rags to riches.[2]

For the first few years of his retirement, Eastland was still known as the one politico whose advice any aspiring candidates made sure to seek. Still, Eastland was more of a listener than a talker, and any wisdom he would dole out would emerge in a few sentences as opposed to a prearranged campaign plan. The few endorsements he made after his retirement came as pieces of gratitude for longstanding friendships. In 1979, the candidate he backed in the initial gubernatorial primary was prosecutor James Herring, an able but generally unknown youthful challenger from the Jackson suburb of Canton. Here, he was motivated primarily by loyalty, for Herring was the son-in-law of Dr. Raymond Zeller, whose campaign for student body president he had managed at Ole Miss more than half a century earlier. The notion that the value of his support was overstated can be seen by Herring's fourth place finish behind Lieutenant Governor Evelyn Gandy and eventual winner William Winter. What may well have been true was the observation by Morton, Mississippi, businessman Jack Stuart that Eastland was the "most overrated man in local politics and the most underrated man in national politics there ever was."[3]

To the great surprise of many, Eastland had grown increasingly comfortable campaigning with African Americans. When President Carter came to Jackson in the midst of his 1980 reelection campaign, then Governor William Winter invited Eastland to the State House to share drinks not just with John Stennis, but Aaron Henry, who by then had been elected to the Mississippi House of Representatives. Not long thereafter, Eastland was happy to join Tennessee Congressman Harold Ford Sr. alongside Vice President Walter Mondale in the back seat of a limousine en route to a campaign event in downtown Memphis.[4]

From time to time, Eastland drove to meetings around the Delta to push for local improvements, particularly expanding Highway 82 from two lanes to four. He continued to take a bit of an interest in politics as late as 1982, a year he helped organize a fundraiser for longtime colleague John Stennis in Bolivar County. And, when his friend David Bowen opted against seeking a sixth term in the House of Representatives, after a court-ordered redistricting plan created a new majority black Second District, Eastland endorsed Patrick "Pete" Johnson, the grandson of the governor who appointed him to the Senate, for the vacancy. When Johnson's bid fell short, Eastland met with both Democratic nominee Robert G. Clark, the state's first African-American state legislator since Reconstruction, and GOP counterpart Webb Franklin, a lawyer from Greenwood, but declined to endorse either man. He matter-of-factly let reporters know he thought Ronald Reagan had performed fairly well as president up until that point, but made it clear that there were some positions in which he disagreed with the Gipper and that he expected his fellow Democrats to pick up seats in the House that year. Still, if there was a subject that consumed him, it was agriculture. He was quick to explain that the future of the Delta lay in the production of more rice and soybeans, for they had already become more profitable than cotton. He made these observations ruefully, for the white gold of the Delta had governed not only the heritage of his homeland but the foundation of his own prosperity.[5]

In 1982 Eastland's health began to fade. That year, he underwent nearly three hours of surgery to restore sight in his right eye. He regained some of his vision, but his energy waned thereafter, and he did not like those outside of his family to see that he was increasingly dependent on others. Some friends in the Delta had died, and others had moved away. State and local politicos would come to visit, but were less likely to ask for his advice or blessing. He would hold his cigars and chew on them, but would not light them. He no longer drank the scotch and waters he so relished. He had abbreviated the long hikes across his plantation that had been his routine during his first few years of retirement to treks of a few hundred yards. Often, he ventured down to his farm office and sat for an hour or two. Occasionally, he took calls from people who wanted his help securing their Social Security benefits but were not aware that he was ailing. Some days, locals noticed, he would trod the mile down to the graveyard next to the Missionary Baptist church he had helped build, where most of those who were so much a part of the life of his plantation were buried, and peer pensively.[6]

While Eastland did make one final trip to Europe, where, among other things, he toured the distilleries in Scotland that produced Dewar's and his beloved Chivas Regal, he got but one final opportunity to exert and show off his clout. Two of his closest friends, D. A. Biglane and Otha Shurden, both of whom coincidentally died within six months of Eastland, decided they would lead a party to that year's Super Bowl, and they commissioned a private jet to take them to Tampa. Unfortunately, the plane they hired lacked restroom facilities of the sort Eastland preferred. As they neared the airstrip, Eastland felt the call of nature. With dozens of aircraft circling west-central Florida, he grew restive. "Put my boy up," he ordered his cohorts. All on the plane knew that the only one of his "boys" who could influence such things any longer was Larry Speakes, who had become Ronald Reagan's acting press secretary. Speakes took the call and within minutes got his new boss to order the Federal Aviation Administration to let Eastland's plane land before all others.[7]

Once they arrived at the Tampa Marriott, they bought a round of drinks and quickly decided that they would be just as happy watching the game on the hotel's big-screen television as they would from the ideal tickets above the 50-yard line that they had purchased. Biglane went to the manager and asked if he could reserve for his crowd the exclusive use of the bar. "Sir," he went on, "I think we're going to be able to talk about this." Biglane began tracing a line with his silver-tipped cane across part of the barroom, then pulled out a money clip and started laying $100 bills on the table by the dozens. Management reconsidered and Eastland's party wound up enjoying the Los Angeles Raiders' 38–9 trouncing of the Washington Redskins as much as anyone at the stadium.[8]

In the spring of 1985, Eastland made his last major appearance seated in a wheelchair as the federal courthouse in Jackson was renamed in his honor. He disliked reliving his past, especially around those he barely knew. He discouraged potential interviewers by telling those he encountered that he had voted his conscience on everything. Two sources who will not be attributed here told the author that Eastland continued to use politically incorrect language to describe African Americans until the very end of his life. Unlike John Stennis, who told Joe Biden that "the civil rights movement did more to free the white man than the black man," as it freed his soul, Eastland never publicly conceded that what he liked to call the Second Reconstruction had been necessary or desirable. He did credit many religious leaders for their work to enact civil rights legislation, but thought any further discussion of the matter counterproductive. "Our state is over the hump now," he would tell people. "I think we oughta forget the battles we had." Still, there were unmistakable cracks in his paternalistic armor. He would show those who visited him in Doddsville the brick homes he had rebuilt for those black families who had once worked his fields. And it was no longer rare for him to publicly applaud those African Americans who had worked with him on measures he believed would benefit all residents of Mississippi. Most notably, in 1985, he sent a $500 check to the state chapter of the NAACP Aaron Henry had chaired since the assassination of Medgar Evers. Although much too frail to attend, Eastland wrote a letter that was read at a dinner honoring Henry and thanked him for helping him to "see the whole picture." "Thousands of us," he wrote, "have been helped by your gallant, dedicated and persistent leadership that has made recognition of a life that includes all mankind possible."[9]

What precipitated Eastland's final decline was his choking on a piece of meat in early February 1986. Long prone to diseases common in the Delta, like malaria and hepatitis, his eyes had been failing and he had suffered several minor strokes. Once taken to the North Sunflower County Hospital in Ruleville, hip trouble seemed to lead to kidney failure. Other ailments reappeared and compounded, and he was slow to respond to any kind of nourishment. He was transported a few days later to the Greenwood-LaFlore County Hospital, where doctors hoped they could provide a higher quality of care. Medical staff placed him in a cubicle within an intensive care unit, but soon recognized that they could treat Eastland's decline, but no longer forestall it. Libby took a room in hospital, and all four children took rooms in Greenwood motels. Doctors sensed that the end was near on the night of Tuesday February 18 and called the immediate family to the hospital. They took turns holding his hand in his cubicle until he passed into eternal rest at 2:00 A.M. the following morning from multiple ailments complicated by a case of pneumonia he had recently contracted.[10]

Funeral services were held at the United Methodist Church of Ruleville the morning after Eastland's passing. His family declined an offer to have his body lie in state in Jackson, and opted to hold rather humble services that effectively marked the end of an era. Never again would as many pivotal figures of the governing class of Mississippi of the mid-twentieth century appear together. Joining Thad Cochran, his successor, were one-time colleagues John Stennis, Roman Hruska, and Dennis DeConcini and the state's congressional delegation. Governor Bill Allain was present, as were most of his predecessors who were still alive, dozens of state and local officials, and hundreds of ordinary Mississippians. A generation earlier, many would have been shocked by the presence of Aaron Henry. But Mississippi, like Eastland, had changed. Those heard talking noted that Ross Barnett had been brought from his nursing home to make what would be his final public appearance, and looked not just a bit shriveled, but far older than his eighty-five years, a true anachronism. Presiding was a preacher who seemed not to be aware of Eastland's wish that no one "holler" over his corpse. His "boys" whom he asked to serve as his pall-bearers—Lieutenant Governor Brad Dye, John Holloman, Bill Simpson, and Jim Ziglar—all grinned knowingly when they heard the prelate erupt into a lengthy hellfire and brimstone sermon they found far better suited for a Delta revival of half a century earlier than this occasion. The eulogy he would have appreciated came from Larry Speakes. Eastland, Speakes said, once told him "he could walk from county line to county line and tell me who would carry the county. And I believed him."[11]

While Eastland's life was celebrated in Ruleville, the town of 3000 or more nearest the Delta hamlet where he was born and claimed as his residence for much of his adulthood, it is Forest where his body is interred, right next to his father's. It was this predominantly white Hill town where he was raised and where he tried his first legal cases. Like many historically conscious Southerners rooted in the lore and the myths of the Confederacy, Eastland longed to be buried near his forbearers. But it was not heritage alone that determined where he would be laid to rest. It was the hopes and aspirations of the white denizens of this and dozens of Mississippi towns of similar size with which he identified above all. And while Eastland rose to one of the highest positions in America, he never ceased to reflect the values of those from whence he sprung, their hopes, and, all too often, their fears.

Conclusion

BIOGRAPHERS EXAMINING THE EFFECTIVENESS OF LEGISLATORS, WHAT-
ever ideological stripe they fall under, often begin by inspecting the value
of projects their subjects brought home to their constituency. Here, Eastland and counterpart John Stennis were uncommonly successful. "They
deal fairly by splitting the appropriations and the proceeds of the federal
government, 50-50," Walter Mondale kidded in 1977. "When they allocate
funds and award contracts, they do it judiciously in that they give fifty
percent to Mississippi and fifty percent for the rest of us." The then vice
president clearly employed a degree of hyperbole, but not as much as
some might think. Over the last half of the twentieth century, Mississippians grew accustomed to a prime return on their tax dollar. Jack A. Travis
Jr., a leader of the state's more traditional Democrats, told an interviewer
in the mid 1970s that Mississippi got a $3.00 to $3.25 return for every tax
dollar their citizens sent to the Internal Revenue Service. To be sure, some
of the largesse did come from subsidies paid to planters like Eastland.
Historian James Cobb found that those owning large farms in the ten
core counties of the Delta received 22 percent of all federal subsidies.[1]
Even more spent in Mississippi while Eastland served with Stennis came
through antipoverty programs that the two opposed ardently. But there
can be no doubt that the great majority of the funding directed to the
Magnolia State emerged from Eastland's and Stennis' hidden hand lobbying of everyone from presidents to the most obscure federal bureaucrats.
Any responsible compendium of the Eastland record should include his
work, among other things, to expedite relief to victims of major natural
disasters, open the Tennessee-Tombigbee Waterway, build a new harbor

at Pascagoula, establish a comprehensive program for fisheries and the seafood industry along the Gulf Coast, negotiate contracts bringing a poultry industry to the state, and establish a NASA test facility between Picayune and Bay St. Louis that later bore Stennis' name.[2]

If asked, Eastland partisans are likely to salute their patron loudest for his work to confirm the more conservative group of justices who filled vacancies opened by the retirements of predecessors on the Supreme Court headed by Earl Warren. Senators who served with Eastland, in contrast, are most likely to hail him for the fairness with which he conducted the business of the Judiciary Committee on issues other than civil rights, as well as the shrewdness he employed to steer the jurists they deemed best for their states to being nominated by a president and confirmed by the full Senate. Their reminiscences are particularly pronounced from the standpoint of the ever more contentious current Senate, which the liberal commentator Chris Matthews likens to a "government by tantrum." California Democrat John Tunney once declared that Eastland used power "as skillfully as anyone" he ever knew in that he could exert that power "without the people around him ever being aware what he was doing." According to James Abourezk of South Dakota, one of the most liberal Democrats ever to serve in the Senate, Eastland had one supreme virtue characteristic of fewer and fewer politicos. "He never tried to fool anyone about himself or his positions," wrote Abourezk, a man who disagreed with him as much as anyone. Eastland's traditional brand of honor led him to admonish one of the new breed of senators first elected in the 1970s that he never put his "word in writing to anyone." To Senate veterans, such a course was unthinkable, as they, as Attorney General Nicholas Katzenbach said, knew that "you could rely absolutely on what Jim Eastland said." Colleagues knew as well that it was rare that Eastland judged people on their ideology rather than, as John Culver of Iowa put it, on how much he "respected their character."[3]

Still, the judgment of history is likely to be harsh upon James O. Eastland. In part, this reflects the locale of his birth. What he was guilty of, Sid Salter, who edited the *Scott County Times* at the time of Eastland's death, was "interjecting the will of the majority of his white Mississippi voting constituents into a volatile national debate." It was never the case in any of his six bids for the Senate that Eastland was elected solely because he was a segregationist, but he would never have been elected if he had not been one. There are many ways to depict the commitment of Mississippi whites in the 1950s and 1960s to preserving the stern inviolability of their state's racial hierarchy. One indicator comes from the December 1954 estimate of Dr. T. M. R. Howard, the chairman of the Regional Council for Negro Leadership, that 75 percent of the state's whites would take up arms in defense of the regional caste system. Here was a guess steep in hyperbole, but one founded on a familiarity with the determination of whites in many parts of the Deep South to preserve their dominance of the racial order. Such a position might be seen when one compares positions taken on race by two somewhat representative southern student bodies. In 1960, the student body president at Drew High School, an institution later known as the home of gridiron icon Archie Manning just ten miles north of Doddsville, wrote Eastland to salute him for a "valiant battle" and vowed that the youth of Mississippi intended to keep their state segregated. Three years earlier, an elected group of students four hours northeast of Sunflower County at Lawrenceburg High School in Tennessee, whose student body included future actor and Senator Fred D. Thompson, arranged an assembly to consider "the pros and cons of segregation, believing that by reasoning, not by force, this problem can be solved."[4]

In fighting throughout much of his first four terms to preserve the static social order so visible in the Mississippi of the post-Reconstruction century, James O. Eastland reflected the wishes of the white electorate that put him in office. He shared their grounding in a mythologized view of a benighted South at the mercy of malevolent Yankees intent upon replacing a way of life they worshiped. His political home was always a state party whose leaders for nearly a century echoed a commitment to preserve the racially hierarchical agrarian society that left them in charge and most blacks in poverty. While we may say we admire those leaders who transform their way of life to one better for all of their people, we are more likely to elect leaders who reflect our often less ambitious or altruistic values at any given time. Such has been true since the dawning of governments resembling any form of democracy. Solon, the Athenian lawgiver of the sixth century B.C., regretted that he could not give his people the best laws he could imagine, but only "the best that they could receive."[5]

In many ways, the outlook of and political path taken by James Eastland on racial issues mirrored that demanded by a majority of Mississippi
whites. In his first bid for the seat in 1942, the notion that whites would
remain supreme across the South was an unspoken matter of agreement
among Eastland and each of his four opponents. Thereafter, he and other
Southerners clung to an ever more defensive posture in the face of an
African-American population emboldened by the appreciation of some
whites for their service over the course of World War II and a growing sense among whites outside the Deep South, particularly those in
the clergy, that their grievances were legitimate. "World War II was the
door that opened up this whole process of new relationships," William
F. Winter, Eastland's onetime driver and a veteran of the war, declared
much later.[6] With a meager number of blacks registered to vote, Eastland's
rhetoric could be sharp and his tactics could be extreme throughout his
first two decades in the Senate. He warned of "mongrelization" in the
1940s, blamed African Americans for the misdeeds of African Arabs in
the alleys of Stuttgart in 1945, and urged defiance in the wake of the 9–0
Supreme Court ruling in the seminal case of *Brown v. Board of Education of Topeka, Kansas* of 1954. He attached his name to the Southern
Manifesto of 1956, which bound signatories to oppose any and all civil
rights legislation, and kept his pledge for the next decade and a half. He
boasted of his willingness to bury bills enforcing the dictates of the Fourteenth and Fifteenth Amendments, both of which he found illegitimate
because of the way they were approved during the Reconstruction era by
Congresses that met without the presence of members elected virtually
entirely from the white populations of the states that had seceded. But
while Eastland made his points early and often in the South and before
even a few northern audiences, he did so without a knack, much less the
flair, for employing the sacred or the vulgar with the demagogic force of
a James "the White Chief" Vardaman or a Theodore "The Man" Bilbo. In
the course of his pronouncements that defiance of decisions mandating
civil rights was a legitimate course of action, Eastland on most occasions
inserted a rejoinder to likeminded audiences that they should refrain
from the use of violence, an admonition not all followed. Many around
him knew that he recognized his need to accumulate some political capital to allow him to get what he wanted in terms of agricultural programs

to benefit his state's farmers or nominations of judges deemed worthy of seats on the federal bench by his colleagues. One who sensed a very real pragmatic streak was Robert F. Kennedy. "You register those people to vote," he told Martin Luther King Jr. in the early 1960s, "and Jim Eastland will change his mind."[7]

Jim Eastland spoke little and wrote down less, so just how much his outlook adapted cannot be discerned with certainty. What is clear is that the readily apparent paternalistic streak that had been such a key tenet of his character took on more of a genteel nature. State NAACP leader Aaron Henry likened his metamorphosis in the 1970s on questions of race relations to that of the Apostle Paul on the road to Damascus. To be sure, there was some hyperbole in Henry's remarks, but what had happened over the course of the 1970s as Democrats tried to reunify their state party after nearly two decades of struggles between those committed to the old Jim Crow order and those loyal to the national party was that Eastland had forged relationships—and with Henry and Charles Evers, very real friendships—with some blacks who had been active in pushing for the civil rights of their people. Such developments were prompted by shifting political realities. The rise in the state Republican Party that began in the 1950s rendered it necessary for traditional Mississippi Democrats to find common ground with the tens, even hundreds, of thousands of new blacks found on Mississippi voter rolls following passage of the Voting Rights Act. "There was a change coming," said Brad Dye, "and if you don't accept change you're gonna get your ass run over bad."[8]

So Jim Eastland found it necessary to adapt to changes in ways that would have seemed revolutionary when he first took his seat in the Senate in July 1941. Delta farmers had switched from cotton to poultry, rice, and soybeans. Others had left the farms altogether for the towns and cities of Mississippi or elsewhere. While there was no longer a black majority, those who remained could and did vote. Jim Eastland's native Delta, his son Woods observed in 2012, had become a venue whose politics were dominated by blacks even if it remained a bastion of white economic power.[9] Statewide, the African-American population was a considerably lower percentage of the whole than it had been a century earlier, but the whites who constituted the ruling class were no longer Bourbon Democrats like Eastland but Republicans like Haley Barbour, Thad Cochran, and Trent Lott, who hailed from more densely populated areas and whose brands of conservatism reflected the economic interests of those communities and, to varying degrees, acceptances of the premises of a biracial society. There is an argument to be made that one loses a bit of the heritage of a region with the departure of too many of those tied to the soil from seats of power. But the paternalistic racial ideology of Jim Eastland so commonly shared in the 1940s and 1950s is, thankfully, increasingly rare in the Mississippi of the twenty-first century.

Letter from James O. Eastland to Theodore G. Bilbo[1]

Dear Senator:

Receipt is acknowledged of your letter of February 19, 1942, imploring me to join the armed forces of our Country without delay.

Of course, senator, you did not expect me to swallow your bait without discovering the barbed hook it so poorly concealed. I thoroughly comprehend the significance of your high-sounding sentiments and professed lofty ideals, and I likewise fully comprehend the political significance of your letter. Therefore, I will first take cognizance of your tearful, pretended interest in my military situation and then attend to the real purpose of your letter.

It is true that I am within the age limits defined by the Selective Service Act, and when my County calls me, I shall gladly answer that call and serve in any designated capacity. I have no excuses or exemptions to plead. My service to my Country will be based upon patriotic motives and not for the contemptible reasons proposed in your letter that I should don my Country's uniform in order to secure political preferences after the war. If I should become a candidate for the United States Senate and fortunate enough to be elected, I would then be in the same category as over one hundred members of the present Congress who are within the age limits and have also registered, subject to call to serve the Country. When their Country calls, these men will answer, and if I am a member of the Congress when called, I shall also answer.

If your line of reasoning were adopted, all Americans between the ages of 20 and 44 would at this time be barred from holding public office, either State, County, or National.

Senator, it comes with poor grace from you to tell any man what his patriotic duty is. In 1898 you were 21 years of age and your Country was at war with the Spanish Empire. That war was fought solely by volunteers. That war was fought before I was born, which was November 28, 1904, yet I killed just as many Spaniards as you killed; I freed just as many Cubans as you freed; I contributed just as much to the defense of my Country as you contributed. In 1917 you did not don a uniform, neither did your candidate, who now occupies the hallowed seat of the great Senator Pat Harrison.

Senator, your advice does not spring from patriotism. Neither does it spring from friendship. It is prompted by your desire to have as your colleague a Senator whom you can dominate and control. The real reason for your solicitude is that you think I will be a candidate for the Senate this year, and you hope by this ill-concealed attempt to becloud the issues to divert attention from the miserable records of Wall Doxey and yourself when, among other things, in utter disregard of the misfortunes and sacrifices of our people, you voted to pension yourselves—to divert money which should be used for the legitimate expenditures of our government and which was sweated from the toil, the privations and the suffering of the American people into a pension fund for the benefit of self-seeking politicians. Then, when an outraged public voiced its protests, both you and your candidate attempted to justify this un-holy scheme and brazen exhibition of greed, but you did not have the moral courage nor the intestinal fortitude to vote your real convictions of the bill to repeal pension-for politicians.

I thank God that I have never subscribed to that brand of patriotism, and I trust that Mississippi will never again elect a Senator whose patriotism is measured by the height of the pension trough.

I have noted with keen and amused interest your fallacious statements regarding the "Democratic custom" and Senator Doxey's committee assignments. You know that I know the inside operation of things in the Senate, you know that I know, as you do, that this committee assignment business is the most overworked political racket in America. I shall turn the truth on this myth if I become a candidate for the Senate. I shall also have something to say about your alleged Democratic custom of giving a full term to a Senator or Congressman who has been elected to an unexpired term—just another myth. Suffice it to say here, I desire to run for the Senate last summer, but could not become a candidate because there would have been no one to represent Mississippi in the upper branch of the Congress. You were absent from your post duty and in Mississippi attempting to dictate to the people of the state how to vote in the election. I had to remain in Washington and make a fight for Mississippi. I made that fight without your support, without your counsel, and without your presence.

You cannot make the people of Mississippi believe that because I stayed on the job in Washington, putting business above politics and made the fight in their interest when you had deserted them, I have forfeited my right to aspire to serve them again as Senator.

You inform me that you will fight me if I should make the race for the Senate this year. As you well know, I have never solicited your support for any office, I have never asked you to vote for me. And, get this straight, I have never asked any politician or would be dictator whether or not I could run for any office which is the people's right alone to give. If Wall Doxey can endure your praise, I can stand your censure.

Of course, you have planned all along to get into the campaign in Mississippi this year up to your eyebrows. These plans were incubating at the Dream House on December 7, and you were not present in Washington when war was declared upon the cowardly assassin of Pearl Harbor.

Leaving your post of duty in Washington is nothing new to you, and it has become a fixed habit of yours to come home and get mixed up in political campaigns that are no affairs of yours. I have reason to remember this very well last summer. I remember when the cotton gins were humming and the farmers needed someone to protect their interest. I was alone in the Senate, so far as Mississippi was concerned, when an effort was made to dump Government-owned cotton on the market and beat down cotton prices below parity, and I remember you were not there when the cotton-freezing bill was called up. We passed that bill by a narrow margin and saved the day for the cotton farmer.

I remember you were in Mississippi when an attempt was made to reduce the price of cottonseed far below the then market value and I had to fight this fight without your help. I don't think you would have been a lot of help but anyhow you were not there.

Last summer when 250,000 bales of Brazilian cotton were coming into the United States via Canada in the form of military supplies, you did not either help me discover the hole or plug the dike. Neither did you attend a single conference with me with officials of the State Department when this unfair practice was stopped by an export subsidy of American cotton to Canada.

You were in Washington when Senators Bankhead and Butler and I introduced an amendment to the Revenue Bill to provide a tariff on foreign fats and oil, which would have guaranteed seventy-five dollars a ton for our cottonseed, but you were not on the floor when the vote was taken and you will remember that I had to look you up and rouse you to get on the floor in time to vote for reconsideration.

Senator, let me tell you that I don't scare easily, and your threats do not fill me with alarm. In fact, the effect is just the contrary—I will be glad for you to come to Mississippi and make as many speeches as possible in behalf of your candidate. And I am sure the people of Mississippi will be interested to hear your explanation of your vote against the repeal of the Neutrality Bill, which President Roosevelt had requested as being vital to our National protection. They will be interested to hear you tell them about your absence from Washington when the declaration against war against Japan was voted, which you no doubt can explain by saying that your presence was required at your Pearl River country estate to supervise the creation of your island hideout, which is said to be a humdinger. They will also be glad to hear how you expect to maintain that luxurious place of rendezvous in view of what you recently said, in trying to wisecrack your way out of your pension grab vote, that you did not know where you would get the $500 to pay your annual dues.

And Senator, I am sure the people of Mississippi would like to learn the inside facts regarding your alliance with Wheeler, Nye, Clark and other isolationists in your fight against the repeal of the Neutrality Law and your threats while acting as the spokesman for the coterie to wage a filibuster against the repeal measure.

In conclusion, let me say that your letter came as no surprise. I knew that whoever dared oppose your candidate for the Senate would incur your wrath. I knew that, regardless of how one might have befriended you in the past, when you no longer could use that friend, you could turn against him with Japanese treachery as you did against the late beloved Pat Harrison, who not only had a fat job created for you when you were down and out, but when you were elected to the Senate made it possible for you to get the little temporary standing that you once had in Washington.

You have your candidate for the Senate. Your hands will be full looking after his campaign, and I predict that it will not be long before he will rue the day he received your kiss of death. If I decide to be a candidate, my friends and I will conduct my campaign, and no matter what grand strategy you and your candidate conduct at your next meeting at your island rendezvous, we will not be deterred. And, if you and your candidate's votes during the coming months should be as damnable as some of those you have cast in recent weeks, the sooner you both quit Washington to inaugurate your defense, the better it will be for the people's welfare.

As a parting word, Senator, if you must butt into the coming Senatorial campaign, why not get into it right by resigning and asking the people of Mississippi for a vote of confidence?

Sincerely yours,
Jim Eastland

P.S. In your letter you tell me that I must "help defeat the Dictators Adolf Hitler of Germany, Tojo of Japan, and Benito Mussolini of Italy." Why did you fail to mention the fourth—Theodore Bilbo of Mississippi?

Notes

KEY TO ABBREVIATIONS

B	Box
CPR	*Clarksdale Press Register*
CQ	*Congressional Quarterly*
CR	*Congressional Record*
DDT	*Delta Democrat Times*
F	Folder
GC	*Greenwood Commonwealth*
JCL	*Jackson Clarion-Ledger*
JDN	*Jackson Daily News*
JMH	*Journal of Mississippi History*
JOE	James Oliver Eastland
MCA	*Memphis Commercial Appeal*
NOTP	*New Orleans Time Picayune*
NYP	*New York Post*
NYT	*New York Times*
OE	*Oxford Eagle*
S	Series
SS	Subseries
WP	*Washington Post*

INTRODUCTION

1. James G. Abourezk, *Advise and Dissent: Memoirs of South Dakota and the U.S. Senate* (Chicago, 1989), 147; James N. Giglio, *Call Me Tom: The Life of Thomas F. Eagleton* (Columbia, MO, 2011), 86–87; interviews with Bennett Johnston, Oct. 4, 2011, Washington, D.C., William Threadgill, Jan. 5, 2012, Columbus, MS, and James W. Ziglar, Dec. 13, 2011, Washington, D.C.

2. Joseph Stanley Kimmitt, transcript, oral history, Feb. 15, 2001, 39; Tom C. Korologos to Terrence O'Donnell, Oct. 30, 1975, White House Name File, B916, Gerald R. Ford Presidential Library, Ann Arbor, MI.

3. Eastland served with but eight women.

4. JOE, address at Neshoba County Fair, Aug. 3, 1978, W. F. "Bill" Minor Papers, Mitchell Memorial Library, Mississippi State University, Starkville.

5. Interview with Hodding Carter III, May 17, 2011, Chapel Hill, NC; *NOTP* and *NYT*, Jun. 13, 1963; Benjamin O. Sperry, "Caught 'Between Our Moral and Material Selves': Mississippi's Elite White Moderates and Their Role in Changing Race Relations, 1945–1956," Ph.D. dissertation, Case Western Reserve University, 2010, 61.

6. Joseph Crespino, *In Search of Another Country: Mississippi and the Conservative Counterrevolution* (Princeton, NJ, 2007), 106; interviews with Steve Patterson, Jun. 22, 2012, Greenwood, MS, and William Winter, Mar. 18, 2010, Jackson, MS.

7. James C. Cobb, *The Most Southern Place on Earth: The Mississippi Delta and the Roots of Regional Identity* (New York, 1992), 146.

8. *Houston Chronicle*, Mar. 19, 1922.

9. *CR*, 95th Cong., 2nd Sess., S4578; JOE to Dave Halle, May 13, 1946, S1, SS7, B1, F1-9, JOE Collection; JOE to Kraus Cleaners, Aug. 20, 1947, S1, SS7, B1, F1-10, JOE Collection; interview with Chip Morgan, Jun. 19, 2012, Stoneville, MS; Neal R. Peirce, *The Deep South States: People, Power and Politics in the Seven Deep South States* (New York, 1974), 226; Larry Speakes to JOE, May 8, 1978, S2, SS4, B20, "May 1978 Eastland Profile" file, JOE collection; Ziglar interview.

10. JOE to E. E. Sims, Jan. 13, 1954, S1, SS19, B15, F15-2; Charlotte Hays, "The Silent Senator from Mississippi," *Midwest*, Feb. 27, 1974, 3–4, 34; telephone interviews with John C. Culver, Dec. 9, 2012, Bethesda, MD, and William Waller, Jul. 15, 2011, Jackson, MS.

11. Interviews with Hiram Eastland Jr., Jun. 22, 2012, Greenwood, MS, Woods Eastland, Jun. 11, 2012, Doddsville, MS, and Craig Shirley, Mar. 25, 2012, Kensington, MD.

12. *Fort Worth Star-Telegram*, Aug. 26, 1962; interviews with Howard H. Baker Jr., Jun. 13, 2011, Huntsville, TN, and Woods Eastland and Anne Eastland Howdeshell, Jun. 18, 2011, Jackson, MS; telephone interviews with Joe Allen, Nov. 21, 2012, Bethesda, OH, Macon Edwards, Jul. 24, 2012, Washington, D.C., and Wallace H. Johnson, Dec. 5, 2011, Cody, WY; *WP*, Dec. 30, 1973.

13. Thoroughly in character, Humphrey later found that the error had been an innocuous one by members of his own staff and treated Eastland aides Brad Dye and Jimmy Walker to dinner at their favorite restaurant in downtown Washington. Telephone interview with Birch Bayh, May 25, 2010, Easton, MD; Adam Clymer, *Edward M. Kennedy: A Biography* (New York, 1999), 47; *CPR*, Feb. 19, 1986; interviews with Brad Dye, Jun. 20, 2011, Ridgeland, MS, David Lambert, Aug. 13, 2012, Alexandria, VA, and Donald A. Ritchie, Jul. 19, 2013, Washington, D.C.; The Ralph Nader Congress Project, *The Judiciary Committees: A Study of the House and Senate Committees* (New York, 1975), 16; undated *Meridian Star* article in B1019, F18, Theodore G. Bilbo Papers, University of Southern Mississippi.

14. Dye interview; interview with Hiram Eastland Jr. and Steve Patterson, Jun. 22, 2012, Greenwood, MS; telephone interview with Walter L. Nixon, Oct. 5, 2011, Biloxi, MS; *NYT*, Jul. 29, 1972; Nick Walters, "The Repairman Chairman: Senator James O. Eastland and His Influence on the U.S. Supreme Court," M.A. thesis, Mississippi College, 1992, 15; Maarten Zwiers, "The Paradox of Power: James O. Eastland and the Democratic Party," M.A. thesis, University of Mississippi, 2007, 8.

15. Interview with Thad Cochran, Apr. 6, 2011, Washington, D.C.; telephone interview with David R. Bowen, Apr. 29, 2011, Jackson, MS.

16. Telephone interview with Lamar Hooker, Jul. 15, 2011, Covington, LA.

17. Telephone interview with Bowen; telephone interview with Bill Minor, Apr. 20, 2011, Jackson, MS.

18. Allen telephone interview.

19. This associate asked not to be named.

20. Hiram Eastland Jr. interview; Larry Speakes, *Speaking Out: Inside the Reagan White House* (New York, 1988), 305.

21. *JCL*, Oct. 18, 1978; *JDN*, Sep. 20, 1978.

22. Interviews with Nell Eastland Amos, Woods Eastland, Anne Eastland Howdeshell, and Sue Eastland McRoberts, Jun. 18, 2011, Jackson, MS, Hiram Eastland, Jan. 1, 2015, Greenwood, MS, and Trent Lott, Sep. 29, 2011, Washington, D.C.; transcript, Brad Dye, oral history A-467, Sep. 20, 1993, Center for Oral History and Cultural Heritage, McCain Library, University of Southern Mississippi, Hattiesburg; Bill Minor, *Eyes on Mississippi: A Fifty-Year Chronicle of Change* (Jackson, MS, 2001), 30; *JCL*, Feb. 20, 1986; *NYP*, Feb. 19, 1956; telephone interviews with Danny Cupit, Jan. 7, 2013, Jackson, MS, and Johnny Morgan, May 8, 2013, Oxford, MS; Waller telephone interview.

23. David Chandler, *The Natural Superiority of Southern Politicians: A Revisionist History* (Garden City, NY, 1977), 305; Michael D. Davis and Hunter R. Clark, *Thurgood Marshall: Warrior at the Bar, Rebel on the Bench* (New York, 1992), 235; McRoberts interview.

24. Some senators on the Appropriations Committee got the Tennessee-Tombigbee appeal from Stennis, who for a long time was their chairman, alone. Baker, Edwards, and Johnston interviews; telephone interview with Ernest F. Hollings, Aug. 23, 2011, Charleston, SC; Michael O'Brien, *Philip Hart: The Conscience of the Senate* (East Lansing, MI, 1995), 142; C. Fraser Smith, *Here Lies Jim Crow: Civil Rights in Maryland* (Baltimore, 1975), 241.

CHAPTER 1

1. Interview with William Winter, Mar. 18, 2010, Jackson, MS; V. O. Key Jr., *Southern Politics in State and Nation* (New York, 1949), 229–253.

2. Chris Myers Asch, *The Senator and the Sharecropper: The Freedom Struggles of James O. Eastland and Fannie Lou Hamer* (New York, 2008), 17, 36; Eastland family tree, S1, SS2, B1, F1-12, JOE Collection; JOE to B. F. Worsham, Jul. 26, 1974, S3, SS1, B140, "1974 Robert E. Lee Citizenship" file, JOE Collection; Justin Glenn e-mail in "Eastland Petty Genealogy" in Alfred Eastland Descendants file in Forest, MS, Public Library; Richard Kleindienst, *Justice: The Memoirs of Attorney General Richard Kleindienst* (Ottawa, IL, 1985), 124; "The Authentic Voice," *Time*, Mar. 26, 1956, 27; Woods C. Eastland to Mrs. J. T. Woodhull, Nov. 12, 1941, S1, SS2, B1, F1-11, JOE Collection; Woods C. Eastland to Bell Eastland, Nov. 7, 1942, S1, SS19, B7, F7-22; John David Smith and J. Vincent Lowery (eds.), *The Dunning School: Historians, Race and the Meaning of Reconstruction* (Lexington, KY, 2013), x, 1–39, 76–77.

3. Asch, *Senator and the Sharecropper*, 36–37; Karen Cox, *Dixie's Daughters: The United Daughters of the Confederacy and the Preservation of Confederate Culture* (Gainesville, FL, 2003), 1; e-mail, Hiram Eastland to author, May 14, 2013; JOE, "Keynote Speech to the Mississippi State Democratic Convention," Jun. 22, 1948, B1, F25, Kenneth Toler Papers, Mississippi State University, Starkville; Dan W. Smith, "James O. Eastland: Early Life and Career, 1904–1942," M.A. thesis, Mississippi College, 1978, 9.

4. Asch, *Senator and the Sharecropper*, 35–38; interview with Woods E. Eastland, Jun. 11, 2012, Doddsville, MS; Marie M. Hemphill, *Fevers, Floods and Faith: A History of Sunflower*

County, Mississippi (Indianola, MS, 1980), 343; *NYP*, Feb. 15, 1956; Smith, "Eastland: Early Life and Career," 6, 8.

5. "Authentic Voice," 27; Henry J. Davis to JOE, Jun. 20, 1942, S1, SS19, B1, F1-14, JOE Collection; J. Todd Moye, *Let the People Decide: Black Freedom and White Resistance Movements in Sunflower County, Mississippi, 1945–1986* (Chapel Hill, 2004), 5; Smith, "Eastland: Early Life and Career," 6.

6. Asch, *Senator to Sharecropper*, 6–9; *GC*, Feb. 13, 2004; Moye, *Let the People Decide*, 3–7.

7. Asch, *Senator to Sharecropper*, 23–28; *GC*, Feb. 13, 2004; Moye, *Let the People Decide*, 7–13.

8. Asch, *Senator and the Sharecropper*, 29–32; *GC*, Sep. 17, 2004.

9. Asch, *Senator and the Sharecropper*, 35, 38; Woods Eastland to Paul B. Johnson, "Family Correspondence" folder, S1, SS2, B1, F1-12, JOE Collection.

10. Asch, *Senator and the Sharecropper*, 38–39; Christopher Myers Asch, "No Compromise: The Freedom Struggles of James O. Eastland and Fannie Lou Hamer," Ph.D. dissertation, University of North Carolina, 25; e-mail, Woods E. Eastland to author, Dec. 27, 2011.

11. Kenneth Archer to Joe Brown, undated, S1, SS19, B5, F5-4, JOE Collection; Lewis Cochran to Courtney Pace, Mar. 28, 1942, S3, SS7, B7, F1-2; *NYP*, Feb. 15, 1956.

12. Bill R. Baker, *Catch the Vision: The Life of Henry L. Whitfield of Mississippi* (Jackson, MS, 1974), 84; Vincent A. Giroux, "The Rise of Theodore G. Bilbo," *JMH* 43:3 (Aug. 1981), 202; interview with Clarence Pierce, Jun. 13, 2012, Vaiden, MS.

13. Asch, *Senator and the Sharecropper*, 39; interview with Anne Eastland Howdeshell, Jun. 18, 2011, Jackson, MS, and David Lambert, Aug. 13, 2012, Alexandria, VA; *MCA*, Jun. 11, 1979; *NYP*, Feb. 15, 1956; Smith, "Eastland: Early Life and Career," 13; "The Authentic Voice," *Time*, Mar. 26, 1956, 27; *WP*, Dec. 30, 1973.

CHAPTER 2

1. *JDN*, Jan. 4, 1976.

2. Biographical press release of JOE office, Jul. 26, 1941, S1, SS1, B1, F1-1, JOE Collection; Dan W. Smith, "James O. Eastland: Early Life and Career, 1904–1942," M.A. thesis, Mississippi College, 1978, 15–16.

3. Larry Thomas Balsamo, "Theodore G. Bilbo and Mississippi Politics, 1877–1932," Ph.D. dissertation, University of Missouri, 1967, 162; Edward Cole, oral history, Jan. 7, 1991, John C. Stennis Oral History Project, John C. Stennis Collection, Mississippi State University, Starkville; JOE to D. H. Class, Jul. 12, 1941, S1, SS19, B1, F1-4, JOE Collection; Reinhard Luthin, *American Demagogues: Twentieth Century* (Boston, 1954), 57–60; Chester M. Morgan, *Redneck Liberal: Theodore G. Bilbo and the New Deal* (Baton Rouge, 1985); Smith, "Eastland: Early Life and Career," 20.

4. *Greenwood (MS) Commonwealth*, Feb. 4, 1976; *JCL*, Feb. 4, 1976; *JDN*, Jan. 4, 1976, Oct. 13, 1977; Morgan, *Redneck Liberal*, 19; Smith, "Eastland: Early Life and Career," 20–22; *Vicksburg Evening Post*, Nov. 12, 1978.

5. Ben Edmundson, "Pat Harrison and Mississippi in the Presidential Elections of 1924 and 1928," *JMH* 33:4 (Nov. 1971), 333–345; Richard C. Ethridge, "Mississippi and the 1928 Presidential Campaign," M.A. thesis, Mississippi State University, 1961, 14, 53, 84; Vincent Arthur Giroux, "Theodore G. Bilbo: Progressive to Public Racist," Ph.D. dissertation, Indiana University, 1984, 51–53; Donald Brooks Kelley, "Of God, Liquor and Politics: The Mississippi Press in the Presidential Election of 1928," M.A. thesis, The University of Mississippi,

1962, 20–23; JOE to Phil Stone, Apr. 28, 1956, "Media: Time Magazine" folder, S3, SS1, B122, JOE Collection.

6. Balsamo, "Bilbo and MS Politics," 180; David Burner, *The Politics of Provincialism: The Democratic Party in Transition, 1918–1932* (New York, 1967), 225; *DDT*, Feb. 23, 1986; Edmundson, "Pat Harrison," 333–345; Richard C. Ethridge, "Mississippi and the 1928 Presidential Campaign," M.A. thesis, Mississippi State University, 1961, 14, 53; Kelley, "Of God, Liquor and Politics," 20–23; JOE to Phil Stone, Apr. 28, 1956, "Media: Time Magazine" folder, S3, SS1, B122, JOE Collection; Morgan, *Redneck Liberal*, 42–43; Michael Newton, *The Ku Klux Klan in Mississippi: A History* (Jefferson, NC, 2010), 95.

7. Woods Eastland to Lester Creidup, Oct. 24, 1942, S1, SS19, B7, F7-22; Woods Eastland to JOE, Aug. 11, 1941, S1, SS2, B1, F1-11, JOE Collection; Vincent A. Giroux, "The Rise of Theodore G. Bilbo: 1908–1932," *JMH* 43:3 (Aug. 1981), 205–207; Morgan, *Redneck Liberal*, 44–45; John Ray Skates, "Fred Sullens: Bourbon out of His Time," *JMH* 49:2 (May 1987), 101.

8. Eastland was probably correct in this instance, as only 38 of the 189 members of the Mississippi House of Representatives served in the next session of the legislature. Roger D. Tate, "Easing the Burden: The Era of Depression and New Deal in Mississippi," Ph.D. dissertation, University of Tennessee, 1978, 38.

9. The third of the "Little Three," Kelly Hammond of Marion County, was defeated in his bid for re-election. Chris Myers Asch, *The Senator and the Sharecropper: The Freedom Struggles of James O. Eastland and Fannie Lou Hamer* (New York, 2008), 41; Balsamo, "Bilbo and Mississippi Politics," 164; Giroux, "Bilbo: Progressive to Public Racist," 39–40, 49; John Holloman, transcript, oral history by Jere Nash, Apr. 7, 2005, Nash and Taggart Collection, J. D. Williams Library, University of Mississippi; Smith, "Eastland: Early Life and Career," 25.

10. *JDN*, Nov. 3, 1978; JOE to M. D. Leatrip, Nov. 11, 1942, S3, SS1, B56, "1942 Eastland Service" file, JOE Collection; Smith, "Eastland: Early Life and Career," 24; Robert E. Snyder, *Cotton Crisis* (Chapel Hill, 1984), 56.

11. Asch, *Senator and the Sharecropper*, 41–42; "The Authentic Voice," *Time*, Mar. 26, 1956, 28; interview with Anne Eastland Howdeshell, Nell Eastland Amos, Sue Eastland McRoberts, and Woods Eastland, Jun. 18, 2011, Jackson, MS, and Hiram Eastland Jr., Jun. 22, 2012, Greenwood, MS; *JDN*, Jan. 4, 1976; *Mississippi: The WPA Guide to the Magnolia State* (New York, 1938), 409; Smith, "Eastland: Early Life and Career," 27, 30.

12. *Chicago Sun-Times*, Feb. 27, 1974; JOE to C. M. Pinson, S1, SS20, B3, "1960" file, JOE Collection; interviews with Thurston Little, Mar. 14, 2012, Corinth, MS, and Fred Smith, Mar. 21, 2013, Jackson, MS; telephone interview with Casey Pace, Apr. 26, 2012, Brandon, MS; Smith, "Eastland: Early Life and Career," 31–32.

13. Asch, *Senator and the Sharecropper*, 42–43; interview with Woods E. Eastland, Jun. 18, 2011, Jackson, MS; JOE to Lucille Eastland, Apr. 8, 1940, S1, SS16, B1, F1-16, JOE Collection; JOE to R. Thomas, Apr. 25, 1942, S1, SS19, B4, F4-19, JOE Collection; W. J. Lusk to Prudential Insurance, Apr. 10, 1937, S1, SS2, B1, F1-7, JOE Collection; Otha Shurden as told to Wilbur Jones, *Cotton: Always King with Me* (Drew, MS, 1985), 27; Smith, "Eastland: Early Life and Career," 32–34.

14. Asch, *Senator and the Sharecropper*, 42–43; interviews with Chris Myers Asch, Aug. 15, 2011, Washington, D.C., Anne Eastland Howdeshell and Nell Eastland Amos, Jun. 18, 2011, Jackson, MS, and Hiram Eastland Jr., Jun. 22, 2012, Greenwood, MS.

15. Asch, *Senator and the Sharecropper*, 42–45.

16. Asch, *Senator and the Sharecropper*, 42–45; Ed C. Breuer to JOE, Nov. 5, 1945, S1, SS3, B1, F1-58, JOE Collection; JOE to Sperry Cole, Dec. 11, 1942, S1, SS19, B5, F5-12, JOE

Collection; JOE to Allen Cox, Nov. 21, 1946, S1, SS3, B1, F1-71, JOE Collection; Scott Ormond to JOE, Jul. 14, 1941, S1, SS3, B1, F1-31, JOE Collection; Woods C. Eastland to B. H. Higdon, Jul. 7, 1942, S1, SS19, B5, F5-12, JOE Collection; Woods C. Eastland to Paul B. Johnson, May 7, 1942, S1, SS21, B1, F1-12, JOE Collection; Woods C. Eastland to George Mitchell, Apr. 26, 1940, S1, SS2, B1, F1-10, JOE Collection.

17. Asch, *Senator and the Sharecropper*, 228–229, 287–288; *GC*, Feb. 18, 1986; *JCL*, Feb. 20, 1986; *WP*, Mar. 23, 1978; see also Chester M. Morgan, "At the Crossroads: World War II, Delta Agriculture, and Modernization in Mississippi," *JMH* 57:4 (Winter 1991), 353–371; John R. Skates, "World War II as a Watershed in Mississippi History," *JMH* 37:2 (May 1975), 131–143.

CHAPTER 3

1. The best biography of Harrison thus far is that by Martha H. Swain, *Pat Harrison: The New Deal Years* (Jackson, MS, 1978).

2. Swain, *Pat Harrison*, 257.

3. Swain, *Pat Harrison*, 257.

4. JOE to James A. Farley, Jul. 12, 1941, S1, SS19, B7, F1-8, JOE Collection; *JDN*, Jun. 30, 1941; Swain, *Pat Harrison*, 246–247.

5. The bulk of this version of an oft-told story comes from Brad Dye, who served as the driver to Eastland in his 1954 reelection campaign as well as to Paul Johnson Jr. in his unsuccessful bid for governor in 1955. Patrick H. "Pete" Johnson heard that Tom Hederman had turned down the appointment before it was offered to either Eastland. Interview with Brad Dye, Jun. 20, 2011, Ridgeland, MS; *JCL*, Jun. 29, 1941; *JDN*, Jun. 30, 1941; telephone interview with Patrick H. "Pete" Johnson, Feb. 22, 2013, Clarksdale, MS; Paul L. Johnson to JOE, Jul. 8, 1941, S1, SS20, B1, "1941" folder, JOE Collection; Dan Smith, "James O. Eastland: Early Life and Career, 1904–1942," M.A. thesis, Mississippi College, 1978, 39.

6. *Chicago Sun-Times*, Feb. 17, 1974; *JCL*, Jun. 29, 1941; *JDN*, Jun. 30 and Jul. 4, 1941; *Montgomery* (AL) *Advertiser*, Jan. 12, 1978; JOE to E. E. Wright, Jul. 7, 1941, S1, SS20, B1, "1941" folder, JOE Collection; Smith, "Eastland: Early Life and Career," 38–40, 58; *WP*, Jul. 22, 1941.

7. Chris Myers Asch, *The Senator and the Sharecropper: The Freedom Struggles of James O. Eastland and Fannie Lou Hamer* (New York, 2008), 102; JOE to Woods C. Eastland, Jul. 22, 1941, S1, SS2, B1, F1-11, JOE Collection; Woods C. Eastland to JOE, Jul. 18, 1941, S1, SS2, B1, F1-11, JOE Collection; Woods Eastland to JOE, Aug. 11, 1941, S1, SS12, B1, F1-11, JOE Collection; Smith, "Eastland: Early Life and Career," 42.

8. John Ray Skates, "Fred Sullens: Bourbon out of His Time," *JMH* 43:3 (May 1987), 93; Smith, "Eastland: Early Life and Career," 43.

9. Asch, *Senator and the Sharecropper*, 92–94; JOE to Tom J. Barnett, Aug. 27, 1941, S1, SS19, B3, F3-10, JOE Collection; JOE to J. A. Rayburn, Sep. 8, 1941, S1, SS19, B5, F5-5, JOE Collection; *NOTP*, Aug. 13, 17, 1941; Smith, "Eastland: Early Life and Career," 46–48, 54.

10. *JDN*, Sep. 3, 1941; JOE to W. Lee O'Daniel, Aug. 28, 1941, S1, SS18, B8, F8-11, JOE Collection; *NYT*, Aug. 17 and Sep. 18, 1941; Smith, "Eastland: Early Life and Career," 55–56; *WP*, Sep. 3, 1941.

11. Asch, *Senator and the Sharecropper*, 94; CR, 77th Cong., 1st Sess., 6292; *JDN*, Aug. 10, 1941; *JCL*, Jul. 27 and Aug. 12, 1941; *NYT*, Aug. 6 and Sep. 1, 1941; Smith, "Eastland: Early Life and Career," 45–51, 56; E. D. Smith to JOE, Oct. 15, 1941, S1, SS18, B9, F9-26, JOE Collection; *WP*, Aug. 12, 1941.

12. *JCL*, Aug. 20, 1941; Courtney Pace to Kelly Hammond, Sep. 4, 1941, S1, SS19, B8, F8-14, JOE Collection; Smith, "Eastland: Early Life and Career," 46–47.

13. JOE to J. C. Bell, S1, SS19, B5, F5-10, JOE Collection; JOE to Earl L. Phillips, Jul. 28, 1941, S3, SS1, B140, "1941 Rural Electrification" folder, JOE Collection; JOE to T. B. Terry, Sep. 4, 1941, S1, SS19, B3, F3-4, JOE Collection; JOE to Will Woods, Sep. 8, 1941, S1, SS19, B5, F5-7, JOE Collection; *JCL*, Nov. 21, 1941; *JDN*, Sep. 21, 1941.

14. JOE to Marcus L. Kaufman, Aug. 15, 1941, S1, SS20, B1, "1941" folder, JOE Collection; JOE to W. Lee O'Daniel, Oct. 14, 1941, S1, SS18, B8, F8-1, JOE Collection; *JDN*, Sep. 5, 6, 21, 1941; Marcus L. Kaufman to JOE, Aug. 15, 1941, S1, SS20, B1, "1941" file, JOE Collection; *NYT*, Sep. 26, 1941; W. Lee O'Daniel to JOE, Sep. 29, 1941, S1, SS18, B8, F8-1, JOE Collection; Courtney Pace to JOE, Oct. 7, 1941, S3, SS7, B1, F1-1, JOE Collection; Smith, "Eastland: Early Life and Career," 54, 76; E. D. Smith to JOE, Oct. 15, 1941, S1, SS18, B9, F9-26, JOE Collection; *JCL*, Sep. 27, 1941.

15. Vincent Arthur Giroux, "Theodore G. Bilbo: Progressive to Public Racist," Ph.D. dissertation, Indiana University, 1984, 56; Courtney Pace to Kelly Hammond, Sep. 4, 1941, S1, SS19, B8, F8-14, JOE Collection; Edward P. Terry to JOE, Sep. 30, 1941, S1, SS18, B1, F1-42, JOE Collection; Maarten Zwiers, "The Paradox of Power: James O. Eastland and the Democratic Party," M.A. thesis, University of Mississippi, 2007, 17.

CHAPTER 4

1. Chris Myers Asch, *The Senator and the Sharecropper: The Freedom Struggles of James O. Eastland and Fannie Lou Hamer* (New York, 2008), 96–97; W. B. Crook to John Lee Gainey, S1, SS19, B5, F5-12, JOE Collection; JOE to Theodore G. Bilbo, Sep. 25, 1934, and Jul. 16, 1940, B1019, F11, Theodore G. Bilbo Papers, University of Southern Mississippi; JOE to Edward P. Terry, B1019, F16, Bilbo Papers; W. Lee O' Daniel to JOE, Sep. 29, 1941, S1, SS18, B8, F8-11, JOE Collection; JOE to W. Lee O' Daniel, Oct. 14, 1941, S1, SS18, B8, F8-11, JOE Collection; *NYP*, Feb. 19, 1956; Dan W. Smith, "James O. Eastland: Early Life and Career, 1904–1942," M.A. thesis, Mississippi College, 1978, 61, 70; W. C. Trotter to JOE, Mar. 21, 1942, S1, SS19, B3, F3-6.

2. *JCL*, Dec. 10, 1941.

3. Vincent Arthur Giroux, "Theodore G. Bilbo: Progressive to Public Racist," Ph.D. dissertation, Indiana University, 1984, 157; Charles Pope Smith, "Theodore G. Bilbo's Senatorial Career: The Final Years, 1941–1947," Ph.D. dissertation, University of Southern Mississippi, 1983, 56, 64; Smith, "Eastland: Early Life and Career," 69, 75, 77.

4. Telephone interview with Patrick H. "Pete" Johnson, Feb. 22, 2013, Clarksdale, MS; Smith, "Bilbo's Senatorial Career," 66–67; Smith, "Eastland: Early Life and Career," 74.

5. Theodore G. Bilbo to JOE, Feb. 18, 1942, S1, SS19, B7, F7-9, JOE Collection.

6. Smith, "Eastland: Early Life and Career," 66; Maarten Zwiers, "The Paradox of Power: James O. Eastland and the Democratic Party," M.A. thesis, University of Mississippi, 2007, 18.

7. Following the death of sitting Senate Majority Leader Joe Robinson of Arkansas, Bilbo had cast the deciding vote against Harrison, which elected Alben Barkley of Kentucky as Robinson's successor.

8. In 1933, Harrison secured for Bilbo a then reasonably plush $6000 a year job within the Agricultural Adjustment Administration, which had him clipping agriculture-related articles for insertion in agency scrapbooks, tasks then leading critics to dub him the

"Pastemaster General." Chester M. Morgan, *Redneck Liberal: Theodore G. Bilbo and the New Deal* (Baton Rouge, 1985), 63.

9. JOE to Theodore G. Bilbo, Feb. 27, 1942, S1, SS19, B7, F7-9, JOE Collection; Weber Ford to JOE, S1, SS19, B14, F4-12; *NOTP*, Mar. 1, 1942.

10. Longtime Bilbo ally C. B. Curlee of Rienzi, for example, later served more than a decade as Eastland's field representative. Theodore G. Bilbo to J. W. Lewis, Mar. 9, 1942, B1019, F11, Theodore G. Bilbo Papers, University of Southern Mississippi; Theodore Bilbo to Orbrey Street, Jul. 10, 1942, S1, SS18, B1, F1-42, JOE Collection; James F. Davis and B. F. McClellan to JOE, Sep. 25, 1940, S1, SS7, B1, F1-13, JOE Collection; James F. Davis to JOE, Jul. 10, 1941, S1, SS7, B1, F1-13, JOE Collection; JOE to Thomas J. Grayson, Jul. 7, 1941, S1, SS7, B1, F1-13, JOE Collection; Smith, "Bilbo's Senatorial Career," 68–69, 75–76; Bob McPeters to John Lee Gainey, Apr. 4, 1942, S1, SS19, B1, F1-2, JOE Collection; *MCA*, Oct. 11, 1942; *NYP*, Feb. 16, 1956.

11. "A Vote for Jim Is a Vote for Them," 1942 JOE pamphlet, S1, SS19, B8, JOE Collection; *JCL*, Sep. 12, 1942; Charles W. Collins, *Whither Solid South: A Study in Politics and Race Relations* (New Orleans, 1947), 77; "Politics and Pictures," Document submitted to and approved by Joe Brown, Campaign Manager, Aug. 25, 1942, "1941–1942" JOE file, William Winter Building, Mississippi Department of Archives and History, Jackson, MS.

12. *JCL*, Feb. 5, May 10, Jul. 4, and Aug. 22, 1942; *JDN*, May 8 and Aug. 20, 1942; *NOTP*, May 10, 1942; Courtney Pace to Richard W. Hogue, May 8, 1942, S1, SS19, B7, F7-2, JOE Collection; Courtney Pace to John C. Satterfield, Jun. 25, 1942, S3, SS7, B3, F3-4, JOE Collection; "Politics and Pictures."

13. Asch, *Senator and the Sharecropper*, 98; *JCL*, Sep. 10, 1942; *JDN*, Sep. 3, 1942; *MCA*, Aug. 22, 1942; "Politics and Pictures"; Smith, "Eastland: Early Life and Career," 80–81.

14. JOE to William A. Winter, Nov. 4, 1942, S1, SS9, B12, "Grenada County" file, JOE Collection; JOE to William Winter, Oct. 30, 1942, S1, SS19, B3, F3-6; telephone interview with Steve Guyton, Feb. 23, 2013, Jackson, MS; Erle Johnston, oral history by Orley B. Caudill, Mississippi Oral History Program of University of Southern Mississippi, 1980, 25, 27; Smith, "Eastland: Early Life and Career," 70–72; interview with William Winter, Mar. 18, 2010, Jackson, MS.

15. Charles W. Bolton, *William F. Winter and the New Mississippi* (Jackson, 2013), 40; JOE to M. D. Leatrip, Nov. 11, 1942, S3, SS1, B58, "1942 Eastland Service" folder, JOE Collection; JOE Announcement Speech, 1942, B1, F21, Kenneth Toler Papers, Mississippi State University, Starkville; *JCL*, Jun. 21, 1942; Smith, "Eastland: Early Life and Career," 73, 78, 82–83, 86.

16. *JDN*, Jun. 21, 1942; John Ray Skates Jr., "A Southern Editor Views the National Scene: Frederick Sullens and the Jackson, Mississippi *Daily News*," Ph.D. dissertation, Mississippi State University, 1965, 10–11; Smith, "Bilbo's Senatorial Career," 81; Smith, "Eastland: Early Life and Career," 91.

17. *JDN*, Aug. 20, 1942; Smith, "Eastland: Early Life and Career," 93; *WP*, Jul. 13, 14, and Aug. 23, 1942.

18. Smith, "Eastland: Early Life and Career," 95; Orbrey Street to Cecil D. Shields, Jul. 16, 1942, S1, SS19, B6, F6-3, JOE Collection; *WP*, Aug. 27, 2012.

19. Otis D. Ashworth to C. L. Milling, Aug. 29, 1942, S1, SS19, B4, F4-13, JOE Collection; John W. Backstrom to Joe Brown, Aug. 29, 1942, S1, SS9, B2, F2-6, JOE Collection; J. S. Hickman to Joe Brown, Sep. 12, 1942, S1, SS19, B3, F3-8, JOE Collection; *JDN*, Sep. 12, 1942; Smith, "Eastland: Early Life and Career," 100; *Additional Report of the Special Committee Investigating the National Defense Program: Resolutions Authorizing and Directing an*

Investigation of the National Defense Program; Transactions between Senator Theodore G. Bilbo and Various War Contractors, 6.

20. For readers of today, Charlie McCarthy was the dummy of Edgar Bergen, the highly popular radio ventriloquist, who now is best-known as the father of actress Candice Bergen. Jack M. Graeves to JOE, Sep. 17, 1942, S1, SS19, B4, F4-3, JOE Collection; *JDN*, Sep. 3, 6, 1942; Smith, "Eastland: Early Life and Career," 96, 102.

21. *JDN*, Sep. 3, 1942; Smith, "Eastland: Early Life and Career," 101–103.

22. *JCL*, Sep. 13, 15, 1942; *JDN*, Sep. 5, 1942; John Ray Skates, "Fred Sullens: Bourbon out of His Time," *JMH* 49:2 (May 1987), 101; Smith, "Bilbo's Senatorial Career," 82; Smith, "Eastland: Early Life and Career," 101.

23. *JCL, Natchez Democrat, NYT, OE*, and *WP*, Sep. 17, 1942; *Kosciusko Star-News*, Sep. 24, 1942.

24. C. D. Bennett to JOE, Oct. 14, 1942, S1, SS19, B2, F2-10, JOE Collection; Theodore G. Bilbo to T. R. King, Oct. 7, 1942, S1, SS18, B1, F1-42, JOE Collection; *Tupelo Daily News*, Sep. 18, 1942.

CHAPTER 5

1. *CR*, 78th Cong., 1st Sess., A2790; *JCL*, Jan. 24, 1943.

2. "Authentic Voice," *Time*, Mar. 26, 1956, 28; *Biloxi-Gulfport Sun*, Nov. 12, 1978; Richard G. Kleindienst, *Justice: The Memoirs of Attorney General Richard Kleindienst* (Ottawa, IL, 1985), 125.

3. Undated handwritten memos, JOE to Courtney Pace, S3, SS7, B1, F1-3, JOE Collection; JOE to Swep J. Taylor, Jan. 13, 1943, S1, SS7, B1, F1-5, JOE Collection; *Picayune Item*, Feb. 11, 1943; Swep J. Taylor, Dec. 26, 1942, S1, SS7, B1, F1-4, JOE Collection; Theodore G. Bilbo to T. R. King, Oct. 7, 1942, S1, SS18, B1, F1-42, JOE Collection.

4. Telephone interview with Clarence Pierce, Jan. 20, 2012, Vaiden, MS; interview with James W. Ziglar, Dec. 13, 2011, Washington, D.C.

5. *Chicago Tribune*, Dec. 23, 1946; *CR*, 78th Cong., 2nd Sess., 1540, 5519–5527; *JCL*, Apr. 6, Jun. 25, Aug. 6, and Dec. 3, 1943, Aug. 17, 1944, Apr. 15, 1945, and Jun. 25, 1946; *JCL*, Jul. 29, 1944; *JDN*, Jan. 6, 1944; *WP*, Jun. 9, 1944; *Washington Times-Herald*, Jun. 9, 1944.

6. *CR*, 78th Cong., 1st Sess., 4141–4142, 5060, 5372, 79th Cong., 2nd Sess., 654, 4296, 5982; *JCL*, Jun. 5, 1943, May 16, 1946; *JDN*, Sep. 16, 1946; Noel Monoghan to Walter Sillers, Jun. 1, 1946, B21, F18, Walter Sillers Papers, Delta State University.

7. *CR*, 78th Cong., 1st Sess., 9812, 10144, 10165–10167, 11064; 78th Cong., 2nd Sess., 223, 908–1013; *JCL*, Nov. 26 and Dec. 4, 1943; Allen Drury, *A Senate Journal, 1943–1945* (New York, 1943), 44, 59, 78, 99, 107, 112; *Pittsburgh Courier*, Feb. 4, 1944; Patricia Sullivan, *Lift Every Voice: The NAACP and the Civil Rights Movement* (New York, 2009), 289; *WP*, Apr. 1, 1944; Roland Young, *Congressional Politics in the Second World War* (New York, 1956), 85.

8. *CR*, 78th Cong., 2nd Sess., 4252–4264, 4313–4314; Drury, *Senate Journal*, 133, 171; JOE to C. B. Curlee, Apr. 6, 1944, S1, SS21, B1, F1-2, JOE Collection; JOE to C. B. Curlee, May 6, 1944, S1, SS21, B1, F1-2, JOE Collection; JOE to John R. King, May 16, 1944, S3, SS1, B30, "1944 Civil Rights" file, JOE Collection; JOE to Dan R. McGehee, May 9, 1944, S1, SS18, B7, F7-21, JOE Collection; undated handwritten memo, JOE to Courtney Pace, S3, SS7, B1, F1-3, JOE Collection; JOE to J. A. Riechman, May 4, 1944, S3, SS1, B30, "1944 Civil Rights" file, JOE Collection; undated Associated Press article, "1944 Communism" file, S3, SS1, B150, JOE Collection; *WP*, Apr. 7, 1944.

9. John H. Bankhead to JOE, Aug. 5, 1944, S1, SS18, B1, F1-25, JOE Collection; Drury, *Senate Journal*, 223; *JCL*, Apr. 18, 1945; *JDN*, Jan. 3, 1973; David McCullough, *Truman* (New York, 1992), 314–320; *MCA*, Apr. 15, 1945; *MCA*, Apr. 14, 1945; *Meridian Star*, Jan. 3, 1973; "Plantation Man," *U.S. News and World Report*, Feb. 27, 1948, 3.

10. JOE to R. I. Ingalls, Aug. 15, 1944, S1, SS20, B1, "1944" file, JOE Collection; JOE to T. M. McDonald, Aug. 15, 1944, S1, SS20, B1, "1944" file, JOE Collection; JOE to W. L. McPheeters, Apr. 25, 1945, S1, SS7, B1, "1945" file, JOE Collection.

11. JOE to Harry F. Byrd, Sep. 25, 1944, B175, "JOE" file, Harry F. Byrd Papers, Albert and Shirley Small Special Collections Library, University of Virginia, Charlottesville; interview with David Lambert, Aug. 13, 2012, Alexandria, VA; Jules Witcover, *Joe Biden: A Life of Trial and Redemption* (New York, 2010), 103.

12. In the early 1930s, Woods Eastland had won $15,000 for Paul B. Johnson in a slander suit against Sullens. John Brunini to Fred Sullens, Mar. 27, 1945, S1, SS7, B1, F1-7, JOE Collection; JOE to Mrs. Walter Sillers, Oct. 7, 1942, S1, SS7, B1, F1-4, JOE Collection; *JDN*, Mar. 5 and 21, 1945; Charles Pope Smith, "Theodore G. Bilbo's Senatorial Career: The Final Years, 1941–1947," Ph.D. dissertation, University of Southern Mississippi, 1983, 81.

13. *JCL*, Feb. 2, 1943, and Apr. 15, 1946; *JDN*, May 13, 1946; JOE to Tom C. Clark, Aug. 16, 1947, S1, SS17, B5, "Department of Justice: Attorney General 1940s" file, JOE Collection; JOE to J. D. Glenn, Jan. 29, 1945, S3, SS1, B135, "1945 Post Office" file, JOE Collection; JOE to Grant Hamilton, Jul. 27, 1944, S3, SS1, B135, "1944 Post Office" file, JOE Collection; *MCA*, Aug. 31, 1947.

14. *CR*, 79th Cong., 1st Sess., 3267–3277; *CR*, 79th Cong., 2nd Sess., 66, 3678–3682, 6630, 6817; JOE to O. W. Phillips, Jul. 26, 1946, S3, SS1, B131, "1946 OPA" file, JOE Collection; JOE to H. G. Saul, Nov. 7, 1946, S3, SS1, B131, "1946 OPA" file, JOE Collection; *JCL*, Jan. 9, 17, Apr. 16, and Nov. 3, 1946.

15. Asch, *Senator and the Sharecropper*, 113–119; *CR*, 78th Cong., 2nd Sess., 6148–6149, 6258, 6277; 79th Cong., 1st Sess., 6991–7005; 79th Sess., 2nd Sess., 86, 91, 114–117, 184, 242–252, 400–403, 697–703, 883–893, 953–955; *JCL*, Jan. 18, 1946, and May 29, 1947; *JDN*, Jun. 6, 1947; JOE to Merle C. Fraser, Feb. 13, 1946, S3, SS1, B32, "1946 Civil Rights" file (2 of 2), JOE Collection; JOE to R. B. Zeller, Jun. 7, 1947, S3, SS1, B132, "1947 Civil Rights" file, JOE Collection; *NYT*, Jun. 30, 1945; Merl E. Reed, *Seedtime for the Modern Civil Rights Movement: The President's Committee on Fair Employment Practices* (Baton Rouge, 1991), 180, 189.

16. *CR*, 79th Cong., 2nd Sess., 7064–7068; JOE to E. T. Davis, Jun. 25, 1946, S3, SS1, B144, "1946 Supreme Court" folder, JOE Collection; *MCA* and *WP*, Jun. 19, 1946; *Roanoke Times*, Jul. 20, 1946.

17. *CR*, 80th Cong., 1st Sess., 10; Robert L. Fleegler, "Theodore G. Bilbo and the Decline of Public Racism, 1938–1947," *JMH*, 68:1 (Spring 2006), 6, 16; Gerald Meyer, *Vito Marcantonio: Radical Politician, 1902–1954* (Albany, 1989), 133–134; Chester M. Morgan, *Redneck Liberal: Theodore G. Bilbo and the New Deal* (Baton Rouge, 1985), 248–253; Enoch Seal, "The Senatorial Career of Theodore G. Bilbo," M.A. thesis, Mississippi State University, 1951, 91.

18. Richard C. Ethridge, "The Fall of the Man: The United States Senate's Probe of Theodore G. Bilbo in December 1946 and Its Aftermath," *JMH* 38:3 (Aug. 1976), 241–260; Fleegler, "Bilbo and Decline of Public Racism," 1; *Time*, Jul. 1, 1946, 23; *WP*, Dec. 15, 1946.

19. *CR*, 80th Cong., 1st Sess., 7, 10, 74–96; *Durant (MS) News*, Jan. 9, 1947; JOE to Joe Bates, Jan. 8, 1947, JOE to K. G. Rayburn, Jan. 8, 1947, and JOE to R. D. Cooper, Jan. 15, 1947, Minutes of Democratic Conference Meeting, Jan. 2, 1947, B9, F2, Felton "Skeeter" Johnston Papers, J. D. Mitchell Library, University of Mississippi; JOE to J. C. Waites, Jan. 15, 1947,

S3, SS1, B132, "1947 Politics: Theodore Bilbo Investigation" file, JOE Collection; *JDN*, Jun. 19, 1946, and Aug. 15, 1954; Alvin Sumerlin, "Theodore Bilbo: The Last Phase," M.A. thesis, Louisiana State University, 1950, 47, 60, 89–90.

20. *CR*, 80th Cong., 1st Sess., 108–109, 10510, 10569; Reinhard Luthin, *American Demagogues: Twentieth Century* (Boston, 1954), 75; *NOTP*, Aug. 23, 1947; *NYT*, Aug. 22, 1947; Bobby Wade Saucier, "The Public Career of Theodore G. Bilbo," Ph.D. dissertation, Tulane University, 1971, 281–284; Sumerlin, "Bilbo," 93–94.

21. *MCA*, Aug. 1, 1947; Billy R. Weeks, "The Pledge 'To Plow a Straight Furrow': The 1947 Senatorial Campaign of John C. Stennis," M.A. thesis, Mississippi State University, 1974; Kenneth H. Williams, "Mississippi and Civil Rights, 1945–1954," Ph.D. dissertation, Mississippi State University, 1985, 124–128.

22. Courtney Pace to John C. Stennis, Nov. 8, 1947, B1, F100, John C. Stennis Collection, Mitchell Memorial Library, Mississippi State University; Weeks, "The Pledge 'To Plow a Straight Furrow,'" 68–69.

23. Interviews with Howard H. Baker Jr., Jun. 13, 2011, Huntsville, TN, Joseph D. Tydings, Feb. 28, 2011, Washington, D.C., and James Ziglar, Dec. 13, 2011, Washington, D.C.; Edmund L. Brunini Sr., oral history, Jun. 9, 1992, 24, John C. Stennis Oral History Project, John C. Stennis Collection, Mississippi State University, Starkville; John Hailman, *From Midnight to Guntown: True Stories from a Federal Prosecutor in Mississippi* (Jackson, 2013), 105, 107; Mark Hazard, oral history by Jere Nash, Oct. 28, 2004, Nash and Taggart Collection, Special Collections, J. D. Mitchell Library, University of Mississippi; telephone interviews with Sid Salter, Apr. 27, 2012, Starkville, MS, and William Waller, Jul. 15, 2011, Jackson, MS; *Scott County (MS) Times*, Feb. 26, 1986; Larry Speakes, oral history, Nov. 14, 1991, 29, John C. Stennis Oral History Project, John C. Stennis Collection, Mississippi State University, Starkville; John C. Stennis to Libby Eastland, Oct. 23, 1953, S1, B100, John C. Stennis Papers, Mitchell Memorial Library, Mississippi State University, Starkville, MS.

24. Baker interview.

CHAPTER 6

1. *CR*, 78th Cong., 1st Sess., 9071; 79th Cong., 1st Sess., 8034, 8084; *JCL*, Nov. 9, 1944; JOE to Rev. Murray Cox, Mar. 10, 1944, S3, SS1, B79, "1944 Foreign Policy: World Peace" file, JOE Collection; *Washington Daily News*, May 7, 1945.

2. *CR*, 79th Cong., 2nd Sess., 805; Jack Temple Kirby, *Media-Made Dixie: The South in the American Imagination* (Baton Rouge, 1978), 23; JOE to Nelson Levings, Apr. 15, 1944, S1, SS6, B1, F1-6; JOE to Dr. J. W. Lucas, Mar. 2, 1945, S3, SS1, B48, "1948 Civil Rights" file (2 of 3), JOE Collection; Frank Lambert, *The Battle of Ole Miss: Civil Rights v. States' Rights* (New York, 2010), 42.

3. Chris Myers Asch, "Revising Reconstruction: JOE, the FEPC, and the Struggle to Rebuild Germany, 1945–1946," *JMH* 67:1 (Spring 2001), 11; *CR*, 79th Cong., 1st Sess., 6991–7002, 7595–7597; *JDN*, Jun. 24, 1945; John Dittmer, *Local People: The Struggle for Civil Rights in Mississippi* (Champaign, IL, 1995), 18; JOE, interview by George Brada, *Rheineschnur Mertin*, Dec. 23, 1973, S2, SS1, B1, F1-25, JOE Collection; *Kansas City Star*, Jul. 6, 1945; Jul. 27, 1945, article in anonymous letter, S3, SS1, B30, "1945 Civil Rights" file, JOE Collection; Morris J. Frank to JOE, Jul. 9, 1945, S3, SS1, B30, "1945 Civil Rights" file (1 of 3), JOE Collection; Robert P. Patterson to JOE, Jul. 30, 1945, S3, SS1, B30, JOE Collection; *PM*, Jul. 6, 1945.

4. Chris Myers Asch, *The Senator and the Sharecropper: The Freedom Struggles of James O. Eastland and Fannie Lou Hamer* (New York, 2008), 105, 308; *JCL*, Jun. 15, 1945; *Richmond Times-Dispatch*, Jun. 18, 1945.

5. Asch, "Revising Reconstruction," 18; Andrei Cherny, *The Candy Bombers: The Untold Story of the Berlin Airlift and America's Finest Hour* (New York, 2008), 97.

6. ACLU to JOE, Dec. 20, 1945, S3, SS1, B79, "1945 Foreign Policy: Germany" file, JOE Collection; *JCL*, Dec. 16, 1945; *Stars and Stripes*, South Germany Edition, Feb. 7, 1946; Wolfgang Schlauch, "Representative William Colmer and Senator James O. Eastland and the Reconstruction of Germany, 1945," *JMH* 34: 3 (Aug. 1972), 202, 205.

7. *CR*, 79th Cong., 1st Sess., 12060; *JCL*, Nov. 22, 1945; JOE to J. S. Broadfoot, Dec. 29, 1945, S3, SS1, B79, "1945 Foreign Policy: Germany" file, JOE Collection; JOE to Frank S. Cannon, Jan. 30, 1946, S3, SS1, B32, "1946 Civil Rights" file (2 of 2), JOE Collection; JOE to Dr. E. A. Copeland, Mar. 29, 1948, S3, SS1, B88, "1948 Foreign Policy: Russia" file, JOE Collection; JOE to Helmut Kohr, Jan. 29, 1946, S3, SS1, B79, "1946 Foreign Policy: Germany" file, JOE Collection.

8. Asch, *Senator and the Sharecropper*, 106–108; *CR*, 79th Cong., 1st Sess., 11371–11379; JOE, *Rheineschnur Mertin*, Dec. 23, 1973; *JCL* and *New York Daily News*, Dec. 5, 1945.

9. *JCL*, Aug. 15, 1946; JOE to Pearl Slater, Apr. 15, 1947, S3, SS1, B80, "1947 Foreign Policy: Greek-Turkish Loan" file, JOE Collection; JOE to Alonzo Westbrook, Oct. 28, 1947, S3, SS1, B80, "1947 Foreign Policy: Russia" file, JOE Collection.

10. Asch, *Senator and the Sharecropper*, 210; *CR*, 80th Cong., 1st Sess., 3324–3325; John C. Culver and John Hyde, *American Dreamer: The Life and Times of Henry A. Wallace* (New York, 2000), 440; JOE to Frank Simmons Jr., Jun. 10, 1947, and JOE to Kay Johnson, Apr. 16, 1947, S3, SS1, B80, "1947 Foreign Policy: Greek-Turkish Loan" file, JOE Collection; *JCL*, Nov. 24, 1946, and Apr. 12, 1947; *JDN*, Nov. 24, 1946, Apr. 16 and Jun. 4, 1947; *WP*, Apr. 12, 1947.

11. *CR*, 80th Cong., 1st Sess., 3923, 6232–6237, 6307–6309, 6331; *JCL*, Apr. 26, 27, 1947; *JDN*, Jun. 4, 1947.

12. Asch, *Senator and the Sharecropper*, 108–111; *CR*, 79th Cong., 1st Sess., 4511; *JCL*, May 18 and Jun. 24, 1947.

13. Greg Behrman, *The Most Noble Adventure: The Marshall Plan and the Time When America Helped Save Europe* (New York, 2007), 45–59; D. Clayton Brown, *King Cotton in Modern America* (Jackson, MS, 2011), 98–99; Gregory A. Fossedal, *Our Finest Hour: Will Clayton, The Marshall Plan, and the Triumph of Democracy* (Stanford, CA, 1993), 221–222; Charles L. Mee Jr., *The Marshall Plan: The Launching of the Pax Americana* (New York, 1984), 78–80, 93, 96–97; Harry S. Truman to JOE, Apr. 8, 1947, Harry S. Truman Papers, B238, File 3465, Harry S. Truman Presidential Library, Independence, MO.

14. JOE to Ira H. Carr, S3, SS1, B80, "1949 Foreign Policy: Russia" file, JOE Collection; *JCL*, Sep. 14, 1947; *JDN*, Dec. 16, 1948, Dec. 22, 1949; *MS*, Dec. 16, 1948.

15. *JCL*, Oct. 1, 1948; *JDN*, Sep. 30, 1948.

CHAPTER 7

1. Kari Frederickson, *The Dixiecrat Revolt and the End of the Solid South, 1932–1968* (Chapel Hill, NC, 2001).

2. James C. Cobb, "World War II and the Mind of the Modern South" in Neil R. McMillen, *Remaking Dixie: The Impact of World War II on the Modern South* (Jackson, MS, 2007), 6.

3. JOE to M. D. Leatrip, S3, SS1, B38, "1942 Eastland Service" folder, JOE Collection; un-dated JOE handwritten memo to Courtney Pace, S3, SS7, B1, F1-3; JOE to Walter Sillers, Jul. 27, 1945, S3, SS1, B31, "Civil Rights 1945" file (3 of 3), JOE Collection; Ben Hilbun, "The Dixiecrat Movement in Mississippi," M.A. thesis, Mississippi State University, 1955, 21; *JCL*, Jul. 23, 1944; Roy H. Ruby, "The Presidential Election of 1944 in Mississippi: The Bolting Electors," M.A. thesis, Mississippi State University, 1966, 20; Walter Sillers to JOE, Dec. 15, 1942, S1, SS7, B1, F1-4, JOE Collection.

4. Richard C. Ethridge, "Mississippi's Role in the Dixiecratic Movement," Ph.D. disserta-tion, Mississippi State University, 1971, 2; Sam H. Jones as told to James Aswell, "Will Dixie Bolt the New Deal?" *Saturday Evening Post*, Mar. 6, 1943, 20–21, 42, 45; "Plain Talk," Box 171, "John U. Barr" file, B171, Harry F. Byrd Collection, MSS3700, Albert and Shirley Smalls Special Collections Library, University of Virginia, Charlottesville.

5. Charles W. Collins, *Whither Solid South: A Study in Politics and Race Relations* (New Orleans, 1947), vii–ix, 77, 229, 261–263, 311–318; telephone interview with Kari Frederickson, May 3, 2012, Tuscaloosa, AL.

6. John U. Barr to Harry F. Byrd, Apr. 20, 1945, B184, "John U. Barr" file, Byrd Collection; John U. Barr to JOE, Jun. 17, 1947, S1, SS7, B1, F1-10, JOE Collection; John U. Barr to JOE, Aug. 18, 1947, S1, SS7, B1, F1-10, JOE Collection; "Undated Byrd for President Committee document," B170, "1943" file, F5, Byrd Collection; JOE to John U. Barr, Dec. 19, 1947, S1, SS7, B1, F1-12, JOE Collection; Ronald L. Heinemann, *Harry Byrd of Virginia* (Charlottesville, 1996), 237–242; Peter J. Kellogg, "Civil Rights Consciousness in the 1940s," *Historian*, 42:1 (Nov. 1979), 25.

7. Helen Fuller, "The Fourth Party," *New Republic*, Mar. 15, 1948, 8–9; Harvard Sitkoff, "Harry Truman and the Election of 1948: The Coming of Age of Civil Rights in American Politics," *Journal of Southern History*, 37:4 (Nov. 1971), 597–600; John Anthony Tuggle, "The Dixiecrats as a Stepping-Stone to Two Party Politics for Mississippi," M.A. thesis, University of Southern Mississippi, 1974, 25.

8. John U. Barr to JOE, Jan. 17, 1948, S1, SS7, B1, F1-11, JOE Collection; JOE to John U. Barr, Mar. 9, 1948, S1, SS7, B1, F1-11, JOE Collection; Elbert Riley Hilliard, "A Biography of Fielding Wright: Mississippi's Mr. States' Rights," M.A. thesis, Mississippi State Univer-sity, 1959; Robert Waite Mickey, "The Decay of Authoritarian Enclaves in America's Deep South, 1944–1972, Ph.D. dissertation, Harvard University, 2006, 234; Gary Clifford Ness, "The States' Rights Democratic Movement of 1948," Ph.D. dissertation, Duke University, 1972, 154; Courtney Pace to Etta, Aug. 27, 1947, S3, SS7, B1, F1-7, JOE Collection.

9. John U. Barr to JOE, Jan. 23, 1948, S1, SS7, B1, F1-11, JOE Collection; John U. Barr to Fielding Wright, Jan. 23, 1948, S1, SS7, B1, F1-11, JOE Collection; *CR*, 80th Cong., 2nd Sess., 466–467.

10. Gary A. Donaldson, *Truman Defeats Dewey* (Lexington, KY, 1999), 111, 116.; JOE, "Jan. 29, 1948 speech to the Mississippi General Assembly," B3, Wilson "Bill" Minor Papers, Mitchell Memorial Library, Mississippi State University; JOE to Charles K. Hickey, S3, SS1, B56, "1948 Eastland Addresses" folder, JOE Collection; *JDN*, Jan. 29, 30, 1948.

11. Frederickson, *Dixiecrat Revolt*, 78–79; Hilliard, "Fielding Wright," 85; John L. McMil-lan to Strom Thurmond, Feb. 13, 1948, and L. Mendel Rivers to Strom Thurmond, Feb. 4, 1948, Gubernatorial Series, B146, F3227, Strom Thurmond Papers, Clemson University.

12. Paul Brown to Strom Thurmond, Feb. 14, 1948, Gubernatorial Series, B146, F3227, Strom Thurmond Collection, Clemson University, Clemson, SC; *Charleston Evening Post*, Feb. 20, 21, 24, 1948; *CR*, 80th Cong., 2nd Sess., 1193, 1199; JOE to Robert W. Frasier, Mar. 3,

1948, S3, SS1, B33, "1948 Civil Rights" folder, JOE Collection; Richard C. Ethridge, "Mississippi's Role in the Dixiecratic Movement," Ph.D. dissertation, Mississippi State University, 1971, 32; *NOTP* and *WP*, Feb. 10, 1948.

13. *CR*, 80th Cong., 2nd Sess., 2377; JOE to Profilet Couillard, Aug. 5, 1948, S3, SS1, B33, "1948 Civil Rights" file (2 of 3), JOE Collection; JOE to A. Willis Robertson, Jun. 26, 1948, S1, SS18, B8, F8-50, JOE Collection; *MCA*, Mar. 10, 1948; *NYT*, Apr. 22, 1948; Robert Penn Warren, *The Legacy of the Civil War* (New York, 1964), 64–76.

14. JOE to E. G. Harpold, Mar. 1, 1948, S3, SS1, B56, "1948 Eastland Addresses" folder, JOE Collection; "High Cotton," *New Republic*, Aug. 30, 1948, 10; "New South: A Political Phenomenon Grips Dixie's Voters," *Newsweek*, Oct. 25, 1948, 32–34; Strom Thurmond to Ben Laney, Apr. 12, 1948, B146, F3228, Strom Thurmond Collection, Clemson University, Clemson, SC; Tuggle, "Dixiecrats," 36, 40.

15. *Anderson* (SC) *Independent*, Mar. 23, 1948; *Atlanta Journal*, Mar. 20, 1948; *Charlotte Observer*, Feb. 25 and Mar. 20, 1948; Richard C. Ethridge, "Mississippi's Role in the Dixiecratic Movement," 131; John Anthony Tuggle, "The Dixiecrats as a Stepping-Stone to Two-Party Politics from Mississippi," M.A. thesis, University of Southern Mississippi, 1974, 53.

16. *CR*, 80th Cong., 2nd Sess., 6577, 8502, 8532; JOE to John P. Conner, Mar. 4, 1948, S3, SS1, B33, "1948 Civil Rights" folder, JOE Collection, *JCL*, Jun. 20, 1948; *MCA*, Jul. 1, 1948.

17. *Atlanta Journal*, Apr. 23, 1948; JOE to John U. Barr, May 14, 1948, S1, SS7, B1, F1-12, JOE Collection; JOE to Howard P. Hill, S1, SS20, B1, "1948" file, JOE Collection; JOE to Fielding Wright, May 10, 1948, S1, SS10, B1, "1948" file, JOE Collection; Kari Frederickson, "The Dixiecrat Movement and the Origins of Massive Resistance: Race, Politics, and Political Culture in the Deep South," Ph.D. dissertation, Rutgers University, 1996, 161; Frederickson, *Dixiecrat Revolt*, 205.

18. *JCL*, Jun. 23, 1948; *Meridian Star*, Jun. 22, 23, 1948.

19. Richard Dallas Chesteen, "Mississippi Is Gone Home: A Study of the 1948 Mississippi States' Rights Bolt," *JMH* 32:1 (Feb. 1970), 59; Richard Dallas Chesteen, "The 1948 States Rights Movement in Mississippi," M.A. thesis, University of Mississippi, 1964, 74, 79; Gilbert Fite, *Richard B. Russell Jr.: Senator from Georgia* (Chapel Hill, 1991), 239–240; Frederickson, *Dixiecrat Revolt*, 128–131; Hilliard, "Fielding Wright," 88; *JCL*, May 10, 1948.

20. Chesteen, "States Rights Movement," 51; Joseph Crespino, *Strom Thurmond's America* (New York, 2012), 69; Frederickson, *Dixiecrat Revolt*, 151–155; *JDN*, Jul. 16, 1948; Zachary Karabell, *The Last Campaign: How Harry Truman Won the 1948 Election* (New York, 2000), 165; *NOTP*, Jul. 17, 1948; David Pietrusza, *1948: Harry Truman's Improbable Victory and the Year That Transformed America's Role in the World* (New York, 2011), 237–239.

21. Crespino, *Thurmond's America*, 70; Donaldson, *Truman Defeats Dewey*, 184; Frederickson, *Dixiecrat Revolt*, 142; *JDN*, Jul. 13, 1948; Sarah McCulloch Lemmon, "The Ideology of the Dixiecrat Movement," *Social Forces*, 30:2 (Dec. 1951), 169–171; Ann Mathison McLaurin, "The Role of the Dixiecrats in the 1948 Election," Ph.D. dissertation, University of Oklahoma, 1972, 182; *NYT*, Apr. 29, 2005; "Tumult in Dixie," *Time*, Jul. 26, 1948, 15–16.

22. Crespino, *Thurmond's America*, 69; Frederickson, *Dixiecrat Revolt*, 237–238; Hilbun, "Dixiecrat Movement," 52; Hilliard, "Fielding Wright," 92; McLaurin, "Role of the Dixiecrats," 174; Pietrusza, *1948*, 238–244.

23. McLaurin, "Role of the Dixiecrats," 177; *MCA*, Jul. 17, 1948; *Savannah Morning News*, Jul. 18, 1948; Maarten Zwiers, "The Paradox of Power: James O. Eastland and the Democratic Party," M.A. thesis, University of Mississippi, 2007, 5.

24. *Charlotte Observer*, Aug. 29, 1948; "High Cotton," *New Republic*, Aug. 30, 1948, 10; *JCL*, Aug. 11, 1948; Pietrusza, *1948*, 238; Tuggle, "Dixiecrats," 73, 78.

25. JOE to Charles G. Neese, Oct. 28, 1948, S1, SS18, B6, F6-3, JOE Collection; JOE to P. E. Whittington, Dec. 21, 1948, S1, SS20, B1, F1-10, JOE Collection; *JCL*, Oct. 5, 17, 1948; *MCA*, Jul. 27, 1948; *Memphis Press-Scimitar*, Sep. 11, 1948; *WP*, Oct. 17, 1948.

26. *MCA*, Jan. 1, 1949; *NYT*, Dec. 13, 1948; Sandra Stringer Vance, "The Congressional Career of John Bell Williams, 1947–1967," Ph.D. dissertation, Mississippi State University, 1976, 65.

27. Frederickson, "Dixiecrat Movement and the Origins of Massive Resistance," 377; *JCL*, Oct. 15, 1948, Jan. 16 and Apr. 30, 1949; *JDN*, Nov. 16, 1948; *MCA*, Jul. 27, 1948, Sep. 18, 1949, and Nov. 12, 1950; *NYT*, Jan. 6, 1951; Sean J. Savage, "To Purge or Not to Purge: Hamlet Harry and the Dixiecrats, 1948–1952," *Political Science Quarterly*, 27:4 (Fall 1997), 783–784; *WP*, Apr. 17, 1949, and Mar. 4, 1951.

28. Chesteen, "States Rights Democrats," 103; JOE to Joseph H. Sasser, Dec. 22, 1948, S3, SS1, B32, "1948 Civil Rights" folder, JOE Collection; Frederickson, *Dixiecrat Revolt*, 258; Strom Thurmond to JOE, Dec. 11, 1948, S1, SS18, B10, F10-10, JOE Collection.

29. *Jackson State Times*, Dec. 16, 1956.

CHAPTER 8

1. Numan V. Bartley, *The Rise of Massive Resistance: Race and Politics in the South during the 1950s* (Baton Rouge, 1997), 240; *CR*, 81st Cong., 1st Sess., 10072; Patricia Webb Robinson, "A Rhetorical Analysis of Senator James O. Eastland's Speeches, 1954–1959, M.A. thesis, Louisiana State University, 1978, 62; *NYT*, Jul. 26, 1949, and Apr. 27, 1950; Duane Tananbaum, *The Bricker Amendment Controversy: A Test of Eisenhower's Political Leadership* (Ithaca, 1988), 43, 92, 168, 176, 181; *WP*, Apr. 17, 1949.

2. *CR*, 80th Cong., 1st Sess., 6803, 6894; 81st Cong., 1st Sess., 1602–1605, 4995, 5043, 14635, 14695; 81st Cong., 2nd Sess., 2910–2911; JOE to Joseph Dean, Feb. 20, 1950, S3, SS1, B81, "1950 Foreign Policy" folder, JOE Collection; *JDN*, Mar. 3, 1950; *MCA*, Mar. 3, 1956; *NYT*, Apr. 25, Jun. 11, Aug. 20, and Oct. 16, 1949, Mar. 4, 1950, Mar. 30, 1956; Text of the Parmer from Washington Broadcast, Jun. 12, 1949, S2, SS12, B1, F1-5, JOE Collection; *WP*, Oct. 12, 1949, Mar. 5, 1950, and Feb. 22, 1956; Michael Ybarra, *Washington Gone Crazy: Pat McCarran and the Great American Communist Hunt* (Hanover, NH, 2004), 462–465, 477–483.

3. *CR*, 81st Cong., 2nd Sess., 16047, 16113; JOE to R. N. Bendel, May 8, 1950, S3, SS1, B81, "1950 Foreign Policy" folder; JOE to L. S. Caudet, S3, SS1, B80, "1950 Foreign Policy: China" folder, JOE Collection; JOE to W. D. Garland, S3, SS1, B80, "1950 Foreign Policy: China" folder, JOE Collection; JOE to E. E. Morgan, Aug. 1, 1953, S3, SS1, B81, "1953 Foreign Policy: Korea" folder, JOE Collection; JOE to M. G. Howard, Dec. 19, 1950, S3, SS1, B57, "1950 Eastland Addresses: Korea," JOE Collection; JOE to Capt. T. W. Sisson, Jan. 22, 1951, S3, SS1, B81, "1951 Foreign Policy: Korea" folder, JOE Collection; John Paton Davies, *China Hand: An Autobiography* (Philadelphia, 2012), 294; *Gulfport Daily Herald*, Dec. 22, 1952; John E. Haynes, *Red Scare or Red Menace? American Communism and Anticommunism in the Cold War Era* (Chicago, 1996), 148–153; Ross Y. Koen, *The China Lobby in American Politics* (New York, 1974), 55; *NYT*, May 2, Jul. 12, 13 and Dec. 6, 1950; *WP*, Jul. 15 and Dec. 6, 1950.

4. *CR*, 81st Cong., 2nd Sess., 1146, 16113; JOE to Mr. and Mrs. S. R. Reed, Apr. 4, 1951, S3, SS1, B81, "1951 Foreign Policy: Korea" folder, JOE Collection; *Hearings Before a Subcommittee of the Committee on the Judiciary, United States Senate*, 81st Cong., 1st Sess., S1194

and S1196, *Bills to Protect the United States against Certain Un-American and Subversive Activities*, 180–181, 215–216; *JDN*, Mar. 4, 1950; *NYT*, Feb. 1, 1950; Kenneth O'Reilly, *Hoover and the Un-Americans: The FBI, HUAC and the Red Menace* (Philadelphia, 1983), 103; Athan G. Theoharis, "Unanswered Questions: Chambers, Nixon, the FBI, and the Hiss Case," in Athan G. Theoharis (ed.), *Beyond the Hiss Case: The FBI, Congress and the Cold War* (Philadelphia, 1982), 271; Allen Weinstein, *Perjury: The Hiss-Chambers Case* (New York, 1978), 6, 357–359, 505.

5. Stephen E. Ambrose, *Nixon: The Education of a Politician, 1913–1962* (New York, 1987), 160–164; Cedric Belfrage, *The American Inquisition, 1945–1960* (Indianapolis, 1973), 101–102; *CR*, 80th Cong., 2nd Sess., 6901–6905, 81st Cong., 2nd Sess., 10144; Thomas W. Devine, *Henry Wallace's 1948 Presidential Campaign and the Future of Postwar Liberalism* (Chapel Hill, 2013), 40; *JDN*, Jun. 14, 1949; *MPS, NYT*, and *WP*, Jun. 11, 1949; *WP*, Jun. 25, 1954; Ybarra, *Washington Gone Crazy*, 331, 334.

6. Interview with Dorothy and Robert G. Baker, Aug. 13, 2013, St. Augustine, FL; O'Reilly, *Hoover and the Un-Americans*, 95, 98; *Orlando Sentinel*, Nov. 15, 1989; Ellen Schrecker, *Many Are the Crimes: McCarthyism in America* (Boston, 1998), 214–215; Ybarra, *Washington Gone Crazy*, 393, 510, 515, 526–534, 720.

7. Robert P. Newman, *Owen Lattimore and the "Loss" of China* (Berkeley, 1992), 316.

8. Chris Myers Asch, *The Senator and the Sharecropper: The Freedom Struggles of James O. Eastland and Fannie Lou Hamer* (New York, 2008), 137–138; Sarah Hart Brown, *Standing against Dragons: Three Southern Lawyers in an Era of Fear* (Baton Rouge, 1998), 122; Laurie B. Green, *Battling the Plantation Mentality: Memphis and the Black Freedom Struggle* (Chapel Hill, 2007), 188–189; *NYT*, Nov. 23, 1951, and Nov. 19, 1955; Robert Sherrill, *First Amendment Felon: The Story of Frank Wilkinson, His 132,000 Page FBI File, and His Epic Fight for Civil Rights and Liberties* (New York, 2007), 159; Gregory S. Taylor, *The Life and Lies of Paul Crouch: Communist, Opportunist, Cold War Snitch* (Gainesville, FL, 2014); *WP*, Nov. 23, 1951, and Jun. 25, 1954; *Washington Times Herald*, May 9, 1949.

9. Asch, *Senator and the Sharecropper*, 137–138; Christopher John Gerard, "'A Program of Cooperation': The FBI, the Senate Internal Security Subcommittee, and the Communist Issue, 1950–1954," Ph.D. dissertation, Marquette University, 1993, 211; *NYT*, Oct. 27, 1951, and Sep. 5, 1952; Victor Rabinowitz, *An Unrepentant Leftist: A Lawyer's Memoir* (Urbana, IL, 1996), 104.

10. Asch, *Senator and the Sharecropper*, 138–139; Girard, "Program of Cooperation," 213–215; Green, *Battling the Plantation Mentality*, 138–139; *Subversive Control of Distributive, Processing and Office Workers of America: Hearings before the Subcommittee to Investigate the Administration of the Internal Security Act and Other Internal Security Laws*, 82nd Cong., 1st Sess., 40–49, 94, 146.

11. Asch, *Senator and the Sharecropper*, 139–140; Girard, "Program of Cooperation," 211–214; *NYT*, Oct. 27, 1951; Rabinowitz, *Unrepentant Leftist*, 108; *Subversive Control of DPOWA*, 90–91.

12. Green, *Battling the Plantation Mentality*, 189; *NYT* and *WP*, Sep. 5, 1952.

13. Brown, *Standing against Dragons*, 114; JOE to W. H. Booth, Mar. 23, 1954, S1, SS19, B17, F17-5, JOE Collection; Irwin Klibaner, *Conscience of a Troubled South: The Southern Conference Educational Fund, 1946–1966* (Brooklyn, 1989), 75; Robert P. Moses and Charles E. Cobb Jr., *Radical Equations: Math Literacy and Civil Rights* (Boston, 2001), 60; *Nashville Banner* Jul. 30, 1945; Linda Reed, *Simple Decency and Common Sense: The Southern Conference Movement* (Bloomington, IN, 1991), xxiii.

14. Virginia Foster Durr, *Outside the Magic Circle: The Autobiography of Virginia Foster Durr* (Tuscaloosa, 1985), 256–257; transcript of oral history by Michael Gillette, Mar. 1, 1975, 46, Lyndon Baines Johnson Presidential Library, Austin, TX; JOE to Eugene D. Cox, Nov. 29, 1955, S4, SS Internal Security Subcommittee, B25, "New Orleans Hearings (1954)" folder, JOE Collection; JOE to Paul Crouch, Mar. 24, 1953, S4, SS Internal Security Subcommittee, B8, "Paul Crouch" folder, JOE Collection; Virginia Van der Veer Hamilton, *Lister Hill: Statesman from the South* (Chapel Hill, 1987), 211. *MPS*, Mar. 8, 1954; *NYT*, Nov. 29, 1955; John A. Salmond, *A Southern Rebel: The Life and Times of Aubrey Willis Williams* (Chapel Hill, 1983), 231–233; John A. Salmond, *The Conscience of a Lawyer: Clifford J. Durr and American Civil Liberties* (Tuscaloosa, 1992), 160–161.

15. Paul Crouch to JOE, Mar. 24, 1953, S4, SS Internal Security Subcommittee, B27, "Southern Conference Educational Fund" file, JOE Collection; Ben Mandel to Senator Jenner, Mar. 18, 1953, S4, SS Internal Security Subcommittee, B27, "Southern Conference Educational Fund" file, JOE Collection; transcripts, Executive Session interviews with Paul Crouch, Feb. 26, 1954, B28, F301, 1–20, and Mar. 1, 1954, F302, 21–32, National Archives, Washington, D.C.

16. Klibaner, *Conscience of a Troubled South*, 79; O'Reilly, *Hoover and the Un-Americans*, 8; *SCEF, Inc.: Hearings before the Subcommittee to Investigate the Administration of the Internal Security Act and Other Internal Security Laws of the Committee on the Judiciary, United States Senate*, 83rd Cong., 2nd Sess., 4–6.

17. Klibaner, *Conscience of a Troubled South*, 79; John A. Salmond, "The Great Southern Commie Hunt: Aubrey Williams, the Southern Conference Educational Fund, and the Internal Security Subcommittee," *South Atlantic Quarterly* 77:4 (Autumn 1978), 436, 440; *SCEF Hearings*, 3, 33–34.

18. Frank T. Adams, *James A. Dombrowski: An American Heretic, 1897–1983* (Knoxville, 1992), 228–229; John M. Glen, *Highlander: No Ordinary School* (Knoxville, 1996), 210–211; Klibaner, *Conscience of a Troubled South*, 80–82; *NYT*, Oct. 11, 1955; John A. Salmond, "The Great Southern Commie Hunt," 436, 440; *SCEF Hearings*, 50–53, 60–66, 75.

19. Glen, *Highlander*, 210–211; *SCEF Hearings*, 84–98.

20. Salmond, *Southern Rebel*, 236–237; *SCEF Hearings*, 101–114.

21. Butler never made his charge again.

22. *NYT*, Mar. 20, 1954; Salmond, "Great Southern Commie Hunt," 442–443; Salmond, *Southern Rebel*, 237–238; *SCEF Hearings*, 116–146.

23. Adams, *Dombrowski*, 198–200; Glen, *Highlander*, 211–213; transcript, Executive Session interview with Myles Horton, B29, F311, Mar. 19, 1954, 2–20; *NYT*, Mar. 21, 23, 1954.

24. Frank T. Adams with Myles Horton, *Unearthing the Seeds of Fire: The Idea of Highlander* (Winston-Salem, 1975), 200; *NYT* and *WP*, Mar. 21, 1954.

25. Paul Crouch to JOE, Apr. 10, 1954, S4, SS Internal Security Subcommittee, B8, "Paul Crouch" folder, JOE Collection; *Daily Worker*, Mar. 24, 1954; Glen, *Highlander*, 214; Klibaner, *Conscience of a Troubled South*, 84; *Montgomery Advertiser-Alabama Journal*, Apr. 5, 1954; telegram to JOE, Mar. 20, 1954, S4, SS Internal Security Subcommittee, B25, "New York Hearings (1954)" folder, JOE Collection; *NYT*, Mar. 25, 1954.

26. Brown, *Standing against Dragons*, 150–151; Durr, *Outside the Magic Circle*, 171–172, 254–256; Hiram Eastland Jr., email to author, Jan. 1, 2013.

27. Brown, *Standing against Dragons*, 131, 143; Pat McCarran to William Jenner, Jul. 15, 1954, B203, "Paul Crouch, 1954" folder, Senate Internal Security Subcommittee Papers,

National Archives, Washington, D.C.; *NYT*, Jul. 9, 10, 1954; telephone interview with Gregory Taylor, Aug. 5, 2013, Murfreesboro, NC; *Washington Daily News*, Jul. 1, 1954.

28. "Communist Infiltration of the American Armed Forces," B202, "Paul Crouch, 1950–1953" folder, Senate Internal Security Subcommittee, National Archives, Washington, D.C.; William Bragg Ewald Jr., *Who Killed Joe McCarthy?* (New York, 1984), 190–194, 370–378; Thomas C. Reeves, *The Life and Times of Joe McCarthy: A Biography* (New York, 1982), 528, 628–632; *Washington Daily News*, Jun. 23, 1954.

29. Wayne Addison Clark, "An Analysis of the Relationship between Anti-Communism and Segregationist Thought in the Deep South, 1948–1964," Ph.D. dissertation, University of North Carolina, 1976, 49; Jerome E. Edwards, *Pat McCarran: Political Boss of Nevada* (Reno, 1982), 147; John Holloman, tape, oral history by Jere Nash, Apr. 7, 2005, Nash and Taggart Collection, Special Collections, J. D. Williams Library, University of Mississippi; Walter Sillers to JOE, Aug. 26, 1954, S3, SS1, B144, "1954 States Rights" folder, JOE Collection; Ybarra, *Washington Gone Crazy*, 750.

30. Robert G. Baker interview; Robert Caro, *The Years of Lyndon Johnson: Master of the Senate* (New York, 2002), 553–556; Paul Clancy, *Just a Country Lawyer: A Biography of Senator Sam Ervin* (Bloomington, IN, 1974), 162–164; Rowland Evans and Robert Novak, *Lyndon B. Johnson: The Exercise of Power* (New York, 1968), 94–97.

31. Robert G. Baker interview; Caro, *Years of Lyndon Johnson*, 554–556; Evans and Novak, *Lyndon B. Johnson*, 96; Edna Lonigan to William Jenner, Dec. 3, 1954, B12, F3, William E. Jenner Papers, Duggan Library, Hanover College, Hanover, IN; Reeves, *Life and Times of Joe McCarthy*, 645–662; *WP*, Dec. 20, 1954.

32. *JCL*, *NYT*, and *WP*, Jun. 27, 28, 1956; Lucas A. Powe Jr., *The Warren Court and American Politics* (Cambridge, MA, 2000), 86.

33. *CR*, 85th Cong., 1st Sess., 14681; Woods Eastland, email to author, Jul. 27, 2013; Arthur Herman, *Joseph McCarthy: Re-examining the Life and Legacy of America's Most Hated Senator* (New York, 2000), 302–303.

CHAPTER 9

1. Kari Frederickson, "Dixiecrat Movement and the Origins of Massive Resistance," Ph.D. dissertation, Rutgers University, 1996, 367; *JDN*, Sep. 18, 1949; *NYT*, Sep. 17, 1949; Maarten Zwiers, "The Paradox of Power: James O. Eastland and the Democratic Party," M.A. thesis, University of Mississippi, 2007, 43.

2. *CR*, 81st Cong., 1st Sess., 7011; Julian M. Pleasants and Augustus M. Burns, *Frank M. Graham and the 1950 Senate Race in North Carolina* (Chapel Hill, 1990), 173; *WP*, May 28 and Jun. 1, 1949.

3. Why Lehman bore any personal enmity toward Eastland prior to coming to the Senate in 1950 to fill the unexpired term of Robert Wagner is unknown. But he and Eastland engaged in a heated debate during a displaced persons bill in early 1950 in which Eastland took the side of those who wanted to institute tighter safeguards to block the admission of any Communists. Eastland pronounced that some in the Truman administration who administered the program were "guilty of moral treason" for allowing some left-of-center applicants to enter. Intelligence officials had told him that Soviets were trying to filter some of their secret police into the country. Lehman, a man understandably focused on the plight of European Jews of any political persuasion, broke in to inquire if Eastland knew that all

displaced persons trying to enter the country were screened. "I deny that," Eastland replied. Days later, Lehman, while Eastland was off of the floor, lambasted Eastland for a dozen errors he had made in the course of his presentation. Eastland, a man with a keen sense of Southern honor, resented that Lehman had waged part of his attack while he was absent. Lehman discounted his retort, saying that "Sometimes a man can be proud of the enemies he makes." *CR*, 81st Cong., 2nd Sess., 2809; *JDN*, Mar. 4, 1950; *NYP*, Feb. 16, 1956; *NYT*, Mar. 3, 8, 1950; *WP*, Mar. 8, 1950.

4. Eastland limited his role in Johnson's second bid for the governorship in 1955 to letting it be known that he would be voting for him both to keep a private pledge to former Governor Fielding Wright that he would never oppose him and another more public one to Democratic primary voters in 1954 that he would not campaign actively for any of the contenders the next year. Tom P. Brady to JOE, Aug. 7, 1955, S1, SS10, B20, F20-4, JOE Collection.

5. Eastland also acted to see that Smith did not have a challenger in 1954, the year he faced his own most serious challenge from Carroll Gartin. Frank D. Barber, transcript, oral history by Reid S. Derr, Sep. 20, 1990, Mississippi Oral History Program of University of Southern Mississippi, 27–30; interview with Brad Dye, Jun. 21, 2011, Ridgeland, MS; telephone interview with Patrick H. "Pete" Johnson, Feb. 22, 2011, Clarksdale, MS; Erle Johnston, *Politics: Mississippi Style* (Forest, MS, 1993), 102–110; Dennis E. Mitchell, *Mississippi Liberal: A Biography of Frank E. Smith* (Jackson, MS, 2001), 132; *NYT*, Aug. 27, 30, 1951; Frank Smith to Clarence Pierce, Feb. 17, 1958, B1, F18, Clarence Pierce Collection, Archives and Special Collections, J. D. Mitchell Library, University of Mississippi.

6. C. B. Curlee to JOE, S1, SS21, B1, F1-10, JOE Collection; JOE to Ferrell Abel, Apr. 7, 1952, S1, SS20, B2, F2-1, JOE Collection; *NYT*, Jun. 27, 1952; Maarten Zwiers, "The Paradox of Power: James O. Eastland and the Democratic Party," M.A. thesis, University of Mississippi, 2007, 43.

7. JOE to Robert J. Burkhardt, Aug. 11, 1952, S1, SS20, B2, "1952" folder, JOE Collection; JOE to Mrs. R. E. Shands and JOE to G. H. King, Oct. 10, 1952, S1, SS20, B2, "1952" folder, JOE Collection; JOE to Walter Sillers, Sep. 29, 1952, B105, File 13, Walter Sillers Papers, Delta State University, Cleveland, MS; interview with Woods Eastland, Jun. 11, 2012, Doddsville, MS; *Indianola Enterprise-Tocsin*, Sep. 9, 1952; *JCL*, Aug. 21, 1952; Thomas R. Melton, "Walter Sillers and National Politics, 1948–1964," *JMH*, 39:3 (Apr. 1977), 222; undated *NOTP* article by Bill Minor in S1, SS19, B20, F20-22, JOE Collection; undated *Pascagoula Enterprise-Star* article, and "Sunflower vote" document in S2, SS4, B4, "Politics: 1952" folder, JOE Collection; Zwiers, "Paradox of Power," 47, 49.

8. 1954 campaign ad, JOE file, William F. Winter Archives and History Building, Mississippi Department of Archives and History, Jackson; *CR*, 83rd Cong., 2nd Sess., 1394–1400; JOE to M. D. Lantrip, S1, SS19, B11, F11-7, JOE Collection; JOE to John C. Stennis, Nov. 13, 1952, S1, SS18, B9, F9-32, JOE Collection; Erle Johnston, *I Rolled with Ross* (Baton Rouge, 1980), 64; *NYT*, May 30, 1953; *WP*, Sep. 11, 1960.

9. Ezra Taft Benson, *Crossfire: The Eight Years with Eisenhower* (Garden City, NY, 1962), 67, 243, 307, 315; *CQ*, May 15, 1953; *CR*, 83rd Cong., 1st Sess., 517, 1046–1053, 2nd Sess., 2233–2235, 13678; *JCL*, Jun. 4 and Jul. 19, 1953, May 13, 1954, and Oct. 27, 1985; *JDN*, Feb. 12, 1953, and Aug. 15, 1954; *MCA*, May 21, 22, 29, and Jun. 4, 1953; *Natchez Democrat*, May 13, 1954; *Neshoba Democrat*, Jan. 21 and May 27, 1954; *NYT*, Feb. 13, 14 and May 28, 1953, Jan. 31, and Jun. 25, 1954; *WP*, Jan. 24 and Feb. 14, 1953, Jan. 8, Feb. 26, Apr. 22, and Jun. 25, 1954.

10. Interview with Woods Eastland, Jun. 11, 2012, Doddsville, MS; Leo Katcher, *Earl Warren: A Political Biography* (New York, 1967), 318; Jim Newton, *Justice for All: Earl Warren and the Nation He Made* (New York, 2006), 282–290; *NYT* and *WP*, Feb. 21, 1954; Courtney Pace to Walter Sillers, Jun. 29, 1953, and Walter Sillers to Courtney Pace, Jul. 2, 1953, B105, F16, Walter Sillers Papers, Delta State University, Cleveland, MS; Walter Sillers to JOE, Oct. 3, 5, 1953, B105. F17, Walter Sillers Papers, Delta State University.

11. Joseph Crespino, "Strategic Accommodations: Civil Rights Opponents in Mississippi and Their Impact on American Racial Politics, 1953–1972," Ph.D. dissertation, Stanford University, 32; Hugh Davis Graham, *Crisis in Print: Desegregation and the Press in Tennessee* (Nashville, 1967), 32; *JDN*, May 17, 1954; *NYT*, May 18, 19, 1954; Reid Sarrett, *The Ordeal of Desegregation: The First Decade* (New York, 1966), 1.

12. *CR*, 83rd Cong., 1st Sess., 7251–7257; *JCL, NYT*, and *WP*, May 28, 1954; *JDN*, Jun. 13, 1954.

13. The Eastlands did buy an eleven-room home in the Kent section of the District of Columbia. W. C. "Chubby" Adams to JOE, Nov. 25, 1952, and Aug. 8, 1953, S1, SS19, B11, F11-2, JOE Collection; *JDN*, Feb. 25, Aug. 23 and Oct. 7, 1953, and May 13, 1954; Mitchell, *Mississippi Liberal*, 77; telephone interview with Clarence Pierce, Jun. 18, 2013, Vaiden, MS; "The Authentic Voice," *Time*, Mar. 26, 1956, 28; Maarten Zwiers, "James Eastland: The Shadow of Southern Democrats, 1928–1966," Ph.D. dissertation, University of Groningen, 2012, 205.

14. Voters did ratify the amendment in a December 1954 special election, but no governor ever asked his legislature to invoke this authority. Erle Johnston, *Mississippi's Defiant Years* (Forest, MS, 1990), 22–24; *Pearl River County Weekly Democrat*, Aug. 12, 1954.

15. C. B. Curlee to JOE, S1, SS19, B14, F14-2, JOE Collection; Aubert Dunn to JOE, Oct. 7, 1953, S1, SS19, B19, F19-97, JOE Collection; Dye interview, Jun. 21, 2011, Ridgeland, MS; JOE to George W. Healy, S1, SS19, B17, F17-12, JOE Collection; JOE to J. S. Hickman, Feb. 18, 1954, S1, SS19, B14, F14-2, JOE Collection; Carroll Gartin ad attached to letter, Mrs. Elmer Walker to JOE, Aug. 8, 1954, S1, SS19, B16, F16-13, JOE Collection; *JDN*, Aug. 11, 1954; *Tupelo Daily Journal*, Jan. 18, 1954.

16. JOE to Ed C. Brewer, May 31, 1954, S1, SS19, B12, F12-2, JOE Collection; JOE to K. G. Shaw, Jul. 19, 1954, S1, SS19, B16, F16-9, JOE Collection; JOE to Dick Mosby, Oct. 15, 1953, S1, SS19, B14, F14-2, JOE Collection; JOE to Railway Brotherhoods, Jul. 7, 1954, S1, SS18, B21, F21-8, JOE Collection; Tom Hederman to JOE, Jul. 7, 1954, S1, SS19, B20, F20-22, JOE Collection; *JDN*, Jun. 29, 1954; Boswell Stevens to JOE, Aug. 16, 1954, S1, SS19, B20, F20-26, JOE Collection.

17. Dye interview; JOE to H. G. Rudner Sr., S1, SS19, B17, F17-12, JOE Collection; *NYP*, Feb. 14, 1956.

18. Erle Johnston, oral history by Orley B. Caudill, Mississippi Oral History Program of University of Southern Mississippi, Jul. 30, 1980, 40; Neil R. McMillen, "Development of Civil Rights, 1956–1970" in Richard Aubrey McLemore, *A History of Mississippi*, Volume II (Hattiesburg, MS, 1973), 156.

19. Chris Myers Asch, *The Senator and the Sharecropper: The Freedom Struggles of James O. Eastland and Fannie Lou Hamer* (New York, 2008), 149; *JCL* and *NOTP*, Jun. 27, 1954; *JDN*, Jun. 26, 27, 1954; Johnston, *Mississippi's Defiant Years*, 17; L. P. B. Lipscomb to Robert Patterson, Jun. 16, 1955, and Oct. 12, 1955, S3, SS1, B34, "1955 Civil Rights" folder 2, JOE Collection; Robert Patterson to L. P. B. Lipscomb, Oct. 11, 1955, S3, SS1, B34, "1955 Civil Rights" folder 2, JOE Collection; Dan Wakefield, "Respectable Racism," *Nation*, Oct. 26, 1955, 339; *WP*, Jun. 27, 1954.

20. "Bilbo Rides Again," *Time*, Jun. 28, 1954, 20; Ira Harkey, *The Smell of Burning Crosses: A White Integrationist Editor in Mississippi* (Jacksonville, IL, 1967), 100; Johnston, *Politics: Mississippi Style*, 114–115; *MCA*, Jun. 13, 1954; *NOTP*, Jun. 16, 1954; *WP*, Jun. 28, 1954.

21. *CR*, 83rd Cong., 2nd Sess., 11510–11517, 13381–13385; C. B. Curlee to JOE, Jun. 16, 1954, S1, SS19, B19, F19-90, JOE Collection; *JDN*, Jun. 6 and Jul. 23, 1954; Johnston, *Politics: Mississippi Style*, 114–115; Johnston, University of Southern Mississippi Oral History, 27–28; "Name the Fight," ad in JOE 1954 file, William F. Winter Archives and History Building, Mississippi Department of Archives and History, Jackson; "The Outstanding Record of Senator Jim Eastland," S1, SS14, B11, F11-4, JOE Collection.

22. President Eisenhower signed this bill after a broad general agreement among southern and western representatives, chiefly Eastland, Clinton Anderson of New Mexico, and Thomas Kuchel of California. *NYT*, Nov. 20, 1953, and Jan. 31, 1954; *WP*, Jan. 11, 1954.

23. Eastland repaid Aiken by casting a vote the Vermonter did not expect for the St. Lawrence Seaway. A majority in Mississippi may have opposed this project, but it was one on which Eastland sensed that few Mississippians would cast their ballots for or against him on in the future. When Aiken told him he did not have to risk hurting his own stature in Mississippi for something that would not benefit his constituents, Eastland responded merely, "I told you I would, didn't I?" George Aiken, transcript, oral history, Jun. 7, 1976, 24, John C. Stennis Oral History Project, John C. Stennis Collection, Mississippi State University, Starkville.

24. George D. Aiken to Louise McCorkel, Jul. 3, 1954, S1, SS19, B14, F14-2, JOE Collection; Dye interview; *JCL*, Aug. 18, 1954; *JDN*, Aug. 8, 1954; G. G. Keith to JOE, S1, SS19, B15, F15-6, JOE Collection.

25. Chris Myers Asch, *The Senator and the Sharecropper: The Freedom Struggles of James O. Eastland and Fannie Lou Hamer* (New York, 2008), 153; JOE to Henry K. Cuon and George C. Wong, Aug. 30, 1954, S1, SS19, B12, F12-5, JOE Collection; JOE to George W. Healy, S1, SS19, B17, F17-12, JOE Collection; *NYP*, Feb. 18, 1956; *NYT*, Aug. 16, 23, 24, 1954; Patricia Webb Robinson, "A Rhetorical Analysis of Senator James O. Eastland's Speeches, 1954–1959," M.A. thesis, Louisiana State University, 1978, 17.

26. JOE to Robert B. Patterson, Jun. 1, 1954, and Robert B. Patterson to JOE, May 12, 1954, S1, SS19, B19, F16-9, JOE Collection.

27. James Wilfred Vander Zanden, "The Southern White Resistance Movement to Integration," Ph.D. dissertation, University of North Carolina, 1957, 344, 346; Clive Webb, *Rabble Rousers: The American Far Right in the Civil Rights Era* (Athens, GA, 2010), 62.

28. Hodding Carter III, *The South Strikes Back* (Garden City, NY, 1958), 43; James P. Coleman, transcript, oral history by Orley B. Caudill, Nov. 6, 1981, and Feb. 12, 1982, Mississippi Oral History of University of Southern Mississippi, 150; James Graham Cook, *The Segregationists* (New York, 1962), 48–50, 52; Brad Dye, transcript, oral history by Jere Nash, Dec. 1, 2004, Nash and Taggart Collection, J. D. Williams Library, University of Mississippi; Johnston oral history, 23; John Bartlow Martin, *The Deep South Says Never* (New York, 1957), 1–4; J. Todd Moye, *Let The People Decide: Black Freedom and White Resistance Movements in Sunflower County, Mississippi, 1945–1986* (Chapel Hill, 1954), 45, 52.

29. Asch, *Senator and the Sharecropper*, 151; Barber, University of Southern Mississippi oral history, 61; E. C. Barksdale, "The Power Structure of Southern Gubernatorial Conservatism," in Harold M. Hollingsworth," *Essays in Recent Southern Politics* (Austin, 1970), 36; Stephen Andrew Berrey, "Against the Law: Violence, Crime, State Repression and Black Resistance in Jim Crow Mississippi," Ph.D. dissertation, University of Texas, 2006, 251;

Hodding Carter III, "Citadel of the Citizens Council," *NYT Magazine*, Nov. 12, 1961, 23, 123–126; Gloster Current to Mr. Moon, Dec. 1, 1955, SII, BA422, "Courts, Gus, shooting of" folder, NAACP Papers, Library of Congress; David Halberstam, "A County Divided against Itself," *The Reporter*, Dec. 15, 1955, 30–32; David Halberstam, "The White Citizens Councils: Respectable Means for Unrespectable Ends," *Commentary*, Oct. 1956, 295, 300; Ruby Hurley to Medgar Evers, SII, BA427, Elizabeth Geyer, "The New Ku Klux Klan," BB84, "Citizens Councils" folder, NAACP Papers, Library of Congress; "Economic reprisals, cases concerning, 1955" folder, NAACP Papers, Library of Congress; Moye, *Let The People Decide*, 68, 80–82; Michael Newton, *The Ku Klux Klan in Mississippi* (Jefferson, NC, 2010), 108–109; Stephanie Renee Rolph, "Displacing Race: White Resistance and Conservative Politics in the Civil Rights Era," Ph.D. dissertation, Mississippi State University, 2009, 47; Sarrett, *Ordeal of Desegregation*, 301; W. J. Simmons to Courtney Pace, May 11, 1961, S3, SS1, B39, "1961 Civil Rights" folder, JOE Collection; Vander Zanden, "Southern White Resistance," 312; "Speech of Roy Wilkins at Belzoni, MS, at memorial meeting for George W. Lee," SII, BA422, "Mississippi Pressures, Lee, George W." folder, NAACP Papers, Library of Congress.

30. Once it became widely known that Sidwell Friends had admitted an African American student, Eastland did transfer his children to private schools in Virginia. *CR*, 84th Cong., 1st Sess., 7119, 7285; JOE to Herman E. Talmadge, Oct. 11, 1956, S1, SS18, B10, F10-3, JOE Collection; John P. Jackson, *Science for Segregation: Race, Law and the Case against Brown v. Board of Education* (New York, 2005), 74; Strom Thurmond to JOE, Feb. 18, 1956, S1, SS18, B10, F10-10, JOE Collection; *WP*, May 26, 1955.

31. *CR*, 84th Cong., 1st Sess., 3013; George Lewis, *Massive Resistance: The White Response to the Civil Rights Movement* (London, 2006), 121; David A. Nichols, *A Matter of Justice: Eisenhower and the Beginning of the Civil Rights Revolution* (New York, 2007), 78–79; *NYT*, Mar. 17, 1955; Tinsley E. Yarbrough, *John Marshall Harlan: Dissenter of the Warren Court* (New York, 1992), 91, 93, 103–110.

32. "Nation Horrified by Murder of Kidnaped [sic] Chicago Youth," *Jet*, Sep. 15, 1955, in jetcityorange.com/Emmett-Till; Stephen L. Whitfield, *A Death in the Delta: The Story of Emmett Till* (New York, 1988), 15–31, 145.

33. Alex A. Alston Jr. and James L. Dickerson, *Devil's Sanctuary: An Eyewitness History of Mississippi Hate Crimes* (Chicago, 2009), 25; JOE to Fred Boon, Nov. 30, 1955, S3, SS1, B34, "1955 Civil Rights" Folder, JOE Collection; JOE to T. W. Graham, S3, SS1, B34, "1955 Civil Rights" Folder, JOE Collection; JOE to William L. Kelley, Nov. 18, 1955, S3, SS1, B34, "1955 Civil Rights" Folder, JOE Collection; Whitfield, *Death in the Delta*, 26, 28, 145.

34. Christopher Myers Asch, "No Compromise: The Freedom Struggles of James O. Eastland and Fannie Lou Hamer," Ph.D. dissertation, University of North Carolina, 2005, 191; Harry Golden, *Mr. Kennedy and the Negroes* (Cleveland, 1964), 125.

CHAPTER 10

1. *NYT*, Oct. 3, 1954; *WP*, Oct. 20, 1954.

2. Frank D. Barber, oral history by Reid S. Derr, May 30, 1990, Mississippi Oral History Program of the University of Southern Mississippi, 16; Gary E. Elliott, *Senator Alan Bible and the Politics of the New West* (Reno, 1994), 70–71; interview with David Lambert, Aug. 13, 2012, Alexandria, VA; telephone interview with Clarence Pierce, Jun. 17, 2013, Vaiden, MS; Michael J. Ybarra, *Washington Gone Crazy: Senator Pat McCarran and the Great American Communist Hunt* (Hanover, NH, 2004), 454.

3. Few people have ever circumnavigated the ideological spectrum as completely or as quickly as Harvey Matusow. Just twenty-one in 1947, he joined a Communist Party cell in Brooklyn and undertook a variety of minor tasks for several left-wing organizations. Within three years, he had grown apprehensive about the work of the Communists and signed with the FBI as a paid informant. By the end of 1951, he had given 181 names of Communists to the House Un-American Activities Committee, including Clinton Jencks, the head of the Mine, Mill and Smelter Operators Union, a body the Congress of Industrial Organizations had expelled as it was Communist-dominated. In 1952, Matusow traveled to Montana and Washington at the behest of Joseph McCarty to carry out, with little effect, a "campaign of lies" against Democratic Senate nominees Mike Mansfield and Henry "Scoop" Jackson, respectively, that they were somehow soft on Communism. A year later, Matusow took a job with McCarthy as a $1 a year consultant charged with compiling a list of all the Communists employed in influential New York media. Within months, he had converted to Mormonism and acknowledged that he had fabricated some of his allegations, apologized to some he had accused of having been Communists, and written a *mea culpa* that was ultimately published by a man he had named as a Communist. Upon learning of Matusow's recantation, Jay Sourwine wrote Eastland that Matusow had even lied about where he had been born. When the subcommittee called Matusow to testify, Eastland told Matusow that he had "lots of experience with vicious liars," but he was the "worst." John Earl Haynes and Harvey Klehr, *Venona: Decoding Soviet Espionage in America* (New Haven, 1999), 15; www.johnearlhaynes.og/page62.htmail; Robert M. Lichtman and Ronald D. Cohen, *Deadly Farce: Harvey Matusow and the Informer System in the McCarthy Era* (Urbana, 2004), 21–27, 31, 47, 51, 69–72, 80–81, 85, 101–104; *NYT*, Feb. 23, 24, 1955; interview with Donald Ritchie, Jul. 19, 2013, Washington, D.C.; Jay Sourwine to JOE, S4, SS Internal Security Subcommittee, B11, "Harvey Matusow" file, JOE Collection; *WP*, Feb. 24 and Apr. 21, 1955.

4. *Daily Worker*, Jan. 5, 1956; Jerome E. Edwards, *Pat McCarran: Political Boss of Nevada* (Reno, 1982), 170; Bob McManus to Jay Sourwine and Ben Mandel, Jan. 14, 1956, S4, SS Internal Security Subcommittee, B17, "Communist Party USA" folder, JOE Collection; David E. Koskoff, *The Senator from Central Casting* (New Haven, 2011), 111; *WP*, Aug. 7, 1965; Ybarra, *Washington Gone Crazy*, 626.

5. *NYT*, Jan. 13, 1956; *WP*, Jan. 8, 13, 1956.

6. Edward Alwood, *Dark Days in the Newsroom: McCarthyism Aimed at the Press* (Philadelphia, 2007), 87, 97–99; *NYT*, Jun. 30 and Jul. 1, 2, 1955; *Strategies and Tactics of World Communism: Recruiting for Espionage, Hearings Before SISS*, 84th Sess., 1st Sess., 1323–1390, 1402–1436; *WP*, Jul. 1, 1955.

7. Alwood, *Dark Days*, 100–102, 104–106, 110–112; J. Edgar Hoover to JOE, Apr. 16, 1956, S4, SS Internal Security Subcommittee, "New Orleans Hearings (1956)" folder, JOE Collection; *NYT*, Jan. 5 and 6, 1956; *WP*, Jan. 5, 1956.

8. Alwood, *Dark Days*, 105, 110–118, 120–121, 128; *CR*, 85th Cong., 1st Sess., 4135, 2nd Sess., 7891; Arthur Gelb, *City Room* (New York, 2003), 258; *NYT*, Mar. 21, 26, 1957; *WP*, Mar. 21, 1957.

9. *JCL*, Mar. 21, 1956; *NYT*, Mar. 20, 1956; *WP*, Apr. 6, 7, 1956; William Rusher, *Special Counsel: An Inside Report on the Senate Investigations into Communism* (New Rochelle, 1968), 37–49.

10. *JDN*, May 25, 1956; *NYT*, Apr. 7, 8, 1956; *WP*, Apr. 7, 1956.

11. *NYT*, Sep. 16, 1956; Rusher, *Special Counsel*, 51, 55–59.

12. "14 from the Times," *Newsweek*, Jan. 16, 1956, 52–53; Turner Catledge, *My Life and the Times* (New York, 1977), 225; *NYT*, Jan. 6, 1956; transcript, Mike Wallace interview with Harry Ashmore, Jun. 29, 1958, S4, SS Internal Security Subcommittee, B7, "Harry Ashmore" file, JOE Collection.

13. Jacob K. Javits with Alfred Steinberg, *Javits: The Autobiography of a Public Man* (Boston, 1981), 213–214, 223; *NYT*, Sep. 2, 1956.

14. For the view of a Morris ally, see Rusher, *Special Counsel*, 105–137. See also *Hearings before SISS: Testimony of Jacob K. Javits*, B13, F1, William Jenner Papers, Duggan Library, Hanover College, Hanover, IN; Javits, *Javits*, 229–238; *NYT*, Sep. 7, 1956.

15. Rusher, *Special Counsel*, 183–208.

16. Roger Bowen, *Innocence Is Not Enough: The Life and Death of Herbert Norman* (Vancouver, 1986), 290–342; *Chicago Tribune*, Apr. 12, 13, and Jul. 22, 1957; *CR*, 85th Cong., 1st Sess., 5607–5613; *NYT*, Apr. 13, 1957; David B. Frisk, *If Not Us, Who? William Rusher, National Review and the Conservative Movement* (Wilmington, DE, 2012), 62–65; Rusher, *Special Counsel*, 198–203, 213–215; Peter Stursberg, *Lester Pearson and the American Dilemma* (Toronto, 1980), 159–213.

17. Frank D. Barber, oral history by Reid S. Derr, Jun. 30, 1993, Mississippi Oral History Program of the University of Southern Mississippi, 17–18; Bowen, *Innocence Is Not Enough*, 325; *CR*, 85th Cong., 1st Sess., 5607–5613; Rusher, *Special Counsel*, 221–225.

18. As late as 1970, SISS published a two-volume study edited by right-wing diplomatic historian Anthony Kubek blaming liberal China hand John Stewart Service for submitting pro-Communist information to Philip Jaffe, the editor of the pro-Communist journal *Amerasia*, that helped to bring the regime of Jiang Jieshi to an end in 1949. But, as Harvey Klehr and Ronald Radosh, two other historians generally seen as part of the conservative side of academia, point out, 69 of the 101 documents SISS published that Service had drafted were found on Service's desk and were never seen by Jaffe. Lynne Joiner, *Honorable Survivor: Mao's China, McCarthy's America and the Persecution of John S. Service* (Annapolis, 2009), 318; Harvey Klehr and Ronald Radosh, *The Amerasia Spy Case: Prelude to McCarthyism* (Chapel Hill, 1996) 3–9, 213.

19. Thomas E. Dodd to JOE, Feb. 8, 1960, S4, SS Senate Internal Subcommittee, B3, "Publications: 1960" folder, and "Staff Summary of Hearing(s)," Feb. 19, 1957, Jul. 11, 1957, S4, SS Internal Security Committee, B2, "Administration (1957)" file, JOE Collection; *JCL*, Jun. 13, 1956; *JDN*, Oct. 30, 1956; *NYT*, Dec. 13, 21, 1956, Feb. 8 and Dec. 7, 1957, May 2, 1959, and May 30, 1960; *WP*, Jun. 16, 1959.

20. Ben Mandel to JOE, Jan. 30, 1958, S4, SS Internal Security Subcommittee, B17, "Communist Party USA" folder, JOE Collection; *JDN*, Jul. 25, 1961; *NYT*, Jun. 24, 1957, Feb. 21, 1958, and May 19, 1959; *WP*, Jul. 5 and Oct. 21, 1956, Jul. 7, 1958, and May 24, 1959.

21. *CR*, 84th Cong., 2nd Sess., 3365; *JCL*, Feb. 29, 1956, and May 11, 1957; JOE to Tom Wood, Mar. 1, 1957, S3, SS1, B82, "1957 Foreign Policy: Middle East" folder, and JOE to Clinton P. Anderson, S1, SS18, B1, F1-2, JOE Collection; *New York Herald Tribune*, Jul. 21, 1958; *WP*, Feb. 28, 1956.

22. *CR*, 86th Cong., 1st Sess., 12580; Anthony DePalma, *The Man Who Invented Fidel: Castro, Cuba and Herbert L. Matthews of the New York Times* (New York, 2006), 155–156, 220; Koskoff, *Senator from Central Casting*, 85; telephone interview with Clarence Pierce, Apr. 26, 2011, Vaiden, MS; *NYT*, Jul. 15, 1959; Stephanie Renee Rolph, "Displacing Race: White Resistance and Conservative Politics in the Civil Rights Era," Ph.D. dissertation, Mississippi State University, 2009, 180; *WP*, Jun. 20, 1950.

23. DePalma, *Man Who Invented Fidel*, 220–227; *JCL*, Sep. 11 and Oct. 14, 1960; *NYT*, Sep. 16, 1960; *WP*, Sep. 11, 1960.

24. JOE to Charlie C. Jacobs Jr., Jul. 29, 1961, and JOE to Maude Simmons, Sep. 21, 1961, S3, SS1, B82, "1961 Foreign Policy: Cuba" folder, JOE Collection; *WP*, Aug. 24, 1961.

CHAPTER 11

1. *NYT* and *WP*, Mar. 7, 1956.

2. "An Issue of 1956: Civil Rights," *Time*, Mar. 19, 1956, 25–26; Percy Greene, transcript, oral history by Neil McMillen, Dec. 14, 1972, Mississippi Oral History Program of University of Southern Mississippi, 40.

3. W. B. Alexander to JOE, Dec. 15, 1955, B61, "Dec. 1–14, 1955" folder, James J. Kilpatrick Papers, Albert and Shirley Small Special Collections Library, University of Virginia, Charlottesville; Harry F. Byrd to JOE, Sep. 26, 1956, S1, SS18, B2, F2-27, JOE Collection; Robert Gaines Corley, "James Jackson Kilpatrick: The Evolution of a Southern Conservative, 1955–1965," M.A. thesis, University of Virginia, 1971, 28; JOE to Walter F. George," Dec. 13, 1955, S1, SS18, B4, F4-20, and JOE to Mrs. Walter Sillers, Dec. 12, 1955, S3, SS1, B144, "1955 Supreme Court" file, JOE Collection; James J. Kilpatrick to Courtney C. Pace, Dec. 22, 1955, James J. Kilpatrick to Robert Patterson, Dec. 14, 1955, and Robert Patterson to James Jackson Kilpatrick, Dec. 14, 1955, B61, "December 15–28, 1955" folder, Kilpatrick Papers; John Frederick Martin, *Civil Rights and the Crisis of Liberalism* (Boulder, CO, 1979), 132; Benjamin Muse, *Virginia's Massive Resistance* (Bloomington, IN, 1961), 20–21; Joseph J. Thorndike, "The Sometimes Sordid Level of Race and Segregation: James J. Kilpatrick and the Campaign against *Brown*" in Matthew D. Lassiter and Andrew B. Lewis, *The Moderates' Dilemma: Massive Resistance to School Desegregation in Virginia* (Charlottesville, 1998), 63.

4. John Kyle Day, *The Southern Manifesto: Massive Resistance and the Fight to Preserve Segregation* (Jackson, 2014), 84–92; Robert Mann, *The Walls of Jericho: Lyndon Johnson, Hubert Humphrey, Richard Russell, and the Struggle for Civil Rights* (New York, 1996), 161–166; Strom Thurmond to JOE, Mar. 2, 1956, S1, SS18, B10, F10-10, JOE Collection; Strom Thurmond to Olin Johnston, Mar. 2, 1956, Subject Correspondence 1956, S18, B12, "Ro to Seg," FIII, Strom Thurmond Collection, Strom Thurmond Institute, Clemson University, Clemson, SC.

5. Privately, Eastland often bashed the NAACP as a "radical, left-wing organization engaged in stirring up racial hatred." After seeing reports from J. Edgar Hoover declaring that Communist attempts to infiltrate the NAACP had been unsuccessful, he defended them from any charges that they received any influence from the Soviet Union. Robert J. Donovan, *Eisenhower: The Inside Story* (New York, 1956), 390; JOE to Percy P. Pounders Jr., Sep. 29, 1955, S3, SS1, B34, "1955 Civil Rights" folder, JOE Collection.

6. Joseph B. Atkins, *Covering for the Bosses: Labor and the Southern Press* (Jackson, MS, 2008), 68–69; Sarah H. Brown, "The Role of Elite Leadership in the Southern Defense of Segregation," *Journal of Southern History* 77:4 (Nov. 2011), 828, 834; Thomas D. Clark, *The Emerging South* (New York, 1968), 201; JOE to John S. Hoggett, Nov. 3, 1955, S3, SS1, B34, "1955 Civil Rights" (1 of 2) folder, JOE Collection; JOE to Walter Sillers, Dec. 20, 1955, B59, F2, Walter Sillers Papers, Delta State University, Cleveland, MS; Elizabeth Jacoway, "Jim Johnson of Arkansas: Segregationist Prototype," in Ted Ownby (ed.), *The Role of Ideas in the Civil Rights South* (Jackson, MS, 2002), 144; *JCL*, Dec. 13, 1955; Walter Lewis, "Dixie Racists to Defy Constitution," *New Leader*, Jan. 16, 1956, 12–13; Neil McMillen, *The Citizens'*

Council: *Organized Resistance to the Second Reconstruction, 1954–1964* (Urbana, IL, 1971), 116–117; *MCA*, Dec. 29, 1955; *NYT*, Dec. 30, 31, 1955; *WP*, Oct. 24, 1955; Patricia Webb Robinson, "A Rhetorical Analysis of Senator James O. Eastland's Speeches, 1954–1959," M.A. thesis, Louisiana State University, 1978, 18.

7. *JCL*, Dec. 1, 1955; *JDN*, Nov. 24, 1955; JOE, "We've Reached the Age of Judicial Tyranny," Dec. 1, 1955, B1, F9, Ed King Collection, J. D. Mitchell Library, University of Mississippi, Oxford.

8. *JCL*, Jan. 29, 1956; *NYP*, Jan. 31, 1956; David James Wallace, "Massive Resistance, Southern Myth, and Media Suppression," Ph.D. dissertation, University of Colorado, 2011, 50; Francis M. Wilhoit, *The Politics of Massive Resistance* (New York, 1973), 81–82.

9. A few members of the North Alabama Citizens' Council faction circulated pamphlets that read, in part, "When in the course of human events it becomes necessary to abolish the Negro race, proper methods should be used. Among these are guns, bows and arrows, sling shots and knives. We hold these truths to be self-evident: All whites are created equal with certain rights, among these are life, liberty and the pursuit of dead niggers. In every stage of the bus boycott we have been oppressed and degraded because of black, slimy, juicy unbearably stinking niggers ... African flesh-eaters." Both Robert A. Caro in *The Years of Lyndon Johnson* and Jere Nash and Andy Taggart in the first edition of their *Mississippi Politics: The Struggle for Power* placed these racist words in Eastland's mouth, and both have since acknowledged their error. Robert A. Caro, *The Years of Lyndon Johnson: Master of the Senate* (New York, 2002), 767; Donovan, *Eisenhower*, 390; interview with Woods E. Eastland, Jun. 24, 2010, Greenwood, MS; Sam Engelhardt to JOE, Jul. 23, 1956, S3, SS1, B37, "1957 Civil Rights" folder 2, JOE Collection; *JDN* and *NYT*, Feb. 11, 1956; John Bartlow Martin, *The Deep South Says Never* (New York, 1957), 40; Martin, *Civil Rights and Crisis of Liberalism*, 134; McMillen, *Citizens' Council*, 44–56; "Montgomery Protest," *South*, Feb. 20, 1956, 13–14; Jere Nash and Andy Taggart, *Mississippi Politics: The Struggle for Power, 1976–2006* (Jackson, 2006), 76; Jere Nash and Andy Taggart, *Mississippi Politics: The Struggle for Power, 1976–2008* (Jackson, 2008), 366; Robert Patterson to L. P. B. Lipscomb, Feb. 16, 1956, S3, SS1, B35, "1956 Civil Rights" folder, JOE Collection.

10. Atkins, *Covering for the Bosses*, 69; JOE to Frank Fair, Apr. 18, 1956, S3, SS1, B35, "1956 Civil Rights" folder 2, JOE Collection; *JDN*, Apr. 27, 1956; Erle Johnston, *I Rolled with Ross* (Baton Rouge, 1980), 27; Howard Smead, *Blood Justice: The Lynching of Mack Charles Parker* (New York, 1986), 68.

11. Connie Lynnette Cartledge, "James P. Coleman: Moderate Politician in an Age of Racial Strife, 1950–1965," M.A. thesis, Mississippi State University, 1984, 26; *JCL*, Dec. 19, 1955; Erle Johnston, *Mississippi's Defiant Years* (Forest, MS, 1990), 63; Michael Newton, *The Ku Klux Klan in Mississippi: A History* (Jefferson, NC, 2010), 109; *NYT*, Dec. 2, 1989, Jan. 30, 1990, and Jan. 20, 2001; Sarah Rowe-Sims, "The Mississippi State Sovereignty Commission: An Agency History," *JMH* 41:1 (Spring 1999), 34–37, 39, 45, 56; Charles Sallis and John Quincy Adams, "Desegregation in Jackson, Mississippi," in Elizabeth Jacoway and David R. Colburn, *Southern Businessmen and Desegregation* (Baton Rouge, 1982), 237; Calvin Trillin, "State Secrets," *New Yorker*, May 29, 1995, 54; Wallace, "Massive Resistance," 56–57; *WP*, Dec. 17, 1989.

12. *CR*, 84th Cong., 2nd Sess., 3815–3822; *JDN*, Mar. 2, 3, 1956; George Godwin Jr., *The Little Legislatures: Committees of Congress* (Amherst, MA, 1970), 121, 123; Scott Huskey, "A Policy History of the Mississippi State Sovereignty Commission," M.A. thesis, Mississippi College, 2005, 12; *MCA*, Mar. 3, 1956; *NYP*, Feb. 29, 1956; Howard E. Shuman, transcript,

oral history, Aug. 3, 1987, 147, Senate Historical Office, Washington, D.C.; *Washington Afro-American*, Mar. 10, 1956; *WP*, Mar. 3, 8, 1956; Maarten Zwiers, "James Eastland: The Shadow of Southern Democrats, 1928–1966," Ph.D. dissertation, University of Groningen, 2012, 209.

13. J. W. Anderson, *Eisenhower, Brownell, and the Congress: The Tangled Origins of the Civil Rights Bill of 1956–1957* (Tuscaloosa, 1964), 53, 63, 134; "In the News by Congressman Thomas Abernethy," Jun. 21, 1956, S1, SS18, B1, F1-3, JOE Collection; Chris Myers Asch, *The Senator and the Sharecropper: The Freedom Struggles of James O. Eastland and Fannie Lou Hamer* (New York, 2008), 156; Steven F. Lawson, *Running for Freedom: Civil Rights and Black Politics in America since 1941* (New York, 1991), 54; *NYT*, Jun. 2 and Oct. 3, 21, 1956; *WP*, Mar. 12, Apr. 25, and Aug. 5, 1956.

14. Jeremiah Bauer, "Eisenhower's Critical Contribution to the Fifth Circuit Court of Appeals," M.A. thesis, University of Nebraska–Omaha, 2010, 126; *CR*, 84th Cong., 2nd Sess., 12854–12857; *JCL* and *NYT*, Jun. 30, 1956; *JDN*, Mar. 7, 1956; David A. Nichols, *A Matter of Justice: Eisenhower and the Beginning of the Civil Rights Revolution* (New York, 2007), 87; J. W. Peltason, *Fifty-Eight Lonely Men: Southern Federal Judges and School Desegregation* (Urbana, IL, 1961), 24–25; *WP*, Apr. 19, Jun. 5, and Jul. 10, 17, 1956.

15. Robert Dallek, *Lone Star Rising: Lyndon Johnson and His Times, 1908–1960* (New York, 1991), 497–498; Mann, *Walls of Jericho*, 128–129; *NYT*, Mar. 14, 1956; *WP*, Jul. 29, 1956; Randall B. Woods, *LBJ: Architect of American Ambition* (New York, 2006), 305.

16. James P. Coleman, transcript, oral history by Orley B. Caudill, Mississippi Oral History Program of University of Southern Mississippi, 1981, 210–211; James P. Coleman, transcript, oral history by John Egerton, Sep. 5, 1990, Southern Oral History Collection, Documenting the American South Collection of the University of North Carolina; JOE to Lyndon Johnson, Aug. 11, 1956, S1, SS18, B5, F5-44, JOE Collection; JOE to Estes Kefauver, Sep. 1, 1956, S1, SS18, B6, F6-3, JOE Collection; *NYT*, Jul. 12, 14, 1956; *Washington Evening Star*, Aug. 23, 1956; *WP*, Aug. 14, 1956.

17. Robert A. Caro, *The Years of Lyndon Johnson: Master of the Senate* (New York, 2002), xv, 842–843; JOE to R. G. Morris, Jan. 17, 1957, S3, SS1, B136, "1957 Civil Rights" folder 2 of 5, JOE Collection.

18. Caro, *Master of the Senate*, 874–875; *CR*, 85th Cong., 1st Sess., 7824–7826; JOE to Harry Parker, Jun. 15, 1957, S3, SS1, B36, "1957 Civil Rights" folder 1 of 5, JOE Collection; *NYT*, Apr. 21, May 21, and Jun. 23, 1957; *WP*, Mar. 26, Apr. 9, May 21, 29, Jun. 4, 20, and Jul. 10, 1957.

19. Asch, *Senator and the Sharecropper*, 172; interview with Robert G. Baker, Aug. 13, 2013, St. Augustine, FL; Caro, *Master of the Senate*, 890–891, 897–904; *NYT*, Jun. 22, 1957; *WP*, Nov. 10, 1956, and Jun. 22, 1957.

20. *CR*, 85th Cong., 1st Sess., 11347–11357; JOE to Walter Sillers, Jul. 15, 1957, S3, SS1, B146, "1957 Supreme Court" file, JOE Collection; *NYT*, Jul. 11, 1957; *WP*, Jul. 12, 17, 1957.

21. Caro, *Master of the Senate*, 910–1012; *CR*, 85th Cong., 1st Sess., 11347–11357, 12880–12890, 16232–16237; Joseph Crespino, *Strom Thurmond's America* (New York, 2012), 118; JOE to J. A. McFadden, Aug. 15, 1957, S3, SS1, B37, "1957 Civil Rights" folder 3 of 5, and JOE to M. W. Swartz, Aug. 13, 1956, S3, SS1, B36, "1957 Civil Rights" folder 1 of 5, JOE Collection; *JCL* and *MCA*, Apr. 28, 1956; *JDN*, Aug. 2, 1957; Erle Johnston, oral history by Orley B. Caudill, Mississippi Oral History Program of University of Southern Mississippi, Jul. 30, 1980, 69; *NYT*, Aug. 31, 1957; Laura Richardson Walton, "Segregationist Spin: The Use of Public Relations by the Mississippi State Sovereignty Commission and the White Citizens Council,

1954–1963," Ph.D. dissertation, University of Southern Mississippi, 2006, 130; *WP*, Jul. 21, 30, and Aug. 29, 30, 31, 1957.

22. Wallace's side is retold in Mike Wallace with Gary Paul Gates, *Between You and Me: A Memoir* (New York, 2005), 70–72, but some details are suspect in a ghostwritten work published forty-eight years after the event.

23. Gordon A. Martin Jr., *Count Them One by One: Black Mississippians Fighting for the Right to Vote* (Jackson: 2010), 3–4; the Mike Wallace interview with JOE, Jul. 28, 1957, Harry Ransom Center, University of Texas at Austin, www.hrc.utexas.edu/collections/film/holdings/wallace/; *MCA*, Oct. 23, 1957; Wallace with Gates, *Between You and Me*, 70–72; *WP*, Apr. 11, 1956.

24. Harry Ashmore, *Hearts and Minds: A Personal Chronicle of Race in America* (Washington, D.C., 1988), 256; *CR*, 85th Cong., 2nd Sess., 8666; JOE to Mrs. J. H. O'Kelley, Oct. 11, 1957, S3, SS1, B37, "1957 Civil Rights" folder 5 of 5, JOE Collection; JOE to Mrs. A. P. Shoemaker, Sep. 30, 1957, S3, SS1, B32, "1957 Politics: Dwight Eisenhower" folder, JOE Collection; press release, containing speech on radio and television by President Eisenhower, Sep. 24, 1957, Speech Series, B22, Integration-Little Rock Ark, Eisenhower Papers; Dwight D. Eisenhower, *The White House Years: Waging Peace, 1956–1961* (Garden City, NY, 1965), 171; *JCL*, Sep. 29, 1957; *WP*, Sep. 25, 1957, and Feb. 26, Aug. 7, 12, 1958.

25. *CR*, 85th Cong., 2nd Sess., 13341–13342; *MCA*, May 11, 1958; *NYT*, Jun. 25, 1957; JOE to R. D. Davis, Nov. 11, 1957, S3, SS1, B144, "1957 Supreme Court" folder, and JOE to John Temple Graves, Mar. 4, 1958, S3, SS1, B144, "1958 Supreme Court" folder, JOE Collection; James F. Simon, *In His Own Image: The Supreme Court in Richard Nixon's America* (New York, 1973), 34; *WP*, May 2, 30, 1958; *Wayne County (MS) News*, Sep. 6, 1962; *Washington Star*, May 3, 1962.

26. Bobby Baker with Larry L. King, *Wheeling and Dealing: Confessions of a Capitol Hill Operator* (New York, 1978), 101; Roger Bell, *Last Among Equals: Hawaiian Statehood and American Politics* (Honolulu, 1984), 176; *CR*, 85th Cong., 2nd Sess., 12175–12186; *JDN*, Jun. 24, 1958; Robert B. Patterson to JOE, Jun. 16, 1958, S3, SS1, B144, "1958 Statehood: Alaska" file, JOE Collection.

27. Baker and King, *Wheeling and Dealing*, 101–102.

28. Bell, *Last Among Equals*, 133–134, 226, 247; JOE to J. S. Kimmel, Mar. 2, 1959, S3, SS1, B144, "1959 Statehood: Hawaii" file, JOE Collection; *CR*, 83rd Cong., 1st Sess., 2987, 4677, 83rd Cong., 2nd Sess., 3314–3315, 86th Cong., 1st Sess., 3869–3875; JOE to Walter R. Permenter, Jan. 14, 1954, S3, SS1, B144, "1954 Statehood: Hawaii" folder, JOE Collection; JOE to L. D. Schoonover, S3, SS1, B142, "1950 Statehood: Alaska and Hawaii" folder, JOE Collection; JOE to Walter Sillers, Mar. 25, 1953, B105, F13, Sillers Papers, Delta State University, Cleveland, MS; *JDN*, Jun. 15, 1953, Dec. 6, 1956; *WP*, Apr. 23 and Dec. 23, 1953; John S. Whitehead, *Completing the Union: Alaska, Hawai'i and the Battle for Statehood* (Albuquerque, 2004), 197, 276.

29. *CQ*, Apr. 24, 1959, 581, and May 8, 1959, 621; *CR*, 86th Cong., 1st Sess., 7452–7464; *NYT*, Apr. 2, 1958, Mar. 8, 19, Apr. 10, and May 6, 1959; Lawrence E. Walsh, *The Gift of Insecurity: A Lawyer's Life* (Chicago, 2003), 173–175; *WP*, Apr. 2, 1958, and Apr. 30, 1959.

30. *CQ*, Feb. 5, 1960, 182; *NYT* and *WP*, Jan. 30, 1960.

31. *CR*, 86th Cong., 2nd Sess., 3186–3191; Keith M. Finley, *Delaying the Dream: Southern Senators and the Fight against Civil Rights, 1938–1965* (Baton Rouge, 2008), 203–206; *MCA*, Feb. 24, 1960; *NYT*, Feb. 24 and Mar. 3, 1960; *WP*, Feb. 24, 1960.

32. Don Colburn, *James O. Eastland: Democratic Senator from Mississippi* (Washington, D.C., 1972), 15; *CR*, 86th Cong., 2nd Sess., 4008, 4020–4032; *JDN* and *WP*, Mar. 2, 1960; *NYT*, Mar. 2, 3, 1960.

33. *CR*, 86th Cong., 2nd Sess., 4572–4592, 5387–5391; Finley, *Delaying the Dream*, 218; *JDN*, Mar. 5, 1960; *NYT*, Mar. 3, 1960.

34. *CR*, 86th Cong., 2nd Sess., 6454; Finley, *Delaying the Dream*, 222; *NYT*, Mar. 20, 1960; *WP*, Mar. 25, 1960.

35. *CR*, 86th Cong., 2nd Sess., 7814; Finley, *Delaying the Dream*, 222–227; *WP*, Apr. 1, 9, 1960.

36. JOE to Elmore D. Graeves, Apr. 8, 1960, S3, SS1, B39, "1960 Civil Rights" folder 2, JOE Collection; *WP*, Apr. 9, 1960.

37. On the Eisenhower lower court judges, see Jack Bass, *Unlikely Heroes* (New York, 1981). Herbert Brownell with John P. Burke, *Advising Ike: The Memoirs of Attorney General Herbert Brownell* (Lawrence, KS, 1993), 183; Robert Fredrick Burk, *The Eisenhower Administration and Black Civil Rights* (Knoxville, 1984), 193–194; Edwin O. Guthman and Jeffrey Shulman (eds.), *Robert Kennedy in His Own Words: The Unpublished Recollections of the Kennedy Years* (New York, 1988), 77.

CHAPTER 12

1. Dewey W. Grantham, *The Life and Death of the Solid South: A Political History* (Lexington, KY, 1988), 102; *Jackson State Times*, Oct. 4, 1960; JOE to W. P. Kretschmer, S1, SS20, B3, "1960 Political" file, JOE Collection; JOE to M. W. Swartz, Sep. 7, 1960, S1, SS20, B3, "1960 Political" file, JOE Collection; *NOTP*, Jul. 17, 1960; *WP*, Oct. 17, 1960.

2. Eastland's support for Johnson reflected no enmity towards John F. Kennedy or any other contender. Indeed, he and John Stennis had helped Governor J. P. Coleman arrange for the Massachusetts senator to stay at the governor's mansion and even sleep in the bed once used by Theodore Bilbo while on a tour of Mississippi in 1957. Nick Bryant, *The Bystander: John F. Kennedy and the Struggle for Black Equality* (New York, 2006), 86.

3. Bryant, *Bystander*, 86. *CQ*, Jul. 17, 1959, 968; JOE, transcript, interview by Martha Rountree, Jun. 24, 1957, 17, S2, SS12, B1, F1-10, JOE Collection; JOE to W. P. Kretschmer, S1, SS20, B3, "1960 Political" file, JOE Collection; JOE to M. W. Swartz, Sep. 7, 1960, S1, SS20, B3, "1960 Political" file, JOE Collection; Grantham, *The Life and Death of the Solid South*, 102; *Jackson State Times*, Oct. 4, 1960; *NOTP*, Jul. 17, 1960; Thomas R. Melton, "Walter Sillers and National Politics, 1948–1964," *JMH* 39:3 (Apr. 1977), 224; *NOTP*, Jul. 17, 1960; Courtney Pace to Breck Moss, Jul. 6, 1960, S1, SS20, B3, "1960" file, JOE Collection; Stanley Posposil to JOE, Apr. 16, 1960, S3, SS1, B132, "1960 Politics" file, JOE Collection; Walter Sillers to Harry F. Byrd, Jun. 1, 1960, S3, SS1, B132, "1960 Elections" file, JOE Collection; Frank Smith, *Congressman from Mississippi: An Autobiography* (New York, 1964), 216; *WP*, Oct. 17, 1960; Maarten Zwiers, "James Eastland: The Shadow of Southern Democrats, 1928–1966," Ph.D. dissertation, University of Groningen, 2012, 259.

4. Ross R. Barnett, transcript, oral history interview by Dennis O'Brien, May 16, 1969, 8, John F. Kennedy Presidential Library, Boston, MA; James O. Eastland, transcript, oral history interview by Joe B. Frantz, Feb. 19, 1971, 9, Lyndon Baines Johnson Presidential Library, Austin, TX; W. J. Rorabaugh, *The Real Making of the President: Kennedy, Nixon, and the 1960 Election* (Lawrence, KS, 2009), 83.

5. Rorabaugh, *Real Making of the President*, 124–125; *WP*, Jul. 28 and Aug. 17, 1960.

6. Carl M. Brauer, *John F. Kennedy and the Second Reconstruction* (New York, 1977), 55; JOE and John C. Stennis, "Joint Statement," Aug. 19, 1960, S1, SS20, B3, "1960" file, JOE Collection; *JCL, JDN*, and *Jackson State Times*, Oct. 4, 1960; *JCL*, Oct. 3, 1982; Lady Bird and Lyndon Baines Johnson to JOE, S1, SS18, B5, F44, JOE Collection; David Pietrusza, *1960: LBJ vs. JFK vs. Nixon: The Epic Campaign That Forged Three Presidencies* (New York, 2008), 264–265; *WP*, Aug. 9 and Oct. 5, 1960.

7. Paul Douglas promised Illinoisans often during his 1960 campaign that he would vote, if reelected, to remove Eastland from his chairmanship. Eastland was on good terms with Douglas personally, but he took umbrage at the persistence of Douglas' pledge and felt compelled to approach him on the Senate floor. Were Douglas to continue to vow to join a move to oust him, Eastland pledged that he would travel to Chicago to endorse Douglas, a move that might serve to discredit him with some of his more liberal constituents. *CQ*, Jan. 13, 1961, 51; Alan Draper, *Conflict of Interests: Organized Labor and the Civil Rights Movement in the South, 1954–1968* (Ithaca, NY, 1994), 129–130; JOE to Felton M. Johnston, Nov. 6, 1960, JOE file, U.S. Senate Historical Office, Washington, D.C.; *JDN*, Nov. 29, 1960, and Jan. 11, 1961; interview with Herb Montgomery, Jun. 19, 2013, Oxford, MS; Rorabaugh, *Real Making of the President*, 137; http://uselectionatlas.org/RESULTS/state.php?year=1960&fip s=288f=08off=08elect=0.

8. *CR*, 87th Cong., 1st Sess., 1027–1029.

9. Telephone interview with Walter L. Nixon, Oct. 5, 2011, Biloxi, MS.

10. *CQ*, Jan. 13, 1961, 51, and Apr. 6, 1962, 548; *CR*, 87th Cong., 1st Sess., 13943–13944; Robert Dallek, *An Unfinished Life: John F. Kennedy, 1917–1963* (Boston, 2003), 494–495; JOE to John F. Kennedy, Mar. 7, 1961, S1, SS16, B1, "John F. Kennedy Administration: White House Correspondence" file, JOE Collection; JOE to Walter Sillers, Feb. 20, 1961, B105, F13, Walter Sillers Papers, Delta State University, Cleveland, MS; Burton Hersh, *Bobby and J. Edgar* (New York, 2007), 37; *JDN*, Jan. 11, 1961; Robert F. Kennedy oral history #4 by John Bartlow Martin, May 14, 1964, New York, 303–305, JFK Library; Robert F. Kennedy to JOE, Sep. 3, 1964, S1, SS17, B5, "Department of Justice: Attorney General" file, JOE Collection; Victor Navasky, *Kennedy Justice* (New York, 1971), 48; Arthur Schlesinger Jr., *A Thousand Days: John F. Kennedy in the White House* (Boston, 1967), 37; *WP*, Mar. 30, 31, 1962.

11. *Chicago Sun-Times*, Feb. 17, 1974; interview with Brad Dye, Jun. 20, 2011, Ridgeland, MS; Charles L. Fontenay, *Estes Kefauver: A Biography* (Knoxville, 1980), 384; William H. Frist and J. Lee Annis Jr., *Tennessee Senators, 1911–2001: Portraits of Leadership in a Century of Change* (Lanham, MD, 1999), 96; Joseph Paul Gorman, *Kefauver: A Political Biography* (New York, 1971), 183, 354.

12. *CQ*, Jul. 27, 1962, 1257; *CR*, 87th Cong., 2nd Sess., 10106–10111; Fontenay, *Kefauver*, 379–393; Frist and Annis, *Tennessee Senators*, 96–97; Gorman, *Kefauver*, 354, 359; *WP*, Aug. 24, 1962.

13. *CR*, 87th Cong., 1st Sess., 3067–3070, 3156–3217; Anne Emanuel, *Elbert Parr Tuttle: Chief Judge of the Civil Rights Revolution* (Athens, GA, 2011), 148; Dennis J. Hutchinson, *The Man Who Once Was Whizzer White: A Portrait of Judge Byron R. White* (New York, 1998), 288; Robert F. Kennedy to JOE, Sep. 3, 1964, S1, SS17, B5, "Department of Justice: Attorney General" file, JOE Collection; Lawrence E. Walsh, *The Gift of Insecurity: A Lawyer's Life* (Chicago, 2003), 176.

14. The oft-told tale that Eastland and Cox were college roommates is not true. Cox was older than Eastland and was in law school while Eastland had just begun matriculating at Ole Miss. Chris Myers Asch, *The Senator and the Sharecropper: The Freedom Struggles of*

James O. Eastland and Fannie Lou Hamer (New York, 2008), 269; Jack Bass, *Unlikely Heroes* (New York, 1981), 152, 164; Emanuel, *Tuttle*, 231; Hutchinson, *Man Who Once Was Whizzer White*, 291.

15. Bass, *Unlikely Heroes*, 164–165; Nick Bryant, *Bystander*, 286; Hutchinson, *Man Who Once Was Whizzer White*, 291–292; Erle Johnston, *Mississippi's Defiant Years, 1953–1973: An Interpretive Documentary with Personal Experiences* (Forest, MS, 1990), 280–281; Gordon A. Martin Jr., *Count Them One by One: Black Mississippians Fighting for the Right to Vote* (Jackson, MS, 2010), 54–57; Frank R. Parker, *Black Votes Count: Political Empowerment in Mississippi after 1865* (Chapel Hill, NC, 1990), 84.

16. Lucas A. Powe, *The Warren Court and American Politics* (Cambridge, MA, 2000), 290; interview with Curtis Wilkie, Jan. 12, 2010, Oxford, MS; Juan Williams, *Thurgood Marshall: American Revolutionary* (New York, 1998), 299.

17. Michael D. Davis and Hunter R. Clark, *Thurgood Marshall: Warriors at the Bar, Rebel on the Bench* (New York, 1992), 234; Nicholas Katzenbach, *Some of It Was Fun: Working with RFK and LBJ* (New York, 2008), 88.

18. John A. Carroll, Thomas J. Dodd, Philip A. Hart, and Edward V. Long to JOE, Aug. 23, 1962, S3, SS1, B158, "1962 Eastland Addresses" file, JOE Collection; JOE to Robert H. Garrison, Sep. 20, 1962, S3, SS1, B58, "1962 Eastland Addresses" file, JOE Collection; Mark Tushnet (ed.), *Thurgood Marshall: His Speeches, Writings, Argument, Opinions, and Reminiscences* (Chicago, 2001), 485–486; *WP*, Sep. 12, 1962; Williams, *Marshall*, 299–303; David Alastair Yalof, *Pursuit of Justices: Presidential Politics and the Selection of Supreme Court Justices* (Chicago, 1999), 78.

19. Bryant, *Bystander*, 136; *CR*, 87th Cong., 2nd Sess., 4199–4200, 4202, 4209, 4246, 4364–4377, 4408–4410, 4511–4512, 4559–4568, 4660, 4937–4955; telephone interview with Nicholas Katzenbach, Apr. 11, 2011, Princeton, NJ; memo, Mike Manatos to Laurence F. O'Brien, May 23, 1961, James O. Eastland Name File, John F. Kennedy Library, Boston, MA; *NYT*, Jun. 4, 2003.

20. Raymond Arsenault, *Freedom Riders: 1961 and the Struggle for Racial Justice* (New York, 2006), 140–225, 280–281, 346–348; interview with W. Hodding Carter III, May 17, 2011, Chapel Hill, NC; JOE to Herbert O. Murdaugh, S3, SS1, B39, "1961 Civil Rights" file, JOE Collection.

21. Arsenault, *Freedom Riders*, 28–29, 256–257, 276–280, 316–317, 325–327, 348–365; Catherine Barnes, *A Journey from Jim Crow* (New York, 1984), 184–185; John Dittmer, *Local People: The Struggle for Civil Rights in Mississippi* (Champaign, IL, 1995), 93; Edwin O. Guthman and Jeffrey Shulman (eds.), *Robert Kennedy in His Own Words* (New York, 1988), 96–97; Wesley C. Hogan, *Many Minds, One Heart: SNCC's Dream for a New America* (Chapel Hill, NC, 2007), 49, 313; Robert F. Kennedy and Burke Marshall, oral history #5 by Anthony Lewis, McLean, VA, 386–388, JFK Library; G. V. Sonny Montgomery with Michael B. Ballard and Craig S. Piper, *G. V. "Sonny" Montgomery: The Veterans Champion* (Jackson, MS, 2003), 38–43; *NYP*, May 28, 1961; *NYT*, May 26, 1961; *Scott County Times*, Feb. 26, 1986; Harris Wofford, *Of Kennedys and Kings* (New York, 1980), 155; telephone interviews with John Herbers, Mar. 25, 2011, Bethesda, MD, John Seigenthaler, Feb. 24, 2014, Nashville, TN, and Kathleen Kennedy Townsend, Jul. 12, 2013, Washington, D.C.; *WP*, May 29, 1961.

22. Bill Minor, *Eyes on Mississippi: A Fifty-Year Chronicle of Change* (Jackson, MS, 2001), 30.

23. Thomas G. Abernathy, Jamie L. Whitten, W. Arthur Winstead, John Bell Williams, William M. Colmer, JOE, and John C. Stennis to John F. Kennedy, Sep. 28, 1962, S1, SS16, B1,

JOE Collection; *CR*, 87th Cong., 2nd Sess., 20804–20806, 21033; William Doyle, *An American Insurrection: The Battle of Oxford, Mississippi, 1962* (New York, 2001), 76–77; Robert F. Kennedy, "Desk Diary: 1962," entries for Sep. 28, 29, 1962, Robert F. Kennedy Attorney General Papers, JFK Library; telephone interview with Sue Eastland McRoberts, Jan. 12, 2012, Jackson, MS; *WP*, Sep. 27, 1962.

24. There are several first-rate accounts of the battle of Oxford. Among the best are Nadine Cohodas, *The Band Played Dixie: Race and the Liberal Conscience at Ole Miss* (New York, 1997); William Doyle, *An American Insurrection: The Battle of Oxford, Mississippi* (New York, 2001); Charles W. Eagles, *The Price of Defiance: James Meredith and the Integration of Ole Miss* (Chapel Hill, 2009); Yasuhiro Katagiri, *The Mississippi State Sovereignty Commission: Civil Rights and States' Rights* (Jackson, MS, 2001), 95–139; Nicholas Katzenbach, *Some of It Was Fun: Working with RFK and LBJ* (New York, 2008), 70–84; and Frank Lambert, *The Battle of Ole Miss: Civil Rights v. States Rights* (New York, 2010); See also George B. Leonard, T. George Harris, and Christopher S. Wren, "How a Secret Deal Prevented a Massacre at Ole Miss," *Look*, Dec. 31, 1962, 20.

25. Leonard et al., "Secret Deal," 20; Arthur M. Schlesinger Jr., *Robert Kennedy and His Times* (Boston, 1978), 319; unsigned four-page memorandum of Sep. 30, 1962 in "Subject File: Correspondence Regarding Enrollment of James Meredith at Ole Miss," John Bell Williams Papers, S2416, B10391, Mississippi Department of Archives and History, Jackson; Sandra Stringer Vance, "The Congressional Career of John Bell Williams, 1947–1967," Ph.D. dissertation, Mississippi State University, 1976, 217–220.

26. Leonard et al., "Secret Deal," 20; Arthur M. Schlesinger Jr., *Robert Kennedy and His Times* (Boston, 1978), 319; unsigned four-page memorandum of Sep. 30, 1962 in "Subject File: Correspondence Regarding Enrollment of James Meredith at Ole Miss," John Bell Williams Papers, S2416, B10391, Mississippi Department of Archives and History, Jackson; Sandra Stringer Vance, "The Congressional Career of John Bell Williams, 1947–1967," Ph.D. dissertation, Mississippi State University, 1976, 217–220. See also *Fayette (MS) Chronicle*, Mar. 11, 1965; Leonard et al., "Secret Deal," 29; J. D. Williams, "Another Mississippi Story," document in John C. Satterfield Papers, B34, F201.2 (Meredith Case), Volume 2, Special Collections, J. D. Mitchell Library, University of Mississippi.

27. Dye interview; John Holloman, tape, oral history by Jere Nash, Apr. 7, 2005, Nash and Taggart Collection, Special Collections, J. D. Williams Library, University of Mississippi; Katagiri, *Mississippi State Sovereignty Commission*, 105.

28. David G. Sansing, *Making Haste Slowly: The Troubled History of Higher Education in Mississippi* (Jackson, 1990), 188.

29. Katzenbach, *Some of It Was Fun*, 81; McRoberts interview.

30. Dye interview; Holloman oral history; Steve Patterson, tape, oral history by Jere Nash, May 11, 2004, Nash and Taggart Collection, Special Collections, J. D. Williams Library, University of Mississippi; Bill Spell, tape, oral history by Jere Nash, Sep. 16, 2004, Nash and Taggart Collection, Special Collections, J. D. Williams Library, University of Mississippi; Curtis Wilkie, *Dixie: A Personal Odyssey Through Events that Shaped the Modern South* (New York, 2001), 130.

31. Eastland would also quietly raise funds for GOP friends, if they were wrapped up in tight contests. One 1962 beneficiary of the generosity of Eastland friends like textile magnate Roger Milliken was Milton Young of North Dakota, a regular Eastland ally on agricultural issues. Virginia Van der Veer Hamilton, *Lister Hill: Statesman from the South* (Chapel Hill, 1987), 253; Luther Ingalls to JOE, Oct. 22, 1962, S1, SS18, B5, F5-12, JOE Collection;

Wallace Malone to JOE, Oct. 22, 1962, S1, SS18, B5, F5-12, JOE Collection; Roger Milliken to Milton Young, Nov. 1, 1962, S1, SS18, B10, F10-56, JOE Collection; George W. Polhemus to JOE, Oct. 16, 1962, S1, SS18, B5, F5-12, JOE Collection; Robert M. Shelton to JOE, Oct. 18, 1962, S1, SS18, B5, F5-12, JOE Collection; WP, Nov. 8, 1962.

32. Hodding Carter interview; interview with James Flug, Oct. 18, 2011, Washington, D.C.; telephone interview with Mark G. Hazard Jr., Apr. 28, 2013, West Point, MS; Edward M. Kennedy, *True Compass: A Memoir* (New York, 2009), 191–195: Roy L. McGhee, transcript, oral history by Donald A. Ritchie, Feb. 26–28, 1992, 94, Harry S. Truman Presidential Library, Independence, MO.

33. Kennedy, *True Compass*, 194.

34. Adam Clymer, *Edward M. Kennedy: A Biography* (New York, 1999), 46–47; Kennedy, *True Compass*, 194–195.

35. Bobby Baker with Larry L. King, *Wheeling and Dealing: Confessions of a Capitol Hill Operator* (New York, 1978), 101; Clymer, *Kennedy*, 46–47.

36. James McGregor Burns, *Edward Kennedy and the Camelot Legacy* (New York, 1976), 130; Clymer, *Kennedy*, 70; *CR*, 89th Cong., 1st Sess., 24544–24554; telephone interview with Rufus Edmisten, Mar. 13, 2012, Raleigh, NC; WP, Feb. 8, 1965.

37. Bass, *Unlikely Heroes*, 146; Jack Bass and Marilyn W. Thompson, *Strom: The Complicated Personal and Political Life of Strom Thurmond* (New York, 2005), 186; *CR*, 88th Cong., 1st Sess., 24127.

CHAPTER 13

1. Thomas Borstelmann, *The Cold War and the Color Line: American Race Relations in the Global Arena* (Cambridge, MA, 2001), 176; Hiram Eastland Jr., e-mail to author, Sep. 12, 2012; interviews with Woods Eastland, Jun. 18, 2011, Jackson, MS, and Herb Montgomery, Jun. 12, 2013, Oxford, MS; Lyndon Baines Johnson to JOE, Nov. 22, 1972, "LBJ, Post-Presidential Correspondence" file, S1, SS16, B1, JOE Collection.

2. Robert A. Caro, *The Years of Lyndon Johnson: The Passage of Power* (New York, 2012), 440; telephone conversation between President Johnson and James Eastland, Nov. 28, 1963, 3:21 PM, K6311.04 PNO 2, Lyndon Baines Johnson Library; telephone conversation between President Johnson and James Eastland, Nov. 29, 1963, 7:03 PM, K6311.04 PNO 3, Lyndon Baines Johnson Library; WP, Nov. 26, 30, and Dec. 5, 1963.

3. *CQ*, Mar. 6, 1964, 457, Mar. 13, 1964, 467; JOE to J. F. Barbour, Feb. 25, 1964, S3, SS1, B43, "1964 Civil Rights" folder 1 of 6, JOE Collection; *Hearings before the Committee on the Judiciary, United States Senate*, 89th Cong., 1st Sess., *Nomination of Abe Fortas of Tennessee to Be an Associate Justice of the Supreme Court of the United States*, 11; Laura Kalman, *Abe Fortas: A Biography* (New Haven, 1990), 248; MPS, Mar. 3, 1964; WP, Feb. 29, 1964.

4. Edward D. Berkowitz, "The Great Society," in Julian E. Zelizer (ed.), *The American Congress: The Building of Democracy* (Boston, 2004), 580; *CQ*, Dec. 19, 1963, 1542–1543; *CR*, 87th Cong., 1st Sess., 8970–8983; John Holloman, tape, oral history by Jere Nash, Apr. 7, 2005, Nash and Taggart Collection, Special Collections, J. D. Williams Library, University of Mississippi; MCA, May 26, 1961; Courtney C. Pace to Walter Jenkins, Dec. 19, 1963, S1, SS16, B1, "Lyndon Baines Johnson Administration: White House Correspondence" file, JOE Collection.

5. *CQ*, Jun. 21, 1963, 1000, Aug. 9, 1964, 1404; JOE to Roy D. Barnett, Jun. 3, 1963, S3, SS1, B41, "1963 Civil Rights" file (1 of 8), JOE Collection; JOE to Horace Evans, Jun. 21, 1963, S3,

SS1, B41, "1963 Civil Rights" file (1 of 8), JOE Collection; Robert D. Loevy, *To End All Segregation: The Politics of the Passage of the Civil Rights Act of 1964* (Lanham, MD, 1990), 43–47; *WP*, Aug. 1, 9, and Sep. 23, 1963.

6. Francis R. Valeo, transcript, oral history, Sep. 18, 1985, 311–313, Senate Historical Office, Washington, D.C.; Charles and Barbara Whalen, *The Longest Debate: A Legislative History of the 1964 Civil Rights Act* (Cabin John, MD, 1989), 133.

7. Sarah H. Brown, "The Role of Elite Leadership in the Southern Defense of Segregation," *Journal of Southern History* 77:4 (Nov. 2011), 851; *NYT*, Aug. 3, 1986; Sally Russell, *Richard Brevard Russell Jr.: A Life of Consequence* (Macon, GA, 2011), 232.

8. Interview with Hiram Eastland Jr., Jun. 22, 2012, Greenwood, MS; JOE to Mr. and Mrs. John Cain, Feb. 17, 1964, S3, SS1, B43, "1964 Civil Rights" folder, JOE Collection; JOE to M. E. Richardson, Jul. 22, 1968, S3, SS1, B45, "1968 Civil Rights" folder, JOE Collection.

9. *CR*, 88th Cong., 2nd Sess., 5587, 7265; C. Alexander Heard, "Notes on Interview of Hodding Carter Jr.," Nov. 4, 1947, B9, "Jul. 3, 1947 to Nov. 4, 1947" folder, Southern Politics Collection, Jean and Alexander Heard Library, Vanderbilt University, Nashville, TN; Hubert H. Humphrey, *The Education of a Public Man: My Life and Politics* (Garden City, NY, 1976), 272–287.

10. *CR*, 88th Cong., 2nd Sess., 3710–3712, 3830, 5857–5874; telephone interviews with Rufus Edmisten, Mar. 13, 2012, Raleigh, NC, and Roger Mudd, Sep. 7, 2012, McLean, VA; Robert Mann, *The Walls of Jericho: Lyndon Johnson, Hubert Humphrey, Richard Russell, and the Struggle for Civil Rights* (New York, 1996), 400–404; *WP*, Mar. 22, 1964.

11. *CR*, 88th Cong., 2nd Sess., 8346–8365, 8703–8750, 9650–9654, 9905, 11081, 11097; *WP*, Apr. 19 and Aug. 5, 1964.

12. *CQ*, Jun. 19, 1964, 1200; *CR*, 88th Cong., 2nd Sess., 5864, 8707, 9644, 14229; JOE to Mary W. Caraway, Jun. 12, 1964, S3, SS1, B43, "1964 Civil Rights" folder, JOE Collection; Neil MacNeil, *Dirksen: Portrait of a Public Man* (New York, 1970), 235; *WP*, Jun. 11, 1964.

13. The two young men, Charlie Eddie Moore and Harry Hezekiah Dee, were eventually found murdered. Klansman James Ford Seale was convicted forty-three years later for one count of conspiring to kidnap the two men and two more for the kidnapping itself. For a very able recent treatment of the Mississippi Klan, see David Cunningham, "Shades of Anti-Civil Rights Violence," in Ted Ownby (ed.), *The Civil Rights Movement in Mississippi* (Jackson, 2013), 180–207; Sally Belfrage, *Freedom Summer* (Charlottesville, 1965), 9; Michael Beschloss, *Taking Charge: The Johnson White House Tapes, 1963–1964* (New York, 1997), 432–433; Taylor Branch, *Pillar of Fire: America in the King Years* (New York, 1998), 366; Reid Stoner Derr, "The Triumph of Progressivism: Governor Paul B. Johnson and Mississippi in the 1960s," Ph.D. dissertation, University of Southern Mississippi, 1994, 366–367; Nick Kotz, *Judgment Days: Lyndon Baines Johnson, Martin Luther King Jr. and the Laws that Changed America* (Boston, 2005), 157–172; Michael Newton, *The Ku Klux Klan in Mississippi* (Jefferson, NC, 2010), 135–141.

14. Branch, *Pillar of Fire*, 367; Newton, *KKK in Mississippi*, 140–141.

15. Derr, "Triumph of Progressivism," 170–171; telephone interviews with Charles E. Cobb Jr., Feb. 16, 2015, Durham, NC, and Patrick H. "Pete" Johnson, Feb. 22, 2013, Clarksdale, MS; Jenny Irons, *Reconstituting Whiteness: The Mississippi State Sovereignty Commission* (Nashville, 2010), 171; *JCL*, Mar. 7, 1965; Erle Johnston, transcript, oral history by Yazohiro Kataguri, Aug. 13, 1993, Mississippi Oral History Program of the University of Southern Mississippi, 10; Rev. Ed King and Trent Watts, *Ed King's Mississippi: Behind the Scenes of Freedom Summer* (Jackson, MS, 2014), Kotz, *Judgment Days*, 188–222; *Los Angeles Times*,

Apr. 3, 2005; Gordon A. Martin Jr., *Count Them One by One: Black Mississippians Fighting for the Right to Vote* (Jackson, MS, 2010), 215; Newton, *KKK in Mississippi*, 141, 148; Sarah Rowe-Sims, "The Mississippi State Sovereignty Commission: An Agency History," *JMH* 61:1 (Spring 1999), 46–47; *WP*, Jan. 31, 1965; Don Whitehead, *Attack on Terror: The FBI against the Ku Klux Klan in Mississippi* (New York, 1970), 71, 79, 94, 101.

16. Belfrage, *Freedom Summer*, 120; Charles C. Bolton, *The Hardest Deal of All: The Battle Over School Integration in Mississippi, 1879–1980* (Jackson, MS, 2009), 122; Hodding Carter III, transcript, oral history, Apr. 11, 1974, Bass-DeVries Collection, Southern Oral History Collection, University of North Carolina, Chapel Hill; *CR*, 90th Cong., 2nd Sess., 21521–21522; Derr, "Triumph of Progressivism," 318; John Dittmer, "The Transformation of the Mississippi Movement, 1964–1968: The Rise and Fall of the Freedom Democratic Party" in W. Martin Dulaney and Kathleen Underwood (eds.), *Essays on the American Civil Rights Movement* (College Station, TX, 1993), 12; Robert Mann, *When Freedom Would Triumph: The Civil Rights Struggles in Congress, 1954–1968* (Baton Rouge, 2007), 219.

17. *CR*, 88th Cong., 2nd Sess., 16593; 89th Cong., 1st Sess., 1943–1953, 5443–5452, 9138–9141, 89th Cong., 2nd Sess., 655–656, 9638–9640; House Un-American Activities Committee to JOE, Dec. 18, 1964, and John Sparkman to JOE, Feb. 18, 1965, SISS files, B220, "Martin Luther King Jr.: 1967" file, National Archives, Washington, D.C.; *JCL*, Jan. 28, 1990; Courtney Pace to Golden R. Lawrence, Oct. 26, 1961, S4, SS Internal Security Subcommittee, B3, "Status Requests, 1961," JOE Collection; *NYT*, Aug. 28, 1961, Jul. 23, and Aug. 1, 1964; Courtney Pace to Alex McKeignay, Mar. 12, 1965, S3, SS1, B44, "1965 Civil Rights" folder 1, JOE Collection; M. B. Pierce to JOE, Jun. 6, 1961, S4, SS Internal Security Subcommittee, B16, "Communism: Civil Rights" folder, JOE Collection; Arthur M. Schlesinger Jr., *Robert Kennedy and His Times* (Boston, 1978), 354–356.

18. Lyndon Johnson, James Eastland, and Robert McNamara in the Oval Office, conversation on Aug. 17, 1964, WH 6408-26-4992, 4993, David G. Coleman, Kent B. Germany, Guian A. McKee, and Marc T. Selverstone (eds.), *Presidential Recordings of Lyndon Baines Johnson*, digital ed. (Charlottesville, VA, 2010); Kotz, *Judgment Days*, 189–212.

19. Lyndon Johnson, James Eastland, and Robert McNamara in the Oval Office, conversation on Aug. 17, 1964, WH 6408-26-4992, 4993, David G. Coleman, Kent B. Germany, Guian A. McKee, and Marc T. Selverstone (eds.), *Presidential Recordings of Lyndon Baines Johnson*, digital ed. (Charlottesville, VA, 2010); Johnson and Eastland, conversations on Aug. 22, 1964, WH 6408-33-5121, 5122, WH 6408-33-5131, WH 6408-32-5117, WH 6408-33-5130; conversations of Aug. 23, 1964, 6408-33-5134, WH 6408-34-5138, WH 6408-33-5133; conversation of Aug. 25, 1964, WH 6408-38-5193; Johnson and Douglas Wynn, conversation of Aug. 25, 1964, 6408-38-5209; Kotz, *Judgment Days*, 209.

20. H. W. Brawley to JOE, Oct. 14, 1964, S1, SS20, B3, "1964" file, JOE Collection; interview with David Lambert, Aug. 13, 2012, Alexandria, VA; Bill Minor, *Eyes on Mississippi: A Fifty-Year Chronicle of Change* (Jackson, MS, 2001), 32; *NYT*, Oct. 9, 1964.

21. Jack Bass, *Unlikely Heroes* (New York, 1981), 147; Nicholas Katzenbach, *Some of It Was Fun: Working with RFK and LBJ* (New York, 2008), 159; Chip Mabry, "Bobby Kennedy's Trip to the Delta," *Delta*, Jul. 8, 2004, 122–123.

22. Taylor Branch, *At Canaan's Edge: America in the King Years, 1965–1968* (New York, 1968), 121; Neil MacNeil, *Dirksen: Portrait of a Public Man* (New York, 1970), 254.

23. *CQ*, Mar. 19, 1965, 435; *CR*, 89th Cong., 1st Sess., 5388; *JCL*, Mar. 17, 1965; Robert Mann, *When Freedom Would Triumph: The Civil Rights Struggle in Congress, 1954–1968* (Baton Rouge, 2007), 238; *WP*, Mar. 16, 19, 1965.

24. Katzenbach, *Some of It Was Fun*, 171; *U.S. Senate Judiciary Committee on the Judiciary, Voting Rights Hearings*, 89th Cong., 1st Sess., S1564 to Enforce the 15th Amendment to the Constitution of the United States, Part 1, 116–117.

25. *CR*, 89th Cong., 1st Sess., 5388, 5871, 9240, 9830–9832, 10028–10032, 10357–10359, 10849–10864, 11739–11740; *MCA*, Mar. 19, 1965, *Senate Judiciary Committee Voting Rights Act Hearings*, 543.

26. Joseph Crespino, "Strategic Accommodation: Civil Rights Opponents in Mississippi and Their Impact on American Racial Politics, 1953–1972," Ph.D. dissertation, Stanford University, 2002, 48; *JCL*, Jun. 21, 1965; *NYT*, May 13 and Jun. 19, 1965; *WP*, Jun. 29 and Jul. 11, 1965.

27. *CQ*, Jul. 9, 1965, 1326, Jul. 16, 1965, 1379–1380; *JCL*, Jun. 18, 19, and Jul. 13, 1965; *WP*, Jun. 30 and Jul. 11, 13, 14, 21, 27, 1965.

28. Jack Bass, *Unlikely Heroes* (New York, 1981), 147; Derr, "Triumph of Progressivism," 480, 489; Nicholas Katzenbach to JOE, Sep. 7, 1965, S1, SS17, B5, "Department of Justice: Attorney General 1960s" file, JOE Collection; Katzenbach, *Some of It Was Fun*, 174; J. Todd Moye, *Let The People Decide: Black Freedom and White Resistance Movements in Sunflower County, Mississippi* (Chapel Hill, NC, 2004), 159; *WP*, Apr. 9, 17, 1966.

29. Chris Myers Asch, *The Senator and the Sharecropper: The Freedom Struggles of James O. Eastland and Fannie Lou Hamer* (New York, 2008), 243–246; David C. Carter, *The Music Has Gone out of the Movement: Civil Rights and the Johnson Administration, 1965–1968* (Chapel Hill, 2009), 36; *CQ*, Mar. 18, 1966, 616; *CR*, 89th Cong., 2nd Sess., 3895–3896, 16563; Joseph Crespino, *In Search of Another Country: Mississippi and the Conservative Counterrevolution* (Princeton, NJ, 2007), 135–136; telephone interview with Kenneth L. Dean, Dec. 12, 2012, Carrolton, GA; John Dittmer, "The Politics of the Mississippi Movement, 1954–1964," in David L. Lewis (ed.), *The Civil Rights Movement in America* (Jackson: 1986), 22–37; *JDN*, Jul. 21, 1966; *MCA*, Aug. 23, 1966; Scott Stossel, *Sarge: The Life and Times of R. Sargent Shriver* (Washington, 2004), 463; *WP*, Jun. 29, 1966; *Winona Times*, May 19, 1966; Maarten Zwiers, "James Eastland: The Shadow of Southern Democrats, 1928–1966," Ph.D. dissertation, University of Groningen, 2012, 318.

30. *Nashville Banner*, Jul. 16, 1966; *New York Herald Tribune*, Apr. 17, 1966; Prentiss Walker, oral history by Orley B. Caudill, Jul. 21, 1976, Mississippi Oral History Program of the University of Southern Mississippi, 31–32; Wirt Yerger, oral history by Jere B. Nash, Jul. 21, 2004, Nash-Taggart Collection, Special Collections, J. D. Mitchell Library, University of Mississippi.

31. The Klan was split on their choice for the Senate. Sam Bowers, the chief of the White Knights of the Ku Klux Klan who was later convicted for both violating the civil rights of Schwerner, Goodman, and Chaney and for the fatal firebombing of the Hattiesburg home of civil rights leader Vernon Dahmer, cast his vote for Eastland in the belief that the Republican Party was "ruled by the Jews," while others thought Bowers had gone soft and sided with Walker. John Drabble, "The FBI, COINTELPRO: White Hate, and the Decline of the Ku Klux Klan Organizations in Mississippi, 1964–1971," *Journal of Mississippi History* 66:4 (Winter 2004), 378.

32. Chris Danielson, *After Freedom Summer: How Race Realigned Mississippi Politics, 1965–1986* (New York, 2011), 23; *DDT*, Sep. 6, 1966; Elivin Livingston to Courtney Pace, S1, SS19, B24, F24-10, JOE Collection; *MCA*, Nov. 15, 1965, and Feb. 8, 1966; Douglas Patrick Munro, "The Nationalization of Southern Politics: Southern Democratic Senators from Eisenhower to Bush," Ph.D. dissertation, Johns Hopkins University, 1992, 605; Walker

University of Southern Mississippi Oral History, 71; *NYT*, Feb. 18, 1966; *WP*, Mar. 19, 1966; telephone interview with Wirt Yerger Jr., May 15, 2012, Jackson, MS.

33. Jack Hatcher to Jimmy Walker, Oct. 11, 1966, S1, SS19, B26, F26-10, JOE Collection; *Laurel Leader Call*, Oct. 8, 1966; *MCA*, Sep. 28, 1966.

34. *DDT*, Dec. 17, 1978; Michael O'Brien, *Philip Hart: The Conscience of the Senate* (East Lansing, MI, 1995), 153.

35. *DDT*, Oct. 14, 1966; Erle Johnston, *Politics Mississippi Style* (Forest, MS, 1993), 188; *Laurel Leader Call*, Oct. 21, 1966; Supplement to *Scott County Times*, Sep. 28, 1966; *WP*, Oct. 20, 1966.

36. *CQ*, Oct. 6, 1966, 236; *JCL*, Oct. 1, 1966; *MCA*, Sep. 30, 1966; "Prentiss Walker Spurns His District," undated document in S1, S18, B10, F10-21, JOE Collection; *Tupelo Daily Journal*, Oct. 5, 1966.

37. Numan M. Bartley and Hugh D. Graham, *Southern Politics and the Second Reconstruction* (Baltimore, 1975), 123; *CQ*, Oct. 6, 1966, 2361; *DDT*, Nov. 2, 1966; *MCA*, Oct. 25, 1966; *MPS*, Oct. 6 and 25, 1966; *Meridian Star* and *NOTP*, Oct. 7, 1966; *Natchez Democrat*, Sep. 30, 1966; Walker University of Southern Mississippi Oral History, 35.

38. *CQ*, Oct. 6, 1966, 2361; JOE to Woodrow McRaney, Aug. 3, 1966, S1, SS19, B23, F23-16, JOE Collection; *JDN*, Oct. 8, 1966; *New York Herald Tribune*, Apr. 7, 1966.

39. Interview with Woods Eastland, Jun. 11, 2012, Doddsville, MS; *JDN*, Oct. 25, 1966; *Leland Progress*, Oct. 27, 1966.

40. *CQ*, Nov. 11, 1966, 2786, May 12, 1967, 757; interview with Hiram Eastland Jr. and Steve Patterson, Jun. 22, 2012, Greenwood, MS; telephone interview with Bill Minor, Apr. 20, 2011, Jackson, MS; *WP*, Nov. 9, 1966.

41. *CQ*, May 5, 1967, 704, Jul. 28, 1967, 1305; *CR*, 90th Cong., 1st Sess., 11016, 24640–24643; JOE to Homer E. Capehart, Dec. 5, 1966, S1, SS19, B27, F27-1, JOE Collection; JOE to W. R. Chisum, S3, SS1, B145, "1967 Supreme Court" File, JOE Collection; *JDN*, May 23, 1969; Neil D. McFeeley, *Appointment of Judges: The Johnson Presidency* (Austin, 1987), 113; *NYT*, Jul. 30, 1967, Jul. 1 and 8, 1969; Lucas A. Powe, *The Warren Court and American Politics* (Cambridge, MA, 2000), 292; *WP*, Jul. 15 and 20 and Aug. 31, 1967; Juan Williams, *Thurgood Marshall: American Revolutionary* (New York, 1998), 336.

42. Asch, *Senator and Sharecropper*, 182, 227; JOE to Margaret Norman, May 8, 1972, S1, SS19, B32, F32-8; *Grenada Daily Sentinel*, Apr. 20, 1972; *NYT*, Jun. 29, 1959; *WP*, Oct. 19, 1963, and Jul. 15, 1971.

43. *CQ*, Jul. 21, 1967, 1233; JOE to Harold R. Regier, Jun. 13, 1968, S3, SS1, B45, "1968 Civil Rights" Folder," JOE Collection; interview with Peter Edelman, Sep. 3, 2013, Washington, D.C.; Peter Edelman, *Searching for America: RFK and the Renewal of Hope* (Washington, 2003), 49–55; *WP*, Jul. 12, 1967; Curtis Wilkie, *Dixie: A Personal Odyssey through Events That Shaped the Modern South* (New York, 2001), 168–169.

44. Hiram Eastland Jr. interview.

45. *CQ*, Sep. 16, 1966, 2141; *CR*, 89th Cong., 2nd Sess., 13553–13557, 19768–19769, 21822, 21853, 22727–22738, 22792–22807, 90th Cong., 2nd Sess., 1027–1033, 4295–4298; JOE to Charles Morelan, Mar. 11, 1968, S3, SS1, B45, "1968 Civil Rights" File, JOE Collection; *JCL*, Jan. 23, 1968; *JDN*, Aug. 16 and 17 and Sep. 7, 1966; MacNeil, *Dirksen*, 284–287, 320–328; *New York Herald Tribune*, Apr. 17, 1966; *WP*, Aug. 26, 1967.

46. Telephone interview with James Biglane, Jan. 31, 2013; Brad Dye, transcript, oral history by Jere B. Nash, Dec. 21, 2004, Nash-Taggart Collection, Special Collections, J.D. Mitchell Library, University of Mississippi; Lady Bird Johnson, *A White House Diary*

(Austin, 1970), 701–702; Otha Shurden as told to Wilbur Jones, *Cotton: Always King with Me* (Drew, MS, 1985), 28–32, 43.

47. Joseph A. Califano Jr., *The Tragedy of Lyndon Johnson: The White House Years* (New York, 1991), 309; Lyndon Baines Johnson, *The Vantage Point: Perspectives of the Presidency, 1963–1969* (New York, 1971), 546–547; Kalman, *Fortas*, 327, 333; Neil D. McFeeley, *Appointment of Judges: The Johnson Presidency* (Austin, 1987), 127; telephone interview with Walter L. Nixon Jr., Oct. 5, 2011, Biloxi, MS; transcript, oral history, James O. Eastland Personal File, Feb. 19, 1971, 18, Lyndon Baines Johnson Presidential Library, Austin, TX; Nick Walters, "The Repairman Chairman: Senator James O. Eastland and His Influence on the U.S. Supreme Court," M.A. thesis, 1992, Mississippi College, 22–23.

48. Interview with James W. Ziglar, Dec. 13, 2011, Washington, D.C.

49. *NYT* and *WP*, Jul. 13 and 14, 1968; Ziglar interview.

50. Ziglar interview.

51. Bruce Alan Murphy, *Fortas: The Rise and Ruin of a Supreme Court Justice* (New York, 1988), 448; Larry Speakes with Robert Pack, *Speaking Out: Inside the Reagan White House* (New York, 1988), 33.

52. *CQ*, Jul. 19, 1968, 1834; JOE to W. R. Johnson, Oct. 15, 1968, S3, SS1, B122, "1968 Media: Pornography" File, JOE Collection; *JCL*, Sep. 26, 1968; Kalman, *Fortas*, 329–356; *Laurel Leader-Call*, Sep. 17, 1968; *MCA*, Sep. 15, 1968; Murphy, *Fortas*, 270–526; *WP*, Sep. 18 and 22, 1968.

53. *CR*, 80th Cong., 1st Sess., 3840; interview with Woods Eastland, Jun. 24, 2010, Greenwood, MS; John Holloman, transcript, oral history by Jere B. Nash, Apr. 7, 2005, Nash-Taggart Collection, Special Collections, J.D. Mitchell Library, University of Mississippi; Doris Kearns, *Lyndon Johnson and the American Dream* (New York, 1976), 367; *MCA*, Oct. 23, 1968; *NOTP*, Jun. 8, 1969.

54. Burns, *Edward Kennedy*, 156.

CHAPTER 14

1. *CR*, 96th Cong., 2nd Sess., 37975; JOE, "The Senate Judiciary Committee," *The Oxford Lawyer* 2:2 (Michaelmas, 1959), 15; Courtney C. Pace to A. S. Coody, Sep. 11, 1959, B83, Archibald S. Coody Papers, Mississippi Department of Archives and History, Jackson; interview with Joseph D. Tydings, Feb. 28, 2011, Washington, D.C.; *WP*, Mar. 27, 1978.

2. Interview with Ben Dixon, Nov. 14, 2012, Washington, D.C.; telephone interviews with Rufus Edmisten, Mar. 13, 2012, Raleigh, NC, and Ernest F. Hollings, Aug. 23, 2011, Charleston, SC.

3. Richard Kleindienst, *Justice: The Memoirs of Attorney General Richard Kleindienst* (Ottawa, IL, 1985), 133; Elliott Richardson, *The Creative Balance: Government, Politics and the Individual in America's Third Century* (New York, 1976), 32.

4. Gerald R. Ford, *A Time to Heal: The Autobiography of Gerald Ford* (New York, 1979), 236–237; *JDN*, Dec. 13, 19, 1974; *NYT*, Jan. 15, 28, 30, and Feb. 6, 1975; *Tupelo Daily Journal*, Jan. 29, 1975; *WP*, Oct. 6, 7, 13, 14, 1955, and Jan. 15, 1975.

5. Norris Cotton, oral history by J. G. Shoalmire, Jun. 7, 1976, John C. Stennis Oral History Project, John C. Stennis Collection, Mississippi State University, Starkville; George Godwin Jr., *The Little Legislatures: Committees of Congress* (Amherst, MA, 1970), 60; Nick Walters, "The Repairman Chairman: Senator James O. Eastland and His Influence on the U.S. Supreme Court," M.A. thesis, Mississippi College, 1992, 19.

6. Telephone interview with Birch Bayh, May 25, 2010, Easton, MD; see Birch Bayh, *One Heartbeat Away: Presidential Disability and Succession* (Indianapolis, 1968) for a complete discussion of the events leading to the passage of the 25th Amendment and its ratification, but particularly the discussions of Eastland's role on pages 29, 126, 211–213.

7. *CQ*, Apr. 10, 1976, 837; Dixon interview; telephone interviews with Joe Allen, Nov. 20, 2012, Bethesda, OH, and William Simpson III, Nov. 19, 2012, Washington, D.C.

8. *CQ*, Sep. 18, 1959, 1294; *CR*, 91st Cong., 2nd Sess., 31157; *NYT*, Apr. 24, 1970; *WP*, Sep. 6, 1970.

9. Bill Christofferson, *The Man from Clear Lake: Earth Day Founder Gaylord Nelson* (Madison, WI, 2005), 192; *CQ*, May 8, 1976, 1123–1124; Kleindienst, *Justice*, 126. Joseph Stanley Kimmitt, transcript, oral history, Feb. 15, 2001, 100, Senate Historical Office, Washington, D.C.; *NYT*, Mar. 22, 1975; Michael O'Brien, *Philip Hart: The Conscience of the Senate* (East Lansing, 1995), 153–154; telephone interview with John Seigenthaler, Feb. 24, 2014, Nashville, TN; Lawrence E. Walsh, *The Gift of Insecurity: A Lawyer's Life* (Chicago, 2003), 173; *WP*, Mar. 8, 1980.

10. Kleindienst, *Justice*, 130–131.

11. Telephone interview with John C. Culver, Dec. 9, 2012, Bethesda, MD; Stanley Kimmitt oral history, 41; interview with Walker Nolan, Oct. 4, 2012, Chevy Chase, MD.

12. *Biloxi-Gulfport Daily Herald*, Oct. 16, 1969; *Meridian Star*, Nov. 4, 1969; Bill Minor, *Eyes on Mississippi: A Fifty-Year Chronicle of Change* (Jackson, MS, 2001), 100–102; Jere Nash and Andy Taggart, *Mississippi Politics: The Struggle for Power, 1976–2008* (Jackson, MS, 2008), 78; *WP*, Oct. 8, 1969.

13. Dennis DeConcini and Jack L. August Jr., *Senator Dennis DeConcini: From the Center of the Aisle* (Tucson, 2007), 99; interview with Orrin Hatch, Feb. 6, 2013, Washington, D.C.

14. Jules Witcover, *Joe Biden: A Life of Trial and Redemption* (New York, 2010), 102–103.

CHAPTER 15

1. *CQ*, Jun. 13, 1969, 1010; *Tupelo Daily Journal*, Jun. 4, 1969; Bob Woodward and Scott Armstrong, *The Brethren: Inside the Supreme Court* (New York, 1979), 23–24.

2. Laura Kalman, *Abe Fortas: A Biography* (New Haven, 1999), 359–370; *MCA*, May 6, 1969; Bruce Alan Murphy, *Fortas: The Rise and Ruin of a Supreme Court Justice* (New York, 1988), 528–577.

3. Not until 1993 would another Democratic president, Bill Clinton, get the opportunity to nominate a justice to the high court.

4. John P. Frank, *Clement Haynsworth, the Senate, and the Supreme Court* (Charlottesville, 1991), 18–20, 26–30; telephone interview with Ernest F. Hollings, Aug. 24, 2011, Charleston, SC; *WP*, Aug. 19, 1969; Woodward and Armstrong, *Brethren*, 57.

5. *CR*, 91st Cong., 1st sess., 25036–25039; Frank, *Haynsworth*, 28–29; Hollings interview; *JDN*, Sep. 4, 1969; William H. Rehnquist to Clarence A. Pierce, Sep. 10, 1985, B1, F30, Clarence A. Pierce Papers, J. D. Williams Library, University of Mississippi; *WP*, Sep. 11, 1969.

6. John Paul Stevens, *Five Chiefs: A Supreme Court Memoir* (New York, 2011), 127.

7. *WP*, Sep. 26, 1969.

8. Joseph D. Tydings saluted Haynsworth as "a fine man" in an interview with this writer, and Birch Bayh echoed his sentiments using different words. Telephone interview with Birch Bayh, May 25, 2010, Easton, MD; interview with Joseph D. Tydings, Feb. 28, 2011, Washington, D.C.

9. Frank, *Haynsworth*, 21, 39; *WP*, Sep. 18, 1969.

10. Bayh interview; Frank, *Haynsworth*, 39, 45; *MCA*, Sep. 21, 1969.

11. Telephone interview with Marlow Cook, May 4, 2011, Sarasota, FL; Frank, *Haynsworth*, 59, 73; H. R. Haldeman, *The Haldeman Diaries: Inside the Nixon White House* (New York, 1994), 110; Clark Mollenhoff, *Game Plan for Disaster: An Ombudsman's Report on the Nixon Years* (New York, 1976), 52–53; *WP*, Oct. 7, 1969.

12. *Baltimore Sun*, Oct. 4, 1969; Gordon S. Brownell to Harry S. Dent, Oct. 10, 1969, B1, F8, Harry S. Dent Papers, Richard M. Nixon Presidential Library, Yorba Linda, CA; Frank, *Haynsworth*, 66–67, 75–76, 78–79; Haldeman, *Diaries*, 110; Mollenhoff, *Game Plan for Disaster*, 63, 65; *WP*, Oct. 7, 1969.

13. *CQ*, Nov. 21, 1969, 2310; *CR*, 91st Cong., 1st Sess., 34049–34054, 35150–35156; Frank, *Haynsworth*, 48, 83; McMahon, *Nixon's Court: His Challenge to Judicial Liberalism and Its Political Consequences* (Chicago, 2011), 133; *WP*, Nov. 14, 1969.

14. Tom Wicker, *One of Us: Richard Nixon and the American Dream* (New York, 1991), 496–497.

15. On these jurists, see Jack Bass, *Taming the Storm: The Life and Times of Judge Frank M. Johnson Jr. and the South's Fight Over Civil Rights* (New York, 1992); Jack Bass, *Unlikely Heroes* (New York, 1981); Anne Emanuel, *Elbert Parr Tuttle: Chief Jurist of the Civil Rights Revolution* (Athens, GA, 2011); Joel William Friedman, *Champion of Civil Rights: Judge John Minor Wisdom* (Baton Rouge, 2009); Robert F. Kennedy Jr., *Judge Frank M. Johnson Jr.* (New York, 1978); Frank T. Read and Lucy S. McGough, *Let Them Be Judged: The Judicial Integration of the Deep South* (Metuchen, NJ, 1978).

16. Richard Harris, *Decision* (New York, 1971), 8–16, 27; *Tupelo Daily Journal* and *WP*, Jan. 20, 1970.

17. Harris, *Decision*, 57; *JCL*, Jan. 31, 1970; *JDN*, Feb. 15, 1970; *Tupelo Daily Journal*, Feb. 3, 1970; Tydings interview; Wicker, *One of Us*, 498.

18. Telephone interview with G. Robert Blakey, Nov. 30, 2011, South Bend, IN; Cook interview; John Ehrlichman, *Witness to Power: The White House Years* (New York, 1982), 125; Harris, *Decision*, 119; Richard Kleindienst, *Justice: The Memoirs of Attorney General Richard Kleindienst* (Ottawa, IL, 1985), 119; Jeb Stuart Magruder, *An American Life: One Man's Road to Watergate* (New York, 1974), 110; John Massaro, *Supremely Political: The Role of Ideology and Presidential Management in Unsuccessful Supreme Court Nominations* (Albany, NY, 1990), 115.

19. Frank, *Haynsworth*, 118–120; *JDN*, Apr. 16, 1970; *Memphis Press-Scimitar*, Apr. 9, 1970; Jere Nash and Andy Taggart, *Mississippi Fried Politics: Tall Tales from the Back Rooms* (Jackson, MS, 2006), 122; Tinsley E. Yarbrough, *Harry A. Blackmun: The Outsider Justice* (New York, 1971), 131–134.

20. *CQ*, Nov. 6, 1971, 2282; John C. Jeffries Jr., *Justice Lewis F. Powell Jr.: A Biography* (New York, 1994), 1–9, Nick Walters, "The Repairman Chairman: Senator James O. Eastland and His Influence on the United States Supreme Court," M.A. thesis, Mississippi College, 1992, 66–68.

21. Interview with Howard H. Baker Jr., Jun. 13, 2011, Huntsville, TN.

22. John W. Dean, *The Rehnquist Choice: The Untold Story of the Nixon Appointment That Redefined the Supreme Court* (New York, 2001), 216–264; *NYT*, Oct. 22, 1971; Larry Speakes, *Speaking Out: Inside the Reagan White House* (New York, 1988), 33–34; Walters, "Repairman Chairman," 66–68.

23. Telephone interview with Marlow W. Cook, May 4, 2011, Sarasota, FL; Speakes, *Speaking Out*, 34–35; Walters, "Repairman Chairman," 68.

24. Christopher Myers Asch, "No Compromise: The Freedom Struggles of James O. Eastland and Fannie Lou Hamer," Ph.D. dissertation, University of North Carolina, 2005, 300; Jeffries, *Justice Lewis F. Powell Jr.*, 232; telephone interview with Wallace H. Johnson, Dec. 1, 2011, Cody, WY; Kleindienst, *Justice*, 123; *NYT*, Oct. 28, 1971; Walters, "Repairman Chairman," 69–71; *WP*, Nov. 5, 1971; Woodward and Armstrong, *Brethren*, 162; interview with James W. Ziglar, Dec. 13, 2011, Washington, D.C.

25. *CQ*, Nov. 27, 1971, 2451, Dec. 11, 1971, 2532; *CR*, 92nd Cong., 1st Sess., 44862–44868, 45440–45446; *Hearings before the Senate Committee on the Judiciary on the Nominations of William H. Rehnquist, of Arizona, and Lewis F. Powell Jr., of Virginia, to be Associate Justices of the Supreme Court of the United States*, Nov. 3, 4, 8, 9, and 10, 1971, 289–349; *NYT*, Nov. 10, 11, 13, 24, and Dec. 7, 1971; *WP*, Nov. 13, 18, 19, and Dec. 1, 7, 1971; Tinsley Yarbrough, *The Rehnquist Court and the Constitution* (New York, 2000), 7.

26. Johnson and Ziglar interviews.

27. *DDT*, Nov. 30, 1975; *JCL*, Dec. 2, 1975; *Meridian Star*, Nov. 30, 1975; *MCA*, Nov. 27, 1975; *NYT*, Dec. 18, 1975; Stevens, *Five Chiefs*, 127, 133; David Alastair Yalof, *Pursuit of Justices: Presidential Politics and the Selection of Supreme Court Justices* (Chicago, 1999), 129.

CHAPTER 16

1. *JCL*, Feb. 20, 1986; Clarke Reed, transcript, Apr. 2, 1974, Bass-DeVries Collection, Southern Oral History Collection, University of North Carolina, Chapel Hill.

2. Charlie McKellar, transcript, oral history by Jere Nash, Sep. 14, 2004, Nash and Taggart Collection, J. D. Williams Library, University of Mississippi.

3. *CR*, 91st Cong., 1st Sess., 24090–24094; *Federal Response to Hurricane Camille: Hearings before the Special Subcommittee on Disaster Relief of the Committee on Public Works, U.S. Senate*, 91st Cong., 2nd Sess., Part One, 107, Part Two, 490; Ernest Zebrowski and Judith A. Howard, *Category 5: The Story of Camille—Lessons from America's Most Violent Hurricane* (Ann Arbor, 2005), vii, 123–134, 143–158.

4. *CR*, 91st Cong., 1st Sess., 24031–24032, 24090–24094, 26096–26099; JOE to James E. McFie and JOE to William Skellie, Sep. 10, 1969, S3, SS1, B55, "1969 Disaster Relief: Hurricane Camille Relief" folder, JOE Collection; *Federal Response to Hurricane Camille Hearings*, 118–119, 129.

5. Telephone interview with Birch Bayh, May 14, 2012, Easton, MD; *CR*, 91st Cong., 2nd Sess., 26096–26099; *Federal Response to Hurricane Camille Hearings*, Part One, 2; *McComb Enterprise Journal*, Sep. 4, 1969; *Mississippi Coast Daily Herald*, Sep. 3, 1969; undated memo to JOE, S3, SS1, B55, "1969 Disaster Relief: Hurricane Camille Relief" folder, JOE Collection; Larry Speakes, undated telegram, S3, SS1, B55, "1969 Disaster Relief: Hurricane Camille Relief" folder, JOE Collection.

6. Hiram Eastland Jr., e-mail to author, Sep. 26, 2012; interview with Hiram Eastland Jr., Jun. 22, 2012, Greenwood, MS; JOE to Albert L. Hopkins, Sep. 10, 1969, S3, SS1, B55, "1969 Disaster Relief: Hurricane Camille Relief" folder, JOE Collection; Harry M. Lackey to Richard M. Nixon, Sep. 12, 1969, S3, SS1, B55, "1969 Disaster Relief: Hurricane Camille Relief" folder, JOE Collection; interview with Trent Lott, Sep. 29, 2011, Washington, D.C.; *NYT*, Sep. 9, 1969; interview with Clarence Pierce, Jun. 13, 2012, Vaiden, MS; John B. Sandifer to JOE, Sep. 9, 1969, "1969 Disaster Relief: Hurricane Camille Relief" folder, JOE Collection; Leo Seal Jr.,

oral history, Nov. 1, 1991, John C. Stennis Oral History Project, John C. Stennis Collection, Mitchell Library, Mississippi State University, Starkville; undated Larry Speakes memo to Mississippi TV, "1969 Disaster Relief: Hurricane Camille Relief" folder, JOE Collection; *Tupelo Daily Journal*, Sep. 8, 1969.

7. The law enacted required Mississippi counties to comply with desegregation orders by December 1, 1969. The 2012 Bayh interview; JOE to R. W. Smart, Oct. 9, 1969, S3, SS1, B55, "1969 Disaster Relief: Hurricane Camille Relief" folder, JOE Collection; *JCL* and *MCA*, Aug. 28 and Sep. 19, 1969; undated JOE statement, S3, SS1, B55, "1969 Disaster Relief: Hurricane Camille Relief" folder, JOE Collection; Mark M. Smith, *Camille, 1969: Histories of a Hurricane* (Athens, GA, 2011) 28–34, 50–51.

8. Christopher Myers Asch, "No Compromise: The Freedom Struggles of James O. Eastland and Fannie Lou Hamer," Ph.D. dissertation, University of North Carolina, 2005, 251; *CQ*, May 17, 1970, 1327; *CR*, 91st Cong., 2nd Sess., 15524–15525, Oct. 2, 1971, 2018; JOE to Clarence McGovern, Jul. 29, 1971, S3, SS1, B46, "1971 Civil Rights" folder, JOE Collection; John Holloman, transcript, oral history by Jere Nash, Apr. 7, 2005, Nash and Taggart Collection, J. D. Williams Library, University of Mississippi; *JCL*, May 17, Sep. 8, and Nov. 25, 1970; *JDN*, Jul. 17, 1954; *MCA*, Mar. 30, 1969; *MPS*, Aug. 12, 1971; *NOTP*, May 30, 1972; Thomas Noer, "Segregationists and the World: The Foreign Policy of the Resistance" in Brenda Gayle Plummer (ed.), *Window on Freedom: Race, Civil Rights and Foreign Policy, 1945–1988* (Chapel Hill, NC, 2003), 146; *Pascagoula Chronicle*, Oct. 20, 1966; *Tupelo Daily Journal*, Sep. 28, 1970, *WP*, May 10 and Oct. 3, 1972, and Jan. 11, 1973.

9. Interview with Steven Patterson, Jun. 22, 2012, Greenwood, MS.

10. *CR*, 89th Cong., 2nd Sess., 20541; JOE to A. E. Bland, Apr. 9, 1974, "1974 Foreign Policy: Rhodesia," S3, SS1, B84, "1974 Foreign Policy" folder, JOE Collection; JOE to Thomas E. Coulter, Sep. 3, 1974, "1974 Foreign Policy: Rhodesia" folder, JOE Collection JOE to R. B. Snowden, Mar. 23, 1971, S3, SS1, B83, "1971 Foreign Policy: Rhodesia" folder, JOE Collection; interview with Jason David Ward, Jun. 12, 2012, Starkville, MS; *JCL*, Mar. 27, 1966, Mar. 9, 1969, Mar. 12, 24, 1970; *Tupelo Daily Journal*, Aug. 26, 1966, and Mar. 20, 1969; *WP*, Feb. 11, 1969.

11. James Abourezk, e-mail to author, Apr. 17, 2012; *CQ*, Apr. 13, 1962, 605; *CR*, 86th Cong., 2nd Sess., 17405–17412, 18993–18995; JOE to Max Yergan, Dec. 19, 1961, S3, SS1, B82, "1961 Foreign Policy: Congo" folder, JOE Collection.

12. *CR*, 91st Cong., 1st Sess., 11411–11414, 2nd Sess., 5946; JOE to J. C. Brown, Jan. 8, 1970, S3, SS1, B46, "1970 Civil Rights" folder, JOE Collection; JOE to Reuben Lott, Mar. 3, 1969, S3, SS1, B45, "1969 Civil Rights" folder 1 of 3, JOE Collection; JOE to Mrs. J. H. O'Kelley, Feb. 20, 1969, S3, SS1, B46, "1969 Civil Rights" folder 2 of 2, JOE Collection; *JCL*, May 6, 1969; JOE to Roy M. Moffett, Mar. 3, 1969, S3, SS1, B45, "1969 Civil Rights" folder 1 of 2, JOE Collection; JOE to M. M. Randolph, Mar. 20, 1969, S3, SS1, B46, "1969 Civil Rights" folder 2 of 2, JOE Collection; Bryce Harlow to JOE, Aug. 16, 1969, S1, SS16, B1, "Richard M. Nixon Administration" folder, JOE Collection.

13. Chris Myers Asch, *The Senator and the Sharecropper: The Freedom Struggles of James O. Eastland and Fannie Lou Hamer* (New York, 2008), 273; *CR*, 91st Cong., 2nd Sess., 2883–2886; Harry Dent, *The Prodigal South Returns to Power* (New York, 1978), 133; JOE to A. D. Ellison Jr., Jun. 25, 1970, S3, SS1, B46 "1970 Civil Rights" folder, JOE Collection; *MCA*, Jun. 15 and Sep. 30, 1969; *NOTP*, May 17, 1970; *NYT*, Oct. 31, 1969; Leon Panetta with Jim Newton, *Worthy Fights: A Memoir of Leadership in War and Peace* (New York, 2014), 41; *WP*, Jan. 15 and Aug. 9, 1970.

14. *CR*, 91st Cong., 1st Sess., 39353, 2nd Sess., 2555; Joseph Crespino, *In Search of Another Country: Mississippi and the Conservative Counterrevolution* (Princeton, NJ, 2007), 11–14; Joseph Crespino, "Strategic Accommodation: Civil Rights Opponents in Mississippi and Their Impact on American Racial Politics, 1953–1972," Ph.D. dissertation, Stanford University, 2002, 265; Dent, *Prodigal South*, 148–153; Dean J. Kotlowski, *Nixon's Civil Rights: Politics, Principle, and Policy* (Cambridge, MA, 2001), 31–37; *MCA*, Feb. 10, 1970; Clarke Reed to *Baltimore Sun*, Aug. 13, 1970, and James M. Moye to Harry S. Dent, Aug. 13, 1970, Harry S. Dent Papers, B5, F20, White House files, Richard M. Nixon Presidential Library, Yorba Linda, CA.

15. J. Lee Annis Jr., *Howard Baker: Conciliator in an Age of Crisis* (Lanham, MD, 1994), 59; *CR*, 91st Cong., 1st Sess., 39353; 2nd Sess., 1125–1126, 5376, 21211–21227, 92nd Cong., 1st Sess., 11511–11514, 2nd Sess., 35315; JOE to Mrs. J. L. Christman, S3, SS1, B46, "1970 Civil Rights" folder, JOE Collection; *JCL*, Mar. 21, 1972, Mar. 29, 1973; *JDN*, Feb. 9, 1970, Oct. 30, 1971, Feb. 24, 1974; *WP*, Apr. 11, 15, 1973.

16. Interview with Brad Dye, Jun. 20, 2011, Ridgeland, MS.

17. *JCL*, Aug. 14, 1971; Jere Nash and Andy Taggart, *Mississippi Fried Politics: Tall Tales from the Back Rooms* (Jackson, MS, 2006), 102; *Pearl Press*, Sep. 4, 1975; Bill Waller, *Straight Ahead: The Memoirs of a Mississippi Governor* (Brandon, MS, 2007), 107–122; telephone interview with William Waller, Jul. 15, 2011, Jackson, MS.

18. Erle Johnston, *Politics: Mississippi Style* (Forest, MS, 1993), 224–225; *MCA*, Oct. 26, 30, 1971; Waller, *Straight Ahead*, 110, 126.

19. Telephone interview with David R. Bowen, Apr. 29, 2011, Jackson, MS; James P. Coleman, transcript, oral history by John Egerton, Sep. 5, 1990, Southern Oral History Collection, Documenting the American South Collection of the University of North Carolina; interview with Trent Lott, Sep. 29, 2011, Washington, D.C.; *MCA*, Jun. 4, 1972.

20. *Chicago Tribune*, Oct. 2, 1972; *DDT*, Apr. 27, 1972; *JCL*, Jun. 8, 1972; Erle Johnston, *Politics Mississippi Style* (Forest, MS, 1993), 233, 241; *Laurel Leader Call*, Apr. 27, 1972; *MCA*, Apr. 7, 17, and Jun. 11, 1972; Taylor Webb ad, *Meridian Star*, May 19, 1972; Larry Speakes, *Speaking Out: Inside the Reagan White House* (New York, 1988), 28; telephone interview with Taylor Webb, Aug. 23, 2012, Leland, MS; *Winona Times*, Apr. 27, 2012.

21. *CPR*, Jun. 7, 1972; *DDT*, May 11, 1972; draft of letter, JOE to Hugh D. Scott Jr., Feb. 9, 1976, S1, SS18, B9, F9-18, JOE Collection; *JCL*, May 23, 1972; *JDN*, May 31, 1972; *Leland Progress*, Jun. 1, 1972; *Natchez Democrat*, Jun. 5, 1972; Clarke Reed, transcript, Apr. 2, 1974, Bass-DeVries Collection, Southern Oral History Collection, University of North Carolina, Chapel Hill.

22. One of Carmichael's backers was State Representative Robert Clark, the first African American to sit in the legislature since Reconstruction. Michael Barone, Grant Ujifusa, and Douglas Mathews, *The Almanac of American Politics, 1974* (Boston, 1973), 535; interview with Gilbert E. Carmichael, Mar. 17, 2010, Meridian, MS; Gilbert E. Carmichael, press release, BI-7, F257, Gilbert E. Carmichael Papers, MSS 338, Mississippi State University, Starkville; *Daily Mississippian*, Aug. 3, 1972; Thomas S. Giordano, oral history by Orley B. Caudill, May 1, 1980, Mississippi Oral History Program of the University of Southern Mississippi, 12; *Grenada Sentinel Star*, Oct. 24, 1972; *McComb Enterprise Journal*, Jun. 7, 1972; *Meridian Star*, May 21, 1972; *NYT*, Nov. 9, 1972; *Pascagoula Press*, May 28, 1972; Neil R. Peirce, *The Deep South States of America: People, Politics, and Power in the Seven Deep South States* (New York, 1974), 97; interview with Clarence Pierce, Jun. 13, 2012, Vaiden, MS; *WP*, May 30 and Jun. 7, 1972; Maarten Zwiers, "The Paradox of Power: James O. Eastland and the Democratic Party," M.A. thesis, University of Mississippi, 88.

23. Waller, *Straight Ahead*, 183; *WP*, Mar. 16, 1975; Zwiers, "Paradox of Power: Eastland and the Democratic Party," 82.

24. Giordano oral history, University of Southern Mississippi, 12–13; *Gulfport Daily Herald* and *JCL*, Aug. 11, 1972; *WP*, Nov. 3, 1972.

25. Hunter M. Gholson to Gil Carmichael, Sep. 5, 1972, S1, SS19, B13, F37-13, JOE Collection; *JDN*, Aug. 22, 1972; *Tupelo Daily Journal*, Aug. 12, 1972; Prentiss Walker to Gil Carmichael, Jul. 30, 1972; BI-6, F161, Gilbert E. Carmichael Papers, Mississippi State University, Starkville.

26. *JDN*, May 26, 31, and Jun. 4, 1972; *MCA* and *OE*, May 30, 1972; *NOTP*, Jun. 11, 1972.

27. JOE to L. B. Porter, Aug. 10, 1972, S1, SS19, B33, F33-7, JOE Collection; JOE to Roger Pryor, Jul. 21, 1972, S1, SS19, B32, F32-12, JOE Collection; *Grenada Daily Sentinel*, Aug. 11, 1972; *JCL*, Oct. 27, 1985; interview with David F. Lambert III, Aug. 14, 2012, Alexandria, VA; *Meridian Star*, Aug. 1, 1972; *NOTP*, Aug. 22, 1972; telephone interview with William Simpson III, Nov. 19, 2012, Washington, D.C.; Larry Speakes to Charles Sims, Sep. 29, 1972, S1, SS19, B37, F37-22, JOE Collection.

28. Carmichael interview; Chris Danielson, *After Freedom Summer: How Race Realigned Mississippi Politics, 1945–1986* (Gainesville, FL, 2011), 84; *JCL*, Aug. 6, 1972; *CPR* and *Picayune Item*, May 31, 1972; Lambert interview; *Lexington Banner*, Oct. 13, 1972; *Meridian Star*, Sep. 10, 1972.

29. *DDT*, May 11 and Oct. 18, 1972; *Hattiesburg American*, Oct. 24, 1972; *JCL*, Sep. 28, 1972; *Meridian Star*, Sep. 7, 1972; *MCA*, Sep. 22, 1972; *Daily Mississippian*, Apr. 13, 1972; *MCA*, Sep. 22, 1972; *NOTP*, Aug. 18, 1972; *OE*, Aug. 4, 1972; *Vicksburg Post*, May 2 and Oct. 25, 1972.

30. *Chicago Tribune*, Oct. 2, 1972; *JDN* and *Tupelo Journal*, Sep. 30, 1972; William D. Mounger and Joseph L. Maxwell III, *Amidst the Fray: My Life in Politics, Culture and Mississippi* (Brandon, MS, 2006), 140–143; *WP*, Oct. 1, 1972.

31. *Biloxi-Gulfport Daily Herald*, Oct. 15, 28, 1972; Harry S. Dent to Julie Eisenhower, Oct. 25, 1972, Harry S. Dent Papers, B12, F29, Nixon Library, Yorba Linda, CA; H. R. Haldeman, *The Haldeman Diaries: Inside the Nixon White House* (New York, 1994), 504; *JCL* and *McComb Enterprise Journal*, Oct. 25, 1972; *Tupelo Journal*, Oct. 26, 1972; *Vicksburg Evening Post*, Oct. 14, 1972; Wirt A. Yerger Jr. to Barry Goldwater, Oct. 6, 1972, B1-6, F153, Gilbert E. Carmichael Papers, Mississippi State University, Starkville.

32. Gil Carmichael, transcript, Mar. 31, 1974, Bass-DeVries Collection, Southern Oral History Collection, University of North Carolina, Chapel Hill; Gilbert E. Carmichael to Joseph A. Bosio, Oct. 20, 1973, BI-6, F163, Carmichael Papers; Chris Danielson, *After Freedom Summer: How Race Realigned Mississippi Politics, 1965–1986* (Gainesville, 2011), 86; Erle Johnston, *Politics: Mississippi Style* (Forest, MS, 1993), 240; *Purple and White* (Millsaps University), Jan. 26, 1973; *JCL*, Oct. 29, 1972; *Tupelo Journal*, Nov. 3, 1972; Wayne Weidie to Charles L. Sullivan, Oct. 23, 1972, BI-6, F153, Carmichael Papers; *West Point Times-Leader*, Oct. 20, 1973.

33. John W. Dean, *Blind Ambition* (New York, 1976), 49; Mark Feldstein, *Poisoning the Press: Richard Nixon, Jack Anderson, and the Rise of Washington's Scandal Culture* (New York, 2010), 225–231; interview with James F. Flug, Oct. 18, 2011, Washington, D.C.; *WP*, Feb. 16, 24, and 25, 1972.

34. *CQ*, Mar. 4, 1972, 510–511; Mar. 11, 1972, 627–630, Apr. 29, 1972, 972; Feldstein, *Poisoning the Press*, 231–263; Mark Felt and John O'Connor, *The FBI, Being "Deep Throat," and the Struggle for Honor in Washington* (New York, 2006), 137–142; Flug interview.

35. Adam Clymer, *Edward M. Kennedy: A Biography* (New York, 1999), 194; telephone interview with Rufus Edmisten, Mar. 13, 2012, Raleigh, NC; Lewis L. Gould, *The Most Exclusive Club: A History of the Modern United States Senate* (New York, 2005), 262; L. Patrick Gray, *In Nixon's Web: A Year in the Crosshairs of Watergate* (New York, 2008), 103–236; *Lake Charles American Press*, Mar. 20, 1973; interview with Walker Nolan, Oct. 4, 2012, Chevy Chase, MD; *Pascagoula Press*, Mar. 13, 1973; *WP*, Mar. 2, 10, 13, 14, 15, and 20, 1973.

36. JOE to Tom Buchanan, Aug. 6, 1973, S3, SS1, B133, "1973 Politics: Richard Nixon" Folder, JOE Collection; JOE to Frank R. Elliott, Feb. 27, 1973, S3, SS1, B133, "1973 Politics: Richard Nixon" Folder, JOE Collection; Larry Speakes, *Speaking Out* (New York, 1988), 46; *WP*, Mar. 1, 1972; Bob Woodward and Carl Bernstein, *The Final Days* (New York, 1976), 349.

37. Interview with Hiram Eastland Jr., Jun. 22, 2012, Greenwood, MS.

38. Dom Bonafede, "Anti-impeachment Plans Focus on Law, Politics, and Media," *National Journal*, May 11, 1974, 688; *Chicago Sun-Times*, Apr. 17, 1974; *CQ*, Apr. 27, 1974, 1063; *CR*, 93rd Cong., 2nd Sess., 8090–8091, 11373–11383; JOE to Kenneth N. Causey, Apr. 19, 1974, S3, SS1, B56, "1974 Disaster Relief" Folder, JOE Collection; JOE to Richard Nixon, Apr. 30, 1974, S1, SS16, B1, "Richard Nixon Administration: Correspondence" Folder, JOE Collection; *NYT* and *WP*, Apr. 26, 1974.

39. Telephone interview with Joe Allen, Nov. 21, 2012, Bethesda, OH; Lambert interview; Speakes, *Speaking Out*, 46; *WP*, Sep. 29, 1974; Woodward and Bernstein, *Final Days*, 349.

40. Conrad Black, *Richard M. Nixon: A Life in Full* (New York, 2007), 985; Hiram Eastland Jr. interview; *JDN* and *WP*, Aug. 9, 1974; *McComb Enterprise Journal*, May 11, 1977; Samuel Shaffer, *On and Off the Floor: Thirty Years as a Correspondent on Capitol Hill* (New York, 1980), 297.

41. Lambert interview; *MCA*, Aug. 8, 1974; *Vicksburg Evening Post*, Nov. 12, 1978; Barry Werth, *31 Days* (New York, 2006), 74, 162.

42. JOE to Jack McInerney, Sep. 25, 1974, S3, SS1, B134, "1974 Politics: Richard Nixon" folder (2 of 3), JOE Collection; JOE to Doris O'Bryant, Aug. 22, 1974, S3, SS1, B134, "1974 Politics: Richard Nixon" folder (2 of 3), JOE Collection; JOE to Ernie Sparks, Sep. 12, 1974, S3, SS1, B134, "1974 Politics: Richard Nixon" folder (2 of 3), JOE Collection; JOE to Robert L. Watkins, Aug. 15, 1974, SS3, S1, B134, "1974 Politics: Richard Nixon" folder (3 of 3), JOE Collection; Werth, *31 Days*, 74, 136.

CHAPTER 17

1. JCL, MCA, *Meridian Star, San Diego Union, Washington Evening Star*, and *WP*, Jul. 29, 1972; *DDT*, Jul. 30, 1972.

2. *CR*, 92nd Cong., 2nd Sess., 25905; *Detroit News*, Jul. 28, 1972; Michael O'Brien, *Philip Hart: The Conscience of the Senate* (East Lansing, MI, 1995), 189; Francis R. Valeo, transcript, oral history, Oct. 2, 1985, 428, Senate Historical Office, Washington, D.C.

3. *CQ*, Nov. 10, 1973, 2987; *CR*, 93rd Cong., 1st Sess., 36125; *JDN*, Jan. 11, 1973; *National Journal*, Jan. 27, 1973, 137; *NYT*, Oct. 25, 1973.

4. Eventually, two teenaged brothers were convicted of the shooting. *CQ*, Mar. 10, 1973, 524; telephone interview with William "Eph" Cresswell, Apr. 20, 2012, Oxford, MS; JOE and Bob Dole, "Dear Colleague" letter, Feb. 1, 1973, S1, SS18, B9, F9-39, JOE Collection; JOE to Rev. and Mrs. E. H. Blumer, Feb. 27, 1973, S3, SS1, B133, "1973 Politics: John Stennis Shooting" file, JOE Collection; *NYT* and *WP*, Jan. 31, 1973; John M. Stennis to JOE, Feb. 14, 1973, S3, SS1, B133, "1973 Politics: John Stennis Shooting" file, JOE Collection; Mark O. Hatfield as told

to Diane N. Solomon, *Against the Grain: Reflections of a Rebel Republican* (Ashland, OR, 2001), 177.

5. *JCL*, Aug. 18, 1974.

6. *DDT*, Nov. 22, 1973; *JCL*, Nov. 21, 1973, Aug. 18, 1974; *JDN*, Oct. 11, 1973; *MCA*, Nov. 15, 1973.

7. James Cannon, *Time and Chance: Gerald Ford's Appointment with History* (New York, 1994), 229–258; *CQ*, Oct. 13, 1973, 2695–2696; JOE to True D. Morse, Nov. 19, 1973, and JOE to Johnny Thomas, Oct. 18, 1973, S3, SS1, B133, "1973 Politics: Gerald Ford" folder, JOE Collection; *JCL*, Aug. 6, 1976.

8. Jimmy Breslin, *How the Good Guys Finally Won: Notes from an Impeachment Summer* (New York, 1975), 178; telephone interview with Macon Edwards, Jul. 24, 2012, Washington, D.C.

9. JOE to Mrs. Jack Haviland, S3, SS1, B47, "Civil Rights: 1974" file, JOE Collection; JOE to Nelson A. Rockefeller, Feb. 17, 1977, S1, SS16, B1, "Gerald R. Ford Administration: Office of the Vice President" folder, JOE Collection.

10. *CQ*, Dec. 6, 1975, 2642, Apr. 10, 1975, 739, 836; JOE to Royce B. Caughman, Mar. 20, 1975, S3, SS1, B85, "1975 Foreign Policy: Southeast Asia" folder, JOE Collection; JOE to Joe Mark McKenzie, May 29, 1975, "1975 Foreign Policy: Cambodia" folder, JOE Collection; *JCL*, May 14, 1975; *MCA*, Feb. 20, 1976; telephone interview with Robert B. Morgan, Sep. 25, 2012, Lilington, NC; *WP*, Sep. 11, 1975.

11. Telephone interview with Birch Bayh, May 14, 2012, Easton, MD; George McGovern, *Grassroots: The Autobiography of George McGovern* (New York, 1977), 246.

12. Joe Biden, *Promises to Keep: On Life and Politics* (New York, 2007), 92; Joseph Biden to JOE, Jan. 15, 1973, and Jan. 17, 1975, S1, SS18, B1, F1-41, JOE Collection.

13. Durkin eventually ended the New Hampshire dispute by agreeing to a new election, and he easily defeated Wyman when that contest was held in September 1975. Dewey Bartlett to JOE, Mar. 30, 1977, S1, SS18, B1, F1-28, JOE Collection; Henry Bellmon to JOE, Mar. 7, 1976, S1, SS18, B1, F1-35, JOE Collection; Richard E. Cohen, "A New Look for Judiciary," *National Journal*, Mar. 6, 1976, 311; *CQ*, Jun. 21, 1975; JOE to Edward J. Gurney, Feb. 4, 1977, S1, SS18, B2, F4-41, JOE Collection.

14. *CQ*, Jun. 28, 1975, 1409, Jul. 26, 1975, 1595–1596; JOE to Jim Johnson, Oct. 7, 1975, S1, SS7, B2, F2-13, JOE Collection; Gerald R. Ford to JOE, Aug. 7, 1975, and Feb. 21, 1976, JOE Name File in White House Congressional Mail Collection, B15, and Jack Marsh to Russ Rourke, Jul. 8, 1975, B100, John O. Marsh Papers, Gerald R. Ford Presidential Library, Ann Arbor, MI; *NYT*, Jul. 9, 1975; Courtney C. Pace to Homer E. Capehart, S3, SS1, B140, "1975 Robert E. Lee Citizenship" folder, JOE Collection; *Tupelo Daily Journal* and *WP*, Jul. 17, 1975.

15. *JDN*, Jul. 10, 1975; *Meridian Star*, Sep. 28, 1975; Jere Nash and Andy Taggart, *Mississippi Politics: The Struggle for Power, 1976–2006* (Jackson, MS, 2006), 32; *NYT*, Aug. 23 and Oct. 20, 1975.

16. JOE to C. A. Tate Jr., Sep. 24, 1975, and JOE to Robert Caviness and JOE to N. S. Morrison, Oct. 20, 1975, S3, SS1, B85, "1975 Foreign Policy: Russia" folder, JOE Collection; Gerald R. Ford, *A Time to Heal: The Autobiography of Gerald Ford* (New York, 1979), 312–313; *JCL*, Mar. 27, 1975, and Oct. 5, 1975.

17. *CPR* and *Tupelo Daily Journal*, Nov. 6, 1975; interview with Gil Carmichael, Mar. 16, 2010, Meridian, MS; *JCL*, Oct. 26, 1975; Johnston, *Politics Mississippi Style*, 267; *MCA*, Nov. 3, 1975; *MPS*, Nov. 6, 1975; *Meridian Star*, Nov. 5, 1975; *Natchez Democrat*, Oct. 13, 1975; *NOTP*, Oct. 6, 1975; *NYT*, Aug. 18 and Nov. 6, 1975.

18. Frank T. Adams, *James A. Dombrowski: An American Heretic, 1897–1963* (Knoxville, 1992), 262–275; William F. Buckley Jr., "Death of a Committee," *National Review*, Jan. 23, 1976, 52; *CR*, 90th Cong., 1st Sess., 13366; Adam Fairclough, *Race and Democracy: The Civil Rights Struggle in Louisiana, 1915–1972* (Athens, 1995), 323–325; *Grenada Sentinel-Star*, May 6, 1976; *JCL*, Apr. 1, 1977; *MCA*, Oct. 7, 1970; *NYT*, Apr. 11, 1976; Robert Sherrill, *First Amendment Felon: The Story of Frank Wilkinson: His 132,000 Page FBI Files and His Epic Fight for Civil Rights* (New York, 2005), 162; *The Attempt to Steal the Bicentennial: The Peoples' Bicentennial Commission, Report of SISS*, 94:2 (May 1976), 1–3; *WP*, Jul. 12, 1967, Mar. 9, 1972, and Apr. 11, 1976; *WP*, Jul. 12, 1967; Jeff Woods, *Black Struggle Red Scare: Segregation and Anti-Communism in the South, 1948–1968* (Baton Rouge, 2004), 181–190, 192–193.

19. Courtney Pace to Dick and Alix [sic], Jan. 15, 1975, S3, SS7, B3, F3-4, JOE Collection.

20. Kenneth L. Dean, oral history, Jun. 9, 1992, 24, John C. Stennis Oral History Project, John C. Stennis Collection, Mississippi State University, Starkville; telephone interview with Kenneth L. Dean, Dec. 12, 2012, Carrolton, GA.

21. *CPR*, Jan. 21, 1976; interview with Charles Evers, Jun. 21, 2012, Jackson, MS; *JCL*, Mar. 28, 1978.

22. Will D. Campbell, *Robert G. Clark's Journey to the House: A Black Politician's Story* (Jackson, MS, 2009), 127; interview with Robert G. Clark, Sep. 11, 2012, Ebenezer, MS.

23. Such suspicions are evaluated both by Francoise M. Hamlin, a recent chronicler of Henry's hometown of Clarksdale, and by Minion K. C. Morrison, Henry's most thorough biographer. Francoise N. Hamlin, *Crossroads at Clarksdale: The Black Freedom Struggle in the Mississippi Delta after World War II* (Chapel Hill, 2012), 99; Minion K. C. Morrison, *Aaron Henry of Mississippi: Inside Agitator.* (Fayetteville, AR, 2015), 35, 61–63, 259–260.

24. Interview with Curtis Wilkie, Jan. 12, 2010, Oxford, MS; Curtis Wilkie, *Dixie: A Personal Odyssey through Events That Shaped the Modern South* (New York, 2002), 253.

25. Interview with Owen Brooks, Jan. 11, 2012, Jackson, MS; *Greenwood Commonwealth*, Mar. 14, 1976, and Oct. 17, 1977; *JCL*, Mar. 9, 27, 1976; *McComb Enterprise Journal* and *MCA*, Mar. 12, 1976; Mark Newman, *Divine Agitators: The Delta Ministry and Civil Rights* (Athens, GA, 2004), 206.

26. *NOTP*, Jun. 14, 1975; *NYT*, Apr. 13, 1975; William M. Simpson, "The Birth of the Mississippi Loyalist Democrats, 1965–1968," *JMH* 42:1 (Feb. 1982), 28–31; William M. Simpson, "The 'Loyalist' Democrats of Mississippi: Challenge to a White Majority, 1965–1968," M.A. thesis, Mississippi State University, 109.

27. Telephone interview with Danny E. Cupit, Jan. 7, 2013, Jackson, MS; *NOTP*, Apr. 13, 1975; *NYT*, Jun. 14, 1975.

CHAPTER 18

1. JOE and John C. Stennis, statement supporting Jimmy Carter, Jun. 10, 1976, S1, SS20, B4, "1976 Politics" file, JOE Collection; JOE, fundraising letter for Robert C. Byrd, Mar. 20, 1976, S1, SS20, B4, "1976 Politics" file, JOE Collection; JOE to James H. Payne, Dec. 30, 1975, S3, SS1, B135, "1975 Politics: Jimmy Carter" file, JOE Collection; J. Herman Hines to JOE, Mar. 26, 1976, S1, SS20. B4, "1976 Politics" folder, JOE Collection; *Mississippi Press*, Jun. 11, 1976; *Mobile Register*, Jan. 17, 1976; undated 1976 column, Bill Minor, S1, SS18, B5, F5-34, JOE Collection; interview with Herb Montgomery, Jun. 11, 2013, Oxford, MS; *NYT*, Jan. 23, 26, 1976.

2. *Biloxi-Gulfport Sun-Herald, JCL, NYT,* and *WP,* Sep. 18, 1976; JOE to Mrs. Don Terrell, Oct. 6, 1976, S1, SS20, B4, "1976 Politics" folder, JOE Collection; *JDN,* Nov. 3, 1976; *Mississippi Press,* Jul. 16, 1976; *Pearl Press,* Sep. 23, 1976; *Tupelo Journal,* Sep. 20, 1976.

3. Telephone interviews with Danny E. Cupit, Jan. 7, 2013, Jackson, MS, and James Free, Jul. 13, 2012, Washington, D.C.; *Grenada Sentinel Star,* Oct. 25, 1976; *Hattiesburg American,* Oct. 30, 1976; *JCL, Meridian Star,* and *Yazoo Daily Herald,* Jul. 22, 1977; *JDN,* Oct. 26, 1976; *Mobile Register,* Oct. 30, 1976; *Pearl River Journal,* Jan. 19, 1977; *Stone County Enterprise,* Oct. 21, 1976; *Tupelo Daily Journal,* Oct. 28, 1976; *West Point Times Leader,* Oct. 26, 1976.

4. Griffin Bell with Ronald G. Ostrow, *Taking Care of the Law* (Atlanta, 1986), 40, 95, 207–208; Reg Murphy, *Uncommon Sense: The Achievement of Griffin Bell* (Atlanta, 1999), 168–169; *NYT,* Mar. 9, 1978; Dennis DeConcini and Jack L. August Jr., *Senator Dennis DeConcini: From the Center of the Aisle* (Tucson, 2007), 128; David M. O'Brien, *Storm Center: The Supreme Court in American Politics* (New York, 1990), 70: *WP,* Feb. 2, 1978.

5. *CQ,* Jan. 15, 1977, 93, and Jan. 29, 1977, 169; *CR,* 95th Cong., 1st Sess., 2120–2121; Murphy, *Uncommon Sense,* 171–182; *Starkville Daily News,* Dec. 21, 1976; *WP,* Jan. 26 and Mar. 12, 1977.

6. Cupit interview; telephone interview with Mark G. Hazard Jr., Apr. 28, 2013, West Point, MS; Mark Hazard, transcript, oral history by Jere Nash, Oct. 2, 2004, Nash and Taggart Collection, J. D. Williams Library, University of Mississippi.

7. Interview with Hodding Carter III, May 17, 2011, Chapel Hill, NC.

8. *JCL-Daily News,* Aug. 7, 1977; Rochelle Jones and Peter Woll, *The Private World of Congress* (New York, 1979), 132; *Natchez Democrat,* Aug. 21, 1977; *South Mississippi Sun,* Aug. 1, 1977.

9. *Columbus (MS) Dispatch,* Apr. 17, 1977; *CR,* 78th Cong., 2nd Sess., 8726–8727, 8732–8733, 79th Cong., 2nd Sess., 8318; *DDT,* Oct. 28, 1976, Mar. 25 and May 5, 1977; JOE to Gerald R. Ford, Oct. 2, 1975, White House Congressional Mail File, Gerald R. Ford Presidential Library, Ann Arbor, MI; Mark Hazard, transcript, oral history by Jere Nash, Oct. 2, 2004, Nash and Taggart Collection, J. D. Williams Library, University of Mississippi; *JCL,* Sep. 28, 1976; *JDN,* Mar. 29, 1977; *Natchez Democrat,* Apr. 8, 1977; *NYT,* Apr. 6, 16, 1977; Jeffrey Stine, *Mixing the Waters: Environment, Politics, and the Building of the Tennessee-Tombigbee Waterway* (Akron, OH, 1993), 28–31, 164–175, 187; Don Waldon, oral history by Jeff Broadwater, Feb. 20, 1992, John C. Stennis Oral History Project, 13–16, John C. Stennis Collection, Mississippi State University, Starkville; *West Point Times Leader,* Mar. 30, 1977.

10. *CQ,* May 29, 1959, 741, Mar. 25, 1972, 692–695; *CR,* 87th Cong., 2nd Sess., 12324; JOE to Harry Beemon, Jan. 9, 1973, S3, SS1, B84, "1973 Foreign Policy: Russia" folder, JOE Collection; JOE to Mrs. George A. Borst, Aug. 27, 1971, S3, SS1, B135, "1971 Population Control" folder, JOE Collection; JOE to Mrs. Dorothy C. Bragg, Sep. 19, 1961, S3, SS1, B39, "1961 Civil Rights" folder, JOE Collection; JOE to Martha Gerald, Jun. 11, 1956, S3, SS1, B135, "Equal Rights Amendment" folder: JOE to Liz Carpenter, Mar. 23, 1972, S3, SS1, B75, "1972 ERA" folder, JOE Collection; JOE to Young Married Sunday School Class, Mt. Pisgah Baptist Church, Oct. 10, 1977, S3, SS1, B135, "1977 Pornography" folder, JOE Collection; Carl Hayden to JOE, Oct. 22, 1968, S1, SS18, B5, F5-4, JOE Collection; *JCL,* Sep. 18, 1975; *NYT,* Jun. 29, 1972; *WP,* Jun. 30, 1968.

11. *Biloxi-Gulfport Sunday Herald,* Jan. 22 and Jul. 10, 1977; *DDT,* Sep. 1, 1977; JOE to Thomas E. Anderson, Jan. 27, 1977, S2, SS1, B135, "1977 Politics: Jimmy Carter" folder, JOE Collection; JOE to Mrs. Felix Howard Webster, Oct. 10, 1977, S3, S1, B85, "1977 Foreign Policy" folder, JOE Collection; *Hattiesburg American, JDN,* and *Meridian Star,* Aug. 27, 1977;

New Albany Gazette, Jul. 7, 1977; *JCL*, Aug. 27 and Oct. 27, 1977; *Vicksburg Evening Post*, Nov. 3, 1977.

12. Telephone interview with Britt Singletary, Jan. 13, 2014, Biloxi, MS; *Vicksburg Evening Post*, Apr. 25, 1977.

13. Barnie T. Bramlett to JOE, Nov. 4, 1977, S1, SS19, B39, F42, JOE Collection; *Capital Reporter*, Oct. 20, 1977; Thad Cochran, transcript, oral history by Orley B. Caudill (Part II), Aug. 30, 1982, Oral History Program of the University of Southern Mississippi, 154–155; *Daily Corinthian*, Jul. 11, 1977; *GC*, Mar. 24, 1978; *MCA*, Nov. 5, 1977 and May 13, 1978; Jere Nash and Andy Taggart, *Mississippi Politics: The Struggle for Power, 1976–2006* (Jackson, MS, 2006), 77, 81; *NYT*, Mar. 2, 1978.

14. John Holloman, tape, oral history by Jere Nash, Apr. 7, 2005, Nash and Taggart Collection, Special Collections, J. D. Williams Library, University of Mississippi; *JDN*, Jan. 19 and Mar. 28, 1978; *MCA*, Oct. 2, 1977.

15. Gil Carmichael, transcript, oral history, Apr. 2, 1974, Bass-DeVries Collection, Southern Oral History Collection, University of North Carolina, Chapel Hill; JOE to F. Carlton Pugh, Nov. 30, 1977, S3, SS1, B85, "1977 Foreign Policy" file, JOE Collection; *GC*, Dec. 18, 1977; Aaron Henry, Introduction of Senator James O. Eastland, Apr. 30, 1978, Jackson Mississippi, S1, B2, F30, Aaron Henry Collection, Mississippi Department of Archives and History, Jackson; *JDN*, Feb. 9, 1978; Erle Johnston, *Mississippi's Defiant Years, 1953–1973: An Interpretive Documentary with Personal Experiences* (Forest, MS, 1990), 386–387; interview with Herb Montgomery, Jun. 19, 2013, Oxford, MS; *Ocean Springs Record*, Jun. 23, 1977; *South Mississippi Sun*, May 17, 1978.

16. *GC*, Dec. 18, 1977; Owen H. Brooks to friend, "Shall We Give Eastland a Chance," Jan. 26, 1978, Aaron Henry, Report before Mississippi State Convention of the NAACP, Nov. 3, 1977, and Aaron Henry, Jan. 1, 1978, letter to NAACP leader and civil and human rights supporter, with Dec. 20, 1977, speech of JOE to fundraising letter for Mississippi Industrial College attached, B1, F9, Edwin H. King Collection, Special Collections, J. D. Mitchell Library, University of Mississippi; *Daily Corinthian*, Mar. 1, 1978; *JCL*, Feb. 28, 1978; *MCA*, Feb. 19, 1978; *Meridian Star*, Feb. 21, 1978.

17. *Biloxi-Gulfport Daily Herald*, Jan. 13, 1978; Cupit interview; interview with Hiram Eastland, Jun. 22, 2012, Greenwood, MS; *DDT*, Jun. 15, 1977; Wayne Edwards, transcript, oral history by Jere Nash, Jun. 23, 2004, Nash and Taggart Collection, J. D. Williams Library, University of Mississippi; *Grenada Sentinel-Star*, Nov. 23, 1977; *JCL*, Mar. 22, 1978; *JDN*, Apr. 21, 1978; Nash and Taggart, *Mississippi Politics*, 79–80; *MCA*, Mar. 22 and Apr. 2, 1978; *NYT*, Mar. 23, 1978; Steve Patterson, transcript, oral history by Jere Nash, May 11, 2004, Nash and Taggart Collection, J. D. Williams Library, University of Mississippi; *Tupelo Daily Journal*, Jan. 30, 1978; Bill Waller, *Straight Ahead: The Memoirs of a Mississippi Governor* (Brandon, MS, 20076), 184–187.

18. Chris Myers Asch, *The Senator and the Sharecropper: The Freedom Struggles of James O. Eastland and Fannie Lou Hamer* (New York, 2008), 287–288; *DDT*, Mar. 22, 1978; *MCA*, Mar. 26, 1978; *MPS*, Mar. 27, 1978; *South Mississippi Sun*, Mar. 23, 1978.

19. Interviews with Hiram Eastland, Jun. 22, 2012, and Jan. 10, 2013, Greenwood, MS, and Woods Eastland, Jun. 24, 2010, Greenwood, MS, and Jun. 11, 2012, Doddsville, MS; *JCL*, Mar. 28, 1978.

20. Telephone interview with Maurice Dantin, Apr. 29, 2011, Columbia, MS; interviews with Brad Dye, Jun. 20, 2011, Ridgeland, MS, and Hiram Eastland, Jun. 22, 2012, Greenwood, MS; *Picayune Item*, Apr. 6 and May 14, 1978.

21. *Bolivar Commercial*, May 22, 1978; Connie Lynnette Cartledge, "James P. Coleman: Moderate Politician in an Age of Racial Strife," M.A. thesis, Mississippi State University, 1984, 17; *Columbus (MS) Commercial Dispatch*, Mar. 23, 1978; *JCL*, Apr. 9, May 9, 10, 24, and Jun. 9, 1978; *Grenada Sentinel Star*, Apr. 16, 1978; *MCA*, May 9, 10, 29, 1978; Nash and Taggart, *Mississippi Politics:*, 80; *Natchez Democrat*, Apr. 20, 1978; *NYT*, May 15 and Jun. 29, 1978; *South Mississippi Sun*, May 23, 1978; *Tupelo Daily Journal*, Apr. 16, 1978.

22. *GC*, Jul. 16, 1978; *Hattiesburg American, JCL, JDN*, and *Vicksburg Evening Post*, Jun. 28, 1978; Erle Johnston, *Politics: Mississippi Style* (Forest, MS, 1993), 280–284; *Mississippi Press*, Jun. 28, 1978.

23. Interview with Hiram Eastland and Steve Patterson, Jun. 22, 2012, Greenwood, MS.

24. *Bolivar Commercial*, May 17, 1978; 2012 Hiram Eastland interview; Edward M. Kennedy to JOE, undated handwritten letter of May 1978, S1, SS18, B6, F6-7, JOE Collection; Nash and Taggart, *Mississippi Politics*, 79; interview with Curtis Wilkie, Jan. 12, 2010, Oxford, MS.

25. *CPR*, Oct. 23, 1978; *JCL*, Jun. 29, Jul. 8, and Aug. 17, 1978; *Jackson Reporter*, Sep. 21, 1978; *Mississippi Press*, Oct. 22, 1978.

26. *JCL*, Aug. 16 and Oct. 23, 1978; Nash and Taggart, *Mississippi Politics*, 82–83.

27. JOE to Thad Cochran, Nov. 7, 1978, S1, SS17, B3, F3-9, JOE Collection; Holloman oral history; *Indianola Enterprise-Tocsin*, Sep. 21, 1978; *JCL, Pearl Press*, and *South Mississippi Sun*, Nov. 2, 1978; *JDN*, Sep. 22, 1978; *MCA*, Oct. 21, 1978.

28. Only two years after Eastland's retirement would Congress split the Fifth into two circuits. Mississippi was included with Louisiana and Texas in a smaller Fifth Circuit. The states of the lower Southeast would be constituted in a new Eleventh Circuit. *Atlanta Journal*, May 21, 1978; Richard E. Cohen, "Commission Proposes Boundary Changes, Seeks to Ease Workload of Appeals Courts," *National Journal*, Dec. 29, 1973, 1948–1949; *CQ*, Jul. 22, 1948, 1854; *CR*, 95th Cong., 2nd Sess., 34531, *DDT*, Nov. 3, 1978; *JDN*, Apr. 22, 1971 *MCA*, Oct. 1, 1978; *Mobile Register*, Sep. 4, 1975; Murphy, *Uncommon Sense*, 212; *National Journal*, Sep. 30, 1978, 1567; *NOTP*, Aug. 3, 1978; *NYT*, Oct. 2 and Nov. 7, 1963, May 6, 1964, Mar. 27, 1978, Sep. 1 and Oct. 2, 1980; *WP*, Jul. 28, 1978; *West Point (MS) Times Leader*, Nov. 20, 1973.

29. JOE to Walter F. Mondale, Dec. 27, 1978, S1, SS16, B2, F2-7, JOE Collection; telephone interviews with Seymour Johnson, Jun. 20, 2012, Indianola, MS, and Frank Mitchener, Jun. 29, 2012, Sumner, MS.

30. 2012 Hiram Eastland interview.

CHAPTER 19

1. Interview with Hiram Eastland Jr. and Steve Patterson, Jun. 22, 2012, Greenwood, MS; telephone interviews with Sid Salter, Apr. 27, 2012, Starkville, MS, and John Sobotka, Mar. 29, 2012, Brandon, MS.

2. Roman Hruska to Clarence R. Pierce Jr., Apr. 26, 1985, B1, F23, Clarence R. Pierce Jr. Collection, J. D. Mitchell Library, University of Mississippi; *JCL*, Sep. 5, 1982; *JDN*, Sep. 10, 1979; *MCA*, Jun. 11, 1979; interviews with Chip Morgan, Jun. 19, 2012, Stoneville, MS, and Donald A. Ritchie, Jul. 19, 2013, Washington, D.C.

3. Telephone interview with James Herring, Apr. 5, 2012, Canton, MS; *JCL*, Oct. 27, 1985.

4. Telephone interview with Walter F. Mondale, Mar. 28, 2012, Minneapolis, MN; interview with William Winter, Mar. 18, 2010, Jackson, MS.

5. Franklin won the Second District seat narrowly. Telephone interview with Webb Franklin, May 23, 2012, Greenwood, MS; *JCL*, Jun. 3, Sep. 5, and Oct. 3, 1982, Oct. 27, 1985; *MCA*, Jun. 11, 1979.

6. *MPS*, Jun. 22, 1982; *NYT*, Feb. 20, 1986; Maarten Zwiers, "The Paradox of Power: James O. Eastland and the Democratic Party," M.A. thesis, University of Mississippi, 2007, 2.

7. Interview with Hiram Eastland Jr., Jun. 22, 2012, Greenwood, MS.

8. Hiram Eastland Jr. interview.

9. Chris Myers Asch, *The Senator and the Sharecropper: The Freedom Struggles of James O. Eastland and Fannie Lou Hamer* (New York, 2008), 289–290; Jack Bass and Marilyn W. Thompson, *Strom: The Complicated Personal and Political Life of Strom Thurmond* (New York, 2005), 342; *CPR*, Feb. 19, 1986; *MCA*, Feb. 21, 1986; *MPS*, Jun. 11, 1979; Sobotka interview; *WP*, Mar. 6, 1986.

10. E-mail, Woods Eastland to the author, Jul. 13, 2012; *GC*, Feb. 18, 21, 1986; *JCL*, *JDN*, and *NYT*, Feb. 20, 1986.

11. *DDT*, Feb. 19, 20, 21, 1986; *GC*, Feb. 21, 1986; *Scott County Times*, Feb. 26, 1986; Salter interview; interview with James Ziglar, Dec. 13, 2011, Washington, D.C.

CONCLUSION

1. James C. Cobb, *The South and America since World War II* (New York, 2011), 166; Don Colburn, *James O. Eastland: Democratic Senator from Mississippi* (Washington, 1972), 9; Walter F. Mondale address, Dec. 1, 1977, Jackson, MS, S1, SS16, B2, "Office of the Vice President" file, JOE Collection; *South Mississippi Sun*, Dec. 2, 1977.

2. Sources not previously cited on Eastland's pork barrel work include *Columbia (MS) Progress*, Apr. 27, 1972; *CQ*, Jun. 24, 1960, 1085; *CR*, 93rd Cong., 1st Sess., 3794–3795; *National Journal*, Apr. 24, 1971, 869–871; *CQ*, Jun. 24, 1960, 1085; JOE, "Address at Neshoba County Fair," Aug. 3, 1978, W. F. "Bill" Minor Papers, B80, F3, Mississippi State University; *Natchez Democrat*, Mar. 21, 1973.

3. Interview with Woods Eastland, Jun. 24, 2010, Greenwood, MS; telephone interviews with John C. Culver, Dec. 9, 2012, Bethesda, MD, and Nicholas Katzenbach, Apr. 11, 2011, Princeton, NJ; *Los Angeles Times*, Nov. 8, 1977; Chris Matthews, *Tip and the Gipper: When Politics Worked* (New York, 2013), xvi.

4. Gloster Current, memo to Roy Wilkins, Dec. 13, 1954, NAACP Papers, S11, BC98, F2, Library of Congress; *Lawrenceburg High School Yearbook: 1957*, 73, Lawrence County Public Library, Lawrenceburg, TN; Charlie McGuffee to JOE, Mar. 31, 1960, S1, SS19, B22, F22-10, JOE Collection; *Scott County Times*, Feb. 26, 1986.

5. Will Durant, *The Life of Greece* (New York, 1939), 117.

6. William Winter, transcript, oral history by Orley B. Caudill, Aug. 9 and Aug. 16, 1978, Mississippi Oral History Program of the University of Southern Mississippi, 8.

7. James W. Hilty, *Robert Kennedy: Brother Protector* (Philadelphia, 1997), 313.

8. Brad Dye, transcript, oral history by Jere Nash, Oct. 2, 2004, Nash and Taggart Collection, J. D. William Library, University of Mississippi; *MCA*, Feb. 20, 1986.

9. Interview with Woods Eastland, Jun. 11, 2012, Doddsville, MS.

APPENDIX

1. James O. Eastland to Theodore G. Bilbo, Feb. 27, 1942, S1, SS19, B7, F7-9, JOE Collection, Archives and Special Collections, J. D. Mitchell Library, University of Mississippi.

Sources Consulted

MANUSCRIPT COLLECTIONS

Albert and Shirley Small Special Collections Library, University of Virginia, Charlottesville, VA
Harry F. Byrd Papers
James J. Kilpatrick Papers
Hugh D. Scott Papers

Charles H. Capps Archives, Delta State University, Cleveland, MS
Walter Sillers Papers

Duggan Library, Hanover College, Hanover, IN
William E. Jenner Papers

Dwight D. Eisenhower Presidential Library, Abilene, KS
James O. Eastland Name File
John W. Hanes Papers
Maxwell M. Rabb Papers

Franklin D. Roosevelt Presidential Library, Hyde Park, NY
James O. Eastland Name File
Henry Morgenthau Jr. Papers
Aubrey Williams Papers

Gerald R. Ford Presidential Library, Ann Arbor, MI
James O. Eastland Name File
Gerald R. Ford Papers
John O. Marsh Papers
Ron Nessen Papers

Harry S. Truman Presidential Library, Independence, MO
Edward J. Foley Papers
Harry S. Truman Papers

Howard H. Baker Jr. Center for Public Policy, University of Tennessee, Knoxville, TN
Howard H. Baker Jr. Papers
Estes Kefauver Papers

Jean and Alexander Heard Library, Vanderbilt University, Nashville, TN
Notes of C. Alexander Heard in researching *Southern Politics* for V. O. Key of interviews
    with
    Sam V. Anderson
    Allen Bridgeforth
    Wilburn Buckley
    Hodding Carter Jr.
    George Nolan Fortenberry
    A. D. Friend
    H. V. Howerton
    Leroy Percy
    Walter Sillers
    Kenneth Toler
    Cecil S. Travis
Southern Political Collection

Jimmy Carter Presidential Library, Atlanta, GA
Jimmy Carter Presidential Papers
James O. Eastland Name File

John D. Mitchell Library, Special Collections, University of Mississippi, Oxford, MS
Thomas G. Abernethy Papers
James O. Eastland Papers
Joseph Howorth Papers
Clarence Pierce Papers
John Satterfield Papers

John F. Kennedy Presidential Library, Boston, MA
James O. Eastland Name File
John F. Kennedy Papers
Robert F. Kennedy Papers
Lawrence F. O'Brien Papers

Lyndon B. Johnson Presidential Library, Austin, TX
James O. Eastland Name File
Lyndon Baines Johnson Papers
Mike Manatos Papers
Drew Pearson Papers

Mississippi Department of Archives and History, William Winter Building, Jackson, MS
Archibald S. Coody Papers
Aaron Henry Papers
John Bell Williams Papers

Mitchell Memorial Library, Mississippi State University, Starkville, MS
Gil Carmichael Papers
W. Hodding Carter III Papers
Wilson F. "Bill" Minor Papers
Mississippi Republican Party Papers
John C. Stennis Papers
Kenneth Toler Papers

New Orleans Public Library, New Orleans, LA
Leander H. Perez Papers

Richard Nixon Presidential Library and Museum, Yorba Linda, CA
Charles Colson Papers
John W. Dean III Papers
Harry Dent Papers
Bryce Harlow Papers
Fred Malek Papers

Southern Historical Collection, University of North Carolina, Chapel Hill, NC
Sam J. Ervin Jr. Papers

Strom Thurmond Institute, Clemson University, Clemson, SC
James F. Byrnes Papers
Harry S. Dent Papers
J. Strom Thurmond Papers

University of Southern Mississippi, Hattiesburg, MS
Theodore G. Bilbo Papers
Johnson Family Papers

ORAL HISTORIES

Dwight D. Eisenhower Presidential Library, Abilene, KS
True D. Morse

Harry S. Truman Presidential Library, Independence, MO
Roy L. McGhee

J. D. Williams Library, University of Mississippi, Oxford, MS
Danny Cupit
Brad Dye
Wayne Edwards
Mark Hazard
John Holloman
Charlie McKellar
Steve Patterson

Bill Spell
Wirt Yerger Jr.
Joe Zucarro

John F. Kennedy Presidential Library, Boston, MA
Ross R. Barnett
Robert F. Kennedy

Lyndon Baines Johnson Presidential Library, Austin, TX
Clifford and Virginia Durr
James O. Eastland
Charles Evers
Strom Thurmond

Mississippi Department of Archives and History, Jackson, MS
James W. Silver

Mitchell Memorial Library, Mississippi State University, Starkville, MS
George Aiken
Haley Barbour
Edmund L. Brunini
Edward Cole
Norris Cotton
Kenneth Dean
Patricia M. "Patt" Derian
John R. Salter Jr.
Leo Seal Jr.
Fred Slabach
Larry Speakes
Don Waldon

Southern Oral History Program, University of North Carolina, Chapel Hill, NC
Harry Bowie
Gil Carmichael
Hodding Carter III
Robert Clark
Thad Cochran
James P. Coleman
Patricia M. "Patt" Derian
Aaron Henry
Paul Johnson Jr.
Eugene McLemore
W. F. "Bill" Minor
Jerry O'Keefe
Claude Ramsey
Clarke Reed
George Rogers

William Simmons
Charles Sullivan
John Bell Williams

Mississippi Oral History Project of the University of Southern Mississippi, Hattiesburg, MS
Thomas P. Abernethy
Bidwell Adam
Frank D. Barber
Haley W. Barbour
Ross Barnett
Thomas Brady
Gil Carmichael
Thad Cochran
James P. Coleman
William Myers Colmer
Thomas S. Giordano
Percy Greene
Charles A. Griffin
Aaron Henry
Paul B. Johnson III
Pete Johnson
Erle Johnston
Heber Ladner
Billy Mounger
Mike Retzer
Frank Ellis Smith
Prentiss Walker
John Bell Williams
William F. Winter
Wirt A. Yerger Jr.

Senate Historical Office, Washington, D.C.
Roy Elson
Joseph Stanley Kimmitt
Howard E. Shuman
Francis R. Valeo

ARTICLES

Ader, Emile. "Why the Dixiecrats Failed." *Journal of Politics*, Aug. 1953, 356–370.

Arsenault, Raymond. "The Folklore of Southern Demagoguery," in Charles W. Eagles (ed.), *Is There a Southern Political Tradition?* Jackson: University Press of Mississippi, 1996, 79–137.

Asch, Chris Myers. "Revisiting Reconstruction: James O. Eastland, the FEPC, and the Struggle to Rebuild Germany, 1945–1946." *Journal of Mississippi History*, 67:1 (Spring 2002), 1–28.

"The Authentic Voice." *Time*, Mar. 26, 1956, 26–29.

Badger, Tony. "Brown and Backlash," in Clive Webb (ed.), *Massive Resistance: Southern Opposition to the Second Reconstruction*. New York: Oxford University Press, 2005, 39–55.

Barksdale, E. C. "The Power Structure and Southern Gubernatorial Conservatism," in Harold W. Hollingsworth (ed.), *Essays in Recent Southern Politics*, Austin: University of Texas Press, 1970.

Bendiner, Robert. "Dixie's Fourth Party." *Nation*, Feb. 14, 1948, 174–175.

Berkowitz, Edward D. "The Great Society," in Julian E. Zelizer (ed.), *The American Congress: The Building of Democracy*. Boston: Houghton-Mifflin, 2004, 566–583.

Bolton, Charles C. "William F. Winter and the Politics of Racial Moderation in Mississippi." *Journal of Mississippi History*, 70:4 (Winter 2008), 335–382.

Boulard, Garry. "'The Man' versus 'The Quisling': Theodore Bilbo, Hodding Carter, and the 1946 Democratic Primary." *Journal of Mississippi History*, 51:3 (Aug. 1989), 201–219.

Brown, Sarah Hart. "Congressional Anti-Communism and the Segregationist South: From New Orleans to Atlanta, 1954–1958." *Georgia Historical Quarterly*, 80:4 (Winter 1996), 797–816.

Brown, Sarah Hart. "Redressing Southern 'Subversion': The Case of Senator Eastland and the Louisiana Lawyer." *Louisiana History*, 43:3 (Summer 2002), 295–314.

Brown, Sarah Hart. "The Role of Elite Leadership in the Southern Defense of Segregation, 1954–1964." *Journal of Southern History*, 77:4 (Nov. 2011), 827–865.

Buchanan, Charlotte. "Woods Eastland: A Distinguished Deltan." *Delta Business Journal*, Jan. 2012, 32–37.

Buckley, William F., Jr. "Death of a Committee." *National Review*, Jan. 23, 1976, 52.

Carter, Hodding. "The Civil Rights Issue Seen in the South." *New York Times Magazine*, Mar. 21, 1948, 15, 52–57.

Carter, Hodding. "A Southern Liberal Looks at Civil Rights." *New York Times Magazine*, Aug. 8, 1948, 10, 20.

Carter, Hodding. "The Court's Decision and the South." *Reader's Digest*, Sep. 1954, 51–57.

Carter, Hodding, III. "Citadel of the Citizens Council." *New York Times Magazine*, Nov. 12, 1961, 23, 125–127.

Chesteen, Richard D. "'Mississippi Is Gone Home': A Study of the 1948 Mississippi States' Rights Bolt." *Journal of Mississippi History*, 32:1 (Feb. 1970), 43–59.

Clark, Mary L. "Carter's Groundbreaking Appointment of Women to the Federal Bench: His Other 'Human Rights' Record." *Journal of Gender, Social Policy and the Law*, 11:3 (Nov. 2003), 1131–1163.

Cobb, James C. "World War II and the Mind of the Modern South" in Neil R. McMillen (ed.), *Remaking Dixie: The Impact of World War II on the American South*, Jackson: University Press of Mississippi, 3–21.

Cohen, Richard E. "Commission Proposes Boundary Changes, Seeks to Ease Workload of Appeals Courts." *National Journal*, Dec. 29, 1973, 1948–1949.

Cohen, Richard E. "A New Look for Judiciary." *National Journal*, Mar. 6, 1976, 311.

"The Counterattack Begins." *Nation*, Dec. 27, 1948, 9.

Cunningham, David. "Shades of Anti-Civil Rights Violence," in Ted Ownby (ed.), *The Civil Rights Movement in Mississippi*. Jackson: University Press of Mississippi, 2013, 180–203.

Davies, David R., and Judy Smith. "Jimmy Ward and the *Jackson Daily News*," in David R. Davies (ed.), *The Press and Race: Mississippi Journalists Confront the Movement*. Jackson: University Press of Mississippi, 2001, 86–109

Dittmer, John. "The Politics of the Mississippi Movement, 1954–1964," in David L. Lewis (ed.), *The Civil Rights Movement in America*. Jackson: University Press of Mississippi, 1986, 65–93.

Dittmer, John. "The Transformation of the Mississippi Movement, 1964–1968: The Rise and Fall of the Freedom Democratic Party," in W. Marvin Dulaney and Kathleen Underwood (eds.), *Essays on the American Civil Rights Movement*. College Station: Texas A&M University Press, 1993, 1–38.

Drabble, John. "The FBI, COINTELPRO: White Hate, and the Decline of the Ku Klux Klan Organizations in Mississippi, 1964–1971." *Journal of Mississippi History*, 66:4 (Winter 2004), 353–402.

Eagles, Charles W. "The Fight for Men's Minds; The Aftermath of the Ole Miss Riot of 1962." *Journal of Mississippi History*, 71:1 (Spring 2009), 1–54.

Edmundson, Ben G. "Pat Harrison and Mississippi in the Presidential Elections of 1924 and 1928." *Journal of Mississippi History*, 33:4 (Nov. 1971), 333–350.

Ethridge, Richard C. "The Fall of The Man: The United States Senate's Probe of Theodore G. Bilbo in December 1946, and Its Aftermath." *Journal of Mississippi History*, 38:3 (Aug. 1976), 241–262.

Faulkner, William. "A Letter to the North." *Life*, Mar. 5, 1956, 51–52.

Fite, Gilbert C. "Mechanization of Cotton Production since World War II." *Agricultural History*, 54:1 (Jan. 1980), 190–207.

Fleegler, Robert L. "Theodore G. Bilbo and the Decline of Public Racism, 1938–1947." *Journal of Mississippi History*, 68:1 (Spring 2006), 1–27.

Fortenberry, Charles N., and F. Glenn Abney. "Mississippi: Unreconstructed and Unredeemed," in William C. Havard (ed.), *The Changing Politics of the South*. Baton Rouge: Louisiana State University Press, 1982, 472–524.

Fuller, Helen. "The Fourth Party." *New Republic*, Mar. 15, 1948, 9.

Giroux, Vincent A., Jr. "The Rise of Theodore G. Bilbo." *Journal of Mississippi History*, 43: 3 (Aug. 1981), 180–209.

Graves, John Temple. "Revolution in the South." *Virginia Quarterly Review*, 26:2 (Spring 1950), 190–197.

Green, Fletcher M. "Resurgent Southern Sectionalism, 1933–1955." *North Carolina Historical Review*, 33:4 (Apr. 1956), 222–241.

Halberstam, David. "A County Divided against Itself." *The Reporter*, Dec. 15, 1955, 30–32.

Halberstam, David. "The White Citizens Councils: Respectable Means for Unrespectable Ends." *Commentary*, Oct. 1956, 293–302.

Hall, Kermit. "The Constitutional Lessons of the Little Rock Crisis," in Elizabeth Jacoway and C. Fred Williams (eds.), *Understanding the Little Rock Crisis: An Exercise in Remembrance and Reconciliation*. Fayetteville: University of Arkansas Press, 1999, 123–140.

Hays, Charlotte. "The Silent Senator from Mississippi." *Midwest*, Feb. 27, 1974.

"High Cotton." *New Republic*, Aug. 30, 1948, 10.

Jacoway, Elizabeth. "Jim Johnson of Arkansas: Segregationist Prototype," in Ted Ownby (ed.), *The Role of Ideas in the Civil Rights South*. Jackson: University Press of Mississippi, 2002, 137–155.

"James O. Eastland." *Current Biography: 1949*, 184–185.

Jones, Sam H., as told to James Aswell. "Will Dixie Bolt the New Deal?" *Saturday Evening Post*, Mar. 6, 1943, 20–21, 42, 45

Kelley, Donald Brooks. "Deep South Dilemma: The Mississippi Press in the Presidential Election of 1928." *Journal of Mississippi History*, 25:2 (Apr. 1963), 63–92.

Kellogg, Peter J. "Civil Rights Consciousness in the 1940s." *Historian*, 42:1 (Nov. 1979), 18–41.

Klarman, Michael J. "Brown and Backlash" in Clive Webb (ed.), *Massive Resistance: Southern Opposition to the Second Reconstruction*. New York: Oxford University Press, 2005, 21–38.

Land, Gary Paul. "Mississippi Republicanism and the 1960 Presidential Election." *Journal of Mississippi History*, 40:1 (Feb. 1978), 33–48.

Lapidary, Charles J. "Ol Massa Jim Eastland." *Nation*, Feb. 9, 1957, 151.

Lemmon, Sarah McCulloch. "The Ideology of the Dixiecrat Movement." *Social Forces*, 30:2 (Dec. 1951), 162–171.

Leonard, George B., T. George Harris, and Christopher S. Wren. "How a Secret Deal Prevented a Massacre at Ole Miss." *Look*, Dec. 31, 1962, 19–36.

Lewis, Walter. "Dixie Racists to Defy Constitution." *New Leader*, Jan. 16, 1956, 17–18.

Mabry, Chip. "Bobby Kennedy's Visit to the Delta." *Delta*, Jul. 8, 2004, 122–123.

McGill, Ralph. "Will the South Ditch Truman?" *Saturday Evening Post*, May 22, 1948, 15–17, 78–90.

McMillen, Neil R. "Development of Civil Rights," in Richard Aubrey McLemore (ed.), *A History of Mississippi*, Volume II. Hattiesburg: University and College Press of Mississippi, 1973, 154–176.

McMillen, Neil R. "Perry W. Howard, Boss of Black-and-Tan Republicanism in Mississippi, 1924–1960." *Journal of Southern History*, 48:2 (May 1982), 205–224.

Melton, Thomas R. "Walter Sillers and National Politics, 1948–1964." *Journal of Mississippi History*, 39:3 (Apr. 1971), 213–226.

Morgan, Chester M. "At the Crossroads: World War II, Delta Agriculture, and Modernization." *Journal of Mississippi History*, 57:4 (Winter 1995), 353–371.

Nash, Jere, and Andy Taggart. "Education Transforms the Mississippi Legislature." *Journal of Mississippi History*, 68:3 (Fall 2006), 169–193.

"The New Chairman." *Time*, Mar. 12, 1956, 26–31.

"New South: A Political Phenomenon Grips Dixie's Voters." *Newsweek*, Oct. 25, 1948, 32–34.

Noer, Thomas. "Segregationists and the World: The Foreign Policy of the Resistance," in Brenda Gayle Plummer (ed.), *Window on Freedom: Race, Civil Rights, and Foreign Policy, 1945–1988*. Chapel Hill: University of North Carolina Press, 2003, 141–162.

Odum, Howard W. "Social Change in the South." *Journal of Politics*, 10:2 (May 1948), 242–258.

Percy, Walker. "Mississippi: The Fallen Paradise" in Willie Morris (ed.), *The South Today: 100 Years After Appomattox*. New York: Harper & Row, 1965, 66–79.

"Plantation Man." *U.S. News and World Report*, Feb. 27, 1948, 3.

Rowe-Sims, Sarah. "The Mississippi State Sovereignty Commission: An Agency History." *Journal of Mississippi History*, 61:1 (Spring 1999), 29–58.

"Rule by Demagogues." *Time*, Jul. 9, 1945, 15.

Sallis, Charles, and John Quincy Adams. "Desegregation in Jackson, Mississippi," in Elizabeth Jacoway and David R. Colburn (eds.), *Southern Businessmen and Desegregation*. Baton Rouge: Louisiana State University Press, 1982, 236–256.

Salmond, John A. "The Great Southern Commie Hunt: Aubrey Williams, the Southern Conference Educational Fund, and the Internal Security Subcommittee." *South Atlantic Quarterly*, 77:4 (Autumn 1978), 433–452.

Sancton, Thomas. "White Supremacy: Crisis or Plot." *Nation*, Jul. 24, 1948, 95–98.

Savage, Sean J. "To Purge or Not to Purge: Hamlet Harry and the Dixiecrats, 1948–1952." *Presidential Studies Quarterly*, 27:4 (Fall 1997), 773–790.

Schlauch, Wolfgang. "Representative William Colmer and Senator James O. Eastland and the Reconstruction of Germany, 1945." *Journal of Mississippi History*, 34:3 (Aug. 1972), 193–213.

Shannon, J. B. "Presidential Politics in the South." *Journal of Politics*, 10:3 (Aug. 1948), 464–489.

Simpson, William H. "The Birth of the Mississippi Loyalist Democrats, 1965–1968." *Journal of Mississippi History*, 42:1 (Feb. 1982), 27–45.

Sitkoff, Harvard. "Harry Truman and the Election of 1948: The Coming of Age of Civil Rights in American Politics." *Journal of Southern History*, 34:3 (Nov. 1971), 597–616.

Skates, John Ray. "Fred Sullens: Bourbon out of His Time." *Journal of Mississippi History*, 49:2 (May 1967), 92–104.

Skates, John Ray. "From Enchantment to Disillusionment: A Southern Editor Views the New Deal." *Southern Quarterly*, 5:4 (Jul. 1967), 367–380.

Skates, John Ray. "Mississippi History: A Theme." *Southern Quarterly*, 6:1 (Oct. 1967), 1–12.

Skates, John Ray. "World War II as a Watershed in Mississippi History." *Journal of Mississippi History*, 37:2 (May 1975), 131–143.

"Southern Revolt." *Time*, Oct. 11, 1948, 24–27.

Theoharis, Athan G. "Unanswered Questions: Chambers, Nixon, the FBI, and the Hiss Case," in Athan G. Theoharis (ed.), *Beyond the Hiss Case: The FBI, Congress and the Cold War*. Philadelphia, PA: Temple University Press, 1982, 246–308.

Thompson, Don Harris. "Senator John Cornelius Stennis: Mississippi Statesman: The Early Years." *Journal of Mississippi History*, 72:2 (Summer 2008), 125–146.

Thorndike, Joseph J. "The Sometimes Sordid Level of Race and Segregation: James J. Kilpatrick and the Campaign against *Brown*," in Matthew D. Lassiter and Andrew B. Lewis (eds.), *The Moderates' Dilemma: Massive Resistance to School Desegregation in Virginia*. Charlottesville: University Press of Virginia, 1998, 51–71.

Trillin, Calvin. "State Secrets." *New Yorker*, May 29, 1995, 63.

"Tumult in Dixie." *Time*, Jul. 26, 1948, 15–16.

Wakefield, Dan. "Respectable Racism." *Nation*, Oct. 22, 1955, 339–341.

"War between the Democrats." *Newsweek*, Jul. 26, 1948, 21–22.

Weill, Susan M. "Mississippi's Daily Press in Three Crises" in David R. Davies (ed.), *The Press and Race: Mississippi Journalists Confront the Movement*. Jackson: University Press of Mississippi, 2001, 17–53.

Weill, Susan M. "The Dixiecrats and the Mississippi Daily Press." *Journal of Mississippi History*, 64:3 (Winter 2002), 259–282.

"Where Segregation Is Legal: Mixed Marriage Ban Is About All That Remains." *U.S. News and World Report*, Nov. 18, 1955, 28.

Winter, William F. "Politicians and the Press." *Journal of Mississippi History*, 49:2 (May 1987), 83–92.

Zellner, Dorothy. "Red Roadshow: Eastland in New Orleans, 1954." *Louisiana History*, 31:1 (1992), 31–60.

Ziker, Ann K. "Segregationists Confront American Empire: The Conservative White South and the Question of Hawaiian Statehood, 1947–1959." *Pacific Historical Review*, 76:3 (Aug. 2007), 439–465.

BOOKS

Abourezk, James G. *Advise and Dissent: Memoirs of South Dakota and the U.S. Senate.* Chicago: Lawrence Hill, 1989.

Abraham, Henry J. *Justices and Presidents: A Political History of Appointments to the Supreme Court.* New York: Oxford University Press, 1974.

Adams, Frank T., with Myles Horton. *Unearthing the Seeds of Fire: The Idea of Highlander.* Winston-Salem: John F. Blair, 1975.

Adams, Frank T., with a foreword by Arthur Kinoy. *James A. Dombrowski: An American Heretic, 1897–1983.* Knoxville: University of Tennessee Press, 1992.

Ader, Emile B. *The Dixiecrat Movement: Its Role in Third Party Politics.* Washington, D.C.: Public Affairs Press, 1955.

Aiken, Charles S. *The Cotton Plantation South since the Civil War.* Baltimore, MD: Johns Hopkins University Press, 1998.

Alston, Alex A., Jr., and James L. Dickerson. *Devil's Sanctuary: An Eyewitness History of Mississippi Hate Crimes.* Chicago: Lawrence Hill Books, 2009.

Alwood, Edward. *Dark Days in the Newsroom: McCarthyism Aimed at the Press.* Philadelphia, PA: Temple University Press, 2007.

Ambrose, Stephen E. *Eisenhower: The President,* Volume II. New York: Simon & Schuster, 1984.

Ambrose, Stephen E. *Nixon: The Education of a Politician, 1913–1962.* New York: Simon and Schuster, 1987.

Anderson, J. W. *Eisenhower, Brownell, and the Congress: The Tangled Origins of the Civil Rights Act of 1956–1957.* Tuscaloosa: University of Alabama Press, 1964.

Annis, J. Lee, Jr. *Howard Baker: Conciliator in an Age of Crisis.* Lanham, MD: Madison Books, 1994.

Arsenault, Raymond. *Freedom Riders: 1961 and the Struggle for Racial Justice.* New York: Oxford University Press, 2006.

Asbell, Bernard. *The Senate Nobody Knows.* Garden City, NY: Doubleday & Co., 1978.

Asch, Chris Myers. *The Senator and the Sharecropper: The Freedom Struggles of James O. Eastland and Fannie Lou Hamer.* New York: The New Press, 2008.

Ashmore, Harry S. *Hearts and Minds: A Personal Chronicle of Race in America.* Washington, D.C.: Seven Locks Press, 1988.

Atkins, Joseph B. *Covering for the Bosses: Labor and the Southern Press.* Jackson: University Press of Mississippi, 2008.

Baker, Bill R. *Catch the Vision: The Life of Henry L. Whitfield of Mississippi.* Jackson: University Press of Mississippi, 1974.

Baker, Bobby, with Larry L. King. *Wheeling and Dealing: Confessions of a Capitol Hill Operator.* New York: W. W. Norton & Co., 1978.

Baker, Ross K. *Friend and Foe in the U.S. Senate.* New York: The Free Press, 1980.

Ball, Howard. *Murder in Mississippi: United States v. Price and the Struggle for Civil Rights.* Lawrence: University Press of Kansas, 2004.

Ball, Howard. *Justice in Mississippi: The Murder Trial of Edgar Ray Killen.* Lawrence: University Press of Kansas, 2006.

Barnes, Catherine A. *Journey from Jim Crow: The Desegregation of Southern Transit.* New York: Columbia University Press, 1983.

Barone, Michael, Grant Ujifusa, and Douglas Matthews. *The Almanac of American Politics, 1974*. Boston: Gambit, 1973.

Barone, Michael, Grant Ujifusa, and Douglas Matthews. *The Almanac of American Politics, 1978*. New York: E. P. Dutton, 1977.

Barrett, Russell H. *Integration at Ole Miss*. Chicago: Quadrangle Books, 1968.

Bartlett, Bruce. *Wrong on Race: The Democratic Party's Buried Past*. New York: Palgrave MacMillan, 2008.

Bartley, Numan V. *The New South: The Story of the South's Modernization*. Baton Rouge: Louisiana State University, 1969.

Bartley, Numan V. *The Rise of Massive Resistance: Race and Politics in the South during the 1950s*. Baton Rouge: Louisiana State University Press, 1997.

Bartley, Numan V., and Hugh D. Graham. *Southern Politics and the Second Reconstruction*. Baltimore, MD: Johns Hopkins University Press, 1975.

Bass, Jack. *Unlikely Heroes*. New York: Simon & Schuster, 1981.

Bass, Jack. *Taming the Storm: The Life and Times of Judge Frank M. Johnson Jr. and the South's Fight over Civil Rights*. New York: Doubleday, 1992.

Bass, Jack, and Walter DeVries. *The Transformation of Southern Politics: Social Change and Political Consequence since 1945*. New York: Basic Books, 1976.

Bass, Jack, and Marilyn W. Thompson. *Strom: The Complicated Personal and Political Life of Strom Thurmond*. New York: Political Affairs, 2005.

Bayh, Birch. *One Heartbeat Away: Presidential Disability and Succession*. Indianapolis: The Bobbs-Merrill Co., 1968.

Becnel, Thomas. *Senator Allen Ellender of Louisiana: A Biography*. Baton Rouge: Louisiana State University Press, 1995.

Behrman, Greg. *The Most Noble Adventure: The Marshall Plan and the Time When America Helped Save Europe*. New York: The Free Press, 2007.

Beito, David T., and Linda Royster Beito. *Black Maverick: T. R. M. Howard's Fight for Civil Rights and Economic Power*. Urbana: University of Illinois Press, 2009.

Belfrage, Cedric. *The American Inquisition, 1945–1960*. Indianapolis: The Bobbs-Merrill Co., 1973.

Belfrage, Sally. *Freedom Summer*. Charlottesville: University of Virginia Press, 1965.

Bell, Griffin, with Ronald J. Ostrow. *Taking Care of the Law*. Atlanta: Mercer University Press, 1986.

Bell, Roger. *Last Among Equals: Hawaiian Statehood and American Politics*. Honolulu: University of Hawaii Press, 1984.

Benson, Ezra Taft. *Crossfire: The Eight Years with Eisenhower*. Garden City, NY: Doubleday & Co., 1962.

Berman, Daniel M. *A Bill Becomes A Law: Congress Enacts Civil Rights Legislation*, 2nd ed. London: The MacMillan Co., 1969.

Berman, William J. *The Politics of Civil Rights in the Truman Administration*. Columbus: Ohio State University Press, 1970.

Berry, Jason. *Amazing Grace: With Charles Evers in Mississippi*. New York: Saturday Review Press, 1979.

Berry, Mary Frances. *Black Resistance, White Law: A History of Constitutional Racism in America*. New York: Penguin Press, 1994.

Berry, Mary Frances. *And Justice for All: The United States Commission on Civil Rights and the Continuing Struggle for Freedom in America.* New York: Alfred A. Knopf, 2009.

Beschloss, Michael R. (ed.). *Taking Charge: The Johnson White House Tapes, 1963–1964.* New York: Simon & Schuster, 1997.

Beschloss, Michael R. (ed.) *Reaching for Glory: Lyndon Johnson's Secret White House Tapes.* New York: Simon & Schuster, 2001.

Biden, Joe. *Promises to Keep: On Life and Politics.* New York: Random House, 2007.

Biles, Roger. *Crusading Liberal: Paul H. Douglas of Illinois.* DeKalb: Northern Illinois University Press, 2002.

Black, Conrad M. *Richard M. Nixon: A Life in Full.* New York: Public Affairs, 2007.

Bolton, Charles C. *The Hardest Deal of All: The Battle over School Integration in Mississippi, 1870–1980.* Jackson: University Press of Mississippi, 2009.

Bolton, Charles C. *William F. Winter and the New Mississippi: A Biography.* Jackson: University Press of Mississippi, 2013.

Borstelmann, Thomas. *The Cold War and the Color Line: American Race Relations in the Global Arena.* Cambridge, MA: Harvard University Press, 2002.

Bowen, Roger. *Innocence Is Not Enough: The Life and Death of Herbert Norman.* Vancouver, BC: Douglas & McIntyre, 1986.

Branch, Taylor. *Parting the Waters: America in the King Years, 1954–63.* New York: Simon & Schuster, 1988.

Branch, Taylor. *Pillar of Fire: America in the King Years, 1963–65.* New York: Simon & Schuster, 1998.

Branch, Taylor. *At Canaan's Edge: America in the King Years, 1965–68.* New York: Simon & Schuster, 2006.

Brauer, Carl M. *John F. Kennedy and the Second Reconstruction.* New York: Columbia University Press, 1977.

Brendan, Piers. *The Decline and Fall of the British Empire.* New York: Alfred A. Knopf, 2008.

Breslin, Jimmy. *How the Good Guys Finally Won: Notes from an Impeachment Summer.* New York: Viking Press, 1975.

Brooke, Edward W. *Bridging the Divide: My Life.* New Brunswick, NJ: Rutgers University Press, 2007.

Brown, D. Clayton. *King Cotton in Modern America: A Cultural, Political, and Economic History since 1945.* Jackson: University Press of Mississippi, 2011.

Brown, Sarah Hart. *Standing against Dragons: Three Southern Lawyers in an Era of Fear.* Baton Rouge: Louisiana State University, 1998.

Brownell, Herbert, with John P. Burke. *Advising Ike: The Memoirs of Attorney General Herbert Brownell.* Lawrence: University Press of Kansas, 1993.

Bryant, Nick. *The Bystander: John F. Kennedy and the Struggle for Black Equality.* New York: Basic Books, 2006.

Burk, Robert Fredrick. *The Eisenhower Administration and Black Civil Rights.* Knoxville: University of Tennessee Press, 1984.

Burner, David. *The Politics of Provincialism: The Democratic Party in Transition, 1914–1932.* New York: W. W. Norton & Co., 1967.

Burns, James McGregor. *Edward Kennedy and the Camelot Legacy.* New York: W. W. Norton & Co., 1976.

Burns, Stewart (ed.). *Daybreak of Freedom: The Montgomery Bus Boycott.* Chapel Hill: University of North Carolina Press, 1997.

Bustbee, Westley A., Jr. *Mississippi: A History*. Wheeling, IL: Harlan Davidson, 2005.

Byrnes, James F. *All in One Lifetime*. New York: Harper & Brothers, 1958.

Cagin, Seth, and Philip Dray. *We Are Not Afraid: The Story of Goodman, Chaney and Schwerner*. New York: Macmillan, 1988.

Califano, Joseph A., Jr. *The Triumph of Lyndon Johnson: The White House Years*. New York: Simon & Schuster, 1991.

Campbell, Karl E. *Senator Sam Ervin: Last of the Founding Fathers*. Chapel Hill: University of North Carolina Press, 2007.

Campbell, Will D. *Robert G. Clark's Journey to the House: A Black Politician's Story*. Jackson: University Press of Mississippi, 2003.

Canellos, Peter S. (ed.). *Last Lion: The Fall and Rise of Ted Kennedy*. New York: Simon & Schuster, 2009.

Cannon, James. *Time and Chance: Gerald Ford's Appointment with History*. New York: Harper Collins, 1994.

Caro, Robert A. *The Years of Lyndon Johnson: Master of the Senate*. New York: Alfred A. Knopf, 2002.

Caro, Robert A. *The Years of Lyndon Johnson: The Passage of Power*. New York: Alfred A. Knopf, 2012.

Carter, Dan T. *The Politics of Rage: George Wallace, the Origins of the New Conservatism, and the Transformation of American Politics*. New York: Simon & Schuster, 1995.

Carter, David C. *The Music Has Gone out of the Movement: Civil Rights and the Johnson Administration*. Chapel Hill: University of North Carolina Press, 2009.

Carter, W. Hodding, III. *The South Strikes Back*. Garden City, NY: Doubleday & Co., 1958.

Catledge, Turner. *My Life and the Times*. New York: Harper and Row, 1971.

Chandler, David Leon. *The Natural Superiority of Southern Politicians: A Revisionist History*. Garden City, NY: Doubleday & Co., 1977.

Chappell, David L. *A Stone of Hope: Prophetic Religion and the Death of Jim Crow*. Chapel Hill: University of North Carolina Press, 2004.

Chappell, David L. *Inside Agitators: White Southerners and the Civil Rights Movement*. Baltimore, MD: Johns Hopkins University Press, 2006.

Cherny, Andrei. *The Candy Bombers: The Untold Story of the Berlin Airlift and America's Finest Hour*. New York: G. P. Putnam's Sons, 2008.

Christofferson, Bill. *The Man from Clear Lake: Earth Day Founder Senator Gaylord Nelson*. Madison: University of Wisconsin Press, 2004.

Clancy, Paul R. *Just a Country Lawyer: A Biography of Senator Sam Ervin*. Bloomington: Indiana University Press, 1974.

Clark, Thomas D. *The Emerging South*, 2nd ed. New York: Oxford University Press, 1968.

Clymer, Adam. *Edward M. Kennedy: A Biography*. New York: William Morrow, 1999.

Cobb, Charles E., Jr. *This Nonviolent Stuff'll Get Us Killed: How Guns Made the Civil Rights Movement Possible*. New York: Basic Books, 2014.

Cobb, James C. *The Most Southern Place on Earth: The Mississippi Delta and the Roots of Regional Identity*. New York: Oxford University Press, 1992.

Cobb, James C. *The Selling of the South: The Southern Crusade for Industrial Development, 1936–1990*, 2nd ed. Champaign: University of Illinois Press, 1993.

Cobb, James C. *The South and America since World War II*. New York: Oxford University Press, 2011.

Cohn, David L. *The Life and Times of King Cotton*. New York: Oxford University Press, 1956.

Cohodas, Nadine. *Strom Thurmond and the Politics of Southern Change*. New York: Simon & Schuster, 1993.

Cohodas, Nadine. *The Band Played Dixie: Race and the Liberal Conscience at Ole Miss*. New York: The Free Press, 1997.

Colburn, Don. *James O. Eastland: Democratic Senator from Mississippi*. Washington, D.C.: Grossman, 1972.

Collins, Charles W. *Whither Solid South: A Study in Politics and Race Relations*. New Orleans: Pelican, 1947.

Comiskey, Michael. *Seeking Justices: The Judging of Supreme Court Nominees*. Lawrence: University Press of Kansas, 2004.

Cook, Gay, and Ann Adamiewicz. *John C. Stennis: Democratic Senator from Mississippi*. Washington, D.C.: Grossman, 1972.

Cook, James Graham. *The Segregationists*. New York: Appleton Century Crofts, 1962.

Cox, Karen L. *Dixie's Daughters: The United Daughters of the Confederacy and the Preservation of Confederate Culture*. Gainesville: University Press of Florida, 2009.

Craig, R. Bruce. *Treasonable Doubt: The Harry Dexter White Spy Case*. Lawrence: University Press of Kansas, 2004.

Crespino, Joseph. *In Search of Another Country: Mississippi and the Conservative Counterrevolution*. Princeton, NJ: Princeton University Press, 2007.

Crespino, Joseph. *Strom Thurmond's America*. New York: Hill and Wang, 2012.

Crispell, Brian Lewis. *Testing the Limits: George Armistead Smathers and Cold War America*. Athens: University of Georgia Press, 1999.

Crosby, Emilye. *A Little Taste of Freedom: The Black Freedom Struggle in Claiborne County, Mississippi*. Chapel Hill: University of North Carolina Press, 2005.

Culver, John C., and John Hyde. *American Dreamer: A Life of Henry A. Wallace*. New York: W. W. Norton & Co., 2000.

Curry, Constance, with an introduction by Marian Wright Edelman. *Silver Rights*. Chapel Hill: Algonquin Books, 1995.

Dallek, Robert. *Lone Star Rising: Lyndon Johnson and His Times, 1908–1960*. New York: Oxford University Press, 1991.

Dallek, Robert. *Flawed Giant: Lyndon Johnson and His Times, 1961–1973*. New York: Oxford University Press, 1998.

Dallek, Robert. *An Unfinished Life: John F. Kennedy, 1917–1963*. Boston: Little, Brown & Co., 2003.

Daniel, Pete. *Standing at the Crossroads: Southern Life in the Twentieth Century*. New York: Hill and Wang, 1986.

Daniels, Jonathan. *A Southerner Discovers the South*. New York: MacMillan Co., 1938.

Danielson, Chris. *After Freedom Summer: How Race Realigned Mississippi Politics, 1945–1986*. Gainesville: University Press of Florida, 2011.

Dattel, Gene. *Cotton and Race in the Making of America: The Human Costs of Economic Power*. Chicago: Ivan R. Dee, 2009.

Davies, John Paton. *China Hand: An Autobiography*. Philadelphia: University of Pennsylvania Press, 2012.

Davis, Michael D., and Hunter R. Clark. *Thurgood Marshall: Warrior at the Bar, Rebel on the Bench*. New York: Birch Lane Press, 1992.

Day, John Kyle. *The Southern Manifesto: Massive Resistance and the Fight to Preserve Segregation.* Jackson: University Press of Mississippi, 2014.

Dean, John W. *Blind Ambition.* New York: Simon & Schuster, 1976.

Dean, John W. *The Rehnquist Choice: The Untold Story of the Nixon Appointment That Redefined the Supreme Court.* New York: The Free Press, 2001.

DeConcini, Dennis. *Senator Dennis DeConcini: From the Center of the Aisle.* Tucson: University of Arizona Press, 2006.

DeLoach, Cartha D. *Hoover's FBI: The Inside Story by Hoover's Trusted Lieutenant.* Washington, D.C.: Regnery Publishing, 1995.

D'Emilio, John. *Lost Prophet: The Life and Times of Bayard Rustin.* New York: The Free Press, 2003.

Dent, Harry S. *The Prodigal South Returns to Power.* New York: John Wiley & Sons, 1978.

DePalma, Anthony. *The Man Who Invented Fidel: Castro, Cuba and Herbert L. Matthews of the New York Times.* New York: Public Affairs, 2006.

Devine, Thomas W. *Henry Wallace's 1948 Presidential Campaign and the Future of Postwar Liberalism.* Chapel Hill: University of North Carolina Press, 2013.

Dittmer, John. *Local People: The Struggle for Civil Rights in Mississippi.* Champaign: University of Illinois Press, 1995.

Dobbs, Ricky F. *Yellow Dogs and Republicans: Allan Shivers and Texas Two-Party Politics.* College Station: Texas A&M University Press, 2005.

Donaldson, Gary A. *Truman Defeats Dewey.* Lexington: University Press of Kentucky, 1999.

Donovan, Robert J. *Eisenhower: The Inside Story.* New York: Harper & Brothers, 1956.

Douth, George. *Leaders in Profile: The 94th Senate.* New York: Sperry & Douth, 1975.

Doyle, William. *An American Insurrection: The Battle of Oxford, Mississippi, 1962.* New York: Doubleday, 2001.

Draper, Alan. *Conflict of Interests: Organized Labor and the Civil Rights Movement in the South, 1954–1968.* Ithaca, NY: ILR Press, 1994.

Drury, Allen. *A Senate Journal, 1943–1945.* New York: McGraw-Hill Book Co., 1963.

Dunbar, Tony. *Delta Time: A Journey through Mississippi.* New York: Pantheon Books, 1990.

Durant, Will. *The Life of Greece.* New York: Simon and Schuster, 1939.

Durr, Virginia Foster. *Outside the Magic Circle: The Autobiography of Virginia Foster Durr.* Tuscaloosa: University of Alabama Press, 1985.

Eagles, Charles W. *The Price of Defiance: James Meredith and the Integration of Ole Miss.* Chapel Hill: University of North Carolina Press, 2009.

Edwards, Jerome E. *Pat McCarran: Political Boss of Nevada.* Reno: University of Nevada Press, 1982.

Egerton, John. *Speak Now against the Day: The Generation Before the Civil Rights Movement in the South.* New York: Alfred A. Knopf, 1994.

Ehrlichman, John. *Witness to Power: The Nixon Presidency.* New York: Simon & Schuster, 1982.

Eisenhower, Dwight D. *The White House Years: Waging Peace, 1956–1961.* Garden City, NY: Doubleday & Co., 1965.

Elliott, Gary E. *Senator Alan Bible and the Politics of the New West.* Reno: University of Nevada Press, 1994.

Emanuel, Anne. *Elbert Parr Tuttle: Chief Jurist of the Civil Rights Revolution.* Athens: University of Georgia Press, 2011.

Emmerich, J. Oliver. *Two Faces of Janus: The Saga of Deep South Change*. Jackson: University and College Press of Mississippi, 1973.

Ervin, Sam J., Jr. *Preserving the Constitution: The Autobiography of Sam J. Ervin Jr.* Charlottesville, VA: The Michie Co., 1984.

Evans, Rowland, and Robert Novak. *Lyndon B. Johnson: The Exercise of Power*. New York: The New American Library, 1966.

Ewald, William Bragg, Jr., *Who Killed Joe McCarthy?* New York: Simon and Schuster, 1984.

Fairclough, Adam. *Race and Democracy: The Civil Rights Struggle in Louisiana, 1915–1972*. Athens: University of Georgia Press, 1995.

Federal Writers Project of the Works Progress Administration. *Mississippi: The WPA Guide to the Magnolia State*. New York: The Viking Press, 1938.

Finley, Keith. *Delaying the Dream: Southern Senators and the Fight against Civil Rights, 1938–1965*. Baton Rouge: Louisiana State University Press, 2008.

Finzsch, Norbert, and Jurgen Martschukat. *Different Restorations: Reconstruction and Wiederaufbau in the United States and Germany, 1865-1945-1989*. Providence, RI: Berghahn Books, 1996.

Fite, Gilbert. *American Farmers: The New Minority*. Bloomington: Indiana University Press, 1981.

Fite, Gilbert. *Richard B. Russell Jr.: Senator from Georgia*. Chapel Hill: University of North Carolina Press, 1991.

Fleming, Harold C., with Virginia Fleming. *The Potomac Chronicle: Public Policy and Civil Rights from Kennedy to Reagan*. Athens: University of Georgia Press, 1996.

Foley, Michael. *The New Senate: Liberal Influence on a Conservative Institution, 1959–1972*. New Haven, CT: Yale University Press, 1980.

Fontenay, Charles L. *Estes Kefauver: A Biography*. Knoxville: University of Tennessee Press, 1980.

Ford, Gerald R. *A Time to Heal: The Autobiography of Gerald Ford*. New York: Harper & Row, 1979.

Fosl, Catherine. *Subversive and Southern: Anne Braden and the Struggle for Racial Justice in the Postwar South*. New York: Palgrave, 2002.

Fossedal, Gregory A., with a foreword by Paul Nitze. *Our Finest Hour: Will Clayton, the Marshall Plan, and the Triumph of Democracy*. Stanford, CA: Hoover Institution Press, 1993.

Frank, John P., with a foreword by Lewis F. Powell Jr. *Clement Haynsworth, the Senate and the Supreme Court*. Charlottesville: University Press of Virginia, 1991.

Frederickson, Kari. *The Dixiecrat Revolt and the End of the Solid South, 1932–1948*. Chapel Hill: University of North Carolina Press, 2001.

Freidin, Seymour K. *Sense of the Senate*. New York: Dodd, Mead & Co., 1972.

Fried, Richard. *Nightmare in Red: The McCarthy Era in Perspective*. New York: Oxford University Press, 1990.

Friedman, Joel William. *Champion of Civil Rights: Judge John Minor Wisdom*. Baton Rouge: Louisiana State University Press, 2009.

Frisk, David B. *If Not Us, Who? William Rusher, National Review and the Conservative Movement*. Wilmington, DE: ISI Books, 2012.

Frist, William H., and J. Lee Annis Jr. *Tennessee Senators, 1911–2001: Portraits of Leadership in a Century of Change*. Lanham, MD: Madison Books, 1999.

Garrow, David J. *The FBI and Martin Luther King Jr.: From "Solo" to Memphis*. New York: W. W. Norton & Co., 1981.

Gelb, Arthur. *City Room*. New York: Berkley, 2003.

Gentry, Curt. *J. Edgar Hoover: The Man and the Secrets*. New York: Penguin Books, 1991.

Giggle, John M. *After Redemption: Jim Crow and the Transformation of African American Religion in the Delta, 1875–1915*. New York: Oxford University Press, 2008.

Giglio, James N. *Call Me Tom: The Life of Thomas F. Eagleton*. Columbia: University of Missouri Press, 2011.

Gilmore, Glenda Elizabeth. *Defying Dixie: The Radical Roots of Civil Rights, 1919–1950*. New York: W. W. Norton & Co., 2008.

Glen, John M. *Highlander: No Ordinary School*. 2nd ed. Knoxville: University of Tennessee Press, 1996.

Godwin, George, Jr. *The Little Legislatures: Committees of Congress*. Amherst: University of Massachusetts Press, 1970.

Golden, Harry. *Mr. Kennedy and the Negroes*. Cleveland, OH: The World Publishing Co., 1964.

Goldman, Eric F. *The Tragedy of Lyndon Johnson*. New York: Alfred A. Knopf, 1968.

Goodwin, George, Jr. *The Little Legislatures: Committees of Congress*. Amherst: University of Massachusetts Press, 1970.

Gore, Albert, Sr., with a new introduction by Al Gore. *Let the Glory Out: My South and Its Politics*. Athens, GA: Hill Street Press, 2000.

Gorman, Joseph Paul. *Kefauver: A Political Biography*. New York: Oxford University Press, 1971.

Gould, Lewis L. *The Most Exclusive Club: A History of the Modern United States Senate*. New York: Basic Books, 2005.

Graham, Allison. *Framing the South: Hollywood, Television, and Race during the Civil Rights Struggle*. Baltimore, MD: Johns Hopkins University Press, 2001.

Graham, Hugh Davis. *Crisis in Print: Desegregation and the Press in Tennessee*. Nashville, TN: Vanderbilt University Press, 1967.

Grantham, Dewey. *The Life and Death of the Solid South: A Political History*. Lexington: University Press of Kentucky, 1988.

Grantham, Dewey. *The South in Modern America: A Region at Odds*. New York: Harper Collins, 1994.

Gray, L. Patrick, with Ed Gray. *In Nixon's Web: A Year in the Crosshairs of Watergate*. New York: Times Books, 2008.

Green, A. Wigfall. *The Man Bilbo*. Baton Rouge: Louisiana State University Press, 1963.

Green, Laurie B. *Battling the Plantation Mentality: Memphis and the Black Freedom Struggle*. Chapel Hill: University of North Carolina Press, 2007.

Greenhaw, Wayne. *Elephants in the Cottonfields: Ronald Reagan and the New Republican South*. New York: MacMillan Publishing Co., 1982.

Gruening, Ernest. *The Battle for Alaskan Statehood*. College: University of Alaska Press, 1967.

Gruening, Ernest. *Many Battles: The Autobiography of Ernest Gruening*. New York: Liveright, 1973.

Guthman, Edwin O., and Jeffrey Shulman (eds.). *Robert Kennedy in His Own Words: The Unpublished Recollections of the Kennedy Years*. New York: Bantam Books, 1988.

Hailman, John. *From Midnight to Guntown: True Stories from a Federal Prosecutor in Mississippi*. Jackson: University Press of Mississippi, 2013.

Halberstam, David. *The Fifties*. New York: Villard Books, 1993.

Haldeman, H. R., with an introduction and afterword by Stephen E. Ambrose. *The Haldeman Diaries: Inside the Nixon White House*. New York: G. P. Putnam's Sons, 1994.

Hamilton, Virginia Van der Veer. *Lister Hill: Statesman from the South*. Chapel Hill: University of North Carolina Press, 1987.

Hamlin, Francoise M. *Crossroads at Clarksdale: The Black Freedom Struggle in the Mississippi Delta after World War II*. Chapel Hill: University of North Carolina Press, 2012.

Hampton, Henry, and Steve Fayer, with Sarah Flynn. *Voices of Freedom: An Oral History of the Civil Rights Movement from the 1950s through the 1980s*. New York: Bantam Books, 1990.

Harkey, Ira. *The Smell of Burning Crosses: A White Integrationist Editor in Mississippi*. Jacksonville, IL: Harris-Wolfe, 1967.

Harris, J. William. *Deep Souths: Delta, Piedmont and Sea Island Society in the Age of Segregation*. Baltimore, MD: Johns Hopkins University Press, 2001.

Harris, Richard. *Decision*. Boston: E. P. Dutton & Co., 1971.

Hartmann, Susan. *Truman and the 80th Congress*. Columbia: University of Missouri Press, 1971.

Hatfield, Mark O., as told to Diane N. Solomon, *Against the Grain: Reflections of a Rebel Republican*. Ashland, OR: White Cloud Press, 2001.

Havard, William C. *The Changing Politics of the South*. Baton Rouge: Louisiana State University Press, 1972.

Haygood, Wil. *Showdown: Thurgood Marshall and the Supreme Court Nomination That Changed America*. New York: Alfred A. Knopf, 2015.

Haynes, John E. *Red Scare or Red Menace? American Communism and Anticommunism in the Cold War Era*. Chicago: Ivan R. Dee, 1996.

Haynes, John Earl, and Harvey Klehr. *Venona: Decoding Soviet Espionage in America*. New Haven, CT: Yale University Press, 1999.

Heard, Alex. *The Eyes of Willie McGee: A Tragedy of Race, Sex, and Secrets in the Jim Crow South*. New York: Harper Collins, 2010.

Hederman, Robert M. *The Hederman Story: A Saga of the Printed Word in Mississippi*. New York: The Newcomer Society in North America, 1966.

Heinemann, Ronald L. *Harry Byrd of Virginia*. Charlottesville: University Press of Virginia, 1996.

Hemphill, Marie M. *Fever, Floods and Faith: A History of Sunflower County, Mississippi, 1844-1976*. Indianola, MS: Marie M. Hemphill, 1980.

Herman, Arthur. *Joseph McCarthy: Reexamining the Life of America's Most Hated Senator*. New York: The Free Press, 2000.

Hersh, Burton. *The Education of Edward Kennedy: A Family Biography*. New York: Dell, 1980.

Hersh, Burton. *Bobby and J. Edgar: The Historic Face-Off between the Kennedys and J. Edgar Hoover That Transformed America*. New York: Carroll & Graf, 2007.

Hilty, James W. *Robert Kennedy, Brother Protector*. Philadelphia, PA: Temple University Press, 1997.

Hogan, Wesley C. *Many Minds, One Heart: SNCC's Dream for a New America*. Chapel Hill: University of North Carolina Press, 2007.

Holley, Donald. *The Second Great Emancipation: The Mechanical Cotton Picker, Black Migration, and How They Shaped the Modern South.* Fayetteville: University of Arkansas Press, 2000.

Honey, Michael K. *Going Down Jericho Road: The Memphis Strike, Martin Luther King's Last Campaign.* New York: W. W. Norton & Co., 2007.

Horne, Gerald. *Communist Front? The Civil Rights Congress, 1946–1956.* Rutherford, NJ: Fairleigh Dickinson Press, 1996.

Huey, Gary. *P. D. East, Southern Liberalism, and the Civil Rights Movement, 1953–1971.* Wilmington, DE: Scholarly Resources, 1985.

Hulsey, Bryan C. *Everett Dirksen and His Presidents: How a Senate Giant Shaped American Politics.* Lawrence: University Press of Kansas, 2000.

Humphrey, Hubert H. *The Education of a Public Man: My Life and Politics.* Garden City, NY: Doubleday & Co., 1976.

Hurst, Louis, as told to Francis Spatz Leighton. *The Sweetest Little Club in the World: Memoirs of Louis Hurst.* Englewood, Cliffs, NJ: Prentice-Hall, 1980.

Huss, John E. *Senator for the South: A Biography of Olin D. Johnston.* Garden City, NY: Doubleday & Co., 1961.

Hustwit, William P. *James J. Kilpatrick: Salesman for Segregation.* Chapel Hill: University of North Carolina Press, 2013.

Hutchinson, Dennis J. *The Man Who Once Was Whizzer White: A Portrait of Justice Byron R. White.* New York: The Free Press, 1998.

Hutchinson, Earl Ofari. *Blacks and Reds: Race and Class in Conflict, 1919–1990.* East Lansing: Michigan State University Press, 1995.

Irons, Jenny. *Reconstructing Whiteness: The Mississippi State Sovereignty Commission.* Nashville: Vanderbilt University Press, 2010.

Jackson, John P. *Science for Segregation: Race, Law, and the Case against Brown v. Board of Education.* New York: New York University Press, 2005.

Jacoway, Elizabeth. *Turn Away Thy Son: Little Rock, The Crisis That Shocked the Nation.* New York: The Free Press, 2007.

Javits, Jacob K., with Alfred Steinberg. *Javits: The Autobiography of a Public Man.* Boston: Houghton-Mifflin, 1981.

Jeansonne, Glen. *Leander Perez: Boss of the Delta,* 2nd ed. Lafayette: Center for Louisiana Studies, University of Southwest Louisiana, 1995.

Jeffries, John C., Jr. *Justice Lewis F. Powell Jr.* New York: Fordham University Press, 1994.

Johnson, Lady Bird. *A White House Diary.* Austin: University of Texas Press, 1970.

Johnson, Lyndon Baines. *The Vantage Point: Perspectives on the Presidency: 1963–1969.* New York: Holt, Rinehart and Winston, 1971.

Johnson, Robert David. *All the Way with LBJ: The 1964 Presidential Election.* New York: Cambridge University Press, 2009.

Johnston, Erle. *I Rolled with Ross.* Baton Rouge: Moran Publishing Corp., 1980.

Johnston, Erle. *Mississippi's Defiant Years, 1953–1973: An Interpretive Documentary with Personal Experiences.* Forest, MS: Lake Harbor, 1990.

Johnston, Erle. *Politics: Mississippi Style.* Forest, MS: Lake Harbor, 1993.

Joiner, Lynne. *Honorable Survivor: Mao's China, McCarthy's America, and the Persecution of John S. Service.* Annapolis: Naval Institute Press, 2009.

Jones, Rochelle, and Peter Woll. *The Private World of Congress.* New York: The Free Press, 1979.

Kalman, Laura. *Abe Fortas: A Biography*. New Haven, CT: Yale University Press, 1990.

Kaplan, Fred. *1959: The Year Everything Changed*. Hoboken, NJ: John Wiley & Sons, 2009.

Karabell. Zachary. *The Last Campaign: How Harry Truman Won the 1948 Election*. New York: Alfred A. Knopf, 2000.

Katagiri, Yasuhiro. *The Mississippi Sovereignty Commission: Civil Rights and States' Rights*. Jackson: University Press of Mississippi, 2001.

Katcher, Leo. *Earl Warren: A Political Biography*. New York: McGraw Hill, 1967.

Katzenbach, Nicholas. *Some of It Was Fun: Working with RFK and LBJ*. New York: W. W. Norton & Co., 2008.

Kaufman, Robert G. *Henry M. Jackson: A Life in Politics*. Seattle: University of Washington Press, 2000.

Kaye, Harvey J. *Thomas Paine and the Promise of America*. New York: Hill and Wang, 2005.

Keady. William Colbert. *All Rise: Memoirs of a Mississippi Federal Judge*. Boston: Recollections Bound, 1988.

Kearns, Doris. *Lyndon Johnson and the American Dream*. New York: Harper & Row, 1976.

Keeling, Ralph. *Gruesome Harvest: The Costly Attempt to Exterminate the People of Germany*. Chicago: Institute of American Economics, 1947.

Kennedy, Edward M. *True Compass: A Memoir*. New York: Twelve, 2009.

Kennedy, Robert F., Jr., *Judge Frank M. Johnson Jr.* New York: Putnam, 1978.

Key, V. O., Jr. *Southern Politics in State and Nation*. New York: Alfred A. Knopf, 1949.

King, Rev. Ed, and Trent Watts. *Ed King's Mississippi*. Jackson: University Press of Mississippi, 2014.

Kirby, Jack Temple. *Media-Made Dixie: The South in the American Imagination*. Baton Rouge: Louisiana State University Press, 1978.

Klarman, Michael J. *From Jim Crow to Civil Rights: The Supreme Court and the Struggle for Racial Equality*. New York: Oxford University Press, 1964.

Klehr, Harvey, and Ronald Radosh. *The Amerasia Spy Case: Prelude to McCarthyism*. Chapel Hill: University of North Carolina Press, 1996.

Kleindienst, Richard. *Justice: The Memoirs of Attorney General Richard Kleindienst*. Ottawa, IL: Jameson Books, 1985.

Klibaner, Irwin. *Conscience of a Troubled South: The Southern Conference Educational Fund, 1946–1966*. Brooklyn, NY: Carlson, 1989.

Kluger, Richard. *Simple Justice: The History of Brown v. Board of Education and Black America's Struggle for Equality*. New York: Alfred A. Knopf, 1976.

Koen, Ross Y., edited and with an introduction by Richard C. Kagan. *The China Lobby in American Politics*. New York: Macmillan, 1974.

Koskoff, David E. *The Senator from Central Casting: The Rise, Fall, and Resurrection of Thomas J. Dodd*. New Haven, CT: New American Political Press, 2011.

Kotlowski, Dean J. *Nixon's Civil Rights: Politics, Principle, and Policy*. Cambridge, MA: Harvard University Press, 2001.

Kotz, Nick. *Judgment Days: Lyndon Baines Johnson, Martin Luther King Jr., and the Laws that Changed America*. Boston: Houghton Mifflin, 2005.

Krane, Dale, and Stephen D. Shaffer. *Mississippi Government and Politics: Modernizers Versus Traditionalists*. Lincoln: University of Nebraska Press, 1992.

Kyvig, David E. *Explicit and Authentic Acts: Amending the U.S. Constitution, 1776–1995*. Lawrence: University of Kansas Press, 1996.

Lambert, Frank. *The Battle of Ole Miss: Civil Rights v. States' Rights*. New York: Oxford University Press, 2009.

Larrowes, Charles P. *Harry Bridges: The Rise and Fall of Radical Labor in the U.S.* New York: Laurence Hill & Co., 1972.

Lawson, Steven F. *Running for Freedom: Civil Rights and Black Politics in America since 1941*. New York: McGraw-Hill, 1991.

Lee, Chana Kai. *For Freedom's Sake: The Life of Fannie Lou Hamer*. Urbana: University of Illinois Press, 1999.

Leuchtenberg, William E. *The White House Looks South: Franklin D. Roosevelt, Harry S. Truman, Lyndon B. Johnson*. Baton Rouge: Louisiana State University Press, 2005.

Lewis, Andrew B. *The Shadows of Youth: The Remarkable Journey of the Civil Rights Generation*. New York: Hill and Wang, 2009.

Lewis, Finley. *Mondale: Portrait of an American Politician*. New York: Harper & Row, 1980.

Lewis, George. *The White South and the Red Menace: Segregationists, Anticommunists, and Massive Resistance, 1945–1965*. Gainesville: University of Florida Press, 2004.

Lewis, George. *Massive Resistance: The White Response to the Civil Rights Movement*. London: Hodder Arnold, 2006.

Lichtman, Robert M. *The Supreme Court and McCarthy Era Repression: One Hundred Decisions*. Urbana: University of Illinois Press, 2012.

Lichtman, Robert M., and Ronald E. Cohen. *Deadly Farce: Harvey Matusow and the Informer System in the McCarthy Era*. Urbana: University of Illinois Press, 2004.

Link, William A. *Righteous Warrior: Jesse Helms and the Rise of Modern Conservatism*. New York: St. Martin's Press, 2008.

Loevy, Robert D. *To End All Segregation: The Politics of the Passage of the Civil Rights Act of 1964*. Lanham, MD: University Press of America, 1990.

Longley, Kyle, with a foreword by Al Gore Jr. *Senator Albert Gore Sr.: Tennessee Maverick*. Baton Rouge: Louisiana State University Press, 2004.

Lord, Walter. *The Past That Would Not Die*. New York: Harper & Row, 1965.

Lowitt, Richard. *Fred Harris: His Journey from Liberalism to Populism*. Lanham, MD: Rowman & Littlefield, 2002.

Lowndes, Joseph E. *From the New Deal to the New Right: The Southern Origins of Modern Conservatism*. New Haven, CT: Yale University Press, 2008.

Luthin, Reinhard. *American Demagogues: Twentieth Century*. Boston: Beacon Press, 1954.

MacKenzie, C. Calvin, and Robert Weisbrot. *The Liberal Hour: Washington and the Politics of Change in the 1960s*. New York: Penguin Press, 2008.

Maclean, Harry N. *The Past Is Never Dead: The Trial of James Ford Seale and Mississippi's Struggle for Redemption*. New York: Basic Books, 2009.

MacNeil, Neil. *Dirksen: Portrait of a Public Man*. New York: The World Publishing Co., 1970.

Madison, Frank. *A View from the Floor: The Journal of a U.S. Senate Page Boy*. Englewood Cliffs, NJ: Prentice-Hall, 1967.

Magruder, Jeb Stuart. *An American Life: One Man's Road to Watergate*. New York: Atheneum, 1974.

Malsberger, John W. *From Obstruction to Moderation: The Transformation of Senate Conservatism, 1938–1952*. Selmsgrove, PA: Susquehanna University Press, 2000.

Mann, Robert. *Legacy to Power: Senator Russell Long of Louisiana*. New York: Paragon Press, 1992.

Mann, Robert. *The Walls of Jericho: Lyndon Johnson, Hubert Humphrey, Richard Russell, and the Struggle for Civil Rights.* New York: Harcourt Brace, 1996.

Mann, Robert. *When Freedom Would Triumph: The Civil Rights Struggle in Congress, 1954–1968.* Baton Rouge: Louisiana State University Press, 2007.

Mars, Florence, with the assistance of Lynn Eden. *Witness in Philadelphia.* Baton Rouge: Louisiana State University Press, 1977.

Marshall, James P., with a Foreword by Staughton Lynd. *Student Activism and Civil Rights in Mississippi: Protest Politics and the Struggle for Racial Justice, 1960–1965.* Baton Rouge: Louisiana State University Press, 2013.

Martin, Gordon A., Jr. *Count Them One by One: Black Mississippians Fighting for the Right to Vote.* Jackson: University Press of Mississippi, 2010.

Martin, John Bartlow. *The Deep South Says Never.* New York: Ballantine Books, 1957.

Martin, John Frederick. *Civil Rights and the Crisis of Liberalism.* Boulder: University of Colorado Press, 1979.

Mason, Gilbert R., M.D., with James Patterson Smith. *Beaches, Blood and Ballots: A Black Doctor's Civil Rights Struggle.* Jackson: University Press of Mississippi, 2000.

Massaro, John. *Supremely Political: The Role of Ideology and Presidential Management in Unsuccessful Supreme Court Nominations.* Albany: State University of New York Press, 1990.

Massengill, Reed. *Portrait of a Racist: The Man Who Murdered Medgar Evers.* New York: St. Martin's Press, 1994.

Matthews, Chris. *Tip and the Gipper: When Politics Worked.* New York: Simon and Schuster, 2013.

Matthews, Donald. *U.S. Senators and Their World.* New York: W. W. Norton & Co., 1973.

McFeeley, Neil D. *Appointment of Judges: The Johnson Presidency.* Austin: University of Texas Press, 1978.

McGovern, George. *Grassroots: The Autobiography of George McGovern.* New York: Random House, 1977.

McMahon, Kevin J. *Nixon's Court: His Challenge to Judicial Liberalism and Its Political Consequences.* Chicago: University of Chicago Press, 2011.

McMillen, Neil R. *The Citizens' Council: Organized Resistance to the Second Reconstruction, 1954–64.* Urbana: University of Illinois Press, 1971.

Mee, Charles L., Jr. *The Marshall Plan: The Launching of the Pax Americana.* New York: Simon & Schuster, 1984.

Meyer, Gerald. *Vito Marcantonio: Radical Politician, 1902–1954.* Albany: State University of New York Press, 1989.

Michie, Allan A., and Frank Ryhlick. *Dixie Demagogues.* New York: The Vanguard Press, 1939.

Mills, Kay. *Changing Channels: The Civil Rights Case That Transformed Mississippi.* Jackson: University Press of Mississippi, 2004.

Mills, Nikolaus. *Like a Holy Crusade: Mississippi 1964—The Turning of the Civil Rights Movement in America.* Chicago: Ivan R. Dee, 1992.

Minchin, Timothy J., and John A. Salmond. *After the Dream: Black and White Southerners since 1965.* Lexington: University Press of Kentucky, 2011.

Minor, Bill. *Eyes on Mississippi: A Fifty-Year Chronicle of Change.* Jackson, MS: J. Prichard Morris Books, 2001.

Mitchell, Dennis E. *Mississippi Liberal: A Biography of Frank E. Smith*. Jackson: University Press of Mississippi, 2001.

Mollenhoff, Clark R. *Game Plan for Disaster: An Ombudsman's Report on the Nixon Years*. New York: W. W. Norton & Co., 1976.

Mondale, Walter F., with David Hage. *The Good Fight: A Life in Liberal Politics*. New York: Scribner, 2010.

Montgomery, G. V. Sonny, with Michael B. Ballard and Craig S. Piper. *G. V. "Sonny" Montgomery: The Veterans Champion*. Jackson: University Press of Mississippi, 2003.

Morgan, Chester M. *Redneck Liberal: Theodore G. Bilbo and the New Deal*. Baton Rouge: Louisiana State University Press, 1985.

Morrison, Minion K. C. *Aaron Henry of Mississippi: Inside Agitator*. Fayetteville: University of Arkansas Press, 2015.

Moses, Robert P., and Charles E. Cobb Jr. *Radical Equations: Math Literacy and Civil Rights*. Boston: Beacon Press, 2001.

Mounger, William D., with Joseph L. Maxwell III. *Amidst the Fray: My Life in Politics, Culture, and Mississippi*. Brandon, MS: Quail Ridge Press, 2006.

Moye, J. Todd, *Let the People Decide: Black Freedom and White Resistance Movements in Sunflower County, Mississippi, 1945–1986*. Chapel Hill: University of North Carolina Press, 2003.

Mudd, Roger. *The Place to Be: Washington, CBS, and the Glory Days of Television News*. New York: Public Affairs, 2008.

Mullins, Andrew P., Jr. *The Measure of Our Days: Writings of William F. Winter*. Oxford: William F. Winter Institute for Racial Reconciliation at the University of Mississippi, 2006.

Murphy, Bruce Alan. *Fortas: The Rise and Ruin of a Supreme Court Justice*. New York: William Morrow & Co., 1988

Murphy, Reg. *Uncommon Sense: The Achievement of Griffin Bell*. Atlanta: Longstreet, 1999.

Muse, Benjamin. *Virginia's Massive Resistance*. Bloomington: Indiana University Press, 1961.

Muse, Benjamin. *Ten Years of Prelude: The Story of Integration since the Supreme Court's 1954 Decision*. New York: The Viking Press, 1964.

Nash, Jere, and Andy Taggart. *Mississippi Fried Politics: Tall Tales from the Back Rooms*. Jackson, MS: Red/Blue Publications LLC, 2006.

Nash, Jere, and Andy Taggart. *Mississippi Politics: The Struggle for Power, 1976–2006*. Jackson: University Press of Mississippi, 2006.

Naske, Claus M. *Edmund Lewis "Bob" Bartlett of Alaska*. College: University of Alaska Press, 1979.

Navasky, Victor. *Kennedy Justice*. New York: Atheneum, 1971.

Nelson, Jack. *Terror in the Night: The Klan's Campaign against the Jews*. Jackson: University Press of Mississippi, 1993.

Nelson, Jack. *Scoop: The Evolution of a Southern Reporter*. Jackson: University Press of Mississippi, 2013.

Newman, Mark. *Divine Agitators: The Delta Ministry and Civil Rights*. Athens: University of Georgia Press, 2004.

Newman, Robert P. *Owen Lattimore and the "Loss" of China*. Berkeley: University of California Press, 1992.

Newton, Jim. *Justice for All: Earl Warren and the Nation He Made*. New York: Riverhead Books, 2006.

Newton, Michael. *The Ku Klux Klan in Mississippi: A History*. Jefferson, NC: McFarland & Co., 2010.

Nichols, David A. *A Matter of Justice: Eisenhower and the Beginning of the Civil Rights Revolution*. New York: Simon & Schuster, 2007.

Nixon, Richard M. *RN: The Memoirs of Richard Nixon*. New York: Grosset & Dunlap, 1978.

Norrell, Robert J. *The House I Live In: Race in the American Century*. New York: Oxford University Press, 2005.

Nossiter, Adam. *Of Long Memory: Mississippi and the Murder of Medgar Evers*. New York: Da Capo Press, 1994.

Oates, Stephen B. *Let the Trumpet Sound: The Life of Martin Luther King Jr*. New York: Harper & Row, 1982.

Oberdorfer, Don. *Senator Mansfield: The Extraordinary Life of a Great American Statesman and Diplomat*. Washington, D.C.: Smithsonian Books, 2003.

O'Brien, David M. *Storm Center: The Supreme Court in American Politics*, 2nd ed. New York: W. W. Norton, 1990.

O'Brien, Michael. *Philip Hart: The Conscience of the Senate*. East Lansing: Michigan State University Press, 1995

O'Reilly, Kenneth. *Hoover and the Un-Americans: The FBI, HUAC, and the Red Menace*. Philadelphia, PA: Temple University Press, 1983.

O'Reilly, Kenneth. *Nixon's Piano: Presidents and Racial Politics from Washington to Clinton*. New York: The Free Press, 1995.

Oshinsky, David. *"Worse Than Slavery": Parchman Farm and the Ordeal of Jim Crow Justice*. New York: Free Press Paperbacks, 1997.

Panetta, Leon, with Jim Newton. *Worthy Fights: A Memoir of Leadership in War and Peace*. New York: Penguin Books, 2014.

Parker, Frank R. *Black Votes Count: Political Empowerment in Mississippi after 1965*. Chapel Hill: University of North Carolina Press, 1995.

Parmet, Herbert S. *Eisenhower and the American Crusades*. New York: The MacMillan Co., 1972.

Parmet, Herbert S. *Jack: The Struggles of John F. Kennedy*. New York: The Dial Press, 1980.

Parmet, Herbert S. *JFK: The Presidency of John F. Kennedy*. New York: The Dial Press, 1983.

Patterson, James T. *Brown v. Board of Education: A Civil Rights Milestone and Its Troubled Legacy*. New York: Oxford University Press, 2001.

Pearson, Drew, and Jack Anderson. *The Case against Congress: A Compelling Indictment of Corruption on Capitol Hill*. New York: Simon & Schuster, 1968.

Peirce, Neil R. *The Deep South States of America: People, Politics and Power in the Seven Deep South States*. New York: W. W. Norton & Co., 1974.

Peltason, J. W. *Fifty-Eight Lonely Men: Southern Federal Judges and School Desegregation*. Urbana: University of Illinois Press, 1961.

Perman, Michael. *Pursuit of Unity: A Political History of the American South*. Chapel Hill: University of North Carolina Press, 2009.

Pettit, Lawrence K., and Edward Keynes. *The Legislative Process in the United States Senate*. Chicago: Rand McNally & Co., 1969.

Pietrusza, David. *1920: The Year of the Six Presidents*. New York: Carroll & Graf, 2007.

Pietrusza, David. *1948: Harry Truman's Improbable Victory and the Year That Transformed America's Role in the World*. New York: Union Square Books, 2011.

Pietrusza, David. *1960: LBJ vs. JFK vs. Nixon: The Epic Campaign That Forged Three Presidencies*. New York: Union Square Press, 2008.

Pleasants, Julian M., and Augustus M. Burns. *Frank Porter Graham and the 1950 Senate Race in North Carolina*. Chapel Hill: University of North Carolina Press, 1990.

Plummer, Brenda Gayle (ed.). *Window on Opportunity: Race, Civil Rights, and Foreign Affairs, 1945–1988*. Chapel Hill: University of North Carolina Press, 2003.

Powe, Lucas A., Jr. *The Warren Court and American Politics*. Cambridge, MA: The Belknap Press of Harvard University Press, 2000.

Price, Polly J., with a foreword by Ruth Bader Ginsburg. *Judge Richard S. Arnold: A Legacy of Justice on the Federal Bench*. Amherst, NY: Prometheus Books, 2009.

Pryor, David, with Don Harrell. *A Pryor Commitment: The Autobiography of David Pryor*. Little Rock: Butler Center Books, 2008.

Rabinowitz, Victor. *Unrepentant Leftist: A Lawyer's Memoir*. Urbana: University of Illinois Press, 1986.

Ralph Nader Congress Project. *The Judiciary Committees: A Study of the House and Senate Judiciary Committees, 1975*. New York: Grossman, 1975.

Read, Frank T., and Lucy S. McGough. *Let Them Be Judged: The Judicial Integration of the Deep South*. Baton Rouge: Louisiana State University Press, 1978.

Reed, Linda. *Simple Decency and Common Sense: The Southern Conference Movement*. Bloomington: Indiana University Press, 1991.

Reed, Merl. *Seedtime for the Modern Civil Rights Movement: The President's Committee on Fair Employment Practices, 1941–1946*. Baton Rouge: Louisiana State University Press, 1991.

Reed, Roy. *Faubus: The Life and Times of an American Prodigal*. Fayetteville: University of Arkansas Press, 1997.

Reeves, Richard. *President Kennedy: Profile of Power*. New York: Simon & Schuster, 1993.

Reeves, Thomas C. *The Life and Times of Joe McCarthy: A Biography*. New York: Stein and Day, 1982.

Reeves, Thomas C. *A Question of Character: A Life of John F. Kennedy*. New York: The Free Press, 1991.

Richardson, Elliott. *The Creative Balance: Government, Politics and the Individual in America's Third Century*. New York: Holt, Rinehart and Winston, 1976.

Ripley, Randall B. *Power in the Senate*. New York: St. Martin's Press, 1969.

Roberts, Gene, and Hank Klibanoff. *The Race Beat: The Press, the Civil Rights Struggle, and the Awakening of a Nation*. New York: Alfred A. Knopf, 2006.

Roland, Charles P. *The Improbable Era: The South since World War II*. Lexington: University Press of Kentucky, 1975.

Rorabaugh, W. J. *Kennedy and the Promise of the Sixties*. Cambridge, UK: Cambridge University Press, 2002.

Rorabaugh, W. J. *The Real Making of the President: Kennedy, Nixon, and the 1960 Election*. Lawrence: University Press of Kansas, 2009.

Rosen, James. *The Strong Man: John Mitchell and the Secrets of Watergate*. New York: Doubleday, 2008.

Rusher, William A. *Special Counsel: An Inside Report on the Senate Investigations into Communism*. New Rochelle, NY: Arlington House, 1968.

Russell, Sally. *Richard Brevard Russell Jr.: A Life of Consequence.* Macon, GA: Mercer University Press, 2011.

Sabin, Arthur. *In Calmer Times.* Philadelphia: University of Pennsylvania Press, 1999.

Salmond, John A. *A Southern Rebel: The Life and Times of Aubrey Willis Williams, 1890–1965.* Chapel Hill: University of North Carolina Press, 1985.

Salmond, John A. *The Conscience of a Lawyer: Clifford J. Durr and American Liberties, 1899–1975.* Tuscaloosa: University of Alabama Press, 1990.

Sandbrook, Dominic. *Eugene McCarthy: The Rise and Fall of Postwar American Liberalism.* New York: Alfred A. Knopf, 2004.

Sansing, David G. *Making Haste Slowly: The Troubled History of Higher Education in Mississippi.* Jackson: University Press of Mississippi, 1990.

Sansing, David G., and Carroll Waller. *A History of the Mississippi Governor's Mansion.* Jackson: University Press of Mississippi, 1977.

Sarrett, Reid. *The Ordeal of Desegregation: The First Decade.* New York: Harper & Row, 1966.

Savage, David G. *Turning Right: The Making of the Rehnquist Supreme Court.* New York: John Wiley & Sons, 1992.

Saxbe, William B., with Peter D. Franklin. *I've Seen the Elephant: An Autobiography.* Kent, OH: The Kent State University Press, 2000.

Schapsmeier, Edward L., and Frederick H. Schapsmeier. *Dirksen of Illinois: Senatorial Statesman.* Urbana: University of Illinois Press, 1985.

Schlesinger, Arthur M., Jr. *A Thousand Days: John F. Kennedy in the White House.* Boston: Houghton-Mifflin Co., 1965.

Schlesinger, Arthur M., Jr. *Robert Kennedy and His Times.* Boston: Houghton-Mifflin Co., 1978.

Schmitt, Edward R. *President of the Other America: Robert Kennedy and the Politics of Poverty.* Amherst: University of Massachusetts Press, 2010.

Schrecker, Ellen. *Many Are the Crimes: McCarthyism in America.* Boston: Little, Brown & Co., 1998.

Schwartz, Bernard, with Stephan Lesher. *Inside the Warren Court.* Garden City, NY: Doubleday & Co., 1983.

Shaffer, Samuel. *On and off the Floor: Thirty Years as a Correspondent on Capitol Hill.* New York: Newsweek Books, 1980.

Shapiro, Ira. *The Last Great Senate: Courage and Statesmanship in Times of Crisis.* New York: Public Affairs, 2012.

Sherrill, Robert. *Gothic Politics in the Deep South: Stars of the New Confederacy.* New York: Grossman, 1968.

Sherrill, Robert. *First Amendment Felon: The Story of Frank Wilkinson, His 132,000 Page FBI File, and His Epic Fight for Civil Rights and Liberties.* New York: Nation Books, 2007.

Short, R. J. *The Centennial Senator: True Stories of Strom Thurmond from the People Who Knew Him Best.* Washington, D.C.: Office of Juvenile Justice and Delinquency Prevention, 2006.

Shurden, Otha, as told to Wilbur Jones. *Cotton: Always King with Me.* Drew, MS: self-published, 1985.

Silver, James W. *Mississippi: The Closed Society.* New York: Harcourt, Brace & World, 1963.

Simon, James F. *In His Own Image: The Supreme Court in Richard Nixon's America.* New York: David McKay Co., 1973.

Sitkoff, Harvard. *The Struggle for Black Equality, 1954–1980.* New York: Hill and Wang, 1981.

Skipper, John C. *Showdown at the 1964 Democratic Convention: Lyndon Johnson, Mississippi and Civil Rights*. Jefferson, NC: McFarland & Co., 2012.

Smead, Howard. *Blood Justice: The Lynching of Mack Charles Parker*. New York: Oxford University Press, 1986.

Smith, C. Fraser. *Here Lies Jim Crow: Civil Rights in Maryland*. Baltimore, MD: Johns Hopkins University Press, 2008.

Smith, Frank E. *Congressman from Mississippi: An Autobiography*. New York: Capricorn Books, 1964.

Smith, John David, and J. Vincent Lowery (eds.), with a foreword by Eric Foner. *The Dunning School: Historians, Race and the Meaning of Reconstruction*. Lexington: University of Kentucky Press, 2013.

Smith, Mark M. *Camille, 1969: Histories of a Hurricane*. Athens: University of Georgia Press, 2011.

Snyder, Robert E. *Cotton Crisis*. Chapel Hill: University of North Carolina Press, 1984.

Sokol, Jason. *There Goes My Everything: White Southerners in the Age of Civil Rights, 1945–1974*. New York: Alfred A. Knopf, 2006.

Sorenson, Theodore C. *Kennedy*. New York: Harper & Row, 1965.

Sowell, Thomas. *Black Rednecks and White Liberals*. San Francisco: Encounter Books, 2003.

Speakes, Larry, with Robert Pack. *Speaking Out: Inside the Reagan White House*. New York: Charles Scribners Sons, 1988.

Stern, Mark. *Calculating Visions: Kennedy, Johnson, and Civil Rights*. New Brunswick, NJ: Rutgers University Press, 1992.

Stevens, John Paul. *Five Chiefs: A Supreme Court Memoir*. New York: Little, Brown & Co., 2011.

Stine, Jeffrey. *Mixing the Waters: Environment, Politics and the Building of the Tennessee-Tombigbee Waterway*. Akron, OH: University of Akron Press, 1993.

Stoper, Emily. *The Student Nonviolent Coordinating Committee*. Brooklyn, NY: Carlson Publishing, 1989.

Stossel, Scott. *Sarge: The Life and Times of Sargent Shriver*. Washington, D.C.: Smithsonian Books, 2004.

Stubbs, Steven H. *Mississippi's Giant House Party: The History of the Neshoba County Fair: 115 Years (and Counting) of Politicking, Pacing, Partaking and Partying in Philadelphia, Mississippi*. Philadelphia, MS: Dancing Rabbit Press, 2005.

Stursberg, Peter. *Lester Pearson and the American Dilemma*. Toronto: Doubleday, 1980.

Sullivan, Patricia. *Lift Every Voice: The NAACP and the Civil Rights Movement*. New York: The New Press, 2009.

Summers, Cecil L. *The Governors of Mississippi*. Gretna, LA: Pelican Publishing Co., 1980.

Sundquist, James L. *The Decline and Resurgence of Congress*. Washington, D.C.: The Brookings Institute, 1981.

Swain, Martha H. *Pat Harrison: The New Deal Years*. Jackson: University Press of Mississippi, 1978.

Talmadge, Herman E., with Mark Royden Winchell. *Talmadge: A Political Legacy, A Politician's Life*. Atlanta: Peachtree, 1987.

Tananbaum, Duane. *The Bricker Amendment Controversy: A Test of Eisenhower's Political Leadership*. Ithaca, NY: Cornell University Press, 1988.

Taylor, Gregory S. *The Life and Lies of Paul Crouch: Communist, Opportunist, Cold War Snitch*. Gainesville: University Press of Florida, 2014.

Thayer, George. *The Farther Shores of Politics: The American Political Fringe Today*. New York: Simon & Schuster, 1967.

Thompson, Julius. *Percy Greene and the Jackson Advocate: The Life and Times of a Radical Conservative Black Newspaperman*. Jefferson, NC: McFarland & Co., 1994.

Threadgill, William James. *Evolving Perspectives: Reflections of a Mississippi Lawyer*. Columbus, MS: unpublished memoir, 2005.

Tushnet, Mark (ed.). *Thurgood Marshall: His Speeches, Writings, Arguments, Opinions and Reminiscences*. Chicago: Lawrence Hill Books, 2001.

Umoja, Akimyole Omowale. *We Will Shoot Back: Armed Resistance in the Mississippi Freedom Party*. New York: New York University Press, 2013.

Valelly, Richard M. *The Two Reconstructions: The Struggle for Black Enfranchisement*. Chicago: University of Chicago Press, 2004.

Vieira, Norman, and Leonard Gross. *Supreme Court Appointments: Judge Bork and the Politicization of Senate Confirmations*. Carbondale: Southern Illinois University Press, 1998.

Vollers, Maryanne. *Ghosts of Mississippi: The Murder of Medgar Evers, the Trials of Byron De La Beckwith, and the Haunting of the New South*. Boston: Little, Brown & Co., 1995.

Waldron, Ann. *Hodding Carter: The Reconstruction of a Racist*. Chapel Hill: Algonquin Books of Chapel Hill, 1988.

Walker, Anders. *The Ghosts of Jim Crow: How Southern Moderates Used Brown v. Board of Education to Stall Civil Rights*. New York: Oxford University Press, 2009.

Wallace, Mike, with Gary Paul Gates. *Between You and Me: A Memoir*. New York: Hachette Books, 2005.

Waller, Bill. *Straight Ahead: The Memoirs of a Mississippi Governor*. Brandon, MS: Quail Ridge Press, 2007.

Walsh, Lawrence E., with a foreword by Nina Totenberg. *The Gift of Insecurity: A Lawyer's Life*. Chicago: American Bar Association, 2003.

Ward, Brian. *Radio and the Struggle for Civil Rights in the South*. Gainesville: University of Florida Press, 2004.

Ward, Jason Morgan. *Defending White Democracy: The Making of a Segregationist Movement and the Remaking of Racial Politics, 1936–1965*. Chapel Hill: University of North Carolina Press, 2011.

Ware, Gilbert. *William Hastie: Grace under Pressure*. New York: Oxford University Press, 1984.

Warren, Robert Penn. *The Legacy of the Civil War*. New York: Vintage, 1964.

Watson, Bruce. *Freedom Summer*. New York: Viking, 2010.

Webb, Clive. *Rabble Rousers: The American Far Right in the Civil Rights Era*. Athens: University of Georgia Press, 2010.

Weinstein, Allen. *Perjury: The Hiss-Chambers Case*. New York: Alfred A. Knopf, 1978.

Werth, Barry. *31 Days*. New York: Nan A. Talese, 2006.

Whalen, Charles, and Barbara Whalen. *The Longest Debate: A Legislative History of the 1964 Civil Rights Act*. Cabin John, MD: Seven Locks Press, 1989.

White, William S. *Citadel: The Story of the United States Senate*. New York: Harper & Brothers, 1956.

Whitehead, Don. *Attack on Terror: The FBI against the Ku Klux Klan in Mississippi*. New York: Funk and Wagnalls, 1970.

Whitehead, John S. *Completing the Union: Alaska, Hawai'i, and the Battle for Statehood.* Albuquerque: University of New Mexico Press, 2004.

Whitfield, Stephen J. *A Death in the Delta: The Story of Emmett Till.* New York: The Free Press, 1988.

Wicker, Tom. *One of Us: Richard Nixon and the American Dream.* New York: Random House, 1991.

Wilhoit, Francis M. *The Politics of Massive Resistance.* New York: George Brazilier, 1973.

Wilkie, Curtis. *Dixie: A Personal Odyssey through Events That Shaped the Modern South.* New York: Scribner, 2002.

Wilkie, Curtis. *The Fall of the House of Zeus: The Rise and Ruin of America's Most Powerful Trial Lawyer.* New York: Crown, 2010.

Wilkins, Roy, with Tom Mathews. *Standing Fast: The Autobiography of Roy Wilkins.* New York: The Viking Press, 1982.

Wilkinson, J. Harvie. *Harry Byrd and the Changing Face of Virginia Politics, 1945–1966.* Charlottesville: University of Virginia Press, 1968.

Wilkinson, J. Harvie. *From Brown to Bakke: The Supreme Court and School Integration.* New York: Oxford University Press, 1979.

Williams, J. Earl. *Plantation Politics: The Southern Economic Heritage.* Austin, TX: Futura Press, 1972.

Williams, Juan. *Eyes on the Prize: America's Civil Rights Years, 1954–1965.* New York: Viking-Penguin, 1987.

Williams, Juan. *Thurgood Marshall: America's Revolutionary.* New York: Times Books, 1998.

Williams, Michael Vinson. *Medgar Evers: Mississippi Martyr.* Fayetteville: University of Arkansas Press, 2011.

Wirt, Frederick M., with a foreword by Gary Orfield. *"We Ain't What We Was": Civil Rights in the New South.* Durham, NC: Duke University Press, 1997.

Witcover, Jules. *Joe Biden: A Life of Trial and Redemption.* New York: William Morrow, 2010.

Wittes, Benjamin. *Confirmation Wars: Preserving Independent Courts in Angry Times.* Lanham, MD: Rowman and Littlefield, 2006.

Wofford, Harris. *Of Kennedys and Kings: Making Sense of the Sixties.* New York: Farrar Straus Giroux, 1980.

Woodruff, Nan Elizabeth. *American Congo: The African American Freedom Struggle in the Delta.* Cambridge, MA: Harvard University Press, 2003.

Woods, Jeff. *Black Struggle, Red Scare: Segregation and Anti-Communism in the South.* Baton Rouge: Louisiana State University Press, 2004.

Woods, Randall Bennett. *Fulbright: A Biography.* Cambridge, UK: Cambridge University Press, 1995.

Woods, Randall Bennett. *LBJ: Architect of American Ambition.* New York: The Free Press, 2006.

Woodward, Bob, and Scott Armstrong. *The Brethren: Inside the Supreme Court.* New York: Simon & Schuster, 1979.

Woodward, Bob, and Carl Bernstein. *The Final Days.* New York: Simon & Schuster, 1976.

Yalof, David Alastair. *Pursuit of Justices: Presidential Politics and the Selection of Supreme Court Justices.* Chicago: University of Chicago Press, 1999.

Yarbrough, Tinsley E. *John Marshall Harlan: Great Dissenter of the Warren Court.* New York: Oxford University Press, 1992.

Yarbrough, Tinsley E. *The Rehnquist Court and the Constitution*. New York: Oxford University Press, 2000.

Yarbrough, Tinsley E. *Harry A. Blackmun: The Outsider Justice*. New York: Oxford University Press, 2008.

Yates, Gayle Graham. *Mississippi Mind: A Personal Cultural History of an American State*. Knoxville: University of Tennessee Press, 1990.

Ybarra, Michael J. *Washington Gone Crazy: Senator Pat McCarran and the Great American Communist Hunt*. Hanover, NH: Steerforth Press, 2004.

Yerger, Wirt A., Jr., with Joseph L. Maxwell III. *A Courageous Cause: A Personal Story of Modern Republicanism's Path from 1956 to 1966 in Mississippi*. Jackson: Life Story Publishing, 2010.

Young, Roland. *Congressional Politics in the Second World War*. New York: Columbia University Press, 1956.

Zebrowski, Ernest, and Judith A. Howard. *Category 5: The Story of Camille—Lessons Unlearned from America's Most Violent Hurricane*. Ann Arbor: University of Michigan Press, 2005.

Zelizer, Julian (ed.). *The Building of Democracy*. Boston: Houghton-Mifflin Co., 2004.

Zinn, Howard. *SNCC: The New Abolitionists*. Boston: Beacon Books, 1968.

Zwiers, Maarten. *Senator James Eastland: Mississippi's Jim Crow Democrat*. Baton Rouge: Louisiana State University, 2015.

DISSERTATIONS AND THESES

Asch, Christopher Myers. "No Compromise: The Freedom Struggles of James O. Eastland and Fannie Lou Hamer." Ph.D. dissertation: University of North Carolina, 2005.

Balsamo, Larry Thomas. "Theodore G. Bilbo and Mississippi Politics, 1877–1932." Ph.D. dissertation: University of Missouri, 1967.

Baskin, Bethany Lamar. "The Rise of William Forrest Winter." M.A. thesis: Mississippi State University, 1992.

Bauer, Jeremiah. "Eisenhower's Critical Contribution to the Fifth Circuit Court of Appeals." M.A. thesis: University of Nebraska–Omaha, 2010.

Berrey, Stephen Andrew. "Against the Law: Violence, Crime, State Repression and Black Resistance in Jim Crow Mississippi." Ph.D. dissertation: University of Texas, 2006.

Campisano, Charles. "The Confirmation Process and a Senatorial Nomination: Historical Quantification and Analysis of the Senate Blue Slip Process." Sr. thesis: The Ohio State University, 2009.

Cartledge, Connie Lynnette. "James P. Coleman: Moderate Politician in an Age of Racial Strife, 1950–1965." M.A. thesis, Mississippi State University, 1984.

Chesteen, Richard Dallas. "The 1948 States Rights Movement in Mississippi." M.A. thesis, University of Mississippi, 1964.

Clark, Wayne Addison. "An Analysis of the Relationship between Anti-Communism and Segregationist Thought in the Deep South, 1948–1964." Ph.D. dissertation: University of North Carolina, 1976.

Corley, Robert Gaines. "James Jackson Kilpatrick: The Evolution of a Southern Conservative, 1955–1965." M.A. thesis: University of Virginia, 1971.

Crespino, Joseph. "Strategic Accommodation: Civil Rights Opponents in Mississippi and Their Impact on American Racial Politics, 1953–1972." Ph.D. dissertation, Stanford University, 2002.

Derr, Reid Stoner. "The Triumph of Progressivism: Governor Paul B. Johnson and Mississippi in the 1960s." Ph.D. dissertation, University of Southern Mississippi, 1994.

Ethridge, Richard C. "Mississippi and the 1928 Presidential Campaign," M.A. thesis, Mississippi State University, 1961.

Ethridge, Richard C. "Mississippi's Role in the 1948 Dixiecratic Movement." Ph.D. dissertation, Mississippi State University, 1971.

Finley, Melissa Lynn. "But I Was a Practical Segregationist! Erle Johnston and the Mississippi State Sovereignty Commission, 1960–1968," M.A. thesis, University of Southern Mississippi, 2010.

Frederickson, Kari. "The Dixiecrat Movement and the Origins of Massive Resistance: Race, Politics, and Political Culture in the Deep South." Ph.D. dissertation: Rutgers University, 1996.

Gerard, Christopher John. "'A Program of Cooperation': The FBI, the Senate Internal Security Subcommittee, and the Communist Issue, 1950–1954." Ph.D. dissertation, Marquette University, 1993.

Giroux, Vincent Arthur. "Theodore G. Bilbo: Progressive to Public Racist." Ph.D. dissertation, Indiana University, 1984.

Hilbun, Ben F. "The Dixiecrat Movement in Mississippi." M.A. thesis: Mississippi State University, 1955.

Hilliard, Elbert Riley. "A Biography of Fielding Wright: Mississippi's Mr. States' Rights." M.A. thesis: Mississippi State University, 1959.

Huskey, Scott. "A Policy History of the Mississippi State Sovereignty Commission." M.A. thesis: Mississippi College, 2005.

Katagiri, Yasuhiro. "The Mississippi State Sovereignty Commission: Civil Rights and States' Rights in a Deep South State, 1956 to 1977." Ph.D. dissertation: International Christian University, 1997.

Kelley, Donald Brooks. "Of God, Liquor and Politics: The Mississippi Press in the Presidential Election of 1928." M.A. thesis: University of Mississippi, 1962.

Kelly, Gregory David. "You Don't Need a Rope for a Lynching: George Lee, Gus Courts and Racial Violence in Humphreys County." M.A. thesis: Mississippi College, 2000.

Klinetobe, Charles. "The Best Laid Plans: Southern Legal Efforts to Preserve Segregation." M.A. thesis: University of Nebraska–Omaha, 2007.

Luce, Phillip Abbott. "The Mississippi White Citizens' Council, 1954–1959." M.A. thesis: The Ohio State University, 1960.

McLaurin, Ann Mathison. "The Role of the Dixiecrats in the 1948 Election." Ph.D. dissertation: University of Oklahoma, 1972.

McWhite, S. Leigh. "Echoes of the Lost Cause: Civil War Reverberations in Mississippi from 1865–2001." Ph.D. dissertation: University of Mississippi, 2002.

Melton, Thomas R. "Mr. Speaker: A Biography of Walter Sillers." M.A. thesis: University of Mississippi, 1972.

Mickey, Robert Waite. "The Decay of Authoritarian Enclaves in the Deep South, 1949–1972." Ph.D. dissertation: Harvard University, 2005.

Munro, Douglas Patrick. "The Nationalization of Southern Politics: Southern Democratic Senators from Eisenhower to Bush." Ph.D. dissertation: Johns Hopkins University, 1992.

Ness, Gary Clifford. "The States' Rights Democratic Movement of 1948." Ph.D. dissertation: Duke University, 1972.

Nichols, Kimberly Ellen. "The Civil Rights Underground: The Movement for Compliance with the Civil Rights Acts of 1964." Ph.D. dissertation: University of Memphis, 2009.

Robinson, James E. "Hodding Carter: Southern Liberal, 1907–1972." Ph.D. dissertation: Mississippi State University, 1974.

Robinson, Patricia Webb. "A Rhetorical Analysis of Senator James O. Eastland's Speeches, 1954–1959." M.A. thesis: Louisiana State University, 1978.

Rolph, Stephanie Renee. "Displacing Race: White Resistance and Conservative Politics in the Civil Rights Era." Ph.D. dissertation: Mississippi State University, 2009.

Ruby, Roy H. "The Presidential Election of 1944 in Mississippi: The Bolting Electors." M.A. thesis: Mississippi State University, 1966.

Saucier, Bobby Wade. "The Public Career of Theodore G. Bilbo." Ph.D. dissertation, Tulane University, 1971.

Seal, Enoch. "The Senatorial Career of Theodore G. Bilbo." M.A. thesis: Mississippi State University, 1951.

Simpson, William M. "The 'Loyalist Democrats' and Mississippi's Challenge to a White Majority, 1965–1968." M.A. thesis: Mississippi State University, 1974.

Skates, John R., Jr. "A Southern Editor Views the National Scene: Frederick Sullens and the Jackson, Mississippi *Daily News*." Ph.D. dissertation: Mississippi State University, 1965.

Smith, Charles Pope. "Theodore G. Bilbo's Senatorial Career: The Final Years, 1941–1947." Ph.D. dissertation: University of Southern Mississippi, 1983.

Smith, Dan W. "James O. Eastland: Early Life and Career, 1904–1942." M.A. thesis: Mississippi College, 1978.

Sperry, Benjamin O. "Caught 'Between Our Moral and Material Selves': Mississippi's Elite Moderates and Their Role in Changing Race Relations, 1945–1956." Ph.D. dissertation: Yale University, 2010.

Stockhem, Aaron J. "Lack of Oversight: The Relationship between Congress and the FBI." Ph.D. dissertation: Marquette University, 2011.

Sumerlin, Alvin. "Theodore Bilbo: The Last Phase." M.A. thesis: Louisiana State University, 1950.

Tate, Roger D. "Easing the Burden: The Era of Depression and New Deal in Mississippi, 1978." Ph.D. dissertation: University of Tennessee, 1978.

Tuggle, John Anthony. "The Dixiecrats as a Stepping-Stone to Two-Party Politics from Mississippi." M.A. thesis: University of Southern Mississippi, 1974.

Vance, Sandra Stringer. "The Congressional Career of John Bell Williams, 1947–1967." Ph.D. dissertation: Mississippi State University, 1976.

Vander Zanden, James Wilfred. "The Southern White Resistance Movement to Integration." Ph.D. dissertation: University of North Carolina, 1957.

Wallace, David James. "Massive Resistance, Southern Myth, and Media Suppression." Ph.D. dissertation: University of Colorado, 2011.

Walters, Nick. "The Repairman Chairman: Senator James O. Eastland and His Influence on the U.S. Supreme Court." M.A. thesis: Mississippi College, 1992.

Walton, Laura Richardson. "Segregationist Spin: The Use of Public Relations by the Mississippi State Sovereignty Commission and the White Citizens Council, 1954–1963." Ph.D. dissertation, University of Southern Mississippi, 2006.

Ward, Jason M. "Saving Segregation: Southern Whites, Civil Rights, and the Roots of Massive Resistance, 1936–1954." Ph.D. dissertation, Yale University, 2010.

Weeks, Billy R. "The Pledge 'To Plow a Straight Furrow': The 1947 Senatorial Campaign of John C. Stennis." M.A. thesis: Mississippi State University, 1974.

Wells, Raymond B. "The States Rights Movement of 1948: A Case Study." M.A. thesis: Mississippi State University, 1965.

Williams, Kenneth H. "Mississippi and Civil Rights, 1945–1954." Ph.D. dissertation: Mississippi State University, 1985.

Zwiers, Maarten. "The Paradox of Power: James O. Eastland and the Democratic Party." M.A. thesis, University of Mississippi, 2007.

Zwiers, Maarten. "James Eastland: The Shadow of Southern Democrats, 1928–1966." Ph.D. dissertation, University of Groningen, 2012.

Index